The Exceptional Student
in the
Regular Classroom

Sixth Edition

Bill R. Gearheart
Professor Emeritus, University of Northern Colorado

Mel W. Weishahn
Southern Oregon State College

Carol J. Gearheart
University of Northern Colorado

Merrill, an imprint of
Prentice Hall
Englewood Cliffs, New Jersey   Columbus, Ohio

Library of Congress Cataloging-in-Publication Data

Gearheart, Bill R. (Bill Ray)
    The exceptional student in the regular classroom / Bill R. Gearheart,
    Mel W. Weishahn, Carol J. Gearheart.—6th ed.
      p. cm.
    Includes bibliographical references (p.) and indexes.
    ISBN 0-13-352204-0
    1. Handicapped children—Education—United States. 2. Main-
    streaming in education—United States.   I. Weishahn, Mel W..
    II. Gearheart, Carol J. (Carol Jean).   III. Title.
LC4031.G4   1996
371.91'0973—dc20
                                       94-47473
                                           CIP

Cover art: Petrina Haven, courtesy of Southeast School, Columbus, Ohio
Editor: Ann Castel Davis
Developmental Editor: Carol S. Sykes
Production Editor: Sheryl Glicker Langner
Text Designer: STELLARViSIONS
Cover Designer: Anne Flanagan
Production Buyer: Pamela D. Bennett
Electronic Text Management: Marilyn Wilson Phelps, Matthew Williams, Karen L. Bretz

This book was set in Kuenstler 480 by Prentice Hall and was printed and bound by R.R. Donnelley
and Sons Company. The cover was printed by Phoenix Color Corp.

© 1996 by Prentice-Hall, Inc.
A Simon & Schuster Company
Englewood Cliffs, New Jersey 07632

Earlier editions, copyright © 1992 by Macmillan Publishing Co., © 1988, 1986 by Merrill Publishing
Company, and © 1984, 1980, 1976 by the C. V. Mosby Company.

Photo credits: pp. 3, 68, 195 by Tom Watson/Merrill/Prentice Hall; p. 7 by Harvey Phillips/PPI; pp. 12,
19, 46, 57, 63, 102, 109, 114, 121, 145, 151, 166, 172, 214, 221, 311, 319, 327, 331, 352, 363, 415,
421, 429, 449 by Anne Vega/Merrill/Prentice Hall; pp. 25, 225, 242, 245, 246, 259, 301, 343, 363,
365 by Scott Cunningham/Merrill/Prentice Hall; pp. 37, 383 by Todd Yarrington/Merrill/Prentice Hall;
pp. 42, 82, 157, 191, 451 by Barbara Schwartz/Merrill/Prentice Hall; p. 160 by Fritz Locke/Edgar Bernstein; p. 209 by Tom Hubbard; pp. 230, 231, 232, 233 by William Williamson; pp. 237, 239 by
Ronald Stewart; p. 261 by Andy Brunk/Prentice Hall; p. 284 by Tom Tondee; p. 294 by Prentke
Romich Company; p. 296 by David Strickler/Strix Pix; p. 304 by Bruce Johnson.

Printed in the United States of America

10 9 8 7 6 5 4 3 2 1

ISBN: 0-13-352204-0

Prentice-Hall International (UK) Limited, *London*
Prentice-Hall of Australia Pty. Limited, *Sydney*
Prentice-Hall of Canada, Inc., *Toronto*
Prentice-Hall Hispanoamericana, S. A., *Mexico*
Prentice-Hall of India Private Limited, *New Delhi*
Prentice-Hall of Japan, Inc., *Tokyo*
Simon & Schuster Asia Pte. Ltd., *Singapore*
Editora Prentice-Hall do Brasil, Ltda., *Rio de Janeiro*

preface

This sixth edition of *The Exceptional Student in the Regular Classroom* comes at a time of reevaluation of a variety of efforts to provide more effective educational programs for students with disabilities, and those who are gifted or talented. The term *mainstreaming* has been replaced by *inclusion*, although each has its origins in the concept of the "least restrictive environment." However, the focus of this text remains the same: to help general education teachers better understand their role in the education of exceptional students.

We are convinced that teachers will teach exceptional students with greater success if they possess three types of knowledge or information: (a) knowledge of the laws and regulations that govern educational provisions for exceptional students, (b) understanding of the nature of the various exceptionalities, and (c) understanding of those instructional strategies most likely to be effective with students with special needs.

In this edition, we have continued to respond to ideas and suggestions from teachers, and from professors who have used earlier editions. Chapters 1 through 4 concentrate on information applicable to all exceptionalities, while the remainder of the text examines eight specific exceptionalities.

Features of the Sixth Edition

The sixth edition continues to build on the strengths of previous editions, establishing a foundation on which future teachers can develop both competence and confidence. Readers will find the following in this edition:

- Emphasis on the influence of the positive personal interactions between teacher/student and student/student in the learning process.
- Teaching strategies that have proved to be effective with exceptional students.
- Basic information about various exceptionalities.
- Information about both legislation and litigation that have shaped special education programs of today, and will continue to influence their development.

New Features of the Sixth Edition

This edition reflects the dynamic, evolving nature of special education. We have revised and updated each chapter to reflect current thinking and practices.

- Additional emphasis has been given to the influence and potential of technological advances, in providing adaptations that will enhance educational programs for exceptional students.
- We discuss the trend toward adoption of the concept of *talent*, as opposed to *giftedness*, along with theories that have led to this consideration.
- Additional emphasis is given to the concept of planning for transitions within the educational program, and the need to plan more carefully for the transition to adulthood.
- We explore the influence of the concepts of inclusion and total inclusion, plus concerns of some professional educator groups.
- Chapter 3, which outlines generally applicable instuctional strategies, has been reorganized and expanded, with additional emphasis on monitoring and reporting student performance and the use of technology in the classroom.
- Greater attention has been given to the needs of students with limited English proficiency, and the need to understand and relate educational practices to cultural and ethnic differences/diversity.
- We emphasize the need to give additional attention to the importance of interactions between the teacher and family members.
- We review litigation influencing education of programs for students who are gifted or talented.
- We have added an additional appendix, featuring journals or newsletters that can provide useful information and insight.

Acknowledgments

Many individuals have assisted in preparing this edition, and we want to acknowledge the specific assistance of certain individuals. We offer sincere appreciation to Barbara Garralda Rhine, who wrote Chapter 10. Her ideas and insights about learning disabilities will be of value to readers. In addition, we offer sincere thanks to Fredricka Weishahn, who assisted with several chapters and the instructor's resource manual, and to John Luckner, for assistance with Chapter 5.

We appreciate the guidance of our reviewers, who were contacted by our editor and responsible to our publisher; namely Robert J. Evans, Marshall University; Anne Y. Gallegos, New Mexico State University; Patrick James Powers, University of Wisconsin—Superior; and Qaisar Sultana, Eastern Kentucky University.

Finally, we thank those individuals at Merrill/Prentice Hall whose understanding, assistance, and encouragement helped us over the "rough spots," when writing became more a chore than a pleasure. These include Ann Castel Davis, Senior Editor, and Sheryl Langner, Production Editor. We consider them our quiet partners in Columbus, Ohio. Their unconditional support and professional attitudes are appreciated more than they may know.

Bill R. Gearheart
Mel W. Weishahn
Carol J. Gearheart

a note to readers

Because we believe that simple is better than complex (if either will achieve the intended purpose), we use a minimum of technical terms in this text. Certain terms, however, require special comment. *Regular classroom teachers* or *general educators* are the dedicated professionals to whom we have addressed this text. We really mean *educators who are not trained special educators,* but that is very cumbersome, so we are using the shorter forms. We ask readers to understand that we are not implying ordinariness. We simply needed short descriptive ways to discuss the teachers who are most important in vitalizing the process of inclusion.

Our major interest is to help classroom teachers better understand and more effectively teach exceptional students. The term *exceptional students* is meant to include all students whose educational needs are not effectively met through use of the usual, or standard, curriculum; thus, they may also be called students who have special needs. In common practice (including most state and federal laws and regulations), such students are identified as hearing impaired, visually impaired, gifted, mentally retarded, and so forth, but these labels can be misleading. Although certain characteristics apply to each exceptionality (that is, all students with hearing impairments have some hearing loss), each student is an individual, with unique characteristics and learning abilities. As we discuss the major characteristics associated with the various exceptionalities, remember that these are generalizations.

One other misconception is sufficiently important that we want to guard against it in advance. Because of the manner in which this text is written, we sometimes speak of the exceptionalities in a manner that might lead readers to think that each is always separate and discrete. This, too, is inaccurate. Even though we may discuss the exceptionalities separately, they often overlap. For example, a student with a moderate hearing loss may also be mentally retarded, or a student who is orthopedically impaired may also have a speech impairment. We ask readers to understand and accept this in advance so that we do not need to repeat it every time we consider any particular exceptionality.

contents

P A R T

one

The Foundation for Education of Exceptional Students

Part I (chapters 1 and 2) provides the framework for a better understanding of educational programs for exceptional students (students with disabilities, and those who are gifted or talented). Chapter 1 reviews the historical bases on which present-day educational programs are founded. It also outlines litigation that has shaped existing legislation, and that continues to interpret and expand our concept of societal responsibility for a free, appropriate education for all students, regardless of their special needs. Finally, it defines the special populations in need of modified programs or educational interventions, and outlines a philosophy of education for exceptional students.

Chapter 2 presents the major legislation shaping the nature of education of exceptional students, with emphasis on the Individuals With Disabilities Education Act (IDEA). It describes educational programs and services commonly available to students with special needs, outlining the manner in which such students are identified, and the process through which their individualized educational programs are planned and implemented. It also addresses certain special concerns, such as the unique challenges involved in identifying and planning appropriate programs for students from culturally and linguistically diverse populations.

chapter 1

- What factors led to concern regarding most special class programs? When and on what bases are special programs justified?

- When might a student be considered mainstreamed without membership in a regular classroom?

- How did the basic thrust of the litigation that preceded PL 94–142 differ from that of the litigation that followed it?

- In your opinion, which disability is the simplest to successfully accommodate in regular classrooms? Which is the most difficult to accommodate in regular classrooms? On what experiences or other bases did you answer these two questions?

- What type of special educational programming is provided in your state for students called gifted or talented?

- Can you develop an unambiguous, practical definition of *talented*? How would you differentiate between giftedness and talent?

Education of Students with Special Needs

■■■■■■■■■■■■

In this chapter we describe the manner in which special education programs and services have evolved, emphasizing historical origins and the litigation that has shaped present programs. Discussions of the manner in which special education is defined, the prevalence of exceptional students in our schools, and the factors that continue to influence the scope and quality of special education programs provide further understanding of the population whose needs are targeted in this text. Also included are a statement of philosophy for the education of students with disabilities and those at risk, and a separate statement of philosophy for the education of students who are gifted, talented, or creative.

■■■■■■■■■■■■

■ Historical Origins of Present Programs

The following history of early efforts to assist individuals with disabilities, to eliminate the disabililty, or, in some cases, to eliminate individuals with disabilities, provides a perspective for understanding present educational efforts. This historical overview examines four eras:

Early history—before 1800
Era of institutions—1800 to 1900
Era of public school special classes—1900 to 1960/70
Era of growth and reevaluation—1960 to present

These eras overlap to some extent. In many cases, a new era started in some parts of the nation or world while an older era still existed in others.

All events before 1800 are considered early history. In much of the pre-1800 period, individuals were not recognized as having disabilities unless the disability was severe. This was particularly true with respect to mental retardation, partly because of a lack of any type of universal educational effort.

Early History—Before 1800

In Western culture, the early history of societal involvement with individuals with disabilities is primarily one of misunderstanding and superstition. It is likely that blindness, deafness, and mental retardation have existed since the beginning of the human race, and early documents clearly refer to abandonment of infants who had disabilities. Roman history repeatedly refers to "fools" kept by the wealthy for entertainment.

It was almost universally held that individuals who were considerably different from normal in appearance or behavior were possessed by demons or evil spirits. Historical writers such as Zilboorg and Henry (1941), Pritchard (1963), and Kanner (1964) provide comprehensive accounts of the manner in which society has related to individuals with disabilities, mainly accounts of inhumanity that developed as a result of fear and ignorance. This section is based on documentation found in the preceding three sources and in Gearheart and Litton (1979).

Most early records refer to individuals with disabilities or defects in ways that make it difficult to determine whether those referred to were mentally retarded, mentally ill, or deaf and unable to communicate. In many societies, a father could determine whether he wanted to keep a newborn infant. If he indicated he did not, it might be thrown off a cliff, left in the wilderness, or left by a roadside. Such infanticide was supported by the common belief that individuals who were different were possessed by demons or evil spirits and that the actions taken were not directed against human infants but against demons. At one time, the Romans even extended this absolute rule of the father over infants to include the possibility that any female infant might be so disposed of. There were, of course, short periods of time during which specific rulers imposed more humane practices, but the foregoing, repugnant as they may seem today, were general practices in much of the "civilized" Western world for centuries.

The Middle Ages and the rise and development of Christianity brought about varied effects, depending on the type of disability, the geographic location, and the specific era. Although the idea of love and concern for others gained headway, individuals with disabilities were variously viewed as fools, nonhumans, or witches (an obvious throwback to earlier demonology). The belief that individuals with mental illness or mental retardation were possessed by demons or evil spirits led to the offering of prayers or the practice of exorcism. On many occasions, the exorcism was rigorous but not nearly so final as later treatment of witches, such as burning at the stake.

Although there were some bright spots, all the more bright for their infrequent appearance, until the 16th century the general picture was bleak. Individuals with disabilities were not accepted as totally human and thus were misunderstood, mistreated, or put to death. Leading philosophers, national governments, and organized churches shared responsibility for this attitude.

Then, slowly and with frequent backsliding, the picture began to change. During the latter part of the 16th century, a Spanish monk, Pedro Ponce de León, was successful in teaching a small group of pupils who were deaf to speak, read, and write. This major breakthrough led to a reversal of the official position of the church that individuals who were deaf could not speak and were uneducable, a position based on the writings of Aristotle. In the following century, Juan Bonet developed an early version of fingerspelling for individuals who were deaf. In 1760, the Abbé de l'Épée opened a school in Paris for individuals who were deaf, and organized education for individuals who were deaf became a reality.

An associate of the Abbé de l'Épée, Valentin Huay, became interested in individuals who were blind. Huay, who had associated with such intellectuals as Voltaire and Rousseau, vowed to improve the lot of individuals who were blind after the traumatic experience of witnessing the exploitation for public entertainment of 10 men who were blind. By 1784, Huay had established a school for individuals who were blind, the National Institution of Young Blind People, also in Paris.

Only a few years later, in 1789, a boy of 11 or 12 years of age was found roaming "wild" in the woods near Aveyron, France. Discovered by hunters, the boy was unable to speak and bore the scars of years of encounters with wild animals. He bit and scratched all who approached, chose his food by smell, and was more animal than human in nearly all respects. This boy, eventually named Victor, was taken to Paris to be observed by students who were studying the development of primitive faculties. There, Phillipe Pinel, a renowned scientist, declared the boy to be an incurable idiot, but Jean Marc Gaspard Itard, who also saw the boy, thought otherwise. Itard obtained custody of Victor and launched an involved program to civilize and educate him, hoping to make him normal. Unfortunately, although the boy showed improvement, he did not become normal in any sense. The record of Itard's work, *The Wild Boy of Aveyron* (Itard, 1962), is an important classic in the education of individuals with mental retardation.

Thus, we see that educational programs for individuals with hearing impairments, visual impairments, and mental retardation had their beginnings within less than a half-century, all in or near Paris. Perhaps the most fitting comment on the long era brought to a close by the new efforts is that the change, the opening of a new chapter in the history of treatment of individuals with disabilities, was long overdue.

Era of Institutions—1800 to 1900

The manner in which the institutional movement swept Europe and the United States is a reflection of the combination of a critical need on the part of the population of persons with disabilities, an awareness of this need on the part of professionals (both physicians and educators), and changing attitudes among the general population. However, considerable support for institutionalization seems to have come from the fact that such a practice kept undesirable or physically unattractive persons out of the public eye and thus off the public conscience. This attitude, though unacceptable today, was a vast improvement over infanticide or the use of prisons as holding centers for individuals with disabilities.

Institutions for individuals with hearing and visual impairments were initiated at about the same time. Institutions for individuals with mental retardation came 50 to 60 years later. The first institutional programs for individuals with disabilities were initiated in Europe, with France, Germany, Scotland, and England leading the way. By 1800, recognized programs for individuals with visual impairment existed in France, England, and Scotland, and programs for individuals with hearing impairment existed in France, Germany, Scotland, and England. Institutions specifically for individuals with mental retardation were not begun until 1831, when the first such program was initiated in France, but multipurpose institutions, such as the Bicetre and Salpetriere in Paris, had housed a variety of societal outcasts—individuals with visual impairment, senility, mental illness, and mental retardation, as well as prostitutes— since the 17th century.

Institutions were *the* way to provide for individuals with disabilities throughout the 19th century, but as the century came to a close, new voices and new ideas began to be heard. For example, in an address to the National Education Association in 1898, Alexander Graham Bell suggested forming an annex to the public schools to provide special classes for individuals with hearing impairment, visual impairment, and mental retardation. In 1902, he further urged that this "special education" be provided so that such children would not have to leave their homes

Fifty years ago, this student with a visual impairment would not have been included in the public school.

to attend institutions and that the National Education Association actively pursue such educational provisions. As a result, the NEA officially formed a Department of Special Education, thus originating a name that remains to this day (Gearheart, 1974). These efforts by Bell and the actions of the public schools, which soon followed, ushered in a new era.

Era of Public School Special Classes—1900 to 1960/70

Educational efforts designed specifically for students with disabilities originated before 1900, but such efforts were sporadic, met with limited acceptance, and had limited success. The order of introduction of special programs into public schools was reversed compared with that of institutional programs, with public school classes for individuals with mental retardation coming before those for individuals with hearing and visual impairments. Such classes were attempted in New York, Cleveland, and Providence, Rhode Island before 1900, but they tended to be classes provided for "problem children" and probably included more nonretarded students than students with mental retardation.

Early in the 20th century, several cities tried gathering groups of students who had been previously unschooled and who for the most part were mentally retarded. Like the institutions, the schools were interested in a return to normalcy, including normal learning ability, but they were generally unsuccessful. Later in the century, particularly after the appearance of a more adequate way to determine degree of mental retardation (Lewis Terman's revision of the Binet test of intelligence—the Stanford-Binet), classes for students with mild mental retardation were started and were successful enough to warrant continuation.

Day school classes for students with visual or hearing impairment were slower in starting, but they did not follow quite so much the start-and-stop pattern that characterized early classes for students with mental retardation, because institutions for students with hearing or visual impairment were more truly schools, and parents were more likely to accept and support residential settings. With the enactment of compulsory school attendance laws in the early part of the century came the problem of providing for *all* minors, including those with disabilities. It should be noted that since most states provided residential schools for students with visual or hearing impairments and students with severe mental retardation, who were often institutionalized at an early age, the real problem was providing for students with mild mental retardation. Thus, the public schools concentrated on special classes for students with mild mental retarda-

tion. However, some of these classes included children whose problems were mostly behavioral, resulting in low academic performance, because no other programs were available.

After about 1920, as special classes for students with mental retardation (later called *educable mentally handicapped* to differentiate them from *trainable mentally retarded*) continued to grow in popularity, there was similar growth in special programs for students with less-than-normal visual acuity (called *visually handicapped*, *visually impaired*, or *partially seeing*) and classes for those with less-than-normal hearing (called *deaf* or *hearing handicapped*). In addition, there were special programs for students with speech problems and often special rooms for students with heart problems or orthopedic disabilities. Some classes for students whose major problems were unacceptable or antisocial behaviors were also initiated, but as often as not, if the problems were not too severe, these students were placed in classes for students with mental retardation, and those who could not get along in this obviously special setting were expelled from school.

The close of this era is given a dual date because although there was a considerable increase in the use of service delivery plans other than special classes during the 1960s, many special classes remained in 1970. By calling this the era of special classes, we do not mean that other means of serving students with disabilities were not in use during this time. Many students with physical disabilities, visual impairments, or hearing impairments were included in regular classrooms with success.

It must also be recognized that a special class may be either a full-time or part-time special class. For example, speech therapy has been conducted for years in small groups of two to four students in totally segregated special settings, often for periods of only 30 to 40 minutes per day, 2 or 3 days per week. Programs for students with visual impairments sometimes consist of segregated special classes at the preschool level, where students learn special skills such as braille, but these same students are almost totally integrated into regular classrooms from second grade on.

In the first 60 to 70 years of the 20th century, special classes were the major means whereby students with disabilities were served. This era represented a definite evolution beyond the institutional era. General educators happily sent problem students to special classes, and special educators accepted a number of students who should not have been so placed. Toward the end of the era, a variety of studies as well as court cases suggested that special classes were sometimes used as dumping grounds, vehicles of segregation, and in some geographic areas, convenient ways to do something for children who were culturally or linguistically different.

As the special class era came to a close, a great deal of ambivalence was expressed when discussing "special classes." Overuse and misuse of special classes was an established fact, but the assumption that special class programs were never appropriate was questionable. This will become more evident as we review litigation and federal legislation, later in this chapter and in Chapter 2.

Era of Growth and Reevaluation—1960 to the Present

Rapid growth in services, in both quality and quantity, began sometime soon after midcentury. Changes taking place in society as a whole accelerated change already underway in the rapidly developing field of special education. There was generally increased acceptance of persons with disabilities as individuals and all educators began to take a more positive attitude regarding their responsibility for stu-

dents with disabilities. Legislation at the federal level encouraged parallel legislation in the individual states. Court cases made it clear to school boards and educators that students with disabilities were the direct responsibility of public education. What emerged was a clear mandate that all children and youth be provided a free, appropriate education.

Nationally recognized individuals joined with parent advocates, organized parent groups, and professional groups as catalysts for this change, but the U.S. Congress provided the major impetus. The pattern through which Congress become involved with the education of students with disabilities was similar to that of its entering any new and unfamiliar arena. At first, legislation was limited in scope and funding. Then, after positive results, Congress enacted broader laws in a sequence that led to Public Law (PL) 94–142: the Education for All Handicapped Children Act of 1975, and eventually to PL 101–476: the Individuals with Disabilities Education Act (IDEA) in 1990. Thus, the end result of strong, continuing interest on the part of key national legislators and well-organized advocates was a comprehensive legislative framework for the education of students with disabilities. In Chapter 2, we discuss in detail this legislation, and the federal guidelines designed to define and shape it, as we consider the implementation of services to exceptional students.

It might seem that with a strong, comprehensive federal mandate, the question of how students with disabilities should be educated, and which agencies are responsible, should be settled. However, as is the case with respect to much legislation, further interpretation was required. In the following section we will consider litigation that influenced the passage of key legislation, and additional litigation that helped to define and interpret it. In fact, considerable litigation continues today, further defining, and often expanding, on the educational and financial responsibilities of the public schools to provide a free, appropriate education for all students, regardless of the type and degree of their special needs.

■ Litigation: Shaping the Course of Special Education

Litigation in the 1950s established the right to nonsegregated education and equal educational opportunities for all children, providing the basis for special education–related litigation in the 1970s that had several major emphases (see Table 1–1). The first such litigation alleged that special education classes (often classes for individuals who were classified educable mentally retarded) led to stigma, inadequate education, and irreparable injury. These lawsuits alleged that special education programs as they existed were a disservice to many students and resulted in a reduction in the numbers of students served by special education in certain parts of the nation.

A second type of litigation involved students who were not served through special education but who were in serious need of such service. These suits led to the initiation of a number of new programs and the addition of students to special education rolls in some areas. Other litigation related to who should pay the cost of private schooling for students with disabilities, recovery (by parents) of attorney fees incident to court proceedings relating to students with disabilities, and the conditions under which students with disabilities can be suspended or expelled from school. Some of these cases are summarized in Table 1–1, and the rest of this section further considers the effect of litigation on programs for students with disabilities.

Much of the special education–related litigation of the 1960s and 1970s was based on the U.S. Supreme Court ruling in *Brown v. Board of Education* (1954), which declared that separate schools for black and white students were unconstitutional. The essence of this decision was that segregation solely on the basis of race deprives minority children of equal educational opportunities, even if various tangible factors appear to be equal (Zirkel, 1978). Parents of children with disabilities later sued school systems in relation to segregated facilities for their children, basing their arguments in part on *Brown v. Board of Education*. Such litigation started in the 1960s but reached previously unheard-of proportions in the 1970s.

Diana v. State Board of Education, used as a basis for similar suits, alleged that intelligence tests used for placement were culturally biased and that class placement based on these inadequate tests led to inadequate education. This suit also claimed that, as a result, the stigma of mental retardation was suffered by children who were not mentally retarded. In the *Diana* case, the plaintiffs sought relief from existing practices of identification and placement. They also sought compensatory damages.

Diana v. State Board of Education was settled out of court with the following points of agreement: (a) children whose primary language is not English must be tested in their primary language and English, but verbal (as opposed to performance) questions, which by their very nature are unfair to children whose primary language is not English, cannot be used in testing such children; (b) all Mexican American and Chinese children already enrolled in special education classes must be retested in accordance with the preceding principle; (c) every school district in the state must develop and submit to the court a plan for retesting and reevaluating Mexican American and Chinese children in classes for students classified as educable mentally retarded, and as a part of this plan, the district must show how it will place back into regular classes children whom this reevaluation indicates were misplaced; (d) school psychologists must develop more appropriate testing devices and measures to reflect Mexican American culture; and (e) any school district that has a significant disparity between the percentage of Mexican American children in regular classes and the percentage in classes for students who are educable mentally retarded must submit an acceptable explanation for this discrepancy. The *Diana* case is similar to many filed against the schools. Most were settled in a manner similar to that in the *Diana* case.

Litigation also demanded more special education classes and services in the public schools for students with disabilities. The following description of two cases, one in Pennsylvania and the other in Washington, DC, illustrates this effort. Although the first affected only mental retardation, the second specifically related to all disabilities and, because it was based on the U.S. Constitution, has ramifications for all areas of the United States.

Two major cases appear to have established the right of access to public education for the school-age students classified as trainable mentally retarded. The first, *The Pennsylvania Association for Retarded Children v. the Commonwealth of Pennsylvania*, questioned educational policies of the state of Pennsylvania. The suit alleged that certain policies led directly to practices that denied appropriate education at public expense to children of school age who were mentally retarded. This case was filed on January 7, 1971, by the Pennsylvania Association for Retarded Children on behalf of fourteen specifically named children and all other children similarly situated. This was a typical *class action suit*, filed to affect the fourteen children named, all others of a similar class now residing in the state, and all children similarly situated who will be living in Pennsylvania in the future.

Pennsylvania, like a number of other states, had compulsory school attendance laws, provided certain types of special classes for children who had disabilities within the public schools and provided residential schools for some children with disabilities. Within the Pennsylvania School Code, children who were trainable mentally retarded could be excluded from public education in two ways. First, if a qualified psychologist or personnel from a mental health clinic certified that a given child could no longer profit from public school attendance, the child could be excluded. Second, because the law provided that the local board of education could refuse to accept or retain children who had not reached the mental age of 5 years, most children classified as trainable retarded were never admitted to the public schools. Even if a child were not excluded under either of these provisions, a third provision permitted the local board to provide training outside the public schools "if an approved plan demonstrates that it is unfeasible to form a special class."

The Pennsylvania Association for Retarded Children (PARC) set out to establish three main points in their case: (1) children who are mentally retarded can learn if an appropriate educational program is provided, (2) "education" must be viewed more broadly than the traditional academic program, and (3) early educational experience is essential to maximize educational potential. After considerable testimony by the state and a variety of "expert witnesses," PARC won the case.

The Pennsylvania Association for Retarded Children v. Pennsylvania suit, like many suits that followed, was settled on the basis of a *consent decree*, which is an out-of-court agreement, usually formally approved by the court. In this suit, the state was ordered to provide free public education appropriate to the learning capabilities of children with mental retardation and the decree provided the working framework. To make certain that the consent decree was carried out, the court established a time schedule for implementation and appointed two masters to oversee the total process.

Mills v. the Board of Education of the District of Columbia is of unusual significance because it

These students belong in public schools.

applied to *all* children with disabilities. To a certain extent, it established a principle that tended to lead to the inclusion in future class action suits of all students with disabilities. This case led to a judgment that required the public schools to provide for students with disabilities even if they did not fit the educational mold. As in the Pennsylvania case, the court appointed masters to oversee the operation.[1]

In addition to the preceding litigation, which established the rights of students and parents and the broad framework within which programs were to be provided, later litigation served to settle more specific questions. For example, *Stuart v. Nappi* (1978) and *Honig v. Doe* (1988) addressed the question of suspension and expulsion of students with disabilities.

Other questions, such as who makes the final decision as to how much special service is provided (*Board v. Rowley*, 1982), who pays for private school costs (*Burlington School Committee v. Department of Education of Massachusetts*, 1985), and the conditions under which parents can recover attorney fees incident to litigation on behalf of their child (*Smith v. Robinson*, 1984), have shaped the direction of special education programs in our schools.

Finally, we should note that litigation continues today. Turnbull (1993) lists over 450 specific cases that have influenced the nature of special education services for students with disabilities. In addition to those cases presented in Table 1–1, other cases have led to such conclusions as (a) students with infectious diseases, including AIDS, who have special education needs are entitled to a free appropriate education, and should not be excluded from school unless they represent a clear, direct health danger to others, (b) cost considerations may be

---

[1]From *The Trainable Retarded: A Foundations Approach*, 2nd ed. (pp. 17–18) by B. R. Gearheart and F. Litton, 1979, St. Louis: C. V. Mosby. Copyright 1979 by B. R. Gearheart. Adapted by permission.

Table 1–1
Court cases that have greatly influenced special education*

Court Case	Summary of Ruling or Settlement
Brown v. Board of Education (1954)	School segregation solely on basis of race deprives children of equal educational opportunities and thus violates the equal protection clause of the 14th Amendment.
Diana v. State Board of Education (1970)	(Settled through consent decree.) State of California agreed to change its evaluation practices with respect to the language in which students are tested and to eliminate certain test items. It also agreed to develop tests designed to reflect minority cultures and to reevaluate all Mexican-American and Chinese students enrolled in EMR classes.
Pennsylvania Association for Retarded Children v. Commonwealth of Pennsylvania (1972)	(Settled through consent decree.) The state must provide access to free, appropriate public education for children who are mentally retarded. *Education* was redefined to include activities that the state had earlier held were not educational. Other benefits for students with mental retardation were also gained.
Mills v. D.C. Board of Education (1972)	Students cannot be excluded from school because they have been found to be behavior problems, emotionally disturbed, mentally retarded, etc. Students must have a hearing before exclusion or placement in a special program. *All* students have a right to an appropriate education.
Frederick L. v. Thomas (1977)	Philadelphia schools were directed to search systematically for students with learning disabilities. (They had claimed the existing differentiated program provided adequately for such students and that such screening was thus unnecessary.)
Stuart v. Nappi (1978)	Disciplinary expulsion may constitute denial of appropriate education. Due process procedures must be followed.
New York State Association for Retarded Children v. Carey (1979)	Retarded children with hepatitis-B, a disease that can be contained, cannot be placed in separate, self-contained programs, based on existence of the disease.
Drycia et al. v. Board of Education of the City of New York (1979)	Students must be evaluated by school-based teams using bilingual evaluation procedures. Appropriate bilingual programs were required in a full continuum of placement options, and parents involved in both evaluation and development of the IEP.

* These thirteen cases include many of those which have been significant in shaping the nature of special education services. Turnbull (1993) lists over 450 pertinent cases.

Table 1–1, *continued*

Court Case	Summary of Ruling or Settlement
Board v. Rowley (1982)	Amy Rowley, a deaf student with excellent speechreading skills, was provided limited instruction by a tutor for the deaf and the services of a speech pathologist, plus amplification equipment. Amy was performing at an academic level above average for her grade and class. Her parents (also deaf) requested a qualified sign-language interpreter for all academic classes. This request was denied. Supreme Court affirmation of this decision supported comparable, appropriate education, but not necessarily maximum opportunity for each student with disabilities.
Roncker v. Walters (1983)	Cost of services may be considered since spending on one student with disabilities may deprive another student with disabilities; however, a proper continuum of placements must be provided.
Smith v. Robinson (1984)	After varying decisions and reversals, the U.S. Supreme Court ruled that parents are not entitled to recover attorney fees. (PL 94–142 amendments now include a provision for some recovery of attorney fees.)
Burlington School Committee v. Department of Education of Massachusetts (1985)	Eight-year-old Michael Panico was enrolled in a private school for students with learning disabilities without school approval. A hearing officer ruled this an appropriate placement, and ordered the parents reimbursed. School officials appealed the ruling. The U.S. Supreme Court eventually ruled that parents may be reimbursed, *if* the court ultimately rules that the placement is appropriate. PL 94–142 provisions were cited.
Honig v. Doe (1988)	Two students who were emotionally disabled were enrolled in the San Francisco Unified School District and received special education services. They were suspended indefinitely during expulsion proceedings. The U.S. Supreme Court held that students with disabilities cannot be expelled for misbehavior that is a manifestation of the disability. Shorter-term suspensions must be used. PL 94–142 does not compel districts to place students with disabilities in regular classrooms, only in the least restrictive setting consistent with their needs and the needs of other students. However, students who are disabled *may* be expelled if their misbehavior is not a manifestation of their disability.

taken into account when providing an appropriate program, (c) a more restrictive environment (favored by the parents) may be more appropriate than one originally selected by school authorities, (d) catheterization is a "related service" (school health service) and must be provided by the school, and (e) the residential component of a psychiatric hospital placement is medical, not educational, and the school district is not compelled to pay for such service (in slightly different cases, psychotherapy was considered part of a treatment program for mental disorders, and the school had to pay the costs of psychotherapy). In a number of instances, apparent contradictions (as in the case of financial responsibility for psychotherapy) appear when we review the separate court cases.

Litigation and Students Who Are Gifted or Talented

Although many states have special provisions for students who are gifted or talented, there is no federal mandate for appropriate education, such as that which applies to students with disabilities. There has been some litigation with respect to the lack of appropriate educational services, but it has been limited in scope, and has not led to decisions by the U.S. Supreme Court with influence on national educational provisions. We will review this litigation in Chapter 12, when we consider the unique status of students who are gifted, talented, or creative; students whose special needs are more often neglected than those of any other exceptionality.

■ Defining Special Education

There is some national acceptance of a common definition of special education, but because education is primarily a state func-

tion, a degree of variation continues. Two national groups have, in effect, defined special education, and with the exception of students who are gifted, talented, or creative, there is growing agreement among the states. The two national definitions are primarily operational in nature and are provided by the Council for Exceptional Children (an organization of professionals who work with exceptional children) and the division of the federal government responsible for programs for students with disabilities (the Office of Special Education).

The Council for Exceptional Children has 17 divisions or affiliates, 7 of which relate to recognized categories of exceptionality. These 7 exceptionalities are (a) gifted, (b) behavior disorders, (c) communication disorders, (d) learning disabilities, (e) mental retardation/developmental disabilities, (f) physical and health disabilities, and (g) visual disabilities. In this text, the term *disability* refers to all recognized categories of disability, and the term *exceptional* includes all categories of disability and giftedness.

Federal agencies and offices that monitor special education programs have one major function: to be certain that the dictates of federal legislation are followed. In a related subfunction, these agencies provide reports to Congress relative to existing services for students with disabilities. These reports have used essentially the same terminology as the Council for Exceptional Children, reporting on the same categories of disability. Thus, the scope of special education—at least the part of special education related to disabilities—has been defined in practice by these two organizations. It has been further defined in terms of the services that may be required by students with disabilities through the regulations of IDEA and the states. The major differences between state definitions of special education involve terminology with respect to the various disabilities, but the range of students served is essentially the same. There are, however, other differences related to the quality of services; differences that, we hope, will be reduced in the direction of better services in all states.

Although specialized educational provisions for students who are gifted are not mandated by federal law, there is a steadily growing interest in such programming in most of the nation. Classroom teachers should plan for students who are gifted or creative, because they will sooner or later make their presence known.

Target Populations

At the federal level, IDEA spells out the target populations for services for students with disabilities. State laws and regulations further define these populations on a state-by-state basis, and the targets are the same (although given varying names in the various states). Whatever the terminology, it may be said that the intent is that *all* children and youth with disabilities be provided a free, appropriate education by some agency of the state, usually the public schools. As for students who are gifted or talented, most states provide some sort of statement of intent to provide services, although there is no national mandate similar to IDEA.

Tables 1–2 and 1–3 provide two different types of data about the prevalence of exceptional students in schools. Table 1–2 presents information regarding prevalence as it has been presented for the past 30 or 40 years. This information is based on U.S. government agency estimates, which in turn are based on estimates provided by recognized authorities. These prevalence estimates are reasonably good, given the variable nature of definitions of many of the exceptionalities. The prevalence ranges probably reflect ranges in how severe disabilities must be in order to qualify.

Table 1–3 provides information regarding the percentage of students with disabilities

actually receiving services in the public schools, as reported by the states in annual reports to the federal government, pursuant to the requirements of the Individuals With Disabilities Education Act of 1990. The totals from which these percentages were derived vary slightly from year to year; Table 1–3 provides a general representation of these reports during the 1985 to 1995 time period. Note that for the area of learning disabilities, a higher percentage of students has been reported as identified and served than the upper range of the theoretical prevalence would predict. For all other disabilities, the percentage identified and served is near the lower end of the estimated range of prevalence, in some cases below that minimum estimate. As we discuss the various areas of disabilities in later chapters, possible reasons for this over- and/or underreporting should become evident. With respect to the area of giftedness and talent, no comparable national data are available.

In addition to the disabilities listed in Tables 1–2 and 1–3 (those for which all states report data), IDEA recognizes and specifically directs services to children identified as having autism, traumatic brain injury, deaf-blindness or multiple disabilities. Further, it includes children with disabilities age 3 through 5 who are experiencing developmental delays, as defined by the state in one or more of the following areas: physical development, cognitive development, communication development, social or emotional development, or adaptive development, and thus need special educational assistance. The federal guidelines define the various terms used as follows:

(1) "Austism" means a developmental disability significantly affecting verbal and nonverbal communication and social interaction, generally evident before age 3, that adversely affects a child's educational performance. Other characteristics often associated with autism

Table 1–2

Target population of exceptional children (theoretical prevalence of exceptional children in the United States)

Exceptionality	Percentage of Population
Learning disability	2.0–4.0
Speech disability	2.0–4.0
Mental retardation	1.0–3.0
Emotional disturbance	1.0–3.0
Hearing impairment (including deafness)	0.5–0.7
Orthopedic and other health impairments	0.4–0.6
Visual impairment (including blindness)	0.08–0.12
Giftedness and talent	2.0–3.0

Note: Based on U.S. government agency estimates and estimates by recognized authorities.

Table 1–3

Exceptional children, ages 6–17, identified and receiving services

Exceptionality	Percentage of National Public School Enrollment Receiving Services
Learning disability	4.5 – 5.0
Speech disability	2.2 – 2.8
Mental retardation	1.2 – 1.6
Emotional disturbance	0.8 – 1.0
Hearing impairment (including deafness)	0.1 – 0.2
Orthopedic and other health impairments	0.1 – 0.2
Visual impairment (including blindness)	0.05 – 0.06
Giftedness and talent	No comparable national data

Note: Based on annual reports to the Federal Government, by individual states, pursuant to the requirements of PL 94–142 and IDEA, 1985–1995.

are engagement in repetitive activities and stereotyped movements, resistance to environmental change or change in daily routines, and unusual responses to sensory experiences. The term does not apply if a child's educational performance is adversely affected primarily because the child has a serious emotional disturbance, as defined in paragraph (b)(9) of this section.

(2) "Deaf-blindness" means concomitant hearing and visual impairments, the combination of which causes such severe communication and other developmental and educational problems that they cannot be accommodated in special education programs solely for children with deafness or children with blindness.

(3) "Deafness" means a hearing impairment that is so severe that the child is impaired in pro-

cessing linguistic information through hearing, with or without amplification, that adversely affects a child's educational performance.

(4) "Hearing impairment" means an impairment in hearing, whether permanent or fluctuating, that adversely affects a child's educational performance but that is not included under the definition of deafness in this section.

(5) "Mental retardation" means significantly subaverage general intellectual functioning existing concurrently with deficits in adaptive behavior and manifested during the developmental period that adversely affects a child's educational performance.

(6) "Multiple disabilities" means concomitant impairments (such as mental retardation-blindness, mental retardation-orthopedic impairment, etc.), the combination of which causes such severe educational problems that they cannot be accommodated in special education programs solely for one of the impairments. The term does not include deaf-blindness.

(7) "Orthopedic impairment" means a severe orthopedic impairment that adversely affects a child's educational performance. The term includes impairments caused by congenital anomaly (e.g., clubfoot, absence of some member, etc.), impairments caused by disease (e.g., poliomyelitis, bone tuberculosis, etc.), and impairments from other causes (e.g., cerebral palsy, amputations, and fractures or burns that cause contractures).

(8) "Other health impairment" means having limited strength, vitality or alertness, due to chronic or acute health problems such as a heart condition, tuberculosis, rheumatic fever, nephritis, asthma, sickle cell anemia, hemophilia, epilepsy, lead poisoning, leukemia, or diabetes that adversely affects a child's educational performance.

(9) "Serious emotional disturbance" is defined as follows:

(i) The term means a condition exhibiting one or more of the following characteristics over a long period of time and to a marked degree that adversely affects a child's educational performance—

(A) An inability to learn that cannot be explained by intellectual, sensory, or health factors;

(B) An inability to build or maintain satisfactory interpersonal relationships with peers and teachers;

(C) Inappropriate types of behavior or feelings under normal circumstances;

(D) A general pervasive mood of unhappiness or depression; or

(E) A tendency to develop physical symptoms or fears associated with personal or school problems.

(ii) The term includes schizophrenia. The term does not apply to children who are socially maladjusted, unless it is determined that they have a serious emotional disturbance.

(10) "Specific learning disability" means a disorder in one or more of the basic psychological processes involved in understanding or in using language, spoken or written, that may manifest itself in an imperfect ability to listen, think, speak, read, write, spell, or to do mathematical calculations. The term includes such conditions as perceptual disabilities, brain injury, minimal brain dysfunction, dyslexia, and developmental aphasia. The term does not apply to children who have learning problems that are primarily the result of visual, hearing, or motor disabilities, of mental retardation, of emotional disturbance, or of environmental, cultural, or economic disadvantage.

(11) "Speech or language impairment" means a communication disorder such as stuttering, impaired articulation, a language impairment, or a voice impairment that adversely affects a child's educational performance.

(12) "Traumatic brain injury" means an acquired injury to the brain caused by an external physical force, resulting in total or partial functional disability or psychosocial impairment, or both, that adversely affects a child's educational performance. The term applies to open or closed head injuries resulting in

Not all disabilities are visible.

impairments in one or more areas, such as cognition; language; memory; attention; reasoning; abstract thinking; judgment; problem-solving; sensory, perceptual and motor abilities; psychosocial behavior; physical functions; information processing; and speech. The term does not apply to brain injuries that are congenital or degenerative, or brain injuries induced by birth trauma.

(13) "Visual impairment including blindness" means an impairment in vision that, even with correction, adversely affects a child's educational performance. The term includes both partial sight and blindness.[2]

---

[2]Code of Federal Regulations (CFR) 34 (1993), Section 300.7, Office of the Federal Register. Washington, DC, U.S. Government Printing Office.

Variations in the Quality and Scope of Programs and Services for Exceptional Students

Although federal law and regulations apply across the nation, a number of factors lead to considerable variation in both the quality and scope of programs and services offered to exceptional students. With respect to programs and services for students with disabilities, several factors interact to determine which students are served, and how effectively they are served. Some of this variation is a result of differences among state laws regulat-

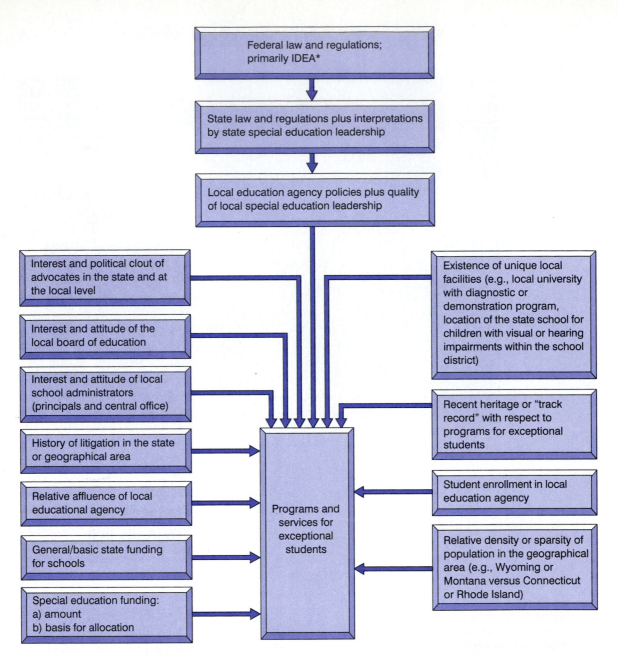

Federal law and regulations; primarily IDEA*

State law and regulations plus interpretations by state special education leadership

Local education agency policies plus quality of local special education leadership

Interest and political clout of advocates in the state and at the local level

Interest and attitude of the local board of education

Interest and attitude of local school administrators (principals and central office)

History of litigation in the state or geographical area

Relative affluence of local educational agency

General/basic state funding for schools

Special education funding:
a) amount
b) basis for allocation

Programs and services for exceptional students

Existence of unique local facilities (e.g., local university with diagnostic or demonstration program, location of the state school for children with visual or hearing impairments within the school district)

Recent heritage or "track record" with respect to programs for exceptional students

Student enrollment in local education agency

Relative density or sparsity of population in the geographical area (e.g., Wyoming or Montana versus Connecticut or Rhode Island)

* Applies to programs and services for students with disabilities, not to the gifted and talented.

Figure 1–1

Factors that determine the quality and scope of programs and services for exceptional students

Source: From *Exceptional Individuals* (p. 27), by B. R. Gearheart, R. C. Mullen, and C. J. Gearheart. Copyright © 1993 by Brooks/Cole Publishing Company. Reprinted by permission.

ing education. Additional variation exists within states because of differences in the financial ability of local education agencies, and such factors as relative density of population, unique local facilities, interest and attitudes of members of the local board of education, or the political clout of local advocates. These factors are illustrated in Figure 1–1.

As for programs and services for students who are gifted, talented, or creative, all but one of these same factors apply. That one is the influence of IDEA, the federal mandate applying to students with disabilities. As a result, there is much greater variation in the quality and scope of programs and services for these students.

■ Other Significant Factors

Two additional factors merit specific mention with respect to influence on educational programs for exceptional students. Each will be discussed in more detail in later chapters. The first is the influence of increasing recognition of and attention to cultural and language diversity. Such diversity demands additional attention as regards identification procedures and when planning appropriate educational interventions. In Chapter 2, we address a variety of considerations with respect to programs for students from culturally diverse populations.

A second factor, unrelated to the first, is the influence of technological advances on society, on education as a whole, and on special education in particular. There is much potential inherent in the use of interactive CD-ROM systems and computers and a variety of other computer-related programs with all students with disabilities. Researchers have developed specific technological adaptations for individuals with physical, visual, and hearing disabilities. There is the additional fact that if we are interested in meaningful posteducational

employment for students with disabilities, we must not only educate them through the use of technology, but we must educate them to effectively *use* technology themselves.

■ A Philosophy of Education for Exceptional Students

It is essential to serve the needs of students with specific, verified disabilities and those at risk. It is equally essential to meet the special needs of students who are gifted, talented, or creative. The following two statements of philosophy, and related principles, provide an overview of the beliefs of the authors, and thus the point of view from which this text has been written.

Education of Students with Disabilities and Those At Risk

Federal law and related regulations mandate programs and services for students with disabilities and those at risk, and it would appear that it is also practical and effective in the long term from an economic point of view. However, there are differences of opinion as to how, and in what setting(s), such services should be provided. We believe that it is therefore important to establish principles upon which to base such service. To this end, we have developed the following statement of philosophy and related principles.

We believe that students with disabilities, and those at risk, have the right to an education that will permit them to develop their abilities to the fullest possible extent. We believe that if the students have unique needs, educational programs should be modified and specialized to meet these needs, and that the public, tax-supported educational systems of the nation should adapt existing educational programs and services to make this possible.

We believe that educational planning should emphasize learning strengths and abilities, and that labeling according to disability should be avoided whenever possible. We believe that children and youth should be taught in regular classrooms whenever possible, but the most important consideration in *all* planning should be their ultimate educational, social, and physical well-being.

The following related principles are of great importance:

1. Collaborative efforts between regular educators and special educators are critical in both the planning and implementation of programs and services for students with special needs.
2. All individuals involved must consider differences related to language or cultural diversity in both assessment and program planning.
3. Early intervention is essential.
4. Some disabilities may be more appropriately viewed as symptoms, rather than specific disorders, and may exist at one time in life and not at another.
5. Even in the case of a specific, irreversible disability, the need for special educational services may vary from full-time, special class service at one time in a student's life to little or no service at another time.
6. A wide variety of services and the total spectrum of service delivery capabilities are essential.
7. Services for a broad age range, infancy through high school, are essential.
8. Career education and transition-related efforts are essential for many students with disabilities, and for some individuals, efforts must extend many years into adulthood.
9. A broad, flexible assessment program should include provisions for initial and ongoing assessment and formal and informal evaluation.
10. Parents must be involved in both assessment and program planning. A certain amount of involvement is required by law and regulation, but in many instances, even more involvement will be of great benefit.

Education of Students Who Are Gifted, Talented, or Creative

The states vary widely in their recognition of the special needs of gifted, talented, or creative students. Some states provide limited financial incentives, many give lip service, and some seem to reject such special provisions on the basis of elitism. States that do provide such services often do so on the basis of a single score, IQ, a practice rejected by nearly all leaders in the field of education of the gifted. The authors reject the single-score paradigm of giftedness, and support the position articulated by Piirto (1994):

The gifted, for the purposes of the schools, are those individuals who, by way of learning characteristics such as superior memory, observational powers, curiosity, creativity, and the ability to learn school-related subject matters rapidly and accurately with a minimum of drill and repetition, have a right to an education that is differentiated according to these characteristics. These children become apparent early and should be served throughout their educational lives, from preschool through college. They may or may not become producers of knowledge or makers of novelty, but their education should be such that it would give them background to become adults who do produce knowledge or make new artistic and social products. (p. 34)

The following principles will guide the implementation of this philosophy:

1. All educators must be encouraged to develop an expanded concept of giftedness, talent, and creativity; specific inservice educational efforts should target this goal.
2. All individuals involved must consider differences related to language or cultural diversity in both assessment and program planning.
3. Financial incentives for the development of special programs for students who are gifted, talented, or creative should be developed at both the state and federal levels.
4. Parents must be involved in both identification and program planning.
5. Identification should include both traditional and nontraditional assessment and both formal and informal procedures. Where appropriate, assessment should include outside "experts" in various fields of endeavor.
6. Programs should be provided from preschool through high school, and should include modified, regular class programs, separate class programs, and advanced placement programs. Programs involving acceleration should be considered viable options.

■■ Summary

In this chapter, we reviewed the historical origins of treatment of individuals with disabilities, and the educational programs that evolved out of these earlier times. Major emphasis was given developments since the mid-20th century, when parents and professional special educators began to actively advocate for more comprehensive services. The U.S. Congress passed a series of legislation, culminating with the Individuals with Disabilities Education Act (IDEA) of 1990, which mandates that school districts provide a complete range of programs and services for students with disabilities.

We discussed a variety of litigation including that leading up to the first meaningful legislation, and a great deal more that served to interpret existing legislation and stimulate the passage of additional laws. Information about the definition of special education, and the prevalence of exceptional students, and factors explaining continuing variations in the quality and scope of programs and services were also presented.

We stated this text's philosophy of education of students with disabilities and a parallel philosophy of education of students who are gifted, talented, or creative. These philosophies provide the foundation for the information included in the rest of the book.

chapter 2

- In what ways are the rights of students with disabilities different from the rights of nondisabled students? How can such differences be justified?

- What placements other than the regular classroom might be inferred by the "most appropriate, least restrictive environment"?

- In what circumstances might a residential school be an appropriate, viable placement for students with disabilities?

- Given that the IEP is not a contract in the legal sense, what is it?

- How and when must parents of students with disabilities be involved in the assessment, planning, and program implementation process?

- What are the responsibilities of regular classroom teachers in program planning and placement?

- What problems are inherent in the assessment of students from culturally diverse backgrounds? How have court decisions influenced such potential problems?

The Legislative Framework
for Services

■■■■■■■■■■■

Litigation shapes the manner in which students with special needs are served, but state and federal legislation provide the legal framework. The Individuals with Disabilities Education Act (IDEA), a federal enactment, plays a major role in shaping both the type and quality of educational services provided for children and youth with disabilities. Rehabilitation and civil rights legislation led to the Americans with Disabilities Act (ADA), which parallels IDEA in many ways. Although not an education act, ADA has considerable effect on educational planning, and

great effect on the potential success of individuals with disabilities, after they complete their formal education.

In this chapter, we outline and discuss in detail the various provisions and requirements of IDEA and other disability-related legislation and the system for provision of educational services that has evolved as a result of its implementation. We also consider education of students who are gifted, talented, or creative, and the challenge of planning and providing appropriate services when cultural and/or language differences are involved.

■■■■■■■■■■■

Significant Federal Legislation

While all legislation that influences the manner in which educational programs and services are provided to exceptional students is significant, in this review we will highlight only selected legislation. Table 2–1 summarizes various federal legislative enactments directly targeting the question of more effective, appropriate education for exceptional students. Table 2–2 summarizes federal legislation relating to rehabilitation or civil rights that impacts the rights and/or treatment of individuals with disabilities. In total, these laws have resulted in great changes in the schools, the workplace, and in the community in general. The major focus in this chapter will be the regulations related to or derived from IDEA. As will be seen, these dictate to a considerable extent how and where students with disabilities receive their education. We will also review in some detail the Americans with Disabilities Act (ADA), for it has considerable impact in relation to employment, transportation, telecommunications, and other areas of adult life. We end with a brief discussion of legislation that has encouraged more effective educational programs for students who are gifted, talented, or creative.

Individuals with Disabilities Education Act (IDEA)

The Individuals with Disabilities Education Act (IDEA) of 1990 (PL 101–476) was originally titled the Education of the Handicapped Act Amendments of 1990. It was renamed, emphasizing use of the word disabilities, in place of handicaps. It reaffirmed the earlier goals of (a) free, appropriate public education, including special education and related services, (b) guarantees of students rights and the rights of their parents, (c) assistance to the states to carry out these basic goals, and (d) establishing a means to assess and ensure the effectiveness of the efforts of the schools in meeting these basic goals.

IDEA specifically directs service to children with certain disabilities, including mental retardation, hearing impairments including deafness, speech or language impairments, visual impairments including blindness, serious emotional disturbance, orthopedic impairments, autism, traumatic brain injury, other health impairments, specific learning disabilities, deaf-blindness, or multiple disabilities. The law clearly provides for all special programs and services required by students between 3 and 21 years of age who are disabled. PL 94–142 was limited in application to children who were 3 to 5 years of age, but amendments in 1986 (PL 99–457) provided that children of 3 to 5 years of age be served, even in states that do not provide public education for other children that young. Thus, IDEA includes ages 3 to 21.

In an analysis of the law and its influences on education of children and youth with disabilities, Turnbull (1993) considers six primary principles of special education law:

1. Zero reject—the right of every child to receive an appropriate, publicly supported education
2. Nondiscriminatory evaluation—the right to an accurate, meaningful evaluation so that proper educational planning and placement may be accomplished
3. An individualized educational program (IEP) established specifically for the special needs of each student
4. Placement in the least restrictive environment that will permit an appropriate

Table 2–1
Federal legislation directly targeting education of exceptional students

Year	Legislation
1975	PL 94–142 Education for All Handicapped Children Act (EHA)—pulled together most legislative efforts that preceded it and established the principle of free, appropriate education in the least restrictive environment for all children with disabilities, parents' rights, and the right to due process, appropriate assessment and fair hearing and appeal. EHA also required that each child with a disability have an Individualized Education Program (IEP).
1978	PL 95–561 Gifted and Talented Children's Act—provided funds to state educational agencies to assist in planning and improving programs for students who are gifted and/or talented.
1983	PL 98–199 Amendments to EHA—emphasized planning for transition of secondary students and provided incentives for services for children from birth to age 3, including parent training and information centers.
1986	PL 99–457 Amendments to EHA—created new incentives for early intervention, including programs for infants and toddlers and their families. Required an Individualized Family Service Plan (IFSP) for each child/family served.
1988	PL 100–297 Amendments to EHA—Included the Jacob K. Javits Gifted and Talented Students Education Act of 1988, which reestablished federal involvement in programs for the gifted with demonstration grants, a national research center, and various national leadership activities.
1988	PL 100–407 Technology-Related Assistance for Individuals with Disabilities Act (the Tech Act)—Recognized the needs of individuals with disabilities for a wide variety of assistive technology, and assisted the states to establish programs.
1990	PL 101–392 The Carl D. Perkins Vocational and Applied Technology Education Act—required vocational education in the least restrictive environment for individuals with disabilities who need such programming.
1990	PL 101–476 Individuals with Disabilities Education Act (IDEA)—Actually an amendment to EHA, replaced the term *handicapped* with *disabilities* in EHA and earlier EHA amendments and reaffirmed EHA's requirement of a free, appropriate education. IDEA designated assistive technology a related service in IEPs, required a transition plan at least by age 16 in the IEP, and strengthened the commitment to inclusion in community schools. IDEA retained the requirement of a full continuum of placements.

Table 2–2
Rehabilitation and civil rights legislation affecting individuals with disabilities

Year	Legislation
1973	PL 93–112 The Rehabilitation Act—Section 504, commonly called the Bill of Rights for the Handicapped, provided that individuals with disabilities could not be discriminated against in any program or activity receiving federal funds. This included public housing, government jobs, public transportation, hospitals, and schools. For schools, the most relevant concerns were those of access; however, it also provided support for EHA in a wide variety of key litigation.
1990	PL 101–336 The Americans with Disabilities Act (ADA)—Extended many of the protections of the Civil Rights Act of 1964, which barred discrimination based on gender, religion, race, and national origin. It also extended, amended, and clarified Section 504 provisions of the Rehabilitation Act of 1973, and applies to private entities, whether or not they receive federal funds. It regulated public and private employment, public services, public accommodations, public and private transportation, and telecommunications, and has had an ongoing effect on awareness of the special needs of individuals with disabilities.

education—opportunity to associate with nondisabled students when possible
5. Due process of law—a system that permits parents and advocates to challenge educational planning when that seems necessary
6. Parent participation in planning and implementation of the educational program

Turnbull's first principle—the right of every child to receive an appropriate, publicly supported education—is the basic intent of all of the laws that have led to the present status of education of children with disabilities. Principles 2 to 6 provide the guidelines through which we are to accomplish the basic principle of appropriate, publicly supported education. The following sections discuss Turnbull's principles 2 to 6.

Protection in Evaluation Procedures

The various court cases that preceded the passage of IDEA established the minimum basic requirements for nonbiased, meaningful evaluation procedures. The rules and regulations for IDEA outline the following minimum evaluation procedure requirements:

State educational agencies and local education agencies (LEAs) shall ensure at a minimum, that

(a) Tests and other evaluation materials:
   (1) Are provided and administered in the child's native language or other mode of communication, unless it is clearly not feasible to do so;
   (2) Have been validated for the specific purpose for which they are used; and
   (3) Are administered by trained personnel in conformance with the instructions provided by their producer.

(b) Tests and other evaluation materials include those tailored to assess specific areas of educational need and not merely those which are designed to provide a single general intelligence quotient.

(c) Tests are selected and administered so as best to ensure that when a test is administered to a child with impaired sensory, manual, or speaking skills, the test results accurately reflect the child's aptitude or achievement level or whatever other factors the test purports to measure, rather than reflecting the child's impaired sensory, manual, or speaking skills (except where those skills are the factors which the test purports to measure).

(d) No single procedure is used as the sole criterion for determining an appropriate educational program for a child.

(e) The evaluation is made by a multidisciplinary team or group of persons, including at least one teacher or other specialist with knowledge in the area of suspected disability.

(f) The child is assessed in all areas related to the suspected disability, including, if appropriate, health, vision, hearing, social and emotional status, general intelligence, academic performance, communicative status, and motor abilities. . . .

Note: Children who have a speech or language impairment as their primary disability may not need a complete battery of assessments (e.g., psychological, physical, or adaptive behavior). However, a qualified speech-language pathologist would (1) evaluate each child with a speech or language impairment using procedures that are appropriate for the diagnosis and appraisal of speech and language impairments, and (2) if necessary, make referrals for additional assessments needed to make an appropriate placement decision. (34 CFR 300.532, 1993)

The various states have adopted regulations consistent with these minimum requirements and in many cases more specific. The federal evaluation requirements are intended as a base, and the states have made their regulations consistent in terminology with their own laws and regulations.

Individualized Education Programs (IEPs)

An individualized education program (IEP) is required for students who are identified as having a disability and who will be served through special education programs. This was initiated with the passage of PL 94–142. The original five requirements were continued in IDEA, with the addition of a sixth, a statement of needed transition services. These minimum requirements, as required by regulations, are as follows:

1. A statement of the present levels of educational performance
2. A statement of annual goals, including short-term instructional objectives
3. A statement of the specific educational services to be provided to this handicapped student and the extent to which such student will be able to participate in regular educational programs
4. The projected date for initiation and anticipated duration of such services
5. Appropriate, objective criteria and evaluation procedures and schedules for determining, on at least an annual basis, whether instructional objectives are being achieved. (*Federal Register*, August 23, 1977, p. 42491)
6. A statement of the needed transition services for students beginning no later than age 16 and annually thereafter (and, when determined appropriate for the individual, beginning at age 14 or younger), including, when appropriate, a statement of the interagency responsibilities or linkages (or both) before the student leaves the school setting. (PL 101–476, Oct. 30, 1990, 104 Stat. 1103)[1]

The IEP was designed primarily to provide instructional direction and help remedy the "cookbook" approach, as a basis for evaluation, and to encourage and facilitate improved communication among teachers,

---

[1] The transition plan is often called an Individualized Transition Plan (ITP).

other staff members, and parents (Polloway & Patton, 1993).

IEPs developed by state and local education agencies have many elements in common. Some states provide considerable guidance regarding the content of the IEPs used in local agencies within their state. However, many districts want to develop distinctive, locally oriented IEPs, and with over 33,000 local education agencies in the nation, many variations in format exist. Figure 2–1 outlines the kind of information most often found in an IEP. It is the responsibility of special educators to see that the legal requirements of the state are fulfilled; regular classroom teachers are not absolutely required by federal regulations to know the details of IEP development. On the other hand, regular classroom teachers are involved in IEP planning meetings and certainly may be involved in implementing IEPs for students with disabilities. Therefore, it is prudent for all teachers to understand the basic requirements for and the purposes of this important management tool. A careful review of the 12 basic components of an IEP should provide a basic concept of the information actual IEPs contain.

IEPs range from 2 to 10 or 12 pages, but their value is not always related to their length. It is not as much a question of length as of the nature of the information and planning provided and the degree to which the information truly reflects an *individualized* program. If assessment is planned with care, assessment tools are appropriate and administered properly, and assessment information and other related information are considered thoughtfully by professionals and parents, a meaningful program can be developed.

The IEP form—the paper on which the IEP is recorded—provides a structured format with which to record both the basis for educational deliberations and the long-range program through which teachers plan to assist the student. The format is important in that it is a reminder to consider a variety of factors and to be as specific as possible in planning. It may also be important in case of controversy, to provide evidence concerning whether school officials have followed the requirements of the law. See Table 2–3 for a list of facts and fallacies concerning IEPs.

Related Services

"Related services," which can be specified in the IEP, include the following:

1. assistive technology services
2. audiology
3. counseling services
4. early identification and assessment of disabilities in children
5. medical services
6. occupational therapy
7. parent counseling and training
8. physical therapy
9. psychological services
10. recreation
11. rehabilitation counseling services
12. school health services
13. social work services in schools
14. speech pathology
15. transportation

Each of these services is further spelled out in the regulations; for example, "transportation" includes travel to and from and between schools, travel in and around school buildings, and specialized equipment such as special or adapted buses, lifts, and ramps, as required.[2]

---

[2]The rules and regulations for IDEA and for all federal laws are not part of the actual legislation. They are guidelines for implementation, spelled out after the law is enacted and usually developed with input and assistance from professionals in the field. As such, they are also subject to modification.

1. IEP development checklist and procedural checklist.

2. Identification and background information. This should include the student's name; parents' names, address, telephone numbers; sex; birth date; and primary language.

3. IEP committee members. These should include the names and functional titles of IEP committee members.

4. Assessment information. This is all information (obtained by school personnel through formal or informal assessment procedures) that was considered in developing the IEP. This information should *always* include a definitive statement of present level of academic functioning in pertinent areas and information about nonacademic areas (such as social skills) if the information in any way applies to targeted learning problems or concerns.

5. Other information. This may include medical information, health history, information from community agencies, and historical information about school attendance and academic performance. When this information is included, the source must be fully documented.

6. Prioritized statement of goals. This is a statement of academic and social performance goals to be attained by the close of the school year and how they are to be evaluated.

7. Statement of short-term objectives. These are specific objectives, indicated on a monthly or quarterly basis. These objectives must be consistent with annual goals and should include at least the following: (a) who will provide the required services, (b) where the services will be provided, (c) special materials or media required, and (d) any special information, such as reinforcers to be used.

8. Educational services provided. Examples include occupational therapy or speech therapy services, resource room instruction, and instruction in a special vocational setting.

9. Educational placement recommendations. These should include settings (for example, resource room and regular classroom), time spent in each placement (for example, 2 hours each day in a resource room and the remainder in a regular classroom), and rationales (for example, rationales for such placement).

10. A statement of needed transition services for all students age 16 and older. This usually will include a description of interagency responsibilities and linkages. In individual cases, transition services statements may be necessary at younger ages.

11. Time frame for special services. Time frames should include significant dates, including at least (a) service initiation dates (may be different dates for different services), (b) duration of services, (c) approximate dates for evaluations, and (d) approximate dates for additional conferences when applicable.

12. Signatures. These should include IEP conference participants' or IEP developers' signatures and parents' signatures indicating acceptance or rejection of various aspects of the program.

Figure 2–1
Major components of an individualized education program (IEP)

Table 2–3
IEPs—Facts and fallacies

Commonly Accepted Fallacy	Fact
If the parent says *no* to a proposed educational plan the school has no alternative but to honor the parent's wishes.	The parent(s) must be a part of all deliberations regarding the educational programming and may say *no* to a given plan. The school may decide to go along with the parent's stand, but when this does not work out, in certain clear-cut cases, school officials have the responsibility to initiate an appeals procedure in which outside authorities are involved in final determinations about placement.
The IEP is a contract, and if the student does not reach the educational goals described in the IEP, the teacher and other school authorities may be liable to lawsuit for breaking or not living up to the contract.	The IEP is an educational management plan or tool. It does require good faith efforts to achieve the goals and objectives listed in the IEP, and the parent(s) can ask for revisions, but federal regulations specifically note that the IEP does not constitute a guarantee that the student will progress at a specified rate or achieve specific academic levels.
If a student does not reach the goals and objectives outlined in the IEP, the teacher will be blamed by the administration at teacher evaluation time.	As noted above, the IEP is recognized in the federal regulations as a plan, not a contract. The local school district can establish whatever means of teacher evaluation it deems feasible, but a strong NEA stand on this issue makes such use of the IEP highly unlikely.

The Least Restrictive Environment

Since the passage of PL 94–142, in 1975, the least restrictive environment (LRE) principle has been a matter of federal policy. Figure 2–2 provides the pertinent IDEA regulations with regard to the general LRE principle; the previous discussion of the IEP provides a more detailed consideration of the factors and variables that should be taken into account in an actual placement decision.

Very soon after the promulgation of regulations relating to the least restrictive environ-ment, various authors noted the misunderstandings the LRE concept sometimes generated. Ballard and Zettel (1977), leading advocates for students with disabilities and supporters of the LRE concept, noted that the concept of the least restrictive environment "does not mandate that all handicapped children will be educated in the regular classroom," and that "it does not abolish any particular educational environment, for instance, educational programming in a residential setting" (p. 183). Turnbull, a recognized expert legal advocate for the rights of students with

(a) Each SEA shall ensure that each public agency establishes and implements procedures that meet the requirements of §§ 300.550–300.556.

(b) Each public agency shall ensure—

(1) That to the maximum extent appropriate, children with disabilities, including children in public or private institutions or other care facilities, are educated with children who are non-disabled; and

(2) That special classes, separate schooling or other removal of children with disabilities from the regular educational environment occurs only when the nature or severity of the disability is such that education in regular classes with the use of supplementary aids and services cannot be achieved satisfactorily.

Figure 2–2
Least restrictive environment
Source: From 34 CFR 300.550 (1993).

disabilities, more recently commented as follows: "No requirement of the right-to-education movement and the federal law that codified the cases was as likely at the outset to generate as much heat as light as the requirement that children with disabilities be educated in the least restrictive placement. Given the inaccurate code name 'mainstreaming,' this requirement had the potential for encountering the same levels of opposition, misunderstanding, and ill will as the earlier constitutional and legislative/judicial requirements for racial desegregation of the public schools" (1993, p. 157). In fact, Turnbull encourages the expanded concept of "least restrictive appropriate educational place-

ment," one that is consistent with federal regulations. Fortunately, the law and related regulations provide a comprehensive set of guidelines relating to implementation of educational programs for students with disabilities, including decisions about the least restrictive appropriate placement. Fundamental to these guidelines is the right of due process of law.

The Right to Due Process

IDEA and related regulations detail precisely how the law must be implemented. Most of its legal requirements are the responsibility of local special education personnel or state officials, but certain aspects of the law and related regulations are important to regular classroom teachers. One of the more important areas is the assurance of due process in all of the proceedings involved with identifying students who require special educational services and with planning and implementing those services.

IDEA extends due process to include any matter relating to the provision of free, appropriate education and specifically provides parents the right to, and a specific procedure whereby they can present concerns or complaints. Specifically, the law requires or provides for the following:

1. Notification in writing before evaluation (in language parents can understand)
2. Parental consent before initiating evaluation
3. The right to an interpreter or translator when needed
4. A school district outline of all anticipated evaluation
5. The right of the parent to inspect all educational records

6. The right of the parent to obtain an independent evaluation
7. Written notice when a change of placement is planned or when the district refuses to make a change in placement
8. Parental consent to changes in placement
9. A specific procedure for an impartial due process hearing in cases of disagreement, including the following:
    a. The right to a specific, timely notice of hearing
    b. Limitations on who can serve as the hearing officer (to prevent bias)
    c. The right of the parents to legal counsel or other representative
    d. The right to require witnesses to attend and the right to confront and cross-examine witnesses
    e. The right to present evidence
    f. The right to appeal to the state educational agency if either party is aggrieved by the results of the first hearing
    g. The right to bring civil action if either party so desires after the state educational agency review and decision

The rules and regulations describe the provisions in detail, along with other related procedural matters.

In addition, each state is required to outline its specific regulations, which must be consistent with the requirements of IDEA. In actuality, the due process hearings provide additional protection for students in that school districts also have the right and the responsibility to appeal parental decisions that are in violation of the educational rights and needs of students; however, the fact that the law provides parents the right of due process has received most of the attention of those commenting on this aspect of the law.

Parental Consultation and Involvement

Although no major section of IDEA separately considers parental consultation and involvement, this consideration may be found throughout the regulations. We feel certain that this was a major intent of the law, as may be seen from the following provisions:

1. The native language of the parents must be used, with an interpreter or a translator provided as needed. Communications must be in the native language.
2. Parental permission is required to initiate assessment.
3. Parents must be informed about a conference in which assessment results are considered.
4. Because parents should be involved in the IEP meeting, the meeting time must be established far enough in advance to permit opportunity for parents to attend, and the meeting must be in a convenient place at a convenient time. If parents cannot attend, the public agency must use other methods to obtain parental participation (such as a conference phone call).
5. School records must be made available to parents.
6. Parents may ask for amendment of records they feel are inaccurate.
7. Parents may ask for independent evaluation of their child.
8. An involved, detailed procedure for appeals of educational decisions is pro-

vided by the law and must be fully explained to parents.

The intent of IDEA regarding parents is clear: Parents can play a significant role in the education of their children. The law and regulations guiding implementation of the law indicate rights and responsibilities. Thus, the law makes it necessary for educators to do all possible to involve parents in planning for children with special needs and demands increased sensitivity on the part of educators to the potential value of help from the parents. It does not mean that parents should dominate such planning, however. More often, it is necessary to *encourage* parents to provide information and ideas, and it is the responsibility of educators to do this. Educators must ask parents to provide information in both initial planning and continued program evaluation. This is clearly the intent of the law, and in most instances, the results have been positive, leading to better, more effective, more appropriate programs.

The Individual Family Service Plan (IFSP)

The Individual Family Service Plan (IFSP) is the early intervention parallel of the IEP. According to PL 99–457, the IFSP must include the following:

1. A statement summarizing the child's present level of development in language and speech, cognition, physical and psychosocial development, and self-help skills.
2. A statement summarizing the family's strengths and needs as they relate to enhancement of the infant's or child's development.
3. A list of major outcomes to be achieved, and the procedures planned to accomplish these outcomes. Criteria and

deadlines must be included, to permit meaningful evaluation of progress.
4. A list of intervention services required to meet the infant/toddler/child's needs, and those of the family. This must include an indication of intensity and frequency of such interventions, and how such services will be delivered.
5. Dates of initial implementation for each service and duration of service.
6. The name of the case manager who will be responsible for implementation and coordination of the plan.
7. Specific steps to be used to transfer the toddler to services provided through IDEA, if the need for services continues.

The IFSP is less formal than the IEP and is more family focused. In practice, IFSPs are more likely to be purposely written by hand, in part to emphasize this informal nature (Gearheart, Mullen, & Gearheart, 1993). The IFSP must be reviewed every 6 months, but in most cases should be reviewed more frequently. This is essential, due to the rapid developmental changes occurring in early childhood, and the fact that family needs and abilities may also change quite rapidly and unexpectedly. Early intervention programs may be home or center based, and may include a variety of intervention strategies. In all instances, assistance to the family is an important facet of such programs.

■ Planning Special Education Services

The regulations governing the implementation of IDEA establish which disabilities should be considered for special education services, define special education services, and provide

Decision making involves parents and school personnel.

guidelines regarding where such services are provided. In addition, these regulations are quite specific with respect to the assessment process, the manner in which parents and educators jointly determine whether services are required, and how and where they will be provided. In the following sections, we will consider how referrals are made, the assessment and classification process, staffing, development of the IEP, and actual placement. First, however, we discuss prereferral intervention.

Prereferral Intervention

When a teacher feels the need for assistance with a given student, after trying a number of potentially viable alternatives, it should be possible to gain assistance from colleagues in the school, so as to more adequately meet that student's needs. Such intervention or consultation takes different forms in the various states, with mandated prereferral activities, commercially published checklists, manuals, and other assistance for schools in implementing prereferral activities. The purpose of all such activities is to collect information that will help decide the next strategies to use, to attempt to solve existing problems. This procedure may involve several meetings, followed by use of newly determined strategies, followed by meetings for further evaluation and planning. Strickland and Turnbull (1990) note that a variety of formats have been established to promote the principle of prereferral. Strickland and Turnbull outline three possible models: (a) the teacher-assistance team, (b) the resource consultation model, and (c) the special education teacher as part-time consultant model. The teacher-assistance team approach involves the appointment of a group of individuals responsible for providing recommendations and strategies to be implemented by classroom teachers. In most cases, to be successful, such teams must be administratively appointed, provide release time and training, and be composed of individuals who believe in prereferral intervention. The actual makeup of such teams, which may also be called educational management teams or instructional strategies teams, varies from district to district. Such teams should have continuity, however. That is, the team composition should not change each semester.

The resource consultation model involves appointment of an individual who has a high degree of consultation skill in addition to broad knowledge of alternative educational strategies. In this model, consultation should be the primary responsibility of the resource person. As compared with teacher-assistance teams, this model has the disadvantage of becoming a one-on-one situation (teacher and consultant) as opposed to team interaction. Its strength lies in the full-time commitment of the consultant.

Special education teachers were the first prereferral intervention specialists, and they may prove every bit as effective as either of the other two resources cited. The disadvantage of this model is that the assignment often is added on to an already too-busy schedule. In addition, special education teachers may not have the necessary consultation skills.

Whatever model or combination of models is in place in a given school, the success of prereferral strategies relies on the support and belief in the process by all involved, including administrators, regular classroom teachers, and consultants or special education teachers. However, all must also recognize that prereferral strategies do not work for all students. Thus, some students must be referred for further evaluation.

Referral for Evaluation

When efforts initiated as a result of prereferral intervention are ineffective, teachers should refer students for further assessment and consideration of more specialized programming.

Such formal referrals lead to a specific sequence of procedures, which may vary from LEA to LEA. (It should be noted that referrals may also come from parents, physicians, or professionals in other community agencies.)

In most LEAs, the regular classroom teacher completes a form that has been developed for such purposes by the school district. In addition to the student's name, age, grade, and sex, most referral forms ask questions about (a) grade level in academic areas (usually, grade equivalent on a standardized achievement test), (b) data on behavior (such as relations with other students and teachers), (c) specific reading strengths and deficits (such as word attack skills, memory for words, and ability to read orally), (d) ability (relative to others in class) in class discussion and interaction, (e) specific strengths and deficits in arithmetic/mathematics, (f) strengths and weaknesses in nonacademic areas, (g) unusual family data that might be pertinent, and (h) a summary of any methods or approaches that have been unusually successful or unsuccessful for the student.

Students should be formally referred when appropriate, but overreferral should be avoided. Since parents must be contacted to gain information and obtain permission for further assessment, the matter of referral must not be approached lightly. If a student is referred when there is no need, the parents may become upset, and many people will spend time and effort needlessly.

In cases where there is an apparent (or verified) problem with hearing or vision, or where classroom adaptations are required due to physical problems, the major question is not classification of disability (although there may be multiple disabilities), but rather the best way to provide the most effective educational program, given the disability. However, whether the problem is mental retardation, behavior disorder, or learning disability, the matter of classification is important for effec-tive planning, and both schools and parents must consider the various legal requirements.

Assessment and Classification

Figure 2–3 indicates graphically what takes place after formal referral. Parents must give permission for assessment, and must be informed of their rights under due process procedures. If they give permission (and most do, if the referral is appropriate and the student's needs explained), the various parts of the interdisciplinary assessment are completed. It is important that such assessment include the elements outlined in Figure 2–3, including formal and informal assessment, health information, historical data, and information from other agencies that have worked with the child or the family. It is very important that all possible information be obtained from family members.

Assessment personnel then schedule a conference; parents must be invited and efforts must be made to encourage them to attend. If conference participants determine that a student's problems result from a disability, they then agree on a classification, and schedule an IEP meeting.

Developing the IEP

The individualized education program is developed; normally it will include the components outlined in Figure 2–1. Parents must be involved in the development of the IEP and must sign it, indicating their involvement and approval.

The content of an IEP commonly determines both the type and extent of special services provided a student and whether the student receives any services outside regular classes. Parents must approve any placement outside regular classes as well as modifications to be implemented in the regular classroom. The range of possible services that

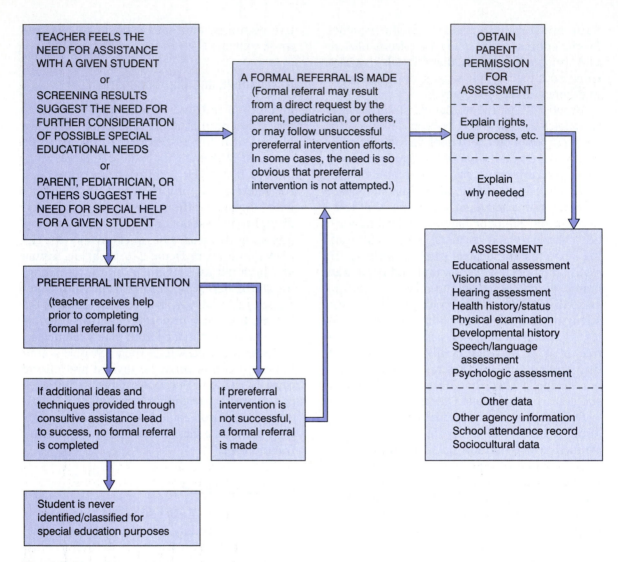

Figure 2–3
The referral assessment staffing IEP placement process
Source: Adapted from *Special education for the 80's* by B. R. Gearheart, 1980, Columbus, OH: Merrill. Copyright © 1980. Reprinted by permission of the author.

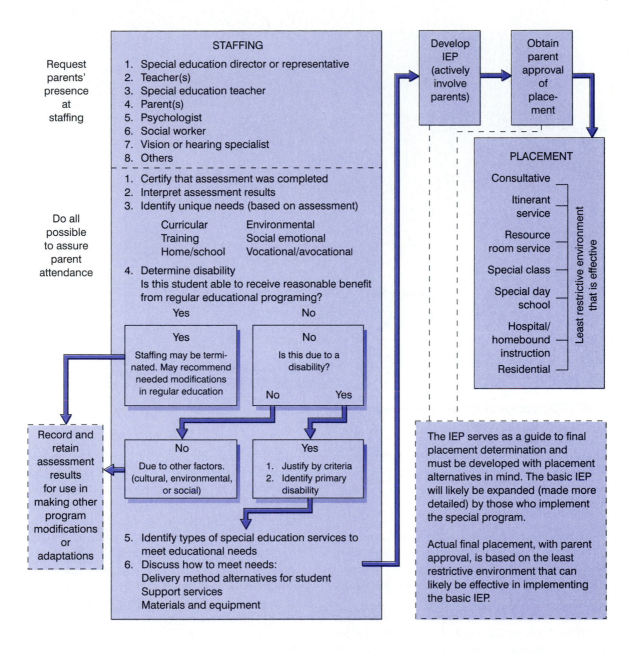

Request parents' presence at staffing

Do all possible to assure parent attendance

Record and retain assessment results for use in making other program modifications or adaptations

STAFFING

1. Special education director or representative
2. Teacher(s)
3. Special education teacher
4. Parent(s)
5. Psychologist
6. Social worker
7. Vision or hearing specialist
8. Others

1. Certify that assessment was completed
2. Interpret assessment results
3. Identify unique needs (based on assessment)

Curricular	Environmental
Training	Social emotional
Home/school	Vocational/avocational

4. Determine disability
   Is this student able to receive reasonable benefit from regular educational programing?

   Yes | No

   Yes
   Staffing may be terminated. May recommend needed modifications in regular education

   No
   Is this due to a disability?

   No | Yes

   No
   Due to other factors. (cultural, environmental, or social)

   Yes
   1. Justify by criteria
   2. Identify primary disability

5. Identify types of special education services to meet educational needs
6. Discuss how to meet needs:
   Delivery method alternatives for student
   Support services
   Materials and equipment

Develop IEP (actively involve parents)

Obtain parent approval of placement

PLACEMENT

Consultative

Itinerant service

Resource room service

Special class

Special day school

Hospital/ homebound instruction

Residential

Least restrictive environment that is effective

The IEP serves as a guide to final placement determination and must be developed with placement alternatives in mind. The basic IEP will likely be expanded (made more detailed) by those who implement the special program.

Actual final placement, with parent approval, is based on the least restrictive environment that can likely be effective in implementing the basic IEP.

Appropriate assessment is required by IDEA.

should be available to meet a student's needs is the continuum of educational services.

The Placement Decision

Determination that a student requires a specialized program should follow identification and classification of special needs. Then, a decision must be made as to where the school can best meet the student's needs.

What should be considered in making this decision? Logically enough, these variables relate to, in order of importance, the student, parents, teachers, and administration.

Students

For a student, the variables include (a) chronological age, (b) type and degree of impairment or disability, (c) age at onset of disability (congenital or acquired), (d) level of academic achievement, (e) measured intellectual ability, (f) social maturity and skills, (g) presence of multiple disabilities (need for related noneducational services), (h) ambulation or mobility (particularly when considering orthopedic and other health disabilities and visual impairment), (i) success of past and present educational programs, (j) speech and language ability, and (k) wishes of the student and the student's parents.

Parents

Before the passage of PL 94–142 and IDEA, parents were primarily passive consumers of educational services and had limited input. They were occasionally involved in program and placement decisions, but generally, they were receivers of information from professionals. For example, they were told their child would be assigned to a particular room. Today, as a result of federal legislation that came about because of parental demands and litigation, parents are participants in educational decision making. This is evidenced not only by mandatory participation in due process procedures but also by parental involvement in the development of IEPs. Such involvement may include contributing information about their child, discussing potential educational plans, and helping evaluate programs in progress.

Teachers

After preliminary placement determinations based on specific student characteristics, the next step is consideration of existing programs and services relative to the needs of a student. In most cases, some intervention by the school staff is effective. Where this is not the case, the possibility of initiating new programs or obtaining services by contract or some tuition arrangement with another school district must be considered.

There is little question that regular class teachers have major influence on the success of students. Some teachers readily accept the challenge of serving students with disabilities, whereas others have considerable difficulty making the adjustments necessary to be effective with such students. Among the most important variables are the following:

1. Professional preparation or inservice education concerning students with disabilities (not a prerequisite but highly desirable)
2. Previous experience with students who have disabilities (not a prerequisite but highly desirable)
3. Willingness to work cooperatively with resource personnel and parents (resource personnel must be readily available)

4. Willingness to accept variations in scheduling, teaching assignments, and classroom structure
5. Ability to assess individual learning needs, set goals and objectives, plan and implement teaching strategies, and evaluate student progress
6. Acceptance of the basic premise that *all* students have the right to the most appropriate education in the least restrictive environment

Administration

Administrative commitment to serve all students regardless of learning abilities or disabilities is important. Administrative staff from the superintendent to the principal must have real commitment to developing the most appropriate, least restrictive alternative.

A very high correlation exists between administrative commitment to the concept of serving students with disabilities in regular classrooms and the attitudes of teachers and students. In other words, if the principal is sincerely interested in serving all students, the commitment has a positive influence on the attitudes of teachers toward such students. If, however, the principal's attitude toward students with disabilities is essentially negative, often, teachers also exhibit this attitude. The commitment must go beyond a willingness to merely comply with federal and state regulations. It must acknowledge the inherent abilities and potential of all students.

■ A Continuum of Alternative Placements

IDEA requires that a "continuum of alternative placements be available to meet the needs of children with disabilities for special education and related services" (34 CFR 300.551). It specifies that this continuum must "include

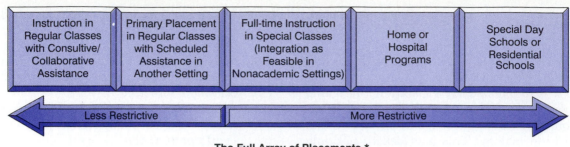

Instruction in Regular Classes with Consultive/ Collaborative Assistance	Primary Placement in Regular Classes with Scheduled Assistance in Another Setting	Full-time Instruction in Special Classes (Integration as Feasible in Nonacademic Settings)	Home or Hospital Programs	Special Day Schools or Residential Schools

Less Restrictive ← → More Restrictive

The Full Array of Placements *

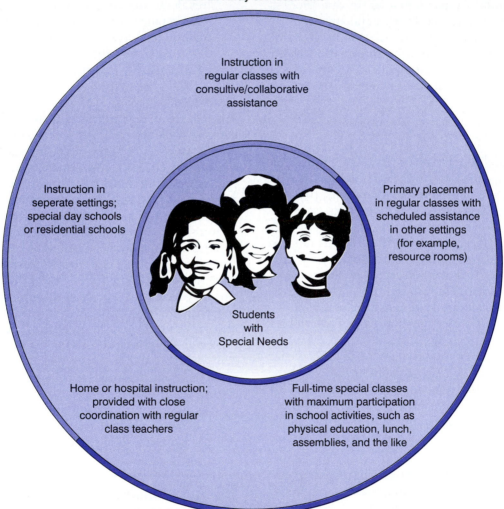

* Beginning with instruction in regular classes – at the top of the circle – each placement clockwise involves more restriction/less contact with age peers in the regular class.

Figure 2–4
A continuum of educational placements for students with disabilities

instruction in regular classes, special classes, special schools, home instruction, and instruction in hospitals and institutions." It further requires that LEAs "make provision for supplementary services (such as resource room or itinerant instruction) to be provided in conjunction with regular class placement" (34 CFR 300.550). A graphical representation of this continuum (see Figure 2–4) includes the major placement alternatives. The following discussion outlines these educational alternatives.

Instruction in Regular Classes with Consultive or Collaborative Assistance

When various prereferral intervention strategies do not provide the desired results, a student should be referred for special education assistance. When it is determined that the student is eligible for and should have such assistance, the principle of the least restrictive environment dictates that instruction in a regular classroom be the first alternative considered. This placement alternative might involve a wide combination of services. Classroom intervention may prove to be quite successful. Depending on the situation, special educators may do such things as provide special materials, assist a teacher in developing special materials, provide assistance in task analysis (leading to modified instructional ideas), develop student contracts, or in some instances, do demonstration teaching. Such assistance may be relatively indirect or direct. Whenever the regular classroom teacher can be assisted in providing appropriate instruction in a regular class setting, this is the placement of choice.

Primary Placement in Regular Classes with Regularly Scheduled Assistance in Another Setting

When a full-time program in a regular class is not effective, the next alternative to be con-

sidered is part-time assistance in a resource room or special class. The original plan for a student may be full-time instruction in a regular class (with consultive or collaborative assistance), but after a reasonable period of time, it may become clear that this is not sufficient. After reevaluation, and with the consent of the parents, part-time assistance in a resource room or special class may be implemented. In other cases, it may be evident from the beginning that this level of special assistance is required. *In all cases, remember that movement within the continuum after the original program is implemented may be necessary.* Whenever possible, such movement should be in the direction of a less restrictive setting, with a student spending more time with his or her peers; however, the major determinant must be the overall appropriateness of the educational program.

Instruction in a Special Class

Instruction in a special class may be the most appropriate, effective program for some students. This may be part-time or full-time. This is true more often in the case of severe disabilities, but even here, some time should be spent with nondisabled students in school activities such as assemblies or athletic events, or in other nonacademic areas. In each of the previous placement alternatives, the primary responsibility for a student's educational program remains with the regular class teacher, supported by the special educator in whatever manner is indicated in the IEP. In the special class alternative, the special class teacher will have the major responsibility for the student, but continuing contact between the regular class teacher and the special educator is important. Therefore, the special educator must maintain a continuing, realistic understanding of the regular class set-

Consultation among teachers leads to better programs for students.

ting and the requirements for a student to function in that setting.

Home and Hospital Programs

Home- and hospital-based programs may be provided in a variety of ways, depending on existing resources, age of the student, the special needs, and related factors. For example, programs for a homebound student may be provided via telephone or electronic hookup in which the student actually participates in class proceedings. Instruction may be provided by a full-time teacher of the homebound, or by a regular class teacher on a contract basis. In a few cases, other students may carry home assignments and materials. Then, they or a parent of the homebound student may return them.

Hospital programs may be carried out in a similar manner; however, some large hospital and children's clinic programs have teaching staffs whose members work with regular class teachers.

Special Day Schools and Residential Schools

These programs may serve students with profound hearing impairments, blindness, severe levels of mental retardation or emotional disturbance, or with multiple disabilities; however, many students with similar levels of disability are served in the regular public schools. It is possible that rural area school districts may need to contract with such programs, due to lack of local facilities and/or inability to obtain specialized service professionals. Such placements are many times alternatives of last resort, but both the law (IDEA regulations) and common sense dictate that they be available when no other alternative is effective.

Services Provided by Related Services Personnel

Earlier in this chapter we offered a list of "related services," as defined by IDEA. Some, such as transportation services, must be scheduled in conjunction with overall educational planning, so as to support and enhance the educational program. These services have minimal direct impact on instruction, other than to make it more practical or available. Other services, such as those of the speech pathologist or physical therapist, may have much greater direct impact on instruction. In this type of related service, the teacher remains continually involved, in fact becoming an integral part of the service. Still others, such as early identification services, may not be ongoing in the case of a given child, as is the case with transportation and speech/language pathology services. Other services might include assistive technology, such as a braille typewriter, counseling for an acquired missing limb, or assistance related to job preparation, provided by rehabilitation personnel at the secondary school level. Whatever the related service, such services have been found to be absolutely essential to support the basic educational program, and thus assist the student with disabilities to gain maximum benefit from special education.

Role of the Special Educator

Regular classroom teachers and special educators must plan together to meet the needs of the student. Although no major section or subsection of IDEA separately targets such collaborative efforts, this is clearly the intent of the law. For example, IDEA requires that each state have a planned, comprehensive system of personnel development that includes training for both regular and special educators. The regular class teacher must participate in IEP meetings, which are intended to be collaborative efforts. After comprehensive, appropriate assessment has been completed, school personnel must develop strategies to assist the student to develop the skills essential to success in the classroom environment (Welch & Link, 1991). This is best accomplished when it is the result of collaborative efforts on behalf of regular and special educators (Edgar & Polloway, 1994). Welch and Link (1991) suggest the use of a TASK (teacher, administrator, "stratistician," "kid") planning strategy, which requires the sharing of instructional information about the student, and joint decisions about such matters as grading (often shared grading), use of contracts, and specific instructional modifications. Polloway and Patton (1993) recommend ongoing, active inservice training, emphasizing a cooperative problem-solving approach to instructional issues. In Chapter 3, we will examine actual educational interventions growing out of such collaborative efforts. Other chapters will address the unique needs of students identified as having specific disabilities.

The process of collaboration may have been carried out in the relationship between the speech-language pathologist (SLP) and the regular classroom teacher over a longer period of time than is true with respect to any other disability. In a simple description, Polloway and Patton (1993) indicate that in this joint effort, "the SLP interacts with the general or special education teacher, who, in turn, instructs the students. Typically the (speech-language pathologist) does not provide direct language instruction to students on a regular basis, but rather in collaboration with the teacher, designs and evaluates interventions. Each person has his or her roles that are jointly determined, and each accepts responsibility for student improvement or lack of improvement" (p. 194). In this case, Polloway and Patton are referring primarily to language improvement services; the speech-language pathologist may also provide direct, one-on-one or small-group therapy on a pull-out basis. This is a good example of the manner in which special education personnel may work with some students on a direct service basis, and others through collaborative efforts with their regular teacher.

Because individualized instruction is the only effective way to reach some students with disabilities (Bateman, 1994), this will be provided by the special educator. Such instruction is often provided in a resource room setting by a teacher who may or may not be called a resource room teacher. Resource room programs vary considerably from state to state, and within states. For example, in some instances, a resource teacher may serve a student on a temporary basis while carrying out additional assessment and planning instructional strategies to be implemented primarily in the regular class.

In the more typical plan, a student spends a planned time in the resource room, receiving individual or small-group instruction consistent with his or her needs. This separate placement must be approved by the parent(s), and to be truly effective, it must include considerable communication between the resource room teacher and the regular classroom teacher. The resource room teacher must have the time, materials, and specific training required to discover effective ways to teach students with special needs. Resource room teachers have two functions: (a) to discover and initiate strategies that will help the student experience success in the resource room and (b) to develop concrete ideas that

will assist the regular classroom teacher. In addition to instruction in a resource room and collaborative consultation between the regular classroom teacher and the resource room teacher with respect to a targeted student's work in the regular class, a resource room teacher may provide unofficial assistance to other teachers to prevent the need for future special education assistance for certain children.

Students may perform in different ways or at different levels when part of a full-size class as compared to their performance in individual or small-group settings. In recognition of this possibility, a resource room teacher may work at times with students in regular classrooms. Such work permits greater insight into interventions that may be required in regular classes.

At times, a student may be assigned to a special class on a part-time basis; however, some students are in the special class full time, with limited contact with other students. Such placement alternatives must be deemed absolutely necessary by a multidisciplinary committee that makes such placement decisions. As with other placements, the parent(s) must agree and the least restrictive placement should be considered.

■ Mainstreaming and Inclusion

The term *mainstreaming* emerged and gained general usage almost immediately following the passage of Public Law 94–142 (1975); the term *inclusion* was not used until several years later. Though many educators apparently believe that their personal or school district concept of mainstreaming or inclusion is specifically mandated by PL 94–142 or its successor, IDEA, some of these concepts vary considerably. In fact, the terms do not appear in the pertinent federal laws, although the concept they represent is clearly part of this legislation. Some educators use these two terms synonymously; others are upset when they are so used. In the following discussion, we will consider mainstreaming first, because it gained popularity first.

Mainstreaming

The term *mainstreaming* is derived from the concept of retaining students with disabilities in the "mainstream" of education, rather than placing them in separate programs. Mainstreaming relates to the requirement in the law that whenever possible, the student with disabilities be educated in the school, in the classroom he or she would attend if he or she had no disability. However, the law and related regulations recognize that in some situations an alternative setting may be necessary to provide the best possible individualized educational program (see Figure 2–5). If an alternative educational setting is necessary, the school district must be able to show that the student could *not* be provided an appropriate program in the regular environment, through the use of supplementary aids and services. The law does require a continuum of alternative placements, thus recognizing the possible need to place a student somewhere other than in the home school district.

Inclusion

The term *mainstreaming* acquired various interpretations, and in general, provided more effective, advantageous educational programs for students with disabilities. However, it also led to misunderstandings, and in some few instances, disadvantageous settings and programs for some students. Eventually, various factors played a role in extending the concept of mainstreaming. One such factor was the

Regular Education Initiative (REI), which recommended a restructuring of the relationship between special education and regular education. This concept, supported by Will (1986), led to a call by some special educators to "merge" special and regular education, in effect eliminating special education as a separate entity (Stainback & Stainback, 1987). However, REI was actually proposed and led by special educators, not regular educators, as the title would seem to indicate, and did not receive significant support from regular educators. It was also questioned by some special educators (Heller & Schilit, 1987; Keogh, 1988). It did, however, help accelerate the use of the term *inclusion*.

Like mainstreaming, the concept of inclusion grew out of interpretations of the "least restrictive environment" requirement in IDEA. That aspect of IDEA clearly requires that the schools attempt to find an "inclusive" program for each child. Rogers (1993), in a discussion entitled "The Inclusion Revolution," directed primarily at non-special educators, defines inclusion as "the commitment to educate each child, to the maximum extent appropriate, in the school and classroom he or she would otherwise attend. It involves bringing the support services to the child (rather than moving the child to the services) and requires only that the child will benefit from being in the class (rather than having to keep up with the other students)" (p. 1). She then defines "full inclusion" as a term referring to "the belief that instructional practices and technological supports are presently available to accommodate all students in the schools and classsrooms they would otherwise attend if not disabled. Proponents of full inclusion tend to encourage that special education services generally be delivered in the form of training and technical assistance to 'regular' classroom teachers" (p. 2).

In their discussion of developing curriculum for inclusive classrooms, York, Doyle,

§ 300.552 Placements.

Each public agency shall ensure that:

(a) The educational placement of each child with a disability—
   (1) Is determined at least annually;
   (2) Is based on his or her IEP; and
   (3) Is as close as possible to the child's home.

(b) The various alternative placements included at § 300.551 are available to the extent necessary to implement the IEP for each child with a disability.

(c) Unless the IEP of a child with a disability requires some other arrangement, the child is educated in the school that he or she would attend if nondisabled.

(d) In selecting the LRE, consideration is given to any potential harmful effect on the child or on the quality of services that he or she needs.

(Authority: 20 U.S.C. 1412(5)(B))

NOTE: Section 300.552 includes some of the main factors that must be considered in determining the extent to which a child with a disability can be educated with children who are nondisabled. The overriding rule in this section is that placement decisions must be made on an individual basis. The section also requires each agency to have various alternative placements available in order to ensure that each child with a disability receives an education that is appropriate to his or her individual needs.

The requirements of § 300.552, as well as the other requirements of §§ 300.550–300.556, apply to all preschool children with disabilities who are entitled to receive FAPE. Public agencies that provide preschool programs for nondisabled preschool children must ensure that the requirements of § 300.552(c) are met. Public agencies that do not operate programs for nondisabled preschool children are not required to initiate such programs solely to satisfy the requirements regarding placement in the LRE embodied in §§ 300.550–300.556. For these public agencies, some alternative methods for meeting the requirements of §§ 300.550–300.556 include—

(1) Providing opportunities for the participation (even part-time) of preschool children with disabilities in other preschool programs operated by public agencies (such as Head Start);

(2) Placing children with disabilities in private school programs for nondisabled preschool children or private school preschool programs that integrate children with disabilities and nondisabled children; and

(3) Locating classes for preschool children with disabilities in regular elementary schools.

In each case the public agency must ensure that each child's placement is in the LRE in which the unique needs of that child can be met, based upon the child's IEP, and meets all of the other requirements of §§ 300.340–300.350 and §§ 300.550–300.556.

The analysis of the regulations for Section 504 of the Rehabilitation Act of 1973 (34 CFR part 104—Appendix, Paragraph 24) includes several points regarding educational placements of children with disabilities that are pertinent to this section:

1. With respect to determining proper placements, the analysis states: "it should be stressed that, where a handicapped child is so disruptive in a regular classroom that the education of other students is significantly impaired, the needs of the handicapped child cannot be met in that environment. Therefore regular placement would not be appropriate to his or her needs."

Figure 2–5
Placement guidelines provided in federal regulations*
Source: From 34 CFR 300.552 (1993).

2. With respect to placing a child with a disability in an alternate setting, the analysis states that among the factors to be considered in placing a child is the need to place the child as close to home as possible. Recipients are required to take this factor into account in making placement decisions. The parents' right to challenge the placement of their child extends not only to placement in special classes or separate schools, but also to placement in a distant school, particularly in a residential program. An equally appropriate education program may exist closer to home; and this issue may be raised by the parent under the due process provisions of this subpart.

§ 300.553 Nonacademic settings.

In providing or arranging for the provision of nonacademic and extra-curricular services and activities, including meals, recess periods, and the services and activities set forth in § 300.306, each public agency shall ensure that each child with a disability participates with nondisabled children in those services and activities to the maximum extent appropriate to the needs of that child.
(Authority: 20 U.S.C. 1412(5)(B))
NOTE: Section 300.553 is taken from a requirement in the final regulations for Section 504 of the Rehabilitation Act of 1973. With respect to this requirement, the analysis of the Section 504

Regulations includes the following statement: "[This paragraph] specifies that handicapped children must also be provided nonacademic services in as integrated a setting as possible. This requirement is especially important for children whose educational needs necessitate their being solely with other handicapped children during most of each day. To the maximum extent appropriate, children in residential settings are also to be provided opportunities for participation with other children." (34 CFR part 104—Appendix, Paragraph 24.)

§ 300.554 Children in public or private institutions.

Each SEA shall make arrangements with public and private institutions (such as a memorandum of agreement or special implementation procedures) as may be necessary to ensure that § 300.550 is effectively implemented.
(Authority: 20 U.S.C. 1412(5)(B))
NOTE: Under section 612(5)(B) of the statute, the requirement to educate children with disabilities with nondisabled children also applies to children in public and private institutions or other care facilities. Each SEA must ensure that each applicable agency and institution in the State implements this requirement. Regardless of other reasons for institutional placement, no child in an institution who is capable of education in a regular public school setting may be denied access to an education in that setting.

* *Note:* We have included these guidelines and related notes from the Code of Federal Regulations in their entirety because they are crucial to interpretations of federal directives as they relate to inclusion.

and Kronberg (1992) describe inclusion as meaning that children attend the schools they would attend if they had no disabilities, in classes with chronological age-appropriate classmates, but having the necessary special support and relevant, individualized learning objectives. They further note that "inclusion does not mean that students must spend

every minute of the school day in general education classes (no student should), that students never receive small-group or individualized instruction, or that students are in general education classes to learn the core curriculum only" (p. 2).

Rogers (1993) notes that the strength of the inclusion movement is the result of two different lines of reasoning. First, there is the belief that segregated education is inherently unequal, and thus a violation of the civil rights of children who are segregated. Second, there is the belief that many special education programs, as they have been provided, have not resulted in the expected benefits in academic, social, or vocational skills. She notes, however, that problems have developed as a result of misunderstandings of the true meaning of inclusion, and from attempts to use inclusion as a means to effect budget savings. Rogers uses as an example a school claiming to be using inclusion in which 44 second graders were "taught" science, by one teacher, through observation of a filmstrip. The group of 44 included several special education students and a group of limited English proficiency students, in addition to what would normally have been considered a large second-grade class of "regular" students. Rogers observes that this cannot be considered true inclusion, just as it could not be defended as science instruction. She believes that true inclusion is characterized by the commitment of a teaching staff to effectively accommodate the full range of individual differences among students, not simply by a set of practices or procedures. The Council for Exceptional Children (CEC) Policy on Inclusive Schools and Community Settings (1993), presented in Figure 2–6, outlines the official position of the council.

Inclusion, whether considered a concept, a philosophy, or a process, must be considered a worthwhile goal for all students with disabilities. Most of the timeworn arguments about the inability of regular class teachers to educate children with disabilities, the high cost of including some children who require special assistance to remain in the regular class, and even the disruptive effect of certain children in the regular class have been struck down by the courts. On the other hand, the courts have also supported some parental demands that local school districts pay the cost of non-inclusive education in private schools in cases when the needs of the student indicated this type of service. However, a critical aspect of the concept of inclusion is that, as stated by the CEC, "Such settings should be strengthened and supported by an infusion of specially trained personnel and other appropriate supportive practices according to the individual needs of the child" (1993, CEC Policy).

Advantages and Disadvantages of the Least Restrictive Environment/Mainstreaming/Inclusion Concept

There are few, if any, educational philosophies or constructs that do not have both advantages and disadvantages. What has happened in regular classrooms as a result of the principle of appropriate education in the least restrictive environment is no exception. Every teacher knows that an additional student with behavior problems or one requiring a good deal of additional, individualized planning and attention means a busier, perhaps more trying, school day. As one teacher said, "Too much is just too much." We agree. In fact, that is why we—and the law—have never indicated that all students with disabilities should be in regular classrooms. Yet, if this concept is properly implemented, there can be benefits to students without disabilities and to teachers.

One major advantage of educating students with disabilities in regular classrooms is that all students then have a broader range of experiences with individuals who are different from themselves. They can gain respect for and appreciation of human differences while recognizing inherent similarities. Students must be exposed to differences if they are to reach their full personal potential.

The Council for Exceptional Children (CEC) believes all children, youth, and young adults with disabilities are entitled to a free and appropriate education and/or services that lead to an adult life characterized by satisfying relations with others, independent living, productive engagement in the community, and participation in society at large. To achieve such outcomes, there must exist for all children, youth, and young adults a rich variety of early intervention, educational, and vocational program options and experiences. Access to these programs and experiences should be based on individual educational need and desired outcomes. Furthermore, students and their families or guardians, as members of the planning team, may recommend the placement, curriculum option, and the exit document to be pursued.

CEC believes that a continuum of services must be available for all children, youth, and young adults. CEC also believes that the concept of inclusion is a meaningful goal to be pursued in our schools and communities. In addition, CEC believes children, youth, and young adults with disabilities should be served whenever possible in general education classrooms in inclusive neighborhood schools and community settings. Such settings should be strengthened and supported by an infusion of specially trained personnel and other appropriate supportive practices according to the individual needs of the child.

Policy Implications

Schools. In inclusive schools, the building administrator and staff with assistance from the special education administration should be primarily responsible for the education of children, youth, and young adults with disabilities. The administrator(s) and other school personnel must have available to them appropriate support and technical assistance to enable them to fulfill their responsibilities. Leaders in state/provincial and local governments must redefine rules and regulations as necessary, and grant school personnel greater authority to make decisions regarding curriculum, materials, instructional practice, and staffing patterns. In return for greater autonomy, the school administrator and staff should establish high standards for each child and youth and should be held accountable for his or her progress toward outcomes.

Communities. Inclusive schools must be located in inclusive communities; therefore, CEC invites all educators, other professionals, and family members to work together to create early intervention, educational, and vocational programs and experiences that are collegial, inclusive, and responsive to the diversity of children, youth, and young adults. Policy makers at the highest levels of state/provincial and local government, as well as school administration, also must support inclusion in the educational reforms they espouse. Further, the policy makers should fund programs in nutrition, early intervention, health care, parent education, and other social support programs that prepare all children, youth, and young adults to do well in school. There can be no meaningful school reform, nor inclusive schools, without funding of these key prerequisites. As important, there must be interagency agreements and collaboration with local governments and business to help prepare students to assume a constructive role in an inclusive community.

Professional Development. And finally, state/provincial departments of education, local educational districts, and colleges and universities must provide high-quality preservice and continuing professional development experiences that prepare all general educators to work effectively with children, youth, and young adults representing a wide range of abilities and disabilities, experiences, cultural and linguistic backgrounds, attitudes, and expectations. Moreover, special educators should be trained with an emphasis on their roles in inclusive schools and community settings. They also must learn the importance of establishing ambitious goals for their students and of using appropriate means of monitoring the progress of children, youth, and young adults.

Figure 2–6
CEC policy on inclusive schools and community settings

Perhaps today's adults were disadvantaged to some extent because when they were in school, they did not have the opportunity to know classmates with disabilities or differences. This disadvantage may be observed in many ways. For example, why do adults today express so many misconceptions about individuals with disabilities? Could it be that they have had little opportunity to learn about such differences? Is it that they never sat next to a braille-reading classmate or a classmate in a wheelchair? If the less-than-desirable attitudes often reflected by society are an indication of lack of experience with different persons, then integrated classrooms may be of great benefit to *all* students.

There are also certain obvious advantages to teachers. Most evidence indicates that today's teachers are in general the best prepared and the most competent ever. The trend to include as part of every teacher's professional preparation specific coursework and skills or competencies for working with students who have disabilities greatly increases the ability of teachers to work with such students and special educators. After many years of separation, general and special educators are beginning to assume cooperative teaching roles. Each discipline has unique skills and competencies, and both are seeking insights and specific suggestions about how best to meet the needs of all students. Regular classroom teachers now have opportunities for cooperative learning experiences for themselves and their students, including those who present special challenges.

Teachers must have challenges to grow personally and professionally. A student with special needs presents one such challenge. We have had considerable experience with regular classroom teachers who express concern when they are informed that they will have a student with a disability in their classroom. It has been encouraging, however, to see these

same teachers grow personally and professionally, and at the end of the year, they indicate this has been one of the most exciting and challenging experiences of their teaching career. Often, such teachers ask if they may have another student with special needs the following year.

■ The Americans with Disabilities Act (ADA)

The Americans with Disabilities Act of 1990 (PL 101–476) was the logical instrument through which gains for students with disabilities were carried through to provisions for these same students after graduation, along with all other adults. Some of its provisions (for example, required accessibility to public transportation, museums, parks, etc.) have a direct influence on programs for children with disabilities. An introduction to a pamphlet describing the ADA, prepared by the Civil Rights Division of the U.S. Department of Justice and the U.S. Equal Employment Opportunity Commission, reads as follows:

Barriers to employment, transportation, public accommodations, public services, and telecommunications have imposed staggering economic and social costs on American society and have undermined our well-intentioned efforts to educate, rehabilitate, and employ individuals with disabilities. By breaking down these barriers, the Americans with Disabilities Act will enable society to benefit from the skills and talents of individuals with disabilities, will allow us all to gain from their increased purchasing power and ability to use it, and will lead to fuller, more productive lives for all Americans.

The Americans with Disabilities Act gives civil rights protections to individuals with disabilities similar to those provided to individuals on the basis of race, sex, national origin, age and religion.

It guarantees equal opportunity for individuals with disabilities in public accommodations, employment, transportation, State and local government services and telecommunications (1991).

The ADA applies to all employers with 15 or more employees, state and local governments, employment agencies, and labor unions. Details of its requirements are beyond the scope and intent of this chapter, but in summary (a) it protects against discrimination in employment, (b) it requires that employers provide specialized equipment as needed by workers with disabilities and modify facilities to make them accessible to individuals with disabilities, (c) it requires various modifications in public buildings to make them more accessible, (d) it requires at least some provision for accessibility on public transit, and (e) it includes various provisions to make telecommunication more accessible. Its provisions extend to such entities as restaurants, hotels, theaters, retail stores, libraries, parks, and museums. Private clubs and religious organizations are exempt from ADA's requirements for public accommodations. ADA was a giant step forward for individuals with disabilities in the United States.

■ Legislation and Programs for Students Who Are Gifted, Talented, or Creative

Discussion of federal legislation that has encouraged or influenced educational programs for students who are gifted, talented, or creative has been left to the end of this chapter, not because such programs are less important, but because there is little legislation to report, and it has had limited influence on the development of more effective programs for such students. In fact, even when federal legislation

provides for some recognition of the need to enhance educational opportunities for students who are gifted, talented, or creative, there is often limited follow-through on the original intent. A case in point is the establishment of the Office of Gifted and Talented in the U.S. Office of Education in 1976, and the closing of this office in 1982. Eventually this office was reopened in 1989, as the result of new legislation (the Javits Gifted and Talented Students Education Act, enacted in 1988), but this type of inconsistent recognition of the special needs of students would never have been tolerated by interested parents and advocates with respect to students with disabilities.

There are two major reasons why laws relating to the gifted, talented, and creative have had far less impact than, for example, PL 94–142 and IDEA. These reasons are that (a) federal laws relating to students with disabilities *require* expanded, appropriate programs, whereas laws relating to students who are gifted or talented merely *encourage* such programs, and (b) laws relating to students with disabilities provide massive amounts of money for programs, whereas laws relating to students who are gifted and talented provide minimal dollars that tend to be spent by state agencies, not at the local level. Only in cases where students who are gifted and talented also have disabilities (for example, students who are gifted and also blind) have PL 94–142 and IDEA directly affected students who are gifted or talented. However, they have led at least some parents of such students to pressure their legislators for better programs, an effort that has had different degrees of success in different states.

PL 91–230 (1970) mandated that the U.S. commissioner of education study the needs of gifted and talented students of the nation and report to Congress. As a result of this report (often called the Marland Report), additional attention was focused on the unmet needs of such students, and important momentum was gained. Later, federal efforts led to the development of the National/State Leadership Training Institute on the Gifted and Talented (NSLTIGT), which has played an important role in developing training programs at local and state levels and in increasing public interest in education of gifted and talented children.

PL 95–561, the Gifted and Talented Children's Act, provided a modest amount of federal financial assistance to plan, develop, and improve programs for gifted and talented children and youth. It was part of the slow but continuing encouragement from the federal level for state and local agencies to develop better opportunities for students with gifts or talents. However, it made no serious attempt to mandate appropriate programs or provide educational guarantees for students with gifts or talents parallel to the programs provided for students with disabilities.

Who, then, speaks for students who are gifted and talented? How are their educational needs met, and who governs and monitors programs established on their behalf? The laws, regulations, and policies of the states determine whether there are special programs, which students are served, the qualifications of teachers who teach such students, the percentage of the state's educational resources committed to this task, and all other related questions. Therefore, there is much variation between states. Sometimes, there is also confusing or misleading information about state practices and policies.

It is difficult to generalize about programs for students who are gifted and talented, however, the following statements reflect the current situation:

1. There has been a slow but steady increase in the number of states that had specific legislation related to education of students with gifts and talents.

2. Special reimbursement for local education agencies to provide programs for such students is apparently an incentive to some school districts (in states that provide for such reimbursement), but not to others. Therefore, reimbursement alone (as it is presently structured and funded) does not appear to be sufficient for all students who are gifted and talented.

3. Apparently, an increased number of school districts support the concept of early identification of students who are gifted or talented.

4. Definitions designed to guide identification of such students vary widely.

5. The scope and quality of programs for students who are gifted and talented vary widely.

■ An Overlying Concern: Cultural and Language Diversity

We have deliberately titled this discussion "an overlying concern" because it influences all planning for special education services when the students involved are members of culturally or linguistically diverse populations. And, although it applies in somewhat different ways to students at risk or with disabilities, and those who are gifted, talented, or creative, it does apply to both groups. Problems generated by difficulties in conducting meaningful assessment of such students were major factors in litigation that contributed to the passage of PL 94–142. These problems have not been fully addressed, and other problems remain with respect to (a) the teacher's ability to make meaningful referrals, (b) gathering background information from parents, (c) conducting meaningful parent conferences, (d) recognizing talent and abilities in students who are from culturally diverse populations, (e) developing modified curricula consistent with cultural interests, and that enhance cultural values, and (f) developing effective ways to provide special education programs that address the needs generated by the student's disability, concurrent with an effective bilingual program.

Wood (1989) lists the following major broad categories of culturally different populations in the schools: (a) Asians or Pacific Islanders, (b) African Americans, (c) Hispanics, and (d) Native Americans. We would add at least two other groups, which overlap these four categories but also include students not included in these four: (e) students from migrant families and (f) students from very low socioeconomic families, primarily from inner-city locations. We believe that the last two categories include a significant number of Anglo students whose cultural background is just as unique and who have special needs just as great as those of students who are more commonly referred to as minority students.

Artiles and Trent (1994) suggest that three theories have been used to explain why and/or how minority students often tend to fail in the school environment. One, advanced by Jensen (1969) and Murray and Herrnstein (1994), maintains that they may be inherently inferior, and that school difficulties are the result of innate deficits. We, and nearly all educators today, reject that point of view. The other two theories, however, have potential merit, and either or both may apply in many instances. One suggests that the home culture shapes behavior, learning, and cognitive styles, and that the school culture is too often oblivious of these differences. This dissonance between home and school cultures leads to problems for culturally and linguistically different children.

The second theory suggests that the school failure of many minority students can be

Friends

explained, in part, by values such as competition and evaluation, which are institutionalized in schools, reflecting the stratification of society in general. Social status in the classroom "is mutually constructed and constantly negotiated during the school day, and political differentials are an integral part of these negotiations. Examples of these transactions are the determination of status in the classroom, the degrading connotations attached to the use of other languages and dialects, and the establishment of communicative code differences to reaffirm group membership and cultural identity. The resulting dissonance in communicative processes (e.g., perceptions, assumptions, gestures, turn-taking procedures) contributes to the development of communication gaps and misunderstandings" (Artiles & Trent, 1994, p. 423). Greater awareness and further investigation of these theories may lead to more effective ways to counteract the dissonance they generate.

Collier (in Baca & Cervantes, 1989) suggests that educational planning for bilingual exceptional children consider such factors as social maturity in both the native and second culture, level of competence in both languages, and degree of acculturation and cultural identity. She also suggests that intellectual ability be measured in both languages.

The challenge involved in providing the most effective educational programs for different exceptional populations is great. Regular classroom teachers should ask for and expect assistance from special educators and other consultants in the local educational agency.

Although we attempt to avoid closing any discussion on a negative note, we feel it may be valuable to list five difficulties associated with identification and programming for students from different populations who are also suspected to have disabilities or to be gifted:

1. Given existing definitions and assessment techniques, it is possible to identify some students as mentally retarded or learning disabled when the problems relate more to cultural or language differences than to what most authorities recognize as mental retardation or learning disabilities.
2. Given existing definitions and assessment techniques, it is possible to identify some students as behaviorally disordered because of misunderstanding of cultural origins of their behavior, inappropriate assessment techniques, or a school organization that does not deal with their needs.
3. Because of the cost and bad public relations associated with mistakes in identification and placement of students from different cultural, ethnic, or lin-

guistic backgrounds, school officials may decide to not search with any real diligence among the minority populations for students in need of special services.
4. Identification procedures in existing programs for students with gifts or talents undoubtedly lead to not finding many potentially gifted or talented students among minority populations.
5. Special education programs have traditionally been viewed as ways to take care of "kids with special problems." Thus, there is a tendency to substitute special education programs for other programs to assist students who have special needs but are obviously not mentally retarded, learning disabled, or emotionally disturbed. This tendency is encouraged by the fact that programs for students with disabilities receive substantial state funding, whereas many other programs do not.

The problems associated with providing the best possible program for culturally diverse exceptional students are many, but with increased attention, more effective programs are growing in number. As a concept, cultural pluralism has been accepted by most national educational groups and much of the nation. The multicultural education program this concept demands must become part of special education.

■ Summary

In this chapter, we reviewed the significant federal legislation that has shaped the implementation of services to students with disabilities, emphasizing the major provisions of the Individuals with Disabilities Education Act

(IDEA). Central to this law is the concept of free, appropriate education in the least restrictive environment, which has led to generalized use of the terms *mainstreaming* and *inclusion*. IDEA emphasizes (a) protection in the process of evaluation, (b) the development of an individualized education plan (IEP) for each student who is to receive special education services, (c) the right to due process of law, and (d) parental consultation and involvement throughout this process. Also included is a discussion of the requirement that the school have a comprehensive continuum of placement options, to be used as required to provide an appropriate education for students with disabilities.

In this chapter, we considered the potential advantages and disadvantages of mainstreaming/inclusion, and the great need for consultation and collaboration between regular and special educators. We discussed legislative provisions for students who are gifted, talented, or creative. We ended by outlining the difficulties inherent in special education programming for students from culturally diverse and/or bilingual populations.

P A R T
two

Effective Instruction and Affective Sensitivity

Chapter 3 provides guidelines for more effective instruction that apply to all areas of exceptionality, along with suggestions more applicable to specific disabilities. In this chapter, we emphasize three stages or components of effective instruction: preparation for instruction; the actual instructional process; and monitoring and recording student performance. Chapter 4 addresses affective aspects of teaching—feelings and expectations that influence the quality of classroom interactions. In this chapter, we provide procedures and techniques for monitoring and evaluating such interactions, and suggestions for enhancing them. Chapter 4 may be the most important single chapter in the text, particularly for teachers who have not fully understood the motivational power of good personal interactions in the teaching–learning process.

chapter 3

- What are the advantages of an informally arranged classroom as compared with a traditionally arranged classroom?

- How does curriculum-based assessment differ from formal assessment?

- What are the advantages and disadvantages of learning centers?

- How do preferred learning styles influence instructional approaches?

- What are the major types of peer systems? What are the potential advantages and disadvantages of each type?

- What are advance organizers? How may they be used to facilitate the learning of students with disabilities?

- In what ways may all students profit from teacher presentation alternatives designed for students with special needs?

- What grading alternatives might be considered for use with students who have disabilities? Could these alternatives also be used with nondisabled students?

Effective Instruction

■■■■■■■■■■■

As the teacher in a classroom, you find yourself in the position of orchestrating the varied dynamics of the learning environment. Quality instruction does not just happen. Effective teaching depends on systematic planning, managing content and teaching/learning activities, and monitoring the progress of the students while meeting the needs of students with different strengths, personalities, cultural backgrounds, and attitudes. The learning and affective environment of the classroom interacts with the individual learners and the teacher and it is within this context that learning takes place. What a challenge!

Teaching practices that appear to be helpful with students with special needs are, for the most part, general practices rather than special techniques. They are simply good practices that are systematically integrated into the instructional process. In a discussion of the dramatic changes taking place in the entire educational system, Gable and Warren (1993) suggest that "the most enlightened social and educational policy is no substitute for effective instruction" (p. 1). As the teacher, you manage that instructional process.

This chapter is organized into major sections (see Figure 3–1), although they are not as separate and distinct as the figure may indicate. Certain activities we have placed in the "Before You Teach" section, such as the physical arrangement of the classroom, must remain flexible throughout the teaching/learning process. Similarly, assessment, that is, monitoring by various methods the progress of the students, may have actually begun prior to the student entering your classroom and will continue throughout the year. Information gleaned from the evaluation procedures given in "Monitoring and Recording Student Performance" may affect the methods you use as described in the "As You Teach" section; you must continually reevaluate the effectiveness of your presentation. The section on technology introduces possible ways to enhance the teaching/learning interaction. Subsequent chapters describe in more detail the varied applications of these technologies.

Before you teach	As you teach	Monitoring and recording student performance
Physical arrangement of the classroom	Maintaining student interest	Checklists and rating scales
Grouping	Principles for teaching	Graphing
Peer systems	Managing a classroom	Assessment alternatives
Learning centers	Learning styles	Grading alternatives
Scheduling	Task analysis	Mastery learning
	Collaboration	Outcome-based education
	Skills that enhance learning	
	Presentation alternatives	

Figure 3–1
Some considerations for effective instruction

■■■■■■■■■■■

■■ Before You Teach

Teachers and students learn within a framework of physical environments, schedules, and student groupings. Students with varying needs and learning styles learn through interactions with teachers, other students, and instructional methods and materials. Educators must plan and manage all of these variables to provide the best possible learning situations for students with special needs.

Planning for any student must relate to the unique needs of that student, but certain factors in the total instructional environment are likely to require adaptation, modification, or at the very least careful consideration of their effect on both teaching and learning. When teachers plan and organize well, students are more secure in the school environment, and more satisfied with their own efforts. The educational environment is a major determinant in how effectively a student learns.

Physical Arrangement of the Classroom

The teacher is able to modify and rearrange many physical aspects of the classroom. Aspects such as the size of the room, location of doors, windows, and storage cupboards or shelves are among those that the teacher cannot readily adjust. It is, however, the teacher's responsibility to recognize the effects that the physical arrangement of the classroom has on the attitudes and social behavior of the students. In addition, it is the teacher's responsibility to ensure a safe and barrier-free classroom for all students. This may affect the choice of arrangement of the desks, tables, and chairs as accommodations are made for wheelchairs, and the storage of braille materials or other special equipment necessary for some students. It may also relate to seating arrangements to prevent glare from windows or to establish proximity to

the teacher for behavioral control or more advantageous hearing or vision. Chapters 5 through 12 contain specific suggestions for the physical arrangement of the classroom to facilitate the learning of the students. This section provides more general considerations.

The arrangement of the desks, tables, and chairs should be flexible and should complement the activities of the particular lesson. Large-group arrangements are appropriate for class lectures and student or teacher presentations or demonstrations while small-group arrangements facilitate interactive and cooperative learning and hands-on activities. If space allows, it is ideal to have both small- and large-group arrangements. Figure 3–2 illustrates various arrangements of tables and desks.

The most advantageous location of the teacher and teacher's desk also depends on the various activities and on the teaching style of the teacher. Some teachers use their desk as only an area on which to store books or a place for students to put papers. They rarely sit at their desk, preferring to stand at the front of the room or to walk among the students.

Seating arrangements may affect both achievement and behavior of the students (Kellough, 1994). Low-achieving students may improve academically when seated near the front of the room, perhaps because of proximity to the teacher or to the stimuli to which they should attend. Similarly, disruptive students may improve their behavior when seated nearer the teacher and/or with well-behaved students. Students with low verbal communication can be seated across from highly verbal students to promote verbal interaction (Hendrickson & Frank, 1993; Heron & Harris, 1987; Stainback, Stainback, & Froyen, 1987).

Grouping

The physical arrangement of the desks or tables also both affects and is dependent on

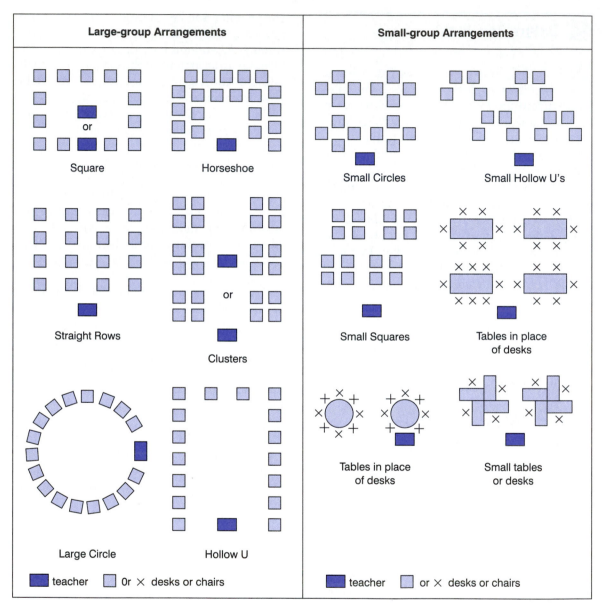

Figure 3–2
Classroom arrangements

instructional practices. Grouping for instruction should always be considered fluid because student learning rates are not static. Provisions for students to move from group to group for various reasons should be a part of the planning in the establishment of groups.

Grouping students by instructional level is probably the most common method. It is based on the desire to reduce the range of abilities by dividing a class according to learning ability, rate, and style. Students in a group are generally expected to progress through learning materials at about the same rate. Although grouping does reduce the number of students being taught at one time, it does not accommodate differing skill needs that must be addressed. An alternative to instructional-level grouping is skill-specific grouping.

Skill-specific grouping challenges teachers because it takes longer to organize initially, but once organized it more directly addresses individual student needs. In a skill-specific arrangement, students are grouped on the basis of short-term objectives established after initial testing to determine the skills needed. Group size varies depending on how many students need instruction in a specific skill. As students move from initial acquisition of a skill to mastery of it, they move on to a different group. This arrangement also allows students to interact with different peers throughout the year. Thus, students may avoid the stigma of continued placement in a low group.

With the skill-specific system, teachers develop a master list or chart of target skills. Such a list may also originate from basal material or a commercial publisher. Teachers should analyze the tasks involved with a specific skill and then provide instruction in tasks that help the student meet the designated objective. A chart or file system that cross-references students and specific skills to be developed helps a teacher know precisely what to teach next and which students to place in a particular skill group.

Instructional-level and skill-specific groupings emphasize placing students with similar abilities and skills together to form homogeneous groups. Heterogeneous grouping is another grouping procedure. It is used in certain activities, such as checking comprehension, completing social studies projects, or reviewing math. With heterogeneous grouping, students with varying abilities and skill levels are placed in the same group. Teachers may use this grouping to ask specific questions, at various levels of comprehension, about a subject the group has studied. The teacher may ask a student with low ability, "What was the main character's name?" and a student with high ability, "What would be another title for this story?" or "If you were the author, how would you have written the story?" Although the teacher should be careful not to confuse a student with low ability by presenting information that interferes with learning a new concept, heterogeneous grouping is an excellent way for students with learning problems to be a part of a different group.

Another grouping system, creating cooperative learning groups, is described in Chapter 4. Such groups encourage interaction among students with disabilities and their peers without disabilities.

Peer Systems: Buddies, Advocates, and Tutors

In peer systems, regular education students work with students who have disabilities to assist in academic learning, social learning, and the building of friendships or understanding on the part of nondisabled students. A peer buddy is one who accompanies the student with the disability during the activities of the day (Eichinger & Woltman, 1993). This role is not conceptualized as direct tutoring,

Peer tutoring is effective.

although it may involve modeling or general assistance with social behaviors.

The peer advocate system involves a nondisabled peer volunteering to assist and offer support to a student who has disabilities. This system includes such functions as accompanying the student on a shopping trip, serving as a source of information to the teacher on the conduct of the student (and others) in activities that the teacher cannot directly observe, or speaking to other students on behalf of the student with the disability. This advocacy role is more likely to be appropriate in middle school or high school, and it relates primarily to severe disabilities.

Peer tutors are students who interact with other students for some specific learning objective. Peer tutoring is not a new concept. It has been widely used with considerable success. In one-room schoolhouses, in which one teacher provided multigrade instruction, older or more able students often taught younger or

less able students in certain subjects for specific parts of the school day. The term *peer tutoring* is used here to refer to both cross-age tutoring, in which older students provide instruction to younger children, and same-age tutoring.

Peer tutoring has many benefits for both students with special learning problems and students who are achieving adequately. Often, regular classroom teachers say that they do not have sufficient time to provide the instructional assistance needed to help students with disabilities without neglecting other students in their classroom. In such cases, peer tutoring can help, if used properly.

Students with disabilities may also be peer tutors for younger children. In several programs, students with low skills have instructed younger children (Delquadri, Greenwood, Whorton, Carta, & Hall, 1986). Although there may be considerable advantage to using students with disabilities as tutors—

and we hope that teachers consider this method—the following discussion involves students with disabilities as recipients of peer tutoring.

Peer tutoring is most effective when a teacher introduces the new concepts to be learned and a tutor provides the necessary review. The teacher should maintain full responsibility for the program and monitor it by periodically observing sessions. Tutors must also report the performance of learners on a routine basis. Probably, the most common form of peer tutoring occurs when the teacher spontaneously asks one student to help another, but such assistance may or may not be helpful. Benefits are more likely to result from a carefully planned program with (a) precise instructional objectives, (b) careful selection of the tutors, (c) specific tutor training, and (d) careful pairing of the tutor and student tutored.

The selection of tutors depends on the nature of the program, the subject, and the age of the students. Teachers can choose any of the following as tutors: (a) all students who volunteer, (b) students who excel in school, (c) well-behaved students who have some academic difficulties, and (d) students who meet the criteria established for the proposed program. Students selected as tutors should have good skills in listening, prompting, modeling, and reinforcing. Above all other criteria, sincerity, genuineness, and commitment are perhaps the most important. The amount and nature of training for a tutor depend on the teacher's time, the materials available, and objectives of the tutoring program.

A teacher inexperienced in the use of peer tutoring may think that a considerable amount of time is required for training before implementation. This is often true, but careful planning usually results in significant benefits. When deciding which students to place in a tutoring program, inexperienced teachers may feel that many students need extra time and instruction. Some students, however, have needs so great that they require special assistance from the teacher, an instructional aide, or special education personnel. A peer tutoring program should not be used as a substitute for a carefully planned program delivered by a competent professional. Students who would not be good candidates to receive peer tutoring include students with severe behavior problems and students who are aware of their academic deficiencies and might openly reject assistance from peers, feeling that such assistance calls further attention to their learning difficulties.

Pairing the tutor with the student to be tutored must be carefully considered. The requirements of the program and the specific objectives influence this decision. The final decision concerning pairing is best made by a teacher who is well acquainted with the students and can predict how well they will cooperate. Of course, pairings are not final and should be changed as needed.

Learning Centers

Although there is considerable misunderstanding of the purpose and instructional usefulness of learning centers, they do provide alternatives to traditional instruction and can be organized to meet individual needs.

Although it is not our purpose to advocate learning centers for all teachers, we think that many teachers do not fully understand how learning centers can enhance teaching effectiveness and ultimately increase the performance of students. To fully understand the potential of learning centers, teachers should first identify how they view themselves. If they view themselves as disseminators of information, then they will have considerable difficulty with learning centers. If, however, teachers view themselves as orchestrators or facilitators, who serve as guides and direct learning, then they will readily understand the advantage of instructional alternatives such as learning centers.

Learning centers may be used for skill development, independent study, reinforcement, practice, followup of teacher-introduced concepts, enrichment, or substitute assignments. Following are significant advantages of learning centers:

1. They provide alternatives to pencil-and-paper seatwork.
2. They allow students to work at their own rate.
3. They provide opportunities to learn through various modes.
4. They can provide instruction in a student's preferred learning style.
5. They allow teachers time to work with other students.
6. They help develop responsibility and self-discipline through accomplishment and success.
7. They provide immediate self-evaluation.

One of the most common problems associated with learning centers is the time required to develop them. Initially, development takes extra time and effort, but once developed, learning centers may be modified easily and used in subsequent years (or at the secondary level with more than one section of the same course). Some teachers seek assistance from students in setting up special interest centers, and in some instances, students with high ability help teachers develop them. Other teachers have had considerable success with jointly establishing and sharing centers with teachers in the same grade or content area.

There are essentially four types of learning centers:

1. *Skills centers*. A skills center can include practice sheets, drill cards in mathematics, sentence completion activities, and dictionary skills.
2. *Discovery and enrichment centers*. Such a center might include science activities, brainteasers, or advanced mathematics activities.
3. *Listening centers*. Such a center may provide lessons on tape, supplemental instruction in another mode, or leisure listening.
4. *Creativity centers*. Such a center may include art, music, crafts, mathematics, or language arts activities.

A learning center has several essential components, varying, of course, depending on the objectives and topics, the age of the students, and the teacher. Each learning center should have clearly stated objectives to structure the activities. Understandable directions should specify what should be done, where and which materials should be used, and how the work is to be evaluated. Samples of student work should be provided to give additional direction and serve as motivators. If media are to be used, instruction in their use should be provided.

The teacher should be certain to introduce each center in such a way that students fully understand the directions, use of the media, the available activities, the evaluation procedures, and the return of materials. A schedule should be established to inform students when they may use the center and how many may use it at one time. There must also be a record-keeping procedure so that the teacher knows who uses the center, for what purpose, and for how long. If the teacher carefully demonstrates use of the center and periodically monitors the use, many problems may be avoided.

Some individuals believe that learning centers lack sufficient structure and may not provide enough teacher involvement to be advantageous for students with learning problems. We believe that if carefully planned and designed, learning centers can be effective, allowing students the freedom to work at their own pace and skill level while learning through a variety of sensory modalities. Although there are some disadvantages, we believe that the advantages far outweigh the disadvantages.

Scheduling

A concern of many regular classroom teachers is scheduling resource services. Students with disabilities may be required to leave regular classrooms one or more times each day to receive assistance from resource or itinerant teachers, speech or language specialists, or physical or occupational therapists. The most common problems identified by regular classroom teachers are generally related to (a) the optimum time for resource services, (b) completion of work missed while the student was in the resource program, (c) the leaving and returning of students on time, (d) the transition to and from the resource room, and (e) lack of continuity in programming.

A student who attends a resource room obviously misses some of the activities in the regular classroom. There is generally no single best time for the student to be absent, but the advantage of receiving intensive instruction or therapy for a short time outweighs the need for continuous regular classroom attendance. Therefore, the issue involves which activity should be missed. It is tempting to send a student to the resource room during noncore activities, such as art, music, or physical education. However, such activities may be the activities in which the student finds his or her greatest success. Often, a student is sent to the resource room during practice or seatwork periods, but this time may be crucial to the student's success in the regular classroom.

The relative advantages and disadvantages of missing particular regular classroom activities must be carefully weighed, and each student's needs must be considered. Of course, the scheduling needs of resource personnel must also be considered. Often, the decision of the optimum time to be absent from the regular classroom is "the least of several evils." Close communication and cooperative planning between resource personnel and the regular teacher can help alleviate this problem.

The question of whether a student should be expected to complete regular assignments made while the student was attending resource services relates to the question of the time when the student is absent. Expecting completion of a missed assignment may place an unnecessary burden on a student who already has difficulty completing assignments. This problem should also be discussed with the resource teacher.

Resource teachers and the regular classroom teachers must respect each other's schedules. Once a schedule has been agreed to by a regular teacher and resource personnel, every effort must be made to send and return the student on time. Failure to follow the schedule can be extremely frustrating to the teachers and the student and can adversely affect the quality of a student's instruction. This matter may seem trivial, but 10 minutes of tardiness multiplied by 180 school days can amount to a considerable problem for both a student and the teachers.

The movements of a student to and from a resource room should be closely supervised. Some students abuse this "free time" unless teachers take specific efforts to ensure that the students take only a minimum of time in moving between rooms. It is unreasonable for either teacher to accompany a student; thus, the student must assume this responsibility. A system of reinforcement should be used to encourage the student to be on time.

The final area of concern involves a possible discontinuity between the regular and special programs and possible disagreement about the responsibility of the resource teacher. Regular teachers may believe that resource teachers should provide tutorial help for subjects with which the student is having difficulty in their class. This may be part of the assignment, but for the most part, resource teachers must devote time to interventions directed at remediation or compensatory-skill development. This potential problem may be circumvented by close communication between the resource teacher and regular classroom teacher and an understanding of the educational objectives.

Continuity can also be accomplished by the regular classroom teacher's sending seatwork with a student to be completed during free times; however, this work must be carefully supervised so that the student does not become caught between the two teachers and their expectations. Some teachers use help notes to communicate areas requiring assistance and thereby facilitate cooperation. Help notes may be placed in the teacher's mailbox or carried by the students. Communication is essential to assure cooperation.

■ As You Teach

In the previous section, we discussed several factors you must consider prior to teaching, and that you will likely need to reconsider from time to time during the school year. This section describes additional factors that effective teachers consider while they are teaching. Some of these issues demand frequent reconsideration, such as that of a student who has little or no interest in school. Rarely will you quickly determine all of the influences related to the feelings of the student and those that

will change the attitude of the student. As you receive feedback concerning the progress of the students through the use of various monitoring systems, you will find that some modifications in the teaching and learning process will be necessary.

Maintaining Student Interest

Authorities in educational psychology disagree on many topics, but they seem to agree that motivation has considerable influence on learning. Mehring and Colson (1990) discuss three motivation theories and the implications of each. They also outline six factors associated by various authorities or in research with linkage between motivation and academic success. These factors are (a) anxiety, (b) self-concept, (c) teacher expectations, (d) the learning process, (e) the goal structure, and (f) incentives for learning.

Anxiety can have a variety of effects on learning. Highly anxious students often engage in failure-avoiding strategies because they cannot emotionally handle failure. Such efforts then take the place of efforts and attention that might lead to learning. Anxious students may not attend to many academic tasks because they are preoccupied with worry and feelings of inadequacy. They may have unusual difficulty in learning material that is not well organized, and when given a choice, may choose easier tasks (in which success is more certain) to avoid negative evaluations.

A student with low self-concept may avoid learning activities and begin a cycle of self-perpetuated failure. The problems of some students may be caused entirely by lack of good self-concept. Obviously, self-concept may be closely related to anxiety.

Chapter 4 discusses teacher expectations extensively. Such expectations are critical to learning, and they may be especially critical to students with disabilities.

The learning process has many dimensions. Mehring and Colson (1990) mention several factors in the learning process that have considerable effect on motivation: (a) interest (learner curiosity); (b) relevance, or meaningfulness, of the learning task; (c) expectancy of success (does the student feel that task is possible and under his or her control?); and (d) satisfaction. As discussed in Mehring and Colson, goal structure refers to three basic structures: (a) cooperative, (b) competitive, and (c) individualistic. It is important to note, "All three goal structures are effective under certain conditions and are relevant to specific goals and objectives of a lesson" (p. 7).

Incentives for learning certainly affect motivation, and teachers must plan incentives with individual students in mind. Intrinsic interest may be sufficient, but extrinsic rewards are often necessary, particularly when a student has a history of failure. Too many external rewards, however, may undermine or reduce the likelihood of building natural interest in the subject under consideration.

Occasionally, a student's failure may result more from instructional methods than from inadequate skills on the part of the student. Therefore, teachers should watch for opportunities to provide success. Success may be encouraged, for example, by decreasing the amount of written work required, making certain that language or other assignments are on the appropriate reading level, encouraging group projects, allowing students to choose from among a variety of carefully planned activities, using learning contracts, or other techniques.

Fernald (1943) worked with students who had experienced considerable academic difficulty and systematically planned positive reconditioning before actually starting a remedial program. She described four conditions to carefully avoid:

1. Avoid calling attention to emotionally loaded situations.
2. Avoid using methods that experience suggests are unlikely to be effective.
3. Avoid conditions that may cause embarrassment.
4. Avoid directing attention to what the student cannot do.

These principles can be applied to almost all remedial situations, and they are particularly important for a student who has failed many times over a period of several years.

In addition to these specific suggestions, teachers should question their teaching methods to increase the likelihood of their students meeting with success. For instance:

1. Do I emphasize and build on the student's strengths rather than weaknesses?
2. Do I ask the student to perform tasks that are clearly too difficult for him or her to perform?
3. Do I systematically plan for small increments of successful performance?
4. Do I permit my students to make mistakes?
5. Do I provide genuine feedback?
6. Do I look for positive rather than negative aspects of a student's work?
7. Do I provide a sufficient amount of assistance and encouragement to students with learning problems?
8. Do I take special opportunities to provide positive reinforcement?
9. Do I structure honest experiences of success for my students?
10. Do I identify areas of the student's interest and capitalize on them?
11. Do I allow low-achieving students to perform tasks given to high-achieving students?

Another dimension of providing success is to encourage students to assume responsibility for succeeding. Often, students who have experienced considerable failure blame external factors for their difficulties. Students must be taught that they have much control over their own success or failure. They must enter into learning activities believing they will be successful. Joint planning between teachers and students can greatly assist students in understanding that they *can* achieve and be successful. Contracting, for example, gives students responsibility for succeeding, and realistically established contracts, with input from the teacher, may give students opportunities to assume responsibility and achieve much-needed success. As students achieve success, they gain confidence and come to view themselves as successful. "Nothing succeeds like success" should be the motto of every teacher.

The authors of most basic educational psychology texts provide lists of techniques to promote motivation. Curriculum guides provided by various major public school districts include suggestions based on what educational psychologists have said and the personal experience of consultants. The list in Figure 3–3 is a composite from the above sources, plus the experience of the authors. The most important thing to remember is to regularly consider and plan for motivation-building activities as part of the teaching–learning process.

Principles for Teaching

The general guidelines that follow are adapted from recommendations provided by Wallace and Kauffman (1986). They provide a yardstick against which teachers may measure their own teaching strategies and procedures. The first five principles are sequential; that is, teachers should start at principle 1 in planning instruction for students with disabilities and continue with principles 2, 3, 4, and 5 in the

sequence given. Principles 6 and 7 are general, applying throughout the teaching process.

1. *Base initial teaching strategies on assessment information.* This objective means more than the use of test results obtained by a psychologist or educational diagnostician. It includes the results of careful observation, tests given by the teacher, information from school records and parents, and all other available sources. The goal is to establish an overall picture of the student, which will provide a beginning point for planning instructional strategies.

2. *State instructional goals and specific performance objectives and allocate sufficient time to carry them out.* Appropriate goals providing general parameters for instructional planning should come first. Specific instructional objectives, stated in terms of student performance, should follow. In some cases, subobjectives must be added. The purpose is to know where we are heading and to have a means to determine the extent to which we have achieved what we are trying to accomplish. This strategy is important in the education of all students but is particularly important with students with learning problems.[1]

3. *Analyze the student's performance of specific tasks to pinpoint learning problems more precisely.* Careful analysis of the manner in which a student completes learning tasks permits more precise information as to what the student can and cannot do. Error analysis provides guidance as to what must be

---

[1]Specific performance objectives may not be regularly used by regular educators, but the IEP may require them, and they are essential to plan effectively for instruction for students with special needs.

Figure 3–3

Planning to enhance motivation

1. Determine what motivates, and then, initiate a lesson by providing a reason to be motivated.

2. Specify exactly what should be accomplished. Establish clear, specific goals in the simplest possible terms.

3. Relate new learnings to past learnings.

4. Be certain that students are at the proper level of readiness for what they are about to undertake.

5. Make every effort to make learning relevant to students. Use familiar materials in examples.

6. Use humor, suspense, and exploration to arouse and maintain curiosity.

7. Do the novel, unusual, or unexpected at times. Be somewhat unpredictable, but not in a manner that is inconsistent with goal achievement.

8. Use praise, both verbal and written. Look for actions or accomplishments to praise.

9. Use a variety of teaching techniques, such as games, simulations, and group projects. Remain alert to the possibility that some techniques may require special adaptations for students with disabilities.

10. Carefully monitor student responses. Be ready and willing to adjust both type and rate of instruction.

11. Set objectives that challenge but do not intimidate.

12. Show respect for both effort and accomplishment.

13. Speak of what you expect students to do or learn in a positive way. Indicate expectation of success.

14. Avoid trick questions or questions that might be interpreted as punishment. Ask questions to find out what students know, not what they do *not* know.

15. Suspend judgment when students respond to questions. Use exploratory questioning and obtain responses from various members of a group.

16. Use positive reinforcement.

17. Maintain your role as teacher (that's your professional responsibility), but whenever possible, also be a friend.

taught next. Analysis may lead to modification of initial plans or may verify them. In any event, it is an essential step in the instructional process.

4. *Present a new set of tasks, designed to help the student overcome performance deficits.* In expanding on this step in the process, Wallace and Kauffman (1986) suggest the following: (a) organize tasks for efficient presentation, (b) be directive—tell, don't ask, (c) get student attention before attempting to start the task, (d) provide sufficient time for student response, (e) if the student does not respond, repeat and simplify the directions given, (f) cue responses (with a word, gesture, or other signal), (g) use prompts, (h) provide a model for the student to follow, (i) present only those tasks essential to the concept being taught, (j) present tasks in logical sequence, and (k) provide opportunity for practice until mastery is achieved.

5. *Provide feedback on task performance.* Such feedback should be unambiguous, immediate, and corrective (reinforce correct responses, which should reduce incorrect responses).

6. *Structure the learning environment for success.* Later sections of this chapter will provide more information on this topic.

7. *Monitor student performance and keep records of progress.* This objective would include keeping a log of teaching activities, maintaining a chart of student progress, and testing what is being taught. Though such record keeping does take time, we believe it may *save* time, in the long run, for those one or two students who may be having significant difficulties.[2]

---

[2]Abbreviated and adapted from *Teaching Students with Learning and Behavior Problems*, 3d ed. (pp. 126–147) by G. Wallace and J. Kauffman, 1986, Englewood Cliffs, NJ: Prentice Hall/Merrill. Used with permission of Prentice Hall Publishing Company.

Managing a Classroom

McDaniel (1986) compiled a list of 10 principles for teachers who want to "modify their own behaviors in ways that will yield effective group management and control" (pp. 63–67). Briefly consider McDaniel's list (which was meant for all teachers, not only those of exceptional students). It is an excellent compilation of principles that McDaniel aptly describes as "traditional and modern, practical and theoretical, pedagogical and psychological" (p. 63):

1. *Focusing.* If you do not have the attention of students, little learning will take place. Trying to teach over the noise of students who are talking to each other or running around the room is essentially useless. To maximize learning, focus the attention of the students on the learning activities.

2. *Direct instruction.* Tell the students what to do, how to do it, and when it should be done. To *keep* students on task, consider topic interest, relevance, and individual needs.

3. *Monitoring.* Monitoring means regular, planned checking to see what students are doing and whether they need assistance or encouragement. It is student accountability, and as students learn they are accountable, classroom control is more easily achieved.

4. *Modeling.* McDaniel emphasizes modeling with respect to using a soft, low-pitched voice, and suggests that soft reprimands (for example) keep a problem private and discourage loud denials or protests. This point is particularly important with students who are frustrated or those with behavior disorders, who have low tolerance for criticism.

5. *Cueing.* As discussed by McDaniel, cues are nonverbal reminders of rules or expectations. Cues may involve facial expressions, raising one's hand,

pointing, or clearing one's throat. Some cueing is done automatically, without deliberate planning. Other cueing must be learned, and students must learn what cues mean. It is possible that students with learning disabilities or below-average intelligence will have more difficulty with cues than the rest of a class, and some direct instruction regarding the meaning of specific nonverbal reminders may be required.

6. *Environmental control*. Grouping, scheduling, organization of classroom furniture, and noise control are examples of environmental control.

7. *Low-profile intervention*. This involves intervening to prevent trouble, catching off-task behavior before it becomes a serious problem, and other, less direct kinds of intervention. This principle overlaps, and is consistent with, principles 3–5.

8. *Assertive discipline*. Chapter 11 discusses this principle in some detail.

9. *I-messages*. McDaniel points out that there are at least two different types of *I*-messages. For the assertive-discipline advocate, it is a matter of indicating that "I want you to _____ " or some such absolutely clear message regarding your expectation. For the humanistic-discipline advocate, the *I*-message principle suggests that you communicate how the student's behavior affects you. It is a matter of communication of feelings. The *I*-message principle requires teachers to communicate clearly and consistently.

10. *Positive reinforcement*. This principle is much discussed in the popular press and is applicable in various realms of life. See Chapter 11 for further discussion.

McDaniel's 10 principles provide a starting point for the development of better classroom discipline (control) and are valuable as applied to teaching exceptional students. Various aspects of these principles are woven into the fabric of much of the remainder of this text.

Common Learning and Behavioral Problems

Throughout this text, we emphasize that many factors contribute to poor student performance in school. Among the more common are educational materials, the environment, the teacher, and the peer group. At times, however, the primary problem involves the student. This section identifies several student-centered problems that interfere with performance. Among the more common problems are limited attention to tasks, negative school attitudes, minimal reading ability, poor comprehension, poor written expressive ability, high rate of absenteeism, withdrawn or passive behavior, unusually high activity level, and failure orientation. Although these characteristics apply to students, we believe that teachers can greatly reduce the effects of these behaviors and problems by offering specific alternatives to students who have these difficulties. The following suggestions are viable alternatives.

Limited Attention to Academic Tasks

Many students have a relatively short attention span, appear to be disinterested, demonstrate poor organizational ability, and fail to see the relevance of subjects. These characteristics may be related to a variety of causes, but the following teaching techniques may be of value:

1. Show the relevance of the subject to the student's life.
2. Teach the student the following listening formula:
   a. Focus your attention on the speaker.
   b. Ask yourself what you should be learning from the speaker.
   c. Listen carefully and attempt to relate what the speaker is saying to

what you already know about the topic.

d. Review in a way that works best for you, such as discussion with a classmate or reading.

3. Consider contracting with the student to provide structure and reinforcement.
4. Use outlining to divide tasks into small units.
5. Give short, sequential assignments, one at a time, as they are completed.
6. Use high-interest materials.
7. Pair the student with a peer who can stay on the task for a longer time.
8. Provide immediate feedback on work completed.
9. Provide systematic rewards, such as free time or special interest projects (reading, listening to tapes, photography).
10. Change activities frequently. Know when to accelerate or decelerate assignments and activities.

Negative School Attitude

A negative attitude may result because a student perceives the subject matter as irrelevant or to disguise an inability to succeed. Often, students who have experienced considerable failure in school attempt to compensate for their failure through consistent noninvolvement. The following suggestions may help overcome such an attitude:

1. Provide alternative assignments. Relate the alternative assignments to the content of the course while focusing on the interests of the student. For example, if the primary assignment for a unit of study concerning the Civil War is to describe the major battle sites, a possible alternative for a student interested in automobiles or transportation might be to describe how supplies were transported to battle sites. For a student

interested in music, an alternative assignment might be to describe the influence of music on the morale of soldiers during the Civil War.
2. Provide for small successes and attainable goals.
3. Teach to the personal interests of students.
4. Incorporate relevant information into instruction.
5. Find areas in which students can experience success and capitalize on them.
6. Look for areas in which students feel good about themselves, such as music, drama, or athletics, and advocate increased involvement in those areas by contacting the music teacher, coach, or other teacher to generate interest. Follow through by reinforcing the student.
7. Arrange brief conferences with students to listen to their problems and communicate that you care about them.
8. Conduct an open class discussion with various students to identify why they do or do not like school. As other students mention positive aspects, an apathetic student may discover or realize similar interests.

Minimal Reading Ability

Many students have difficulty with reading. The following suggestions may help overcome this difficulty:

1. Minimize tedious reading assignments.
2. Be certain that the students understand the purpose of reading assignments.
3. Divide large assignments into small assignments.
4. Use topical outlines, advanced organizers, and glossaries.
5. Use few timed tests and tightly timed assignments, or provide additional time.

6. Tell the students in advance about an interesting part of the reading and ask them to find it.
7. Maintain a chart that shows reading progress.
8. Consider tape-recorded materials and presentations using other media.
9. Provide summaries of key concepts to be read.
10. Consider peer teaching and group projects.

Poor Comprehension

Many students have difficulty comprehending what they read or hear. The following suggestions may help overcome this difficulty:

1. Provide direct instruction in needed areas.
2. Provide a summary before directed reading.
3. Divide assignments and tasks into small parts.
4. Control the number of verbal directions.
5. Alternate activities.
6. Maintain realistic performance expectations.

Poor Written Expression

Many students have difficulty expressing themselves in writing. The following suggestions may help overcome this difficulty:

1. Attempt to change a student's attitude by providing experiences that lead to success in writing.
2. Initially encourage a student's productivity—not structure, spelling, grammar, punctuation, or capitalization.
3. Provide free-writing opportunities in which students select their own topics. Ask them to write as much as they can for 10 minutes, encouraging them *not* to stop or correct.

4. Consider nonverbal and dramatic activities before writing. Discuss these activities before the students write about them.
5. Provide a wide range of interesting writing topics, such as firsthand experiences, unusual pictures, films, or music.
6. Encourage each student to keep a personal diary or journal.
7. Provide opportunities for the students to record their ideas on a tape and to hear the tape played back before they begin to write.
8. Have the students write captions for cartoons related to something of interest.

High Rate of Absenteeism

For various reasons, many students miss school frequently. The following suggestions may help overcome this difficulty:

1. Be willing to negotiate makeup work.
2. Reinforce good attendance with appropriate rewards.
3. When a student returns after an absence, attempt to involve him or her immediately in class activities.
4. Meet with students and discuss with them the reasons for their high rate of absenteeism.
5. Contact parents and attempt to work closely with them.
6. Make classroom activities interesting and relevant.

Withdrawn or Passive Behavior

For various reasons, many students refuse to take an active part in class. The following suggestions may help overcome this difficulty:

1. Provide opportunities for self-expression through drama or role playing that involves aggressive or assertive roles.

2. Structure group participation to emphasize the strengths of withdrawn or passive students.
3. Reward participation in group activities or projects.
4. Try to become aware of the students' interests and develop conversations and projects around these interests.
5. Put the students in charge of special projects, such as preparing lab materials, taking roll, and handing out and collecting materials.

Unusually High Activity Level

Unusually active students may have difficulty in a classroom environment. The following suggestions may help overcome this difficulty:

1. Discuss with the student the release of tension and restlessness and agree on appropriate outlets.
2. Allow the student to move around, sharpen a pencil, or get a drink when necessary.
3. Send the student on errands.
4. Establish short-term goals and shorten assignments.
5. Provide a change of activity to help focus the student's attention.
6. Reward accomplishments frequently and as soon as possible.
7. Build expectations gradually.
8. Be aware of tension as it is building and provide assistance or a change of pace.
9. Do not accept destructive actions.

Failure Orientation

Some students are so accustomed to failure that they expect it. The following suggestions may help overcome this difficulty:

1. Discuss with the student what he or she needs to do to function well in the classroom.

2. Work out a success plan to help the student cope with problems.
3. Be committed to continue with or change plans, but not to give up.
4. Try to accept and understand the student's feelings without being overly judgmental.
5. Reinforce small successes.
6. Help the student achieve self-discipline and self-control.
7. Deal with immediate problems and mutually work out short-range plans.
8. Formulate realistic expectations.
9. Assist the student in coping with failure.

Inappropriate Behavior

An often verbalized concern about teaching students with special needs is managing inappropriate behavior. Some teachers appear to have few problems in this arena, but others seem to have many. Kameenui and Simmons (1990) believe that teachers must not interpret the various individual acts or elements of a student's behavior as independent, isolated, or neutral events. They emphasize that teachers must interpret behavior in relation to the context in which it occurs. They agree that teachers must maintain order to teach effectively but suggest that teachers think of all behavior as providing potentially valuable information. A student's behavior can be viewed as communication; the question is whether the teacher is able to interpret what the student is saying.

Consistent with this point of view, Kameenui and Simmons (1990) suggest five assumptions designed to provide teachers with a "foundation for managing children within the broader context of instruction" (p. 471):

1. A child's inappropriate behavior is not random or evil.
2. Inappropriate behaviors are learned and predictable.

3. A learner's inappropriate behavior is the learner's best effort to be intelligent.
4. There is no place for ridicule or humiliation of children in the process of managing behaviors.
5. A teacher's mere presence influences how children behave.

Teachers must work to attain and maintain order and structure in their classrooms. They must manage student behavior so as to maximize student learning. When teachers are asked what factors most contribute to successful classroom learning, they tend to mention such qualities as teacher's open and honest communication, knowledge of subject matter, sincere interest in and caring about young people, enthusiasm, and consistency. The quality most frequently mentioned is consistency. Clear expectations for the students, carefully planned classroom rules and procedures, and natural consequences are closely related to consistency. Unquestionably, the teacher is the most critical influence on classroom atmosphere, and the degree of consistency in a classroom depends on the teacher. When the teacher establishes certain expectations for performance and behavior, both the students and the teacher must adhere to them. Posting these expectations or writing them on the chalkboard can provide continuity. The teacher should also allow students to discuss and possibly modify these expectations so that they may feel some ownership, but when the expectations are finally established, they must be followed by everyone.

Learning Styles

Learning styles are the ways "in which *each* learner begins to concentrate on, process, and retain new and difficult information" (Dunn & Dunn, 1992, p. 2). Everyone has their own multidimensional characteristics that determine what will most likely attract and maintain their concentration, engaging their own processing style so that these efforts result in learning. Each student has a learning style that differs from that of his or her peers, and teachers need to be aware of these unique styles. Dunn and Dunn group factors influencing an individual's learning style into five major areas: (a) immediate environment, (b) own emotionality, (c) sociological preferences, (d) physiological characteristics, and (e) processing inclinations.

Environmental elements have different effects on students. Noise is important in terms of a student's ability to tolerate sounds while learning. Some students are able to block out extraneous noises, whereas others may need a quiet environment. Lighting may also affect students in different ways—some students prefer a brightly lit area, whereas others prefer subdued light. Some students prefer an easy chair when tackling a difficult learning task, whereas others prefer a straight-back chair and desk. Although teachers may not be able to modify all aspects of the environment significantly, they should consider its effects. If a student's difficulty seems to be related to an environmental problem, attempts should be made to adapt or modify conditions as necessary.

Elements in the emotional realm include persistence, motivation, responsibility for learning, and need for structure. Some students need well-defined guidelines and structure, whereas others are more creative and respond better when given considerable freedom in carrying out assignments. Teachers should recognize these elements and make adjustments to accommodate each student's needs.

The sociological dimension involves the ability of a student to learn from or with others. Some students prefer to work alone, but others choose to work in pairs, in small groups, or with an adult. Few prefer to work

There are many ways to learn.

the same way all of the time. Therefore teachers should consider varying their instructional approaches to fit individual learning styles and preferences.

Elements in the physical dimension include a student's best time of day for active involvement and learning (early birds or night owls), mobility needs (to move or change positions), and preferred perceptual strengths. Students vary considerably in the ways that they learn. Some students learn better by listening to a teacher (auditory learners). Other students prefer to read or see the material (visual learners), and still others learn more readily by touching and interacting with the material (tactile and kinesthetic learners).

Processing inclinations relate to the student's preference for sequential presentations of information that lead to an understanding of a concept or for a more global understanding first with later examination of the details. They also may relate to the primary use of the right or left side of the brain. This possibility is raised by cognitive theories that suggest different hemispheres of the brain have different functions (Dunn & Dunn, 1992). According

to such theories, verbal and sequential abilities tend to be associated with the left hemisphere while emotions and spatial processing inclinations are associated with the right hemisphere.

Nearly all students learn better when they are actively involved in the instructional process and are using all of their senses. This multisensory learning approach is preferable to a more limited sensory approach such as lecturing. If it is not practical to offer multisensory instruction, it is often advantageous to present new material through a student's strongest perceptual mode while reinforcing through the other senses. By teaching to a student's strength, the teacher can increase the student's attention, success, and achievement, whereas focusing on the student's weakest perceptual mode may have the opposite effect.

Teachers can assess student learning styles by using a questionnaire (see Figure 3–4). The questionnaire may be administered orally in a personal interview with one student at a time or be given to a small group of students. The statements on the questionnaire should be short, direct, and simply stated. Teachers may add other statements to learn the preferred general learning climates of students.

To assess a student's perceptual strengths, the teacher should observe the student's behaviors. Visual learners may close their eyes or look at the ceiling when they try to recall a visual image or picture. Auditory learners may subvocalize or move their lips when they are attempting to memorize information. Tactile or kinesthetic learners may use their fingers to count off items or write in the air with their fingers. Analysis of these behaviors is subjective, of course, and such behaviors may or may not indicate preferred learning style. However, observation at least provides preliminary information on which the teacher may base continued observation and assessment.

Another informal assessment procedure that may provide insight into the perceptual strengths and preferred learning styles of students involves presentation of three lists of words and numbers as follows:

1. Tell the students that you will give them a test to determine whether they are visual, auditory, or tactile-kinesthetic learners.
2. Write a list of five to seven words on the blackboard while the students are watching. Use everyday words, such as *toothpaste, soap, salt, comb*, and *milk* (the number of words you should use depends on the age of the students).
3. Allow the students to view the list of words for approximately one minute.

	True	False
Environmental Statements		
1. I like to have it quiet when I'm working.	☐	☐
2. I work best when there is a little noise in the classroom.	☐	☐
3. I prefer rock music in the background when I am studying.	☐	☐
4. Music of any kind makes it difficult for me to work.	☐	☐
5. I can study when people are talking.	☐	☐
6. I prefer bright light when studying.	☐	☐
7. I learn best in the morning.	☐	☐
8. I learn best in the afternoon.	☐	☐
9. I like to study while sitting in a comfortable chair.	☐	☐
Emotional and Social Statements		
1. I prefer to work with the teacher.	☐	☐
2. I learn best when I work alone.	☐	☐
3. I need specific rules and directions about what I should do.	☐	☐
4. I prefer to work in a small group.	☐	☐
5. I prefer to work in a traditional instructional situation.	☐	☐
6. I like to work with one friend.	☐	☐
7. I need a lot of reinforcement to complete a task.	☐	☐
8. I have a lot of difficulty completing assignments.	☐	☐

Figure 3–4

Questionnaire to assess preferred learning styles

4. Erase the list, and then ask the students to write down the words.

5. Ask for a volunteer to repeat the list of words. Volunteering may be an additional indication of strong visual learners.

6. Ask the students to score their papers.

7. Dictate orally a different list of similar words, such as *automobiles, bicycles, birds, pencil, paper,* and *shoes.* Dictate the list a second time; neither you nor the students should be writing at this time. Then, ask the students to write down the words.

8. Use the same process of correction you did as with the written presentation in steps 5 and 6.

9. Dictate a different list of words of approximately the same length and ask the students to write the words while you are dictating them. When you are finished dictating, ask the students to copy the list; they may look at their initial lists if they wish. Next, ask them to turn their papers over and rewrite the words from memory. Follow the correction procedures used with both earlier lists.

10. Repeat all nine of these steps using a series of numbers, such as 8, 6, 4, 3, and 9, instead of words. Present the numbers visually, auditorily, and tactile-kinesthetically.

When this process is completed, ask the students to total their scores of the word and number parts for each of the three tests. Explain to the students that there may be some relationship between their scores on the three types of tests and the ways they learn. Teachers who observe definite patterns may want to note these observations for future planning. This informal method is for general assessment of students' preferred learning styles and is not intended to be precise, but an informal assessment such as this may provide insight into the reasons that some students perform better in some situations than in others. Dunn and Dunn (1992) describe more formal assessment procedures.

The characteristics of learning styles apply to gifted students as well as students with learning problems. Research has indicated that students who are gifted differ in their learning styles from their peers who are not gifted (Yong & McIntyre, 1992). A high percentage of students who are gifted appear to prefer a tactile-kinesthetic learning style to auditory learning. Additional research has indicated that there are also differences in the learning preferences of gifted students who are from diverse backgrounds (Dean, Salend, & Taylor, 1993). For example, gifted African American students seem to prefer a visual learning modality while gifted Mexican American students prefer a kinesthetic modality.

This information suggests that teachers must consider the learning styles of all the students, those who have been identified as gifted, those from diverse cultures, those with learning or behavior problems and those who appear not to "fit" any of these categories.

Task Analysis

Task analysis is the process of dividing various academic tasks into smaller steps. The steps then become separate objectives. Many teachers routinely use this approach without thinking of it as task analysis and without actually writing the subparts.

Task analysis is based on the assumption that a student may not be able to accomplish a given task or assignment because of an inability to accomplish one or more of its parts. The following nonacademic analogy roughly illustrates this concept. A person has a flat tire on an automobile trip. Like some individuals, this individual has difficulty changing the flat tire to resume the trip. Is it sufficient to simply state that the person cannot change the flat tire? No, it is more helpful to analyze the necessary steps of the tire change to determine the actual problem. Does the person know how to use the jack? Should the person loosen the nuts on the wheel before or after using the jack? Is the automobile on a level surface? Is the problem related to the spare tire?

The process of changing an automobile tire may be divided into several steps. To be able to change a tire, one must understand each of the steps that must be taken and the order in which they must be taken. In total, these steps make up the task of changing the tire. A

lack of ability in or understanding of just one of these steps may make it impossible for the person to change the tire and resume the trip.

Nearly every learning situation can be divided into as many components as necessary to understand the whole. The essential subskills are identified and taught to allow completion of the larger task or assignment. The goal or task may be a portion of the regular curriculum of the students, or it may be from the student's IEP (see Figure 3–5).

Task analysis may help teachers identify (a) what steps are necessary to accomplish the targeted task, (b) where students are having difficulty with a task, (c) what should be taught next, and (d) what adaptations may assist students with task accomplishment

Figure 3–5
Example of a goal and objectives

Goal: Jana will improve her accuracy and rate in computing addition problems that involve regrouping.

Objectives:

1. Jana will write the answers to addition fact problems with sums from 1 to 10 on a worksheet with 100% accuracy.

2. Jana will write the answers to addition fact problems with sums from 1 to 10 on a worksheet with 100% accuracy and at the rate of 35 per minute.

3. Jana will write the answers to two-digit plus one-digit (13 + 5) problems without regrouping addition problems on a worksheet with 100% accuracy at the rate of 40 per minute. (Objectives such as this can be subdivided into one related to accuracy and another related to rate.)

4. Jana will write answers to two-digit plus one-digit problems with regrouping (12 + 8) on a worksheet with 100% accuracy at the rate of 35 per minute.

5. Jana will write answers to two-digit plus two-digit (12 + 11) problems without regrouping on a worksheet with no errors.

6. Jana will write answers to addition problems with regrouping on a worksheet with no errors at the rate of 35 per minute.

7. Jana will write the answers to real-life problems involving addition, such as adding the cumulative mileage of a trip, while maintaining accuracy and maintaining or improving rate.

(Bigge, 1991). As mentioned, many teachers routinely use this approach to instruction without thinking of it as task analysis. Good teachers continually use an analytic or diagnostic approach to instruction to enhance the success of both the students and themselves.

Collaboration

As mentioned in Chapter 2, the collaborative efforts of regular classroom teachers, frequently the student, special education teachers, and other personnel such as physical therapists, physical education teachers, media specialists, or paraprofessionals are imperative if students with disabilities are to receive the services necessary for effective learning (Simpson, Whelan, & Zabel, 1993; Nowacek, 1992). This group focuses their attention on a problem and jointly works together to solve it. The collaborative team may consist of only the classroom teacher and the special education teacher and their meetings may be very informal, but the goal is the same. When the collaborative team is larger, the meetings may follow a more structured procedure so as to make the most efficient use of the time available, usually involving the following steps:

1. Problem analysis—This includes a definition of the problem, information regarding when and where the problem occurs, environmental factors that may relate to the problem, and other pertinent data. All members share information and reach consensus on the major issues to be addressed.
2. Generation of interventions—Team members brainstorm possible interventions or solutions to the problem and evaluate them. The team then agrees on the order in which approved ideas will be implemented, setting specific goals, objectives, timelines, and criteria

for determining if the problem has been solved. The team determines roles and responsibilities of its members.
3. Implementation—The agreed-upon interventions are implemented by the personnel responsible (this may include the student).
4. Evaluation and Follow Up—At the designated time, or earlier if any team member feels the need, the team meets to discuss the effectiveness of the interventions. The interventions may be discontinued because the problem no longer exists, continued with modifications, or completely changed. Other problems may be selected from the prioritized list. When new ones are proposed, the team follows previous steps (Sugai & Tindal, 1993; West & Idol, 1990).

The key to a successful collaborative approach is the equal empowerment of each of the team members. The group must reach consensus regarding the problem, interventions, and clear evaluation procedures consistent with the expertise of each member. An atmosphere of mutual trust and professionalism must pervade the meetings if they are to be effective (Morsink & Lenk, 1992; Field, LeRoy, & Rivera, 1994).

Collaborative or team teaching is an outgrowth of the collaboration among teachers to solve learning and behavior problems. The special education teacher and the regular class teacher jointly teach the instructional program in the regular classroom. Each teacher's areas of expertise are employed in the teaching/learning process. The teachers involved in collaborative teaching meet first to clarify roles and then regularly to develop joint lesson plans. The teaching roles and responsibilities may vary day to day depending on the objectives of the lesson. The students see cooperative efforts modeled and benefit from having two adults in the room. The principles of equal empowerment of each teacher with respect for the expertise of each apply in such an arrangement (White & White, 1992; Lowenthal, 1992; Reeve & Hallahan, 1994).

Each of the chapters in Part Three contain additional suggestions concerning how the regular class teacher and the special education teacher may work together for the benefit of the student.

Skills that Enhance Learning

The following skills relating to self-management, listening, systematic plans for studying, preparation for examinations, and critical thinking are important, but are not the only skills that enhance learning. In subsequent chapters we offer examples of additional skills and suggestions for how to teach them.

Self-Management Skills

Academic achievement appears to be closely related to self-management skills. Students with good self-management skills tend to do well in school, to persist with assignments, to seek assistance from teachers and peers when appropriate, and feel better about themselves (Carter, 1993). Many low-achieving students, however, do not have the self-management skills that are obvious prerequisites to learning. When given a task, low-achieving students tend to use their poor organizational strategies consistently regardless of whether they are effective. In other words, they impulsively and hurriedly complete the assignment without the prerequisite organization. Students who do not possess the necessary self-management skills must be taught how to search for useful information, order this data, and organize it for learning and retention.

An environment that encourages students to develop self-management skills generally results in greater independence, increased task completion, and ultimately greater achievement. Teachers should be alert for students who do not have the necessary organizational strategies and should provide specific instruction in this area.

When assisting a student who does not have self-management skills, the teacher must serve as a model, actually demonstrating the skill. The teacher should talk while the student watches the strategy. The teacher should identify a series of steps (organizational skills) through which to proceed. Then, the teacher should ask the student to perform the task while instructing himself or herself aloud with assistance from the teacher. The student should verbally follow the steps with statements such as, "First, I must do this, and then this, and this." In the next step, the student should perform the task, still speaking aloud but without assistance from the teacher. In the next step, the student should whisper to himself or herself the necessary tasks. In the final step, the student should subvocalize the tasks. Essential to the success of teaching self-management skills are (a) teacher modeling through talking, (b) student self-talk, and (c) praise from the teacher.

Listening Skills

Assisting students in the development of listening skills may be one of the most overlooked areas in planning for students with special needs. Reading and written expression are major areas of curriculum. Often, a teacher first recognizes that a student (who may be later identified as having a learning disability or mild mental retardation) has special needs as a result of lack of achievement in reading or written expression. Standardized achievement tests attempt to measure achievement in various aspects of reading or written expression, and teachers assign grades or provide other types of evaluation with respect to reading and written expression, but they often overlook listening.

Why is listening important? Listening is the foundation of all of the other language arts. Language arts authorities suggest that in most school programs, more classroom time is spent listening than in any other activity. According to Rakes and Choate (1989): "Through listening activities, students build language skills, expand vocabularies, enrich experiences, learn concepts, understand the mechanics for specific tasks, develop readiness skills for particular lessons, appreciate the joys of spoken and written language, and even relax. Listening is a set of learned skills, incidentally acquired by some students but mastered only through direct instruction by many" (p. 30).

Measurement of listening skills is best accomplished through nonstandardized measures, for example, some variations of informal reading inventories (IRIs). Many standardized tests do not even attempt to measure listening skills. Although measuring listening skills is not so simple as measuring other skills, teachers can learn to look for indications of underdeveloped listening skills, use informal means to verify their existence, and then proceed to help students listen more efficiently. One of the more obvious descriptions of poor listeners is "inattentive." Another is "distractible." Yet, many students with poor listening skills are not so easily recognized.

Rakes and Choate provide a simplified format for determining if students have special listening needs and a series of practical suggestions for remediation in the classroom. In addition to the more typical focus on attention and recognition of auditory stimuli and auditory memory (following directions, remembering general information, recalling in sequence, and listening critically), they suggest a listening area that is not always a major concern of educators. This area, auditory appreciation, relates to skills involved in comfortable listening as well as interactions with other people and good literature.

Wallace, Cohen, and Polloway (1987) believe that "although listening is the most used language arts skill, it is the least taught skill. Teachers assume that children listen, and that if speaking is taught, listening will follow" (p. 67). Wood (1989) believes listening is a skill that must be taught and many slow students prefer to learn from listening rather than from reading. If this is the case, then listening skills are unusually important to many students with special needs.

Since listening skills provide much of the basis for reading and the other language arts, and a great deal of formal school time is spent in listening activities, evaluation of the listening skills of students with special needs and planned listening activities (when indicated) are essential, as is an awareness of the importance of listening skills. See Figure 3–6 for a recorded guided activity to promote listening skills.

Study Skills

Many, perhaps most, students with learning problems have not developed all of the study skills necessary for success in the academic setting. Some school districts are so convinced of the need to systematically teach study skills that they have initiated systemwide programs as part of secondary school mainstreaming. Smith and Smith (1989) provide a description of such a program in the Mesa, Arizona, schools. This program involves a teacher training phase, a synchronized teaching phase, and a followup phase. The training phase includes inservice sessions on multisensory teaching, alternative teaching strategies, note-taking skills, organization and time management, memory skills, listening skills, reading in content areas, vocabulary development, and test taking. The synchronized teaching schedule divides the school year into one-month periods, emphasizing skills one at a time and reinforcing them in classwork

Figure 3–6

A recorded guided activity to promote listening skills

1. Prerecord a lesson involving information new to the class and pertinent to topics that you will read or discuss in the near future in the instructional sequence. Adjust the time and length of the recording for the grade level.

2. Tell the students that they must listen carefully, remembering all they can about the lesson.

3. After playing the audiotape, ask the students to tell what they heard. Write their contributions on the board as the students give them with no comments by or questions from you.

4. Direct the students to listen for additions and corrections and play the audiotape again.

5. Make additions and corrections on the board as necessary.

6. Ask the students to organize the information on the board into some logical sequence and to indicate the major parts and subparts of the presentation. Establish some type of outline (number and letter designations) for this purpose.

7. Ask the class for ideas of how you might have organized and presented this information to make it easier to understand and remember.

8. Conclude the lesson with a discussion of the total lesson. Target the information and concepts that you wish to emphasize.

when possible. This prevents confusion that might result from trying to learn too many skills at one time and provides maximum reinforcement of new learning. The followup phase provides evaluation of effectiveness and helps teachers incorporate instruction of study skills into their specific content areas.

Whatever the approach to teaching study skills to students with special needs and whether regular classroom teachers or special educators teach the skills, they should assess the skills informally to make students aware of and responsible for their study patterns. Teachers may construct an easily administered checklist or questionnaire of study skills (see Figure 3–7). After students complete the questionnaire, discuss the answers. The objective of this activity is to provide information to each student about his or her study skills and

general classroom behavior so that both student and teacher can develop a plan of specific strategies to enhance the skills. Students must understand their desirable and undesirable behaviors and assume responsibility for them.

Teachers may need to take time to teach some of the essential skills related to their subject areas, including time scheduling, note taking, and outlining. Encourage students to use index cards to record their assignments, and check these cards periodically to make necessary revisions. Teachers may also find it necessary to use outlines and advance organizers to give students structure for note taking. Additional skills include using the dictionary and reviewing reading materials.

The question of what should be considered study skills is open to differences in interpretation, but authorities agree that study skills

	Almost always	Sometimes	Never
1. Do you listen to directions or instructions provided in class?	☐	☐	☐
2. Do you take notes regarding assignments?	☐	☐	☐
3. Do you ask questions when you don't understand?	☐	☐	☐
4. Do you pay attention to class lectures and discussions?	☐	☐	☐
5. Do you keep up with assigned readings?	☐	☐	☐
6. Do you feel disorganized most of the time?	☐	☐	☐
7. Do you participate in class discussions?	☐	☐	☐
8. Do you find it difficult to complete assignments in class?	☐	☐	☐
9. Do you feel adequately prepared most of the time?	☐	☐	☐
10. Do you find the vocabulary too difficult?	☐	☐	☐

Figure 3–7
Questionnaire to help teachers assess study skills

are important and may require direct instruction. Hoover (1988) has written a book on teaching study skills to students with disabilities. Other authors, such as Devine (1987), have developed texts that relate specifically to teaching study skills, but they target all students. Hoover and Devine accept a broad interpretation of study skills, while Sheinker and Sheinker (1989) emphasize skimming, summarizing, note taking, and outlining.

Preparation for Examinations
In addition to not having adequate study skills, many students with learning problems do not have good skills in preparing for and taking examinations. Teachers may want to provide direction and instruction in this area with some of the following suggested methods:

1. Help students understand examination directions and terms such as *define, list, compare, contrast,* and *defend.*

2. Teach students to watch for cue words, such as *never, all,* and *always.*
3. Tell students what you expect. Is your emphasis content, organization, spelling, grammar, mechanics, or creative expression?
4. Provide students with a copy of a previous test, talk about it, and use it as a teaching tool.
5. With objective tests, encourage students to read all questions carefully and answer first the questions whose answers they know immediately. Then, students may consider more carefully the remaining questions.
6. With essay examinations, encourage students to outline their answers before writing.
7. Encourage students to answer all questions unless there is a penalty for incorrect answers.
8. Encourage students to write clearly and distinctly.

9. Encourage students to leave sufficient time to reread their answers, paying attention to such things as punctuation and spelling.

Some of these suggestions are not appropriate for all courses, but these methods generally provide students with the assistance they need to be more successful when taking examinations.

Critical Thinking Skills

A major objective in planning for students with special needs is to help them improve their thinking skills. Development of study skills involves critical thinking skills, but study skills represent just one specific type of thinking. The focus here is a need to plan activities that promote the development of thinking skills, emphasizing activities that work for students with special needs.

Tiedt, Carlson, Howard, and Watanabe (1989) introduce certain assumptions for teaching critical thinking. These assumptions relate to learning through language skills (listening, speaking, reading, and writing) and include the following: (a) children want to learn, (b) children learn more effectively when self-motivated, (c) children learn from each other (they do not require adult instruction), (d) children naturally apply discovery methods, making and testing hypotheses as they learn language, and (e) children like to play with language, showing both humor and creativity. In a discussion of thinking as a major goal of education, Costa (1987) observes: "Many educators are forming a new understanding of what is a basic skill. We are realizing that there is a prerequisite to the 'basics'—the ability to think" (p. 17).

McTighe (1987) suggests teaching *for* thinking, *of* thinking, and *about* thinking. In teaching *for* thinking, he recommends a variety of questioning techniques, including those requiring basic recall: (a) interpretation, and (b) judgment, hypothesizing, or analogical reasoning. In addition, he suggests "interpretive reading and discussion, writing, laboratory experiments, problem solving, debates, simulations" (p. 26). McTighe believes that the previous activities provide opportunities to practice thinking. To McTighe, teaching *of* thinking means direct instruction that can help students develop specific thinking skills, for example, how to compare. To teach comparing (or any thinking skill), first define the skill and illustrate it in simple examples that are familiar to all students. One emphasis might be that comparisons involve finding similarities and differences. Then, develop a series of steps to use when comparing in the class setting and outline them on the board. After it is certain that all students understand how to apply these steps in simple comparisons (such as comparing a football to a basketball or an automobile to an airplane), present a lesson that involves more complex comparisons and help the class work through these comparisons. For example, after studying the Civil War and the Revolutionary War, compare the two. In working through such comparisons in class, involve all students. Devise a similar procedure for whatever thinking skills you want to target.

The third approach suggested by McTighe, teaching *about* thinking, involves helping students develop metacognitive abilities (discussed in more detail in Chapter 10). Such abilities are also a part of the recommendations made by Sheinker and Sheinker (1989).

There is a resurgence of interest in the direct teaching of thinking skills, and such teaching works with students who have special needs. Such instruction can take place in a group setting where students with special needs learn cooperatively with other students. We suggest the following two books on this topic: (a) *Teaching Thinking in K–12 Class-*

rooms: Ideas, Activities, and Resources (1989) by Tiedt, Carlson, Howard, and Watanabe and (b) *Thinking Skills Instruction: Concepts and Techniques* (1987) by Heiman and Slomianko, editors.

Presentation Alternatives

Teachers should systematically consider alternative ways of providing meaningful instruction. The following suggestions are relatively easy to implement and do not require substantial time. They effectively promote teacher enthusiasm while providing an effective instructional environment.

Study Guides

A study guide may provide direction for students with learning problems and should be of some value to all students. A guide can include statements of objectives, assignment requirements, suggested readings or media to be used, and evaluation criteria used in the course. It can provide direction regarding time, resources, and peer teaching opportunities. Learning contracts can be established in combination with a guide. A teacher and a small group of capable students can develop a study guide cooperatively and then share it. Once developed, a study guide may be used in subsequent courses.

Topic Outlines

A topic outline is less formal than a study guide and takes less time to develop, so a topic outline can be considered a condensed study guide. It provides a general flow of course content and may help students organize their lecture notes. Like a study guide, a topic outline can be developed by students.

Technical Vocabularies and Glossaries

Technical vocabularies or glossaries can be tremendous aids for nearly all students. Effec-

tively used, they may eliminate many of the problems resulting from inability to understand the content of a lecture because students do not understand the vocabulary. These aids can be used in peer teaching and tutoring situations. Alternatively, vocabulary information can be tape recorded and made available. A technical vocabulary or glossary may be written, typed, or recorded by students.

Advance Organizers

Advance organizers are easy to develop with a minimum of teacher time. An example of an advance organizer is an outline of key points or topics to be learned. Another example is presentation of questions to students before presentation or independent study of the material. Advance organizers give direction and structure and tell students what is important.

Summaries

A summary is an overview in one or two paragraphs about a topic. It may be provided in advance to clearly establish the importance of the concepts to be studied. Alternately, many teachers assign a section of a chapter or unit of study and ask the students to summarize their findings, sharing this summary in turn with other groups who have similarly prepared summaries. Different summaries may be assigned to individuals who then collectively overview the lesson. Students who have difficulty with detailed reading may be required only to develop a list of key words or concepts.

Media

Tape recordings of portions of a textbook or chapter summaries may be helpful for students who have reading problems. A tape or multimedia presentation may also be developed to overview a course or specific units of study. Naturally, commercially available films and media can also be used. More capable individual students or a group of students may help develop media presentations. School district or building media specialists are often pleased to assist in the development of media presentations.

Special Texts

Although special modified or adapted texts are generally not popular with students, some individuals may profit from their use. An abridged text is one alternative. Another alternative is a distillation of the material in key concepts or a two- to three-page chapter synopsis. The preparation of such abstracts can be excellent training for academically advanced students in a class.

Alternative Responding

Typically, students respond with written reports, oral presentations, and examination answers. Alternatives include tape-recorded responses, drawings, and peer interpretations of examinations and recording of responses.

Modified Lectures

Many teachers have found that suspending a lecture after a specified time encourages independence and responsibility by students. Students may then be assigned group projects related to the topic being studied. After completing the projects, each group may provide a report to the rest of the class.

■■ Monitoring and Reporting Student Performance

The performance of students can be monitored and recorded in many ways, including anecdotal records, grades, test scores or rankings, numerical values, charts, and graphs. At times, recording student performance may be considered informal assessment. Although frequently of less value in determining what to teach, more formal testing is also a means of monitoring and reporting student progress. Unfortunately, too often the monitoring and recording of achievement or other progress culminates in little more than a letter grade or number recorded in a book. The teacher assumes that the grade is what the student "gets" and the student assumes that is what the teacher "gave."

A monitoring system provides important information about general performance and skill development and direction for program modification. The modification can be more teacher oriented (for example, modifying the style of presentation) or it may involve a discussion with the student to determine the modifications he or she may need to make. Often, teachers think they do not have enough time to use precise measurement systems. However, they may use other approaches, such as the assistance of volunteers, parents, paraprofessionals, older students in another grade (such as members of Future Teachers of America), peers, or the students themselves. Student self-monitoring can provide considerable reinforcement, meaning, and purpose to learning activities.

Checklists and Rating Scales

Checklists and rating scales may be used to document progress toward objectives or the achievement of the objectives. In its simplest form, a *checklist* lists descriptors and the informant marks a yes or no column indicating the presence or absence of the descriptor. The descriptors may be detailed or global depending on the purpose of the checklist. Figure 3–8 is an example of a brief checklist and, in Chapter 11, Figures 11–1 and 11–2 are examples of checklists of behavioral descriptors.

A *rating scale* is also a list of descriptors; the informant indicates agreement or disagreement with predetermined statements

Figure 3–8
A brief checklist of study skills

Study Skill	Yes	No
Schedules time for study		
Estimates time needed for long-term assignments		
Takes notes in class		
Uses active listening strategies in lecture classes		

regarding the descriptor. Figure 3–9 provides examples of two brief rating scales using different types of ratings. A rating scale provides more information than a checklist and usually requires more judgment on the part of the informant.

Checklists and rating scales are useful for keeping records of the accomplishment of specific objectives or of progress toward the objectives. They may also serve as a basis for discussion with students or with parents during conferences. Asking students to rate themselves provides the teacher with information regarding the student's insight into his or her own development.

Graphing

Graphing is an example of a potentially useful recording system. Without such a visual chart the teacher may not be fully aware of the value of any given new approach to instruction and practice (See Figure 3–10). In this instance, the chart provides feedback that assists the teacher in evaluating the new approach. It should be noted that such a recording system might have indicated that the new approach resulted in more spelling errors and it would be important to know this, too. Measurement and charting procedures are particularly helpful for students with behavior disorders.

Assessment Alternatives

In most cases, teachers have little difficulty in identifying students who have learning problems. Specifying a problem, however, may be more difficult because of overlapping problems. The basic difficulty may be intellectual, social, or emotional, or it may be the result of inadequate instruction, lack of opportunity to learn, or some combination of factors. Through a combination of formal and informal assessment, teachers can more precisely define the nature of the problems and determine procedures to assist the student in the learning process.

Norm referenced assessment involves the use of tests in which a large representative sample of the population has been tested and becomes the "norm group" (Gearheart & Gearheart, 1990). Norm referenced tests are used to compare an individual with the norm group. The individual being assessed through the use of a norm referenced test must be similar to the norm group in age, grade, primary language, geographic region (south, north, urban, rural, etc.), economic background, and other salient factors if the comparison is to be of value. Norm referenced tests may be used for initial screening of students, determination of eligibility for services, general measures of progress, and to provide a broad description of comparison with other students. Such measures do not provide

Study Skill	1 Always	2 Sometimes	3 Never

Schedules time for study
Estimates time needed for long-term
  assignments
Takes notes in class
Uses active listening strategies in
  lecture classes			

Study Skill	Agree	Not sure	Disagree

Knows how to schedule time for study
Estimates time needed for long-term
  assignments
Takes notes in class
Uses active listening strategies during
  lecture classes			

Figure 3–9
Brief rating scales using different types of rating

teachers with the type of information required for instructional planning (Stiggins, 1994; Mercer & Mercer, 1993).

Criterion referenced assessment involves measurement that compares a student's level of mastery of specific aspects of the curriculum. Criterion referenced tests are not designed to compare a student with others but to determine mastery of skills. A criterion referenced test might indicate, for example, that a student is able to add and subtract three-digit math problems but is not able to multiply them. This type of information assists the teacher in selecting the next objectives and often provides a more meaningful vehicle for communication between teachers, parents and teachers, and students and teachers. It also illustrates the progress or lack of progress of the student (Wiggins, 1993; Shriner, Ysseldyke, & Thurlow, 1994).

Curriculum-based assessment is informal assessment directly related to classroom curriculum. Salvia and Hughes (1990) effectively state the rationale for curriculum-based assessment: "The fundamental problem with using published tests is the . . . content. If the content of a test—even content prepared by experts—does not match the content that is taught, the test is useless for evaluating what a student has learned from school instruction" (p. 8). The eight steps in the Salvia and Hughes curriculum-based assessment model are (a) specify reasons for assessment, (b) analyze curriculum, (c) formulate behavioral objectives, (d) develop appropriate assessment procedures, (e) collect data, (f) summarize data, (g) display data, and (h) intrepret data and make decisions. As conceptualized by Salvia and Hughes, the steps in this model are both interactive and dynamic. That is, decisions at any one step

Figure 3–10
Student performance recording system

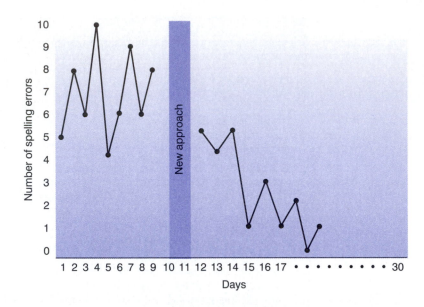

may affect decisions at other steps, and decisions may be modified as instruction and continuing assessment take place.

In its most simplified form, curriculum-based assessment might include the following steps:

1. List skills in targeted material, making certain that all essential skills are listed.
2. Arrange skills in logical order.
3. Develop a written objective for each skill listed.
4. Develop items and prepare materials to test for each objective.
5. Give the test as a pretest, before teaching the targeted material.
6. Evaluate pretest results. Determine which students have already mastered which skills and whether teaching of prerequisite skills is required. (The question of prerequisite skills may have to be further investigated before proceeding.)
7. Initiate instruction, based on information obtained in step 6.

8. After completion of instruction, readminister the test to determine which students have mastered which skills.
9. Modify instruction as indicated, and repeat the procedure.

Anecdotal records are another form of informal assessment for identifying problems. Anecdotal records help teachers clarify the events leading to behavioral or learning problems by providing factual descriptions of events. A factual record should describe (a) the antecedent (the event that occurred immediately before the behavior), (b) the behavior (quoting the student and using action verbs), and (c) the consequences of the behavior. In describing behavior, teachers should attempt to use quantitative statements. It may not be sufficient to state, "He is always out of his seat" or "He never turns in his assignments." Preferred statements are "During a 50-minute period, he was out of his seat four times" or "During the last 3 weeks he turned in only two of the nine assignments."

Anecdotal records are commonly used to describe disruptive student behavior and can help teachers analyze more accurately what is actually happening. Often, teachers develop anecdotal records before discussing a problem with a resource person or school counselor.

Interviews are assessment techniques that enable the teacher to learn the student's perspective. The steps in interviewing are (a) establish rapport by being sincere and honest and showing interest; (b) present reasons for the interview; (c) formulate open-ended questions, avoiding questions calling for only a *yes* or *no* response; (d) listen to the student in an accepting environment to gain information and insight into the problem, rather than offer suggestions or point out what you think is wrong; and (e) terminate the interview with a goal or a plan of action. Preferably, the plan should be established by the student with the teacher's input, including an agreed time when the student and teacher can meet again to modify or evaluate the plan.

Portfolios have been used by artists and photographers to provide others with examples of their work. Portfolios for students are similar in that they are collections or examples of the student's work. The work included in a portfolio may have been evaluated and reworked by the student, may be work in progress, or both. An organized collection of a student's work is more personal than other types of assessment and is a natural outcome of whole language and process writing methodology, thematic math and science, and collaborative or cooperative learning (Feuer & Fulton, 1993). The creation of the portfolio requires the student to be actively engaged in the evaluation process rather than passively accepting grades "given" by teachers.

Teacher observations may also be part of the documentation included in a portfolio. Such observations may be anecdotal, based on checklists or rating scales, be related to inter-views with the student, or may include any other relevant information the teachers and student agree is valuable. These are more than subjective recordings; they can be made relatively objective through conformity to established criteria. They should be collected and maintained with the purpose of the portfolio in mind. A portfolio to document the progress of a sixth-grade student has a different purpose than the portfolio of a junior in high school who will use the portfolio in job interviews or in applying for admission to a college.

Portfolios may be primarily collections of paper documents, they may be video or audio tapes, or combinations of all three. Computer software is available that is useful for both teachers and students in managing, storing, and retrieving information in the portfolio. The use of software facilitates the collaboration of teachers in different departments in documenting achievements in varied situations, for example, the application of writing skills in the completion of a research paper in science class or use of mathematic competencies in art class. Video and audio recordings completed by the teacher, student, teacher and student, or several students provide information that may either take the place of paper documents or provide enhancements and dimensions that are unavailable through written documents alone.

Student portfolios may serve as invaluable documentation to be discussed during parent conferences (Stiggins, 1994). They contain information regarding progress toward specific goals as well as a record of goals achieved.

Evaluation Alternatives

Regular classroom teachers are faced with the difficult task of fairly evaluating the progress of all students in their classes. Teachers are often concerned about whether they should alter their established grading practices for students with special needs. We believe that if a student with disabilities is appropriately placed and instruction is provided at a level commensurate with the student's ability, it is not necessary to significantly alter the usual grading practices. Certain alternatives, however, may be appropriate for all students.

Cumulative Point System

All assignments are given a predetermined number of points, and students are offered several options for earning the points that determine the final grade. This system gives the students the responsibility to do as many assignments as they choose. Some optional assignments may be modified to give a student with special learning problems additional opportunity to succeed.

Contracts

Students select the grade they want to earn and negotiate the nature of the assignments and the expected quality of the work. This approach gives students the opportunity to select assignments with teacher guidance and generally encourages greater commitment. A student with learning problems can be given reinforcement at structured intervals to help ensure success.

Alternative Assignments

Giving credit for extra or alternative work related to course objectives but completed in a different format is often helpful for students with special needs. This approach gives a student with learning problems options for completing course requirements in manners appropriate to his or her needs.

Individualized Educational Program (IEP)

The individualized educational program with the goals and objectives indicated may be the criterion for evaluation. The documentation of the goals and objectives achieved indicate

the progress of the student. Such a plan would likely be discussed at the meeting convened to develop the IEP.

Pass/Fail

When such a system is used, the basic competencies to achieve a "pass" are delineated. If the student does not meet those minimum competencies a "fail" grade is given. Sometimes levels are indicated such as "high pass" or "low pass."

Descriptive

Evaluation consists of descriptions written by the teacher, similar to those discussed regarding portfolios.

Cooperative

Cooperative grading may be used when two or more teachers collaborate in teaching the student. The teachers share information regarding insights, observations, and criteria for measuring performance resulting in the assignment of one grade.

Other Considerations

Factors, related to evaluation, that teachers may consider include the following:

1. When scoring a student paper, be careful not to limit yourself to negative aspects. Attempt to point out something the student did well.
2. Consider providing prompts to students who do not understand an examination. With prompts, you are not giving answers, but merely rephrasing questions to help students better understand.
3. Accept that students make errors and provide feedback about what they did incorrectly. Use a test as a teaching tool, not as punishment.
4. Consider giving a free grade. At the beginning of the term record an A in

every student's folder or your grade book. This procedure may have a positive effect for a student who has never received an A. It serves as a strong motivational tool, and a student may work diligently to maintain higher grades.

5. Consider giving a test more than once if you really want to know what students do or do not know and how much they have learned.

6. Consider an advance-warning system. When 3 or 4 weeks remain in the term, meet with students and tell them what their final grades will be. If a grade is low, give the student several alternatives to earn a higher grade.

7. Consider joint planning with students for the relative value of course assignments. A student may want, for example, a special project to determine half of a term grade and examinations and class participation to determine the other half.

8. Allow sufficient time for teacher-student discussions of evaluation alternatives and self-evaluation by students.

Teachers must be willing to examine the purposes underlying their evaluation procedures. Grading and evaluation should be teaching tools that assist students in achieving goals and objectives, not merely a basis for entering grades in a grade book.

Mastery Learning

Mastery learning was apparently first suggested by Benjamin Bloom and discussed in a text on mastery learning in 1971 (B. S. Bloom, in J. H. Block). The concept has been expanded, modified, and applied by a number of authors, including Madeline Hunter (1994) and others who have worked with Dr. Hunter.

More recently, it has been recommended as a potentially valuable approach for use with students with disabilities (Cicchelli & Ashby-Davis, 1986; Stainback, Stainback, & Forest, 1989; Wood, 1984, 1989).

According to Wood (1989), "Mastery learning methods require mastery at the end of a particular unit of instruction, whereas nonmastery methods allow students to move into a subsequent unit of instruction regardless of their performance at the end of the preceding unit" (p. 156). Cichelli and Ashby-Davis (1986) view mastery learning as highly Skinnerian (behaviorist) "in that it breaks down a complex behavior into a chain of component behaviors and ensures student mastery of each link in the chain" (p. 155). Salvia and Hughes (1990) indicate that there are two different paradigms of instruction, equal opportunity to learn and mastery learning. They say, "In equal opportunity to learn paradigms, all students are given equal exposure to material, and levels of mastery are allowed to vary" (p. 16). In contrast, "in mastery learning all students are expected to learn the same objectives to the same levels of proficiency, and the time and procedures required to attain mastery are allowed to vary" (p. 16).

Cummings (1980) provides guidelines for mastery teaching in her book *Teaching Makes a Difference*, although she does not specifically label her approach mastery teaching. Cummings believes that teachers make instructional decisions in four major areas, which in turn have a profound influence on student achievement:

1. *Objective selection*. Has the level of complexity of the objective been identified, and is it appropriate to the level of readiness of the learner?

2. *Teaching to the objective*. Have the student and teacher behaviors that will lead to the objective been identified?

3. *Monitoring and adjusting*. Has the student behavior been monitored to determine whether learning has taken place, and are appropriate adjustments being made, based on student responses?
4. *Principles of learning*. Are known principles of learning being utilized (that is, principles relating to motivation, rate and degree of learning, retention of learning, and so on)?

Outcome-based Education

Outcome-based education is based on premises similar to those of mastery learning. Goals, competencies, or outcomes for the various grade levels and in each of the subjects are established by the school district or school building staff. These goals or outcomes are the minimum requirements that the students are expected to achieve. General procedures to follow after establishing outcomes are similar to the following:

1. Define objectives for each area.
2. Teach the skill or concept in the objective by whatever methods or strategies are appropriate.
3. Evaluate the mastery of the targeted skill or concept.
4. Provide additional instruction if mastery was not accomplished or proceed to additional objectives if the targeted skill was mastered.

Some students will be able to progress rapidly through the objectives to the general outcomes and others will require additional time and reteaching. Proponents suggest that concepts such as these will ensure the achievement of basic skills by all students (Kennedy, 1992; Worthen, 1993).

Technology

Depending on one's perspective, everything from electric pencil sharpeners to artificial intelligence systems may be considered "technology" in the classroom. In the past, overhead and filmstrip projectors, slide projectors, record players and 16 mm film projectors were considered innovative instructional technology. Today, microcomputers, compact discs, and videodiscs, also once considered innovative and novel, are being combined with each other and with the older technologies into hypermedia systems. It is impossible to predict what technology will be considered innovative in the next ten years.

Microcomputers or personal computers are common in classrooms, and instructional programs are commercially produced at reasonable prices. Hypermedia systems and programs are also commercially produced but (at the time of this printing) are considered somewhat expensive. Other instructional programs and hypermedia systems are produced by teachers and students both individually and collaboratively.

Microcomputers are used regularly in classrooms to provide drill and practice, tutorials, games, simulations, and problem-solving activities. They can be useful in including students with disabilities or, if improperly used, to exclude students. It is possible for students to be engaged in computer activities throughout much of the day and, through the physical location of the computer and the nature of the tasks assigned or because of adaptations used with the computer that are misunderstood by other students, be isolated both physically and psychologically from classmates. The same student in another classroom may be included through the use of a buddy working at the same terminal, by using a program that

Box 3–1   *Supporting Inclusion with Technology*

Pat Shubert.   A specialist in special education technology for the Norfolk, Va., School District, works with teachers, students, and parents to successfully include special education students in regular classes. Here are her suggestions for how to use technology to support inclusion.

1. No one teacher, parent, or technology specialist should determine what technology solution should be prescribed for a student. Determining appropriate inclusive technologies must be a team decision.

2. Explore ways to adapt the regular curriculum and setting before prescribing alternate curricula, programs, or settings. Use technology as a tool to accommodate or modify the regular curriculum.

3. Use and build on the technologies and teacher expertise you have already, rather than pushing for newer, higher-tech equipment. Equipment doesn't drive inclusion as much as innovative applications do.

4. Technology support services must be site-based. Don't educate teachers about equipment at a center and expect them to install and implement it with students back in their classrooms. The technology support person should work in the classroom with the teacher and students.

5. Technology support personnel should familiarize themselves with all exceptionalities and regular education practices to be effective.

6. Because the needs of students with disabilities vary so greatly, the usual type of inservice training doesn't work with inclusive technology. Demonstrate several different software packages and discuss how each could be adapted for various needs and disabilities.

7. Use training funds to send teachers to state or national conferences. They will get an education in state-of-the-art technology. Also, see if you can raise money to help them develop their own applications. The best innovations come from the people who work most directly with the students.

From "Supporting Inclusion With Technology," by T. Wall, (1994) *Electronic Learning, 13*(6) p. 34. Used with permission.

encourages or requires the interaction of students at other terminals, or by ensuring that students understand the adaptations. Children as young as kindergarten ages are casual with technology when they understand its use while adults are often in awe (Oddone, 1993). Box 3–1 presents suggested ways educators and administrators may support using technology as a means to include exceptional students in regular classrooms.

Evaluation is a continuing process.

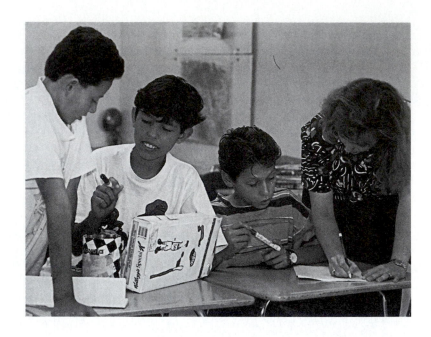

Common Uses of Computers in the Classroom

Drill and practice activities are among the most common uses of computers in the classroom and are used to assist the learner in increasing fluency in new skills or to refresh existing skills. Drill and practice activities are based on the assumption that the learner has received previous instruction regarding the concept, principle, or procedure and will now benefit from practice and drill. An advantage of using the computer for such activities is that it never gets tired, frustrated, or bored with the number of repetitions needed. Disadvantages are that students may practice errors or may not receive the appropriate type of feedback. Carefully developed software that has been evaluated by the teacher and judged appropriate for the student can usually overcome such disadvantages. A variety of software is produced commercially, addressing most content areas and necessary skills at varying degrees of difficulty.

Tutorial software provides instruction, practice, and feedback with the computer acting as teacher. The underlying pattern of the tutorial is information presented in small units followed by a question. The response of the learner is analyzed by the computer, which then supplies reteaching or advances the student to new information. Many networks of pathways or branches to reteach or to present more information may be programmed into the software, making it easier or more difficult, depending on student responses. Tutorial software can be useful in individualizing learning if it is programmed appropriately.

Games may be recreational or instructional. *Recreational* games are unrelated to specific academic skills and are often used as rewards for other accomplishments. Some nonacademic but essential skills such as eye–hand coordination or sharing may be taught or reinforced by recreational games. *Instructional* games are those related to instructional goals or objectives such as math facts, spelling, or development of language skills.

Computer-based simulations provide real-life situations in which students assume roles that require them to interact with other people or elements of the simulated environment. Among the most well-known programs are those used by astronauts and pilots to simulate weightlessness or emergencies. Available software that includes simulations may help develop academic skills, as well as social and behavioral skills, such as those required in interviewing for jobs.

Problem-solving computer-assisted instruction requires the learner to use previously mastered skills to solve problems. The student examines the material presented, defines the problem, and generates a solution. Depending on the complexity of the program, the computer may accept the solution and proceed, it may add information to further assist the learner, or it may furnish additional information that provides another dimension to the problem that the student must consider before generating a solution. The computer may manipulate data or perform calculations while the student seeks a solution. The student learns about the content under study and also must use cognitive processes such as reasoning skills, and logical and critical thinking skills (Seels & Richy, 1993).

Computer Hardware

The physical equipment or hardware of a computer is essentially the same regardless of the size or complexity of the system. (See Figure 3–11).

Input devices are the means of getting information into the computer. Typewriterlike keyboards, trackballs, mice, joysticks, paddles, graphic or digitalized tablets, voice recognition systems, and touchscreens are among the common devices. The central processing unit (CPU) is the brain of the computer that controls the total system.

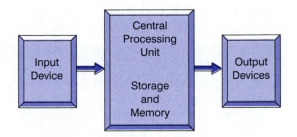

Figure 3–11

Basic elements of a personal computer

Personal computer control instructions are stored in two types of memory. Read-only memory (ROM) includes the instructions that are a permanent part of what the computer needs, such as the programming language(s) and internal monitoring functions. Random access memory (RAM) is the flexible part of the memory. The particular part of the program or set of data manipulated by the user is temporarily placed in RAM and then stored on a separate disc or erased for the next use of the computer.

The memory capacity (RAM) of the CPU varies and is described in terms of how many bytes it can store at one time. A megabyte—one million bytes—of memory can hold approximately 2,000 pages of text. Current personal computers process only one program at a time, with other programs stored for future use outside of the computer, although many newer programs are being designed to run simultaneously, sharing data, storage memory, and CPU software. Storage disks may be flexible (floppy), rigid (hard), and CD-ROM (Compact Disc—Read Only Memory). The basic differences between the disks relates to the amount of information each can hold and the speed with which it can be accessed. Program operations and data are displayed on a television-type monitor or printed as data on paper sheets.

Both input and output devices may be adapted for use by individuals with special

Table 3–1
Adaptations for personal computers

Alternate or Adapted Input Devices	Alternate Interface Devices	Alternate or Adapted Output Devices
• Keyboards may be smaller or larger in size, have more or less than the standard number of keys, be pressure sensitive • Switches that can be released by pushing, pulling, tilting, sipping, puffing, muscle movement, specific noise, glance or look, blink, or touch with no pressure • Pointing devices such as head wands or sticks, mouthsticks, or chin wands • Mouse or trackball that is hand or foot manipulated, varied in size, used by left or right hand or foot • Touch screens that are attached to the monitor, placed in the lap or on a flat surface • Voice or utterance activation	• Interface cards • RAM software • Ports • Game connectors	• Monitor adaptations to enlarge text, variations in color, white on black text • Magnification attached to the monitor • Synthesized or digitized speech • Print in larger fonts or in braille

requirements. These adaptations are summarized in Table 3–1 and will be described in greater detail in later chapters. The applications of the adaptations that are appropriate for the individual needs of the students will also be discussed.

Multimedia and Hypermedia Systems

Multimedia systems available in classrooms range from a simple audiocassette and slide projector combination to hypermedia systems that involve sound, graphics, motion and still images, and text. The degree to which the learner is involved with the various media systems also varies. The type of media used in the classroom usually depends on the topics of study, expertise of the teacher, and the individual needs of the student.

Sound-slide sets of media combine still images and voice or music. These can be presented to an individual or class through the use of a slide projector and audiocassette tape or transferred to a videocassette. Motion may be added if the images are either modified from still images or produced by a video camera. Multi-image projections usually consist of two or more images presented simultaneously and often as a combination of still and motion. These presentations likely include voice or music. Multimedia presentations incorporate slides, overhead transparencies, filmstrips, and motion pictures. They can illustrate comparisons, time sequences, and wide angle panoramic views and may create moods.

Interactive video combines features of both television and computer-assisted instruction. The video portion of interactive video, presented at any speed, is provided through a videocassette, videodisc, or compact disc. The interactive aspect of interactive video is provided through computers that have decision-making abilities. Various levels of interactivity range from essentially linear video to learner-directed instructions. Interactive video can combine text, audio, graphics, and still and motion pictures in one system. Individualization can be provided if branching has been programmed. The branching may provide remedial instruction or enrichment material. Skills that previously would have required role playing or real-life interactions can be developed with individual, self-paced simulation exercises through the use of interactive video.

Computer multimedia systems are similar to interactive video except that computer multimedia systems begin with a computer, and therefore assume the use of basic text and graphics. Digitalized audio, still images, and video may be added. The purpose of computer multimedia systems is to facilitate interaction between the learner and the subject matter. Computer multimedia systems lend themselves to discovery-oriented instruction rather than drill and practice, tutorials, or programmed instruction. A discovery program consists of a database of information, directions to guide the learner in locating the desired information, and the tools for manipulating the information. Students working in groups or individually develop a product such as visually illustrated text or narrated video. Computer multimedia allows students to set their own pace and view the material as many times as is necessary for understanding. It also allows for demonstrating complex processes such as the nuclei of living cells or the dynamics of the solar system, processes that are too fast (action of waves) or too slow (effects of glacial movement) to be observed. The computer tools remove many of the tech-

nical obstacles, allowing the students to concentrate on thinking and organizing the ideas and information. Computer hypermedia, similar to computer multimedia, combines text, audio, and visual information stored in a computer. The computer is used to link and annotate individual items (called *nodes*) of stored information into larger networks or paths of information. There are no paths that users must follow, but the system provides a map of the paths connecting the nodes and a method to travel the routes. Onscreen icons or buttons are activated by the user and the monitor displays the requested information. Each information node has several more icons or buttons that provide access to other units of related information. Hypermedia systems allow students to browse through databases in a nonlinear fashion, choosing the specific aspects of the information and the degree of detail they wish to pursue. Students are also able to create their own presentations using the tools of the hypermedia systems. Learning that comes from creating links among verbal, audio, and visual information, problem solving, and drawing conclusions is likely to be retained and applied in real-life situations (Wishnietsky, 1992).

Virtual Reality

Virtual reality places an individual in a computer-generated universe while being actually present somewhere else. A head-mounted display (HMD) with tiny video displays for each eye provides a three-dimensional view. Datagloves provide hands-on interaction with the virtual world and headphones or speakers provide computer-generated sound. Sensors attached to the head, hands, and feet feed information regarding body movement to a computer, which alters the visual image based on the information received. All the sensors report the positions of the HMD and dataglove to the computer, which calculates what the world would look like from that angle, draws it in a three-demensional projection, combines it with appropriate audio, and displays it on the screens in the HMD (Gayeski, 1993). Students using virtual reality curricula can travel inside of a single cell of the body or through the streets of London at the time of Charles Dickens. The trip may be made as a group or individuals may wander at will (Lewis, 1993). Pilots who train in flight simulators are in a type of virtual reality room. The computer-generated graphics, movement, sound, and video create a sense of flight as the system reacts to the actions of the pilot.

The varied uses of multimedia systems depend on the resources available in the school and the teacher in the classroom. The most advanced and best designed technologies do little by themselves to assist the learning of the students but the application of such systems may provide for individualization that will enrich the learning of all students. Certain of the multimedia combinations are particularly helpful to students who learn best through multisensory methods and interaction with the environment. Specific applications and adaptations for individual students are discussed in subsequent chapters.

Summary

In this chapter, we included suggestions and considerations relating to preparation for instruction (what to do "before you teach"), to the instructional process (ideas to consider "as you teach"), and suggestions for monitoring and recording student performance. We also included a brief section on applications of technology in the education of students with special needs. Ideas relating to the physical arrangement of the classroom, grouping, scheduling, the use of learning centers, and various peer systems, have broad applicability in meeting the instructional needs of all students. Sections on managing a classroom, common learning problems, learning styles, skills that can enhance learning, and various presentation alternatives may be applicable at different grade and age levels. Many of these ideas have application across areas of exceptionality.

The major goal of these various strategies is simple: a better, more meaningful learning environment. A more satisfying teaching experience for the regular classroom teacher is a related subgoal. To accomplish these goals, we urge teachers to remember the power of motivation and to strive for instructional flexibility.

chapter 4

- What is the difference between a student with a disability and a disabling situation?

- How may teachers evaluate their interactions with students?

- Can you provide several examples of student–materials interaction? How may any potential negative results of such interactions be minimized?

- What are the major advantages of cooperative learning? What are the disadvantages?

- How may racial or ethnic minority group membership influence teacher expectations?

- How may talk in the teachers' lounge influence the behavior and academic progress of students?

- What are the major influences on the self-perception of students who have disabilities?

Feelings, Expectations, and Interactions

■■■■■■■■■■■

The philosophy and practices of inclusion and mainstreaming require the least restrictive educational placement for students with disabilities, as does federal, and in many cases state, law. Mere placement, or presence in regular classrooms, does not mean inclusion or acceptance. For a student to truly become part of a class, there must be acceptance, modeled by the teacher and practiced by the students. Information about content and teaching strategies alone does not necessarily lead to effective instruction. Without positive feelings, optimistic and realistic expectations, and warm accepting interactions, students with or without disabilities do not receive appropriate instruction. This chapter emphasizes the importance of positive interactions among the students—disabled, nondisabled, gifted, talented; in short, every student—with each other and with the teacher.

■■■■■■■■■■■

The Impact of Teacher–Student Interactions

Teachers do not always know how they are affecting the life of a student, and sometimes the emphasis on academic performance overshadows the interactions the student values most. Because anecdotes vividly illustrate the potential impact of personal interactions, this chapter begins with a story about a high school student who was experiencing difficulties in school and in his personal life. It illustrates the manner in which a biology teacher's awareness of the student's potential *outside* the classroom made a major difference in the student's life.

A Teacher Who Really Cared

Mel, a teenage student in a midwestern state, was in many respects just like any other high school student. He had grown up in a small, rural community of some five hundred people, where he had enjoyed all the activities of his peers. He was active in Boy Scouts, he enjoyed hiking and swimming in the creek and particularly liked competitive athletics. He excelled in some areas of athletics and might have been called a standout athlete in his community. He definitely had promise and was well known and liked by almost everyone.

As Mel was about to enter high school, there was a family move to the city, and for the first time he had to break into a new group, namely, the boys who were involved in competitive sports. He tried to become a part of this group but was not accepted. This nonacceptance was a new experience and was devastating until he saw that there was another group that would accept him. This accepting group was a group of troublemakers whose like can be found in almost any school or community. To be accepted, all that was necessary was to do one better (or worse) than the next guy. If another member of the group fought someone 6 feet tall, you only needed to fight someone taller. If another member stole something worth $20, you had to steal something worth $30. The rules were clear and simple and acceptance was assured if you played by the rules.

Another sure way to be accepted was to become a thorn in the side of teachers, counselors, and school administrators. Even if part of the group was not enrolled in school, this type of behavior was very visible and highly respected. Mel wanted to be the best and he quickly moved in that direction, finding solid acceptance with his new friends. Drinking and street fighting became a routine part of his life and he was a regular troublemaker in school. Teachers came to know his problem behavior and most concluded that he was a loser. His records indicated his problems, and through coffee-room talk, even teachers who had not had Mel in their classes knew what to look for. Mel's school attendance became sporadic, and he was suspended at various times, permitting him to spend more time with his out-of-school friends. Mel was on his way down.

At this point in his life, Mel might have been considered "behavior-disordered." The school counselor suggested that he should think about what type of work he could do at age 16; the assumption was that he would quit school after his 16th birthday. But then an outside influence intervened. At about the same time as the possibility of quitting school became more realistic, Mel got to thinking about something he had noticed over the 18 months he had been in high school. As he walked down the halls, he noticed that one teacher (Mr. S.) often had a group of students, primarily boys, gathered around him in the hall outside his classroom door. Mel was curious about what was going on. Mr. S., who taught biology, would sometimes greet Mel as he walked down the hall, and if he was not engaged in conversations with other students, would ask how Mel was doing. Mel was intrigued by this unteacherlike behavior, and would stop and talk if he was alone. He couldn't do this in front of his friends because it might be seen as fraternizing with the enemy.

Before long Mel found ways to spend more time in that group around Mr. S.'s door. At first he was a little uneasy, particularly when Mr. S. looked him straight in the eye in a friendly, nonjudgmental manner, engaging in person-to-person conversation. Mr. S. did not leave his role as a teacher, but somehow came across as a teacher who was also a friend.

Several weeks after deciding that maybe Mr. S. was all right—for a teacher—Mel took something out of another student's locker just as he was entering the wing of the school that included Mr. S.'s room. As he passed Mr. S., he got a look that made him wonder if his behavior had been seen. He avoided Mr. S. for some time, then stopped by when no one else was there.

After a few moments of conversation, Mr. S. said, "I see that you're pretty fast with your hands," at which point Mel thought, "Here it comes, he's just another teacher." But Mr. S. followed quickly with, "Are you fast with your feet, too?" Before Mel could reply, he continued, "Track is going to start in a couple of weeks; are you interested in going out?" Mel

wanted to go out, but athletic participation was not acceptable in his group, so he replied that as far as he was concerned, track was for sissies, and left.

In the next few days, Mel saw Mr. S. a number of times, who told him he should think more about going out for track. Then he was given a handout telling when track tryouts were to be held and other such details. Mr. S. didn't give up easily, and somehow Mel found himself in that wing of the school with greater frequency. Just before the day for tryouts, Mr. S. said, "Why don't you come out for three days? If you don't like it, quit, but promise me you'll give it a try for three days." And Mel did try out.

Mel found success in track, which led him to give both football and basketball a serious try. He made the team in all three sports and became a different person. His grades improved in the remainder of high school, and after graduation he entered college, in part on the strength of a track scholarship. While in college, Mel worked part time, making deliveries for a laundry. One of his stops was a school for students with disabilities. He became interested in these students and changed his major from physical education to special education in his junior year. Mel completed his undergraduate degree and became a teacher of students with disabilities.

Mel continued to teach students with disabilities, later completed a master's degree, and still later a doctorate in special education. Now, 30 years after a teacher took time to encourage a teenage boy to believe in himself, Mel is involved in teaching teachers. He regularly emphasizes the importance of advocacy for students, along with the importance of teaching basic skills and content in the subject

areas. He maintains that "good personal interaction is what teaching is all about."[1]

[1]"Mel," in this vignette, is Dr. Mel Weishahn, one of the authors of
this text. He is sorry today for all the problems he caused his parents but will be forever grateful for Mr. S., a teacher who cared. He
believes that student advocacy, *really caring*, is of prime importance for all teachers.

■■■■

There is little doubt about the appreciation of
this student for the efforts her teacher has
made on her behalf. The student is a bright
tenth grader, who is a good softball player and
who has learning disabilities.[2]

Mrs. W,

Thanks for giving me those
huges when I need them. It sure
helps me out. And to those relax-
ing bit. School any more is bring me down I
guess I want school out and 2nd softball.

I just about gave up a couple of times but if
it wasn't for you I'm hanging in there. Will yesterday I wanted to leave my first hour. and call
it Quiets. but Im half way there. Pluse Im not a
Quieter either

If my spelling is off im sorry but Im trying to
get it done before I got to class.

You have a heart.

Will you do me a favor. Keep doing your
job and Ill make it though.

I hope.

Thanks. your my best teacher.

I wish All my teachers were like you.

Love
C.J.

■■■■

[2]From a note received by "Freddie, an excellent teacher
who cared," by permission.

This teacher was clearly affected by her student. After his death she wrote this tribute to
him, which was published in the local news-
paper.

The World Is Less Without Steven's Splendid Spirit[3]

He was much younger than other
boys his age. He was full of
unbounded joy in life's small pleasures. He
could not hear music without singing or dancing in response. He never faced a challenge
without enthusiasm. He never received even a
slight indication of affection without a wriggle
of delight and full-hearted return of it. He
never knew the disappointment of a lost love,
the independence of living on his own, the
satisfaction of a first paycheck, the pride of
high school graduation. The world was so full
of him—and then he was gone.

Despite many stereotypical features, Steven
was first of all Steven, not a Down's syndrome
child. He was squarely built but amazingly
agile and a lithe dancer. He had the blond,
rosy-cheeked moon face so often characteristic of the people we used to call Mongoloids.

The schools called him someone with "Significantly Limited Intellectual Capacity" and
placed him in special classrooms and, finally,
in a special school. But there was nothing limited about Steven's capacity for learning, living,
or loving. These he embraced with vigor
throughout his too short time with those who
loved him.

Steven died young. Like many people born
with Down's syndrome, he had a fragile respiratory system and heart. Pneumonia was a
deadly threat to this smiling, pre-teenager
who appeared so robust. A cold quickly

Respect earns respect.

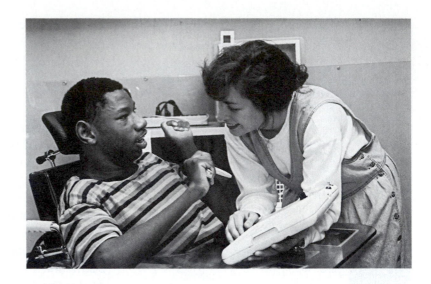

became something more and overwhelmed him quietly in the night.

Once, Steven and I sat in the school lobby waiting for our respective rides. We were laughing and joking and his belly laughs carried down the hall. A person, who was a fleeting acquaintance, walked by and with a distressed look said, "Oh, is this your son?" I remember her surprise and then relief when I told her he was my student. But, most of all, I remember my pride that the affection we held for each other was so apparent. When Steven held you in his heart, it was a privileged position.

Remembering him now, I think about his friends in class. When he was absent, they asked after him in their halting speech. One boy, who loved him especially well, sat beside his chair patting the seat and, with head tilted to one side, kept saying quizzically, "Huh? Huh?" When Steven returned, the room would ring with shouts of his name and squeals of delight. I wonder what they did when he didn't come back. I know how they felt.

I am a teacher. I was trained to plan for the future, to push toward that better tomorrow. I wanted to put my students on the fastest possible track to successful integration into the real world. Nothing in my training ever prepared me for the death of one so young and full of unfulfilled promise. The loss of this joyful boy reshaped my perspective on life—and on teaching.

Now when I look at someone younger than myself, I still see a future full of possibilities. But I see something more. I see a whole person, complete in the here and now, with a present to celebrate. I no longer see a person in waiting, a small adult, a grownup in training. I realize that a critical part of my job as a teacher is to nurture the present person and enrich the present moment. I know now that the journey is as precious as the destination.

Steven was not presidential material, nor could he have been a nuclear physicist, but I was proud to know him. I know he would have been a fine and honorable adult. He would have been productive and carried his own weight. He would have crowed to see how much he has taught his teacher, but he wouldn't have been surprised. He was my friend, my teacher, my beloved boy. The world is so much less without his pure and splendid spirit.

[3]From the *Greeley Tribune* by Vicki Heisler, July 11, 1993, p. A 11. Copyright 1993 by the *Greeley Tribune*. Reprinted by permission.

■■■■

Unfortunately, not all interactions between teachers and students are positive. The vignettes following illustrate some of the negative feelings students may have regarding their school experiences.

The Poor Scholar's Soliloquy[4]

No, I'm not very good in school. This is my second year in the seventh grade and I'm bigger and taller than the other kids. They like me alright though even if I don't say much in the classroom because outside I can tell them how to do a lot of things. They tag around me and that sort of makes up for what goes on in school.

I don't know why the teachers don't like me. They never have very much. Seems like they don't think you know anything unless you can name the book it comes out of. I've got a lot of books in my room at home—books like *Popular Science Mechanical Encyclopedia*, and the Sears' and Ward's catalogues—but I don't very often just sit down and read them through like they make us do in school. I use my books when I want to find something out, like whenever Mom buys anything secondhand I look it up in Sears' or Ward's first and tell her if she's getting stung or not. I can use the index in a hurry.

In school though we've got to learn whatever is in the book and I just can't memorize the stuff. Last year I stayed after school every night for two weeks trying to learn the names

of the Presidents. Of course, I knew some of them like Washington and Jefferson and Lincoln, but there must have been thirty altogether, and I never did get them straight.

I'm not too sorry though because the kids who learned the Presidents had to turn right around and learn all the Vice Presidents. I am taking the seventh grade over but our teacher this year isn't so interested in the names of the Presidents. She has us trying to learn the names of all the great American inventors.

I guess I just can't remember names in history. Anyway, this year I've been trying to learn about trucks because my uncle owns three and he says I can drive one when I'm sixteen. I already know the horsepower and number of forward and backward speeds of 26 American trucks, some of them Diesels and I can spot each make a long way off. It's funny how that Diesel works. I started to tell my teacher all about it last Wednesday in science class when the pump we were using to make a vacuum in a bell jar got hot but she said she didn't see what a Diesel engine had to do with our experiment on air pressure so I just kept still. The kids seemed interested though. I took four of them around to my uncle's garage after school and we saw the mechanic, Gus, tear a big truck Diesel down. Boy, does he know his stuff!

I'm not very good in geography either. They call it economic geography this year. We've been studying the imports and exports of Chile all week, but I couldn't tell you what they are. Maybe the reason is I had to miss school yesterday because my uncle took me and his big trailer truck down state about 200 miles and we brought almost 10 tons of stock to the Chicago market.

He had told me where we were going, and I had to figure out the highways to take and also the mileage. He didn't do anything but drive and turn where I told him to. Was that fun! I sat with a map in my lap and told him to turn south, or south-east or some other direction. We made 7 stops, and drove over 500 miles round trip. I'm figuring now what his oil cost and also the wear and tear on the truck—he calls it depreciation—so we'll know how much we made.

I even write out all the bills and send letters to the farmers about what their pigs and beef cattle brought at the stockyards. I only made three mistakes in 17 letters last time, my aunt said, all commas. She's been through high school and reads them over. I wish I could write school themes that way. The last one I had to write was on "What a Daffodil Thinks of Spring," and I just couldn't get going.

I don't do very well in school arithmetic either. Seems I just can't keep my mind on the problems. We had one the other day like this:

"If a 57 ft. telephone pole falls across a cement highway so that $17\frac{3}{5}$ feet extend from one side and $14\frac{9}{17}$ feet from the other, how wide is the highway?"

That seemed to me like an awfully silly way to get the width of a highway. I didn't even try to answer it because it didn't say whether the pole had fallen straight across or not.

Even in shop I don't get very good grades. All of us kids made a broom holder and a bookend this term and mine were sloppy. I just couldn't get interested. Mom doesn't use a broom anymore with her new vacuum cleaner, and all our books are in a bookcase with glass doors in the parlor. Anyway I wanted to make an end gate for my uncle's trailer, but the shop teacher said that meant using metal and wood both, and I'd have to learn how to work with wood first. I didn't see why, but I kept still, and

made a tie rack at school and the tail gate after school at my uncle's garage. He said I saved him ten dollars.

Civics is hard for me, too. I've been staying after school trying to learn the "Articles of Confederation" for almost a week, because the teacher said we couldn't be good citizens unless we did. I really tried because I want to be a good citizen. I did hate to stay after school, because a bunch of us boys from the south end of town have been cleaning up the old lot across from Taylor's Machine Shop to make a playground out of it for the little kids from the Methodist home. I made the jungle gym from old pipe, and the guys made me Grand Mogul to keep the playground going. We raised enough money collecting scrap this month to build a wire fence clear around the lot.

Dad says I can quit school when I am fifteen and I am sort of anxious to because there are a lot of things I want to learn how to do, and as my uncle says, I'm not getting any younger.

[4]From "The Poor Scholar's Soliloquy," 1944, *Childhood Education*, 20, pp. 219–220. Copyright 1944 by the Association for Childhood Education International. Reprinted by permission.

■■■■

I Taught Them All[5]

Naomi J. White

I have taught in high school for ten years. During that time I have given assignments, among others, to a murderer, an evangelist, a pugilist, a thief, and an imbecile.

The murderer was a quiet little boy who sat on the front seat and regarded me with pale blue eyes; the evangelist, easily the most popular boy in school, had the lead in the junior play; the pugilist lounged by the window and let loose at intervals a raucous laugh that startled even the geraniums; the thief was a gay-hearted Lothario with a song on his lips; and the imbecile, a soft-eyed little animal seeking the shadows.

The murderer awaits death in the state penitentiary; the evangelist has lain a year now in the village churchyard; the pugilist lost an eye in a brawl in Hong Kong; the thief, by standing on tiptoe, can see the windows of my room from the county jail; and the once gentle-eyed little moron beats his head against a padded wall in the state asylum.

All of these pupils once sat in my room, sat and looked at me gravely across worn brown desks. I must have been a great help to these pupils—I taught them the rhyming scheme of the Elizabethan sonnet and how to diagram a complex sentence.

---

[5]From "I Taught Them All" by Naomi J. White, 1937, *The Clearing House*, 12, pp. 151, 192. Copyright 1937 by The Clearing House. Reprinted by permission.

■■■■

About School[6]

This poem was handed to a high school English teacher the day before the writer committed suicide.

He always wanted to explain things,
  but no one cared.
So he drew.

Sometimes he would just draw
  and it wasn't anything.

He wanted to carve it in stone
  or write it in the sky
  and the things inside him that needed
  saying.

And it was after that he drew the picture.
It was a beautiful picture.
He kept it under his pillow
  and would let no one see it.
And he would look at it every night
  and think about it.
And it was all of him and he loved it.

When he started school he brought it with him.
Not to show anyone, but just to have it with
  him
  like a friend.

It was funny about school.
He sat in a square brown desk
  like all the other square brown desks
  and he thought it would be red.

And his room was a square brown room
  like all the other rooms.
And it was tight and close. And stiff.

He hated to hold the pencil and chalk
  with his arm stiff and his feet flat on the
  floor,
  stiff,
  with the teacher watching and watching.

The teacher came and spoke to him.
She told him to wear a tie like all the other
  boys.
He said he didn't like them
  and she said it didn't matter.
After that he drew. And he drew all yellow
  and it was the way he felt about morning.
And it was beautiful.

The teacher came and smiled at him.
"What's this?" she said.

*"Why don't you draw something
      like Ken's drawing?*

Isn't it beautiful?"
*After that his mother bought him a tie
      and he always drew airplanes and rockets
      like everyone else.*

And he threw the old picture away.
*And when he lay out alone looking at the sky,
      it was big and blue, and all of everything,
      but he wasn't anymore.*

*He was square and brown inside
      and his hands were stiff.*
And he was like everyone else.
*All the things inside him that needed saying
      didn't need it anymore.*

It had stopped pushing. It was crushed.
Stiff.
Like everything else.

---

[6]Original source unknown.

PAIN IN SCHOOL IS having an indifferent teacher[7]

My unhappy experience was when I was—well—just last year. I worked on a project for about two weeks 'cause my parents didn't think I was doing enough extra projects for school. So, they wanted me to do one. So I did it. Then, when I brought it to school (these were the last few days) my teacher told me that—well—she didn't really tell me—but she didn't pay very much attention to my project. I

made a map. And it just sat in the back of the room for a few days and I finally brought it home. I never got a grade on it, or anything.

PAIN IN SCHOOL IS learning to feel embarrassed

While in the second grade a question was asked and I raised my hand with much anticipation because I knew the answer and I was the only one who had any idea of the correct answer.

I was wrong and the teacher proceeded to tell me how dumb I was to think that I could do better than her more well-versed students. This tirade went on for about ten minutes while she told me to go to the head of the class and talk about why I had made such a "stupid" answer. At the end of this she told me my zipper was down which gave me much more embarrassment.

PAIN IN SCHOOL IS traveling a lonely road with a hurt that takes many years to heal

"I am sure you will be better off in the service. The service can teach you a trade. Maybe you can finish high school while in the service."

Seventeen years old and my world had just completely collapsed around me. I had just been told by my counselor that I would be better off in the service than in school.

He was polite, very sympathetic but he was still saying "Sorry, boy, you are too dumb for school!" Even today I would like to tell him to stick his advice in his ear! My work in school had not been good, but I felt much of that was due to the fact that I did more playing than studying.

When I left school that day I wondered what I would tell my parents. What could I tell myself? How could I fight a gnawing, cancerous emotion of worthlessness? I wondered how I could face my buddies. I remember having an overwhelming urge to run, to hide, to get away. But, where does a seventeen-year-old boy hide? The only hiding place I could find was the service. That day, I enlisted in the Navy before I went home. There was only one paper to be signed before I left for the service, that was a parental permission paper for men under eighteen years of age— they signed!

The hurt I felt that day almost twelve years ago has actually helped me today. When I am working with a boy who is called stupid, can't read, maybe he feels like he isn't worth much, I can go a little further than just sympathizing with him, I can feel what he feels. . . .

Some refer to such feeling as sensitivity. Call it what you will, but I can simply tell my students to "move over, brother, you have company. I've been down this road before once by myself. It's a lonely road, let me travel with you."

---

[7]From *Pain and Joy in School* by E. Schultz, C. Heuchert, and S. Stampf, 1973, Champaign, IL.: Research Press. Copyright 1973 by Research Press. Used with permission.

■■■■

Cipher in the Snow[8]

Jean E. Mizer

It started with tragedy on a biting cold February morning. I was driving behind the Milford Corners bus as I did most snowy mornings on my way to school. It veered and stopped short at the hotel, which it had no business doing, and I was annoyed as I had to come to an unexpected stop. A boy lurched out of the bus, reeled, stumbled, and collapsed on the snowbank at the curb. The bus driver and I reached him at the same

moment. His thin, hollow face was white even against the snow.

"He's dead," the driver whispered.

It didn't register for a minute. I glanced quickly at the scared young faces staring down at us from the school bus. "A doctor! Quick! I'll phone from the hotel . . . "

"No use. I tell you he's dead." The driver looked down at the boy's still form. "He never even said he felt bad," he muttered, "just tapped me on the shoulder and said, real quiet, 'I'm sorry. I have to get off at the hotel.' That's all. Polite and apologizing like."

At school, the giggling, shuffling morning noise quieted as the news went down the halls. I passed a huddle of girls. "Who was it? Who dropped dead on the way to school?" I heard one of them half-whisper.

"Don't know his name; some kid from Milford Corners," was the reply.

It was like that in the faculty room and the principal's office. "I'd appreciate your going to tell the parents," the principal told me. "They haven't a phone and, anyway, somebody from school should go there in person. I'll cover your classes."

"Why me?" I asked. "Wouldn't it be better if you did it?"

"I didn't know the boy," the principal admitted levelly. "And in the last year's sophomore personalities column I note that you were listed as his favorite teacher."

I drove through the snow and cold down the bad canyon road to the Evans place and thought about the boy, Cliff Evans. His favorite teacher! I thought. He hasn't spoken two words to me in two years! I could see him in my mind's eye all right, sitting back there in the last seat in my afternoon literature class. "Cliff Evans," I muttered to myself, "a boy who never talked." I thought a minute.

"A boy who never smiled. I never saw him smile once."

The big ranch kitchen was clean and warm. I blurted out my news somehow. Mrs. Evans reached blindly toward a chair. "He never said anything about bein' ailing."

His stepfather snorted. "He ain't said nothing about anything since I moved in here."

Mrs. Evans pushed a pan back off the stove and began to untie her apron. "Now hold on," her husband snapped. "I got to have breakfast before I go to town. Nothing we can do now anyway. If Cliff hadn't been so dumb, he'd have told us he didn't feel good."

After school I sat in the office and stared bleakly at the records spread out before me. I was to close the file and write the obituary for the school paper. The almost bare sheets mocked the effort. Cliff Evans, white, never legally adopted by stepfather, five young half-brothers and sisters. These meager strands of information and the list of D grades were all the records had to offer.

Cliff Evans had silently come in the school door in the mornings and gone out of the school door in the evenings, and that was all. He had never belonged to a club. He had never played on a team. He had never held an office. As far as I could tell, he had never done one happy, noisy kid thing. He had never been anybody at all.

How do you go about making a boy into a zero? The grade-school records showed me. The first and second grade teachers' annotations read "sweet, shy child"; "timid but eager." Then the third grade note had opened the attack. Some teacher had written in a good, firm hand, "Cliff won't talk. Uncooperative. Slow learner." The other academic sheep had followed with: "dull"; "slow-witted"; "low (IQ)." They became correct. The boy's IQ score in the ninth grade had been listed at 83. But his IQ in the third grade had been 106. The score didn't go under 100 until the seventh grade. Even shy, timid, sweet children have resilience. It takes time to break them.

I stomped to the typewriter and wrote a savage report, pointing out what education had done to Cliff Evans. I slapped a copy on the principal's desk and another in the sad, dog-eared file. I banged the typewriter and slammed the file and crashed the door shut, but I didn't feel much better. A little boy kept walking after me, a little boy with a peaked, pale face; a skinny body in faded jeans, and big eyes that had looked and searched for a long time and then had become veiled.

I could guess how many times he'd been chosen last to play sides in a game, how many whispered child conversations had excluded him, how many times he hadn't been asked. I could see and hear the faces and voices that said over and over, "You're a nothing, Cliff Evans."

A child is a believing creature. Cliff undoubtedly believed them. Suddenly it seemed clear to me: when finally there was nothing left at all for Cliff Evans, he collapsed on a snowbank and went away. The doctor might list "heart failure" as the cause of death, but that wouldn't change my mind.

We couldn't find ten students in the school who had known Cliff well enough to attend the funeral as his friends. So the student body officers and a committee from the junior class went as a group to the church, being politely sad. I attended the services with them, and sat through it with a lump of cold lead in my chest and a big resolve growing through me.

I've never forgotten Cliff Evans nor that resolve. He has been my challenge year after year, class after class. I look up and down for veiled eyes and bodies slumped into a seat in an alien world, "Look, kids," I say silently, "I may not do anything else for you this year, but not one of you is going to come out of here a nobody. I'll work or fight to the bitter end doing battle with society and the school board, but I don't want to have one of you coming out of here thinking himself a zero."

Most of the time—not always, but most of the time—I've succeeded.

[8]From "Cipher in the Snow" by Jean Mizer, 1964, *N.E.A. Journal, 53*, pp 8–10. Copyright 1964 by the N.E.A. Journal. Reprinted by permission.

■■■■

We believe that all teachers who work with young people should devise some system for recalling the *absolutely profound influence* they have on their students. Teachers have the potential to greatly enhance or seriously limit their students' feelings of self-worth, achievement, and behavior. After reading the last vignette, "Cipher in the Snow," a teacher we know placed a drawing of a large zero under the glass cover of her desk, to be clearly visible every school day, and pledged that each day it would remind her of her influence so that none of her students would be a "zero" in her class.

Teachers must recognize that all students need to be acknowledged as individuals in their own right and to know that significant others in their lives care about what they do and how they feel. It is easy to become trapped in an atmosphere that is primarily mechanical, that emphasizes achievement, test scores, and rules and regulations. We fully appreciate the tremendous demands on today's teachers, but a perspective that recognizes the worth of every individual is essential to the achievement of basic educational goals. Throughout, this text emphasizes that the teacher is the single most important factor in the successful mainstreaming of students

with disabilities. There is little question that teachers have a profound influence on the students' behavior and achievement. We want to encourage every teacher to be aware of this influence and to make certain that it is a *positive* influence.

Student with Disabilities or Disabling Situation?

Problems with specific students (perhaps only one or two in a classroom) are a major factor in teacher dissatisfaction. Such problems are among the reasons that teachers leave the teaching profession. These problems are *real* and cannot be ignored or forgotten. Sometimes, the problem *is* Jimmy Smith or Mary Jones. The problem is attributable directly to a student. At other times, the problem has multiple sources, and they are difficult to isolate and identify.

Students with disabilities have certain limitations imposed *as a result of their disabilities*. By the very nature of a condition, the teacher can predict a need for certain modifications or adaptations of curriculum, materials, teaching

Partners in learning

strategies, or a combination of these factors. Students with impaired vision, for example, must have modified materials to participate fully in regular classrooms. Students with hearing impairments need adapted approaches and the specialized services of support personnel, and students with orthopedic or other health impairments may need to have architectural barriers removed and special equipment provided if they are to be educated in regular classrooms.

With another group of students, teachers cannot clearly establish the reason for school difficulties, and it is not educationally sound to assume that in every case internal factors are the major cause. In many cases, the failure or difficulty is the result of a number of interacting external factors, or *disabling situations*.

If a student is having difficulty in reading or math, for example, or is withdrawn or acts out in class, the teacher must consider a number of variables that may be influencing the student's poor achievement or unusual behavior. These variables include (a) the student, (b) the materials being used, (c) the environment, (d) the teacher or teachers, and (e) the student's peers. The influence of these variables is depicted in Figure 4–1. Although the student may be the primary cause of the problem, more commonly the interaction of several factors produces a disabling situation. To determine if this is so, teachers must learn to analyze the interactions among various factors.

Figure 4–1
Ingredients of a disabling situation

actual reading level of the student; the student may be "required" to read a text or some other material that is far beyond his or her skill level. Teachers should administer an informal reading inventory to determine whether students have sufficient skills to successfully read assigned materials. The readability of the materials being used must also be assessed. Studies have indicated that intermediate texts for third to sixth grades may have readability levels anywhere from second to tenth grades. When the readability level of a particular textbook is far beyond the instructional reading level, it is not safe to assume that the problem is exclusively with the student. This may then be a disabling situation for the student. There is also evidence that students have preferred learning styles—auditory, visual, tactile, and kinesthetic—and that if assessment is made of the preferred learning channel or style and materials are matched to this preferred channel, the students' learning rate and achievement can be increased.

Student–Materials Interactions

The appropriateness of educational materials may greatly influence a student's achievement or behavior. Although this influence may seem obvious, often, not enough time and effort are given to observation, planning, and evaluation of educational materials. For example, the reading materials required for a particular subject may not be appropriate to the

Student–Environment Interactions

Poor student–environment interactions occur when a student is highly distracted by a noisy or visually distracting classroom. As a result, this student may not be able to attend to tasks or assignments. Most students can filter out distractions, but some cannot. For example, the last time you studied for an examination, did you seek an area free of auditory distractions (such as a quiet corner of the library) or were you able to listen to hard rock and sit at a table with your friends who were laughing and having a good time? Some individuals have little or no difficulty studying among considerable distractions, whereas others prefer a relatively quiet atmosphere. If you prefer an environment that is free of distractions but were unable to get away from them and as a result did poorly on the examination, who or what should be blamed? In this instance, you might feel that you could not concentrate because there were so many distractions. This situation is similar to that of a student who is distracted by extraneous visual or auditory signals in a classroom environment. In such a case, is it safe to assume that the problem lies within the student? In all likelihood, it is not. The difficulty undoubtedly involves a disabling situation and interactions between the student and environmental factors.

The five-point interaction matrix (Figure 4–1) should be considered when the teacher analyzes the needs of any student. It is not safe to assume that failure of a student is primarily the fault of the student. Rather, it may result from a disabling situation related to inadequacies in the environment, educational materials, instructional techniques, or interactional patterns in the classroom. This situation may be particularly true with a student who is exhibiting only mild problems and for whom there is no known reason for the difficulty. Objectively consider which factors are contributing to a particular student's difficulty and make the necessary adjustments to correct the situation.

Student–Student Interactions

Probably, all teachers understand that some of any student's difficulties are the result of interactions with peers. In fact, many teachers label students' difficulties as "problems with peers."

In some cases, such difficulties can be reduced by changing seating, by some specific program of behavior management, or simply by modification of the teacher's attitude. Student–environment interactions, discussed previously, can be the key to reducing negative interactions between students. Interactions with peers, *combined* with other factors, may best explain the problems under consideration and provide meaningful bases for intervention.

Teacher–Student Interactions

There is little question that teachers have profound influences on the students' behavior, achievement, and feelings of self-worth. The ways in which the teacher interacts with a student can either seriously impede or greatly facilitate the student's success in school. Such interactions should be considered with all students, but they have even more implications for students who are not achieving or who are apathetic, nonconforming, or acting out in the classroom. In addition, teachers should consider such interactions with students who are identified as disabled.

The nature and quality of the interactions between a teacher and student can be strongly influenced by the expectations of the teacher. The teacher's expectations may be too low, and the teacher may expect only minimal achievement or little acceptable behavior. In contrast, the teacher's expectations may be too high, and the teacher may pressure a student to achieve beyond her or his capabilities, resulting in discouragement, behavior problems, or failure. Expectations are not in themselves bad if teachers are willing to modify their initial expectations as a result of additional information and experience. However, adjustment of expectations does not always occur. Some teachers form inappropriate initial expectations and do not change them even when they obtain disconfirming information. To some extent, everyone forms expectations on the basis of preconceived information or as a result of initial interactions, but teachers must maintain a flexible attitude concerning these expectations and be willing to change them.

Teacher Expectations

The classic research study on teacher expectations is that conducted by Rosenthal and Jacobson (1968). Their main purpose was to determine if favorable teacher expectations could be responsible for significant IQ test score gains of students. A group-administered test (with which all of the students were unfamiliar) was given to all students who would be returning to a particular school. On completion, 20 percent of the students were selected to participate in the study, randomly assigned to an experimental group, and labeled "late bloomers." The researchers gave teachers a list of students in their classroom who would likely exhibit marked intellectual growth during the coming year. From this information, the teachers erroneously assumed that the students not on the list of those expected to exhibit significant intellectual growth did not have the potential for such growth. The results of the study indicated that the students labeled as late bloomers, and of whom the teachers had higher expectations, did evidence significant gains in total IQ scores.

A second example of the influence of teacher expectations, although not in any respect a scientific study, provides an interesting dramatization of a self-fulfilling prophecy.

The setting was a large urban junior high school. In an attempt to establish a sense of community and to increase the interaction of students to a level that might be expected in a smaller school,

several pods were established. Approximately 100 students were assigned to a pod, with roughly four homerooms in each pod. By design, each pod was established to serve as a school within the larger school.

Several weeks after school began, teachers received a random listing of students assigned to their pod. Preceding each student's name was an assigned number, with numbers ranging from 50 to 150. It was assumed by some teachers that the numbers were the results of group intelligence tests, and accordingly, many teachers established groups on the basis of the number.

After several weeks, it was learned that the numbers were not IQ test results, but locker numbers. The ironic side effect was that the students with high locker numbers tended to be doing very well in their classes and teachers highly valued their interactions; students with relatively low locker numbers were not doing as well.

This may be an extreme example of the influence of student data, but it further illustrates our concern. In all fairness, however, we must say that further investigation of this real-life situation revealed that a number of teachers were quick to question the "IQs" on the student listing. Our concern is for the potentially damaging effects of teachers who could not objectively observe and evaluate their students even after several weeks.

Teachers' expectations can definitely influence student behavior. Students who are viewed negatively by their teachers and others tend to behave inappropriately. This inappropriate behavior may promote negative self-evaluations and further negative evaluations by others. The following anecdote illustrates the point.

A discussion among teachers in the teachers' lounge centered on the unacceptable, disruptive behavior of a number of children from the Jones family. Teachers who had previously taught students from this family said that they *all* were troublemakers and in general were the most disruptive members of their classes. As a result of this discussion, Mr. Carlson, the sixth-grade teacher, had a preconceived notion about the behavior of Jimmy Jones, a new arrival in his classroom. Mr. Carlson was ready and waiting for disruptive behavior from Jimmy. Whenever Jimmy was the least bit disruptive (even though his behavior was not significantly different from that of other students), Mr. Carlson saw his prophecy as fulfilled: "I knew Jimmy was going to be a problem, and I'm going to stop it before it gets started." Mr. Carlson was so certain that he would observe disruptive behavior that he interpreted minor problems as disruptive. If this situation continued, Jimmy might also fulfill his prophecy—by becoming disruptive.

In this illustration, the prophecy was initiated by a conversation in the teachers' lounge, but expectations concerning a particular student may also be influenced by information contained in the student's cumulative file. Although many discussions in faculty lounges are professional and in the best interests of students in the majority of cases, they can be demeaning and damaging at times. Discussions may concern poorly achieving students or extreme behavior problems. Teachers must vent their feelings, of course, and often the teachers' lounge is the most logical place to do so, but teachers should consider the influence that such discussions may have on other teachers and the possible effect on the students being discussed.

In one particular teachers' lounge where negative comments about students' behavior had become a serious problem, the faculty decided to post a readily observable sign: "If it's not good, don't bother!" When asked what the sign meant, they were quick to say, "If you don't have something positive to say about students (or any other matter), don't say it. If it is necessary to discuss a particular student, attempt to do so outside the teachers' lounge." This concern may seem trivial compared with other problems in schools, but we believe that often teachers' attitudes and interactions with students are influenced by talk in the teachers' lounge.

The following short story by Rosella Reeves is not about the effect of expectations on students with disabilities. It's about the influence of teacher expectations *on every student in the classroom*. It is also about the influence of expectations *on the teacher*.

Stages of Insight: A Short Story[9]
Rosella Reeves

I did my student teaching in a heterogeneously grouped first grade class. The school was in a low socio-economic area, and the teacher was a veteran master.

When I arrived in February, I observed the most advanced group of first graders I had ever seen; some were reading on a third or fourth year level and most were at least on grade level. Textbooks were only one resource in this classroom; they were supplemented by many and varied materials. Much independent reading was done. Writing instruction included composing sentences and writing creative stories and poems. There was an abundance of math manipulatives. The children could multiply and divide as well as add and subtract. The scientific method of problem solving was used in science projects. The class listened to classical recordings and recognized many famous paintings. The painting easel was in daily use by the children. The absence rate in the class was low because the children were afraid they would miss something exciting. The children were well disciplined, interested, and mature.

I taught from February through May; the critic teacher was concerned that I hadn't seen the procedures for starting a first grade in September. She asked that I copy or construct some of her games and charts. In private conferences I was instructed in detail on how to start a first grade class and was given advice on good materials to purchase.

I experienced success as a student teacher. The supervising teacher wanted to be sure that I developed confidence and experienced self-esteem in my practice teaching. She told me that it is impossible for a teacher to help instill self-confidence and self-esteem in children if she hasn't developed these characteristics herself. I was given maximum positive feedback in the classroom and volunteered as hostess to visitors and mistress of ceremonies for a school talent show. I was also a regular solo teacher when the critic teacher found it "necessary" to be out of the classroom on a regular basis. This solo teaching gave me increased opportunities to make decisions independently. I left the student teaching environment feeling confident and excited about starting to teach in my own classroom.

My horizons were enriched and broadened by my observation and practice experiences in this class. Groups of student teachers from the university, classroom teachers, and instructional supervisors were regular observers in this class while I was there. It was a rare privilege to be exposed to a situation where children who had not come from an enriched background were experiencing such a high level of success in school.

When I arrived in the following September as a first year teacher, I was informed by some colleagues that I had been assigned to teach a "not-ready" class. I had never heard of such a class. All the first year pupils in the school had been given a readiness test. My class was composed of children who had fallen below the passing mark on the readiness test.

I was told by some colleagues that with the not-ready class I probably wouldn't need all those materials from student teaching. I was depressed and concerned that I would be unhappy teaching such a class after having completed student teaching in an enriched situation. My fear was that I might be teaching a few letter sounds, color words, number words, and other readiness skills for an entire year.

After some thought, I called my former critic teacher to apprise her of the situation and to get some advice. She made me feel much better by reminding me that I hadn't seen her class in the fall when they were beginners and much less "advanced" than when I saw them in February; that even though her class had not been grouped according to scores on a readiness test, they were from a low socio-economic area and lacking in many experiences usually thought to be necessary for success in school. She said there was no reason I couldn't use the many materials I had collected during student teaching and indeed, have a situation much like the one I had experienced in her classroom. I was told to keep an open mind, ignore negative comments about what to expect from the children, expect that everybody in the class could learn to some degree, and realize that even in this so-called homogeneous group there would be differing levels of ability. The critic teacher also suggested that I work with the children in small groups to determine what they already knew and didn't know, and use this information to group them for instruction. Then, I was to start teaching, using all the materials I had.

That first year, I taught everything as if I expected everybody in the class to be a successful learner. There was some concern in the school about whether my intensive teaching was geared too high for the class. The supervisor visited the class more often than was usual to determine if the children were really understanding what I was teaching. She became very enthusiastic about the amount of teaching material I had as well as the progress and understanding of the class as a whole. The supervisor later commented that if an experienced teacher had looked at the test scores and cumulative folders of this class, she probably would have said, "Forget it!"

There was additional surprise and doubt in the school toward the end of the year when I suggested that a few members of the "not-ready" class be tested for the school system's advance program. The surprise intensified when one or two of the children tested actually passed the test and were admitted to the advance program the next year.

My first year of teaching was stressful and hard at times, but it was also invaluable to me in the formation of a positive attitude toward people with a label. My motivation to teach was improved because I knew if I could successfully teach that class, I could teach anywhere. Because of the experiences I had then, I have never been able to stand before a class without wondering if I am getting maximum effort from each child. I tried to exhibit belief in each child, enrich his learning environment, and communicate to him my expectations for his success. If a child really tried for an entire year and still didn't experience success, I was ready to consider help from a spe-

cial education class; I wanted to be sure that I wasn't responsible for having a child labeled "special education" who had just not been applying himself in class.

I believe that most children can learn in a regular classroom if they have a teacher who is a builder. A builder:

- has awareness. The educator who has awareness knows that he may be contributing to a child's learning problems if he and the child come from different backgrounds; this educator will seek to gain experiences that will help him successfully teach all children.
- has belief and expectation. The educator who has belief in a child and high expectations for a child to learn, will emphasize what the pupil is doing right and minimize what he is doing wrong; the educator will use this approach to help the child build self-esteem and independence.
- observes learning styles and laws of learning. A teacher who determines a child's learning style and observes the laws of learning will know if a child learns best from a visual, auditory, or kinesthetic approach, or from a combination of these and will teach each child moving from the concrete to the abstract.
- is interesting. The interesting teacher will be colorful and interested in many things, and will provide an interesting, enriched program.
- provides repetition and involvement. The effective educator will provide repetition in teaching and practice work for the purpose of achieving mastery and will concentrate on getting pupils involved in whatever is happening in class.

[9]From "Stages of Insight: A Short Story" by Rosella Reeves, 1989, *Kappa Delta Pi Record, 25,* pp. 12–13. Copyright 1989 by Kappa Delta Pi. Reprinted by permission.

■■■■

The Influence of Labels

When a teacher refers a student for further evaluation and that student is eventually classified as disabled, the teacher should have learned a good deal about the student's strengths as well as weaknesses. Objectivity should overcome possible tendencies to expect too little and thus begin the cycle of self-fulfilling prophecy. When a student arrives with a label, the teacher may respond with unreasonably low expectations. Students labeled disabled may be stereotyped on the basis of the teacher's preconceived attitude or experience with individuals who have disabilities. Although a stereotype may reflect either positive or negative expectations, it generally reflects a negative attitude about a population as a whole. The labels "mentally retarded," "emotionally disturbed," and "learning disabled" have negative connotations and often result in low levels of expectation.

In a series of related studies, teachers were shown videotapes of children labeled learning disabled or mentally retarded, or unlabeled. The teachers had lower expectations for labeled students than for unlabeled students with *identical* behaviors (Coleman & Gilliam, 1983; Foster, Algozzine, & Ysseldyke, 1980; Minner, 1982; Simpson, 1981; Taylor, Smiley, & Ziegler, 1983). The influence of such labels is obvious. Just as success breeds more success, failure and negative thinking are powerful forces for continued failure. An effect of labeling is that it is often difficult to remove the label. Just as removing a paper label from a jar may be difficult and tedious, and often part of the label remains, so removing a label from a student is also difficult, and some of the label often stays with the student.

Achievement Expectations

Teachers who have high expectations of students tend to teach more than teachers whose expectations of their students' ability to achieve is low (Kellough, 1994). Studies that report the influence of teacher expectations on the academic achievement of students with disabilities support the notion that students perform better on test scores and in daily work when the teacher's expectations are high but realistic (Fad & Ryser, 1993; Lancelotta & Vaughn, 1989). Similarly, teachers interact more frequently, more positively, and more facilitatively with students they perceive as high achievers than with those they perceive as low achievers (Roberts & Zubrick, 1993; Tal & Babad, 1990). Interestingly, this is often the case with teachers who believe themselves to be very good at disguising their feelings (Babad, Bernieri, & Rosenthal, 1991).

One possible result of low achievement scores may be some sort of grouping, or tracking, based on inferred ability. Although an important historic court case relating to the Washington, DC, schools, *Hobson v. Hanson* (1967), rejected the claims of the school district that tracking was beneficial to all and ordered it to end the practice, some versions of tracking remain today. (In *Hobson v. Hansen,* the court concluded that tests used to make the track placements reflected economic and social backgrounds, not ability, and resulted in de facto segregation of black children.) Ability/achievement level grouping is intended to promote more homogeneity and thus permit more effective instruction. Although this practice may be viable in providing instruction, caution must be exercised in its use. Grouping must be flexible, and it should reflect the particular subject being studied. A given student may be placed in the low reading group but belong in a high group in another subject.

A general problem related to grouping is a type of spread phenomenon. A student is placed either in a high group for all activities regardless of achievement in that subject or all low groups on the basis of achievement in one particular subject. Teachers must make every effort to maintain flexibility when grouping students for instructional purposes (Jenkins et al., 1994).

Membership in Minority Groups

Membership of students in racial or ethnic minority groups may contribute to lowered expectations by teachers. These expectations are usually based on generalizations that minority or poor students do not perform well (Baron, Tom, & Cooper, 1985). While educators must overcome negative expectations, they should not overcompensate for minority students by lowering standards. Teachers may provide assignments that are drill/practice oriented and tend to be dull to students for whom they have low expectations, yet provide students for whom they have high expectations with assignments that actively engage the participants in meaningful activities (Good, 1987). Students often tend to behave in a manner that is compatible with the expectations placed on them. Teachers must recognize all students as worthy individuals and expend all possible effort to make each student an integral part of the class, with status equal to that of all other students.

Other Factors Influencing Teacher Expectations

A number of other student characteristics and attitudes on the part of teachers may lead to lower expectations and less desirable interac-

tions between teachers and students. The more common such characteristics are gender, speech and language, physical attractiveness, and personality (Costa, 1991). Expectations stem from preconceived notions or misinformation rather than from actual experience. For example, consider the message communicated when students are asked to line up according to gender, or girls are asked to hand out papers while boys are asked to move chairs. It also has been established that boys frequently receive more attention from teachers than girls, are asked more open-ended questions, and receive extended directions to facilitate independence (Brophy & Good, 1974; Good & Brophy, 1987). Verbal and nonverbal cues may be misinterpreted, especially when the teacher and students are from different cultural backgrounds. This misinterpretation may lead to fewer opportunities for participation and/or more frequent criticism and disciplining for breaking rules (Brophy & Good, 1974).

The first step in attempting to avoid this type of situation is for teachers to recognize that their preconceived attitudes and expectations can significantly influence the behavior, achievement, and self-concepts of students. Some school faculties have addressed this concern by conducting inservice meetings or open discussions concerning characteristics that may negatively influence the expectations of teachers. In this way, teachers recognize that their feelings are not unique and that their colleagues share similar feelings. Often, a student characteristic identified by a colleague seems quite trivial or humorous, although it is very real to the teacher identifying it. By sharing their feelings, teachers may come to recognize the absurdity of some of their feelings about student characteristics and learn to overcome such feelings.

One other type of interaction between teachers and students must be considered—

the interaction between teachers and students with physical impairments. Rather than rejective interactions, teachers may demonstrate pitying or oversolicitous attitudes. These attitudes are revealed by such comments as "Isn't it wonderful that a blind student can do so well!" or "I think, because she's in a wheelchair, she deserves a B." Such attitudes and interactions may defeat the very purpose of regular classroom placement. To set a student up as someone so special that he or she becomes the class pet may do serious disservice to that student. Teachers must be aware of the influence of their attitudes, be they negative, pitying, or positive.

Figure 4–2 presents thoughts from successful teachers that relate to teacher expectations and teacher behaviors. These teachers believe that such factors contribute to their success and enable them to be accepting of all stu-

Figure 4–2

What makes me a good teacher?

> We asked teachers what they thought made them successful. While this list is neither all inclusive nor ranked, each statement was mentioned by several teachers.
>
> Show that you are interested in the students and that they belong in your classroom.
>
> Employ active listening; avoid judging, moralizing, or pulling rank.
>
> Treat students as individuals, not as subjects to be taught.
>
> Avoid criticism.
>
> Maintain an open-door policy before and after school.
>
> Model respect, empathy, social responsibility, enthusiasm, and pride in learning.
>
> Demonstrate optimism about each student's ability and confidence that each student will work to the best of his or her ability.
>
> Use both nonverbal and verbal cues to show awareness and acceptance of each student.
>
> Make the classroom psychologically safe for each student.
>
> Emphasize the positive in feedback to the entire class, small groups, and individuals.
>
> Systematically plan successful experiences for each student.
>
> Anticipate possible disruptive behavior and have alternate plans.
>
> Learn to recognize the need for shifts in activities, the need for transitions that boost student interest, and the need to pace lessons to move smoothly and briskly, but allow time for thinking and reflection.
>
> At times (and within limits) be a ham, an entertainer; demonstrate enthusiasm for teaching.
>
> Model problem-solving skills and rational thinking processes.

dents in their classroom. Successful teachers recognize that it is essential to remain open and flexible to different ideas, attitudes, and beliefs and to objectively evaluate them.

■ Monitoring and Evaluating Interactions

The influence of teacher expectations on the students' behavior and achievement appears to be well established. Educators must go beyond the mere identification of attitudes and expectations, however, and make specific efforts to change their biases. The first step in changing expectations is to analyze interactions with students. Teachers can assess their interactions in a number of ways. Some methods are informal and do not require specific instruments or extensive training. Other methods are the product of research studies and provide very specific information concerning interactions. We would suggest the following informal techniques. Teachers are encouraged to modify these procedures to fit their individual needs.[10]

Time Analysis

The time analysis technique can provide information concerning teacher interactions with students. The checklist and set of directions in Figure 4–3 is an example of this technique. The teacher may add any number of questions to increase the time analysis findings, depending on the specific purpose of the analysis. The time analysis technique is simple to use and interpret and can provide considerable information concerning how the teacher spends time and the nature of the interactions.

Teacher-made Checklists

The teacher may develop a checklist to fit almost any situation. The items on a checklist can involve verbal or nonverbal behaviors or general classroom procedures. Such checklists seem to be popular with teachers, and we provide two examples (Figures 4–4 and 4–5). Figure 4–4 is for elementary students, and Figure 4–5 is more appropriate for secondary students. These are merely examples, and teachers are encouraged to modify the lists or add statements of particular interest or concern. Students should not be asked to sign their names, since this may inhibit their openness and sincerity.

The teacher should analyze the results by averaging the responses and plotting the averages to get a picture of teacher interactions. Checklists may be administered several times during the year to measure changes.

Peer–Teacher Observers

A trusted colleague can come into the classroom and observe the teacher in action. The colleague should keep running notes on the teacher's interactions during a period of several days. Often, it is helpful if the observing teacher has a checklist or an indication of specific behaviors to be recorded; otherwise, at the end of the period only very general comments may be shared. The teachers may later change roles if this is agreeable to both.

Videotapes

The teacher may arrange to have his or her teaching videotaped. The teacher should view the videotape alone, noticing interactions with different students. Next, if desired, the

---

[10]Our thanks to Clifford Baker, who provided many of the informal techniques presented in this discussion.

	1 Students	2 How Is Time Spent?	3 Pleasurable or Nonpleasurable?
Most Time 1. 2. 3. 4. 5.			
Least Time 1. 2. 3. 4. 5.			

Column 1. List the five students in the class with whom you spend the most time. List the five with whom you spend the least time.

Column 2. Identify what you do with the child during that time—how is the time spent?

Sample Key

XH = extra academic help
BM = behavior management
 L = listening to the student
 T = talking to the student
PL = playing with the student

Column 3. Write "P" if the time spent is pleasurable and "NP" if it is nonpleasurable.

Analyze the Results. Answer the following questions.
1. At what kinds of activities do you spend most of your time?
2. Is most of your time spent with these 10 students pleasurable?
3. What is different about the students with whom you spend the most time?
4. Do the students with whom you spend more time need you more?
5. What are the differences between the students with whom the time is pleasurable and the students with whom the time is nonpleasurable?

Figure 4–3
Time analysis for teachers

	Always 3	Seldom 2	Never 1
1. I can get extra help from the teacher when I need it.	☐	☐	☐
2. The teacher praises me when I do well.	☐	☐	☐
3. The teacher smiles when I do something well.	☐	☐	☐
4. The teacher listens attentively.	☐	☐	☐
5. The teacher accepts me as an individual.	☐	☐	☐
6. The teacher encourages me to try new things.	☐	☐	☐
7. The teacher respects the feelings of others.	☐	☐	☐
8. My work is usually good enough.	☐	☐	☐
9. I am called on when I raise my hand.	☐	☐	☐
10. The same students always get praised by the teacher.	☐	☐	☐
11. The teacher grades fairly.	☐	☐	☐
12. The teacher smiles and enjoys teaching.	☐	☐	☐
13. I have learned to do things from this teacher.	☐	☐	☐
14. When something is too hard, my teacher makes it easier for me.	☐	☐	☐
15. My teacher is polite and courteous.	☐	☐	☐
16. I like my teacher.	☐	☐	☐

Figure 4–4
Teacher-made interaction checklist for elementary students

teacher can also view and discuss the videotape with a colleague. It may be necessary to tape several sessions to record typical patterns of behavior and interaction. Also, it may be helpful to arrange for a series of taping sessions, for example, once every two or three months. Nearly every school district has videotaping equipment, and local instructional media personnel may be able to assist with the taping.

Figure 4–6 illustrates an example of the type of evaluation form that can be completed by a colleague observing in the classroom and used as a basis for discussion after the observation. It may also be used for self-evaluation during viewing of videotapes made in the classroom. Colleagues and teacher may both view the videotape and compare their observations.

Role Playing

For role playing to be most effective, it is advisable for the regular teacher to switch classes with another teacher so that the students are not inhibited by the presence of their own teacher. The students may be asked to act out the roles of a good teacher and a poor teacher. Other role questions include the following:

1. How does your teacher act when he is happy or sad?
2. How does your teacher look and what does she say when interrupted?
3. How does your teacher look and what does he say when asked to repeat the directions for an assignment?

	Always 5	Often 4	Sometimes 3	Seldom 2	Never 1
The teacher					
1. is genuinely interested in me	☐	☐	☐	☐	☐
2. respects the feelings of others	☐	☐	☐	☐	☐
3. grades fairly	☐	☐	☐	☐	☐
4. identifies what he or she considers important	☐	☐	☐	☐	☐
5. is enthusiastic about teaching	☐	☐	☐	☐	☐
6. smiles often and enjoys teaching	☐	☐	☐	☐	☐
7. helps me develop skills in understanding myself	☐	☐	☐	☐	☐
8. is honest and fair	☐	☐	☐	☐	☐
9. helps me develop skills in communicating	☐	☐	☐	☐	☐
10. encourages me and provides time for individual help	☐	☐	☐	☐	☐
11. is pleasant and has a sense of humor	☐	☐	☐	☐	☐
12. has "pets" and spends the most time with them	☐	☐	☐	☐	☐
13. encourages and provides time for questions and discussion	☐	☐	☐	☐	☐
14. respects my ideas and concerns	☐	☐	☐	☐	☐
15. helps me develop skills in making decisions	☐	☐	☐	☐	☐
16. helps me develop skills in using time wisely	☐	☐	☐	☐	☐

Figure 4–5
Teacher-made interaction checklist for secondary students

4. How does your teacher look and what does she say when you make a mistake?

5. How does your teacher look and what does he say when you misbehave?

6. How does your teacher look and what does she say when you do something well?

Teachers may add other situations about which they are most interested in obtaining feedback. The role playing may be taped on a video or audio recorder so that the teacher receives a firsthand evaluation. Again, it may be helpful for the teacher to exchange classes with a colleague so that the students will not be inhibited by their own teacher's presence. Although the initiation of such role playing may require different introduction and presentation at the elementary level than at the secondary level, it works at both levels with just a little innovation.

Teacher _____ Grade _____ Class _____

Date _____ Class size _____ Observer _____

Unit or lesson _____

Section I: General Evaluation

Indicate the extent to which you agree or disagree with each statement concerning the observed teacher: 1 = strongly agree; 2 = agree; 3 = disagree; 4 = strongly disagree; 5 = uncertain or not applicable.

A. Structure and Goals

_____ 1. The teacher clearly conveyed the purpose for each activity of the class period.

_____ 2. The stated purposes were consistently followed throughout the period.

_____ 3. The lesson seemed carefully planned and organized.

_____ 4. The various elements of the class period were effectively integrated.

_____ 5. The lesson built toward one or more basic concepts, processes, or attitudes that the students seemed to understand.

B. Teacher-Student Rapport

_____ 1. The teacher demonstrated fair and equal concern for all students.

_____ 2. The teacher answered student questions in a straightforward and understandable manner.

_____ 3. The teacher encouraged and facilitated quality interaction among the students.

_____ 4. The teacher appeared open to all ideas, suggestions, opinions, and criticisms from the students.

_____ 5. The students seemed genuinely receptive to the ideas of the teacher.

C. Instruction

_____ 1. The teacher conveyed enthusiasm about teaching.

_____ 2. The teacher presented material that was appropriate for this class.

_____ 3. The teacher demonstrated appropriate command of the subject.

_____ 4. The teacher introduced topics in a manner that was stimulating and meaningful to the students.

_____ 5. Transitions between topics and activities were efficiently and effectively implemented.

_____ 6. Major points were effectively reviewed by the teacher.

_____ 7. The teacher effectively implemented several checks for student comprehension as the lesson unfolded.

_____ 8. The teacher asked questions that required students to express their opinions, prior experiences, knowledge, and thoughts.

_____ 9. The teacher used student responses to encourage or to bring others into the discussion.

_____ 10. Questions were used throughout the lesson.

_____ 11. Students were attentive throughout the lesson.

_____ 12. Audiovisuals and supplementary materials were effectively managed by the teacher.

Figure 4–6

Sample evaluation form for classroom observation or videotape viewing

Section II: The Teacher

For each word or phrase listed below, indicate the extent to which it accurately describes the teacher you observed: 1 = this word or phrase does not describe this teacher; 2 = this word or phrase partially describes this teacher, 3 = this word or phrase accurately describes this teacher.

_____ 1. Effective use of gestures
_____ 2. Effective use of pauses and silence
_____ 3. Varied pitch and tone of voice
_____ 4. Clear presentations
_____ 5. Use of vocabulary appropriate for the students

_____ 6. Effective use of teacher mobility
_____ 7. Effective use of eye contact with students
_____ 8. Flexible in responses to students
_____ 9. Warm and accepting of all students

Section III: Strategies

Read the brief descriptions of each teaching strategy below, and then indicate the extent to which you observed the strategy being employed during this lesson. If possible, also provide concrete examples of how each strategy was used during the observation.

Encouragement of the students: In various ways, the teacher encourages student participation (e.g., with a smile, a nod, eye contact, or body position and gestures).

_____ a. I observed no encouragement.
_____ b. I observed a moderate amount of encouragement.
_____ c. I observed the effective use of encouragement.

Evidence _____

Awareness of student attentiveness: The teacher steadily monitors the class, demonstrating withitness and overlapping behaviors, and redirecting a student whose attention is beginning to wane. The teacher demonstrates this awareness by observing students' facial expressions and their involvement in class activities.

_____ a. The teacher did not demonstrate awareness.
_____ b. The teacher seemed to be moderately aware.
_____ c. The teacher was effectively aware of student attention.

Evidence _____

Section IV: Final Comments

1. What part(s) of the class period and lesson seemed to enhance the learning process?

_____

2. What behavior(s) on the part of the students demonstrated their acceptance of each other?

_____

3. What did the teacher do that encouraged acceptance, cooperation, and friendship among the students?

_____

4. What suggestions do you have for improvement?

_____

This teacher evaluation form may be copied and used without the permission of the author or publisher.

Figure 4–6, _continued_

Source: Adapted with the permission of Prentice Hall Publishing Company from _A Resource Guide For Teaching: K–12_ by Richard D. Kellough, pp. 467–472. Copyright © 1994 by Prentice Hall Publishing Company.

The Quality of Student Interactions

Students with disabilities are placed in (or remain in) regular classrooms in the belief that such placements will lead to a variety of positive results. In addition to teacher–student interactions, there are continuous student–student interactions. If physical placement in regular classrooms is to lead to the desired results, there must be *positive* interactions, and several authorities believe that without active teacher efforts, the results are more likely to be negative interactions or rejection.

In a discussion of factors contributing to the development of successful mainstreaming, Salend (1984) notes that nonhandicapped students can facilitate the mainstreaming process through positive interactions and can "aid their handicapped peers' adjustment and ability to function in the mainstream by serving as role models, peer tutors, and friends and by providing assistance to physically disabled and sensory impaired students" (p. 411). However, he cautions that peer contributions may be negatively affected by their attitudes.

At times, students may prove to be forces for improvement in the quality of interaction (see Box 4–1 for a classic example), but for the most part, teachers must provide the impetus. Salend (1984) suggests that all possible effort be expended before students are mainstreamed to increase their social skills, and that teachers employ specific strategies to promote positive attitudes (toward students with disabilities) on the part of nondisabled students. Whatever process or strategy is used—films, books, or discussions—the first requirement is that teachers accept students with disabilities as valued individuals. Various researchers have established that teacher acceptance can be attained through appropriate teacher education (West & Idol, 1990; Morsink, Chase, & Correa, 1991).

Measuring the Status of Students with Disabilities

Researchers have attempted to measure the social development and interactions of students with disabilities and students without them (Goldstein, 1993; Sabornie & Beard, 1990; Fox, 1989; Fiedler & Simpson, 1987). The most commonly used sociometric technique is peer nomination, which requires students to name classmates who fit a particular criterion (e.g., "In working on a project I would like to work with _____ ") (Cartledge & Milburn, 1986). A student's score is the total number of nominations received from classmates. See Figure 4–7 for an example of the nomination method. The directions for administering this nomination questionnaire are as follows:

1. The teacher explains to the class, "Today I am going to ask you to indicate on your paper the name of a classmate with whom you would like to share certain activities. We all work better when we have the opportunity to work with someone we get along with well. I am gathering this information to find out who in this class would work well together. I hope you will be completely honest. No other student will know whom you have chosen."
2. Hand out preference forms with questions similar to those indicated.
3. Give the following instructions:
   a. At the top of this form, write the names of three classmates you would like to work with in school if you had a choice.
   b. In the middle of your paper, write the names of three classmates that you

Box 4–1   *Sensitivity in Student Interactions*

Ian O'Gorman, a fifth-grade student in Vista, California, had a malignant tumor removed from his small intestine, and had to receive chemotherapy. Warned that his hair would fall out, he decided to have his head shaved in advance. Ian's friends and his younger brother decided that they didn't want him to feel different, so ten of them shaved their heads, along with two students from another class. Their teacher, Jim Alter, moved by their simple explanation of why they did it, had his head shaved too. When outsiders enter that classroom, and that school, it's impossible to tell who is undergoing chemotherapy.

would like to be with during breaks. You may write down any or all of the three names used previously.

c. Next, write the names of three classmates you would like to sit near in school if you had a choice. You may write any or all of the names previously used.

d. At the bottom of this form, write the names of classmates with whom you would not like to work.

After the students have made their choices, the teacher can add up the results. Any reasonable status categories may be used to determine the sociometric status of any specific student, for example,

Star. One who was chosen 14 or more times by classmates.

Above average. One who received from 9 to 13 choices.

Below average. One who was chosen between 3 and 8 times.

Neglected. One who was chosen fewer than 3 times.

These status numbers are based on an average classroom enrollment of between 28 and 35 students and should be changed proportionately depending on the size of the class. The use of both positive and negative nomination criteria generally permit more accurate status distinction.

A second method, the rating scale technique, can also be used to measure the sociometric status of students. With this procedure, students are provided a list or classroom roster and are asked to rate each classmate on a numerical scale according to particular criterion. A student's score on the rating scale is the average of all ratings from classmates. The criterion may be the degree to which students would like to play or work with each classmate. They may rate their classmates on a scale from 1 (wouldn't like to) to 5 (would much like to) scale. For ease of administration, the teacher can simply prepare a class roster with the range of numerical values printed next to each name, such that students can circle their ratings.

One advantage of the rating scale technique over the nominating method is that evaluations are obtained for all students in a class rather than only students nominated by others. This factor is important because students with disabilities may not be chosen on a positive nomination measure.

A third method of sociometric assessment is the paired comparison technique. With this technique, students are presented one at a

Figure 4–7

Peer nomination preference form

Questionnaire

Name:

In working on a project I would like to work with:

1. _____

2. _____

3. _____

During breaks, I would like to be with:

1. _____

2. _____

3. _____

I would like to sit next to:

1. _____

2. _____

3. _____

I would not like to work with:

1. _____

2. _____

3. _____

time with all possible pairings of classmates and must choose the most preferred peer for each pairing. Each student obtains a score that reflects the total number of times he or she is selected by classmates. Although regularly mentioned in summaries of sociometric measurements, this method has one serious drawback. It takes a great deal of time in preparation and administration. For example, Vaughn and Langlois (1983) report that it took 20 to 30 hours to complete this procedure in a class of 40 preschool children.

There are many ways to obtain sociometric data and various measures to assess different dimensions of social status. The nomination method measures friendship, and the rating scale can be used to obtain information about general acceptance. Sociometric assessment should be supported by other information, such as behavioral observations and teachers' ratings, to have maximum value.

Certain potential limitations of sociometric measures should be noted. Preferences for same-sex and same-race peers, recent negative experiences, and other similar factors may reflect influences that are either beyond the control of the teacher, or influences that are temporary and not appropriate for long-term, concerted efforts on the part of the teacher. Like other information, sociometric information must be considered as only one part of the total picture.

The use of sociometric information should not stop with the assignment of sociometric status; it should be meaningfully extended. For example, it may help to determine the number of mutual choices (two students who chose each other). It may also be interesting to determine whether students with disabilities were chosen in academic or social areas. Teachers should devise their own methods of analysis for their own situations.

Sociometric information is not the only way to analyze classroom interactions. Most teachers are keenly aware of social interactions in their classrooms. Naturally, they should be aware of their roles as models and the ways in which they interact with students. At times, however, even though teacher interactions with students with disabilities are positive, the students without disabilities do not reflect accepting, empathic, and objective attitudes. In such instances, teachers should structure cooperative learning experiences and open class discussions.

Enhancing Interactions Between Students

Information is contradictory concerning the effects of inclusion of students with disabilities on the attitudes of their peers without disabilities. Studies indicate that placement of students with disabilities in regular classrooms may result in either or both greater prejudice and rejection, or increased acceptance and friendships that extend beyond the classroom (Fox, 1989; Putnam, Rynders, Johnson, & Johnson, 1989; Eichinger, 1990; Stainback & Stainback, 1992; Vaughn, McIntosh, Schumm, Haager, & Callwood, 1993; Fad & Ryser, 1993; Roberts & Zubrick, 1993; McIntosh, Vaughn, Schumm, Haager, & Lee, 1993).

Based on this contradictory evidence, it is quite clear that if a student's status is low and his or her interactions with peers are not positive, the teacher must make specific efforts to modify the situation. This improvement may be gained in three general ways: (a) by structuring a cooperative learning atmosphere; (b) by providing detailed information and awareness of the potential of all persons; and (c) by providing students with opportunities to discuss, question, and clarify their beliefs and attitudes about persons with disabilities. The following sections consider ways in which teachers may use these specific approaches.

Cooperative Learning

There are at least three major emphases that a teacher may build into classroom learning situations. These are (a) positive goal interdependence (cooperation), (b) negative goal interdependence (competition), and (c) no goal interdependence (individualistic efforts) (Johnson & Johnson, 1975). A case may be made for the value of each of these emphases as it applies to students in general, but if mainstreaming is to be truly effective, considerable cooperative learning must take place. Students with disabilities must actually interact with nondisabled students, not simply be in the classroom physically. In addition to increasing the likelihood of acceptance of students with disabilities, cooperative learning may help students with disabilities increase their self-confidence by perceiving themselves as achievers.

Evans (1984) summarized the dynamics of cooperative learning situations as part of a discussion of fostering peer acceptance of students with disabilities. His summary (Figure 4–8) provides ample evidence of the importance of cooperative learning to acceptance of students with disabilities.

Developing and using cooperative learning methods requires teachers to believe that

Figure 4–8

The dynamics of cooperative learning situations

Source: From "Fostering Peer Acceptance of Handicapped Students" by R. J. Evans, 1984, *ERIC Digest, 1406,* p. 1.

A cooperative learning situation benefits all students. Working cooperatively with peers provides:

- More direct face to face interaction among students.
- An expectation that one's peers will facilitate one's learning.
- More peer pressure toward achievement and appropriate classroom behavior.
- More reciprocal communication and fewer difficulties in communicating with each other.
- More actual help tutoring, assisting, and general facilitation of each other's learning.
- More open mindedness to peers and willingness to be influenced by their ideas and information.
- More positive feedback to and reinforcement of each other.
- Less hostility, both verbal and physical, expressed toward peers.

Cooperation also creates perceptions and feelings of:

- Higher trust in other students.
- More mutual concern and friendliness for other students, more attentiveness to peers, more feelings of obligation to and responsibility for classmates, and desire to win the respect of other students.
- Stronger beliefs that one is liked, supported, and accepted by other students, and that other students care about how much one learns.
- Lower fear of failure and higher psychological safety.
- Higher valuing of classmates.
- Greater feelings of success.

cooperation can be as effective as competition. It also requires information about various learning structures that can be used to promote cooperative learning. There are several, research-based, practical cooperative learning structures. We will review the following: (a) cooperative goal structuring, (b) MAPS and the circle of friends, (c) the teams-games-tournament approach, (d) the jigsaw approach, (e) the student teams achievement divisions approach, and (f) the small-group teaching approach. In addition, we will address the use of problem-solving discussions and buddy systems.

Cooperative Goal Structuring

Johnson and Johnson (1986) describe a process called cooperative goal structuring as a way to promote social integration of students with disabilities through cooperative learning. Cooperative goal structuring involves establishing a goal that can be achieved only if *all* group members work toward the goal. A review of research (*Research Brief T1, 1988*) provided by the ERIC Clearinghouse on Handicapped and Gifted Children concludes that this process has application at all grade levels, with students who have various mild and moderate handicaps. The research brief concludes that as a result of use of this process for 2 weeks (ten 45-minute sessions) students with disabilities participated more often and students without disabilities looked at and spoke to their peers with disabilities more often. Cooperative goal structuring is most effective when teachers provide specific instruction in cooperation, make certain that all students understand that the goal is a cooperative (group) effort, and then reward individuals based on group results or products. The steps involved in setting up this process follow:

1. The teacher specifies the instructional objectives in such a way that all group members will master the assignment.
2. The size of the groups is determined. With low-achieving or young students, two or three per group may be best; with older students, four may be preferable.
3. Students are assigned to groups on the basis of a pretest. Generally, one high-achieving student, two average students, and one low-achieving student should form the group.
4. The classroom is arranged so that group members are close together and different groups are some distance from each other.
5. Each group is given appropriate instructional materials.
6. The teacher explains the task and the expected, cooperative goal structure. Each student must understand the task. The teacher should also specify a group goal (completion of the assignment) and the criterion for success (90% correct). The criterion may be based on the combined score of all group members.
7. All group members are taught the following skills: helping, tutoring, teaching, and sharing. The teacher should be

certain to observe the interactions of the group and intervene if necessary.
8. Evaluation should be based on the group products. If a low-achieving student is having considerable difficulty, the teacher may need to modify the student's responsibility by using improvement scores, assigning less material, or using different material.

MAPS

The Map Action Plan was designed to help school personnel successfully integrate new students with disabling conditions into regular classrooms with age-appropriate peers (Forest & Lusthaus, 1990; Polloway, Patton, Payne, & Payne, 1989; Stainback et al., 1989). Its primary use has been to facilitate integration of students who have, prior to this class placement, always been in a special school, special class, or an institutional setting. Although usually used with students at the secondary level, it can be applied with adaptations at any level. Its essential elements are as follows:

1. An integration consultant or resource teacher visits the school where the student to be integrated will attend, to speak with students in the class that the new student will attend. The consultant talks with the students, asking about their perceptions of individuals with disabilities. As a result of this meeting, the class knows of the coming of a new class member and the unique needs of that member. In addition, a potential circle of friends (called by some a *peer network*) is set up. When possible, those who will be part of the circle meet with school counselors, teachers, a consultant, and others as appropriate to talk over and prepare in writing a list of things that they can do

to make the coming of the new student more effective and pleasant for all.

2. A meeting is held after the new student has been in the class for a few weeks to review what is happening and what more can be done to make the setting work. This meeting normally involves the students in the circle of friends, the integrated student, parents, teachers, and consultants. In a case study relating to May, a 12-year-old with Down syndrome, seven questions were asked and discussed:

> What is May's history?
> What is your dream for May? (asked of the parents)
> What is your nightmare?
> Who is May? (her personal traits)
> What are May's strengths, gifts, and talents?
> What are May's needs?
> What would an ideal day for May look like? (Stainback et al., 1989, pp. 51–56)

The circle of friends directly involved with the integrated student is not set; that is, some may wish to discontinue being part of any meeting and planning sessions. Those who participate must want to participate. Some new individuals may wish to join. If students who will be in the class in the fall get to meet the new class-member-to-be in spring, they may plan contacts over the summer.

There can be many variations of MAPS, and in general, MAPS is used with students with severe disabilities. However, the circle of friends aspect of MAPS is generally applicable with all levels of disability. Gaylord-Ross (1989) notes: "One should not assume that every student with severe disabilities will need this degree of formalization (MAPS) in order to build meaningful relationships. The implementation of a MAPS program . . . should be based upon the unique needs of each individual" (p. 29).

Circle of Friends

Unlike the MAPS system, the circle of friends concept is as applicable at the levels of mild and moderate disabling conditions as it is at severe levels. The concept involves informing nondisabled students about the needs of a given student and formally asking them if they would like to be part of making that student feel welcome in the class setting. Participation in the circle must be voluntary, and the grouping should not be static or fixed. When properly carried through, such a structure can lead to expanded understandings on the part of nondisabled students, in addition to more effective programming for students with disabilities.

Forest and Lusthaus (1989) caution that the system is not a buddy system or a "chance for students to do a good deed for the day" (p. 47). It is a flexible, informal network, emphasizing true friendship and acceptance. They note that, for example, peer tutors can become friends, but they need not be. Circles should meet on some regular basis and be facilitated by a "warm and caring teacher who will promote the reciprocal nature of real friendship" (p. 50). The existence of the circles framework makes legitimate the anxieties, questions, and fears of students and teachers, and it provides the possibility of involvement by peers without disabilities in a friendly, caring, support role.

Teams-Games-Tournament

The teams-games-tournament structure involves four or five students assigned to a team to maximize heterogeneity of ability levels, gender, and race (DeVries & Slavin, 1978; Slavin, 1986). Following an instructional presentation by the teacher, the student groups are assigned worksheets covering academic material.

Teammates study and quiz each other to be certain that all members are prepared. Then, students are assigned to three-person tournament tables. The highest-scoring three students in past tournaments are assigned to Table 1, the next three to Table 2, and so on. Questions are asked during the tournament about the material presented by the teacher and studied by the teams. Each student's score is added to an overall team score, thereby allowing all students an opportunity to contribute to the score for their team.

Jigsaw

The jigsaw approach also assigns students to heterogeneous teams. Learning material is divided into several sections according to the number of team members. Each student is responsible for studying one section with one member from each of the other teams. After the students have studied thoroughly, they return to their teams and teach their respective sections. On completion of their study, each team member is quizzed on all aspects of the unit.

With the jigsaw approach, the grading or scoring procedure is different from that of the teams-games-tournament approach in that the quiz scores contribute to individual rather than group grades. Group members are rewarded for their contributions because each member assists other team members in the learning of the various sections (Aronson, 1978). Slavin (1978) has developed a modification of the jigsaw approach that emphasizes team scores rather than individual scores.

Student Teams Achievement Divisions

Like the teams-games-tournament and jigsaw approaches, the student teams achievement divisions approach uses four or five heterogeneously grouped students. The primary difference is that the games and tournaments are replaced by 15-minute quizzes that students

take after studying with their teams. The quiz scores are converted into team scores, which serve to create achievement divisions.

Achievement divisions are formed with six students in each division, and their performance is compared with past quiz scores. With this procedure, the students' scores are compared with those of students of similar ability. Students in each division do not interact with other divisions and are not aware of other division assignments. A bumping procedure is used to change weekly division assignments and to maintain equality. This approach to cooperative learning allows equal opportunities for contributions to the team score.

Small-Group Teaching

Small-group teaching is similar to the other cooperative arrangements except that it is relatively low in group reward interdependence. In this approach, learning is accomplished through group inquiry, discussion, and information gathering by students. Students choose subtopics provided by the teacher and then form small groups of two to six members. If needed, the groups may further subdivide the assignments into individual responsibilities. After completing their respective assignments, the individual students prepare for a group presentation that is evaluated by the entire class and the teacher. This promotes task interdependence and helps build the self-confidence of *all* students (Sharon & Sharon, 1976).

Problem-solving Discussions

Problem-solving discussions may be informational, to discuss the nature and causes of disability, degrees of disability, how a disability affects learning, and levels of realistic expectation. Or, with this information as background, discussions may be held with the intent of generating possible stagies for more effective inclusion of a student into the class (Polloway

Games can be a reward for task completion.

& Patton, 1993). In practice, people often have more negative feelings about intellectual disabilities than about physical ones, so several interrelated discussions may be required.

The teacher must decide, perhaps with the student and parent, whether the student should be present for such discussions. The age of the student, degree of disability, and maturity level of the student and class are considerations in making the decision. Problem-solving discussions may enhance interactions between students, but if not handled properly, may also result in pity or increased divisions. The regular classroom teacher, special education teacher, and perhaps the parents and student should plan for such discussions.

Buddy Systems

With buddy systems, the most important factor is the compatibility of the two students.

This situation must be handled very carefully, and the teacher must observe closely to be certain the student with a disability is gaining independence. The wrong buddy could lead to increased dependence. The responsibilities of a buddy usually depend on the particular disability—auditory, visual, health-related, intellectual, or emotional. The buddy or helper may be rotated every few weeks to give more students the opportunity to assume responsibility.

The consideration of group learning strategies in the preceding sections provides a brief overview of such programs. It is of great value when properly implemented, and a solid research base indicates that cooperative learning has consistent, positive influences on interethnic relationships and mutual concern among students (Slavin, 1980).

Thus far, most of our suggestions emphasize interaction and cooperative working relationships—approaches believed to greatly facilitate interaction among all students. Some evidence, however, indicates that contact alone does not necessarily result in positive attitude changes. This research indicates that students also need specific information and that with specific information and awareness of the potential of individuals with disabilities, individuals without disabilities change their attitudes significantly (Cleary, 1976; Gronberg, 1983; Prillaman, 1981; Scheffers, 1977).

Understanding Students with Disabilities

The next several sections review ways in which teachers can provide specific information to help students without disabilities better understand the abilities of individuals with disabilities.

Books and Films About Individuals with Disabilities

Many trade books about individuals with disabilities are valuable in helping students without disabilities better understand peers who have disabilities. (See Appendix A for an annotated list of such books.) Such materials may be read to a class or placed on the classroom reading shelf or in the school library. Films about individuals with disabilities also may be of interest and value. Reading such books and viewing such films can serve as starting points for discussions. Hildreth and Candler (1992) suggest questions that may guide the discussion:

1. What academic, social, or physical characteristics were portrayed by the main character?

2. What were the reactions of the other characters?
3. What caused the academic, social, or physical problems?
4. How was the main character helped (in school, assistive devices, counseling, etc.)?
5. What was the reaction of the family to the main character's problems?

If properly selected, such books or films will provide insights into the feelings and adjustments of individuals with disabilities.

As new materials are available (either books or films), teachers may wish to consider using them; however, not all are equally valuable and appropriate. Rudman (1984) provides criteria for selecting books that portray persons with special needs. These criteria may also be valuable in film selection. The following list summarizes her criteria. Books (and films) about individuals with special needs should

1. Portray persons in a balanced way, having individual talents and temperaments
2. Show persons of various races, social classes, and economic backgrounds
3. Show individuals as capable of helping themselves and others, not as objects of pity
4. Show individuals as coping with disability, not as receiving some miracle cure because they are good persons
5. Use accuracy in describing settings and situations (i.e., not describe institutions as either torture chambers or ideal havens)
6. Not pair specific disabilities or physical attributes with specific personality traits or mental abilities
7. Not show tragedy or violence as a specific byproduct of disability
8. Show persons with disabilities as capable of loving relationships

Knowledge of Technological Aids

Both teacher and students will find it helpful to hold brief instructional sessions regarding the uses and functions of any special equipment used by the student. Students without disabilities may not understand equipment such as voice synthesizers, braille typewriters, computers that translate standard print into braille, wheelchairs, braces, or hearing aids, and may find them a source of distraction. The teacher, or the student, may alleviate the disruption by briefly explaining the use of the device and perhaps demonstrating how it functions.

For example, a visually impaired student can demonstrate magnification devices and explain their value and use. The student may also explain the rationale for using a regular typewriter, braille materials, or large-type materials. Other aids and appliances, such as tape recorders, tape players, talking book machines, arithmetic aids, and embossed or enlarged maps may also be demonstrated. Units of study on the eye or ear may be presented by the regular classroom teacher or the special education resource teacher in cooperation with a student who is visually or hearing impaired.

The age and willingness of a student with a disability to participate are factors to consider when planning such discussions. If a student is unwilling, the special education teacher (vision specialist or hearing specialist) may conduct them. Regardless of who participates, the session must be handled so that the student is not made to seem too "special." If the presentation implies that the student is someone super or someone to feel sorry for, this may defeat the very purpose of the discussion and demonstration.

Panel of Individuals with Disabilities

Some teachers have had considerable success by inviting guest speakers who are disabled or panels of persons with disabilities to share their experiences. Such presentations should emphasize ways in which these individuals modify or adapt to everyday living situations. Such individuals may also discuss their interests, hobbies, and work experiences. Students should be encouraged to ask questions of the guests. It is important that the teacher invite individuals who will assist in the development of positive attitudes.

Special Materials

Special materials have been developed to help students without disabilities better understand and accept the differences and similarities of their classmates with disabilities. Such materials are similar to values education and clarification materials but have been designed specifically to provide information about individuals with disabilities and to promote positive attitudinal changes. It appears that attitudes of the general public toward individuals with disabilities are changing slowly in a positive direction. Although some telethons and other fundraising projects continue to emphasize the differences of people with disabilities, many other efforts emphasize the inherent similarities in the general needs of all people.

Because attitudes, beliefs, and behaviors toward differences are based on values learned from important others, such as family members, or from meaningful experiences, students without disabilities should have opportunities to participate in discussions, interviews, and presentations by adults and students with disabilities and to view films, filmstrips, and other media about individuals with disabilities. Teachers should provide specific information concerning differences between students with and without disabilities, and this content should be part of every student's education. Interaction is a basic need; therefore, educators must design instruction to help students relate to others in their environment.

 ## Teaching Social Skills

Teachers must encourage positive interactions among all students in the class. Students without disabilities must learn acceptance and students with disabilities must learn to interact in a fashion that is socially acceptable. Researchers have indicated that a lack of social behaviors is one of the reasons why students with disabilities may be physically present in the classroom but not truly included (VanBourgondien, 1987; Lenz, Clark, Deshler, Schumaker, & Rademacher, 1990; Hallenbeck & McMaster, 1991; Kohler & Strain, 1993; Salend, 1994).

In a commonsense definition, Cartledge and Milburn (1986) indicate *social skills* to be "socially acceptable learned behaviors that enable the person to interact with others in ways that elicit positive responses and assist in avoiding negative responses from them" (p. 7). Important social behaviors include greeting others, sharing, asking for assistance when needed, initiating conversations, giving compliments, following game and classroom rules, talking about such things as current movies and television shows, showing a sense of humor, helping classmates, and knowing current slang words. Unacceptable social behaviors include not responding to peer social initiations, misinterpreting the approach behaviors of peers, and entering games or group activities uninvited.

Since many students with disabilities do not have the social skills necessary to interact positively with their peers, it is imperative that teachers assess students' social skills and begin remediation of deficits. Training in social skills may occur before and after placement in

a regular classroom. Gresham (1982) categorizes training in social skills under three major headings (a) manipulation of antecedents, (b) manipulation of consequences, and (c) modeling. Manipulation of antecedents involves having nondisabled students initiate social interactions with statements such as "Come with me," "Let's play a game," and "Come on." By design, these initiations establish occasions for increased interaction. Other examples are sociodramas and cooperative games.

The training approach used most often is manipulation of consequences. This approach involves having the teacher socially reinforce the student with a disability when the student interacts or cooperates with nondisabled peers. This procedure is also used to reinforce students without disabilities when they are interacting or working positively with a student who has a disability.

The third general approach used to teach social skills is modeling. Modeling can be used in film or live formats. With film or videotape presentations, a student observes other students modeling desirable social behaviors. The most practical approach for regular classroom teachers appears to be live modeling, in which a student observes models in natural environments.

Cartledge and Milburn (1986) believe that instruction in social skills "involves many of the same procedures as teaching academic concepts; that is, the exposure of the child to a model of imitation, eliciting an imitative response, providing feedback about the correctness of the response, and structuring opportunities for practice" (p. 115). Regular classroom teachers should consult with special education resource personnel for assistance with specific approaches, but awareness of these principles will involve teachers in informal instruction throughout the school day. For teachers interested in continued study in this area, we suggest the various social skills curricula described by Cartledge and Milburn (1986); Goldstein, Sprafkin, Gershaw, and Klein (1980); and Jackson, Jackson, and Monroe (1983). See Chapter 11 for additional information regarding teaching social skills.

Teacher–Family Interactions

Given the demographics of today's society, the term *family* must include more than the traditional mother, father, children, grandparents, uncles, aunts, and cousins. Today it includes day caregivers, baby sitters, nannies, foster parents, neighbors, and reconstituted or blended families with one or more additional sets of parents, grandparents, and siblings. Just as the term may be extended, it may also refer to smaller groups such as single-parent families and to those families physically or emotionally removed from other relatives who traditionally provided support (Eby & Kujawa, 1994; Daniels-Mohring & Lambie, 1993; Simpson, 1990).

Factors That Influence Interactions

Factors that affect today's families include economic level, geographic location, and cultural heritage. Difficulties with work schedules, transportation, additional child care needs, and time conflicts may be interpreted by teachers from traditional middle-class backgrounds as lack of interest or desire to participate on the part of the parent or family[11] (Gersten & Woodward, 1994; Turnbull & Turnbull, 1990).

---

[11]In the interests of simplification, we will use the terms *parents* and *family*, meaning them to encompass any relatives, neighbors, or other caregivers who assume responsibility for the student.

Geographic factors affect the teacher–family interactions. In small, stable, rural areas teachers and parents know each other from a variety of social contexts (church, social organizations, etc.) unrelated to school; however rural, migrant families may be unknown by the community and may never become acquainted with people in the community. Mobile urban and suburban families and teachers in many urban or suburban schools have minimal opportunities to know each other and few opportunities for chance encounters (Daniels-Mohring & Lambie, 1993; Chrispeels, 1991). The cultural–ethnic heritage and the degree of acculturation of the family will also affect the interactions between teacher and family (Goor & Schwenn, 1993). Some ethnic groups emphasize respect for teachers as authorities and tend to accept whatever they say without question. Others depend on extended family relationships to help them with the socialization and schooling of their youngsters and rely on family interactions more than those with the teacher (Fad & Ryser, 1993; Epstein, 1991). Some feel uncomfortable discussing with any outsider (including school personnel) problems they may experience with their children. This discomfort may relate to or be the result of ethnic background, racial discrimination, or previous disrespectful treatment they have encountered from school personnel (Nagata, 1989). Students with special needs include representations of the same diverse populations as all other students in the school, and affect the dynamics of the family in a variety of ways (see Box 4–2).

Communication

Communication with the families of students may be categorized as face to face, technological, and written (D'Angelo & Adler, 1991). The need for a variety of means of communi-

BOX 4–2   *Difficulties Parents May Experience*

They may be disappointed or ashamed that their child has a disability.

They may be asking "What did I do wrong?"

They may be disappointed with the efforts of the school to meet the needs of their child.

They may have experienced teachers who were unwilling to assist their child.

They may receive only negative reports about their child.

They may have disabilities in reading or understanding.

They may have had misunderstandings with other professionals, such as doctors or social workers, and be angry with all professionals.

They may have given up on themselves, feeling they have done all they can.

cation is dictated by varying family demographics.

Face-to-Face Communication

Face-to-face communications are usually conferences or home visits. Such meetings should be carefully planned. Gronlund and Linn (1990) and Simpson (1990) provide guidelines for the teacher to consider prior to, during, and after a conference:

1. Make notes regarding information to be conveyed. If the student is old enough, this may be a collaborative effort.
2. Determine a convenient time, considering the parent's work schedules, and provide both verbal and written notification of the time and place in their primary language.
3. Arrange for a space or room free of distractions such as telephones, and provide adult-sized chairs. If possible, arrange the furniture so all may see each

other without a desk or table between parents and teacher, but with a space for examining papers or other student work.

4. Begin the conference with positive comments, examination of work samples, shared anecdotes, or similar information designed to put the parents at ease.
5. If there are concerns, focus on what the student can do or does do, what needs to be changed, and why. It is during this part of the conference that the teacher must use skill in asking for and using parental input, listening to parents, paraphrasing parental responses to ensure understanding, and reading nonverbal signs of anxiety, confusion, or understanding. Open-ended questions or statements, such as "How do you see that?" or "You seem to be happy (or unhappy) about that," encourage communication.
6. Collaboratively with the parents and, if present, the student, plan a course of action. This may be a time to meet

Teamwork

again, action to be taken by the teacher (send a copy of the homework assignment home each day), the student (write down the assignment each day), or the parent (look for the written assignment and make sure it is completed). Ensure that all understand, through use of listening and questioning procedures similar to those described in item 5.

7. End the conference on a positive note, summarizing issues discussed, action(s) to be taken, and, when appropriate, the next meeting time.

8. After the conference, evaluate it and be certain to complete a written record. Teachers must evaluate their own participation as honestly as possible (see Box 4–3).

Home visits are time consuming but provide for insights into the dynamics of the family that are impossible to gain in any other manner. They should be arranged in advance and at a time convenient to the family. Conversation will likely be more social in nature than a school-based conference unless it is a specifically scheduled home conference. It is extremely important for teachers to be aware of their own cultural values, and how they may be different from those of the family they are visiting. Teachers must avoid being judgmental, and recognize that their very presence may contribute to both the positive and negative dynamics observed (Cronin, Slade, Bechtel, & Anderson, 1992; Daniels-Mohring & Lambie, 1993).

Written Communication

Written communication includes report cards, contracts, happy notes, handbooks, progress narratives, monthly activity calendars, newsletters, daily or weekly assignment calendars, and records of daily grades or assignments completed. Such forms of written communication vary depending on the age of the students involved. Some are entirely teacher initiated while others are developed with the

Box 4–3   *Things for the Teacher to Think About Before and After Communication with Parents*

Do I listen?

Am I positive and honest?

Do I make promises that I can't keep?

Am I respectful to parents?

Do I avoid arguing?

Do I talk to parents so they can understand, but not condescendingly?

Do I patronize parents?

Am I sensitive to parents' needs?

Do I ever ridicule parents, their beliefs, or parenting practices?

Am I sincere in my association with parents?

Am I judgmental or quick to judge?

Do I accept a student's parents as they are?

Do I feel I have all the answers?

Do I remember they have known their child much longer than I have?

student(s), depending on purpose and the age of the students. In subsequent chapters we will discuss all of these forms of written communication. Policies related to grading, courses required for graduation, course requirements, attendance, and discipline (both school wide and for individual classrooms) are also forms of written communication. Frequently, written communication tends to be directed from the teacher or school to the parents allowing for little feedback; unfortunately, this is the most common communication practice used in schools (Simpson, 1990; Snell, 1993; Gersten & Woodward, 1994). It may be the least beneficial for many

parents because of their own lack of educational background and familiarity with English. Many recent immigrants experience difficulty reading in their primary language and are unable to read English. Teachers must be prepared to address the challenges of establishing and maintaining communication with these parents (Sicley, 1993). Although teachers are not counselors, they must be sensitive to the impact of a variety of family situations, such as blended (or in-process) families, divorce, custody disagreements, live-in male and female friends, and of the effect of such factors as financial deprivation, lack of coping abilities, physical, mental, or substance abuse, or neglect. All have an impact on the student and are compounded when the student has a disability.

Other Forms of Communication

Technological advances have provided the basis for innovators to develop a variety of ways for teachers to maintain communication with students and families. The most common is the telephone. Telephone calls from the teacher, reporting good news as well as negative, will maintain more productive communication than phone calls only to report inappropriate behavior. Parents are more likely to call for clarification regarding homework or to provide other information if the teacher has set the tone with regular phone calls (Warner, 1991). Dial-a-Teacher is a staffed program designed to provide parents and students with homework assistance, albeit one that obviously requires administrative and financial support (Warner, 1991). Telephone answering machines are a less expensive way to provide parents and students with prerecorded messages. The messages may be related to homework, a general statement regarding the topics addressed in class that day or week, progress reports for students who are identified by a code known only to the parent and teacher (Student "J" or "# 9"), or reminders of upcoming events, such as a field trip, and that permission slips are due. Parents may also record questions or comments that the teacher will hear the next day and provide the appropriate followup through written notes, phone calls, or a face-to-face conversation.

Audio- and videotapes developed by teachers for parents to check out can provide information about lessons covered in class, such as a science demonstration or class discussion. Other tapes may target such topics as how to avoid power struggles with youngsters or may provide suggestions regarding how to increase study or organizational skills. Entire classes may be taped so parents and students are able to view them (Chapman, 1991). This can be particularly helpful for students, who, because of illness, are frequently absent from school. Some school districts use public radio and television to provide information regarding general topics being covered in classes, information regarding upcoming events and advice in child rearing practices pertinent to that location (D'Angelo & Adler, 1991).

The demographics of the American classroom are changing dramatically, and teachers must respond to these changes. Students from diverse backgrounds require teachers to develop skills that accommodate language and cultural differences.

■ ■ Summary

In this chapter, we highlighted the facilitative influence of positive interactions between teachers and students, and between exceptional students and their peers. We suggested that teachers examine their feelings and expectations to be certain that they are a consistently positive factor in student success, illustrating this point with anecdotes emphasizing both the positive and negative influence of teacher attitudes and feelings. We suggested specific strategies teachers can use to monitor and evaluate various classroom interactions. We also examined aspects of teacher–family interactions.

The emphases in this chapter included additional awareness of the instructional impact of classroom interactions, learning how to monitor such interactions, and finally, understanding the extent to which positive relationships in the classroom tend to mirror teacher feelings and attitudes. The goal is positive, contagious attitudes that can spread throughout the schools.

P A R T

three

Teaching Exceptional Students

These final eight chapters contain basic information about teaching students with special educational needs, for convenience in discussion considered in relation to eight classifications. These classifications, which are described in federal and state laws and regulations, are used (some in modified form) in all states. Therefore, they may provide the least confusing way to communicate information about exceptional students enrolled in regular classrooms. The definitions, characteristics, and instructional suggestions provided relate to students with hearing impairments, speech and language disorders, visual impairments, orthopedic and health impairments, mental retardation, learning disabilities, emotional and behavior disorders, and giftedness or talent. For ease of presentation, we have elected to consider the lower-incidence, less ambiguous disabilities first. Whatever the order of discussion or consideration, we would hope that reference to classifications such as mental retardation, learning disabilities, and hearing impairment will not detract from what we consider to be our most important message: In the education of students with special needs, the focus of attention must be the *students* themselves.

chapter 5

- What types of behavior indicate possible hearing impairment?

- Why is it sometimes difficult to identify a young student with a mild hearing loss?

- What environmental and instructional modifications are necessary to provide successful hearing experiences for students with hearing impairment?

- Why do students with hearing impairment tend to avoid interactions with hearing students? How can teachers change this situation?

- What are the three major communication systems used by individuals with severe hearing impairment? Why not have and use just one system to reduce potential confusion?

- Is it essential for regular classroom teachers to know how to sign?

- To what extent should hearing individuals exaggerate gestures when communicating with students who have hearing impairment?

- How may regular classroom teachers facilitate the speechreading skills of students with hearing impairment?

Teaching Students Who Are Hearing Impaired

■■■■■■■■■■■■

Controversy and conflict have marked the history of education of individuals with impaired hearing. For example, the issues of how and where these students should be taught are still debated today, more than 200 years after the inception of educational programming. The "how" controversy is most commonly referred to in terms of oral (speechreading and auditory training) versus manual (fingerspelling and manual alphabet) methods of instruction. These differences also relate to the extent to which teachers should employ simultaneous oral–manual instruction. The "where" conflict refers to the extent to which these students should be educated with their hearing peers. Federal legislation, IDEA, requires that a continuum of services be provided, yet some professionals in this field do not advocate regular classroom participation. King (1991) and Thomas (1989) believe we may be doing a disservice to these students by placing them in regular classes. As King (1991) states, "Throughout the U.S. more and more deaf children are being inappropriately placed in mainstream situations. In far too many instances, school placement is marked by disregard for or ignorance of the linguistic backgrounds of the children involved, their specific needs for language development and communication, and the quality of interpreting skills that are supposed to equalize classroom communication" (p. 20).

This controversy may be further exacerbated by some deaf adults who believe it is naive, at best, to think that children with significant hearing loss can be educated in regular schools. They advocate that they should be educated exclusively with other deaf persons. This issue, of course, is related to the "oral versus manual" controversy, and to many other aspects of educational programming.

Luetke-Stahlman and Luckner (1991), in their discussion of deafness and deaf culture, write, "We believe that all hearing-impaired students should be offered a bicultural curriculum in public, private, and residential contained or mainstreamed classes. Our premise for this approach is that, through the study of Deaf culture, hearing-impaired students will develop an affinity for both their hearing and Deaf cultural and linguistic linkages with people throughout the world and will appreciate more fully the value and relevance of their educational experience" (p. 347).

While we respect the feelings and opinions of others regarding these hotly debated issues, we emphasize throughout this text that all placement and other educational programming decisions must be made by a team of professionals *in very close collaboration* with the student and his or her parents.

It is not the purpose of this text to discuss in detail the controversies and conflicts related to the education of individuals with impaired hearing, but we believe that readers should be aware of these issues. The primary purpose of this textbook is to assist regular classroom teachers to better understand and work with students with special needs and to offer specific alternative teaching strategies to successfully accommodate these students in regular classrooms.

Special acknowledgement is due Dr. John Luckner, professor of special education, University of Northern Colorado, for his critical evaluation and assistance in the revision of this chapter.

■■■■■■■■■■■■

The Importance of Hearing to Early Learning

From birth, a child learns to discriminate between loud and soft, high and low, and disturbing and pleasant sounds. An infant also learns to determine the direction, distance, and meaning of sounds. In addition, an infant analyses the human voice and differentiates his or her own babbling and crying from the sounds of others. As a result of interactions with significant others, sometime between the ages of 12 and 24 months, the child begins to learn to speak and to develop language skills. Obviously, if the child has a hearing impairment, speech and language development may be delayed.

Difficulty communicating with the majority population, and underdeveloped speech and language skills are the greatest limitations imposed by hearing impairment. Delayed speech and language influence a child's ability to develop communication skills, such as reading, writing, listening, and speaking. As a result, these skills develop at a slower rate than those of the normally hearing child. A student with a hearing impairment has the most difficulty in the language arts areas, such as reading, spelling, and writing, because of the challenges that exist in developing an understanding of and ability to use language. The extent of difficulty depends on the student's command of the language, degree of hearing loss, age of onset of loss, and age of intervention (hearing aids, systematic language instruction, auditory training).

A student may have no trouble understanding concepts but have difficulty learning the label or language used to describe concepts. For example, the concept of buoyancy may be understood, but the student may have difficulty in writing, saying, or spelling the word *buoyancy*. A student with a hearing impairment may have much less difficulty with science, math, or other non–language arts pro-

grams. Math, with the exception of story problems, is conceptual in nature. Science may also be thought of as conceptual.

In contrast, the reading process involves associating meaning with sounds and written symbols. A hearing impairment that delays language development seriously limits associations between sounds and written symbols; therefore, reading may be an area of considerable difficulty for such a student, particularly for a young child who is in the process of acquiring reading skills while simultaneously developing language. Such a child *can* learn to read; however, a very well-planned program must be offered—a program that reflects close cooperation between regular teachers and the special education resource or itinerant teachers. Although language development is important to success in school, the student with a hearing impairment is able to learn and profit from instruction in regular classrooms.

In addition to academic difficulties that may result from a hearing loss, two other limitations may be imposed by impaired hearing. The first limitation is characterized by inability to hear music. Such a limitation cannot be overcome, but must be compensated for in a manner that is acceptable to the individual. A second limitation may be imposed by society. Such societal limitations, characterized by negative or demeaning interactions with others, including parents, teachers, siblings, and friends, may lead to self-imposed social limitations and restrictions. Teachers may play important roles in reducing this type of limitation.

The Nature of Hearing Impairment

In instances where a hearing impairment has been identified, regular classroom teachers can use a number of methods and techniques. To better understand these methods and techniques, we consider here various other aspects of programs for students with hearing impairment as they are administered in the public schools.

Types of Hearing Impairment

There are two major types of hearing impairment, and different degrees of hearing loss are associated with these two types. One type of hearing impairment affects the loudness, or intensity with which a person hears speech. This type of loss, known as a *conductive hearing loss*, is caused by interference with the transmission of sound from the outer ear to the inner ear. The interference may be caused by some type of blockage, such as a foreign object, or by a malformation. If detected early, most types of conductive losses are correctable by surgery. A student with this type of loss generally can profit from the use of a hearing aid and an auditory trainer, because the aid magnifies sounds at all frequencies.

The other type of loss, a *sensorineural loss*, affects the frequency, intelligibility, and clarity of the sounds the person hears. A sensorineural loss is associated with damage to the sensory end organ or dysfunction of the auditory nerve. This type of hearing loss is not as amenable as a conductive loss to correction by use of a hearing aid because the problem is related to nerve damage. No matter how much the sound is amplified, the nerve damage prevents the sound from reaching the hearing area of the brain. Consequently, a hearing aid will increase the intensity of sound but not improve the quality of the signal.

An analogy to a radio roughly illustrates the two types of hearing loss. By turning the volume down, it is possible to simulate a hearing loss affecting the loudness with which one hears sounds. If one can hear the sounds, one can understand them; they are not distorted. This is similar to a conductive loss. The tun-

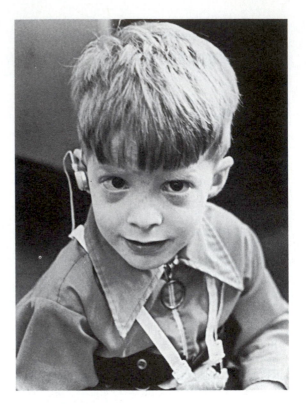

What did you say?

ing dial, which controls the frequency of signals, illustrates sensorineural loss. If the radio is not tuned in correctly, the sounds are not clear and are difficult to understand. Often words are not complete. The sentence "He sat at his desk" may sound like "e a a iz de."

Measurement of Hearing

An instrument known as a pure-tone audiometer is used to measure hearing acuity (sharpness or acuteness of sensory discrimination). An audiometer produces sounds at varying intensities (loudness) and frequencies (pitch). When administering an audiometric examination, an audiologist systematically presents a series of carefully calibrated tones that vary in loudness and pitch. The results are charted on a graph called an *audiogram*, which provides an indication of the person's ability to hear each tone at each of the presented frequencies. An audiometric evaluation assists in determining the extent and type of hearing loss so that the proper remedial or medical steps may be taken.

The unit of measurement used to express the intensity of sound is the decibel (dB), and the frequency is expressed in hertz (Hz). If an individual has a hearing loss, it is indicated in decibels; the more significant the loss, the larger the number. For example, a 60-dB loss is greater than a 25-dB loss. The following common environmental sounds expressed in intensity (decibels) may be of assistance in understanding the nature of hearing loss:

Decibels	Sounds
0	Threshold of hearing
20	Very quiet conversation; watch ticking
40	Outdoor minimum sound level in a city; electric typewriter
60	Average restaurant sounds or normal conversation
80	Loud radio or tape deck music in a home
100	Chainsaw or air hammer at 30 feet
120	Loud thunder
140	Threshold of pain; jet aircraft, 80 feet from tail at takeoff

In addition to information concerning the extent of the loss in decibels, it may be helpful to have information concerning the frequency at which the loss occurs. The audiogram in Figure 5–1 indicates a severe hearing loss in an 11-year-old student. The numbers on the left side of the audiogram indicate the decibels, or loudness of the sound. The zero indi-

cates the degree of loudness necessary for an average person to hear sound, and the other numbers indicate increasing loudness of sound. The lines on the audiogram indicate the degree of hearing loss in each ear at various frequencies. The numbers across the top of the audiogram indicate the frequency in hertz of the sounds. The sounds that are most critical for interpretation of speech (speech range) fall between 500 and 2000 Hz.

The portion of an audiogram shown in Figure 5–2 represents the sounds of speech at the various frequencies. As shown in this figure, many of the voiceless speech sounds (*f, th, s*) are in the higher ranges. A student who has a high-frequency (2000- to 4000-Hz level) loss never hears these sounds when spoken, and since much of speech is imitation, the student may leave them out when speaking.

Severity of Hearing Impairment

Often, attempts to systematically classify hearing acuity in relation to actual hearing efficiency or functional ability do not account for

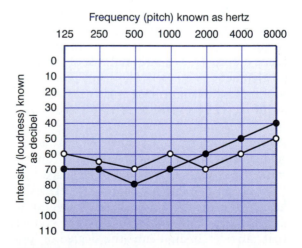

Figure 5–1

Audiogram (○, right ear; •, left ear)

Figure 5–2

Sounds of speech at various frequencies

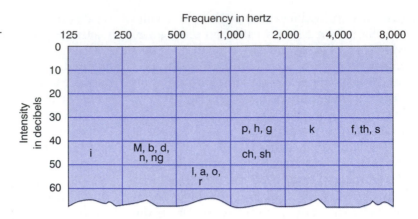

a number of outside factors, such as motivation, intelligence, social maturity, and family background. These variables may influence the functional ability of individuals. Two individuals with the same measured hearing loss do not necessarily have the same type or degree of difficulty in academic or social settings.

One type of classification emphasizes how a student might react to language instruction based on the age of onset of the hearing loss. If the hearing loss occurs at birth or at an early age, before speech and language are developed, it is classified as *congenital*, or *prelingual*, deafness. If the loss occurs after the development of speech and language, it is classified as *acquired*, or *postlingual*, deafness. These definitions emphasize the essential role of language development. A student who has a postlingual hearing loss has an intact language system to build on. Therefore, reading, writing and speech development may come easier for that student compared to a student with a prelingual hearing loss who is struggling to understand the nuances of the English language.

Although it is difficult to classify degrees of hearing impairment on the basis of severity, it is necessary to have a classification system that provides insight into the degree of loss and the potential implications. The following system is commonly used by educators:

Degree	Decibels
Mild	27–40 dB
Moderate	41–55 dB
Moderately severe	56–70 dB
Severe	71–90 dB
Profound	91 + dB

A person who has a hearing loss between 27 and 40 dB has a mild hearing loss and is likely to have difficulty with faint or distant speech. Students with mild losses may need favorable seating; may benefit from speechreading, vocabulary, or language instruction, or a combination of these; and may need speech therapy.

A hearing loss in the 41 to 55 dB range is usually classified as moderate. An individual with such a hearing loss who benefits from the use of amplification most likely can understand conversational speech at a distance of 3 to 5 feet. Such a student probably needs auditory training, speechreading, favorable seating, speech conversation, and speech therapy. The extent of services provided by the resource teacher or consultant may vary considerably, depending on the student's actual achievement in the regular classroom.

An individual with a moderately severe hearing impairment has a hearing loss in the 56 to 70 dB range. For such a student, conversation must be loud to be understood. The student's speech may not be intelligible, and she or he may have a limited vocabulary. This student may have difficulty in group and classroom discussion, can use all the services usually provided students with mild and moderate losses, and, in addition, requires specific assistance from the resource teacher or consultant.

A person who has a hearing loss between 71 and 90 dB has a severe loss and may not be able to hear a loud voice beyond a distance of 1 to 2 feet, but may be able to distinguish some environmental sounds. The student has difficulty with consonant sounds but not necessarily vowels. Such a student needs all of the services required by students with less severe losses and may need to learn many of the techniques used with students who are deaf.

An individual with a hearing loss of more than 91 dB has a profound impairment. Although this individual may be able to hear some loud sounds, he or she probably does not rely on hearing as the primary learning channel. Likely, this student needs all of the previously mentioned services and possibly more intensive services from the resource teacher, consultant for the hearing impaired, and interpreter. A student with a profound hearing loss requires special assistance, with emphasis on language, speech, and auditory training. However, the student may attend regular classes on a part-time basis or attend classes that do not require a significant emphasis on language skills.

Considerable caution must be exercised in using this classification system, because students with nearly identical losses may function differently. In addition to using caution with classification systems, educators must also exercise care in predetermining the extent of special education services needed in relation to the degree of loss. Experts in this field do not agree on the relative importance of various degrees of loss. In any individual

case, a variety of other information must be carefully considered. Characteristics of need may include unintelligible speech, with substitutions, omissions, or distortions; reading problems; underdeveloped language patterns; lower levels of abstraction; and perhaps fewer interpersonal relationships (Marsh, Price, & Smith, 1983). Some students with severe losses are readily served in regular classrooms, whereas other students with moderate loss need extensive special education services for the majority of the school day.

 ## Identification of Students with Hearing Impairment

Research (Davis, Elfenbein, Schum, & Bentler, 1986) indicates that even a mild to moderate hearing loss can significantly affect the learning process. Although not always recognized by the regular classroom teacher, a student's learning or behavior problems may result from a hearing loss. The teacher can misjudge the student as being mentally retarded or emotionally disturbed or as having some type of specific learning disability. In other instances, the teacher may feel the student's problems are caused by some failure in the teacher's methods. Until the teacher recognizes that the student's problem may be the result of a hearing loss, a great deal of time can be wasted on fruitless remedial measures. Therefore, it is important for regular classroom teachers to be aware of some common behaviors that may indicate hearing loss.

Behavioral Indications

Following are the most common behaviors and medical symptoms that may indicate hearing loss.

Lack of Attention

One such behavior is apparent lack of attention. If a student does not pay attention, it is possible that he or she cannot hear what is being said. Another possibility may be that the student hears sounds but they are so distorted that they are difficult to understand. Consequently, the student tunes them out or does not make the effort to attend to them. Occasionally, the opposite behavior is observed. A student may be abnormally attentive—always paying close attention in an attempt to determine what is happening in the classroom. Although this is less frequently seen than inattentive behaviors, it does occur. And when it does occur, it adversely affects the student's stamina.

Lack of Speech Development

Immature, unusual, or distorted speech may be the result of hearing loss. Distorted speech may be an indication of the way the student is hearing—in a distorted manner.

Difficulty in Following Directions

An unusual amount of difficulty in following oral directions is another possible indicator of hearing impairment. A student who has little difficulty with written directions and considerable difficulty with oral directions may have a hearing loss. Also, a student who often loses her or his place in oral reading assignments could have difficulty hearing what the others are reading. Another indication may be that the student asks the teacher and others to speak louder. Some students with mild losses give inappropriate answers to questions, and this too may be an indication of hearing impairment.

Best Work in Small Groups

If a student seems to work best in small groups or in relatively quiet working areas, this may be an indication of a hearing loss. Greater success with tasks assigned by the teacher at a relatively close distance or in an uncluttered auditory area (as compared with tasks assigned at a distance or in a noisy situation) may also be an indication.

Dependence on Classmates for Instructions

Teachers should be aware of a student who watches classmates to see what they are doing before he or she starts working. The student may not have fully heard or understood the directions given and may be looking for cues from classmates or the teacher.

Turning or Cocking of Head

A behavior that may indicate that a student has a hearing loss is an unusual amount of cocking the head to one side. The student may need to turn one ear toward the speaker to hear more adequately. In addition, the student with a hearing loss may make frequent requests for repetitions.

Acting Out, Stubborn, Shy, or Withdrawn Behavior

Have you ever tried to listen to a speaker who was talking so softly you had difficulty hearing? You could see the speaker's lips move but were unable to hear what was being said. Remembering that frustrating experience may help the teacher understand why a student with a hearing loss may seem stubborn, disobedient, shy, or withdrawn. If a student is unable to hear, personality and behavior problems may arise. The student may compensate for inability to hear by acting out in the classroom. Other students with hearing impairment may compensate by withdrawing, acting stubborn, or being shy.

Use of Gestures

Although rare, some students with hearing loss rely on gestures to communicate when speech would be more effective. This is more common with younger children, because they have not developed the necessary language and communication skills.

Disparity between Expected and Actual Achievement

A possible indication of hearing loss is disparity between expected and actual achievement. Obviously, there may be many reasons that students do not achieve in a manner consistent with their ability, but teachers should be aware that one of the reasons may be hearing loss.

Reluctance to Participate in Oral Activities

A less extreme behavior sometimes characteristic of a student with a hearing impairment is reluctance to participate in oral activities. Another possible characteristic is an apparent lack of a sense of humor. A student who often fails to laugh at a joke may not be hearing the joke.

Medical Indications

So far, this chapter has been concerned only with behavior that may indicate that a student has a hearing loss. There are also medical indications of hearing loss that should not be ignored by teachers. These include frequent earaches, fluid running from the ears, frequent colds or sore throats, and recurring tonsillitis.

It is advisable to be aware also of students with allergies. An allergy can produce swollen tissues in the nose and ears, leading to faulty hearing. Signs to watch for include dark circles under the eyes, red eyes, frequent sneezing, and a chronic runny nose. These physical characteristics must be brought to the attention of the school nurse and the parents, who should be urged to contact their physician. Teachers should also be aware of otitis media, an inflammation of the middle ear that, without treatment, can cause a conductive hearing loss. This condition is particularly common among children with hearing problems.

Should the teacher suspect a hearing loss, he or she must compile a list of the specific behaviors noted and refer the student immediately to the school nurse, speech specialist, or audiologist. Any of these professionals will conduct a preliminary screening; and if the results indicate the need, the student will be referred to an otologist (a physician who specializes in diseases of the ear).

It is essential that teachers monitor the referral process. Occasionally, for a variety of reasons, action is extremely slow or no action is taken. In such an unfortunate situation, the classroom teacher may have to ask pertinent questions to determine the status of the referral.

■■ Placement Considerations

As indicated at the beginning of this chapter, there is controversy regarding the most appropriate placement for students with hearing loss. Experts in the field of the education of the hearing impaired feel strongly that the term "least restrictive environment" implies only mainstreaming (King, 1991; Carroll, 1989; Thomas, 1989). Carroll (1989) states, "It appears that the ideal of 'least restrictive environment' has become the sole criteria to justify the placement of deaf children in public school programs. Yet the overwhelming emphasis of PL 94–142 [now IDEA] is on the 'most appropriate education' " (p. 20).

The following student characteristics are not criteria for placement, but are normally discussed in multidisciplinary team meetings:

1. The ability to exchange ideas through spoken, written, and read language (including expressive and receptive auditory–oral communication skills)

The teacher's face should be clearly visible to students with hearing impairments.

2. Social and emotional maturity nearly equal to that of the other students in the classroom, as well as minimal disparity between listening age and academic skills
3. The ability to profit from large-group instruction when new information is presented
4. Independence, self-confidence, and determination to succeed
5. A chronological age close to that of the regular class students (McCartney, 1984)

In addition to the characteristics of a student, other factors, such as availability of sound amplification, presence of support staff, counseling or remediation if necessary, rate of speech and type of voice of the teacher, visibility of the teacher's lip movements, acceptance and understanding level of the teacher, use of visual aids, quality of lighting, degree to which the other students will extend consideration and respect, and the wishes of the parents, must be considered prior to placement.

Such factors relate to a student, parents, and other students. An additional factor is the relationship between regular class teachers and resource personnel, who must establish and maintain a working relationship that enhances the education of the student. Regular class teachers must feel free to ask without reservation for assistance whenever needed. Resource teachers must be allowed to observe in regular classrooms at any time, not in a judgmental manner but as team members. If the working relationship between regular classroom teachers and resource teachers is one of mutual respect and understanding, recognizing that there are no authoritative experts and that neither is self-sufficient, they will be well on the way to the critical factor: open collaboration and communication for the benefit of the student.

Advantages of Regular Classroom Placement

Following are some of the advantages offered by regular classroom placement:

1. An opportunity to continue relationships with hearing classmates, which reinforces the feeling that the student with a hearing impairment is more like than not like other students. The student with a hearing impairment will maintain or gain a feeling of belonging.

2. An exposure to a greater variety of language styles. A regular classroom provides normal, age-appropriate speech, language, and social models.
3. The necessity of establishing a wider variety of communication techniques. A student who is hearing impaired may have to modify his or her communication skills if he or she is not understood by classmates. This may necessitate a reexamination of the student's communication skills.
4. An opportunity for a student with a hearing impairment to compete academically with hearing classmates. The academic pace is faster, and general achievement expectations are raised. However, in the interests of professional objectivity, note that this may be the major reason why some students *cannot* participate with success in regular classrooms.
5. Preparation to function in a hearing world. All individuals interacting with a student who is hearing impaired must remember that the ultimate objective is for the student with the hearing impairment to function as independently as possible in a hearing society.

In addition, an advantage of regular classroom placement is that hearing students have an opportunity to become acquainted with someone who is different. This must be seen as positive, particularly when students must learn to relate with and understand people of different ethnic backgrounds or races or with persons who have disabilities. Placement or retention in a regular classroom works well for some students with hearing impairment and is essentially unsuccessful with others. As noted, we believe that retention in a regular classroom is the best choice, *if it is effective in meeting the educational goals of the student*.

Obtaining Complete Information

Teachers must attempt to obtain complete information about the student's strengths and weaknesses before taking a student with a hearing impairment into a class. Be certain that there is sufficient information concerning (a) the nature of the loss, (b) the amount of residual hearing, (c) how the student communicates, and (d) what support services are appropriate and how they will be provided. The teacher should hold a few brief private sessions with the student to establish a comfortable relationship and begin the communication process. Because the speech of a student who is hearing impaired may be unintelligible, such sessions may familiarize the teacher with the student's speech patterns. The teacher may also find it helpful to discuss the student's speech needs with the speech/language specialist or special education resource person. Most of the information concerning the student can be obtained from special education resource personnel in the school or school district.

By nature of professional preparation and experience, a resource teacher or consultant generally has very good understanding of medical aspects of impairment, audiology, and speech therapy. A resource teacher or consultant may serve as a liaison between the disciplines and regular teachers, interpret the exact nature of hearing loss in relation to medical and audiological evaluations, and provide specific suggestions related to the characteristics of hearing efficiency for a particular student. It is hoped that information concerning the individual's functional ability is emphasized rather than medical or quantitative information. In addition, the resource teacher may interpret a student's development of language and its influence on learning.

Another valuable source of information is the student's parents. Brief conferences with the parents before actual placement and on an ongoing basis thereafter can provide considerable information about a student who has a hearing impairment. The information, support, and participation of the parents in their child's educational program are known to be primary determinants of successful mainstreaming programs (Gearheart, Mullen, & Gearheart, 1993).

■ Specialized Technology/ Assistive Devices

The technology underlying the development of devices to compensate for various degrees of hearing impairment has advanced rapidly in recent years. Broadly speaking, these specialized assistive devices fall into two categories: (a) those that amplify available auditory information; and (b) those that provide alternatives to auditory input. Among these are devices designed as generalized adaptations to daily life that utilize amplification, alternative input, or a combination of methods to provide information for individuals with hearing impairment.

Amplification of Auditory Information

Hearing Aids

A hearing aid is not a complicated piece of equipment. The aid helps compensate for hearing loss by amplifying sound. It cannot replace the natural ability of an ear, and a student who wears an aid should not be expected to hear normally. Limitations in the use of an aid may be imposed by damage to the ear, by the nature of speech sounds, or by the hearing aid itself. Misunderstandings of what a hearing aid can do are common. Many individuals believe, for example, that a hearing aid is like eyeglasses: you simply put them on and you will see—or hear—better. This is not true.

There are basically three parts to a hearing aid: (a) a microphone, which picks up sound and converts the sounds to electrical impulses; (b) an amplifier, which makes sounds louder by increasing the electrical impulses; and (c) a speaker or receiver, which reconverts the electrical signals back into sound and directs them to the ear mold.

There are many types of hearing aids, but hearing aids are generally classified on the basis of where they are worn. The first type is a body aid, which is strapped to the body with a wire connected to the ear mold. These sturdy, compact aids are generally worn by young children. Often, the controls are on the young child's back so that he or she will not play with them. The second type, an ear-level aid, may be mounted in eyeglasses, fit behind the ear, or fit entirely in the ear. Aids are also classified as monaural (one ear) or binaural (both ears).

Care and Maintenance.   Even though the parents or a student have examined a hearing aid prior to the student's coming to school, the aid may not adequately function in school. The teacher can check several things if a student seems not to be hearing well because of a hearing aid malfunction. Although it is not the primary responsibility of the regular classroom teacher to troubleshoot hearing aid problems, it is helpful to be aware of a few minor factors that may cause malfunctions so that the resource teacher or the parents can be alerted. The following suggestions are related to hearing aid malfunctions:

1. Make sure the battery is not dead. Keep a fresh battery at school (changed at least monthly, even though it may not have been used) so that the child does not have to go without the hearing aid on the day the battery goes dead. Often, the resource teacher has an extra supply of batteries and can assist in determining whether other problems might exist.

2. Determine if the battery is installed properly, with the positive and negative terminals in the proper position.
3. Check the cord to see if it is worn or broken or if the receiver is cracked.
4. Be sure the plug-in points are not loose. Check both the hearing aid and the receiver.
5. Check the ear mold to make sure it is not obstructed by wax and that it is inserted properly. An improperly fitted ear mold can cause irritation and feedback (squeaky or squealing sounds that annoy the student wearing the aid and are sometimes heard by other students). Possibly, the student is outgrowing the ear mold, so the parents or the resource teacher should be informed.
6. Examine the tube to determine if condensation has built up. If it has, blow through the tube until it disappears.

Regular teachers should be aware of some additional considerations with respect to the proper care and maintenance of hearing aids.

1. Do not allow the hearing aid to get wet.
2. Serious damage may result from leaving the hearing aid in extremely hot or cold places.
3. Always turn an aid off before removing it from the ear. Removing the aid without turning it off causes a squeal. Whenever an aid is taken off, it should be placed in a safe, padded box.
4. If a student repeatedly removes the aid, this may be an indication that the aid is not working correctly or does not fit properly and causes discomfort. Naturally, if this occurs, the teacher should contact the resource teacher or consultant.
5. Do not allow a student to wear a hearing aid microphone too close to the receiver,

or the aid will make unusual noises. If the student has a unilateral loss (one ear), the receiver should be worn on the side opposite the hearing aid.
6. Do not take an aid apart to attempt to repair it. This should be done by a hearing aid dealer.

Assessing Effectiveness. The resource teacher or consultant can assist in evaluating many aspects of hearing aid problems and hearing aid effectiveness. They can evaluate routinely all aspects of hearing aid operation by checking and replacing wornout batteries and troubleshooting for any other problems. Many teachers obtain a tester for use in the building or make arrangements for assistance from a local hearing aid dealer. Occasionally, the student will own a tester.

A more important role of the resource teacher is to assess hearing aid effectiveness in the classroom situation, particularly if a student has just recently been fitted with an aid. The resource teacher can appraise the effectiveness of an aid by evaluating changes in the ways a student handles everyday situations. The resource teacher should look carefully for (a) changes in social interactions, (b) changes in voice quality and articulation, (c) increased language skills, (d) reactions to sound and amplification, and (e) increased educational achievement. In addition, the resource teacher should observe whether the student is turning the volume down or completely turning it off. Such actions may be indications of an improperly fitted aid. Systematic longitudinal evaluation of a student's hearing aid effectiveness is important, and routine procedures should be established to provide hearing aid maintenance.

Increasing Understanding. Often, hearing students are curious about how a hearing aid works. In cooperation with the resource teacher, consultant, parents, and the student with a hearing impairment, the teacher may present information about the operation of the hearing aid. A brief unit of study may be conducted on the anatomy and physiology of the ear and the basic principles of acoustics. Hearing students can be given an opportunity to listen to a hearing aid (a stethoscope may be used so they do not have to put the ear mold in their ears). This type of experience may provide understanding of amplification devices and problems associated with them.

FM Systems

A conventional hearing aid amplifies all sounds, including background noises, and this often poses a serious problem. Background or environmental sounds may mask or cover up what the teacher is saying. One way to accommodate this problem is the use of frequency modulation (FM) radio equipment. An FM system is similar to a hearing aid and has the same three basic parts, but in addition, the teacher wears a microphone around the neck that sends the teacher's voice directly to the student wearing the FM radio receiver. When the teacher speaks, his or her voice is received by the student as if the teacher were standing right next to the student's ear. FM systems use a wireless microphone that transmits an FM radio signal to a combination hearing aid–FM receiver, bypassing environmental sounds and bringing desired sounds directly to the ear (Lewis, 1992).

Induction Loop Systems

Many hearing aids have a telecoil (T) setting which, when activated, responds to magnetic controls. In this system, a loop of wire is fixed around the inside periphery of a building (classroom, church, theatre). The loop can be connected to the amplifier of a microphone being used by the speaker (teacher, minister, actor), and the changing magnetic fields from the loop of wire can be received and converted

back into sound by the induction coil in a hearing aid. This direct system reduces the amplification of background noises and allows receivers to concentrate directly on the words spoken into the microphone.

Infrared Systems

Infrared systems operate on a similar basis to FM amplification systems. The carrier waves are infrared light rather than radio frequencies. The light waves carry the messages to the ear through a receiver similar in appearance to the earpieces of a stethoscope. These systems are effective in reducing background noises and reverberations and are mainly used to amplify large areas such as theaters, auditoriums, large classrooms, and lecture halls. Such systems can be adversely affected by direct sunlight and can only be used indoors.

Cochlear Implants

A cochlear implant consists of a microphone, transmitter, processor, and receiver. The microphone is attached externally at ear level and picks up sounds, which are transformed into electrical currents and amplified by a battery-operated processor. This energy is sent to the transmitter, which is located behind the ear and held in place magnetically. The electrical current is transformed into magnetic signals to the receiver, which is a small disk planted beneath the skin behind the outer portion of the ear. Two electrodes are attached to this receiver, one placed in the scala tympani and the other grounded in the eustachian tube. As current flows between the two electrodes, the nerve cells of the cochlea are stimulated, so the sensation of hearing occurs.

Variations of this process include use of a percutaneous plug, which provides direct input of electrical energy. Such variations are often referred to as *hardwired*. Some implants have multiple channels to allow for more variation in the sounds that are transmitted. Others use an extra cochlear electrode, which is mounted on the round window rather than the cochlea. Cochlear implants are most effective in a recipient who has lost hearing after already learning speech and language. They are least effective in adults who have been deaf since early childhood (Rennie, 1993). Whatever the type of cochlear implant, a cooperative effort with an audiologist or speech-language specialist is essential.

Since 1985, when the Food and Drug Administration approved cochlear implants for children, increasing numbers of schoolaged children have undergone the cochlear implant procedure. Candidates for cochlear implants usually have a profound sensorineural hearing loss and have not benefited from the usual amplification devices available. The recipient of this device, however, will hear sounds that are different from normal hearing, and there must be a collaborative, rehabilitative effort involving the surgeon, family, and educators to enable the cochlear recipient to understand and use the new sounds. Usually, audiologists and speech-language specialists will also be very helpful. The teacher with a student who has had an implant must collaborate with these professionals in any special training pertinent to the regular classroom.

As indicated previously, there are significant controversies in the area of the education and treatment of individuals with hearing loss. One such controversy concerns the use of cochlear implants. Although there have been many technological gains in the development of cochlear implants there is still a certain degree of unreliability in their effectiveness. Therefore, children in which these implants are somewhat ineffective could conceivably be deprived of their optimal opportunities to learn speech as well as signed language. This could result in feelings of isolation in both the deaf and hearing communities.

Alternatives to Auditory Input

Interpreters

Students enrolled in a total communication program may use interpreters to help them in their regular classrooms. The interpreter is usually located just outside the direct line of sight from the student to the teacher, slightly facing the student, thereby allowing the student to directly speechread the teacher or the interpreter.

The interpreter repeats what the teacher is saying through signs, fingerspelling, and non-vocalized speech. He or she may paraphrase or modify what the teacher is saying if the student is not familiar with the words or concepts being used. Interpreter-tutors are not teachers, but they must be experts in total communication. In some states, they must pass proficiency examinations and be certified.

Using an interpreter is a new experience for many teachers. Initially, it seems unusual to both the teacher and the hearing students. In fact, for the first several days or until the hearing students become comfortable, they may be seriously distracted by the signs, gestures, and expressions of the interpreter.

The following general suggestions may be helpful when using an interpreter:[1]

1. Be aware that you and the interpreter may have to adjust and modify the pace of instruction periodically. Occasionally the interpreter may ask you to stop momentarily, repeat, or slow down. Teamwork between the teacher and interpreter is vital to the student.
2. Be certain there is good lighting wherever the interpreter stands.
3. In using demonstration and visual aids, allow extra time for students to see what is being

---

[1]Adapted from *Guidelines for Interpreting for the Hearing Impaired*, p. 3, 1982. Greeley, Colorado: Office of Resources for the Disabled, University of Northern Colorado.

Interpreter working in the classroom

demonstrated as well as to see what is being said. With hearing students the teacher can turn her back to the class and simultaneously elaborate a point as she demonstrates. With students with hearing impairments this is not possible, since they must turn their attention from the interpreter to the chalkboard to see what the teacher is demonstrating and then turn back again so they will not miss the explanation. The best solution to this problem is first, to be more explanatory as new points are put on the board and second, to pause while maintaining eye contact with the students.

4. When using an overhead projector, slides, videotapes, or films, it is sometimes necessary either to reduce the lighting or to turn off the lights completely in the classroom. In such situations it is important to provide a small lamp or spotlight to focus on the interpreter while discussion or explanation takes place.

5. Because sign language does not contain signs for every word in the English language, the interpreter must fingerspell special vocabulary using the manual alphabet. The interpreter

may also be asked by the student to pause and define the term. It is most helpful to write special vocabulary on the board or give a list to the interpreter before class so that neither the interpreter nor the student misunderstands the concept.

6. Question-and-answer periods may pose problems. If the student is unable to vocalize her question, she must sign the question to the interpreter and the interpreter then vocalizes the question to the teacher.

7. The interpreter cannot interpret more than one speaker at a time. During discussions, remind the other students to speak one at a time.

8. To establish rapport, speak directly to the student, not to the interpreter.

Interpreters should be encouraged to assist with the development of the IEP. They will have information regarding the student's communications needs and, in general, have valuable information to share from their unique perspectives.

Some caution must be exercised to avoid dependency between the interpreter and the student; use an interpreter only when necessary.

Students who do not have good speechreading skills and thus might not be able to participate in regular classrooms may be able to do so with the assistance of an interpreter. It is imperative that every method that may help a student make maximum progress be fully investigated.

Media and Audiovisual Equipment

Audiovisual equipment and personnel can be of particular value to the teacher who has a student with a hearing impairment in the class. Overhead projectors can greatly enhance the student's achievement. The teacher may put important notes or key vocabulary words and phrases on the overhead projector while lecturing. An overhead projector allows the teacher to maintain eye contact with students while writing. When using slides or films, the teacher should be certain there is sufficient light to enable the student to see faces clearly as the narrator or teacher makes comments. In general, supplementary diagrams and pictures should be used as often as possible. Often, the complete narrative script to a filmstrip or audiotape accompanies the materials and, if available, should be given to the student who is hearing impaired.

Many educational films have been captioned so that they can be used in regular classrooms. The resource teacher or consultant may provide the teacher with a detailed listing of materials that are available free of charge. Use of these modified and adapted instructional materials does not interfere with the education of normally hearing students. In fact, it facilitates their achievement as well.

Vibrotactile Devices

A vibrotactile device changes auditory signals into vibrations that are felt on the skin. It is often worn on the wrist or the chest and can be used in conjunction with an FM system. This type of device is fundamentally used with children who are profoundly deaf for the purpose of improving general sound awareness, discrimination of speech sounds, and the production of speech. It may also be used as an alerting device.

Laser Videodiscs

Laser videodiscs are high-capacity storage systems for audio and visual images. Each 12-inch disc can store up to 30 minutes of continuous video display with over 100,000 visual images in the form of still or moving pictures. Information is accessed through a videodisc player linked to a computer with a television or monitor. Those videodiscs designed for education are interactive and allow the user to select desired segments. Some videodiscs come designed with barcoding for easy access in selecting material.

This popular media system has innumerable possibilities for enhancing instruction for students with impaired hearing by providing much-needed visual representation. Discs available range from typical school subjects to the Fun & Games disc by Voyager (see Figure 5–3), which offers many children's activities such as games, lessons in sign language, dancing instruction, and kite building.

Computers/Software

Microcomputers have come to be an invaluable tool in the classroom, offering a multitude of colorful and novel drills, lessons, and games. Software applications for students who are hearing impaired generally teach manual communication, written language, and speech training (Clymer, 1994; Stuckless, 1994).

There are several programs available for teaching manual communication skills. Talking Hands from EBSCO Curriculum Materials (Figure 5–3) specifically teaches fingerspelling. Microtech Consulting Company (Figure 5–3)

CUE Soft-Swap
4655 Old Ironside Dr., Suite 200
Santa Clara, CA 95054

EBSCO Curriculum Materials
P. O. Box 486
Birmingham, AL 35202

IBM Educational Systems
One Culver Road
Dayton, NJ 08810

Laureate Learning Systems, Inc.
110 E. Spring St.
Winooski, VT 05404

Microtech Consulting Company
P. O. Box 521
Cedar Falls, IA 50613

Micro Video Corporation
210 Collingwood, Suite 100
P. O. Box 7357
Ann Arbor, MI 48107

Software To Go
MSSD Box 77
800 Florida Avenue, N.E.
Washington, DC 20002

Ultratec
450 Science Dr.
Madison, WI 53711

Voyager Company
1351 Pacific Coast Highway
Santa Monica, CA 90401

Figure 5–3
Producers of hardware, software, and assistive devices

offers several computer-based applications ranging from fingerspelling to ASL vocabulary building to story comprehension.

Written language skills can be taught with the help of graphics/text programs such as First Words, First Verbs, and Micro LADS (Language Assessment and Development System, see Figure 5–3), which offer instruction in syntax. All are available from Laureate Learning Systems, Inc. HyperStories (CUE Soft-Swap, see Figure 5–3) helps students create stories that branch, making various plots and endings possible. Word processing programs are quite appropriate for students with hearing impairment, provided the students have adequate keyboarding skills and knowledge of the word processing program. Since these students often have difficulty with spelling and word usage, word processors can have an extra benefit. Spell checkers and thesauruses often provided within the program allow the student to focus on the writing process while receiving instant assistance in these troublesome areas.

Programs designed to improve speech skills, such as the IBM Speech Viewer (see Figure 5–3) come with an adapter card, a speaker, microphone, and software. Students are graphically given feedback on various components of their speech such as pitch, voicing, loudness, and timing. A related software offering is the Video Voice Speech Training System (Micro Video Corporation, Figure 5–3) for use with Apple II and IBM computers.

Software to Go (see Figure 5–3), sponsored by Gallaudet University, has cataloged more than 1,000 titles of software available to any educational program or library that serves individuals with hearing impairment (Kurlycheck, 1993). Members who belong to this clearinghouse and lending library may receive printouts of software evaluations and borrow selected titles for up to one month.

Adaptions for Daily Life

Technological advances have allowed developers to create a number of devices to add convenience to the daily lives of individuals with hearing impairment. Following are a few of the devices that have proven to be effective in removing some of the limitations imposed by impaired hearing.

TDDs

TDDs are telecommunication devices for persons who are deaf. They are essentially telephones that allow a conversation to be typed rather than spoken. They are equipped with small keyboards, a coupler or transmitter on which the telephone receiver is placed, and a display screen for incoming and outgoing messages. A hard copy of the message can be obtained from an attachable or built-in printer. TDDs are often portable and come with optional or built-in memory units that allow the user to store short messages for later use or to transmit an entire message from

memory. Most TDDs are connected to household lamps or lights to alert the user of incoming calls.

The Superprint 4420 from Ultratec (see Figure 5–3) enables messages to be received as quickly as they are typed, allowing a more realistic flow in conversation. An automatic identification function alerts an answering party that the caller is using a TDD, a feature which can be extremely helpful in emergencies. If hearing persons should call, a voice message will announce that they have reached a TDD and they will be directed to call a relay service provided by telephone communications companies.

The Intele-Modem, also from Ultratec, can turn a personal computer into a TDD by automatically converting ASCII computer

TDDs (telecommunication devices for the deaf) allow conversations to be typed rather than spoken. (Photo courtesy of Utratec, Inc.)

code to TDD code, allowing contact with various types of TDDs and computers.

Telecaptioning/Other Media

Telecaption adapters, or decoders, enable viewers to read captions, or subtitles, across the bottom of a television screen. Without the adapters, the captions on the screen are invisible. Decoders can be attached to an existing television set or can be installed in newly purchased sets.

Funds for close-captioned television and captioned films for the deaf are available through the Captioning and Adaptations Branch of the U.S. Department of Education to enhance the education and welfare of those individuals with hearing impairment through the use of the media (National Information Center on Deafness, 1989).

Alerting Devices

Alerting devices enable individuals with hearing impairment to monitor everyday sounds in the home such as smoke detectors, alarm clocks, telephones, doorbells, or a baby's crying. A monitored signal is transmitted through FM radio waves to a receiver, which then activates a flashing light or vibrator. Vibrotactile or visual receivers can also be worn on the wrist (Kaplan, 1987).

▚ Methods of Communication

Development of language and communication skills is the primary emphasis of educational programming for students with hearing impairment. Educators have disagreed concerning the most effective and efficient method of communication for such students. Three methods have been advocated: (a) the manual method, (b) the oral method, and (c)

total communication. Each of these is briefly discussed in the following sections.

Manual Communication

Manual communication may be divided into two main categories: sign language and sign systems. The most common sign language is American Sign Language (ASL). It is a set of gestures representing words or concepts (Figure 5–4). It is generally used by the adult deaf population and has been called the "mother tongue." ASL has its own grammar, syntax, idioms, and vocabulary. Educators of students with impaired hearing became dissatisfied with ASL because it did not correspond to English. As a result of this dissatisfaction, they developed alternative manual sign systems that more closely approximate English. Figure 5–5 provides a comparison of ASL with two other sign systems: Pidgin Sign English and Manual English. Fingerspelling, or manual alphabet, is another form of manual communication. In fingerspelling, various finger positions represent individual letters of the alphabet and are used to spell out words (Figure 5–6).

Oral Communication

The oral-aural method of communication makes use of oral and auditory training and speechreading. This method encourages the use of residual hearing while the presentation of material emphasizes the student's visual and auditory attention. Of course, use of amplification is stressed. The oral method emphasizes speechreading and oral speech as the primary means of communication. Gestures and other movements are generally not used other than those ordinarily used by hearing individuals to supplement conversation.

Cued speech is used to augment oral programs, especially speechreading. It includes

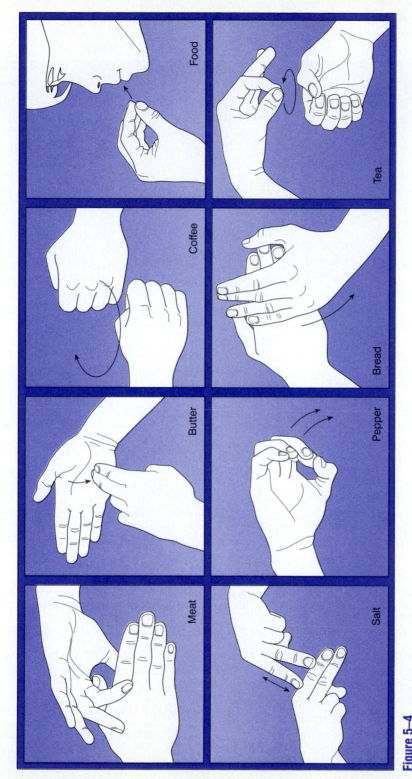

Figure 5–4
American Sign Language

American Sign Language (ASL)	Pidgin Sign English (PSE)	Manual English (ME)*
(Also called: Ameslan, Native sign language)	(Also called: Sign English, Signed English)	(Also called: English) Seeing Essential English (SEE 1) Signing Exact English (SEE 2) Local Sign Systems
• A language separate from English, capable of great subtlety in a visual mode. • Uses different syntax than English. • Cannot be used simultaneously with voiced English. • Many signs are more conceptual than those in English systems. • Used by deaf adults, hearing children of deaf adults, and deaf children.	• A combination of ASL and Manual English. • Usually signed in English word order. Endings and grammatical markers are often not used. • Can be used simultaneously with voiced English. • Borrows a great many signs from ASL. Uses occasional fingerspelling of words. • Used by deaf people and hearing people in social and formal situations. Often said to bridge the gap between deaf and hearing people. • Widely used by sign language interpreters.	• A visual code for the English language that assists deaf children in learning English. • Follows English exactly, using word order and grammatical markers such as endings, suffixes, and prefixes. • Can be used simultaneously with voiced English. • Borrows a great many signs from ASL. Includes invented signs for grammar and vocabulary. Uses occasional fingerspelling of words. • Widely used in public schools. • Used by deaf children in formal situations. • Rarely used by deaf adults or in social situations.

* Manual English is sometimes called Manually Coded English (MCE). Use of the terms English, Manual English, Manually Coded English, Signed English, and Pidgin Sign English varies.

Figure 5–5

Sign language systems

Source: Moser, B. W. (1987). Introducing sign language systems to parents of young deaf children. *Perspectives for teachers of the hearing impaired, 6*(2), 12–15. Reprinted by permission of *Perspectives in Education and Deafness*.

eight hand shapes in four specific positions to represent phonetic elements that are not readily visible (Cartwright, Cartwright, & Ward, 1984; Schwartz, 1984). The cued speech system was deliberately designed so that it cannot be used as an independent or total form of communication, but functions as an adjunct to speech. Consequently, an individual who uses cued speech produces the various hand shapes while simultaneously speaking.

Total Communication

A third approach, called total communication, combines the manual and oral-aural methods according to the abilities, interests, and needs

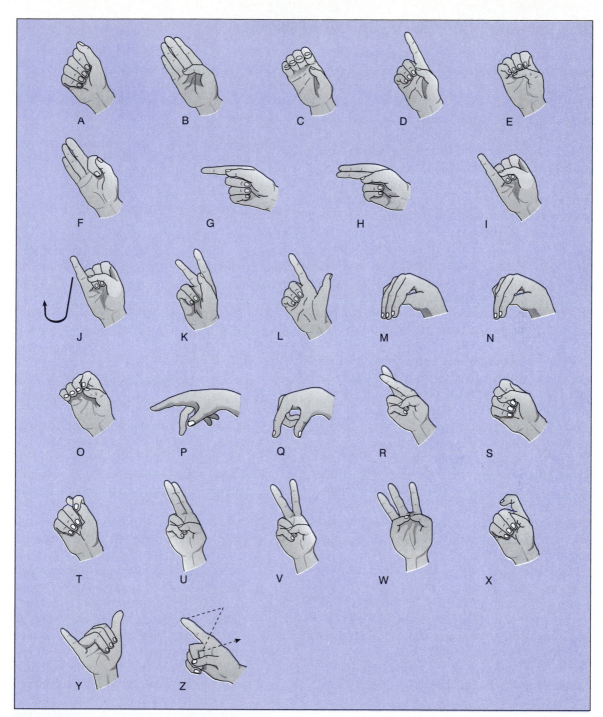

Figure 5–6
Manual alphabet used by the deaf of North America
Source: Courtesy American Foundation for the Blind, New York.

of the student who has a hearing impairment. Total communication is a philosophy of flexibility—a flexibility that encourages and supports the right of these students to choose and use a system that is most appropriate for them. The total communication method teaches the student to use amplification, residual hearing, speechreading, and oral speech in combination with manual systems. Cued speech may also be used as an aid to total communication.

Because of differences between sign languages and English, there has been a proliferation of methods that purport to code English in sign. The most common methods are Seeing Essential English (Anthony, 1971), Signed English (Bornstein, 1974), and Signing Exact English (Gustason, Pfetzing, Zawolkow, & Norris, 1972).

There exists some controversy between advocates of ASL and advocates of coding English in sign. The main point in dispute is whether it is more effective to use ASL as the primary tool for teaching students with hearing impairments and subsequently teach English (reading and writing) as a second language, or to bypass the necessity of learning two languages in favor of one coded-English system or a combination of coded-English systems. If the latter procedure is followed, a student can use one form of English for signing, reading, and writing.

Although manually coded English systems in some form are widely used in the United States (Quigley & Paul, 1984) and ASL was for a time about the only form of sign language used, there still is only "limited information on the educational effectiveness of the various communication forms" (p. 231). Luetke-Stahlman and Luckner (1991) state the following:

These languages or systems must be available to students based on their needs, as determined by assessment and as documented in the Individualized Education Program (IEP). Yet, because this may not be feasible financially, some students who need an ASL, oral English, Cued Speech, or SEE program are assigned to an available placement. As a result, students rely on the integrity and skill level of their teachers to supply them with the language or system that is most beneficial for learning new, unknown information. (p. 11)

Facilitating Speechreading

Most students with hearing impairment have some remaining, or *residual*, hearing, and special efforts must by made to facilitate speechreading because the students may not hear all of the sounds in the environment. Students must learn to closely observe lips, facial gestures, body gestures, and other environmental clues to fully understand what their teachers and classmates are saying. Regular classroom teachers should take the following steps:

1. Allow students with hearing impairment to sit where they can make the most of what they hear and see. Sometimes, young children need guidance in this area. Remember, students with hearing impairments listen with their eyes as well as their ears whenever possible. Such students should be within 5 to 10 feet of the speaker. Do not, however, have students sit so close that they must look up constantly. To aid students in becoming more proficient speechreaders, change the seating arrangement from time to time to give the students practice in watching different speakers in the classroom from different positions. Seating arrangements may depend on the classroom organization. If the class is small, arranging the desks in a semicircle and seating a student with a hearing impairment on the end facilitates speechreading. In a lec-

ture situation, placing the student near the front of the room and off to one side allows the student to readily read the speech of classmates and teachers. Seating arrangements must remain flexible to ensure that the student can observe and participate in class activities. The teacher should observe the student to notice whether she or he seems to be straining or missing important concepts; if so, modification in the seating arrangement may be necessary. It may also be helpful to ask the student periodically if she or he would like to move.

2. Seating should be arranged so that a student does not have to look into a light source. Do not stand in front of windows, for this makes speechreading difficult. Do not stand in a dark area or an area where there are shadows. Generally, speechreading is easier when the light source is behind the student.

3. Try to face the group when speaking and when members of a class are speaking, encourage them to face the student who has a hearing impairment. Also you may have to cue the student and let him or her know who is talking as well. You may need to ask the question twice before accepting a response. When writing on the chalkboard, turn to face the class before speaking. Stay in one place as much as possible when giving oral examinations or while lecturing, so that when the student looks up, you are in the same general location. Some teachers have found it helpful to reserve several seats for the student who has a hearing impairment, with one seat as "home base." Oral examinations requiring written responses may also

cause considerable difficulty for such a student. If the student is writing a response while you are giving another item, the student may miss several items. Overhead projections and transparencies work extremely well in such cases for all students, and visual aids in general are effective with students who are hearing impaired.

4. Call attention to visual aspects of a particular concept to be learned. Phonetic analysis, as an example, may not be helpful. Generally, instruction that emphasizes visual clues is preferred.

5. Do not exaggerate your gestures, for exaggerated gestures may cause considerable confusion. Use gestures as usual, but keep your hands and any objects away from your face whenever possible. Beards and mustaches sometimes distract attention from the lips or make them difficult to see.

6. Speak naturally. Individuals who have not had a lot of experience with the hearing impaired have a tendency to sound out words with exaggerated movements of their mouth. Such exaggeration may have a tendency to confuse the student.

7. Periodic verification may be necessary to ensure that the student with impaired hearing has understood the instruction, assignment, or question. The teacher should also encourage the student to ask questions to verify or clarify oral presentations.

8. Provide a good pattern of speech for a student with a hearing impairment. Distinct articulation is more helpful than speaking louder. Speech patterns should not, however, be exaggerated.

9. Ask questions of the student occasionally to make certain she or he is following the discussion. When present-

ing a new word or asking a question, repeat it if the student does not understand it the first time, looking directly at the student. If the student seems to miss the term or request, rephrase what you originally said and ask a question; for example, "This is a stapler. How could you use a stapler?" or "Who would use a stapler often?"

10. Certain words are not easily understood through speechreading. When possible, write them on the overhead or chalkboard. Encourage the student to ask questions or have statements repeated if he or she does not understand.

11. When providing instruction, in general, it is helpful to paraphrase verbalizations, repeating, and simplifying when the student has difficulty understanding.

12. When presenting isolated words, as in spelling lessons, use the words in context. You may also give spelling tests by providing the contextual words of sentences on a sheet of paper, leaving blank spaces for the spelling words. With this method, a student has the necessary contextual clues. Remember, many words appear alike on the lips and sound alike, for example, *beet* and *bead*. Other examples are *meal* and *peel*, *safe* and *save*, and *pie* and *buy*.

13. When presenting new vocabulary words, present the multiple meanings for these words. Some words have more than five meanings. This can be difficult for a student with a hearing impairment because the student's vocabulary may not be sufficient to understand the multiple meanings. It is also very helpful when presenting new words that they be presented both auditorially and in printed form.

14. Chewing movements should be avoided as much as possible. If students are allowed to chew gum, this may make speechreading difficult, since students with hearing impairment may not be able to differentiate between chewing and speech.

15. When referring to an object in the room, it may be beneficial to point to it, walk over to it and touch it, or actually manipulate the object. This may put the object into the context of the discussion and support what is being discussed. When speaking directly to a student or calling for the student's attention, call the student's name or speak directly to her or him. In nearly all instances, instruction that combines both visual and auditory cues is more effective.

16. Do not seat a student with a hearing impairment close to audiovisual equipment that has a fan or motor noise.

17. If you use pictures with verbal presentations, initially describe the material and then show the illustration. This allows the student to focus on one major stimulus at a time.

Facilitating Language and Speech Development

An essential component of educational programming for students with hearing impairment is speech training. A student's ability to monitor language may be seriously limited by the impairment, thereby limiting the student's expressive language abilities.

Often, the speech specialist working with the student has clearly established goals and objectives related to the student's speech patterns and general articulation. Regular classroom teachers play important roles in facilitating good speech habits. Reinforcement of therapy goals and objectives in the classroom is essential if carryover and maintenance in everyday situations are to be expected. The following suggestions may facilitate carryover and maintenance:

1. Encourage the student to participate in oral discussions and expect the student to use complete sentences when speaking. Be careful, however, not to emotionally load the situation. If proper speech is insisted on and the student is demeaned in front of the entire class for incorrect usage or incomplete sentences, the student may be discouraged from participating in any oral discussion. Be careful not to nag the student. Often, the correction of a mispronounced word may be accomplished by a brief conference at the end of the period or day. Some teachers have had success with keeping a list of words with which the student has had difficulty and then giving them to the student with the correct pronunciation without comment. Also encourage the student to participate in conversation, reading, storytelling, and creative dramatics.

2. Encourage the student to use the dictionary to aid in pronunciation of difficult words. This practice naturally depends on the age and reading level of the student.

3. Don't be afraid to talk with the student about the hearing loss. Students with hearing impairment need to be told when they are speaking too loudly or too softly. Since a student with a hearing impairment may not be able to monitor his or her own speech sounds, the teacher can do a great deal to keep the student from developing dull or expressionless speech habits.

4. Praise and encourage a student who has correctly pronounced a previously difficult word. Children need a great deal of encouragement and success if they are to accomplish this very difficult task.

5. Provide a relaxed language environment. The more relaxed and casual the speech and language styles of teachers and students, the better the opportunity for language acquisition.

Facilitating Social Interactions

One criterion by which mainstreaming may be judged is the extent to which a student with a disability is accepted, chosen as a friend, and liked by other students (Cartwright et al., 1984). There are indications that the social interaction between hearing students and students with hearing impairment is much less than that among hearing students (Lee & Antia, 1992). Such research seems to place responsibility for increased and positive interaction on the student with a hearing impairment. Part of the poor interaction may be attributed to lack of communication skills of the student with a hearing impairment or to insufficient social skills, such as ability to initiate and continue conversations or discuss playground or afterschool activities. Other factors may include the teachers, the environment, and the hearing students.

Teachers

When the regular classroom teacher maintains a supportive climate within the classroom, it is possible for some students with hearing impairment to become dependent on the teacher for positive and rewarding social interactions (Kretschmer & Kretschmer, 1978; Schlesinger, 1985). Teachers must be aware of their influence and the possibility that they are fostering overdependence. They should recognize that overdependence may in fact be negatively influencing the attitudes of the hearing students and limiting the interactions between the hearing students and the students with hearing impairment. Teachers should encourage and develop procedures to enhance such interactions. Resource or itinerant personnel may have specific suggestions to assist in this area.

Environment

The physical and instructional environment of a classroom is another factor that may discourage interactions among students. The teacher may want to change seating arrangements periodically to enhance interactions between hearing students and students with hearing impairment. Of course, cooperative learning strategies and peer tutoring will likely enhance interaction.

Hearing Students

If the objective is to increase interactions with hearing students, then systems must be developed to foster and enhance these interactions. As mentioned, educators may too quickly assume that the problems lie exclusively with the student who is hearing impaired. Quite logically, if there appears to be a breakdown, part of the problem may rest with the hearing students. As a result, specific efforts must be initiated to help hearing students better understand students with hearing impairment. Perhaps a self-fulfilling prophecy is at work here for not only hearing students but also students who are hearing impaired. Students may think, "I don't relate to _____ because I don't know how; so, I guess I can't," and it becomes a self-perpetuating circle involving all of the students. It is the responsibility of regular classroom teachers to design specific interventions to facilitate communication and interactions by helping hearing students become more proficient at commu-

nication skills. Suggestions relating to this topic were included in chapters 3 and 4. This topic is also discussed in "Hearing Students and Communication," later in this chapter.

Suggestions for Regular Classroom Teachers

Students with hearing impairment may find success in regular classrooms if some modifications and adaptations are made. These relate to room arrangement, awareness on the part of teachers, and alternate teaching strategies that do not require substantial teacher time.

Classroom Acoustics

Regular classroom teachers certainly do not have responsibility for the construction of classrooms; however, several factors will improve the acoustics of a room. Hard surfaces such as glass, chalkboards, and tiled floors reflect sound and produce extraneous sound. Soft, porous materials such as fabric, paper window shades, and cork absorb sound. Use of porous materials can reduce noise. If a classroom has a large expanse of chalkboard, portions of it can be used as bulletin boards. Papers taped to it will reduce some noise. Similarly, posters, corkboard, and curtains on the classroom rear wall reduce the amount of reflected sound. Carpets covering all or part of the floor reduce the sound in a room. Desks arranged in staggered fashion allow for the bodies of the students to further reduce reflected sound. Noise and distance are natural enemies of sound amplification. Extraneous noises interfere with the sounds being attended to (primarily voice in a classroom), and distances increase the possibility of interference by extraneous sounds.

Preferential Seating

The appropriate seating of a student with a hearing impairment depends partially upon the type of hearing loss. If the student has a bilateral loss with binaural amplification, seating should be arranged so that the teacher's voice is not directed above the student. Generally, a second row in the center is best. If the student has different levels of loss in each ear, the second-row placement is helpful but should be off center so that the better ear is angled toward the teacher. However, the teacher does not do all of the talking in a classroom, so some experimentation may be required. Different seats for different classes or activities may be the best solution.

Awareness of Student Fatigue

Students with hearing impairment may experience fatigue more easily than other students, and teachers should be aware of this potential problem. Such fatigue may be particularly noticeable in young children near the end of the day, but this is a factor for all students who are hearing impaired. Such fatigue should not be interpreted as boredom, disinterest, or lack of motivation. The fatigue results in part from the continuous strain of speechreading, the use of residual hearing, and the constant watching required to keep up with various speakers while participating in classroom activities. It may be helpful to vary the daily schedule so that the student is not required to attend to academic subjects for an extended period of time. Shorten lesson periods or alternate written and oral work with rest periods. However, the student should be expected to complete all assignments. The teacher should also be aware that the student with a hearing impairment may hear better on some days than on others. This may especially be true if the student has a cold or allergy. Also, some

students experience tinnitus (hearing noises within the head), which can result in nervousness or irritability.

Preteach-Teach-Postteach

The preteach-teach-postteach strategy assumes that the resource teacher and the regular class teacher have a cooperative, mutually respectful working relationship. The regular classroom teacher informs the resource teacher of the lessons or concepts to be taught, and they are presented first to the student with a hearing impairment in a one-to-one or small-group setting. This can be done in the regular classroom as well as having the resource specialist "pull out" the student. One advantage of having the resource specialist work in the regular classroom is that the specialist could work with a few typical students, in addition to the student with impaired hearing, who might benefit from additional practice with vocabulary and concepts. The student then attends the regular classroom, and the unit of study is taught by the regular classroom teacher. After the class, the regular classroom teacher reports to the resource or itinerant teacher by means of a short note, checklist, or personal discussion indicating problems or areas that may need to be retaught in the one-to-one or small-group setting. Ultimately, it is anticipated that the preteaching and postteaching phases may be shortened or eliminated except where the regular classroom teacher or the student specifically requests it (Reynolds & Birch, 1982).

Classmates as Helpers

The use of a listening helper or buddy can be of considerable assistance to a student who has a hearing impairment. This peer may sit next to the student who is hearing impaired to ensure that the student turns to the correct page or takes notes, or this peer may provide other appropriate assistance in adjusting to a new class or school or participating in activities such as physical education. The buddy may clarify something the teacher has said by repeating it while facing the student who is hearing impaired or by writing it down.

At the upper elementary and secondary levels, a listening helper or buddy may assist in note taking by making a carbon copy of class notes. This allows the student who has the hearing impairment to concentrate fully on what the teacher is saying.

The listening helper or buddy may be rotated weekly or monthly, or a few classmates may volunteer for an extended period of time. Some caution must be exercised so that the helper or buddy provides assistance only when needed. Otherwise, the very purpose of the integrated educational experience may be defeated. If the helper provides assistance when it is not necessary, the student with a hearing impairment may become overly dependent on classmates—a dependency that must be carefully avoided.

Demonstration and Team Teaching

If teachers fully appreciate the potential of true integration, they may realize the value of demonstration and team teaching. The presence of two adults in a classroom is valuable for several reasons. First, a model for working cooperatively is provided for all of the students. In addition, the special educator may learn more about large-group instruction and the limitations imposed in modifying and adapting materials, curricula, and teaching strategies. Regular classroom teachers can increase their competency in working with students who are hearing impaired by observing the special educator.

Team teaching involves the regular classroom teacher and the special educator in cooperatively planning the lessons, including the modifications or adaptations necessary to meet the needs of all of the students. Then, they team teach, or co-teach, the lesson, sharing full responsibility. The team approach may be for a specific unit of study or may be ongoing for a semester or an entire year in a content area such as math or social studies.

Demonstration teaching usually involves the special educator in demonstrating a particular strategy or method of meeting the needs of the student who is hearing impaired, for example, in preparing for the use of a captioned film. This arrangement allows the classroom teacher to learn new competencies.

Variations in the roles of the teachers are possible and should be mutually agreed upon. Sometimes, the special educator assumes the role of an aide or tutor and provides assistance to students having problems with a particular concept or assignment, or the classroom teacher may assume this role. Whatever the roles assumed or approaches used, the goal is the same: full integration of the student who is hearing impaired.

Previewing New Materials or Assignments

Whenever possible, the teacher should briefly discuss topics with the student who has difficulty hearing before the actual class presentation. This goal may be accomplished by providing the student with an outline of the material to be discussed. Communicating with resource teachers and employing the preteach-teach-postteach strategy should be given consideration. Allowing the student with a hearing impairment to preread assignments is also helpful. Another possibility worthy of consideration is providing on the board or a piece of paper a list of key vocabulary words that deal with the new material. When giving an assignment, write it on the board in addition to giving it orally. The student's listening helper may check to see that the student has the correct assignment.

Curricular Considerations

As a result of the difficulty in developing language skills and, in turn, reading skills, many students with hearing impairment may have difficulty in reading textbooks in curricular areas such as science, social studies, and literature. The teacher may deemphasize the use of textbooks and focus on hands-on experiences, particularly in content areas such as science. When that is not feasible, books that address the topics with simpler reading levels are alternatives. Easier reading materials combined with captioned films, vocabulary lists presented before verbal presentations, study guides that focus on critical concepts, and visual representations help students who have hearing impairments learn along with their hearing peers. Graphic organizers, information networks, webs, and concept maps are very helpful for students with impaired hearing. These graphic organizers make information more accessible, assisting with comprehension, summarization, and synthesis of complex ideas. Teachers can use graphic organizers to diagram and present important concepts, events, facts, and vocabulary in ways that are usually far more vivid and precise than is possible with a strictly spoken presentation (Luckner & Humphries, 1992).

Hearing Students and Communication

As mentioned, hearing students often do not understand the nature of hearing impairment or how a hearing aid functions. Although many hearing students who have classmates who are hearing impaired learn some of the signs or the manual alphabet, it may be helpful to provide systematic instruction to the hearing students. Unless such instruction is provided, the hearing students often express frustration when attempting to communicate with their classmates who have hearing impairments. Instruction in signing may be offered occasionally after school or during special Saturday morning pro-

grams. Such an elective course may be offered on an ongoing basis and may initially be taught by resource or itinerant teachers or in cooperation with students who are hearing impaired. Hearing students who have gained proficiency may be encouraged to share in the instruction or serve as teaching assistants or peer tutors. There is little question that efforts to help hearing students understand and communicate better with their classmates who are hearing impaired can greatly facilitate interactions. In addition, many regular classroom teachers also learn how to sign.

These suggestions to regular classroom teachers are certainly not all inclusive, but they do represent areas of great concern. It would be helpful to review and discuss them with the resource or itinerant teacher periodically. Ingenuity and creativity in modifying and adapting curriculum, materials, and teaching strategies can make mainstreaming successful for everyone.

The most important consideration is teacher attitude. The teacher is the single most important variable. The teacher must be understanding but not pitying and should treat a student who has a hearing impairment as nearly as possible like any other student in the classroom, being fair and truthful, not lenient, in reporting the progress of the student. The student should be treated as a student who is able, who is an individual, and who, incidentally, has impaired hearing.

■ Specialized Instruction and Assistance from Resource and Itinerant Teachers

A number of special skills should be routinely provided by resource personnel. The specific skills vary, depending on the grade level of the students. At the primary level, the resource teacher may have responsibility for reading instruction or may supplement the material presented in the student's regular class. The reading material used by the resource teacher may be the same as that used in the regular class except that the resource teacher spends considerable more time on vocabulary, comprehension, questioning, and related language activities. At the intermediate level, the resource teacher will probably supplement regular classroom instruction by emphasizing phonetic and comprehension skill and by introducing new vocabulary words before their introduction in class. Students who are hearing impaired also may need to be taught slang words and phrases that are popular with their classmates.

In addition to supplemental instruction, the resource teacher may work in a number of other areas, such as individual and small-group auditory training, vocabulary development, comprehension, questioning, speechreading, and speech correction.

At the secondary level, the resource teacher or consultant may be involved in team teaching or demonstration teaching, may provide adapted or modified materials, or may be part of the preteach-teach-postteach strategy. If activities are planned far enough in advance, teachers may use captioned films, slide-tape presentations, and other tangible materials.

Sometimes, the resource teacher or consultant is an integral part of routine classroom activities. This person may have specific instructional responsibilities to hearing students with instructional needs similar to those of students with hearing impairment. The exact nature of the special educator's role depends on the age or grade level of the students, the number of students, and the extent of hearing impairment. Generally, the role involves providing inservice assistance and instruction to regular education staff, working

closely with parents, functioning as a consultant, tutoring or supplementing instruction, introducing new materials or skills, and instructing in specialized skills that relate to hearing impairment.

Depending on the geographical area to be served (one or more schools), resource or itinerant teachers may be responsible for the inservice education of regular classroom teachers in one or several buildings. Often, the resource or itinerant teacher is called on to acquaint a building staff with the rationale underlying integrated placement of students who have hearing impairment. The nature of an inservice session may be general and relate only to the philosophy of integrated education, or it may be specifically related to techniques for modifying and adapting curriculum, materials, and teaching strategies.

Although it is not necessary for regular teachers to know the manual alphabet, they often are interested in learning it. In this instance, the resource or itinerant teacher may conduct inservice programs for teachers or students or arrange for classes to be taught by another person.

Another role often assumed by the resource teacher is providing selected journal articles, readings, or topics of special interest in relation to a particular student's problem or to specific teaching techniques. The orientation and inservice efforts of the resource personnel are ongoing responsibilities that must be taken seriously. How resource personnel "sell" themselves, the program, and the students with hearing impairment has a tremendous influence on the effectiveness of the program.

Resource teachers, due to their specialized preparation and experience, may assist regular teachers in counseling the student and the student's parents. This counseling may be routinely academic, such as parent-teacher conferences, or relate to specific problems imposed by hearing impairment, such as interpersonal relationships, language and speech problems, or vocational interests.

The resource teacher assists in planning and implementing work-study, vocational education, and vocational-rehabilitation services for students in secondary schools. The resource or itinerant teacher may be responsible for actually initiating these services or may contact others to initiate them. As mentioned, the roles and responsibilities of resource personnel vary considerably. The key to successful resource services is communication between regular teachers and resource personnel.

■■ Summary

As a greater number of students with impaired hearing are included in regular classrooms, and as professionals continue to analyze, share information, and refine their knowledge base, mainstreaming may reach its fullest potential for these students.

In this chapter, we have reviewed the importance of hearing to early learning, the nature of hearing impairment, how hearing is measured, and both behavioral and medical indications of hearing impairment. Placement consideration, and the advantages of regular classroom placement were also considered.

We discussed specialized technololgy and assistive devices, providing detailed information about hearing aid use, care and maintenance; FM systems; induction loop systems; infrared systems; and cochlear implants. In addition, we reviewed the use of interpreters and educational alternatives to auditory input. These alternatives included vibrotactile devices, laser videodiscs, and contemporary use of computers and accompanying software. We also described technological adaptations to daily life including TDDs, telecaptioning, and alerting devices. Communication approaches were presented and illustrated along with information about how classroom teachers can facilitate speechreading, desirable speech habits, and quality interactions between students with hearing impairment and their peers. We provided a variety of practical suggestions, such as preferential seating, use of classmates as helpers, and previewing new materials before class. Finally, we outlined the role of resource teachers and consultants, stressing the importance of cooperative efforts between educators who work together to teach students with hearing impairment.

chapter 6

- How do the language development theories proposed by Bruner, Chomsky, Piaget, and Skinner differ? How is it possible to substantiate such theories? What differences in remedial procedures are inferred by the acceptance of each theory?

- How different must a student's speech be to be considered a disability? How does this interpretation apply to linguistic differences that are likely to be found in students from culturally diverse populations?

- What must teachers know about pragmatics to be able to effectively assist students who have communication problems?

- Why has the major focus of speech specialists shifted away from articulation disorders? How do students with minor articulation disorders overcome such disorders?

- Why has stuttering held such historical interest for speech-language professionals? Which of the present causal explanations appears to be most logical?

- Which speech or voice disorders may be so potentially serious that they require immediate referral? What are the possible prognoses for these disorders?

Teaching Students Who Have Speech or Language Disorders

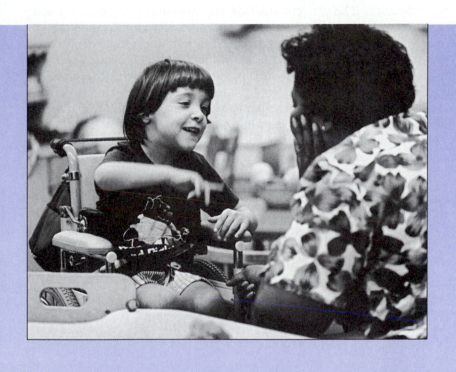

■■■■■■■■■■

This chapter addresses the speech and language disorders that may affect learning and social effectiveness. Such disorders may range from less severe, such as mild hoarseness that affects the quality of voice, to very severe disabilities that prevent any understandable communication. The ability to communicate in a variety of situations is essential to the educational process. The complex human language system that has developed and continues to develop has led to unbelievable accomplishments in technology and medicine. These advances in technology have provided a variety of means of communication for those with communication disorders that will enable them to function effectively in a world where the ability to communicate effectively is of increasing importance.

Over 2.8 million students in the United States speak languages other than English (Salend, 1994). Teachers must heed this when considering the possibility of referring students for special assistance. While students are learning English they may experience articulation difficulties, have limited comprehension of written or spoken material, or make grammatical or syntactical errors. Although teachers must consider these factors in planning what and how to teach these students, they are not synonomous with speech and language disorders.

■■■■■■■■■■

Communication

Communication is a process that involves two or more individuals in the transmission of thoughts or ideas between them. In the simplest form, this involves individual A transmitting an idea to individual B. To do this, individual A must convert the idea into some type of symbol system. This is often referred to as *encoding*. After receiving the message, individual B must *decode* it, or convert the symbols back into the idea. The four major elements of language and their normal relationship in the communication process are illustrated in Figure 6–1. The expressive skills most used by humans are speaking and writing. The receptive skills are listening and reading. The process through which communication takes place may be called an *integrative process*.

This chapter begins the consideration of communication with speech, one aspect of the complex language system. According to Bernstein and Tiegerman (1993), "Speech is . . . the oral verbal mode of transmitting messages and involves the precise coordination of oral neuromuscular movements in order to produce sounds and linguistic units" (p. 4). They note that although speech is the primary mode of communication, it is not the only mode. Writing, drawing, manual signing, and singing are other means of communication.

Language is the code or system in which people normally communicate. According to Bernstein and Tiegerman (1993), "Language encompasses complex rules that govern sounds, words, sentences, meaning, and use. These rules underlie an individual's ability to understand language (language comprehension) and his ability to formulate language (language production)" (p. 5). They further note that language can produce an infinite number of sentences, in a wide variety of settings. Most people cannot explicitly state all of the language rules, but their usage indicates knowledge of most of them.

Two additional statements, from an American Speech-Language-Hearing Association (ASHA) committee report, add further meaning to the Bernstein and Tiegerman description. The first, the core definition provided by the ASHA Committee on Language (1983) is, "Language is a complex and dynamic system of conventional symbols that is used in various modes for thought and communication" (p. 44). The second, one of the statements made in expansion of this core definition, is "Effective use of language for communication requires a broad understanding of human interaction including such associated factors as nonverbal cues, motivation, and sociocultural roles" (p. 44).

Congress has provided a definition of speech or language impairments: "communication disorders such as stuttering, impaired

Figure 6–1
Integrative process

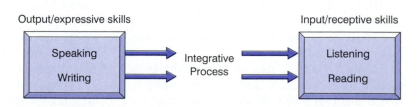

Note: Speaking and writing are the major expressive skills. Gestures (especially as in sign language used by individuals who are hearing impaired) and facial expressions are among the other expressive modes important in communication.

articulation, a language impairment, or a voice impairment that adversely affects a child's educational performance" (34 CFR 300.7 [11]). Language, the fundamental ability that affects all interactions with others, is complex and not fully understood. However, what is understood is that impairments in langage abilities likely lead to impairments in the learning process.

∷ Theories of Language Development

Noam Chomsky (1957, 1965) formulated a theory to explain how native speakers of a language learn all of the variations of the language without having heard them or having learned the rules that govern them. He theorized that there is an inborn capacity to learn language and that human infants have a plan in the brain that enables them to internalize the knowledge necessary to generate words and sentences. According to Chomsky, a baby is predisposed to learn language, and this innate ability is activated when exposed to linguistic input, such as the mother speaking to the baby. This innate ability contains the general principles for forming sentences and applying these principles to the child's native language. Through an explanation of brain structures, Chomsky accounts for the ability of young children to acquire language almost effortlessly, learn the rules governing the language without ever having them explained, and generate an infinite number of sentences never before heard.

Chomsky (1965) also developed the concepts of deep structure and surface structure, which are two levels of the communication process. A thought, idea, or feeling that is to be shared with a listener is generated in the brain (deep structure), and through application of

morphological and syntactic rules of language, a word, phrase, sentence, or series of sentences is generated (surface structure). The surface structure may be modified in a variety of ways to meet the expectations of the interaction or to clarify to the listener the original idea. Chomsky provided a view relating to the language acquisition process in which the child was active rather than passive; however, his view of language development is regarded as incomplete. Chomsky's concepts served as an impetus to further language research, especially in natural settings, examining both normal and disordered language.

Benjamin F. Skinner (1957) developed a theoretical explanation for a variety of types of learning and applied the principles of imitation, practice, and selective reinforcement to the acquisition of language. He suggests that a child gradually, and with increased precision, imitates the vocal symbols and sequences of symbols heard. Parents and caregivers serve as models of appropriate utterances, which the child imitates. The parents and caregivers act as reinforcers by rewarding the child's attempts at imitation and as shapers of the child's utterances by continued modeling and reinforcement.

Skinner based his theory on animal learning and principles of operant conditioning. According to Skinner and other behaviorists, children learn language because their verbal behavior is rewarded by others in the environment. From Skinner's theory, a systematic approach to training techniques has been developed. It incorporates the principles of modeling, imitation, shaping, and reinforcement. Many programs for children with language disabilities are based on these principles.

Critics of this theory believe that the rate of language acquisition is much too rapid to depend on environmental conditioning alone. Also, children apply rules, inappropriately at times, and produce utterances they have never heard ("I wented" or "I goeses"). Furthermore, parents and caregivers do not correct all grammatical errors, but children learn the appropriate structures.

Jean Piaget (1952, 1954, 1962) suggests that language is cognitively based and that unless certain cognitive levels are achieved, language learning cannot proceed. It is generally accepted that attainment of object permanence must be achieved before expression of words with stable meanings. Bloom (1970) suggests that the meaning of a child's utterance is far more advanced than is the child's knowledge of syntax. A child can convey multiple meanings by using the same words, for example, "Daddy hat." In one situation, the child may be indicating the father's ownership and in another indicating the desire for a ride in the car. According to Bloom, children express meanings before they are able to use syntax, and the meanings that they convey are dependent on their cognitive knowledge. He also indicates that children use language to talk about what they know, which is related primarily to their sensorimotor experiences. This implies that children mean more than they are able to say through the use of syntactically correct utterances.

How children figure out the ways in which words, word order, and inflections convey meaning is not fully explained, nor is the ability of children to use increasingly more complex forms and structures to encode meaning. Further, the fact that children with normal intelligence sometimes do not learn to speak or do so at a level much below their cognitive abilities seems to indicate that abilities other than purely conceptual ones are involved in the process of language learning.

Jerome Bruner (1974, 1975) suggests that children learn language to socialize and direct the behavior of others. In social interaction, children develop the framework for understanding and formulating content and form.

The functions of speech acts, the contexts in which they are performed, and the intents of utterances are critical. In general, children learn to talk because they have a reason, and they acquire language only after they learn other forms of communication (such as reaching for a bottle, or leading caregivers to a sink and pointing, indicating the desire for a drink). Language is learned in social interactions in which children are active participants and are able to benefit from the language behaviors of others. This theory partially explains the role of linguistic input, the relationship between gestures and language, and the manner in which children learn complex social devices used by others to make their intentions known. It does not explain how communicative intentions are linked to appropriate linguistic structures in the process of language acquisition.

Each of the theories regarding the development of language may be viewed as describing an aspect of language development, even though no theory provides a complete model. Yet, taken together, the theories illustrate the complexity of language. Language theories may

Listening provides a basis for language development.

serve as a starting point for teachers who have students about whom they have suspicions relating to speech and language disabilities.

Components of Speech

To further understanding of speech and the language process, this chapter considers the major components of speech and language. The theoretical views of language development remain unproven and subject to debate, but the components of speech and language skills described by the American Speech-Language-Hearing Association (ASHA, Committee on Language, 1983) are much less ambiguous. They provide insights that relate to the disorders of speech and language that regular classroom teachers may encounter. Phonology, morphology, syntax, semantics, and pragmatics form the foundation of language. All are rule governed and essential to the normal development of language. Brief definitions and some examples of disorders of each of the components follow. Figure 6–2 illustrates how they are interrelated.

Phonology is the sound system of oral language. The English language consists of 46 sounds, or phonemes, which are either vowels or consonants. These basic units are combined into meaningful sequences. For example, the sounds or *j, a,* and *m* combined form the word *jam.* In this case, each letter stands for a single phoneme; however, in the word *this, th* is pronounced as one sound and is a phoneme. Errors may occur through mispronunciations, omissions, or substitutions.

Morphology refers to the smallest units of language that represent meaning. In general terms, morphology relates to the structure of words, to the stems and the suffixes or prefixes that modify the meaning of a stem in some fashion. Morphemes can be words that stand alone, like *took, was,* or *that,* or be parts of words like *un,* which added to the word *able,* for example, changes the meaning. Similarly, the *s* in *chairs* and the *es* in *dishes* modify the meaning of the stems. Errors may be related to incorrect usage of morphemes, for instance, *goed* and *mostest.*

Syntax refers to the relative subordination of words and clauses. In English, these are often determined by word order. A variety of rules govern word order. If the rules are not followed, the result is either a string of words with no meaning or doubt about the meaning. The sentence "The boy bit the dog" has a significant change in meaning if just two words are transposed, namely, *boy* and *dog.* Examples of syntactic errors (violation of rules) include "My teacher gave a talk on the moon" and "The paper said he died last week due to a reporting error." The rules governing morphology and syntax combined make up the rules of grammar.

Semantics encompasses the meanings assigned to words, groups of words, and sentences. Phonology, morphology, and syntax form the structures of the language system, while semantics refers to the meanings of those structures. Knowledge of semantics is reflected in vocabulary usage, concepts that are developed, and word associations. For example, in the group of words *man, in, lives, the, house,* and *white,* each word has some element of meaning. By grouping the words *the man lives* and *in the white house,* a greater degree of meaning is reflected. And finally, by putting the words together in a sentence, *The man lives in the white house,* additional meaning is attached. Understanding either the lesser meaning attached to the string of words or the more involved meaning of the sentence depends upon understanding of the individual words, appropriate word order, and the concept conveyed in the sentence. Semantic errors may be as simple as misunderstanding the meaning of a word (for example, confusing the noun

Figure 6–2

Components and levels of the speech and language code for communication

Source: Reprinted with permission of Merrill, an imprint of Prentice Hall Publishing Company, from *Language Assessment and Intervention for the Learning Disabled.* 2nd ed. (p. 23) by E. Wiig & E. Semel. Copyright © 1984, 1990 by Prentice Hall.

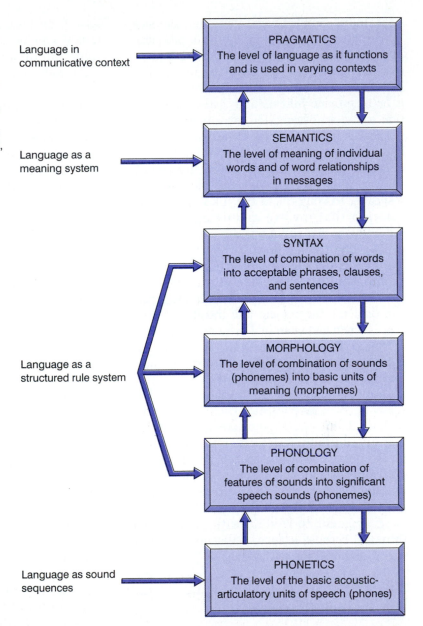

judge in isolation with the verb) or as serious as complete misinterpretation of sentences.

Pragmatics refers to the use of language in varying situations. This includes modifying the choice of words based on the information level of the receiver, on the setting, or on the purpose of communication. For example, simple words might be used with a 3- or 4-year-old, while more enriched vocabulary would be appropriate for a 14-year-old. At the college level, more complex vocabulary and sentence structure might be appropriate for a presentation to a class and more informal language would be used in the cafeteria. Pragmatics also includes the intention of the speaker, whether it be to provide information, gather information, share an observation, or something else. A speaker must be aware of characteristics of listeners, including such aspects as level of understanding, interest, and ability to respond.

In summary, pragmatics refers to ability of a speaker to conform to the rules of communication that involve modifying language according to the situation, the characteristics of listeners, the intent of communication, or some combination of these. In our culture, examples of errors include asking personal questions upon just being introduced to a person or using incomplete and incoherent sentences when giving an oral presentation.

The components just reviewed as separate entities are interrelated. Effective communicators have a command of all of the components even though they may not be able to verbalize many of the rules governing them. Individuals with disabilities in this area are at a disadvantage in communicating their thoughts and ideas effectively. When speech and language are underdeveloped or defective, academic problems almost always result, especially in reading. In the case of serious problems, there is an apparent correlation with problems in thinking, because it appears that for the most part, humans think with words.

Speech Disorders

Teachers regularly ask, How different must a student's speech or language be to be considered a disorder? or When is it appropriate to refer a student? Some questions that teachers might ask in making such determinations have been identified by Culatta and Culatta (1985) and Wood (1989). The questions and some interpretive thoughts related to them are as follows:

1. *Is the student easily understood?* If your answer is no, a referral is in order.
2. *When I compare this student to others in the class, does this student sound strange?* If the answer is yes, analyze why. Is it because the 6-foot-tall male sounds like an 8-year-old girl? Or does an 8-year-old girl have a nasal or hoarse voice? Disorders of articulation are easy to identify and may be reason for a referral, but voice problems may be more serious, because they may indicate need for medical attention.
3. *When I observe the student, are there physical characteristics that seem different?* If the answer is yes, again try to identify what they are. Some examples of what to look for are unusual or unnecessary movements of the mouth, lips, tongue, nose, arms, legs, or head and unusual postural changes during speaking.
4. *When the student speaks, even though I can understand what was said, does the student sound out of place or unable to judge what is appropriate for the situation?* If yes, it may be that the student is unaware that good speakers judge situations and adjust their speaking style. It may also be that the student has some desire to resist conformity. The former may indicate a problem meriting referral, whereas the latter may indicate a problem that is unrelated to speech or no problem at all.
5. *Do I enjoy listening to the student?* If no, why not? If it is because the message is not desirable, that is not a speech problem. However, if it is

because of the quality of the voice (such as hoarseness, pitch, or unpleasant tone), a referral may be in order.

6. *Does it sound as though the student is damaging or has damaged his or her vocal mechanisms?* Does it sound as though the student is straining? Does speaking induce coughing or wheezing?

7. *Does the student appear embarrassed or seem to experience physical discomfort when speaking?* While a teacher cannot judge the inner feelings of a student, some behavioral indicators may lead the teacher to believe the student is experiencing discomfort. The student may blush when required to speak or be reluctant to participate in class discussions. For this to be a problem, it must be beyond the normal shyness or anxiety that many students experience when speaking in front of a class or similar activities in which attention is focused on them.

A different set of questions that teachers might answer in relation to how different a student's speech must be to be considered a speech disorder follow:

1. *Does the speech interfere with communication?*
2. *Does the speech cause the speaker to be maladjusted?*
3. *Does the speech call undue attention to itself at the expense of what the speaker is saying?*

These questions focus on the effects of speech rather than the physiology of speech production. A speech-language specialist is concerned with helping students produce speech in the most normal manner possible and use it effectively in normal communication so that listeners can concentrate on *what* the students are saying, not on *how* they are saying it. This generalization also applies to language disorders, which are often related to speech disorders.

Speech, language, and hearing problems are interrelated and may affect learning. This interrelationship is illustrated in Figure 6–3, and it explains why regular classroom teachers may discuss referral with a speech-language pathologist, teacher of the learning disabled, or teacher of the hearing impaired. If a student is identified as having a speech or language disorder, the IEP should indicate the services to be provided and who is responsible for providing them, as well as who is responsible for providing suggestions and assistance to the regular classroom teacher. Speech disorders may be divided into three broad categories: (a) articulation disorders, (b) stuttering and other speech-flow disorders, and (c) voice disorders. Other speech problems are related to cerebral palsy, hearing loss, and cleft lip or cleft palate.

Articulation Disorders

Articulation errors were once the focus of speech-language pathologists, but the focus shifted because of two major factors: (a) it was increasingly recognized that many young children outgrew minor articulation problems with no specialized assistance and (b) it became obvious that some of the more serious speech disorders required more time and effort from specialists. This shift does not mean that teachers should not refer students if the only obvious difficulty is an articulation problem. Nor does it mean that speech-language pathologists never serve young children who have only articulation problems. In many cases, a combination of evaluation by a speech-language pathologist followed by management suggestions implemented by a regular classroom teacher and the parent proves

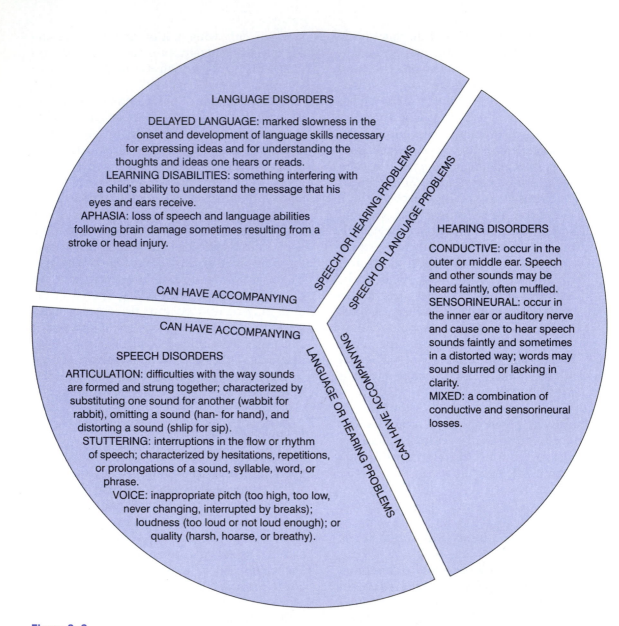

LANGUAGE DISORDERS

DELAYED LANGUAGE: marked slowness in the onset and development of language skills necessary for expressing ideas and for understanding the thoughts and ideas one hears or reads.
LEARNING DISABILITIES: something interfering with a child's ability to understand the message that his eyes and ears receive.
APHASIA: loss of speech and language abilities following brain damage sometimes resulting from a stroke or head injury.

SPEECH OR HEARING PROBLEMS

SPEECH OR LANGUAGE PROBLEMS

CAN HAVE ACCOMPANYING

CAN HAVE ACCOMPANYING

LANGUAGE OR HEARING PROBLEMS

CAN HAVE ACCOMPANYING

HEARING DISORDERS

CONDUCTIVE: occur in the outer or middle ear. Speech and other sounds may be heard faintly, often muffled.
SENSORINEURAL: occur in the inner ear or auditory nerve and cause one to hear speech sounds faintly and sometimes in a distorted way; words may sound slurred or lacking in clarity.
MIXED: a combination of conductive and sensorineural losses.

SPEECH DISORDERS

ARTICULATION: difficulties with the way sounds are formed and strung together; characterized by substituting one sound for another (wabbit for rabbit), omitting a sound (han- for hand), and distorting a sound (shlip for sip).
STUTTERING: interruptions in the flow or rhythm of speech; characterized by hesitations, repetitions, or prolongations of a sound, syllable, word, or phrase.
VOICE: inappropriate pitch (too high, too low, never changing, interrupted by breaks); loudness (too loud or not loud enough); or quality (harsh, hoarse, or breathy).

Figure 6–3

Disorders of speech, language, and hearing and how they interrelate
Source: From public information materials of the American Speech-Language-Hearing Association. Reproduced by permission.

most effective. The need for regular classroom teachers to understand and properly play this partnership role is a theme of this chapter.

Articulation errors are those involving omissions, substitutions, distortions, or additions when pronouncing (articulating) words. The following are examples of articulation errors:

Substitution. wun for *run, dat* for *that, wabbit* for *rabbit, thum* for *some*
Omission. pay for *play, cool* for *school, ift* for *lift, day* for *daddy*
Distortion. shled for *sled*
Additions. buhrown for *brown, cuhow* for *cow, puhlease* for *please, sawr* for *saw*

Certain generalizations applicable in nearly all cases of articulation-error therapy may be used as guidelines for remedial efforts. First, *the student must hear the error*. In most cases, the letter or letters are pointed out to the student in writing or print so that there can be no question as to what letter or letters are in question. Then, the student must learn to hear the sound as properly articulated by the teacher or speech-language pathologist. Often, the student must learn to listen for the sound in initial, medial, and final positions and then must learn to differentiate between the sound properly articulated and the sound as she or he articulates it. This may be done with a tape recorder. The teacher may deliberately mispronounce the sound, and on the playback the student may learn to discriminate the incorrect sound from the correct sound in varying phonetic contexts. After this stage, recordings of both the student and the teacher may be made to assist the student in recognizing the varying sounds. Other methods or materials may be used; however, learning to *hear* errors is an absolute prerequisite to any further work with articulation problems. This is sometimes called auditory training.

When absolutely certain that a child can hear the difference between accurate and inaccurate articulation of the sounds in question, it is necessary that the child learn to produce the correct sound. This may be accomplished through games, exercises, behavior shaping (using approximations of the right sound and slowly approaching the correct articulation), or any method that seems appropriate to the age and interests of the child.

Many young children see little reason to change their speech patterns. This is true with all speech correction but perhaps most often with articulation problems. The children seem to get by, and unless they are embarrassed by the reactions of others, they may not care. In some instances, teachers must make them care enough to hear articulatory differences and then motivate them to learn to make the correct sound. Reward systems may be of considerable value in accomplishing this step.

A third step is to have the student incorporate the newly learned, accurately articulated sound in familiar words. Even though the student learns to hear the difference between accurate and inaccurate articulation and to produce the required sound, until the sound is regularly used in language, the student has not overcome the problem. When an individual has had months or years of practice in saying a sound incorrectly, it takes much repetition to develop new speech habits and patterns. Here again, motivation is highly important, and with young children, games are often valuable.

In addition to the preceding overall rules for remediation, one general rule must be carefully observed by regular classroom teachers. If a student is being seen by a speech-language pathologist, the teacher should consult with the specialist to be certain that any special efforts in the classroom are complementary, not contradictory, to the specialist's efforts.

Stuttering and Other Speech-Flow Disorders

Most speech authorities agree that stuttering has been and remains the most elusive of the speech disorders (Conture & Fraser, 1991; Van Riper & Emerick, 1990). This is true in terms of both cause and treatment, and although new theories and treatments are advocated with some regularity, there seems to be no best theory or treatment.

Stuttering is just one disorder that may be described as a breakdown in the normal flow of speech. Other disorders receive much less attention, and all can be described as relating to difficulties in one or more of the five generally recognized dimensions of speech flow. Those dimensions are (a) sequence, or the order of sounds (for example, the word *cavalry* is often pronounced as *calvary*); (b) duration, or the length of time any phonetic element is produced (a duration problem may lead to confusion through decreased intelligibility and is usually just one part of a more complex problem); (c) rate, or the speed of articulation of speech sounds, syllables, or words (like duration, rate is not often a problem except as combined with other speech problems); (d) rhythm, or the pattern of phonetic elements (when rhythm is faulty, intelligibility and thus comprehension of speech are endangered); and (e) fluency, or the smoothness of articulation of sounds (the extreme example of disfluency is stuttering; other types of disfluency, as in some regional speech-flow patterns, are accepted as normal in some parts of the nation and are at least acceptable in others).

Stuttering, the most recognized of the speech-flow disorders, has been explained by speech experts through various theories. There are many such theories, falling into two major groups: organic and behavioral. Organic theories propose a variety of neurological causes for stuttering, ranging from older theories involving a lack of cerebral dominance to those that liken stuttering to epileptic seizures. In many of these theories, the fact that stutterers do not always stutter is accounted for by postulating a constitutional weakness that tends to give under pressure.

Nonorganic theories about the cause of stuttering may be grouped according to three major points of view, each dictating a somewhat different treatment, as may be seen from the accounts that follow. Each of these descriptions is a generalization of two or three closely related theories.

1. Stuttering is a result of the fact that important individuals in a student's early life label normal disfluencies "stuttering." In response, the child focuses on these disfluencies, attempting to eliminate them. Overreaction, fear, tension, and anxiety lead to maintaining these disfluencies long beyond the time when they would normally be abandoned. Thus, they become actual stuttering.

2. Stuttering is the result of an unusual need of the child to be understood. When the child tries to maintain the attention of listeners, normal disfluencies that might otherwise be overlooked by both speaker and listener lead to more and more frustration. As the speaker struggles (because of internal drives, not outside influence) to become more fluent, tension and frustration lead to continued disfluency.

3. Stuttering is the result of a need to satisfy anal or oral desires, infantile tendencies, or high levels of hostility. In turn, these are the result of inadequate or unsatisfactory relationships with parents. Various psychoanalytic theories of child–parent conflict explain these conflicts.

Various combinations of theories have been constructed to form additional theories, but for nonspecialists, these three are the thrust of stuttering theories. Although various authorities may insist that their approach is based on a specific theory and think that recognition of the cause is highly important, all therapies are notable for their high rate of failure in practice.

Certain recommendations are generally applicable to interactions with persons who stutter. These should be followed unless the speech-language pathologist specifically dictates otherwise. These recommendations, made by the Stuttering Foundation of America (1993), involve an attitude that can be fostered in the classroom and practiced by the teacher and students:

1. Maintain eye contact, waiting until the person is finished.
2. Let the person know by your manner and actions that you are listening to *what* he or she is saying, not *how* he or she says it.
3. Even though tempted to finish sentences or fill in words, try not to.
4. Refrain from making comments such as "Slow down," "Relax," or "Just take a breath." Such simplistic help is demeaning and is not helpful.
5. Use a relaxed rate in your own conversational speech but not so slow as to sound unnatural.

Primary, or beginning, stutterers may overcome the problem if those around them have accurate information and the right attitude. For secondary, or confirmed, stutterers, major goals may include acceptance of stuttering as part of the language pattern and learning to stutter more gracefully.

The speech-language pathologist will be able to offer specific recommendations to the general education teacher after an evaluation of the individual who stutters.

Though speech authorities lack agreement about stuttering, there is general agreement concerning some observations, according to the Stuttering Foundation of America (1993).

- Over three million Americans stutter.
- People who stutter are as intelligent and well-adjusted as nonstutterers.
- Some 25 percent of *all* children go through a stage of development during which they stutter. About 4 percent may stutter for six months or more.
- Stuttering becomes increasingly formidable in the teen years as dating and similar social interactions take place
- People who stutter are self-conscious about their stuttering and let the disability determine the vocation they choose.
- There are no instant miracle cures for stuttering; however, clinicians can help not only children but teenagers and even older adults make significant progress toward fluency.
- Stutterers rarely, if ever, stutter while singing.
- Stutterers rarely stutter while speaking in unison or in synchronization with a rhythmic beat.
- Stutterers rarely stutter while alone or while swearing.
- Stuttering cannot always be induced, even in those who otherwise stutter regularly.
- Stutterers tend to stutter on the same words when reading and rereading the same passage. They may not stutter on these same words in other sentences.
- Stutterers tend to be able to predict their stuttering.
- Time pressure seems to be a factor in causing or increasing stuttering.

Voice Disorders

Voice disorders are not nearly so common as articulation disorders (Van Riper & Emerick,

1990). However, they require immediate attention by classroom teachers. That is, teachers must make prompt referrals to speech-language pathologists if voice disorders are suspected. If a speech-language pathologist is not available, referral to a school nurse or parent is in order.

Voice disorders are generally considered to include disorders of pitch, intensity, quality, and flexibility. For the most part, these problems do not have the same kind of direct effect on the learning of basic skills as, for example, serious articulation problems have. In fact, unless they are very different from the norm, they are often accepted as part of the uniqueness of an individual. The following descriptions of these four voice disorders are presented so that teachers may have an overall view of voice disorders and a base from which to consider referral, to either the speech-language pathologist or, through the parents, to a physician.

Pitch problems seldom cause any serious difficulty for a speaker, with the exception of a high, falsetto voice in an older teenage or adult male. For girls and women, various levels of pitch are accepted, with low voices often regarded as sexy and high ones as feminine. Despite a number of recent societal changes in concepts of masculinity and femininity, there is a stubborn persistence of the belief a man should have a voice that is of low or medium pitch. Therefore, a boy with a high-pitched voice that apparently is continuing into his upper-teenage years may benefit from therapy to help him lower the pitch. Sometimes pitch can be lowered, and sometimes it cannot. The matter is usually a sensitive one, but if assistance can be provided, it may help greatly in the social arena.

Voice intensity, loudness or softness, is not often a problem in and of itself, but very loud speech may mean that the individual does not hear his or her own voice distinctly and should serve as a cue to recheck the possibility of a hearing problem. The teacher should also note that if a child speaks indistinctly (as opposed to too softly) and is asked to speak up, the result may be even more unsatisfactory than before. In speaking up, many students with indistinct speech give voice to very loud vowel sounds, which even further drown out the weaker consonant sounds. Therefore, the teacher or speech-language pathologist must work on more precise consonant production.

Of the four major voice disorders, voice quality is the most common. Three types of quality problems are (a) breathiness, (b) harshness, and (c) nasality. Harshness or breathiness may be caused by vocal abuse (such as occurs at a hard-fought football game) or may be the result of infection or inflammation of the vocal cords. These temporary problems usually go away after a few days of vocal rest.

A more serious problem occurs as a result of continued vocal abuse, causing growths to develop on the vocal cords. Benign growths are fairly common among singers and, to some extent, among those who do a great deal of public speaking. These, too, may go away with vocal rest or with therapy to assist in more normal voice production. However, growths may be malignant. Thus, the advice to seek prompt medical attention is applicable to older students and, of course, to adults. Malignant growths cause the same type of voice quality as do benign growths, but the only way to be sure is referral to a qualified specialist.

A speech-language pathologist should determine whether problems relating to nasality are likely to be long term. Hypernasality (excessive nasal quality) may be a result of unrepaired cleft palate, and remedial action may be possible. In other cases, some reduction of unpleasant speech resulting from nasality may be attained through speech therapy.

The teacher should be alert for voice disorders and should be particularly alert for rapid changes in voice quality, especially hoarseness or breathiness. If the teacher is in doubt, an immediate referral to a specialist or physician is in order.

The fourth voice disorder is flexibility disorder. The most common flexibility problem is exhibited by the monotone speaker. This problem may result from many different causes, such as physical tiredness, emotional difficulties, voice pitch too near the top or the bottom of the vocal range, or a hearing problem. If a voice is very unpleasant because of a flexibility disorder and the problem persists, referral to a speech-language pathologist is the proper course of action. Seldom does the regular classroom teacher possess the technical knowledge and skill to assess and attempt to remediate this type of problem on his or her own.

In summary, most voice problems may be of a minor nature and may be properly overlooked. An exception is the case of unusual voice changes, particularly those typified by hoarseness, harshness, or breathiness. If these persist, even for a few weeks, referral is recommended.

Other Speech Problems

Three other speech problems, with three specific causes, deserve mention: (a) speech problems directly related to cerebral palsy, (b) speech problems related to hearing loss, and (c) speech problems related to cleft lip or cleft palate. Problems related to cerebral palsy can run the gamut from mild to severe. In some cases, they may result in speech that is almost unintelligible, although perhaps as many as one third of all individuals with cerebral palsy have essentially no speech problem. The best general rules to follow with a student whose cerebral palsy leads to speech problems are to provide sufficient time for the student to respond to questions or participate in class discussion and to make every attempt to learn

to decode the student's speech. When a student with cerebral palsy is assigned to a new teacher, a few short one-to-one sessions between the student and teacher can help much toward early understanding of the student's speech. Practical communication is the goal, and speech therapy must be left to the speech-language pathologist except as the specialist provides specific instructions for assistance in the regular classroom.

Problems related to hearing loss may lead to a variety of speech difficulties, depending on various factors, but the major determining factor is the time of onset of the hearing loss. Some speech problems and some language problems are to be expected with students who are hearing impaired, but with proper assistance, such problems can be minimized. Remember that when a student has continued speech or language problems, the possibility of hearing impairment must be fully investigated. In a somewhat similar manner (although for different reasons), students who have mental retardation usually have some difficulties with language and vocabulary development. They may or may not lead to difficulties viewed as speech disorders.

Cleft lip and cleft palate problems vary in their effect on speech, depending on the depth of the cleft and the success of surgical procedures. Since midcentury, most children born with a facial cleft of any severity have been treated surgically during the first few months of life. A cleft lip after surgical treatment seldom causes any serious problem, but a cleft palate is often not completely corrected surgically. The effects of cleft palate commonly include articulation errors and problems with nasality. The correction of these physiologically based speech problems should be left to the speech clinician. As a result of the related problems, students with a cleft palate may avoid speaking and may eventually become retarded in vocabulary and overall language development.

Other less common problems include those related to faulty dentition or abnormal laryngeal structure. In many instances, such students can be helped, but medical assistance and the best efforts of a speech-language pathologist are required for maximum improvement. It is obvious that regular classroom teachers play significant roles in the implementation of speech programs for such students.

Language Disorders

The speech-language pathologist will assess the student to determine whether or not the student's syntactic and semantic production and comprehension are similar to that of the student's peers. This may be accomplished through the use of standardized tests. An analysis of the student's spontaneous language provides additional information regarding pragmatic production and communicative comprehension. This type of analysis of strengths and weaknesses in language may lead to the discovery of disorders broadly classified as (a) delayed language (including impairment of language development), (b) autism, and (c) impairment of acquired language (aphasia).

Delayed Language

Delayed language (also called delayed speech) means simply that an individual is unable to use language in the manner normally expected of that age. This inability may be related to some other known disability, for example, hearing impairment, learning disability, or mental retardation. In such cases, there is usually agreement as to how to pro-

ceed, and a joint effort is required among all professionals of different disciplines working with the child and parents.

One of the more common causes of delayed language is a lack of need for the child to talk. If parents attempt to anticipate a child's every need, so that speech is not required for basic need fulfillment, the attempts may delay language development. Or if parents literally believe that children should be seen and not heard, they may delay speech and language. Fortunately, children usually play with other children in the neighborhood and thus have opportunities and needs to speak to be a successful part of the group.

The term *delayed speech* is often used to refer to the speech patterns of children who have hearing impairment or mental retardation, but these conditions are not the same as delayed speech or delayed language in children who have adequate hearing and normal or above-normal mental ability. Parents who might become overly concerned with the fact that their young child seldom speaks and wonder if something is basically wrong should consider the case of Albert Einstein, who did not speak until after his third birthday. The situation is somewhat different, however, if the child comes to school at the age of 5 years and still has seriously delayed language. This condition may require special attention, and planning should start with a complete physical checkup to eliminate the possibility of physiological defects. If there are no such disabilities and the child's intellectual level appears to be at least normal, then the environmental background should be reviewed.

Autism

Autism is characterized by both disorders in communication and in behavior. Literature regarding emotional disturbance, behavioral disorders, and mental illness include autism as an aspect of these more general disorders (Kauffman, 1993a; American Psychiatric Association, 1994). In 1975, when PL 94–142 was passed, autism was included in the category of severe emotional disturbance. It was later included in the category of other health impaired, and in 1990 was listed in PL 101–476 (IDEA) as a separate category. This reflects the efforts of various organizations to encourage Congress to recognize the unique needs of persons with autism. Speech-language pathologists regard autism as primarily a communication disorder and include discussions regarding causality and treatment in their literature (Reed, 1994; Shames, Wiig, & Secord, 1994; Bernstein & Tiegerman, 1993). Because autism is characterized by communication disorders, we have elected to include our discussion in this chapter, recognizing that it might also be appropriate to include it in Chapter 11. The interventions suggested in Chapter 11 for acting-out behavior that follow a behavioral approach would likely be implemented for students with autism.

The American Psychiatric Association (1994) indicates that essential features of autistic disorders include "the presence of markedly abnormal or impaired development in social interaction and communication and a markedly restricted repertoire of activity and interests" (p. 66). The association's *Diagnostic and Statistical Manual of Mental Disorders* indicates, "The impairment in reciprocal social interaction is gross and sustained" and that "the impairment in communication is also marked and sustained and affects both verbal and language skills." The child may not develop language at all or the language may be echolalic and have immature grammatical construction. The child may have voice quality that is monotonal and monotonous, and be unable to understand abstract terms, jokes,

puns, or sarcasm. Nonverbal communication, such as facial expressions or gestures related to language and communication are not developed and are meaningless to others; although ritual gestures such as hand flapping, grimacing or foot tapping are frequently present. Lack of eye contact, little or no social contact and no apparent interest in social interaction, a preference for sameness, repetition, and rigidity in daily routine, and intense interest in such stereotypic actions as staring at a button, examination of others' fingernails, or insisting on a cup of water being nearby are other characterizations of autism.

Individuals with autism must be considered a heterogeneous group; therefore individualized educational plans (IEPs) are written to address individual needs. In general, interventions center around the development of language and personal interaction skills while reducing ritual behaviors. The phonological development of children with autism appears to be similar to that of nonimpaired children but they demonstrate delays in the development of syntax (Bernstein & Tiegerman, 1993). A normal 3-year-old child begins to use phrases, combining them into sentences and combines sentences into narratives following linguistic rules of word order and tense. They are also developing the concept that ideas are expressed through the use of sentence structures such as questions, negation, sequence, causality, and temporality. The child with autism appears not to develop these syntactical aspects of language and therefore semantic and pragmatic aspects are also underdeveloped.

Older students with autism exhibit continued restricted language usage and understanding and difficulty and disinterest in social relationships. According to standard assessment techniques, most appear to have some degree of mental retardation (Reed, 1994; Smith, 1990). The ritual behaviors with the need for sameness or preoccupation with detail often persist into adulthood.

Impairment of Acquired Language

Impairment of acquired language (aphasia) is more often associated with adults and is known to follow head injuries, strokes, and brain lesions (Shames, Wiig, & Secord, 1994). Thus, aphasia is thought to be a matter of brain injury that leads to a loss of previously functional ability to speak or comprehend the spoken word.

Childhood (developmental) aphasia is a general term used for a language dysfunction in children that many authorities believe is caused by a brain dysfunction in the auditory mechanism for processing speech (Berko Gleason, 1993; Owens, 1988). Most authorities describe several specific types of aphasia, but as is the case with stuttering, there is considerable disagreement among these authorities as to the causes and in some cases, the treatment. What the teacher is likely to observe is a child who appears to be trying desperately to find the language to respond to a question, to participate in a discussion, or to ask a question.

■ Limited English Proficiency and Linguistic Variations

According to the 1990 U.S. Census, nearly 20 million people who call America home were not born here and over 30 million speak a language other than English at home. Exceptional students from culturally diverse backgrounds present unique challenges to teachers in relation to assessment and teaching. Spoken language may be different with respect to morphology, syntax, semantics, and pragmatics, and the differences likely affect writing production and the predictive aspects of reading.

All languages or dialects are created equal from a linguistic point of view in that they all communicate. Dialects such as Appalachian English, Hawaiian Creole, Black English, New York City, Western Pennsylvania, or Southern White Nonstandard English are important dimensions of communication that "maintain the historical, social, and cultural background of the speakers" (ASHA, 1983, p. 24). ASHA states: "Communicative difference/dialect is a variation of a symbol system used by a group of individuals which reflects and is determined by shared regional, social, or cultural/ethnic factors. Variations or alterations in the use of a symbol system may be indicative of primary language interferences. A regional, social, or cultural/ethnic variation of a symbol system should not be considered a disorder of speech or language" (ASHA, 1982, p. 949).

Students who live in homes in which a language other than English is spoken may be *monolingual*, that is, may speak only English or only the language spoken at home, or be *bilingual*, able to speak both languages. When students primarily speak a language other than English they may also be referred to as "language minority" or bilingual individuals. Each of these terms is the subject of considerable discussion regarding definition and classification (Hamayan & Damico, 1991). Monolingual, in general, refers to someone who speaks one language that may or may not be English. Bilingual refers to individuals who speak and understand two or more languages. The debate centers around the degree of proficiency required in both languages to be considered truly bilingual. The degree to which the individual is able to comfortably function in two or more cultures often becomes another aspect of consideration. For example, several students recently arrived from China may have studied English for several years prior to immigration. However, the ability to use English in school (understand the verbal

Dialects are created equal from a linguistic point of view in that they all communicate.

interactions between teacher and students, lecturing of the teacher, reading the material or writing a term paper or taking notes), in social situations, or in purchasing groceries or clothing, will differ greatly among them. Some may regard them all as bilingual because they speak and read and write more than one language, while others would classify them on an individual basis as bilingual, English language minority, or as having limited English proficiency (LEP) based on the individual skills of each (Sleeter & Grant, 1994; Gersten & Woodward, 1994; Hamayan & Damico, 1991; Baca & Cervantes, 1989).

Bilingual programs for teaching students English are also the subject of discussion. Some bilingual programs emphasize the learning of English and use the native language and culture of the students only until they are proficient in English (Ramirez, 1992), while others promote maintaining literacy in the primary language and culture as they become literate and develop proficiency in English (Cummins, 1989). Bilingual programs may have an English as a Second Language (ESL) component. All ESL programs have as a goal the promotion of proficient English, often rely on English as the medium of teaching and learning, and may or may not emphasize the native culture or language (Sleeter & Grant, 1994; Ramirez, 1992; Baca & Carvantes, 1989).

Careful consideration must be given to students who demonstrate speech or language differences so that differentiations may be made between standard English, dialects, limited English proficiency, and speech or language disorders. It must be remembered however, that students with speech or language differences may also have speech or language disorders. For speech disorders to be considered problematic, they must be present in all of the languages the student speaks (Baca &

Cervantes, 1989). The following are indicators of speech disorders:

1. Omissions of initial or final consonants in both languages.
2. Substitutions. However, teachers must identify cultural substitutions and eliminate them from consideration.
3. Reluctance to participate in class discussions in their native language. Reluctance in English may be normal until students are proficient and feel comfortable.
4. Distortions of sound in both languages. Speaking too softly may be related to culture.
5. Disfluency in both languages. As students learn English, some disfluency is normal.

The assessment of students with limited English proficiency poses particular difficulties that are as yet unresolved. There are specific factors that relate to articulation, such as phonemes (sounds) that do not occur in the native language but are present in English or do not occur in English but do occur in the native language. There are also the omissions and substitutions previously mentioned. Some non-Western languages do not have terms that distinguish gender; words are sexless, for example, there is no direct translation for "She's a grand old flag" or "He's as good as his word." Language concepts such as minutes, hours, days, weeks, inches, miles, or rods may be confusing since the student's cultural experience may not place importance on such arbitrary divisions of time and space (Freeman & Freeman, 1992). Some students may be misdiagnosed as having voice problems because of the interference of the native language, for example, the nasal quality of the Navajo language.

General guidelines related to differentiation among students who have a language disability, those who have limited English proficiency, and those who have both, include several factors. The teacher who makes a referral should be knowledgeable about the cultural and linguistic background of the student and attempt to determine their effects on the student's speech and language, also considering the degree to which the student is acculturated. Students who do not yet understand the give and take in an active discussion group may be perceived as having a language deficiency (Dean, Salend, & Taylor, 1993; Schiff-Myers, Djukic, McGovern-Lawler, & Perez, 1994). Similarly, students may be reluctant to express themselves verbally, believing, consistent with their culture, that speaking at length about any topic is self-seeking and self-agrandizing (Gollnick & Chinn, 1994; Langdon, 1989).

Choosing the most appropriate formal and informal assessment tools is a critical issue. Considering the use of interpreters during the administration of tests is helpful but does not resolve all of the concerns, such as the loss of meaning in translation (Figueroa, 1989). Informal measures to determine the student's ability to use each language and to collect and analyze spontaneous language samples in a variety of settings provide additional means that may be employed to resolve an as yet unresolved issue (Venn, 1994).

Teachers can create an atmosphere that will enhance speaking opportunities and support students who have limited English proficiency by considering the following suggestions:

1. Provide learning experiences that are meaningful and congruent with the student's cultural and linguistic knowledge.
2. Use multicultural materials.
3. Provide nonjudgmental and safe opportunities for students to evaluate and

analyze events related to language that are or may be embarrassing for them.

4. Use every opportunity to sensitize other school personnel regarding the language and culture of the students.

5. Present positive contributions of individuals from ethnic groups represented in the class.

6. Avoid negative comments about a student's language. A statement such as, "Can you say that in a way that I can understand?" is more supportive than "I can't understand you."

7. Reinforce language production. Small-group activities allow students more opportunities for speaking and for the teacher to prompt and reinforce students more frequently.

8. Reduce the tension that will likely develop in classes where a high degree of oral participation is expected, thus allowing students to be more productive.

9. Learn to understand nonstandard English dialects. Students who speak nonstandard dialects usually experience less difficulty understanding the teacher than the teacher has in understanding them. However, this is not necessarily true of students who have limited English speaking abilities. They may have significant difficulty comprehending oral English (Adger, Wolfram, & Detwyler, 1993; Trueba, 1991).

Many school districts provide teachers with similar suggestions in handbooks and at staff development meetings. The time a teacher spends in recognizing and meeting the individual needs of the students with diverse cultural and linguistic backgrounds will pay great dividends in teacher satisfaction and in student well-being and achievement.

The Role of Regular Classroom Teachers

Teachers must remain alert to make referrals of students who need special assistance in the area of speech or language. They should be particularly alert to possible voice disorders. Often, when arithmetic or reading skills are obviously quite low, teachers feel more secure in making referrals, for they feel confident in these areas and have considerable training. Many teachers have not had similar training with speech and language problems, and therefore the following guidelines may be of value. The guidelines may require revision to conform with local practices, but in principle, they are generally applicable.

1. For a teacher who is not experienced in evaluating potential speech problems, overreferral may be the best practice. With experience, the number of referrals may be reduced without the risk of overlooking students who require assistance.

2. If a speech specialist is available for conferences with teachers (and one should be, on either an informal or a formally scheduled basis), teachers should confer with the specialist to learn more about the type of information needed and who should or should not be referred. Such conferences usually turn out to be informal inservice training sessions, and as such, they are of great value. The number of such conferences can be reduced as a teacher gains experience.

3. When it appears that a speech or language difficulty is related to other problems, such as hearing impairment or

mental retardation, a teacher should check all records and talk with previous teachers (when possible) to determine if these possibilities have been investigated. Any recent audiological evaluation should receive particular attention in a case of possible hearing impairment.

4. In settings in which the speech specialist is overloaded with cases (a common situation), the teacher may expedite matters by describing the type and extent of the problem in detail. It is not enough to say that the child lisps. Many other factors can be considered, such as how consistently the problem occurs, whether it occurs mainly when the child is under pressure or is tired, and whether it is noticed by other children.

If the teacher's referral leads to speech evaluation and the speech specialist begins to provide assistance to the student, usually the specialist also provides specific suggestions to the teacher. The teacher's role depends on the type and extent of the problem. In general, the role of the classroom teacher relates to the following concepts:

1. Being sure the aims and objectives of the therapy program are fully understood.
2. Demonstrating acceptance of the student with a communication disorder and encouraging other class members to do the same.
3. Reinforcing good speech and language habits in all students, especially in the student with the impairment, so the importance of what is learned in the therapy sessions is transferred to other settings. Modeling appropriate speech and language also communicates the importance of speech and language.
4. Attending to *what* the student is saying more than to *how* it is said.

5. Helping students follow medical instructions relating to vocal rest or other disorders for which there are medical instructions.
6. Recognizing that students with cleft lip or palate may require surgery and thus miss school. Help them either keep up or catch up.
7. Being aware of the strengths as well as the weaknesses of students with cerebral palsy.
8. Keeping records of the students' progress, following a system devised in collaboration with a speech-language specialist.

■ The Role of Speech-Language Pathologists

The speech-language pathologist is the orchestrator of school speech and language services. As such, the pathologist provides direct services to students with severe or difficult problems and advice to teachers who serve students with mild problems. Effective speech programs involve identification, evaluation, and remediation and depend on cooperative working relationships between speech specialists and regular classroom teachers. The American Speech-Language-Hearing Association and others recommend that speech and language programs be organized along a continuum extending from a communicative development component to a communicative disorders component (Figure 6–4).

In respect to communicative development, a speech-language pathologist must make teachers and parents more aware of factors that help students develop good communicative skills, especially factors that can be part of a regular classroom or home environment.

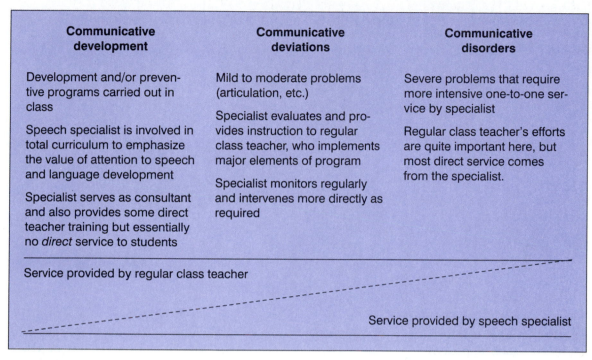

Communicative development	Communicative deviations	Communicative disorders
Development and/or preventive programs carried out in class	Mild to moderate problems (articulation, etc.)	Severe problems that require more intensive one-to-one service by specialist
Speech specialist is involved in total curriculum to emphasize the value of attention to speech and language development	Specialist evaluates and provides instruction to regular class teacher, who implements major elements of program	Regular class teacher's efforts are quite important here, but most direct service comes from the specialist.
Specialist serves as consultant and also provides some direct teacher training but essentially no *direct* service to students	Specialist monitors regularly and intervenes more directly as required	

Service provided by regular class teacher

Service provided by speech specialist

Figure 6–4
The comprehensive speech and language program continuum

Many of the suggestions provided in this chapter would be a part of any program of communicative development, along with efforts to construct a curriculum ensuring experiences that promote maximum communicative skills in all children. This program is primarily developmental and preventive in nature, and except for orienting teachers newly employed in a given school, the speech specialist has minimum visibility once the program is well established.

Communicative deviations are mild to moderate speech and language problems that require some assistance from the speech-language pathologist but with the regular classroom teacher providing much of the direct effort. Instructions, including original instructions and ongoing assistance, are provided by the specialist. If classroom efforts are not successful, the specialist intervenes more directly, as required in individual cases.

Communicative disorders include disorders that obviously require specialized help because of their severity and specific, one-to-one assistance on an ongoing basis. Even here, much cooperation between a regular classroom teacher and specialist is necessary, but this type of service requires much greater time involvement on the part of the speech-language pathologist.

The speech-language pathologist must help teachers recognize situations in which various class proceedings, including certain standardized academic tests, are greatly affected by lack of speech or language ability. The speech-language pathologist must determine the

Collaboration between the class-room teacher and the speech-language pathologist benefits students.

most effective ways to improve a student's speech or language and must involve the teacher in such remediation, providing assistance in carryover activities for the classroom.

Programming for very young children who are autistic may be implemented by the speech-language pathologist in both the regular classroom (to provide the student with a natural milieu and role models) and in individual therapy for speech development, establishing eye contact, and development of communicative intent. As the student develops skills, and verbal and social interaction with others becomes even more critical, the focus of interventions may shift to the development of semantic and pragmatic communication conducted in the regular classroom in small groups. The speech-language pathologist will likely collaborate with the regular classroom teacher regarding the development and implementation of specific interventions such as those described in the next section.

For students whose language is severely impaired, augmentative or alternative communication (AAC) such as communication boards (described in Chapter 8) and sign languages (discussed in Chapter 5) may be used. The use of AAC allows for a variety of means of establishing communicative intent and capability (Prizant et al., 1990). The initial teaching of the use of AAC may be conducted by the speech-language pathologist or teacher of the hearing impaired but the functional use will be implemented in the regular classroom. Figure 6–5 provides some guidelines to facilitate communication with an individual who uses AAC.

Suggestions for Regular Classroom Teachers

Students develop language as an imitative function, so teachers have a special reason to model correct articulation, grammar, and language usage. Regular classroom teachers are regularly involved in promoting speech and language development for all students and may also be

What to do when you meet someone who uses AAC:

- If you do not already know them, introduce yourself.
- Ask them for a demonstration of how their communication system works.
- Wait and watch while they construct a message. Be patient.
- Be prepared for a slower rhythm in the communication process and don't feel you have to fill every silence.
- Don't finish words or sentences unless you are directed to.
- If you don't understand, ask them to repeat.
- Watch facial expressions and gestures.
- Give them opportunities to talk, ask you questions, and make comments.
- Try to be at eye level, using a chair if they use a wheelchair.
- Talk directly to them, not to others who may assist them.

involved in individualized efforts for specific students. Reading to students from texts in content areas, fiction, and nonfiction is interesting to the student. Audiotapes also provide appropriate models of language. In addition, selected television programs that have been videotaped may provide language enrichment. Ideas such as these can easily be incorporated into the daily schedule at any grade level; will provide models of accurate articulation, phrasing, and appropriate speech; and will enhance language usage and comprehension.

In conjunction with a speech-language pathologist and consistent with the particular objectives for a student, structured naturalistic activities may provide opportunities for using the skills learned in therapy. Such activities for younger children may center around recess or involve role playing or puppetry. Language experience approaches in the beginning-to-read stage allow for expansion of vocabulary as well as assist in awareness of relationships between spoken and written language. For older students, activities may be based on clothing or grooming, food preparation, assembling or sorting of materials, and

interviewing. Cognitive rehearsal strategies help students organize their thoughts before speaking. For some students, combining and recombining sentences in oral or written form provides linguistic awareness.

Instructions or oral directions in short, simple sentences, with pauses and restatements of important information, provide appropriate models and help comprehension, which of course is a goal of communication. Discussing speech and language activities and what the student has learned may help reduce negative feelings about therapy. Responding to a student's efforts at communication in a positive manner will encourage the student and model acceptance for others.

Oral communication may be encouraged through activities like expression of feelings, oral reports, and problem solving. However, the teacher must be sensitive to situations that might be threatening to a student (Morsink, 1984).

Seating arrangement may facilitate opportunities for a student to use oral language in the classroom. Having the student near the teacher tends to restrict instead of enhance interactions (Lewis & Doorlag, 1991). Rather, the student should be surrounded by good speech models.

Discuss pronunciation and meanings of new words and provide opportunities for students to use new words orally and in written form. A structured format for teaching vocabulary includes demonstrating appropriate and inappropriate examples, asking for examples from students, providing examples by which students can assess their own performance, and providing definitions for students to identify (Schloss & Sedlak, 1986).

Students lacking conversational skills may be taught the pragmatics of conversation, which, according to Schloss and Sedlak (1986), include the following:

1. Taking turns
2. Initiating
3. Clarifying a point
4. Following the sequential organization
5. Making coherent contributions
6. Maintaining a reasonable social distance (p. 237)

In content areas requiring specific vocabulary (for example, science), quizzes may help ensure understanding of concepts that enhance comprehension of lectures or explanations. Explanations of the derivations of words may help some students comprehend a variety of words more fully. For example, a student who learns the meaning of *inter* as between or among may be able to infer the meanings of *intercolonial, intercultural, intercellular,* and *interdependent*.

Role playing in appropriate situations provides practice of skills in effective communication. An example that is applicable in almost any content area is having a student teach a particular concept or lesson. This requires planning what will be taught and how it will be taught. A student might explain the concept of osmosis with the aid of a chart,

or the correct positioning of the body when holding a bat by using stick figures. Oral presentation might be rehearsed to ensure clarity.

Encouraging active participation in class may be of great value, especially if a student with some particular problem is given notice. For example, the teacher might say, "Tomorrow I am going to ask you to comment on the basic differences between communism and democracy. Let's see if you can challenge the thinking of the rest of the class."

The Language Master, a machine providing visual and auditory information, may be a useful tool. This system uses cards with visual representations (words, pictures, or short phrases) on the top and a magnetic tape near the bottom. As a card is inserted in the machine, a verbal message (which the teacher has prerecorded) is played. The student receives simultaneous auditory and visual stimuli. The Language Master will record the verbal response of the student, allowing for playback. The student may, for example, see a picture of teeth and hear the auditory stimulus "The plural of *tooth* is _____?" The student's response, "*teeth,*" is recorded. On the prerecorded message, the teacher may have left space for the student's response and provided the correct response so that the student receives corrective feedback or immediate verification of a correct answer. The Language Master also provides practice in a variety of other grammatical aspects, vocabulary, and reading enrichment exercises.

To combine oral language and sequencing, the teacher may ask students to provide oral directions for certain activities. For example, the teacher might have a student direct the class as they construct a collage for a bulletin board or perform a specific dance. To practice verbal skills, ask students to interview another student for specific information, such as favorite sports or least favorite subject and the reasons for the choice. It is important for students to phrase their questions in ways that require more than one-word responses.

When targeted skills are being practiced, a tape recorder may be used, and a student allowed time to evaluate his or her performance. For example, when the use of adjectives is the targeted skill, provide an opportunity for a student to prepare and record a short presentation about a topic of interest. After recording, the student would evaluate his or her use of adjectives in the presentation. Videotaping conversations between two students will also allow students to replay the videotape and determine how well they used specific targeted skills.

Listening skills may be enhanced through the use of materials in a content area. The teacher can read a series of paragraphs from the text in a content area and ask the students to either write or provide an oral concluding statement. The statement should be a summary of the content of the paragraphs previously read. Skills related to evaluation and judgment may also be reinforced by asking the students to choose the most appropriate statement from a group of concluding statements. A similar activity related to listening skills is reading a short story, poem, or other selection, not reading the title, then asking the students to provide a title.

The teacher may show a movie or read a story that addresses a topic of interest to students and then provide a list of questions that follows the format of the movie or story. This provides guidance, structure, and practice for students who have difficulty staying on a topic in oral discussions.

Sample sentences may direct students to identify descriptive words (or any other class of words). Students can be asked to suggest other words that will change the meaning of a sentence, or for a more difficult exercise, to suggest words that alter the meaning without completely changing it.

Singing activities may be used to increase oral language and fluency. Choral reading has the same benefits. Time between classes or at the beginning of class may be used by having students tell jokes or ask riddles. Students may be told in advance that they will need to be prepared on a given day. Some ground rules about appropriateness of jokes or riddles may need to be discussed with the students to help them learn how to adjust what they say based on situations and listeners (pragmatics).

Students can be directed to work in pairs, with one the describer, who provides a verbal description of a simple picture, and the other the listener. The listener sketches the picture, based on the words of the describer. After completion of the drawing, the original picture and the sketch may be compared and the roles may be reversed.

Students may be provided with a map of the school building, local area, or the United States (depending on the students' abilities) and taken on an oral trip. The teacher gives directions that must be followed to arrive at the destination. A more complicated version of the same activity is to provide the students with a paper grid and give directions that they must follow to arrive at a specific square. Since a grid is more abstract than a map, it requires considerably more skill on the part of the students. Activities similar to these also provide students with practice in using terms such as *left, right, north,* and *south*.

Videotapes, stories, or another student telling a story provides for a variety of activities in which students must recall what they hear. Students may illustrate what they hear and retell it or sequence pictures that illustrate the major points. To make the task more difficult, allow time to elapse (a few minutes, hours, or days) before asking the students to respond. This emphasizes memory as well as listening.

Music, such as *Peter and the Wolf, The Nutcracker Suite, The Sorcerer's Apprentice,* or *2001: A Space Odyssey,* provides students with a source for describing mental pictures. As an alternative, students can draw or paint pictures or develop creative movement activities related to music (Norton, 1989).

Teachers may provide oral information regarding a specific topic (from a content area) or use a story and develop a cluster diagram with students. A simple cluster diagram related to transportation is presented in Figure 6–6. A cluster diagram enables students to observe a visual representation of what they have heard and to note the organization of the various concepts. More complex cluster diagrams may be used as the students' skills increase. Prior to expecting the students to develop such diagrams, teachers must model the procedure for them.

When students have difficulty with word order or exhibit certain consistent omissions in spoken language, the use of card pictures to make sentences more concrete may be of value. In this activity each card is used to refer to one grammatical function of a sentence (Figure 6–7). Through lengthening the sentence or fad-

ing the visual cues, the students should be able to generalize the rules relating to word order.

A number of abstract concepts are utilized at elementary levels of spoken language. Examples include (a) comparisons of size—big, bigger, biggest, longer, shorter; (b) spatial concepts—on, under, beside, in, in back of, top, middle; (c) ordinal concepts—first, second, third; and (d) directional concepts—left, right, north, west, southeast. When students have difficulty using such abstract concepts correctly, visual aids often provide the concrete experiences necessary for understanding. Physical activities relating to the concepts also develop understanding.

Enhance thinking skills and verbal exchanges by providing opportunities for teacher–student and student–student interactions. Present problems for which there are no "correct" answers, such as the following:

1. What would you do if you found a $20 bill on the floor? Why?
2. If you are driving somewhere and have a flat tire, what can you do?
3. What would you take along with you if you were going to spend 2 weeks on an

Figure 6–6

A cluster diagram (visual representation) about transportation

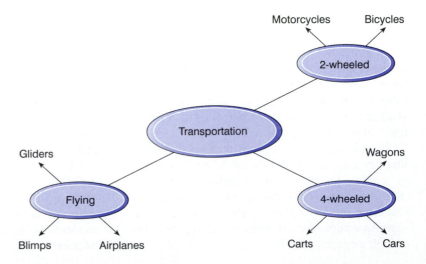

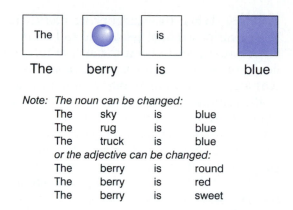

The	●	is	■
The	berry	is	blue

Note: The noun can be changed:

The	sky	is	blue
The	rug	is	blue
The	truck	is	blue

or the adjective can be changed:

The	berry	is	round
The	berry	is	red
The	berry	is	sweet

Figure 6–7

Using card pictures to refer to one grammatical element of a sentence

island? Why did you choose those things?

Students with severe language disabilities may need visual cues (pictures cut from magazines) to elicit initial responses or to broaden responses. Such cues are removed as soon as possible.

Acting out scenes from daily life can provide opportunities for students to practice sequencing skills and to practice skills in communication. Such dramatic play may provide an incentive for some students who otherwise avoid self-expression to exercise spoken language. If the spoken language used in such play is limited, the activity may be expanded to include small-group brainstorming to list different words that might be used. For example, if part of the play concerns baking a cake, the cake might be described as *delicious, yummy, exquisite, super good, moist, dry, burned,* or *lopsided.* Dramatic play provides opportunities for spoken language similar to that provided by written-language experience stories. Topics relevant to the lives of the students provide the motivation. Dramatic play can be used in such content areas as literature

and social studies. Students can develop skits related to *The Diary of Anne Frank* or the three branches of the U.S. government.

Puppets permit the transfer of the identity of students to the characters represented by the puppets. Such substitution encourages many shy students to participate in a variety of discussions, for they can hide behind the puppet. The use of puppets may relate to stories the students have read, stories the students have written, or stories read to the students. Even creation of the puppets is an opportunity for enhancing spoken language among students.

Role playing is a more structured form of dramatic activity. It is better suited to some students and some age-groups than puppetry. Problems of various types can be suggested by the students or the teacher. A discussion of the facets of the problem will provide motivation and time for the students to get into the character. The students assume roles and act out solutions to the problem. After each role-playing session is completed (sessions are brief), the teacher conducts a discussion of the events as well as alternative solutions. The problem-solving aspect and the use of spoken language provide students with opportunities for growth. Some teachers use this type of activity to solve routine classroom discipline problems, such as waiting for others to finish speaking or respecting the property of others. Frequently, students who act, speak, and think as someone else in role playing use a broader range of vocabulary and greater sentence complexity.

Most students learn concepts through experiences—direct teaching of concepts may be quite difficult. Often, students use terms representing abstract concepts without fully understanding them. Concept teaching must include specific language training and use of the concepts in a variety of situations. The following steps are suggested to develop understanding of concepts:

1. Clearly identify the concept to be taught.
2. Identify and discuss critical and noncritical attributes. Take care to note that the critical attributes apply to that concept only.
3. Identify examples and nonexamples of the concept. After you complete several discussions of examples and nonexamples and you feel the students understand, ask the students to provide both examples and nonexamples.
4. After the students master critical and noncritical attributes and examples and nonexamples, discuss finer discriminations and distinctions.
5. Provide opportunities to use the newly acquired knowledge.

Interesting and unusual lost-and-found ads may be selected and brought to class. They may be read to the students if students have difficulty reading, or the students may read them. A discussion of what lost-and-found ads are and purposes for them should follow. Students may develop oral stories about the ads. Dividing the class into small groups should provide all students with opportunities to share their stories. The activity may be varied for older students, using want ads or apartment rental ads. The students might describe the type of person who would perform well at the job, what type of person would desire or would want to sell the objects listed, or who lived in the apartment or wants to live in the apartment described. Such oral discussions promote spoken language development, but the responses may also be written to develop written skills.

The teacher and students may discuss the differences between conversation and interviewing, and develop a list of purposes for interviewing. They may explore appropriate and inappropriate factors relating to interviewing, and interviewing may be discussed and practiced. When the students are proficient, assign various school personnel to be interviewed (the principal, custodians, other students, or teachers). In conjunction with content areas, students may interview individuals in the community. Prior to the interviews, the students should establish purposes for the interviews and develop lists of questions to ask. After the interviews take place, the students should report the results to the entire class. A variation of this activity is to use want ads and role play the interviewer and the interviewee. Students may be required to do some reference work related to the job requirements. An activity such as this is easily incorporated into units on career opportunities or awareness.

In place of the usual written reports, students may design dioramas or television commercials that illustrate the main theme of a book. Dioramas or pictures may be used as visual aids in oral presentations. Television commercials may consist of enactment of portions of a book, with announcers describing the salient aspects. In addition to providing practice in oral language, such activities provide means of synthesizing for students who have difficulty in written expression.

To help students visualize figures of speech or metaphors, provide a list such as "I'll put a bug in his ear" and "She has a frog in her throat." Ask the students to illustrate the literal meanings. As an extended activity, students may illustrate their inferred meanings on the reverse side of the paper.

Teachers may compile a series of direct and indirect questions. In a few instances, questions might be either direct or indirect requests, with other cues the determining factors. Teachers should read the questions with the students, indicating the real meaning of the question. Examples of questions are as follows:

1. What day of the week is this?
2. Can you open the window?

The regular classroom teacher often provides ongoing assistance to students with speech disorders.

3. Won't you stop talking?
4. When does your bus leave?
5. Must you stand there?
6. Is the door open?
7. Can't you sit still?

Students can record stories for younger students. While preparing tapes, they are learning to use appropriate voice inflection, which has benefits for oral language and reading. Rap songs relating to topics addressed in the content areas (safety, nutrition, or health) may be created by older students for younger students (Polloway et al., 1989).

Facilitated communication is a procedure during which an adult provides physical support to the arm and/or hand of the individual who has severe communication difficulties, particularly autism, while that person types on a keyboard (Biklen, 1992). The support may range from actually holding the arm or hand to resting the facilitator's hand on the arm to touching the clothing or shoulder of the individual typing. The premise is that autism has a neuromotor component that can be overcome by stabilizing the hand or arm (Biklen, 1992). The facilitator must be trained in the technique and learn how to fade support as the individual with autism gains skill and confidence. The individual may type on one of a variety of keyboards, such as standard mechanical typewriters, computers, enlarged keys, or communication boards with words, pictures, or phrases (Biklen & Schubert, 1991). According to Biklen (1992), students with autism have acquired linguistic skills but are unable to express them verbally, and facilitated communication provides them with another communication alternative.

Concerns regarding facilitated communication center around questions regarding the prompting of the facilitator and whether the ideas expressed are those of the facilitator or the student. A related concern is the lack of scientific research supporting its effectiveness (Thompson, 1993; Mulick, Jacobson, & Kobe, 1993; Calculator, 1992). However, some suggest that facilitated communication is very similar to other accepted interactive approaches and should be continued to be used and researched (Long, 1994; Miller, 1993).

Many students, including those who are autistic, benefit from structured environments that are consistent and predictable. Disciplinary practices that include clear instructions and rules with consistently enforced consequences stressing positive behavior are beneficial to most students, especially those who are autistic. Frequent communication with the family will increase the likelihood of consistency in disciplinary practices, methods of promoting social interactions and increasing language skills (NICHCY, 1991). Autistic students of all ages may require continued teaching of social skills. For young children, targeted skills may involve being aware of others and playing near them, while for older students the skills will more often center around attentional and conversational skills (Bristol & Shopler, 1989).

Teachers at all grade levels must attend to the manner in which they recognize language usage. This attention requires careful planning, but with practice, such planning becomes second nature and has positive effects on all students in the class. The key concepts in such planning and teaching are exposure, encouragement, variety, opportunity, and innovation. The interest of students must be stimulated and maintained. A reward system must be established, be it grades, praise, or privileges, to encourage students to maintain effort. McCormick (1986) suggests that students with speech or language deficits are more alike than different from their peers in that they "need and can benefit from a range and variety of learning experiences; . . . are interested in and want to talk about the same general objects, events and relationships; and . . . seek the same control over their environment" (p. 124).

The preceding ideas and suggestions are samples of what may be done. They may be modified and thus provide a wide variety of options.

■ Summary

In this chapter, we addressed the speech and language disorders students may experience, particularly noting difficulties in identification and interpretation of such disorders, given the many linguistic variations and the influence of multiple factors that may be related to limited English proficiency. We discussed various theories of language development, and specific consideration of articulation, stuttering, voice, and language disorders to establish a basic understanding of the potential scope of speech-language-related learning problems. We emphasized the role of the speech-language pathologist and the importance of coordinating classroom efforts, and discussed the role of the regular classroom teacher. We then made a number of suggestions for use in the regular classroom, noting the use of augmentative or alternative communication and outlining the pros and cons of facilitated communication. Because students use their speech and language skills throughout their school day, the remedial and development efforts of regular classroom teachers remain essential in any program of intervention.

chapter 7

- To what extent may an individual with a visual impairment further damage residual visual abilities?

- Which students with thick-lensed glasses fit the definition of visually impaired? Which do not fit the definition?

- What behaviors that can indicate impaired vision may be observed in school? What action should be taken when such behaviors are observed?

- How do you think common environmental scenes will appear to someone with glaucoma? cataracts? a detached retina?

- What electronic devices are available to help persons with visual impairments read normal print? What devices are available to help them with travel about the community?

- What is the difference between orientation skills and mobility skills? How can a blind student learn such skills?

- If a blind person needs travel assistance across the street and into a fifth-floor office, would you know how to provide such assistance?

- How do dog guides communicate with their masters? What are their strengths and limitations?

Teaching Students Who Are Visually Impaired

■■■■■■■■■■

In light of the current discussion regarding the relative advantages and disadvantages of including all exceptional students in regular education programs, it is interesting to note that, with respect to students with impaired vision, the concept of inclusion is more than 130 years old. In 1866, Dr. Samuel Gridley Howe advocated that visually impaired students be educated with their sighted peers. Although some of the terminology he used seems strange, his concept predated legislation such as PL 94–142 and PL 101–476 by over a century. His statement also provides insight regarding how persons with visual impairment were treated at that time:

All great establishments in the nature of boarding schools, where sexes must be separated; where there must be boarding in common, and sleeping in congregate dormitories; where there must be routine, and formality, and restraint, and repression of individuality; where the charms and refining influences of the true family relation cannot be had—all such institutions are unnatural, undesirable and very liable to abuse. We should have as few of them as possible, and those few should be kept as small as possible. . . .

With a view to lessening all differences between blind and seeing children, I would have the blind attend the common schools in all cases where it is feasible (depend upon it, one of the future reforms in the education of the blind will be to send blind children to the common schools, to be taught with common children in all those branches not absolutely requiring visible illustrations, as spelling, pronunciation, grammar, arithmetic, vocal music and the like). We shall avail ourselves of the special institutions less and the common schools more. (quoted in Irwin, 1955, p. 128)

This early emphasis on education in the "common schools," led many of the service delivery systems used today with other handicapping conditions to be modeled after successful programs for the visually impaired.

Students with impaired vision cannot readily use the same educational materials as other students, and if they do, they receive information at a slower rate, as with recorded materials, braille, large print, magnification devices, or reading machines. As a result of limited access and the slower rate, the primary features of programming for the visually impaired involve modification and adaptation of educational materials. A related problem for students with impaired vision involves concept development. A concept is often developed and unified through our visual experiences and lends meaning to our perceptions and experiences. For example, abstract concepts such as space and color may present some difficulty for visually impaired students, since they do not have unifying visual referents. Because of the potential problem in concept development, program emphasis must be placed on concrete experiences and on providing input to the other sensory channels: touch, hearing, taste, and smell, using the visual channel whenever appropriate.

In this chapter, we discuss a number of major concerns:

1. Measurement and classification of vision
2. Identification of students who are visually impaired
3. Types of visual impairment
4. Procedures for referral
5. Educational programming
6. Continuum of services
7. Suggestions for regular classroom teachers
8. Specialized instruction and assistance from resource and itinerant teachers.

■■■■■■■■■■

■ Measurement and Classification of Vision

Barraga (1983) noted "a gradual trend to use *blind* and *low vision* to differentiate the population and to use *visually handicapped* as a generic term to refer to the entire population" (p. 21). Using this classification system, the student who is blind is one whose vision is unreliable and who finds it necessary to rely on other senses for functional purposes. Students who are blind cannot use print, even with maximum magnification; they must use braille. A student who can perform visual tasks, but does so with reduced precision and endurance and at reduced speeds would likely be considered a person with low vision. Usually, the student with low vision cannot perform certain detailed tasks, but if there is significant usable vision, the classification should be *low vision* rather than *blind*.

Those individuals who have central visual acuity of 20/200 or less in the better eye after correction or who have a field of vision no more than 20 degrees in diameter are usually considered legally blind.

Ratios such as 20/20, 20/70, and 20/200 are used to express visual acuity. The first number is the distance in feet at which the test is made. The second number is the size of symbols or letters on the Snellen chart, expressed in terms of the distance at which a person with normal vision can comfortably read them. For example, if at 20 feet an individual can read the 20-foot-size symbol or letter on the chart, the measured acuity is 20/20, or normal vision; if an individual can read only the symbol representing the 70-foot-size letter or larger, distance visual acuity is indicated as 20/70; if only the largest, the 200-foot-size letter, then the individual's measured distance visual acuity is 20/200. These figures do not provide information concerning *near-point* vision (the ability to see at close distances, as in reading). There is also considerable variance among individuals with the same measured acuity. For example, two students may have 20/200 measured acuity, but one may be able to read printed material, whereas the other may have to read braille.

The Keystone Telebinocular device may be used to assess near-point vision and depth perception, factors that also affect the student's ability to use vision effectively. A complete evaluation of functional vision will include near vision, far vision, depth perception, and color discrimination (McLoughlin & Lewis, 1990).

The *Federal Register* (1977) defined *visual handicap* as a "visual impairment which even with correction, adversely affects the child's educational performance. The term includes both partially seeing and blind children" (p. 42479). Also referring to an educationally oriented definition rather than a legal one, Barraga (1983) states, "A visually handicapped child is one whose visual impairment interferes with his optimal learning and achievement, unless adaptations are made in the methods of presenting learning experiences, the nature of the materials used, and/or in the learning environment" (p. 25).

Another dimension that should be considered is an individual's *visual functioning* (Barraga & Erin, 1992) which includes not only the physical condition of the eye, but also other factors, such as the motivation, needs, and experiences of the individual. One's *visual efficiency*, however, is more unique to the individual and includes all of the above in reference to the performance of specific tasks with ease, comfort level, and time involved. A student's visual efficiency would be given very strong consideration in designing an educational program.

The student who is visually impaired may be considered in terms of medical, legal, educational, or functional definitions, but our emphasis here involves educational and functional ability. For our purposes, we define the student with impaired vision as one whose vision is limited to such an extent that he or she may require educational modifications and adaptations. Optimum programming for students who are blind enables them to utilize their other senses within the learning environment.

◼ Identification of Students Who Are Visually Impaired

Students with severe visual impairments are usually easily identified before enrollment in school. However, impaired vision in some students goes undetected for many years. Some individuals compensate extremely well for poor vision, and others may not complain about their vision because they assume that everyone sees the way they do. Impairment may be detected by routine visual screening during the primary grades, or it may not be detected until fourth or fifth grade, when the subject matter requires extensive visual work, such as increased reading and map study. Many screening programs are carelessly conducted or not carried out on a routine basis. In addition, tests for near-point vision (ability to read at 12 to 16 inches) are required by only a few states. Most screening programs are concerned with distance vision (ability to see at 20 feet). Although vision screening procedures are improving, even at best they do not identify all students with impaired vision.

Indicators of Possible Vision Problems

When considering the problems associated with vision screening, the role of regular classroom teachers in identifying students with vision problems cannot be overemphasized. Teachers have opportunities to observe students in a variety of conditions and may be in the best position to identify visual difficulties. Regular classroom teachers should be aware of behaviors and observable signs that may indicate a visual problem. Following are some of the most common indicators of possible vision problems.

Poor Handwriting

Some students with an undetected vision problem may demonstrate poor handwriting or difficulty in writing on the line.

Rubbing Eyes

Eye rubbing may be observed in excessive amounts or during close visual work.

Shutting or Covering One Eye

A student who is having difficulty seeing may close one eye or tilt or thrust the head forward.

Inattentiveness

An indicator of a possible vision problem is inattentiveness during activities involving the chalkboard, map reading, or other distant activities.

Light Sensitivity

Some students with an undetected vision problem may demonstrate unusual sensitivity to bright or even normal light by shutting their eyes or squinting.

Losing Place During Reading

A student with a tendency to lose place in a sentence or page while reading may have a vision problem. Teachers should observe carefully to see if the student is demonstrating a mechanical reading problem or one related to a possible visual defect.

Difficulty with Reading

A student who has little difficulty with oral or spoken directions or tasks but experiences an unusual amount of difficulty with reading or other work requiring close use of the eyes may have vision loss.

Achievement Disparity

Obviously, there may be many reasons that a student does not achieve in a manner consistent with ability, but teachers should be aware that impaired vision may be one of the reasons for any disparity between expected and actual achievement.

Unusual Facial Expressions and Behaviors

A student who demonstrates an unusual amount of squinting, blinking, frowning, or facial distortion while reading or doing other close work should be observed and possibly referred for further examination.

Eye Discomfort

The student who complains of burning, itching, or scratchiness of the eyes may be experiencing a vision problem and should be referred to the school nurse for closer examination.

Holding Reading Materials at an Inappropriate Distance

A student with a visual problem may hold reading materials too close or too far or frequently change the distance from near to far or far to near.

Discomfort Following Close Visual Work

A student who complains of pains or aches in the eye, headaches, dizziness, or nausea following close visual work should be observed and possibly referred for further examination.

Body Rigidity

Students who hold their bodies rigidly while looking at near or distant objects or during class activities may have a vision problem.

Difficulty with Distance Vision

A student who experiences difficulty in seeing distant objects or who avoids gross motor activities may have visual loss. Such a student may prefer reading or other academic tasks to playground activities.

Nausea, Double Vision, or Unusual Blurring

A student who complains of nausea, or blurred or double vision should be referred for a visual examination as soon as possible.

Reversals

A tendency to reverse letters, syllables, or words may be an indication of impaired vision.

Letter Confusion

A student who confuses letters of similar shape (o and a, c and e, n and m, h and n, f and t) may have impaired vision.

Poor Spacing

Poor spacing in writing and difficulty in staying on the line may be an indication of visual impairment.

Dislike of Visual Tasks

Disliking tasks that require sustained visual concentration may be related to a visual problem.

Physical Indications

Teachers should not overlook physical indications of impaired vision, including red eyelids, crusts on lids among the eyelashes, recurring styes or swollen lids, watering eyes or discharges, crossed eyes or eyes that do not appear to be straight, pupils of uneven size, eyes that move excessively, drooping eyelids, and excessive blinking.

Types of Visual Impairment

Many types of eye problems may result in reduced visual acuity, restricted field of vision, or disease of the eye. The most common visual defects in students are astigmatism, myopia (nearsightedness), and hyperopia (farsightedness). These defects are called *refrac-* *tive errors* and can usually be corrected by lenses. Among the more common conditions that result in reduced field of vision, blind spots, or blurring of vision are glaucoma, cataract, retinal detachment, retinitis pigmentosa, macular degeneration, corneal pathologic conditions, and diabetic retinopathy.

Figures 7–1 to 7–9 depict the most common visual problems. Figure 7–1 shows a typical street scene as seen by someone with 20/20 visual acuity. The remaining figures represent the same scene as it might appear to persons with various serious vision problems.

Figure 7–1
Normal vision

Figure 7–2
Myopia (nearsightedness)
Note: With myopia, vision is clear when looking at near objects but blurred at far distances.

Figure 7–3

Hyperopia (farsightedness)

Note: With hyperopia, vision is blurred when looking at near objects but clear when looking at a distance.

Figure 7–4

Glaucoma

Note: With glaucoma, there is loss of peripheral vision while retaining most of the central vision.

Figure 7–5

Cataract

Note: With a cataract, there is diminished acuity caused by a density or opacity of the lens. The field of vision is not affected, and there are no significant blind spots. There is an overall haziness (denser in some spots), particularly in glaring light conditions.

Figure 7–6

Retinal detachment

Note: With retinal detachment, a hole in the retina (back of the eye) allows fluid to lift the retina from its normal position. This results in a field defect, seen as a dark shadow. It may be in the upper portion or lower part, as illustrated.

Figure 7–7

Retinitis pigmentosa

Note: Retinitis pigmentosa is a form of tunnel vision. Generally, only a small area of central vision remains.

Figure 7–8

Macular degeneration

Note: Macular degeneration is a breakdown of the central part of the retina that results in an area of decreased central vision called a blind spot or scotoma. Peripheral vision remains unaffected.

Figure 7–9

Corneal pathological condition
Note: With corneal pathological condition, the image may be distorted or
clouded so that clear detail is not dis-
cernible. The field of vision is normal.

Alongside each representation is a brief
description of the condition and its effect on
an individual's vision. These figures are only
illustrative of the various conditions and
should not be interpreted as the actual acuity
because there may be considerable variance in
any of the conditions represented.

Procedures for Referral

When teachers observe any of the behaviors or
signs of visual problems, they should immediately refer the student to the school nurse,
principal, or other individual in the school
designated to receive such referrals. The parents should also be consulted. It is possible
that the student may have a refractive error,
which may be corrected by lenses, but it is
also possible that more serious problems have
developed that require immediate medical
attention.

Teachers may find it helpful to have information concerning the capabilities of the various eye specialists in the community in order
to make the necessary referrals or provide
information to parents. Occasionally, classroom teachers may need to confer with one of

these specialists. Brief descriptions of these
specialties follow:

1. *Ophthalmologist*. A medical doctor who
   specializes in the diagnosis and treatment of diseases of the eye. This physician is also licensed to prescribe glasses.
2. *Optometrist*. A highly trained person
   who specializes in eye problems but
   does not possess a medical degree. This
   individual is licensed to measure visual
   function and prescribe and fit glasses. If
   disease is suspected, a referral will be
   made to an ophthalmologist.
3. *Optician*. A technician who makes
   glasses and fills the prescriptions of
   ophthalmologists and optometrists.
4. *Orthoptist*. A nonmedical technician
   who directs prescribed exercises or
   training to correct eye muscle imbalances and who generally works under
   the direction of an ophthalmologist.

After a complete vision assessment, if the
student has impairments not correctable by
lenses or surgery, a staffing meeting will likely
be called to determine how to meet the student's needs. At this time, reports from the
vision specialist are consulted and an IEP is

developed. The teacher, with the help of others in the school, must obtain information as complete as possible concerning the nature of the student's eye condition, functional vision, effects of diminished vision in other areas (such as motor development, social skills, and intellectual capabilities), lighting needs, and travel limitations. An understanding of the variety of conditions that may affect vision and information relating to the specific abilities and the needs of the student should lead to the most advantageous educational programming.

Educational Programming

For nearly three-quarters of a century, educators have recognized that students with visual impairment could be educated with their sighted peers with only minor modifications and adaptations, and that the limitations imposed by visual disability do not require a special curriculum. Rather, teachers must provide materials in different media or in modified or adapted form so that such students can learn through sensory channels other than vision. For example, if a student is not able to read material in printed form, the material may be presented through the tactile (touch) or auditory channels. If the student can read printed material only with considerable difficulty, the material may be enlarged or the student may use magnification devices or reading machines. The primary function of special education services for students who are visually impaired is modification and adaptation of existing educational materials.

Students who are blind or have low vision follow the same curriculum as their peers but do need additional "plus factors." The student studies reading, math, and social studies, but in addition may need braille instruction; orientation and mobility (travel) training; instruc-

tion in the use of computers and other technology, such as keyboarding; and training in the use of an abacus. Generally, plus factors, or compensatory skills, are taught by the resource or itinerant teacher and are not a responsibility of the regular classroom teacher.

Continuum of Services

There is a definite need for a full continuum of services for students with impaired vision. The following variables should be considered when studying placement options: (a) age, (b) achievement level, (c) intelligence, (d) presence of multiple disabilities, (e) emotional stability, (f) nature and extent of eye condition, (g) wishes of students and parents, and (h) recommendations of the staffing team. Naturally, each student should be considered individually, with certain general considerations taken into account. For example, there seems to be a relationship among the age of the student, the nature and extent of the visual impairment, the student's level of achievement, and the amount of direct special education service and instruction needed. A child who is a young braille reader (ages 5 to 9) will need resource or itinerant assistance on a scheduled daily basis to provide instruction in braille reading and other specialized areas. During early education, a child may spend 1 to 1½ hours each day with a resource or itinerant teacher. A child who has developed braille reading skills (Figure 7–10) and is familiar with the necessary tangible apparatus may attend regular classrooms for most of the school day, and in some instances, the entire day. If the student is able to read printed material with or without an aid, it is not necessary to spend as much time with a resource or itinerant teacher. A student at the secondary level may also require specific instruction from resource or itinerant

Figure 7–10
Braille alphabet

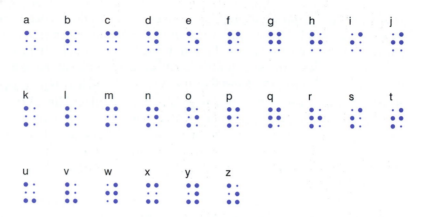

Note: Each letter of the braille alphabet is represented by a pattern of raised dots within a six-dot cell. Additional combinations include letter sequence, numbers, punctuation, and words.

personnel, but this student's needs are not the same as those of younger students. Special teachers may do more counseling relevant to adjustment to secondary school life and transition to career opportunities, training in orientation and mobility, training in the use of advanced technological equipment, and instruction related to independent living skills.

 ## Suggestions for Regular Classroom Teachers

The suggestions that follow may be used for readers of either braille or print, because many techniques and modifications are the same for both groups. The suggestions fall into six categories: (a) adapted educational equipment, (b) educational environment, (c) orientation and mobility, (d) teaching strategies and adaptations, (e) general considerations, and (f) integration of special services. Although some suggestions are loosely categorized, grouping permits easier conceptualization of these techniques and modifications.

Adapted Educational Equipment

As mentioned, educational programming for students who are visually impaired primarily involves modifying and adapting existing educational materials. Most of these materials are available from private agencies at no cost to students. Over their many years of service to individuals who are visually impaired, these agencies have developed an extensive array of helpful materials. It is not practical to review all of the adapted materials and special equipment available for students with impaired vision, for there are several hundred different types. Most of these materials are directed at increasing learning through sensory channels other than vision.

The first section that follows reviews some of the most recent computer-assisted learning devices. The second section provides information regarding other adapted equipment. A list of manufacturers' and suppliers' addresses follows.

Computer-assisted Learning

Speech Synthesizers. Synthesizers are devices attached to computers that are able to read words or numbers displayed on the computer screen. The *Speaqualizer* from APH (American Printing House for the Blind, Inc.), for example, allows the user to hear data being displayed in column form as well as text form.

Braille Computers.   Braille computers are similar to conventional computers except that they have braille keys and a braille display. Some models provide synthesized speech in place of or in addition to a braille display: The *Braille 'n Speak® Classic*,[1] from Blazie Engineering, Inc., functions as a talking note taker and note organizer. The *Braille Lite®*, also from Blazie, a similar device, has a braille display and a memory that will store up to 800 pages of braille. When connected to a modem, the *Braille Lite®* permits worldwide access to host computers. The *Type 'n Speak®* (also from Blazie Engineering), has a standard keyboard and allows output in either braille or regular print. Many options such as talking telephone directories and appointment calendars are available with these models as well.

Text Magnification Software.   Software that is compatible with a variety of brands and types of computers magnifies the text on the computer screen from two to eight times the original width and height.

Braille Printers.   When interfaced with a computer, a braille printer will print in braille the information stored in the computer. With a standard keyboard, users may print in either braille or standard print, thus allowing the teacher to easily provide class outlines, study guides, vocabulary terms, or tests to both students who use braille and those who do not.

The Reading Edge™ (A Kurzweil Reader from Xerox Imaging Systems).   This is a stand-alone reading machine incorporating optical character recognition, synthesized speech, and a book-edge scanner into a single integrated unit that converts printed material into speech. It has nine different reading voices and can recognize and speak eight languages.

Franklin Language Master™ **6000 SE** (Franklin Electronic Publishers).   This device spells words, gives definitions, and reads aloud. There are several orientation keys for users who are blind and a large-type display option, high-contrast screen, and black-on-white keyboard for individuals with low vision.

NOMAD Talking Touch Pad (from APH, American Printing House for the Blind, Inc.).   Pictures placed on the touch-sensitive work surface of the NOMAD can be programmed with speech, enabling the student to more independently learn those subjects requiring graphs, charts, or diagrams.

Computer Software.   The following software, also available from APH, is compatible with Apple II computers equipped with speech synthesizers:

APH Presents the Talking Apple Computer—a demonstration program guiding the user through menu choice, speech settings, and other options

APH Scientific Calculator—a calculating program that handles many types of numerical algorithms

APH/SEI Talking Software Series—a set of 33 different titles from APH and Sliwa Enterprises, Inc. (SEI) covering a wide range of subjects such as literature, history, vocabulary, and government

LetterTALK+—typing and word processing instruction for students who either have low vision or are totally blind

Sensible Speller™ (Sensible Software Inc.)—a spell checker program

Speaking Speller—a program using print or synthesized speech to ask students to spell words generated by the teacher

---

[1]All trademarks are of their respective companies.

Talking Typer—a program that reinforces typing skills and allows lessons to be customized

Teacher's Pet—a user-friendly program allowing the creation of drill and practice exercises as well as tests and quizzes

Textalker™ and *Textalker*™ *-gs* (Echo Speech Corporation)—text-to-speech software programs that make compatible application programs speak

Other Adapted Equipment

Braillewriters, Slates, and Styluses.　A braillewriter is a six-key (corresponding to the six dots in the braille cell) machine that is manually operated and types braille. The slate is a metal frame with openings the size of the braille dots; the stylus is a pointed object used to emboss the dots. The slate and stylus can be carried in a pocket and are often used to take notes (Figure 7–11).

Cassette Tape Recorders.　Tape recorders may be used to take notes, formulate compositions, listen to recorded texts, or record assignments.

Speech Compressors.　A speech compressor is a modified tape recorder. In a speech compressor, the pause between each recorded word is electronically removed, thereby compress-

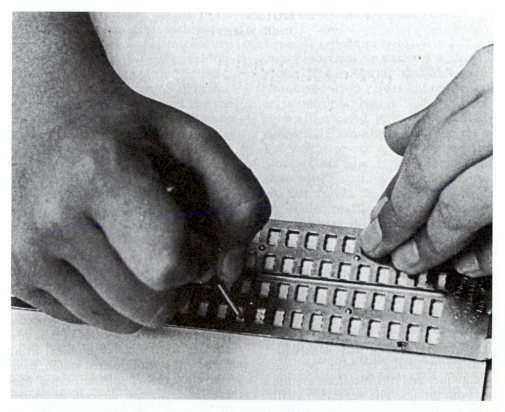

Figure 7–11
Taking notes with a slate and stylus

ing the material and speeding up the listening process without changing the pitch.

Variable-speed Attachments. Variable-speed attachments can be used to vary the speed at which the student listens to a tape, allowing the student to listen to the material at a slower or faster rate (although the speed change alters the pitch).

Talking Book and Other Recorded Programs. The Library of Congress and certain commercial producers provide records, compact discs, or tapes recorded specifically for individuals who cannot use print as their primary means of reading. These sources offer a variety of textbooks and leisure reading on disk and cassette.

Raised-line Drawing Boards. A raised-line drawing board is a board covered with rubber. A piece of acetate is placed on the board and a pen or pointed object is used to "raise" the drawings so that the student may feel them. A teacher may use a raised-line drawing board to draw geometric shapes, script letters, or diagrams.

Raised-line Paper. Special raised-line paper allows students who are visually impaired to write script on a raised line. They also may use raised-line paper to draw a graph.

Tactile Graphics Kit. Tools and heavy gauge aluminum foil are used to create masters of raised-line drawings. These masters can then be used to produce multiple copies on a vacuum-form machine.

Optacon (Optical to Tactual Converter). The Optacon is an instrument that scans printed material electronically, transforming the print into vibrating letter configurations, accomplished through an array of 144 pins. The reader holds a scanner over the print material while placing the index finger of the opposite hand over the raised configuration.

Talking Calculators. A talking calculator is an electronic calculator that presents results visually and auditorily.

Closed-circuit Television. Closed-circuit television systems enlarge printed material on a television screen. As an example, one system uses TV monitors and cameras focused at both teacher and student. The teacher can monitor the student's work, and the student can view an enlarged version of the teacher's blackboard or overhead display. The Big Picture, from American Printing House for the Blind, Inc., creates highly magnified, high quality black and white images of text and pictures that are scanned with its hand-held TV camera.

Other Aids. Often students who have some remaining vision can use a number of optical aids. These aids may be used at all times or for specified tasks. Magnifiers that can be mounted on a desk, held by hand, or head mounted are frequently prescribed by low-vision clinics. Students may also use monoculars (telescopic aids for one eye) that may be mounted on glasses or held in the hand. With a monocular, a student may view the chalkboard, classroom demonstrations, or other distant objects (Figure 7–12). The following list of additional visual aids represents types available from various sources:

1. Geography aids
   a. Braille atlases
   b. Molded plastic, dissected and undissected relief maps
   c. Relief globes
   d. Landform models (a set of three-dimensional tactile maps illustrating 40 geographic concepts)
   e. Teaching tapes
2. Mathematical aids
   a. Abacuses
   b. Raised clockfaces

    c. Geometric area and volume aids

    d. Wire forms for matched planes and volumes

    e. Braille rulers

    f. Talking calculators

3. Writing aids

    a. Raised-line checkbooks

    b. Signature guides

    c. Longhand-writing kits

    d. Script-letter sheets and boards

4. Miscellaneous aids

    a. Audible goal locators, which can be used as goal base, object locators, or warning devices

    b. Special braille or large-type answer sheets

    c. Science measurement kits (containing such items as thermometers, spring balances, gram weights, and gravity specimens), insect identification kits

    d. Sports field kits (containing raised drawings of the playing fields or courts of various sports)

    e. Simple-machine kits, including working models of such simple machines as pulleys and levers, and including planes, wheels, and axles

    f. Games available from the American Printing House for the Blind, Inc., such as *The Ten Spot Game*, *The Baseball Game*, *The Game of Squares*, and *The Game Kit*

    g. Adapted sports equipment (such as audible balls)

    h. Braille clocks, wristwatches, and timers

Resources for Adapted Educational Equipment

American Printing House for the Blind, Inc.
1839 Frankfort Ave.
P.O. Box 6085
Louisville, KY 40206-0085
800-223-1839

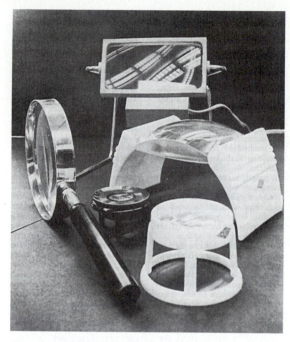

Figure 7–12

Magnification devices used by students with visual impairment

Blazie Engineering, Inc.
105 E. Jarrettsville Rd.
Forest Hill, MD 21050
410-893-9333

Echo Speech Corporation
6460 Via Real
Carpinteria, CA 93013
805-684-4593

Franklin Electronic Publishers
122 Burrs Rd.
Mount Holly, NJ 08060
800-525-9673

Sensible Software, Inc.
335 E. Big Beaver, Ste. 207
Troy, MI 48083
313-528-1950

Xerox Imaging Systems
9 Centennial Dr.
Peabody, MA 01960
800-343-0311

Occasionally, some students are self-conscious about their need for special equipment and are reluctant to use it. A teacher's openness and understanding can do a great deal to help students and classmates appreciate the benefits and need for special equipment.

The American Printing House for the Blind has an extensive offering of adapted materials and educational equipment. In addition, the American Foundation for the Blind has an *Aids and Appliances Catalog* from which materials may be ordered. Several other agencies also have special materials available.

It is generally not the responsibility of regular classroom teachers to obtain materials unless a resource or itinerant teacher is not available. Resource or itinerant teachers are familiar with the agencies that provide adapted materials and equipment. In the event that materials are not available from any of the agencies, the resource or itinerant teacher will have to reproduce these materials or arrange for them to be prepared. For example, a particular reading text may not be available in modified form because it has been published only recently. After all agencies have been queried, the resource or itinerant teacher may have the text reproduced in large type, tape recorded, or transcribed into braille.

In addition to textbooks and adapted materials available from an agency, there is always a need for teacher-made materials, such as teacher-made tests, work sheets, and special games or activities. These must be reproduced in the desired format by the resource or itinerant teacher or by specially trained aides, because it is essential that the materials be the same as the materials of the student's peers.

Regular classroom teachers and resource or itinerant teachers must plan carefully, and must establish a special communication system to provide explanations of the nature of the materials needed and allow sufficient time for their reproduction. This is usually accomplished by the regular classroom teacher leaving the desired materials in the resource or itinerant teacher's mailbox, establishing a routine conference with the resource or itinerant teacher, or sending the material with the student when she or he meets with the resource or itinerant teacher.

Occasionally, regular classroom teachers may have to modify materials. For example, if preparing duplicated materials for class distribution, it may be necessary to darken the letters or figures with a felt-tipped pen so that they can be seen more easily by the student who has only partial vision. Materials duplicated in purple usually cause considerable difficulty for individuals who are visually impaired; black stencils may provide the desired contrast. Yellow acetate placed over the printed page tends to darken the print itself as well as provide greater contrast. It may also be of value to consider preparing handout materials in primary or enlarged type for all students.

Educational Environment

Although not major concerns, several environmental or classroom modifications can facilitate the education of students with impaired vision. Preferred or open seating allows students to sit wherever they are most comfortable. When a teacher is using the chalkboard, when a movie or filmstrip is being shown, or when the teacher is demonstrating a particular concept using tangible materials, a student with impaired vision should be allowed to select the best visual location.

The student's seating should be arranged for the best possible lighting conditions, but this does not mean that all students with low vision should be in brightly lighted areas. Some visual impairments require no special lighting, and others require lower levels of illumination. Resource or itinerant teachers and reports from eye specialists should be of particular value in this matter.

Teachers should not stand in front of a bright light source, such as a window, because students are then looking directly into the light. Writing on a chalkboard where there is considerable glare should also be avoided. When a demonstration is given, a student with low vision should be encouraged to stand near the teacher or actually assist in the demonstration. It may also be helpful to allow the student to handle the demonstration materials before or after the demonstration.

Before the actual placement in the regular classroom, a formal orientation procedure should be conducted. The resource or itinerant teacher or an orientation and mobility specialist can provide additional guidance in structuring this experience. Initially, the student should be familiarized with the general layout of the classroom and be given guided and unguided opportunities to explore. Certain landmarks within the classroom should be established, such as (a) the student's desk, (b) the teacher's desk, (c) cabinets or bookshelves, (d) storage areas for paper and general classroom materials, (e) the wastebasket, (f) bulletin boards and chalkboards, (g) windows, (h) special interest centers, (i) doorways and restrooms, and (j) other classroom equipment.

After the student is oriented to the classroom and the general school building, other areas may be introduced, such as the school offices, gymnasium, cafeteria, auditorium, restrooms, recreation areas, and locker rooms. Often, orientation to the school building and surrounding areas is taught formally by an orientation and mobility specialist or a resource or itinerant teacher.

Teachers who have students who are visually impaired are sometimes reluctant to change the classroom seating or position of desks, tables, and other items because they are afraid the student may become disoriented or sustain an injury. The physical arrangement of the room should be changed as often as normally necessary, but the student must be oriented to the changes. This should take only a few minutes of formal orientation and a few minutes of independent exploring by the student, followed by a brief question-and-answer session concerning the new arrangement. Other students in the class can help by directing the student who is visually impaired through the new arrangement or by describing it.

Safety while traveling independently in the classroom can be a problem if classroom doors and upper cabinet doors are not completely open or closed. Often, a student may think the classroom door is open because of auditory and other cues, when in fact it is only partially open. Keeping the door completely open or closed is difficult to accomplish with 30 other students in the classroom, but it should be attempted.

The noise level of the classroom should be kept reasonably low, since students with low vision must depend on auditory skills for much of their educational program. Braille-reading students need open space and shelves at the side of the room, since braille materials are large and bulky. Braille-reading students may also need room for braillewriters, typewriters, books, and other materials.

Orientation and Mobility

The ability of a student who is visually impaired to move about independently is one of the most important factors in the total educational program.[2] Programming efforts should be directed toward academic and social development, but if the area of travel is

[2]Special acknowledgment is due David Kappan, associate professor of special education, University of Northern Colorado, for his critical evaluation and assistance in the development of the section on orientation and mobility.

*Orientation and mobility special-
ist at work*

neglected, the student may be denied opportunities to move freely and independently in the
school and community.

The concepts of orientation and mobility
are interrelated because mobility cannot be
achieved unless an individual is oriented. *Orientation* refers to an individual's use of the
other senses to establish position and relationship to objects in the environment. *Mobility*
refers to the individual's movement from one
point in the environment to another. In other
words, mobility is getting from point A to
point B, whereas orientation involves knowing
the location, the location of the objective, and
the most efficient way to reach the objective.

Regular classroom teachers are not responsible for formal training in orientation and

mobility. This training is specialized and
should be conducted by an orientation and
mobility specialist or in the case of precane
orientation and mobility, a resource or itinerant teacher whose background includes specific preparation in this area. It is important,
however, that regular classroom teachers
understand the nature of the training and the
major methods or modes of travel. The five
modes of travel used by persons who are visually impaired are (a) the sighted guide, (b) cane
travel, (c) the dog guide, (d) the electronic
travel aid, and (e) independent travel.

Sighted Guide

One of the most common techniques taught is
use of a sighted guide. The student with low

vision grasps the guide's arm just above the elbow, with fingers on the inside and thumb on the outside, and assumes a position approximately a half step behind the guide. The grip is just firm enough to maintain contact. The guide's arm is positioned next to the body. In effect, the person who is visually impaired is "reading" the sighted individual's arm or elbow, and any movement of the guide's body and arm is detected. By following approximately a half step behind, the individual with visual impairment knows when the guide is stepping up or down and turning left or right. This position provides the necessary reaction time.

When ascending or descending stairs, the guide should approach the stairs at a right angle and pause at the first step. The individual who is visually impaired can locate the beginning of the step with one foot and negotiate the stairway, remaining one step behind the sighted guide. The guide's arm position indicates when they have reached the landing or end of the staircase. The classmates of a student with low vision can readily be taught how to serve as sighted guides. Additional methods related to efficient use of this technique would be taught by a resource or itinerant teacher or an orientation and mobility specialist.

All students should be acquainted with the proper procedures used when serving as a sighted guide. A resource or itinerant teacher or an orientation and mobility specialist may want to attend or actually conduct a brief inservice session. The students may want to wear blindfolds to gain a better understanding of traveling without sight. However, some caution should be exercised here, so that the students do not develop a pitying attitude but rather an understanding of travel techniques used by people who are visually impaired.

Cane Travel

Use of a cane is a common systematic method of travel. The age at which a student is introduced to a cane and provided formal training in its use depends on the student's maturity, need for independent travel, and physical and mental ability.

There are several types of canes, but the most common are made of aluminum or fiberglass and are approximately half an inch in diameter. The tip of the cane is usually made of steel or nylon. The length of the cane is prescribed by the orientation and mobility specialist and is determined by the user's height, length of stride, and comfort.

Cane travel is taught on a one-to-one basis by a specialized instructor. It initially involves fundamentals in restricted areas, and later training is applied in outdoor situations, such as residential and business districts. Extensive training is conducted in crossing streets, utilizing public transportation, and dealing with complex navigational situations.

Dog Guide

The third mode of travel uses a dog guide. Generally a dog guide is not recommended until a student is at least 16 years old. Before this age, the student may not have the maturity to handle a dog properly or the need for independent travel. Often, young students want to obtain a dog guide as a pet or companion, not necessarily for independence in traveling. For obvious reasons, a dog guide should not be considered a pet but rather a partner in achieving independent travel. Contrary to popular opinion, only a relatively small percentage of persons who are visually impaired use dog guides. The resource or itinerant teacher or the orientation and mobility specialist may provide specific information concerning dog guide agencies, such as cost and nature of training. It is essential that potential dog guide users investigate the individual program offering dog guide training to ensure that the highest standards are maintained.

Electronic Travel Aid

The electronic travel aid is the fourth mode of travel used by individuals who have visual impairment. A number of devices are available, and most are used to supplement another method of travel. Although it is encouraging to see research being conducted in this area, it does not seem that any one device meets the needs of all individuals. Some of the devices enhance auditory feedback, some detect obstacles, others enable individuals to walk in a straight line, and still others are directed at revealing the specific location of obstacles in the environment.

A Mowat Sensor is a small hand-held device that uses a high-frequency elliptical sound beam to detect obstacles. If an object is present, the entire sensor vibrates, and the vibration rate increases as the person approaches the object. The sensor operates on a rechargeable battery and is small enough to be carried in a purse or coat pocket.

A Sonicguide™ emits a high-frequency sound. It converts detection echoes into audible stereophonic signals and provides information about the distance, position, and surface characteristics of objects within the travel path and immediate environment. The electronic system for the unit is built into special eyeglasses fitted for the individual user.

A Laser Cane emits invisible light beams that strike an object and are reflected back to the receiving unit of the cane. A sound or tone is emitted to warn the person of objects or dropoffs. In addition, a vibrating unit felt by the user's finger signals obstructions ahead. The three beams include upper-, lower-, and midrange signals to provide basic protection for the user's entire body.

A Russell Pathsounder is a chest-mounted device that emits an ultrasonic signal. When the unit locates an object, it offers auditory feedback and/or tactile signals. It provides protection for the upper body and has possible value for a student with both vision and hearing impairments.

The mobility aids or device used, whether cane, dog, electronic aid, or some combination, should be given careful consideration by a student and parents after consultation with the resource or itinerant teacher or the orientation and mobility specialist. Numerous hours of instruction by an orientation and mobility instructor are prerequisite to successful use of these devices.

Independent Travel

A fifth mode of travel is independent, that is, with no aid. Generally, a student with low vision, after becoming familiar with the environment, is able to move about without aid, for instance, in the classroom, short distances in the school building, to the bus, and perhaps on the school campus.

Protective Techniques

A number of protective techniques may be used by a student with visual impairment while traveling with or without the use of other aids. These protective techniques are routinely taught to young children and are normally used only in familiar areas. They may be used in combination with a cane or an electronic aid for additional protection. Three of the basic techniques taught by the resource or itinerant teacher or orientation and mobility specialist are as follows:

1. *Upper hand and forearm technique.* For protection in familiar settings, a student may extend one arm in front of his or her body at shoulder height and parallel to the floor, with the palm outward (Figure 7–13).
2. *Lower hand and forearm technique.* When protecting the lower body, a student extends one arm down and forward toward the midline of the body

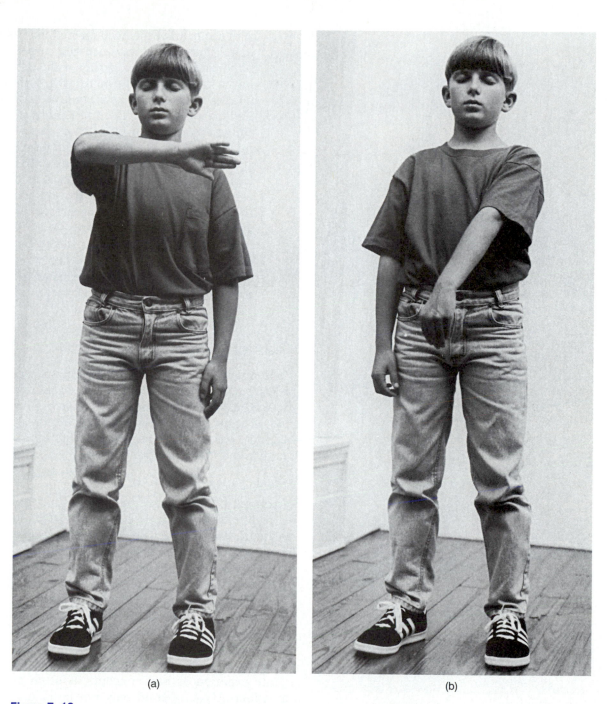

(a)

(b)

Figure 7–13

Use of the upper hand and forearm for protection while traveling independently

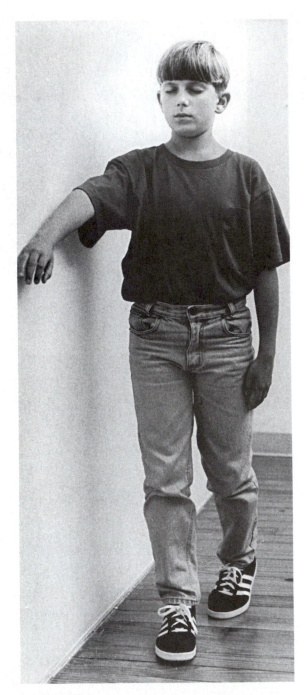

Figure 7–14
Trailing

with the palm of the hand facing him or her. The student may use the upper hand and forearm together with the lower hand and forearm to give both upper and lower body protection.

3. *Trailing technique*. Trailing enables a student to maintain orientation, determine her or his position in space, locate specific objects, and secure a parallel line of travel. The student stands at a comfortable distance from the surface to be trailed, extends one arm forward at hip level, and establishes contact with this surface with the outside of the little finger. The student can then walk along the object using the hand to maintain contact and detect information (Figure 7–14).

Teaching Strategies and Adaptations

It is generally not necessary for regular classroom teachers to significantly change teaching strategies to accommodate a student with visual impairment. However, teachers may consider the following suggestions that others have found to be effective.

Hands-on Learning

Learning by doing and teaching by unifying experiences are certainly not new concepts to regular classroom teachers. These concepts, however, are particularly important to students with impaired vision because such students may not have the same experiential background as other students of the same age. Whenver possible, a student with low vision should be allowed to explore physically rather than have the process explained verbally. Closely related is the need to integrate experiences and concepts as often as possible. A young child may not be able to relate one isolated concept to another because of lack of previous experience with the particular concept.

Concrete Materials

Whenever possible, teachers should begin instruction at a concrete level, moving more to the abstract as students develop the concept. Teachers should avoid totally verbal instructions or lessons, and should use manipulative, tangible, or auditory materials whenever possible. Hands-on learning should be emphasized, remembering that students may need repeated contact with objects. Although a model may be necessary, a real object or situation is much preferred. For example, if a science lesson is concerned with simple pulleys, provide an actual pulley if possible. Local museums are valuable sources for such materials, and they often lend them to school personnel. Resource or itinerant teachers can also assist in obtaining actual objects or making models.

Unified experiences also help students form concepts. The small pieces of information that sighted students are able to organize into meaningful concepts at a mere glance must be unified for students who are blind or have low vision. A trip to a clothing store, for example, provides a basis for reinforcing and unifying concepts related to quantity, percentages, money, sizes, shapes, and social skills. When planning such trips, notify the store's staff in advance. They will frequently allow the student who is visually impaired to go beyond normal barriers.

Extra Time

A student with low vision may need extra time to complete assignments and examinations. Allowing time and a half is usually adequate. The student may complete the work in a resource room or library or at home. If the student understands the concepts being presented, it may be a good idea to shorten the assignment.

Fatigue

A student who has impaired vision may become fatigued if required to perform tasks involving close visual examination for long periods of time. It may be helpful to vary activities as much as possible, as by alternating listening activities, close visual activities, and motor activities. The student should be encouraged whenever possible to take short breaks from activities requiring prolonged periods of visual work.

Physical Education

Lessons in physical education or gross motor activities should be demonstrated by physically moving visually impaired students through the activity. For example, when teaching a particular tumbling routine, the instructor may want to actually move the student through the correct movements rather than merely explain the process. Chapter 8 provides specific physical education adaptation strategies that are equally appropriate for students with impaired vision.

Chalkboard

When writing on the chalkboard, teachers should be certain to explain verbally the concept or actual writing being presented. In general, any visually based instructions or lessons should be supplemented with a verbal explanation. This can become routine with little effort and practice. Some teachers have found it helpful to give a student who is visually impaired a copy of the notes written on the board. To be certain that the best possible dark–light contrast is provided, be certain that the chalkboard is as clean as possible. Allow the student to move as close to the chalkboard as necessary to see it comfortably.

Fire Drills

As the class as a whole is being prepared for a fire drill, instruct a student who is blind or who has low vision to take hold of the nearest student or adult and quickly and quietly follow the others. The principles are the same as those for using a sighted guide. Young students may need practice, especially if they are not used to having a student with visual impairment in the class. For older students, it is routine.

Giving Directions

Teachers should be as specific as possible when giving directions. For example, saying, "Your science project is on the shelf in the back of the room, to the left of and about 2 feet away from the sink" is clearer than, "Your science project is on the back shelf." If giving directions relating to the building as a whole or to some area outside the school, say, for example, "The snack machine is to the left as you leave this room, down four doors, and about three steps to the right," to provide precise directions. It may be necessary to give the directions slowly, to repeat them, or with a young student, even ask the student to repeat the directions.

Media

If a filmstrip being used has subtitles, ask another student to read the titles aloud to the entire class. When a film is used, another student may summarize the key visual concepts or briefly provide a running visual narrative.

Tactile Activities

For the approximately 20 percent of visually impaired students who are blind, art activities should emphasize the tactile sense. Use activities such as clay modeling, finger painting, weaving, paper sculpture, and collage whenever possible. It is important that the students carry out the *process* involved in an art project; the end product should be deemphasized. By completing the process, in whatever medium, the students can achieve the same objectives as peers.

Note Taking

At the secondary level, students are often required to take notes or submit assignments. Naturally, students who have visual impair-

ment should meet these requirements, but the ways in which they do so may be different. Students who are blind or have low vision may use a slate and stylus, braillewriter, or cassette tape recorder. After recording lectures, students may transcribe their notes into braille and finally type them to be handed in. Some teachers allow such students to provide a modified recording of their notes.

Raising Hands

If other students are expected to raise their hands to gain recognition or respond, the student with visual impairment should be expected to do the same. Since such students may not be able to see classmates raising their hands to respond, teachers may need to provide specific instructions on hand-raising procedures.

Test Taking

Testing procedures may have to be modified for students who are visually impaired. Reading braille or large type takes considerably longer than reading standard print, and it may be necessary either to extend the amount of time for completion of tests or reduce the number of test items. Students should not be penalized if they cannot finish tests because of the tools they are using. Of course, time modification depends on whether the purpose of the test is speed or power. If the purpose is speed, a student may have considerable difficulty.

The administration of a test may also have to be modified. For example, it may be necessary to (a) administer the test orally, (b) tape the test in advance and have the student record or type the answers, or (c) send the test home with the student and have a parent read the test while the student types or braillewrites the answers. When taping the examination, the reader should state the total number and type of questions, the value assigned to each item, and time limitations, and should take care to read the examination itself slowly and clearly. Sometimes, a student can braillewrite responses and give them to the resource or itinerant teacher, who in turn, writes in the student's responses and returns the test to the classroom teacher. Some students require few or no modifications and are able to take the tests with the other students.

Achievement tests are administered at the beginning or end of the school year. Because of their relative importance and the amount of time needed to complete them, they may have to be administered by resource or itinerant teachers or aides. Regular teachers should be certain to consult with resource or itinerant teachers in advance to consider the options for testing.

Braille

Teachers often express concern when informed that they will have braille-reading students in their classrooms. Actually, it is not necessary for teachers to learn braille, because resource or itinerant teachers can write or print whatever the student has written directly above the braille dots. If a student completes an assignment and turns it in to the classroom teacher in braille, the teacher should forward it to the resource or itinerant teacher, who can write the student's responses and return the assignment to the classroom teacher. At the upper elementary, middle school, and secondary school levels, students may complete assignments on a conventional typewriter or use a paperless braille system, which provides materials in conventional print.

General Considerations

When speaking to students who are blind or who have low vision, teachers should use normal volume unless distance warrants otherwise. Such students may become frustrated when people raise their voices unnecessarily.

During class discussion, the teacher should be certain to use the name of a student who is blind or has low vision in order to make sure that the student knows the teacher is looking at him or her. Likewise, when entering a room, the teacher should address the student by name and identify himself or herself.[3] Similarly, if the student enters a room where the teacher is alone, the teacher should speak directly to the student or use some other auditory cue.

If a student who is blind or has low vision drops an object, the teacher should allow sufficient time for the student to recover the item without help. If necessary, however, the teacher may use verbal guidance to help the student locate the item. When handing an object such as a book to the student, a teacher and other students should lightly touch the student's hand with the object to let the student know the location of the object.

Unless an eye specialist has indicated that a student should not use her or his vision, every effort must be made to increase the student's visual efficiency. There are several misconceptions concerning the use of residual vision. Contrary to myth, using the vision will not decrease it. In fact, it is not unusual for a student's measured acuity to remain the same over a period of years while visual performance actually increases. Holding a book close to the eyes or reading with a dim light will not further damage the eyesight of a student with low vision. Some students may require a dim light to read more comfortably. Even at the secondary level, it may be necessary to tell other students about this, since

---

[3]Once it becomes clear that a student recognizes the teacher's voice, the teacher should *not* identify himself or herself, but simply address the student by name. Students who are blind or have low vision often pride themselves on voice recognition, and teachers should acknowledge this skill.

they have probably been told by parents and teachers not to hold books too close or to read in dim light. Resource or itinerant teachers will be able to provide guidance relating to reading, postural, and lighting requirements.

Somewhat related to this matter is the use of low-vision or optical aids (such as magnifiers and special glasses). Students who use these aids should be encouraged to use them whenever appropriate. Regular classroom teachers should observe whether the devices seem to be helpful, how often they are used, and under what conditions they are beneficial. Frequent visual fatigue may be an indication of need for larger-print materials or reevaluation of the efficiency of the visual aids being used.

Generally, the length of time a student can use special aids can be determined only after careful classroom observation. Some students may perform well for a short time but tire after several hours of close visual work. Naturally, this information should be shared with resource or itinerant teachers, who in turn may share this information with physicians or specialists in low-vision aids.

Students with impaired vision often develop poor postural habits. This may result from poor muscle tone, lack of knowledge about preferred head or shoulder position, or continual close examination of printed material. Some system of gentle reminders should be established to help students develop good postural habits. Students who are partially sighted may spend a great deal of time bent over, with their heads only a few inches from their desks. This position can obviously result in poor posture and considerable fatigue. Easels and bookrests can enable students to read much more comfortably. Resource or itinerant teachers can suggest specific postural training and adaptations for reading efficiency and comfort.

Teachers should not alter established standards for grading or discipline for students with visual impairment. When an assignment has been given or a classroom rule established, such students should be expected to adhere to the same procedures as the other students. If teachers employ a double standard, one for the class and another for students with visual impairment, the other students will be quick to recognize the difference and resent it. Such resentment may have an adverse effect on interpersonal relationships and cause other students to reject students who have impaired vision.

Students with impaired vision may not be able to see the teacher's positive facial expressions after completing an assigned task successfully or a look of displeasure when they have not. Verbal feedback, a pat on the back, or a touch on the arm may be necessary. Of course, the teacher should praise any student only when the job has been well done, not just because it was done by a student who is blind or has low vision.

Teachers may assign buddies to help with, for example, highly visual assignments, orientation to a new school building, physical education activities, and fire drills. The buddy system is a desirable approach to peer teaching or assistance, regardless of whether or not a student is disabled.

Students who are blind or have low vision often demonstrate unusual mannerisms, such as rocking, head movements, eye pressing, and hand waving. The mannerisms tend to occur when the students are tense or nervous or are listening intently. Although such students are usually unaware of these behaviors, other students notice them. To discourage such mannerisms, teachers should use systematic plans that they have worked out with resource or itinerant teachers.

Independence, freedom of movement, and play are as important for students who have impaired vision as for sighted classmates. More than 100 years ago, Samuel Gridley Howe, a noted educator of children who were visually impaired, offered the following general rules:

Never check the actions of the child; follow him, and watch him to prevent any serious accidents, but do not interfere unnecessarily; do not even remove obstacles which he would learn to avoid by tumbling over them a few times. Teach him to jump rope, to swing weights, to raise his body by his arms, and to mingle, as far as possible, in the rough sports of the older boys. Do not be apprehensive of his safety. If you should see him clambering in the branches of a tree be assured he is less likely to fall than if he had perfect vision. Do not too much regard bumps on the forehead, rough scratches, or bloody noses; even these may have their good influences. At the worst, they affect only the bark, and do not injure the system like the rust of inaction. (quoted in Buell, 1950, p. 37)

It is natural for a teacher who has not had experience with students who have visual impairment to be somewhat overprotective and to be concerned that these students might injure themselves on playground equipment or in traveling around the school building. However, every effort should be made *not* to underestimate the capabilities of students who have impairments. The teacher's responsibility to a student with impaired vision is the same as to other students—helping the student develop socially, emotionally, physically, morally, and intellectually.

Integration of Special Services

When several professionals work with a student, it is important that they consult with each other so that each is aware of the nature of the training provided by the others. It has been suggested that a case manager be named at the time of the development of the IEP to coordinate all of the efforts being made on behalf of the student (Kirk & Gallagher, 1989). The classroom teacher is generally able to observe the student in a variety of settings and under a variety of conditions, as well as provide the specialists with information concerning the transfer and maintenance of desired skills or concepts. Often, a student may be able (especially when first learning) to demonstrate a skill or understanding of a concept when working on an individual basis with a resource or itinerant teacher or an orientation and mobility teacher but be unable to transfer this understanding to classroom activities.

Coordination among the various teachers at the secondary level is also important, although unless visual impairment is newly acquired (by an accident, for example), the student will have learned many of the basic skills. It may be helpful for secondary teachers to know about various technological devices that a student may use to determine how much classroom adaptation is required. The importance of close communication with the parents of a student who is visually impaired cannot be overemphasized, and every effort should be made to work cooperatively with parents.

 ## Specialized Instruction and Assistance from Resource or Itinerant Teachers

The amount and nature of specialized assistance from special educators varies from school district to school district and at times within a single district. The exact nature of assistance from special education resource or itinerant personnel depends on the following factors:

1. *Geographic distance to be traveled between schools.* Some teachers are

responsible for only one school, whereas others have responsibilities extending to two or three schools. In some rural areas, a resource or itinerant teacher may travel to several communities.

2. *Number of students and teachers to be served.*

3. *Age of student.* Generally, the younger the student, the more need for direct service.

4. *The number of braille readers and print readers.* This can vary extensively. Generally, a braille-reading student requires many more direct services.

5. *Availability of orientation and mobility instruction.* If an orientation and mobility specialist is not available, a resource or itinerant teacher may be responsible for this instruction.

6. *Availability of paid or volunteer braille transcribers, large-print typists, and tape transcribers.*

7. *Availability of adapted and special materials.* In states where an instructional materials center for individuals who are visually impaired is available, the acquisition and distribution of educational materials can be greatly facilitated.

Resource or itinerant teachers may provide services directly or indirectly. Direct services involve working directly with students who have visual impairment on a one-to-one basis or in small groups. Indirect services involve working with individuals other than students, such as teachers, administrators, medical personnel, and parents. Most resource or itinerant personnel provide both direct and indirect services. Although it is sometimes difficult to clearly establish that one service is direct and another indirect, the following discussion of specific responsibilities is based on these categories.

Direct Services

Compensatory skills, such as compensatory listening skills, use of a stylus and slate, and use of a braillewriter are taught by special education specialists. If academic lags are *directly attributable* to vision deficits, these are remediated by special education personnel.

Specialized Instruction in Reading

Resource or itinerant teachers provide instruction in braille reading and braillewriting, the use of a slate and stylus, and use of the reading devices like the Optacon or Kurzweil Reading Machine. The amount of time required for instruction in special skills depends on the age of the student. More time is required for young braille-reading students because they are developing these specialized skills, whereas secondary-level students may have already developed these skills. Braille instruction should be provided daily for the first 3 years of the student's education or until the student develops the necessary competency. After the student is relatively proficient at braille reading and braillewriting, daily instruction may no longer be necessary.

If a student is a print reader, the amount of instruction is usually not so great as for a braille reader. However, if the student uses low-vision aids (magnification devices or special reading machines), it may be necessary to provide specific instruction in their use.

Instruction in Listening Skills

It has been estimated that nearly one-half of communication time is spent in listening activities and that approximately two-thirds of a student's school day is spent in activities related to listening. Since listening is one of the most significant avenues of learning for students who have visual impairment, such students must rely on the auditory channel more than their sighted classmates do. As a result, systematic instruction in listening must be provided and incorporated into regular classroom instruction as much as possible. Instruction in listening should include a variety of listening situations, such as environmental situations, formal presentations, informal conversations, talking books, and tape-recorded materials.

Instruction in Techniques of Daily Living

Functioning as a responsible and contributing member of society requires more than being able to complete academic tasks such as reading and math. A student who has low vision or who is blind may not know how to carry out all of the activities of daily living, because many of these skills are learned by watching and with minimal instruction. For example, young children learn about combing hair or shaving by observing these activities carried out by their parents. Such skills, as well as housecleaning, cooking and serving of food, and home repair, must be taught to students who are blind or have low vision. School curriculums must include instruction regarding many of these skills. Other skills for independent living must be taught, too, such as handling money without seeing it and selecting clothing that matches. Teachers at both the elementary and secondary level are involved to some degree in either teaching the skills or reinforcing them. Resource or itinerant teachers can provide information regarding how to adapt or modify these activities and how to use the special equipment that is available for individuals who are blind or who have low vision.

Instruction in Orientation and Mobility

The extent to which resource or itinerant teachers are responsible for direct instruction in orientation and mobility depends on whether orientation and mobility specialists are available and whether resource or itinerant teachers are also certified as orientation and mobility specialists. If available, a specialist is responsible for formal instruction; if not, a resource or itinerant teacher may assume some of this responsibility.

In addition, resource or itinerant teachers are responsible for familiarizing or orienting students to new classrooms or school buildings and supplementing the instruction of orientation and mobility specialists. Throughout the education program, orientation and mobility training should be systematically provided.

Student and Parent Counseling

Many resource or itinerant teachers assume responsibility for student and parent counseling and for seeking appropriate professional counseling when needed. These teachers may work with a student for several years, whereas a classroom teacher may be in close contact with the student for only one year. Resource or itinerant teachers are acquainted with the problems imposed by impaired vision and the relationship of those problems to adjustment and social and emotional growth. Resource or itinerant teachers may also be in the best position to discuss personal problems, interests, and projected vocational plans.

Although the primary responsibility for reporting student progress rests with regular classroom teachers, resource or itinerant teachers should attend parent-teacher conferences to report progress in special areas. Often, it is necessary for a resource or itinerant teacher to meet separately with a student's parents to interpret special programming efforts or special problems related to the student's visual impairment.

Instruction in the Use of Adapted or Special Equipment and Aids

Instruction in the use of special equipment and aids, like tape recorders, tape players, speech compressors, the Optacon, talking calculators, closed-circuit television, and talking-book machines, is necessary for students who are visually impaired. Instruction is also necessary in the use of special mathematical computation devices like the abacus and talking calculator, and of special maps. Generally, instruction in the use of such equipment is introduced as the need arises rather than systematically scheduled.

Development of Visual Efficiency

Through systematic instruction, the visual efficiency of a student with low vision can be increased. Special techniques and materials to determine the amount of visual efficiency and specific techniques to increase visual ability are available. Constant visual stimulation provided through a sequentially planned program can increase the visual efficiency of many students. This instruction should be provided by resource or itinerant teachers on a routine basis. Resource or itinerant teachers may also observe students in regular classrooms to determine if the students are using their vision as much as possible.

Instruction in Handwriting

Instruction in handwriting for a student who is partially seeing should be initiated at the same time as it is introduced to sighted classmates. It may be necessary, however, for a resource or itinerant teacher to provide supplemental assistance in this area. A student who reads braille must gain proficiency at handwriting so that she or he can provide a signature and make brief notations. Special handwriting aids and instruction are necessary.

Keyboarding—with an electric or electronic typewriter or computer if available—is routinely taught to students who are blind or have low vision. Since their handwriting may be difficult to read and braillewriting can be read by only a few individuals, typing can boost their written communication skills. Instruction is generally initiated at about the fourth-grade level. Often, keyboarding is taught along with spelling assignments because there is considerable repetition in both subject areas. As students increase their keyboarding proficiency, they can complete more and more assignments with the aid of a typewriter or computer. The adapted approach to instruction known as touch typing employs a special system that does not require vision. Naturally, accuracy is emphasized rather than speed, since it is difficult for students to check their work. Instruction in this area usually continues throughout the upper elementary and secondary school years.

Supplementary or Introductory Instructions

Because it may take longer for a student who is visually impaired to complete an assignment or because an assignment may be highly visual, it is often necessary for a resource or itinerant teacher to supplement the instruction of the regular classroom teacher. For example, when teaching the process of carrying in mathematical addition, the resource or itinerant teacher may want to introduce the use of a special mathematics aid or supplement the regular classroom teacher's instruction by using a special mental mathematics technique.

Often, the resource or itinerant teacher may want to introduce a particular concept before its introduction in the regular classroom. For example, a unit on the solar system may have considerably more meaning to the student with low vision if the resource or itinerant teacher provides a model of the solar system and introduces the unit to the student first. In physical education, it is often necessary to orient a student to special equipment, games, and activities before the physical education period so that the student acquires a basic understanding of the concept and the physical education instructor does not have to take a disproportionate amount of time when introducing the concept to the class.

Indirect Services

Services other than those that involve face-to-face contact with students are considered indirect services. As mentioned, a number of variables determine the nature and extent of indirect services provided. The following discussion is an overview of indirect services that might be provided by special education personnel.

Preparation of Materials

If an educational material is not available from any agency in the desired format and all sources have been queried, it may be necessary to have a transcriber-reproducer prepare the material. Resource or itinerant teachers serve as liaisons between classroom teachers and transcriber-reproducers to ensure that materials are in the needed formats and that they are completed in sufficient time.

Many day-to-day materials, such as teacher-made tests, work sheets, and special projects, obviously are not available from outside agencies. Therefore, it is the responsibility of the resource or itinerant teacher to have these materials prepared or to prepare them. The materials needed may be varied, ranging from teacher-made mathematics tests to geologic survey maps.

Often, it is not practical or possible to have a text brailled on relatively short notice or for use only once. In this event, the resource or itinerant teacher can assist in arranging for the material to be read aloud by another person. Readers are used frequently for secondary school students. If used properly, they can be tremendous helps to students who are visually impaired.

Acquisition of Materials

The acquisition of educational materials such as braille or enlarged-type texts, tapes, and tangible apparatus is one of the primary responsibilities of resource or itinerant teachers. Such materials must duplicate the content of the materials being used by the other students and must be obtained in the shortest possible time. Several well-established procedures are used by resource or itinerant teachers to obtain materials in the needed formats without duplication of efforts. These procedures involve checking national and state agencies and volunteer groups before actual transcription or production of the desired materials.

Inservice Sessions

Resource or itinerant teachers may be responsible for inservice education of classroom teachers and administrators. They may be expected to acquaint building staffs with the rationales underlying integrated placement of students who are blind or have low vision. In some instances, inservice education is general in nature, relating only to the philosophy of integrated education. In other instances, inservice education is directed at small groups of teachers and specifically relates to techniques for modifying and adapting materials or teaching strategies. Another inservice role often assumed by resource or itinerant teachers is providing journal articles, readings, or films for regular classroom teachers. These materials are directed at providing the competencies needed to work effectively with students who are blind or have low vision.

To ready students for classmates who are blind or have low vision, resource or itinerant teachers may conduct short inservice sessions with students to acquaint them with the nature of blindness or low vision. At other times, student inservice sessions may relate to special materials and techniques.

Coordination of Ancillary Services

Resource or itinerant teachers often assume responsibility for providing and coordinating many services needed in addition to classroom activities. Resource or itinerant teachers may coordinate orientation and mobility services or therapeutic recreation and leisure activities. They may also assist in planning and implementing work-study or vocational education programs. In general, the role is one of student advocacy—providing the services and programs necessary for the complete educational and social development of students with disabilities.

Assistance in Adapting or Modifying Activities

Resource or itinerant teachers may assist physical education, art, music, home economics, or industrial arts teachers in adapting or modifying particular lessons or activities. If resource or itinerant teachers have established routine and ongoing communication with all teachers, it is relatively easy for them to anticipate activities that require modification or adaptation. Resource or itinerant teachers may offer specific suggestions on how to change activities so that students who are visually impaired can meet the objectives of lessons. Sometimes, it is desirable for resource or itinerant teachers to actually attend activities to assist students or teachers.

Interpretation of Medical Information

Often, resource or itinerant teachers are expected to serve as liaisons between medical personnel and regular classroom teachers. They may be asked to interpret medical reports and to explain the nature of eye conditions and the limitations imposed by them. In addition, resource or itinerant teachers must share information concerning seating arrangements, lighting requirements, and levels of visual expectation for students who see only partially. They may also be asked to evaluate the suitability of materials to be used, particularly clarity of pictures, type size, spacing, and margins.

In addition to the specific indirect services already mentioned, there is, of course, ongoing consultation with regular classroom teachers. This includes monitoring the progress of students who have visual impairment, additional vision assessments that may indicate change in the aids used, modifications in programs, and general support to regular classroom teachers.

 ## Summary

Students with impaired vision have been successfully included in regular classrooms for many years, in effect, serving as pioneers for other areas of exceptionality. In this chapter, we discussed the legal definitions of visual impairment, and presented information about how vision is measured and classified. Practical suggestions outlined how teachers may observe indications of visual impairment as students complete classroom tasks, and included referral guidelines. We discussed the major visual impairments, along with other less common impairments.

We emphasized that specialized programming for these students primarily involves the modification and adaptation of existing educational materials. The curriculum for these students is the same as their sighted classmates, but special education personnel also must teach a number of compensatory skills.

We offered a number of suggestions for educational programming, including the use of adapted equipment and modifications in the educational environment, also discussing orientation and mobility techniques. In addition, we reviewed the role and responsibility of special education personnel, providing the regular classroom teacher with insight into their specific functions.

chapter 8

- Why is cerebral palsy often considered a multiple disorder? How should educators prioritize goals for a student with multiple disorders?

- Should students with asthma be allowed to participate in physical education?

- What actions should the teacher take if a student has an insulin reaction while in class?

- Why are absence seizures sometimes not recognized? If they are so minimal, why are they such a problem?

- What actions should the teacher take if a student has a generalized tonic-clonic seizure in class?

- What are the essential components of an official policy relating to medication in the schools?

- What are some ways that a nonverbal or seriously physically disabled student can communicate with others?

- What conditions may likely result from maternal substance abuse?

Teaching Students Who Are Orthopedically or Health Impaired

■■■■■■■■■■■■

Students with orthopedic and other health impairments are one of the most heterogeneous categories in special education. Students grouped in this broad category range from the cerebral palsied (a condition commonly associated with secondary or multiply disabling conditions) to students with asthma, or disability as a result of a head or spinal cord injury. One student may have limited use of the arms but have good use of the legs, another may have use of all extremities but have considerable difficulty breathing, and another may be generally weak because of a progressive condition. One may be completely mobile in the classroom, another mobile with the use of crutches, and still another may require the use of a wheelchair.

This chapter is divided into six major sections. The first is concerned with orthopedic impairments, which is related primarily to disorders of the joints, skeleton, and muscles. The second part reviews the most common health impairments: allergies, asthma, diabetes, epilepsy, cardiovascular disorders, and human immunodeficiency virus (HIV). Also included in this section is a discussion of conditions resulting from maternal substance abuse and traumatic brain injury. In the third section we discuss use of medications in schools. In the final sections we offer information concerning assistive and augmentative devices, adapting physical education, and resources outside schools.

The primary focus of programming for students with orthopedic and health impairments is the modification and, as much as possible, elimination of physical barriers. The phrase "least restrictive environment" in IDEA is concerned with appropriate placement of students who have disabilities. This phrase has special meaning when applied to students with orthopedic and health impairments. The least restrictive environment for these students is an appropriate academic placement in a carefully considered physical environment.

Several other factors should also be given serious consideration before students with orthopedic and health impairments are placed in regular classrooms. Of course, the willingness and ability of regular classroom teachers to accept and make changes for these students are of concern. The availability of support and ancillary personnel (resource teachers and therapists) is another factor. If a student needs daily therapy and must be bused to receive such service, provision must be made. Support from and a close working relationship with parents are essential elements for the success of a mainstreaming program. The degree of acceptance and positive interaction with nondisabled classmates is very important, too.

Specific student variables that should be considered are (a) modes of communication; (b) stamina; (c) intellectual ability; (d) achievement level; (e) personality, (f) relative independence in ambulation and mobility; (g) ability to profit from large-group instruction; and (h) personal interest, motivation, and commitment to being served in a regular classroom setting. These variables are not intended as criteria for placement or success in a regular classroom; they are provided as general guidelines for professionals in making placement decisions.

If it is recommended that a student who is orthopedically impaired be placed in a regular classroom, a resource teacher or consultant must begin specific planning to determine the best possible educational placement and arrange for transportation and therapeutic services as required. The mere presence or placement of the student in a regular classroom and accomplishment of assigned academic tasks may represent only a small part of the total educational need for the individual.

The computer broadens the universe for this student.

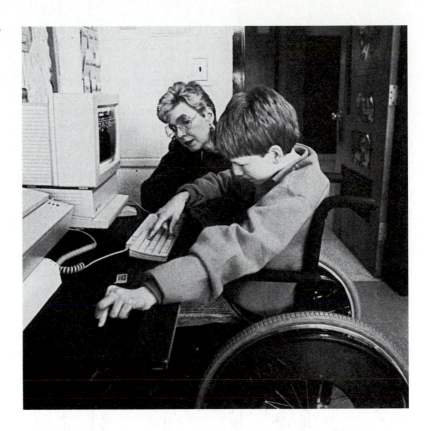

Independent ambulation is an important factor in the total development of students, possibly more important to students than many of the academic challenges. Movement is essential for not only maintaining and improving motor function but also facilitating important psychosocial interactions. Teachers should be aware of the effects that lack of movement has on students and their interactions with peers. Schools and classrooms should be arranged to enable movement to all areas. Independent ambulation must be given priority if students are to be allowed equal opportunities to grow socially, educationally, and emotionally.

Because of the diversity of problems presented by students who are orthopedically or health impaired, a complete continuum of educational services must be offered, ranging from full-time special class placement for students who are multiply disabled or severely physically disabled to full-time regular class placement for those able to function and achieve in a regular class environment. Children temporarily disabled by infectious diseases or accidents may receive hospital or homebound instruction; however, the primary goal should be education in regular classrooms wherever possible.

Today, it is possible for more children to be educated in regular classes than in years past because of the reduction of architectural barriers, as required by PL 93–112, the Rehabilitation Act of 1973 (Section 504). School buildings built around the turn of the century typically had many stairs and second stories, whereas today's schools are generally one-level structures, much more accessible or adaptable for students with limited mobility. However, even modern schools often require modifications. Some modifications include bathroom stalls made wider and deeper, sinks and water fountains lowered to enable individuals in wheelchairs to use them, classroom doors widened to accommodate wheelchairs, and chalkboards lowered and hinged to allow individuals in wheelchairs to write comfortably.

Many variables contribute to the number of students with physical disabilities who attend regular classes. Advanced medical and technological procedures may lessen the degree of disability. For example, children born with congenital heart defects may have these corrected surgically and live without serious restrictions. This was not possible in the past. Similarly, changes in treatment procedures for conditions such as asthma, diabetes, and heart defects allow students more complete participation in normal activities. Students may be fitted with artificial limbs at an early age, and congenital defects such as clubfoot may be corrected earlier, also allowing fuller participation in nearly all endeavors.

The information on disabilities and related adaptations that follows is presented on the basis of medically derived or defined conditions. Although there are disadvantages to discussing a condition on the basis of medical diagnosis rather than educational implications, it is hoped that through this approach, teachers will seek specific suggestions concerning educational procedures on the basis of a particular disability. For example, if a student has epilepsy, teachers are encouraged to seek information concerning the nature of the condition, the treatment procedures, educational implications, and the unique management techniques that they must employ.

■■■■■■■■■■■

Orthopedic Impairments

This section discusses the most commonly found serious orthopedic impairments: (a) arthritis, (b) cerebral palsy, (c) spina bifida, (d) spinal cord injury, (e) muscular dystrophy, (f) scoliosis, and (g) hip disorders. More than two hundred possible conditions are included in the category of orthopedic impairments; this section only discusses the conditions found most commonly in regular classrooms.

Arthritis

Nature of Condition

Although arthritis is a condition that occurs primarily in adults, it can begin at any age. The most common form of arthritis in students is juvenile rheumatoid arthritis. It may have a sudden onset, or it may begin gradually. The effects and complications vary greatly. In some instances, arthritis may last only a few weeks or months and not seriously limit the student. In other cases, it may continue throughout the student's life, becoming worse as time goes on.

Rheumatoid arthritis attacks the joints of the body and may involve many organs, such as the heart, liver, and spleen. There may be a skin rash, inflammation of the eyes, retardation of growth, and swelling and pain in the fingers, wrists, elbows, knees, hips, and feet. As the disease progresses, the joints may stiffen, making movement difficult and painful. Osteoarthritis, or the wear-and-tear type of arthritis, is generally confined to one joint and does not affect the whole body.

Treatment Procedures

There are no cures for rheumatoid arthritis, only ways to control the inflammation and secondary effects. The majority of students with this condition are free of active disease after a period of about 10 years. The major aim of treatment is to allow the students to live as normally as possible. Many times, students with arthritis become "care-cripples." In other words, they are overprotected and not allowed to participate fully in the activities of home or school. Juvenile arthritis is self-limiting, and students ordinarily use good sense in determining whether they should participate in activities.

Treatment procedures are generally individualized, because no two cases are exactly alike. Because of the variance among patients and their individual response to drugs, the drugs prescribed by physicians may be different in each case. Generally, aspirin is the single most effective drug used in the treatment of arthritis because it reduces pain and inflammation of the joints and is among the safest drugs on the market. Usually, large amounts are prescribed on a routine basis, and dosage must be continued even after the swelling and pain have subsided.

Special exercises may be prescribed, involving putting joints through a full range of motion to prevent loss of strength in the muscles and joint deformity. Heat treatments may also be prescribed to enable joints to move more smoothly and with less pain. Heat treatments take a variety of forms. They may be carried out at home or in a clinic. Surgical procedures are also used to prevent and correct deformity caused by this disease. For some children, splints, braces, or plaster casts are prescribed to subdue inflammation and protect the joint or joints.

Educational Implications

The educational modifications necessary for the student with juvenile arthritis depend on the age of the student, severity of condition, independent travel ability, and range of motion in the arms, hands, and fingers. A student with juvenile arthritis probably does not need special methods or materials in the academic areas. If the joints in the upper extremities are severely involved, however, the student may need writing aids, adapted paper, or special pencils. The Arthritis Foundation publishes an illustrated "Self Help Manual for Arthritis Patients." This manual describes aids and devices that may be helpful.[1]

It is likely that a student with arthritis has the most difficulty with walking. The knees, ankles, and hips may be more involved than the upper body, and walking may cause considerable pain. As a result, it may be well to consider somewhat limited movement for many such students. However, some students experience increased joint stiffness during prolonged immobility and may need to get up and walk to relieve the discomfort. Some students need an individualized physical education program or a program carried out by a physical therapist, whereas others need very little modification in their physical education program.

Teachers should watch for any changes in vision, because eye disease is commonly associated with rheumatoid arthritis. Inflammation of the iris (iridocyclitis) is a serious condition and may be found in association with some forms of juvenile rheumatoid arthritis. In particular, pain in the eyes or light sensitivity may indicate need to be seen by an ophthalmologist. It is generally recommended that students with arthritis be checked for changes in vision at least every 6 to 9 months.

Psychological and environmental factors may influence the manifestations of arthritis and its ultimate conclusions; however, they are not causes of arthritis (Hanson, 1983). Teachers need not modify academic and social standards. They should simply be aware of the general emotional climate and its possible effects on the student. Changes in mood or temperament are common for such students and may be related to the amount of pain. Teachers and school counselors can help students cope with the frustration, anger, and pain.

Teachers should be aware of other implications for students who have arthritis. For example, a student may miss a considerable amount of school during arthritic attacks. Faulty posture habits should be avoided, since good body alignment and posture are important in reducing the effects of arthritis. Activities such as extensive and prolonged writing may need to be avoided if they are painful. It may also be necessary to give the student extra time to get to and from classrooms and extra time for completing assignments. Students must learn to live with arthritis and accept the limitations imposed by it. Understanding teachers can do a great deal to help students develop acceptance.

Cerebral Palsy

Nature of Condition

Cerebral palsy is not a disease but a group of conditions that may seriously limit motor coordination. Of the serious crippling conditions, cerebral palsy is the most common. Several years ago, polio was the number one crippling condition among children; today, cerebral palsy is more common. Cerebral palsy is most commonly present at birth, but it may be acquired at any time as the result of a head injury or an infectious disease. It is characterized by varying degrees of disturbance of voluntary movements resulting from brain injury. Because of brain injury, the majority of students with cerebral palsy have multiple disabling conditions, such as mental retardation, hearing impairment, visual difficulties, language disorders, and speech problems.

The two most common types of cerebral palsy are spastic and athetoid. Spastic cerebral

---

[1]Arthritis Foundation, 3400 Peachtree Rd, N.E., Atlanta, GA 30326.

palsy is characterized by jerky or explosive motions when the student initiates a voluntary movement. For example, in a severe type, a student who is asked to draw a line from one point to another may demonstrate erratic or jerky movements such as this:

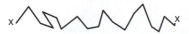

A student with athetosis also has difficulty with voluntary movements, but controlling movement in the desired direction is an added problem. In other words, this student demonstrates extra or purposeless movements. In drawing a line from one point to another, the student may have considerable uncontrolled movement, such as this:

Cerebral palsy and other conditions may be classified on the basis of limb involvement (topographical classification) as follows:

1. *Monoplegia*—one limb
2. *Hemiplegia*—both limbs on same side of body
3. *Paraplegia*—lower limbs only
4. *Diplegia*—major involvement in lower limbs and minor involvement in upper limbs
5. *Triplegia*—three limbs, usually one upper limb and both lower limbs
6. *Quadriplegia*—all four limbs
7. *Double hemiplegia*—both halves of the body, with one side more involved than the other

This classification is generally specified in the diagnostic information and in the student's school records.

Educational Implications

The severity of cerebral palsy dictates where a student would best be served, but the emphasis should be on providing as normal an educational environment as possible. Wherever practicable, students with cerebral palsy should attend regular classes with their nondisabled peers. Classroom modifications vary according to individual needs. Some students need no modifications, whereas others need some minor or major adjustments.

Often, an interdisciplinary approach is required in the care and treatment of individuals with cerebral palsy. It may be necessary for some students to be served on a routine and continued basis by a physical, occupational, or speech therapist or a combination of these. If such therapies are initiated early, they may not be needed as frequently during the upper elementary and secondary school years. Therapy sessions may be attended during the school day or after school hours.

Physical therapists are primarily concerned with the lower extremities and with posture, movements, and prevention of contractures (permanent muscle shortening because of lack of neurostimulation and muscle use). They are trained to evaluate physical development, ability, and movement. Physical therapists work under the direction of physicians in carrying out precise programs. Nonetheless, it is necessary for regular classroom teachers to have a basic understanding of treatment procedures so that they may reinforce desirable movements and postural habits.

Occupational therapists are primarily concerned with the upper extremities and with the routine activities required in daily living, such as buttoning, tying shoes, and eating. Many routine activities may be seriously limited for cerebral palsied students because of lack of muscle coordination. It is important that regular classroom teachers have information concerning the skills being taught so that

Technological advances enhance the lives of individuals formerly limited by the inability to communicate. (Photo courtesy of the Prentke Romich Company.)

they may reinforce them in the classroom. Often, occupational therapists assist in modifying and adapting educational materials to be used by students who have cerebral palsy.

In the past, there has often been a sharp distinction between physical and occupational therapists. This role differentiation is not so distinct now, and many therapists share responsibilities or delineate them according to student needs. The services offered by speech therapists also need to be reinforced by teachers to ensure carryover and maintenance of desired speech habits.

Before actual placement of the student in a regular classroom, it is helpful for the regular classroom teacher to obtain as much information as possible about the student from the parents, resource or itinerant teachers, and therapists. It is helpful to obtain specific infor-mation concerning methods of communication, therapy needs and schedule, reading or writing aids used, and ambulation devices used. If time permits, the teacher will also benefit from actual observation of therapy sessions and a few brief meetings with the student.

If the student with cerebral palsy is placed in the proper educational program, it should not be necessary to offer a curriculum different from that of the student's peers. However, it may be necessary to modify or adapt materials and equipment so that the student can participate more fully in classroom activities. The extent of the modifications necessary varies considerably. For example, some students have limited use of their hands and arms but have no difficulty getting around. As a result of the variance between individuals, it is difficult to offer specific suggestions.

The following list of materials and equipment provides examples of ways that teachers and others may modify materials and equipment:

1. Pencil holders made of clay, Styrofoam™ balls, or plastic golf balls may be helpful for students with fine-motor coordination difficulties.

2. Adapted typewriters may be useful for students with fine-motor coordination difficulties or students with very weak muscles. Electric or electronic typewriters are generally preferred. The student whose condition is seriously disabling may use a pencil, rather than the fingers, to strike the keys. A student who has considerable difficulty writing may use hand calculators in arithmetic computations.

3. Some students have conditions so severe that communication is seriously limited. Assistive and augmentative communication devices are beginning to play a critical role in helping students with cerebral palsy communicate with peers, teachers, and other individuals (Brown, 1993). We will more comprehensively review technology appropriate for these students later in this chapter.

4. Positioning the student so that most of the body is supported may reduce uncoordinated movements, thus allowing the student to concentrate on only one or two body parts.

5. Page turners are useful for students with limited arm use. A turner may be attached to the head, elbow, or hand. A rubber thumb (used by office workers) may also make page turning easier.

6. Weights (such as small sandbags) placed on the wrist or hand can be used to eliminate random or uncontrolled movements. Cursive writing may be easier than manuscript writing for some students with cerebral palsy.

7. Book holders that can be adjusted to any angle are helpful for some students.

8. Desks and tables should be at such height that the student's feet firmly touch the floor and the student's forearms rest on the working surface. Occasionally, the trunk of a student's body may need to be stabilized by straps or a harness.

9. Paper holders may be necessary for students who have the use of only one arm or very limited use of both arms. A clipboard to hold paper in position may be fastened to a desk, or a piece of unbleached muslin cloth may be attached to the desk and sprayed with nonskid fluid. It may be necessary to tape down the paper while the student is writing on it. A large rubber band may also be used to hold paper down.

10. A lip or rim around tables or desks may prevent pencils and other items from rolling off.

11. Some materials originally designed for use by individuals who are blind, such as talking books and cassette recorders, are helpful for students who have difficulty turning pages or balancing a book.

12. Stand-up tables are necessary for many students with cerebral palsy. Since a considerable amount of time is spent sitting, provisions should be made to allow students with cerebral palsy to stand for parts of the school day. Standing is often required to prevent muscle contractures, provide proper circulation, and maintain desired posture. Since standing unaided may be difficult, a stand-up table may be purchased or built inex-

pensively to provide support while the student is standing. An individual stand-up table should normally include a tray for a work area approximately 2 feet square. The table should have a base of the same size so that it does not easily tip over. The height of the table can be changed by raising or lowering the foot platform.

Spina Bifida

Nature of Condition

Spina bifida is a serious birth defect in which bones of the spine fail to close during the 12th week of fetal development. As a result, a cyst, or sack, is present in the lower back when the child is born (Figure 8–1). This protrusion is generally surgically treated during the child's first 24 to 48 hours of life. The extent of the disability resulting from this condition varies enormously. Some individuals have little or

no disability, whereas others have varying degrees of paralysis of the legs and incontinence (lack of bowel and bladder control). In addition to the degrees of paralysis and incontinence, the child may have impaired autonomic nervous system functioning (absence of perspiration) and absence of sensation below the level of the spinal defect.

In some respects, spina bifida is similar to other crippling conditions that cause degrees of paralysis in the legs, but it is complicated by the lack of bowel and bladder control. Because of the deficiency of nerve fibers, a student may not be able to tell when his or her bladder is full. The bladder may overflow, and the student may not be aware of the situation until he or she sees the wetness through the outer clothing. There is a threat of infection from residual urine in the bladder, and the student may also have difficulty with bowel control.

Surgical procedures can assist in accommodating this condition, or artificial devices may

Figure 8–1
Spina bifida

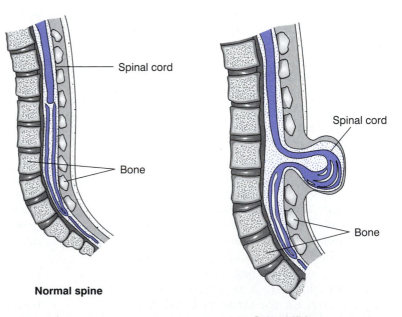

Normal spine

Spina bifida

be worn to collect urine. The student may also regulate fluid intake and adhere to a systematic voiding schedule. Generally, the student is able to take care of toileting needs, but young children may need some assistance from a classroom aide, volunteer, parent, or resource or itinerant teacher.

Educational Implications

It is important for teachers to work closely with medical personnel, especially the school nurses, to ensure proper health care. Teachers must also maintain a close working relationship with physical and occupational therapists. Last, but certainly not least, teachers should discuss the special needs and problems with the parents and should be aware of the symptoms of urinary infection—increased temperature, flushed skin, and excessive perspiration. The parents or the school nurse should be contacted if any of these symptoms occurs. Infections can generally be avoided with proper care, but in the event of infection, the student may have to be hospitalized, necessitating absence from school. Frequent urological, neurosurgical, and orthopedic consultations and procedures are also commonly required, necessitating careful planning between parents, resource teachers, consultants, and regular teachers. A schedule providing specific times for toileting needs should be implemented.

Teachers should be aware of problems associated with the lack of sensation in the legs. The lack of sensation can lead to skin or pressure sores. Teachers should also watch for injuries of which the student is unaware because of the lack of sensation, and should be aware of potential problems imposed by wearing braces or using a wheelchair. It may be necessary to reposition the student or ask the student to sit up straight during the school day to prevent pressure sores, postural problems, and muscle contractures.

If not handled properly, the psychosocial limitations imposed by spina bifida can be serious. The student may bear the brunt of laughter or joking because of odor or accidental urination. Teachers should also be aware that factors such as excitement or spicy foods can cause problems and should allow students with spina bifida to leave the classroom suddenly if an "accident" occurs.

The problems imposed by poor ambulatory skills must be taken into consideration by therapists and teachers. However, this factor is not any more significant for a student with spina bifida than for a student with cerebral palsy or any other major orthopedic impairment. Inasmuch as students with spina bifida have good use of their upper body, arms, and hands, the educational modifications necessary are minimal. Children with spina bifida can profit from regular classroom attendance and instruction with only minor modifications and adaptations.

Spinal Cord Injury

Nature of Condition

Spinal cord injuries occur most frequently in adolescents and young adults and are often the result of motorcycle, automobile, or sport-related accidents. Tumors, abscesses of the spine, or other diseases such as poliomyelitis and arthritis can also cause damage to the spinal cord. The point at which the spine has been damaged (or severed) is a determining factor in the extent of the paralytic conditions. Pressure sores, muscle contractures, or respiratory or urinary infections can also be complications of a spinal cord injury.

Treatment Procedures

Rehabilitative efforts often concentrate on increasing residual strength, building up new muscles, and helping the individual adapt to orthopedic devices, such as braces or splints.

The primary focus of the therapy is to help the individual achieve as much independence as possible in mobility and self-care. In addition to the physical adjustments after the injury, these individuals must also overcome the depression that commonly follows. Psychological help is an integral part of the rehabilitation process.

Educational Implications

Educators who work with individuals who have sustained a spinal cord injury should realize that intellectual capabilities are basically unaffected by this type of injury. Although the educational needs of these individuals are essentially the same as for most other students, there may be continued health care needs related to pressure sores or infection. Assistive technology such as motorized wheelchairs, switches, and voice-activated devices have made a tremendous difference in the extent to which these students can become empowered in physically managing their school and home environments.

Muscular Dystrophy

Nature of Condition

Muscular dystrophy is a progressive condition in which the muscles are replaced by a fatty tissue. The most common and most serious type, Duchenne's disease, occurs almost exclusively in male children. Duchenne's disease, or childhood muscular dystrophy, is a generally fatal disease characterized by a slow deterioration of the voluntary muscles. The onset of the disease generally occurs between a child's first and sixth year and rarely occurs after the first decade of life. Early signs of the condition include a tendency to fall easily, clumsiness in walking, difficulty in climbing stairs, and difficulty in rising from the floor.

There is a progressive decline in the child's ability to walk. The child falls more frequently and eventually needs crutches to move about. As the child continues to lose strength, it is necessary to move from crutches to a wheelchair. Later, nearly all large muscles are involved and the child is bedridden. During the later stages, the child may be unable to raise his arms, sit erect, or hold his head up. Fortunately, the small muscles of the hands and fingers maintain some strength even during the most advanced stages.

Educational Implications

Regular classrooms offer obvious educational advantages as compared to special schools or classes for students with muscular dystrophy. In addition to the educational advantages, there are many recreational and social factors involved in regular school attendance. During the early stages of muscular dystrophy, very few modifications and adaptations are necessary, but as the condition progresses, the educational environment may have to be increasingly modified. Eventually, the student may not be able to attend any educational program and may require homebound instruction; however, every effort should be made to maintain students with muscular dystrophy in regular classrooms as long as possible.

Muscular dystrophy imposes a contradiction in attitude. On the one hand, it is known that it is generally fatal; on the other, students, parents, teachers, and others must carry on as though the students were going to live a rich and full life. This apparent contradiction must be dealt with. Guidance and counseling services can do a great deal to accommodate acceptance of this conflict. There is little question that if children and parents are to accept this contradiction, ongoing counseling must be offered.

Counseling programs should be conducted in cooperation with students, parents, brothers and sisters, therapists, teachers, and physicians. Counseling should center on acceptance of the condition, the best ways in which to utilize the time available, preparation for the inevitability of death, and related matters. Depression and withdrawal are common among individuals who anticipate the loss of a friend or family member. Because of variations in age of onset, speed of deterioration, and other factors, all counseling must be individualized. There are currently nearly 200 clinics throughout the United States sponsored by the Muscular Dystrophy Association of America. These clinics provide no-cost services such as counseling, physical therapy, medical management, diagnostic services, and followup care.

It is important that students with muscular dystrophy attend adapted physical education classes and maintain a balance among diet, activity, and rest, since there is a tendency for such children to become overweight. They should be encouraged to participate as fully as possible in recreational and physical activities. Although the effects of the condition cannot be stopped by physical activity, there is some indication that such activity may delay some of the debilitating effects. Some caution must be exercised, however, because students with muscular dystrophy become very easily fatigued. They should be allowed periods of rest as needed.

Several studies have been conducted to determine whether mental retardation is associated with muscular dystrophy. There have been no indications that there is a greater incidence of mental retardation in students with muscular dystrophy than in the population as a whole. In addition, research studies have attempted to identify particular personality characteristics associated with muscular dystrophy. Although some researchers have found personality patterns unique to students who have muscular dystrophy, others have not been able to do so. Therefore, it is reasonable to assume that differences in personality may be attributed to something other than

the muscular dystrophy. If there is no mental retardation or particular personality configuration associated with muscular dystrophy, then achievement and adjustment in school should be similar to that of other students. Perhaps, the most important role of teachers is to stimulate students who have muscular dystrophy academically, recreationally, and socially and to expect as nearly as possible the same of these students as of others.

Scoliosis

Nature of Condition

Scoliosis means lateral (side-to-side) curvature of the spine (Figure 8–2). The normal spine has several curvatures in a front-to-back direction but no curvature from side to side. The most common type of scoliosis, *idiopathic* (cause unknown), is most commonly but not exclusively found in young adolescent girls. The second most common form, *paralytic*, is often associated with conditions such as cerebral palsy, spina bifida, muscular dystrophy, or poliomyelitis.

Scoliosis screening programs are usually conducted as part of physical education programming or by school nurses. Teachers should watch for a difference in shoulder height, differing contours of normal flanks, or a hump when a child bends over (Figure 8–3).

If curvature is suspected, teachers should inform the school nurse or family so that further testing may be conducted.

Educational Implications

Since there are strong hereditary tendencies for scoliosis, teachers should be alert to signs of the condition in siblings of a student with scoliosis.

Students with scoliosis should be expected to participate in all routine activities, including physical education. Students with other orthopedic impairments may have a more

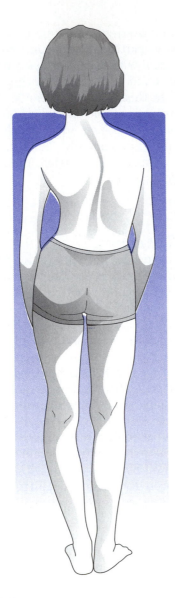

Figure 8–2
Scoliosis

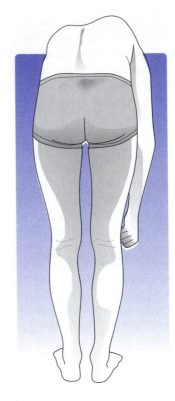

Figure 8–3
Appearance of scoliosis when an individual bends forward

severe form of scoliosis. Often, a brace such as the Milwaukee or Boston brace, to be worn full time, is prescribed to correct the condition. In very severe cases, surgery may be recommended.

Teachers should be particularly watchful for an improperly sized wheelchair, which may result in the student's leaning to one side, thus making scoliosis worse. If a student is wearing a brace, the teacher should also watch for an improper fit, which can cause discomfort, pain, or pressure sores. As indicated, students with scoliosis can be expected to participate in all school activities. A teacher in doubt should consult with the parents or medical specialist. Special care must be taken so that the treatment of the student with scoliosis does not become more of a disability than the condition itself.

Hip Disorders

Nature of Condition

The two most commonly found hip disorders in schoolage children are congenital dislocation of the hip and Legg-Perthes disease. Congenital dislocation of the hip occurs as a result of an abnormally formed hip joint. The hip may be completely dislocated, partially dislocated, or generally unstable. Medical intervention is initiated at an early age by gentle reduction of the misalignment and maintenance in the realigned position through the use of casts or splints. In more severe cases, surgery is required to release tightened tendons in the hip area. Generally, a child with a congenital hip problem has had the condition diagnosed and treated before entering school. In some cases, however, it is not diagnosed until after the child enters school.

Like congenital dislocation of the hip, Legg-Perthes disease is a problem that can be corrected by bracing, casting, or surgery. It is a condition of unknown origin that results from a disruption of the blood supply in the head of the long bone of the thigh (the femur). The lack of blood supply to the growth center of the femur causes disintegration and flattening of the femoral head at the hip joint.

Legg-Perthes disease is more common among males than females and is seen during the elementary school years (3 to 11 years of age). Treatment is directed at reducing weight-bearing pressure on the head of the femur, allowing for bone restoration. The child may be involved with an extensive treatment for as long as 2 years. In some cases, surgery is required to reshape the hip socket or the head of the femur.

Educational Implications

Close communication between teachers and parents is essential in cases of prolonged hospitalization. Hospital and homebound instruction may be necessary to ensure that when the student returns to the regular classroom, he or she will not be significantly behind classmates.

During treatment, the student's legs are usually placed in a position spread wide apart and maintained in this position by a cast, brace, or splint (Figure 8–4). After the cast, brace, or splint is removed, the student may progressively bear weight on the legs. Occasionally, the student may use a creeper (a low platform on wheels, similar to what an automobile mechanic uses to work underneath an automobile) for a period of time. Naturally, the student should avoid physical activities that put weight-bearing stress on the affected hip. Other than this consideration, there need not be any significant modifications or adaptations for students with Legg-Perthes disease.

■ Health Impairments

In this section, we address several of the more common health impairments of schoolage children—allergies, asthma, diabetes, epilepsy, cardiovascular disorders, and human immunodeficiency virus. In addition, we discuss conditions resulting from maternal substance abuse and traumatic brain injury. In each case, the discussion covers the nature of the condition and educational implications. Where applicable, the discussion also includes treatment procedures.

Allergies

Nature of Condition

An allergy is an adverse sensitivity or intolerance to a specific substance that may not be a problem to other individuals. When students who have allergies come in contact with substances to which they are sensitive, they develop reactions, or irritations. Reactions

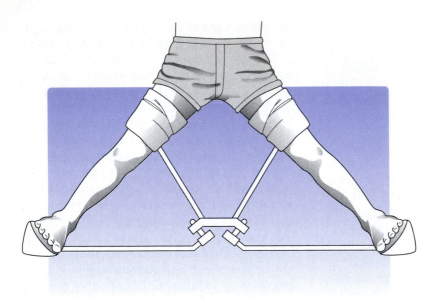

Figure 8–4
Hip abduction orthosis
Source: From Atlas of Orthotics (p. 93) by American Academy of Orthopedic
Surgeons, 1975, St. Louis: C. V. Mosby. Adapted by permission.

may take many forms, such as sneezing, watering eyes, runny nose, tiredness, itching, or rash. The student may react to a number of different substances. Among the most common are inhalants (pollen, smoke, dust, and perfumes, for example), foods (eggs, chocolate, wheat, pork, strawberries, nuts and citrus fruits, for example), infectious agents (bacteria and fungi, for example), substances that come in contact with the skin (poison ivy, poison sumac, fur, leather, animal hair, and dyes, for example), and drugs (vaccines, serums, and antibiotics, for example).

Treatment Procedures

Physicians may prescribe medication for temporary relief, but generally they carefully examine medical history, home surroundings, eating habits, and so on to determine the allergens to which individuals are sensitive. They may conduct specific allergy tests, such as skin tests on the arm or back, to determine substances to which the individuals react. They may also suggest a series of shots to desensitize the individual to a particular substance.

A student with allergies can participate fully in nearly all educational programs. Teachers may, however, assist in identifying specific sensitivities, particularly if the student seems to have more difficulty when at school. If an allergic reaction is suspected, this should be reported to the parents or school nurse, since treatment can do a great deal to ease the effects of the condition. In addition, students with allergies tend to develop asthma, and this should be avoided if at all possible.

Educational Implications

Some students miss school because of their condition, particularly during early fall or in the spring, when pollen levels are highest. It is the responsibility of teachers to make certain that students complete missed assignments. It may also be necessary to provide additional instruction or establish a peer teaching arrangement.

Some students with allergies fatigue more easily than other students when participating in physical activities. As a result, they may withdraw during recess or physical education, while their classmates continue. This behavior must be observed very carefully, since withdrawal may have serious social and emotional results. Because physical fitness is an important component of treatment, teachers may assist by modifying or adapting activities and encouraging students who have allergies to participate as much as possible. Teachers should also carefully observe to see if there is any change in the condition as a result of activity and report this information to the parents or physicians. Students must learn how to live with the limitations caused by allergies and develop a lifestyle that allows a maximum amount of freedom.

Asthma

Nature of Condition

Asthma usually results from an allergic state that causes an obstruction of the bronchial tubes, the lungs, or both. When sensitivity flares into an attack, an excessive amount of mucus is produced and there is a spasm of the bronchial musculature. As a result, breathing becomes difficult, and a student may lose color, wheeze, and perspire excessively. The attack may last for minutes, hours, or days.

Asthma attacks may be frightening because of the labored breathing and other behaviors. An attack may be brought on by a specific sensitivity to an allergen or by excessive physical activity. Asthma attacks can cause emotional stress for the students and those

around them. The arousal of emotions may intensify the frequency and severity of asthma symptoms. The disease and emotional climate are so interrelated that they affect each other (Kraemer & Bierman, 1983).

Treatment Procedures

Treatment procedures are similar to those for allergic individuals. Adrenaline administered by injection or by inhalation usually gives relief for brief periods. However, since asthma is a chronic condition, long-term treatment procedures must be employed.

Educational Implications

Students with asthma should be treated as normally as possible. Caution must be exercised to avoid overprotection from routine classroom activities. If care is not practiced, students may become asthmatic or emotional cripples.

Teachers should be aware of the factors that precipitate asthma attacks and have information concerning the proper course of action should an attack occur. Although the severity of the asthmatic condition of each student is different and there are unique care and treatment procedures for each, teachers should consider some general factors. Mild attacks can sometimes be controlled by asking a student to sit down and breathe easily. Medical personnel occasionally recommend drinking warm water as a way of stopping a mild attack. During an attack, a student may be more comfortable in a standing or sitting position rather than lying down. Teachers should encourage the student to sit forward in a chair, with hands on knees and shoulders forward, while breathing through the mouth.

Students may have to take medicine during school hours to keep mild asthma from becoming severe. If a pressurized aerosol is used, the teacher, after careful consultation with parents, should closely monitor its use to be certain it is not overused.

If a specific food being offered in a classroom party is an allergen, the teacher should check with the parents to identify an acceptable substitute. It is also recommended that classmates be helped to understand this condition to avoid ridicule, which would only add to the problem.

Management of students with asthma should include attention to psychological factors that may aggravate the condition. Teachers should also be aware of possible side effects or behavioral changes related to prescribed drugs. Teachers are in a unique position to observe students during a variety of activities throughout the school day. They can provide an atmosphere that promotes growth, acceptance, and independence. Information provided by teachers may be helpful to parents or physicians in determining subsequent treatment procedures.

Teachers should consider the following general guidelines for students who experience asthma attacks during periods of exercise. Warmup periods are helpful, as are short periods of moderate exercise. Certain types of exercise, such as gymnastics, wrestling, and swimming, are usually less likely to produce asthma attacks (Richards, 1986). Short sprints are also less likely to produce attacks than prolonged running. In addition, exercise in warm, humid conditions is generally less likely to induce attacks than that done in cold, dry air outdoors. With appropriate management (for example, medications taken prior to strenuous exercise), students may effectively compete in activities such as basketball, soccer, or track (Kraemer & Bierman, 1983). It is essential that teachers check with parents or physicians to determine specifically what students can and cannot do.

Diabetes

Nature of Condition

Diabetes is a metabolic disorder wherein an individual's body is unable to utilize and prop-

erly store sugar. This condition is a result of inability of the pancreas to produce a sufficient amount of the hormone insulin. Although diabetes is most commonly seen in adults, it does occur in schoolage children and can become a serious problem if the proper treatment procedures are not adhered to. Symptoms indicative of diabetes include unusually frequent urination, abnormal thirst, extreme hunger, changes in weight (generally a rapid loss), drowsiness, general weakness, possible visual disturbances, and skin infections like boils or itching. If a student shows any of these symptoms, the school nurse and the student's parents should be contacted as soon as possible. Prompt medical diagnosis and treatment are essential in the care of diabetic students.

Treatment Procedures

If diabetes is diagnosed, treatment procedures probably involve daily injections of insulin, adherence to a strict diet to maintain the correct sugar level, and a balance between exercise and rest. Generally, students with diabetes have normal childhood and adolescence and can do almost everything their peers do except fill up on sweets. They must maintain a balance between exercise and rest.

To most of us, daily injections seem a serious problem, but to the student with diabetes, they become as routine as other hygienic practices, such as bathing or brushing teeth. Injections are generally administered at home. In some instances, maintaining glucose may be achieved by use of an insulin infusion pump. The infusion pump is powered by small buttons and provides the necessary amount of insulin on a continuous basis. Often, students and parents attend a clinic that teaches them how to manage daily activities, such as injections, diet, exercise, care of the feet (this can be a definite problem because of poor circulation), and the changes in lifestyle that are necessary to accommodate the condition. As a result of these clinics, students who have diabetes generally know a great deal about the condition and how to manage it.

Educational Implications

Classroom teachers should be aware of several potential problems, such as an insulin reaction (hypoglycemia) and diabetic coma. An insulin reaction may result from anything that increases the metabolic rate, such as too much exercise, too much insulin, too little food, or nervous tension. Reactions may occur anytime during the day, but most often, they occur before meals or after strenuous exercise. For instance, an insulin reaction may occur if a student refuses to finish breakfast and the usual dose of insulin becomes unbalanced by the reduced food intake. Emotional tension about school or personal problems may have variable effects. Occasionally, tension may cause the blood sugar level to fall below normal, resulting in an insulin reaction.

An insulin reaction may follow a typical pattern for each individual, and therefore it is important to consult with students or their parents to determine what these signs may be. Often, general irritability may be the first sign. One student may be despondent and cry readily, whereas another may be exuberant or belligerent. The student may be hungry, perspire excessively, tremble, be unable to concentrate, and complain of being dizzy. Symptoms vary in duration and often disappear after the student is provided with a sugar cube, soft drink, candy, raisins, fruit juice with sugar, or any other carbohydrate. Generally, the symptoms will disappear after 10 to 15 minutes. If they do not, the student's parents or physician should be called.

The opposite of an insulin reaction is a diabetic coma. Although fairly rare, comas do occur and can be serious if not treated immediately. A diabetic coma is the result of failure

to take insulin, an illness, or neglect of proper diet. An individual has too much sugar and must have an injection as soon as possible. Generally, a coma is slow in onset, and the following symptoms may be observed: thirst, frequent urination, flushed face, labored breathing, nausea, and vomiting. Such symptoms should be reported to the parents, school nurse, or physician as soon as possible. Treatment involves rest, injection of insulin, and possible hospitalization.

Table 8–1 is a summary of the indicators, causes, and appropriate actions in cases of diabetic coma and insulin reaction. If in doubt over the symptom, administer sugar, since the body's reaction to an excess of sugar is slower and can be corrected later. However, the body's reaction to too much insulin is sudden and dangerous (Kleinberg, 1982; Winter, 1983). Specific instructions from a physician always take precedence over generalized instructions, but the guidelines in Table 8–1 may be of value until you consult with a physician or school nurse.

Several additional factors should be considered:

1. Check with the student's parents to see if the student should have a midmorning snack. If so, help the student be as inconspicuous as possible about it. It may also be advisable to schedule the student for an early lunch period.
2. Very active or strenuous physical activities should be avoided immediately before lunch. Since the goal in the management of diabetes is to maintain a balance among insulin, food intake, and energy expenditure, it might be well to encourage the student to establish an exercise routine at the same time each day.
3. Keep candy, raisins, or sugar handy in case the student needs them.

Table 8–1

Summary of observable signs, causes, and actions to take for diabetic reaction and insulin reaction

	Insulin Reaction (rapid onset)	Diabetic Coma (slow onset)
Observable signs	Facial Pallor Hunger Impaired/blurred vision Irritability Excessive sweating Weakness Personality/mood change Headache Fainting Trembling Forceful heartbeat	Excessive thirst Abdominal pains Repeated urination Loss of appetite Nausea or vomiting General aches Rapid pulse Weakness
Causes	Reduced intake of food Delayed or missed meals Abnormal amount of exercise Too much insulin	Infections Fever Failure to follow diet Too little insulin Overeating
What to do	Call the parents, doctor, or school nurse Provide sugar or other food with sugar, such as orange juice, candy or a sweetened soft drink	Call the parents, doctor, or school nurse immediately Allow the student to lie down Keep the student warm Provide fluids without sugar

4. Be certain to inform special or substitute teachers that there is a student in the class with diabetes, and record in writing what substitutes should do in case of insulin reaction or diabetic coma. This suggestion is relevant not only in the case of the student with diabetes but for all health impairments.

5. Encourage the parents to have their child's vision routinely checked, because many individuals with diabetes develop retinal problems.

6. Allow the student who has diabetes the flexibility to use the restroom whenever necessary, because students with diabetes may need to urinate more frequently. Inform the parents if there is a sudden increase in use of the restroom or the drinking fountain. Such an increase may be an indication of need for medical attention.

7. With permission of the student and parents, a teacher may present a unit of study concerning endocrine function and energy and their relationship to sugar consumption and nutrition.

8. Above all else, do not panic about having a student with diabetes. Proceed calmly

if the student has an insulin reaction or goes into a coma. The vast majority of the time, the student can be treated like any other student in the class.

Students with diabetes should be expected to participate in all normal school activities unless a physician has advised specific restrictions. Students who have diabetes must learn to live with the condition and to accept the limitations imposed by it. They must develop a lifestyle that allows the greatest possible freedom and still maintains the necessary balance among diet, rest and activity, and medication.

Epilepsy (Seizure Disorders)

Nature of Condition

Epilepsy is a chronic disorder of the brain, accompanied by seizures. Epilepsy has been traditionally classified according to terms such as *grand mal*, *petit mal*, and *psychomotor*. These terms describe both the type and severity of the disorder and continue in common use; however, many doctors use a newer, alternate classification system. The following discussion uses the newer system, indicating the traditional terms parenthetically.

Convulsions, or seizures, are the main symptoms in all types of epilepsy. Many individuals, especially young children, have one or two seizures in their life, but when several seizures occur unrelated to illness or fever, the diagnosis is likely to be epilepsy. Seizures are a result of excessive, uncontrolled electrical discharges in the brain cells. Actually, epilepsy is common, with many cases of seizures never recognized or reported. Estimates of occurrence range from 1 of every 50 to 1 of every 500 children, depending on the criteria established for the study. The most common types of seizures are (a) generalized tonic-clonic (grand mal) seizures, also known as generalized convulsive seizures or major motor seizures; (b) absence (petit mal) seizures; and (c) complex partial (psychomotor) seizures, also known as temporal lobe seizures.

Generalized Tonic-Clonic (Grand Mal) Seizures

Generalized tonic-clonic seizures are the most alarming to school personnel and other students. When such a seizure occurs, an individual loses consciousness, collapses, and has general convulsive movements. The individual may shout or produce a gurgling sound, and saliva may escape from the lips. The muscles first become rigid or stiff, and then there are jerky movements of the arms and legs. An individual may bite the tongue or lose bladder or bowel control. Breathing is often labored and at times seems to have stopped completely. The individual may have a bluish or pale complexion. The seizure may last for several minutes, and afterwards the individual may be confused or drowsy. The individual does not recall what happened during the seizure, and he or she may be very tired and want to sleep for a short time.

There are many misconceptions concerning epilepsy, including the presumption of mental retardation, brain injury, or insanity. But there is even more misinformation about what should be done when an individual has a generalized tonic-clonic seizure. Such a seizure can be frightening unless the teacher knows exactly what to do. The Epilepsy Foundation of America suggests the following steps in the event of a generalized tonic-clonic seizure:

1. Remain calm. Students tend to assume the same emotional reaction as their teacher. The seizure itself is painless to the student.
2. Do not try to restrain the student. Nothing can be done to stop a seizure once it has begun. It must run its course.

3. Help the student lie down, and put something under the student's head.
4. Clear the area around the student so that he or she is not injured on hard, sharp, or hot objects. Try not to interfere with the student's movements in any way.
5. Remove glasses and loosen tight clothing.
6. Do not force anything between teeth. Under no circumstances should a hard object such as a spoon, pen, or pencil be put in the student's mouth. More harm may result from such an action than from doing nothing. Do not put fingers into the mouth.
7. After the seizure, turn the student's head to one side for the release of saliva.
8. Do not offer the student anything to drink until he or she is fully awake.
9. It is not generally necessary to call a physician unless the attack is immediately followed by another major seizure or unless the seizure lasts more than 10 minutes.
10. When the seizure is over, let the student rest if he or she needs to and then resume classroom activities. Having the student remain in the classroom helps the other student learn to accept and become more comfortable with epilepsy.
11. Inform the student's parents of the seizure. Document as precisely as possible what happened before, during, and after the seizure (Figure 8–5).
12. It is generally not necessary to send the student home unless she or he has been injured or if the seizure has been unusually severe.

Absence (Petit Mal) Seizures

Absence seizures are generally short in duration, lasting from 3 to 30 seconds. They are most common in children and can occur between 50 and 200 times a day if untreated. Often a student who experiences absence seizures may be accused of being a daydreamer because he or she loses contact with what is happening in the classroom during the seizure. The student may become pale and may stare into space. The student's eyelids may twitch, or the student may demonstrate slightly jerky movements. After the seizure, the student continues with activities almost as though nothing has happened because he or she is probably not aware of a seizure. Absence seizures have a tendency to disappear before or near puberty but may be replaced by other types.

One of the most significant problems of absence seizure behavior is that it often goes undiagnosed. Teachers can play an important role in identification and should watch for a number of signs that might otherwise elude detection for some time. Repeated occurrences of two or more of the following signs may indicate the presence of this form of epilepsy: (a) head dropping, (b) daydreaming or lack of attentiveness, (c) slight jerky movements of arms or shoulders (ticlike movements), (d) eyes rolling upward or twitching, (e) a seeming inability to hear complete sentences or directions, and (f) dropping things frequently. If any combination of these signs is observed, be certain that the school nurse and the student's parents are contacted to ensure that a proper medical examination is obtained. Once diagnosed, absence seizures are almost always quickly brought under control with medication.

Complex Partial (Psychomotor) Seizures

Complex partial seizures affect not only the motor system but also mental processes. A seizure may last from a few minutes to several hours. Behavior during the seizure varies from person to person, but for any individual, generally the same behavior occurs during each

Student's name _____ Date _____

Time of observation: _____   Activities preceding seizure:

Description of seizure or behavior: _____

_____   _____

_____   _____

_____   _____

_____   Student's behavior after seizure:

_____   _____

_____   _____

_____   _____

Length of seizure?_____   _____

Were there any injuries? ___ Yes ___ No   Follow-up procedure:

If yes, describe: _____   _____

_____   _____

_____   _____

_____   _____

Teacher/observer: _____

Figure 8–5
Seizure observation form

seizure. During a seizure, an individual may chew or smack his or her lips or appear to be confused. In some instances, the individual may carry out purposeless activities, such as rubbing his or her arms or legs. The individual may pick at or take off clothing, or the individual may demonstrate a sudden arrest of activity along with staring. Although this is uncommon, some individuals experience fear, anger, or rage. After the seizure, the individual does not remember what happened and wants to sleep. A teacher who observes any of these behaviors should contact the school nurse and the student's parents.

Educational Implications

All of the three most common types of seizures can cause severe educational problems. Generalized tonic-clonic epilepsy is probably the most serious because of the possibility of bodily injury and because it is so widely misunderstood. Absence seizures can seriously limit a student's achievement because she or he misses the material being covered during a seizure and may be labeled a behavior problem. Although complex partial seizures are relatively uncommon in children, they impose serious limitations on school achievement and adjustment. All three types are serious, and minor modifications and adjustments may be necessary to accommodate a student with any of these conditions.

Special curricular modifications are not necessary for students with epilepsy. Their academic program and materials are the same. We offer here several factors that teachers should be aware of when planning curricular modifications. The extent to which a student's seizures are controlled determines the extent to which teachers should consider each of the following factors and suggestions. If the seizures have been controlled for several years, it is not necessary to make many special provisions. If the seizures are not well controlled or if epilepsy has only recently been diagnosed, however, many of these factors are important.

1. If a seizure occurs, a teacher may turn the incident into a learning experience for the entire class. Explain what a seizure is, that it is not contagious, and that it is nothing to be afraid of. Teach the class understanding of the student—not pity—so that classmates continue to accept the student as "one of the gang." After the seizure and a short rest, the student can generally carry on routinely. The way in which the teacher and students react to the seizure is very important. Overreaction by the teacher can have a negative effect on the student with epilepsy and on other students in the class. However, if the teacher has prepared and informed the students concerning what to do in the event of a seizure, a potentially traumatic and upsetting experience can be a routine matter.

   There is some controversy concerning whether a student's previous history of seizure behavior should be discussed with the class before a seizure occurs in the class. It is possible that seizure may never occur in class. On the other hand, education about the nature of epilepsy as a part of general education may reduce the stigma and provide information for everyday living.

2. A teacher may want to discuss the condition with the student and the student's parents to obtain more complete information concerning how the student feels about the condition, the extent of seizure control, and any individual aspects that need to be considered.

3. A teacher should not lower the level of expectation or set up protective devices that would single out the student with epilepsy. This attitude must be avoided if the student is to develop a feeling of self-worth and a healthy personality.

4. A teacher should inform special or substitute teachers that there is a student in the class with epilepsy and should record in writing what to do in the event of a seizure.

5. School personnel, including other teachers, should be educated about the nature of epilepsy and procedures to be employed in the event of a seizure.

6. In general, a student with a seizure disorder should participate in school sports or games with as few exceptions as possible. When a physician so indicates, sports that in the past were routinely denied to students with epilepsy, such as football, karate, or boxing, are allowed. Swimming is certainly allowed; however, it is recommended that the student not swim alone. The teacher must consult the parents and physician to determine if there are any activities that must be specifically avoided.

7. A teacher should obtain information from state and national agencies concerned with epilepsy. Free information is available from the Epilepsy Foundation of America.[2] Materials from a national agency such as the Epilepsy Foundation can familiarize the class with procedures to employ in the event of a seizure. Students can be assigned specific responsibilities so that care of the student with epilepsy becomes a routine matter. If the class is prepared for a seizure, it should not be a disturbing experience.

The greatest limitation imposed by epilepsy is not the condition itself but the misinformation, antiquated attitudes, and in many cases, consistent rejection in a society that fears what it does not understand.

---

[2]The Epilepsy Foundation of America has a program entitled "School Alert." This program presents a basic educational program for classroom teachers, school nurses, and others in recognizing epilepsy and techniques of management in the school and classroom (Epilepsy Foundation of America, 1828 L St. NW, Washington, DC 20036).

Cardiovascular Disorders

Nature of Condition

There are two major types of cardiovascular disorders in children: congenital and acquired. Congenital heart disease may be the result of maternal rubella (German measles), chromosomal aberrations (such as Down syndrome), or structural abnormalities, including holes in the walls of the heart chambers and problems related to the flow of blood or the valves.

The most common acquired heart disorder in children is caused by rheumatic fever. Permanent heart damage resulting from rheumatic fever is called rheumatic heart disease. Rheumatic fever is brought on by a streptococcal infection, commonly known as strep throat or scarlet fever. This disease can affect many body organs but most commonly affects the valves of the heart. The incidence of heart disorders as a result of rheumatic fever is falling dramatically because of advances made in diagnosis, such as the use of throat cultures to detect strep throat.

Treatment Procedures

Advanced medical technology has significantly decreased the effects of congenital heart disorders. Most congenital heart problems can be corrected surgically, so that students with heart disorders can live normal lives. There are some students, however, who must live with the effects of their condition.

Students with rheumatic fever usually return to normal school activities after a period of hospitalization and home bed rest. Not all attacks of rheumatic fever result in a heart disorder, but if there is a residual effect, it most often involves the heart. Frequent followup medical evaluations for such students are mandatory. Often, such students must receive prophylactic penicillin or other preventive antibiotics indefinitely to prevent a recurrence of strep throat, which might result in rheumatic fever.

Educational Implications

The degree of involvement for students with cardiovascular disorders is different in each situation, and therefore, it is difficult to provide specific recommendations for every student. However, teachers should consider certain general principles or guidelines. Probably the most important consideration is close communication between teachers and parents. Parents can provide specific information concerning appropriate expectations and precautions. Health records should also be consulted to obtain more complete information. Occasionally, the records note that a student's heart condition is self-limiting, which means that the student is able to pace himself or herself, and may do so without teacher reminders.

All students can be included.

If there is an indication that the student's activity should be limited, the student's physician should give specific information as to which physical activities may or may not be appropriate. Generally, students should not engage in competitive athletics unless their physicians specifically approve. Some students may require a shortened school day combined with home instruction, special rest periods, a modified physical education program, or a special diet. Teachers can help parents avoid over-protectiveness (an understandable reaction on the part of parents) by encouraging the student to participate in as many activities as possible. Good communication and a strong relationship between parents and teachers cannot be overemphasized.

Human Immunodeficiency Virus

Nature of Condition

Human immunodeficiency virus (HIV) is a condition wherein a microscopic-sized virus, introduced into the body, attaches itself to helper T cells, which are the coordinators of the body's immune system. Inserting itself into the chromosomes of the cells, the virus directs the cells to produce more viruses. The invaded cells swell and die, releasing many new viruses to continue the attack on other helper T cells. As this process repeats itself, the body's immune system is unable to fight off diseases as a healthy body can do. Various diseases then invade the body, producing a variety of symptoms, each of which makes the individual more ill. Persons infected with HIV are diagnosed as having acquired immune deficiency syndrome (AIDS) if they develop conditions such as Kaposi's sarcoma (a form of cancer), pneumocystis carinii, pneumonia, or other serious diseases. An individual may be infected with HIV for years before developing AIDS, which indicates the latter stages of HIV.

HIV can be spread through sexual intercourse, sharing contaminated needles, and exchange of infected blood. Some infected mothers infect their infants prior to or after birth (through breast milk). HIV cannot be spread through casual contact, such as handshaking, eating food prepared by an infected person, swimming in pools, drinking from fountains, sitting on toilet seats, or handling doorknobs. Students infected with HIV or AIDS are clearly included under the Rules and Regulations of IDEA and an individualized education program must be designed to meet the needs of the student and updated in accordance with the annual review process or as warranted by the condition of the student. Particular care must be taken with regard to confidentiality (Fraser, 1989).

Educational Implications

Students infected with HIV may not require any modifications in expectations or assignments. Should the student develop AIDS, modifications related to the needs of the student may be required, depending on the complications relating to the conditions that develop. Then, students may have frequent absences or need less fatiguing activities.

The procedures for attending to body fluids of persons infected with HIV are not different from those of persons not infected. Teachers and other school personnel must exercise care in maintaining a healthy environment for all who are in school. Body fluids, such as saliva, nasal discharge, urine, blood, and vomit, can transmit a wide variety of infections, such as colds, hepatitis A, and flu, and should be cleaned up following accepted practices. Procedures for cleaning up any body fluids should be in place in the school and include disinfection of mops, brooms, dust pans, rugs, pails, floors, and disposal of infected towels and bandages. The same procedures should apply if a student who is infected with HIV attends the school.

According to the Centers for Disease Control (1989), all school personnel should be trained in preventing the spread of all infectious diseases. The centers suggest that the routine cuts and scrapes, which usually occur in schools, pose little problem and students can be encouraged to wash and bandage their own minor injuries. In case of larger amounts of body fluid, some barrier should be placed between the skin of a person who is in contact and the fluids, as plastic gloves or a thick layer of paper towels. Materials used in cleanup should be disposed of in plastic bags. Clothing and other nondisposable items that have fluids on them should be removed and placed in plastic bags until they can be washed in hot, soapy water. If direct contact with the skin has occurred, the skin areas should be washed. Every school should have liquid soap in dispensers, paper towels, and covered waste receptacles with disposable plastic liners in all bathrooms or classrooms in which there is a sink. Procedures for washing hands are:

1. Wet hands with warm running water.
2. Apply liquid soap and water.
3. Wash hands using a circular motion and friction for 30 seconds, including around the nails, between the fingers, and the wrist.
4. Rinse hands well under warm running water.
5. Repeat steps 2 through 4.
6. Wipe the surfaces around the sink with a paper towel, and discard the towel.
7. Repeat step 4.
8. Dry hands and dispose of the towel.
9. Apply lotion (lotion prevents chapping and serves as a barrier to infections).

Procedures to prevent the spread of infectious diseases should be practiced in all schools, whether or not a student with HIV is enrolled (see Figure 8–6). However, more criti-

Controlling the spread of communicable and contagious diseases within the schools has always been a problem faced by educators, the medical profession, and the public. Effective policies and procedures for managing such diseases in the schools have historically been developed by health agencies and implemented by the schools. These policies and procedures were primarily designed to manage acute, temporary conditions rather than chronic conditions which require continuous monitoring and remove children from interaction with other children while the condition is contagious or communicable.

The increased prevalence of chronic communicable diseases such as hepatitis B, cytomegalovirus, herpes simplex virus, and acquired immune deficiency syndrome have raised public and professional concern, necessitating the reassessment of existing school policies and procedures. The Council believes that having a communicable/contagious disease does not in itself result in a need for special education. Further, the Council believes that in developing appropriate policies for managing communicable diseases, schools and public health agencies should assure that any such policies and procedures:

a. Do not exclude the affected child from the receipt of an appropriate education even when circumstances require the temporary removal of the child from contact with other children.

b. Provide that determination of a nontemporary alteration of a child's educational placement should be done on an individual basis, utilizing an interdisciplinary/interagency approach including the child's physician, public health personnel, the child's parents, and appropriate educational personnel.

c. Provide that decisions involving exceptional children's nontemporary alterations of educational placements or services constitute a change in the child's Individualized Education Program and should thus follow the procedures and protections required.

d. Recognize that children vary in the degree and manner in which they come into contact with other children and school staff.

e. Provide education staff with the necessary information, training, and hygienic resources to provide for a safe environment for students and educational staff.

f. Provide students with appropriate education about communicable diseases and hygienic measures to prevent the spread of such diseases.

Figure 8–6

The Council for Exceptional Children's policy statement on managing communicable and contagious diseases

cal for the inclusion and well-being of a student with HIV is the support of teachers and students.

Students with HIV, AIDS, or AIDS-related conditions may require alterations in nutri-

tion, physical activity, or intake of fluids due to physiological changes resulting from the condition. Such students may also have feelings of powerlessness due to the condition or experience family disturbances because of the

g. Provide, where appropriate, carrier children with education about the additional control measures that they can practice to prevent the transmission of the disease.

h. Enable educational personnel who are medically at high risk in regard to certain diseases to work in environments which minimize such risk.

i. Provide educational personnel with adequate protections for such personnel and their families if they are exposed to such diseases through their employment.

The Council believes that special education personnel preparation programs should:

a. Educate students about communicable and contagious diseases and appropriate methods for their management.

b. Counsel students as to how to determine their level of medical risk in relation to certain diseases and the implications of such risk to career choice.

The Council believes that the manner in which policies for managing communicable and contagious diseases are developed and disseminated is critically important to their effective implementation. Therefore, the following must be considered integral to any such process:

a. That they be developed through the collaborative efforts of health and education agencies at the state, provincial, and local levels, reflecting state, provincial, and local educational, health, and legal requirements.

b. That provision is made for frequent review and revision to reflect the ever-increasing knowledge being produced through research, case data reports, and experience.

c. That policies developed be based on reliable identified sources of information and principles endorsed by the medical and educational professions.

d. That such policies be written in content and format to be understandable to a variety of consumers including students, professionals, and the public.

e. That policy development and dissemination be a continual process and disassociated from pressure associated with precipitating events.

Source: From *Policies Manual* (p. 13) by Council for Exceptional Children, 1989, Reston, VA: Council for Exceptional Children. Copyright 1989 by Council for Exceptional Children. Reprinted by permission.

disease. Students may also experience fear or diminished self-concept because they have a terminal disease. There may be a grieving process related to the loss of good health or a knowledge deficit regarding what HIV is, what AIDS is, the risk of transmission, or how HIV was acquired. If so, the students need strong acceptance from teachers and other students and reassurance, education regarding the illness, encouragement to maintain independence as far as possible, and self-management to maintain or build self-esteem.

Conditions Resulting from Maternal Substance Abuse

Nature of Condition

The increased use of a variety of substances by mothers during pregnancy, such as alcohol, cocaine, crack (a form of cocaine), phenylcyclidine hydrochloride (PCP), heroin, hallucinogens, and other similar drugs has resulted in a growing number of children experiencing a variety of disorders (Van Dyke & Fox, 1990).

Prenatal development is affected by many environmental factors called *teratogens*, which are agents that increase the likelihood of various malformations. Such factors affect a fetus in different ways at different times during pregnancy. For example, a critical time for the central nervous system is weeks 3 through 5, and teratogens ingested during this time affect the central nervous system in a more adverse manner at this time than any other. Similarly, weeks 4 through 7 are important for the normal development of arms. Some teratogens can more easily be avoided, whereas others cannot—for example, medications required by a mother to control seizures or other diseases. The presence of other conditions, such as nutritional deficiencies or metabolic disorders, may intensify the impact of maternal substance abuse.

Children born to mothers who have ingested large amounts of alcohol may be born with fetal alcohol syndrome. Such babies may have distinguishing facial characteristics (including narrow eyelids, low nasal bridges, and short, upturned noses) and may be born with heart defects and joint and limb abnormalities that restrict movement (Leerhsen & Schaefer, 1989; Schiamberg, 1988). They may experience mental retardation from mild to severe, be hyperactive, and have short atten-

tion spans and emotional problems (Behrman, Vaughan, & Nelson, 1987; Creasy & Resnick, 1989; Pueschel, Bernier, & Weidenman, 1988; Van Dyke & Fox, 1990). Babies born to cocaine- or crack-addicted mothers may have already experienced a stroke or neurologic insult, and are likely to be born prematurely (Revkin, 1989). Crack babies, as they are frequently called, are increasing in number, and there is increasing concern regarding their ability to succeed in school.

Cocaine is derived from the leaves of the coca plant, in which it occurs naturally as an alkaloid. When it is sold, it is usually in the form of hydrochloride salt diluted with inert substances. Crack is manufactured by boiling the hydrochloride in water and baking soda, which converts the salt back into the alkaloid and precipitates out of the solution as pure cocaine crystals. Once either substance enters the body, neurons in the brain are stimulated to release the chemicals that carry messages across the gap from one neuron to the next (neurotransmitters). The results are an accelerated heart rate, raised blood pressure, a lower digestive rate, and a feeling of euphoria. Fetuses are particularly vulnerable to cocaine, because it readily passes through the placental barrier. It lingers much longer in fetuses than in adults because the liver in fetuses is insufficiently developed and thus cannot break down the cocaine as quickly. Cocaine use can have significant effects on the developing central nervous system, and the risk increases when cocaine is used frequently.

Cocaine or crack use by mothers may lead to two major negative effects. The first, neurologic insult, may affect learning ability and cognitive processing. Neurologic insult may result in poor organization, reading problems, difficulty in acquiring mathematical skills, and decreased social adjustment (Revkin, 1989; Van Dyke & Fox, 1990). A second effect is less direct and more difficult to determine.

Frequent users of cocaine experience a period of euphoria followed by depression, paranoia, irritability, and loss of appetite, which increases the desire for more cocaine and the resultant high. This cycle becomes the norm, and getting cocaine becomes the most important goal (Morganthau, 1989). A parent who is experiencing this cycle often neglects or abuses the child (Revkin, 1989). Thus, neither the nutritional nor emotional needs of the child are being met, and the child suffers physical abuse as well (Berger, 1987). Additionally, there is some evidence that crack babies do not respond normally to their parents. Therefore, abnormal response on the part of the child may lead to absence of normal bonding even if the parents no longer use cocaine (Van Dyke & Fox, 1990).

Babies born to mothers who ingested phenylcyclidine hydrochloride (PCP) have characteristics different from those of newborns exposed to other drugs before birth. They exhibit sensitivity to touch, sensitivity to environmental sound, and abnormal eye movements. At a later age, they seem to be delayed in language and fine-motor abilities (Pueschel, Bernier, & Weidenman, 1988).

Children born to heroin-addicted mothers are generally slow in growth. They often experience behavior and perceptual problems and difficulties in organizational ability. In addition, they seem to be more susceptible to such complicating factors as infections, malnutrition, and acquired immune deficiency syndrome.

Mothers who are multiple drug users increase the risk for their children. Children born to multiple drug users tend to be more severely retarded, are more likely to have physical abnormalities, and are more likely to have severe neurologic disorders.

Educational Implications

Children prenatally exposed to drugs or alcohol may require educational practices similar to those for children with learning disabilities, mental retardation, or other physical or health impairments. Ultimately, it is the needs of the individual student, not the cause of the disability, that dictates specific educational measures. Understanding the organicity of prenatally drug- and alcohol-affected children will help educators in their goals and expectations for these children. Sufficient longitudinal studies have not been completed to determine how such children will fare when they reach their teens and adulthood (Van Dyke & Fox, 1990).

Traumatic Brain Injury

Nature of Condition

Current advances in medical technology and the increasing number of trauma centers nationally have ensured the survival of a growing number of children and youth with head injuries (Tucker & Colson, 1992).

Traumatic brain injury (TBI) is defined as an injury to the brain caused by an external physical force or by an internal occurrence such as stroke or aneurysm, producing a diminished or altered state of consciousness. The injury can impair functional ability or psychosocial adjustment and can adversely affect educational performance. Impairments can be mild to severe in one or more of the following areas: language, memory, attention, cognition, abstract thinking, judgment, reasoning, problem solving, sensory and motor abilities, physical functions, psychosocial behavior, information processing, and speech. Brain injuries occurring from birth trauma are not included in this term (*Federal Register*, 19 August 1991).

Depending on the extent of the brain trauma, individuals with this injury may appear distractible and impulsive. Their expressive language may show delayed responses or may be inadequate to convey a clear message. They may have trouble with sequencing, analyzing, or integrating information.

Many individuals who suffer from traumatic brain injury were previously successful academically and socially. As they become aware of their new limitations, there often follows a disturbance in their emotional functioning as well as their academic functioning (Reed, 1991). They may show a lower tolerance for frustration or withdraw from group activities. Outbursts of temper, rudeness, and other inappropriate behaviors are also characteristic of this injury.

According to the National Head Injury Foundation, over one million children each year sustain head injuries. The most frequent causes are car or motorcycle accidents, falls, child abuse, gunshot wounds, or other severe blows to the head. While depth and duration of coma can affect prognosis, recovery in children can be astounding and may continue as long as five years (Bigge, 1991).

Educational Implications

A student with traumatic brain injury often needs transitional support from the hospital rehabilitation team as she or he recovers and becomes ready to enter a school setting. The student achieves the most success in school when there is early contact and continued communication between school personnel and the medical facility. Often physical therapists, speech therapists, and psychologists are part of this team.

The standard curriculum may be very frustrating to a student with traumatic brain injury, and classroom placement should take into consideration the student's strengths and skills. Memory compensation strategies, behavior management, and social skills are a few of the areas educators may need to address when the student returns to school.

Fluctuation and variability in the student's process of recovery can be confusing and may require more frequent assessment of progress.

Students with TBI may need modifications in their environment to reduce distractibility and frustration. Teachers may need to use cuing systems such as wall charts, calendars, notebooks, lists, or alarms so that the student may easily understand and remember tasks and assignments. Worksheets may need to be simplified and tests should be untimed or allowed to be taken home. Instructions should be simple and understandable and information should be limited and presented in short units. Peer support is also necessary, and cooperative learning opportunities may be helpful in reducing the stress of interacting with a larger group.

It is important to note that students who have had a traumatic brain injury may continue to change for months or even years after returning to school. Medical and educational personnel will need to be flexible in their plans and expectations as the student goes through these neurological changes.

■ Medication in Schools

Often, students with health impairments must take medication as part of the treatment. For example, students with cerebral palsy may take Lioresal or Dantrium to relieve some of the spasticity associated with cerebral palsy, or students with a seizure disorder may take Dilantin or phenobarbital to control the seizures. Sometimes, students with spina bifida experience bladder problems that result in urinary tract infections, and they take either antibiotics, acidifying agents, or anticholinergic medications or a combination of them. However, most medications have some side effects, such as dizziness, fatigue, lethargy, vomiting, or lack of appetite. Teachers must be aware of and monitor students for the presence of such side effects.

Few states have legislation or formal regulations regarding the administration of prescribed drugs in schools. The American Academy of Pediatrics (AAP) Committee on School Health has published guidelines for the administration of medication in school (1984). They may be summarized as follows:

1. A physician must provide written orders, including the name of the drug, dosage, how often it is to be taken, why it is needed, and the approximate termination date.
2. The parents must request, in writing, that school personnel administer the medication according to the physician's instructions.
3. The medication for use in school must be in a container labeled by a pharmacist.
4. A student who is able to take the medication independently should be encouraged to do so with the written permission of the parents and physician.
5. If the medication is administered by school personnel, proper authorization must be obtained, the medications stored in a locked space, and a record kept (date, time of day, and individual who administered).

Forms that address the authorizations necessary and that are to be used to keep records in school may be developed if the school does not have them.

To avoid legal risks, teachers, principals, and school nurses should work together to ensure adherence to the recommendations of the AAP. The Committee on School Health of the AAP suggests that as school districts develop policies regarding the administration of prescribed medication, they seek the advice of an attorney and that they provide liability coverage for all staff members.

■■ Assistive Devices

Students who have orthopedic or health impairments may require special equipment, classroom aids, and adaptations in order to participate fully in classroom activities. The modifications necessary depend on the age of the student, the severity of the impairment, and the primary use of the classroom. Young students may need more specialized equipment, since they have not yet developed daily living skills or modes of ambulation. They may also require more assistance in the care of crutches, braces, or wheelchairs. The severity of the condition usually dictates the specialized equipment necessary, and the purpose of the classroom usually dictates the need for modifications. For example, if students are expected to move about frequently, as in a biology lab, modifications with regard to mobility may be necessary. However, if the classroom is used primarily for lecture and the students listen and take notes, minimal accommodations are necessary. The following sections describe the care and maintence of braces, crutches, and wheelchairs; specialized furniture and equipment; and classroom aids.

Braces, Crutches, and Wheelchairs

Many students with cerebral palsy, spina bifida, muscular dystrophy, and other orthopedic impairments need braces, crutches, or wheelchairs. Therefore, regular teachers should be acquainted with the purpose, care, and maintenance of this equipment. Braces are classified into three general types: (a) corrective, (b) control, and (c) supportive.

Corrective braces are used for prevention and correction of a deformity during a student's rapid growth. Often, during this period, the tendons (cords that attach muscles to bones) do not keep pace with the growth of the long bones. When this happens, the heel cords may tighten, and surgery may be required to lengthen them to keep up with the long-bone growth. Corrective braces may prevent or delay surgery. *Control* braces are used to prevent or eliminate purposeless movements of the type found in athetoid cerebral palsy or to allow movement in only one or two desired directions. *Supportive* braces are used to provide support for children who need assistance in standing. Often, students in a wheelchair do not have adequate muscle strength or control to support themselves. In this instance, a body brace may be used to support the spine and prevent serious scoliosis. Some students wear braces for only a short time, whereas others need them for many years and perhaps for their entire lives.

It is not the primary responsibility of regular classroom teachers to maintain this equipment. Teachers are assisted by therapists, resource or itinerant teachers, and the parents. However, classroom teachers may have more contact with students than the others do and may be able to spot-check equipment periodically. For example, teachers should be watchful for torn or worn leather pieces and should check to see that a brace is not rubbing against the body and causing pressure sores to develop. Teachers may also want to check periodically for loose or missing screws and the general condition of buckles, locks, and joints.

Crutches are used to stabilize the trunk and to provide support while standing and walking. Generally, crutches do not call for much care or maintenance, but they should be checked periodically for loose screws, worn rubber tips, and proper height adjustments.

Wheelchairs may be either manual or electric. Electric wheelchairs are powered by battery packs, which allow them to be operated by hand, mouth, chin, or breath. Wheelchairs are most commonly used by students who have severe crippling conditions, but some students who attend regular classes need a wheelchair for part or all of the school day because of slowness, fatigue, or lack of independent travel skill. Wheelchairs must be checked periodically for worn or broken parts, and teachers should be aware of posture, fit, and comfort. A teacher who notices any equipment in need of repair should immediately notify a therapist, resource teacher, consultant, or parents.

Specialized Classroom Furniture

Students in wheelchairs often need an adapted writing or work area (Figure 8–7). Tables that can be raised or lowered to different heights permit flexibility. A table with a pedestal base allows greater maneuverability and freedom than does a table with legs. Cutout desk tops attached to existing surfaces or portable lapboards are also beneficial. Traditional classroom arrangements of rows of desks are generally inconvenient unless some provision is made for wider aisles.

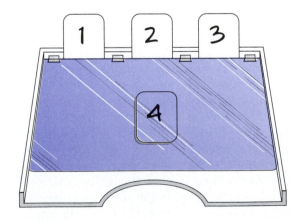

Figure 8–7
A cutout lapboard or desk top that may be fitted over wheelchairs to provide a work area

Chalkboards and bulletin boards may be lowered to be more accessible to students in wheelchairs. Relocating classroom items such as coat hooks, alarms, light switches, some doorknobs, plumbing fixtures, and pencil sharpeners may be advisable in some situations. The practicality of these modifications should be considered in view of cost and necessity.

Many schools built recently follow designs that incorporate modifications to reduce barriers for students who have disabilities, including the following:

1. Floors with nonskid surfaces, such as carpeting
2. Doors with automatic door checks that allow them to remain open for wheelchairs and crutch walkers (at the very least, doors should have a grasping bar rather than doorknobs)
3. Lowered chalkboards (about 24 inches from the floor)
4. Classrooms with two doors, one near the front and another near the back
5. Sinks accessible from three sides
6. Faucets that self-close
7. Toilet facilities near classrooms
8. Facilities for students who need additional rest
9. Sliding doors on storage spaces
10. A variety of equipment, such as standing tables, adjustable seats, and adjustable desks

Such modifications are not prerequisites for successful mainstreaming of students who are orthopedically impaired, but they may facilitate accessibility. When developing exit plans for fire drills or other emergencies, care should be taken to make certain that students in wheelchairs or using crutches or braces are not left unattended or without assistance (if necessary).

Augmentative and Alternative Communication Devices

Many students have the potential to be successful in regular classrooms, but because of serious communication problems, they have been limited in their educational opportunities and placement alternatives to more restrictive educational environments (Light & McNaughton, 1993). For example, many students with cerebral palsy have well-developed receptive language skills but lack the fine-motor coordination needed to express themselves using writing or typewriting. Other students may have speech impairment severe enough to seriously limit their functional oral language. In years past, these students were often relegated to education programs that seriously limited their academic, social, and emotional growth. Today, because of technological advances and alternative communication systems and devices, students with severe motor or communication problems can participate to a much greater extent in regular classrooms.

There are many different types of communication systems, ranging from direct-selection communication boards containing the letters of the alphabet to highly sophisticated microcomputers. Communication boards are an inexpensive way to help nonverbal students express themselves and answer questions (Figure 8–8). When using a manual communication board, a student identifies or is assisted in identifying a selection of numbers, letters, words, or phrases. Other boards employ a scanning procedure, in which a student moves a light to indicate the word selected. Boards may require changes as students develop new vocabulary or pursue new areas of study.

Electronic communication devices offer numerous options to enable the user to communicate spontaneously and effectively. High-quality speech output can be digitized (tape

Figure 8–8
A student with cerebral palsy using a head pointer and communication board

recorded by the teacher, parent, or others and the recorded message is then stored within the communication device) or synthesized to match the user's age and gender. Programmable models can create limitless vocabulary options. The Liberator™ from the Prentke Romich Company[3] is a comprehensive communication system that can be adapted to all ages and cognitive levels (Figure 8–9). The user may access the keyboard by the touch of a finger, a headstick, a mouthstick, or optical pointer, or by a variety of switch-activated scans that can be controlled by a tongue, a chin, sipping and puffing, or a joystick. Audible scanning is available for those with visual impairments, and a built-in printer can produce hardcopy of anything written by the user.

The AlphaTalker™ (Prentke Romich) comes with high-quality digitized speech and can store up to 14 minutes of vocabulary. Environmental controls can be interfaced with this device to turn on lights, switch channels on a television, or dial a telephone. Minspeak Application Programs™ (Prentke Romich) are prestored vocabularies customized to meet specific communication needs. Programs for younger age groups include simple phrases, storybooks, and songs. Other available applications can be word based or sentence based, depending on the level of language competence of the user, and can be modified to increase content and complexity (Kaiser & Goetz, 1993).

Because communicating with alternative communication devices can be time consuming, strategies have become available to enhance the speed of communication. Word prediction systems attempt to guess the word being typed after the user types one letter. The user can then select one of the lighted selections or type another letter to receive a second set of suggestions. Another accelerative device is a message coding system whereby a sequence of keys are programmed to elicit a message more enhanced with meaning than are the individual keys alone.

The communication systems mentioned are only a few examples of the array of devices available. Technological developments continue to strive toward products that are user friendly as well as affordable. It is, indeed, encouraging to see the growth that has occurred in this technology and to know that what lies ahead will provide students with opportunities that were beyond our imagination only a few years ago.

Classroom Aids

Because of difficulty with movement, students who have orthopedic impairments may use a number of learning aids not typically found in

---

[3]Prentke Romich Company, 1022 Heyl Road, Wooster, OH 44691.

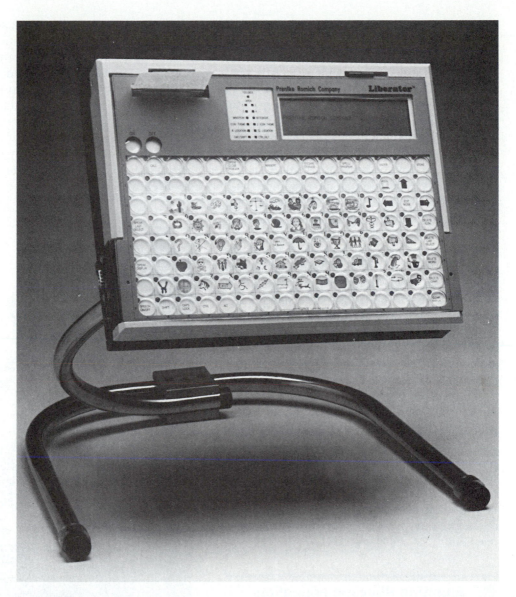

Figure 8–9

The Liberator™, an electronic communication assistive device

Source: Photo courtesy of the Prentke Romich Company.

regular classrooms. The aids may be very simple modifications, such as clay-wrapped pencils to assist with grasping and holding, four-fingered scissors, or clipboards or elastic tape to hold paper on writing surfaces. Page turners are useful for students with limited arm use; wrist or hand weights may assist students who have limited control. Teaching machines such as magnetic-card machines are often used if they do not require complex motor movements. Conventional and modified typewriters are used extensively. Students who have difficulty with movement may use head wands to strike the keys. With light-operated typewriting machines, students use a light source fixed to the hand or head to project a light spot on the control panel.

Talking books, previously available for the blind only, are now available for individuals with impairments that prevent them from handling books comfortably. Talking books and talking book machines are distributed by the Library of Congress at no cost to the users.

Resource or itinerant specialists in consultation with physical and occupational therapists may recommend other ways to modify materials. They can observe the students in regular classrooms and offer suggestions of ways to modify and adapt equipment and materials. Part of their responsibility is to keep abreast of new materials and equipment and share their recommendations with regular teachers.

■▪ Adapting Physical Education

Students with a crippling condition or health impairment can often successfully participate in nearly all curricular areas; however, one area that presents special problems is physical education. Physical educators who have had experience or special preparation in this area often adjust easily to accommodate such students. Physical educators who have not had experience or preparation in this area may have special problems adjusting to students with limited ambulation or health impairment. As mentioned, activity is essential for students who have disabilities, perhaps even more so than for nondisabled students, because nondisabled students routinely get the necessary activity, whereas students with physical problems may be overprotected and not

Together

afforded opportunities to be active. In general, physical education activities can be adapted in at least four ways to allow greater participation for students who have disabilities:

1. Change the way all students participate.
2. Change the way one player of each team participates.
3. Modify the equipment.
4. Make special allowances for students who have disabilities.

The following suggestions are not intended as comprehensive or a detailed program but as items to consider when attempting to modify or adapt programs for students with crippling conditions or health impairments:

1. Consider minor rule modifications of games or contests.
2. Ask the students how to adapt a game or activity. Some physical educators have had considerable success in asking the students to identify ways to modify or adapt an activity.
3. Schedule opportunities for rest. Fatigue may be a factor for students who have disabilities. The number of points required to win a game can be reduced, quarters may be shortened, or distances may be reduced.
4. Use larger balls and pieces of equipment, use lighter balls and racquets, or lower baskets.
5. Use more players on a team, reducing the individual responsibility and activity.
6. Change the way the entire class plays a game—all players on knees, sitting on the floor, using only one hand, or using scooter boards.
7. Have one person on each team assume a functional disability—using a wheelchair, crutches, or brace.
8. Create a special role for the student who has a disability and one other student on the other team, such as to hand out a baton at the end of a relay or catch a basketball after a goal is made and return it to the shooter.
9. Plan a backup activity in the event that the primary activity does not work.
10. Use as many activities as possible that the student with disabilities can do.

We are not advocating that activities be modified every day; daily modification may not provide the activity needed by nondisabled students. We are suggesting, however, that attempts be made to meet the needs of *all* students.

Participation in a regular physical education program can have many benefits and should be encouraged as much as possible. Regular physical education, however, should not preclude physical therapy provided by a physical therapist or individualized or adapted physical education provided by a specialist. We strongly encourage regular physical educators to consult with adaptive specialists, special education resources, or itinerant teachers for additional suggestions.

Resources Outside Schools

The families of students with orthopedic or chronic health impairments may need financial assistance, medical services, or social support systems. While it is not the role of classroom teachers to become or take the place of social workers or counselors, it may be helpful for classroom teachers to provide parents with information regarding services available to them. Teachers often have considerable contact with the parents and therefore know about their particular needs. Unusual financial needs may relate to costs of continued treatment, equipment, or transportation. In addition, families may need information regarding medical management of specific conditions. Social support systems address the issues of counseling, support groups, and recreational opportunities. Prior to contacting any source for assistance, teachers should be sure the family needs the assistance and that *the family is willing to use the resource*.

Resources available to assist families may be at the local, regional, state, or national level. Usually, it is best to begin at the local level; however, the resources may not be available locally, so regional, state, and national resources must often be contacted. Local resources for financial aid include various clubs, such as Lions, Rotary, and VFW; church groups; and businesses. Regional sources (a county or counties) include farm bureaus, clubs such as the Masons, and foundations. State and national resources include Shriners' hospitals, Services for Children with Handicaps, the March of Dimes, the Arthritis Association, and the National Kidney Association.

Resources for medical care at the local level include physicians, nurses, hospitals, and school health services. Regional resources include clinics, specialists, and community (usually county) health services. State and national resources include children's hospitals, university hospitals, and special-purpose clinics.

Social support groups at the local level may include counselors, clergy, church groups, and social service groups such as the Boy or Girl Scouts and Boy's or Girl's Clubs. Many national groups have local chapters that can provide information about local support groups. Regional sources that provide support or information include mental health centers,

county social services, and specialty camps. State or national organizations that provide support or information include United Cerebral Palsy, the Easter Seal Society, and the Association for the Aid of Crippled Children. (See Appendix B for a list of national organizations.) School nurses, public health nurses, referral agencies, clearinghouses, consultants, and social workers are other sources that can provide information about additional resources in a particular locality.

Resources such as those just described can also provide information to teachers about specific conditions and recommended practices. Although this text addresses many of the conditions students may experience, it is not all inclusive. It is the responsibility of professional teachers to continue to gain insights and information regarding the students who are in their classrooms.

■ Summary

Legislation and advocacy in the last few decades have brought about the inclusion of increasing numbers of students with orthopedic impairments. In addition, students with medically complex and fragile conditions are also being appropriately served in regular schools.

As is the case with other disabling conditions, effective communication may be the key to a successful learning experience for these students. The regular classroom teacher may be the crucial element in communication among the parents, therapists, medical personnel, and resource personnel. The teacher also may be in the best position to observe the effects of therapy, medication, diet, and activity and their influence on the student's behavior and growth. Often the teacher has the opportunity to observe the student in a different setting and for a longer period of time than parents or medical personnel, and should immediately communicate with the parents whenever observing a marked change in behavior.

Modification and adaptation may be minimal for a student with an orthopedic or health impairment who attends a regular classroom. In this chapter, we offered suggestions that will be helpful to all involved. Perhaps the most important factor for the regular classroom teacher to understand is the influence of his or her attitude on the attitudes of students, disabled and nondisabled alike. The following adage indicates the need for an objective and sensitive attitude:

What you think of me,
I will think of me,
What I think of me,
Will be me.

When those who daily interact with an individual perceive that individual in a negative way, that perception may be internalized as "fact." If others in the immediate environment—teachers, parents, siblings, and friends—see the individual in a positive way, the individual will probably see herself or himself in this way. Our goal for students with disabilities is that they should see themselves first and foremost as valuable individuals with many abilities, and only incidentally as persons with disabilities.

chapter 9

- What is adaptive behavior? Why is it essential in consideration of mental retardation? Why is it difficult to measure?

- How can one differentiate between academic retardation without mental retardation and academic retardation associated with mental retardation?

- How do individuals with mental retardation differ from their peers who have normal mental abilities with respect to memory abilities and deficits?

- What can be done to correct or adjust for the potential bias in tests of intelligence?

- How does career education differ from vocational education? Why is it essential for students with mental retardation?

- Which environmental influences may have the greatest negative effects on intellectual development?

- How might a referral for suspected mental retardation lead to a permanent negative result? How can educators minimize the chance that this will occur?

Teaching Students with Mental Retardation

■■■■■■■■■■■■

Since the beginnings of recorded history, persons with mental retardation have been sometimes feared, sometimes ridiculed, and almost always misunderstood. Their treatment has varied according to the knowledge, perceptions, and biases of various societies and historic times. Individuals recognized as mentally retarded (called variously fools, morons, imbeciles, idiots, and the like) were primarily those with more profound levels of mental retardation. Those with more mild levels were not considered part of this group, but were more often just regarded as "slow" or "slow learners."

Today we know that many students with mild levels of mental retardation disappear into the mainstream of adult society after completion of formal education. When aided and served through appropriate programs, the percentage who become self-supporting, responsible citizens increases, and all of society benefits. As for most individuals with more severe levels of mental retardation, truly normal participation in society is unlikely, but they may become partially self-supporting. However, this goal can be achieved only if society provides the right opportunities during their formative years and monitors their work and living environments during their adult years.

Since the early 1970s, there have been many changes in the ways in which individuals with mental retardation have been educated. Before that time, most of the children who were then called *educable mentally retarded* were in separate special classes in the public schools, and many of the children who were more severely retarded were housed and educated, to some extent, in large residential facilities. Today, with many of the residential facilities closed and large numbers of individuals deinstitutionalized, more individuals with greater degrees of mental retardation are in local communities. Most of the separate special classes for children with mild mental retardation have been abandoned in favor of more integrated settings.

The main reason for abandoning most special class programs for students with mental retardation was that investigators could not prove that separate special classes were superior to regular classes (Dunn, 1968; Goldstein, Moss, & Jordan, 1965). Along with concerns about stigma and social development, this lack of proof concerning special classes played a significant role in the advent of mainstreaming and the development of the philosophy of inclusion.

Other investigations of programs for the mentally retarded (Semmel, Gottlieb, & Robinson, 1979; Leinhardt & Pallay, 1982; Saint-Laurent, Fournier, & Lessard, 1993) have supported the earlier conclusions of Dunn, and Goldstein, Moss, and Jordan. Today it seems clear that much of the daily educational program for students with mental retardation can be successfully provided in the regular classroom. It seems equally clear that some students with mental retardation will need resource room assistance at some time during their school years, and that all will need to have individualized programs, whether in the regular classroom or another setting.

■■■■■■■■■■■■

■■ Defining Mental Retardation

Definitions of mental retardation have evolved over the years from those primarily reflecting IQ to those rejecting IQ-only definitions and requiring both IQ-related criteria ("subaverage general intellectual functioning") and concurrent/related limitations in adaptive skills (self-care, social skills, health and safety related skills, etc.). In addition, newer definitions specify that for a diagnosis of mental retardation, these characteristics must have been "manifested during the developmental period," generally meaning before age 18. The federal government's definition states, "Mental retardation means significantly subaverage general intellectual functioning existing concurrently with deficits in adaptive behavior and manifested during the developmental period that adversely affects a child's educational performance" (34 CFR, 300.7[5], 1993).

Definitions supported by such groups as the American Psychiatric Association and the World Health Organization are similar, and in general, advocate the use of four "levels" of mental retardation: *mild* (IQ of 50–55 to 70–75); *moderate* (IQ of 35–40 to 50–55); *severe* (IQ of 20–25 to 35–40); and *profound* (IQ below 20–25). In practice, the two lower levels are often combined, and called *severe/profound*. The latest definition advocated by the American Association on Mental Retardation (AAMR, 1992) is quite similar, but rejects these classifications. It also specifies "assumptions essential to application of the definition":

Mental retardation refers to substantial limitations in present functioning. It is characterized by significantly subaverage intellectual functioning, existing concurrently with related limitations in two or more of the following applicable adaptive skill areas: communication, self-care, home living,

social skills, community use, self-direction, health and safety, functional academics, leisure, and work. Mental retardation manifests before age 18. The following four assumptions are essential to the application of the definition:

1. Valid assessment considers cultural and linguistic diversity as well as differences in communication and behavioral factors;
2. The existence of limitations in adaptive skills occurs within the context of community environments typical of the individual's age peers and is indexed to the person's individualized needs for supports;
3. Specific adaptive limitations often coexist with strengths in other adaptive skills or other personal capabilities; and
4. With appropriate supports over a sustained period, the life functioning of the person with mental retardation will generally improve. (p. 5)

In the following section, we outline the diagnosis and classification system related to this definition. Its emphasis is the type of support systems required to maximize the development of individuals with mental retardation. While not using the mild, moderate, severe, profound classifications, it does retain the approximate 70 to 75 IQ as an upper boundary for identification as mentally retarded.

■■ Diagnosis, Classification, and Systems of Supports

In the AAMR system, diagnosis strictly follows the definition. An individual is diagnosed (educators might more likely say identified) as having mental retardation. If his or her IQ is approximately 70 to 75 or below, there are significant disabilities in two or more adaptive skill areas, and the age of onset is below 18. In later sections of this chapter, we will say more about IQ and adaptive skills assessment.

Observation and imitation play a role in social skill development.

Following identification, assessment personnel determine the individual's strengths and weaknesses in reference to psychological/emotional considerations, physical health, and environmental needs. Based on this information, a profile of needed supports is developed, across the dimensions of (a) intellectual functioning and adaptive skills, (b) psychological/emotional considerations, (c) physical health/etiology, and (d) environmental considerations.

Finally, based on this four-dimensional profile, the individual's "Intensity of Needed Supports" is determined. These intensities of supports, from least to greatest, are called intermittent, limited, extensive, and pervasive. Intermittent means support "as needed," and may, for example, relate to episodic short-term support (i.e., in times of acute medical crises or following job loss). Limited supports are characterized by consistency over time, but are not as costly or involved as are the levels of greater intensity. Extensive supports are long-term supports, in at least some environ-

ments, and those needed regularly, for example, daily. Pervasive supports are those that must be constant, across all environments, and potentially life sustaining in nature.

The 1992 AAMR definition and classification system was intended to focus attention on the strengths and weaknesses of individuals and their need for support in various environments. Their previous definition, still in use in some agencies and schools, used the terms mild, moderate, severe, and profound, as described previously. These terms, often related almost exclusively to IQ levels, in too many cases led to service providers overlooking the variability in needs (level of supports) in various environments. According to AAMR, the purpose of their three-step system of definition, classification, and systems of supports is "to provide a detailed description of the individual and his or her needed supports, . . . recognition of all separate areas of need that may require intervention [and] their interdependence" (1992, p. 34). It is hoped that the application of this system may reinforce the concept that individuals do not simply have "moderate" or "profound" mental retardation, but rather may have quite variable adaptive skill needs, requiring varied levels of support. This may increase the chances that educators and service providers will focus on their environment, and the manner in which environmental placement and interventions can enhance their personal lives.

Prior to the 1992 AAMR recommendations, systems based on IQ ranges prevailed. However, the IQ level at which mental retardation "begins" has changed over the years. This has led some to wonder how to determine the existence of "real" mental retardation. With respect to this question, and following their extensive discussion of various definitions, Beirne-Smith, Patton, and Ittenbach (1994) comment that "the lesson is that . . . the definition of mental retardation is totally a social and political one that rests with the powers that be, and not in the minds of the people who experience intellectual deficits" (p. 78).

Developmental Disabilities

The term *developmental disabilities* is often associated with mental retardation, and the two terms may at times be used interchangeably. Developmental disabilities was defined in federal legislation as a mental *or* physical impairment, resulting in substantial functional limitations in three or more major life areas. In addition, it is generally defined as a condition manifested before age 22. Therefore, the condition of an individual with mental retardation might be included under the term developmental disabilities, or in some cases (for example, when limitations are in only two areas), might not. The individual with developmental disabilities might have severe physical impairments and no mental retardation. The two terms, and the condi-

tions they reflect, often overlap, but the terms are not synonymous.

■ Implications of the Work of Piaget, Inhelder, Luria, and Vygotsky

The AAMR definition, or some similar definition and related identification and classification system, is essential to identify and plan for individuals with mental retardation, but as one of our students once asked, "What is mental retardation—really?" Unfortunately, there is no simple answer, but a discussion of the views of such developmental theorists as Piaget, Inhelder, Vygotsky, and Luria may provide additional insight.[1]

The work of Piaget, whose developmental theories have profoundly influenced education, has been interpreted by Inhelder (1968), in relation to individuals with mental retardation. Piaget believed that cognitive development (of normal individuals) progresses through predictable stages in a predictable order. These stages of development for normal individuals, with approximate related age norms are as follows:

1. Sensorimotor—birth to 2 years
2. Preoperational—2 to 7 years
3. Concrete operations—7 to 11 years
4. Formal or abstract operations—11 years and older

---

[1]The following descriptions of the views of Piaget, Inhelder, Vygotsky, and Luria are very brief and do not do justice to the theories they developed. A more lengthy description would not be appropriate to this text, but readers who intend to work with students with mental retardation may wish to further explore the work of these theorists.

Inhelder, applying Piagetian theory, believed that the child who has mental retardation progresses through the same stages as children with normal mental ability, in the same order, but at a different rate. The greater the mental retardation, the slower the rate of progression. Inhelder also believed that individuals with mental retardation may not achieve all stages of development, and predicted there would likely be levels beyond which individuals will not progress. Inhelder's predictions were based on earlier, IQ-related classification systems of mental retardation, but in effect, stated that those with the greatest degree of mental retardation would remain at Piaget's sensorimotor level, while those with the mildest degree of mental retardation would reach the concrete operations stage, but not likely go beyond. Piaget also believed that cognitive development and language are linked developmentally, and that various cognitive achievements are essential prerequisites to certain language behaviors (Long & Long, 1994).

The immediate implications of Piaget's and Inhelder's beliefs are that teachers must be fully aware of the developmental stages and be able to recognize them in a child's actions and performance, and then must plan the activities of a student with mental retardation based on their developmental readiness for a given learning task. Taken more fully, Piaget's and Inhelder's work implies that each individual would be unlikely to exceed a predictable, maximum level of development. This, however, is a dangerous assumption, for it implies that we can determine with accuracy the level of mental retardation. Teachers who make such assumptions may not have sufficiently high expectations, and thus may not provide learning tasks that allow these individuals to achieve their optimal intellectual development.

In contrast to the Piagetian point of view, Luria (1961, 1963) and Vygotsky (1962) believed that language precedes and promotes cognitive development. Luria proposed a three-stage theory describing the manner in which language controls the development of motor behavior. In stage one (0–3 years) children learn to use language to communicate, but do not use it to control their behavior. In stage two (3–4½ years) children use language in relation to motor behavior (to support or prevent their own actions or behaviors), but not to communicate meaning to someone else. This might include, for example, saying "no, no" as they restrain themselves from touching some breakable object, or an electric cord, which they have been told not to touch. They are "talking to themselves," and might use any of various words, such as "bad, bad" or "pow, pow" in the preceding example. The true meaning of the words (to others) may not be important; in fact, children may use almost any word(s) with the same result.

In stage three (4½ years and beyond), the true meaning of the language used directs behavior. For example, children might say aloud, "That's alright to do," or "I better wait to touch that," with respect to various actions they are considering. They can then develop the ability to use language to direct their actions, and their thinking processes.

Luria (1963) suggests that children with mental retardation suffer from deficits in verbal mediation ability, due to separation of neurological systems that should be working together. Their development is arrested at the second stage of the three-stage model, and they therefore have great difficulty in "talking themselves through" more involved problem solving. If language has the lead role in the development of cognitive ability, and if their language development is arrested at the second stage, this would seem to explain some of the difficulties experienced by students with mental retardation.

One facet of Vygotsky's theories provides direct support for the belief that individuals with mental retardation should be integrated with other, nonretarded individuals to the maximum extent practical in existing structures.

Vygotsky (1962) was convinced that individuals and society are interactive components of the system in which we live, and that it is of little value to study the individual without at the same time studying his or her environment. He further believed that social contacts facilitate cognitive development in two ways: (a) interacting with others permits sharing and practicing cognitive processes, through which those with less experience and ability can modify their current performance; and (b) in joint activities, more advanced peers or adults take on the role of metacognitive control and monitoring, helping the less experienced (or those with mental retardation) learn how to learn. Thus, in addition to those values that are more often mentioned with respect to integration of individuals with mental retardation—growth in social skills—this social contact may also provide growth in cognitive abilities.

The developmental theories of Piaget, Vygotsky, Luria, and others who have researched and interpreted these theories, have many implications. Because of the wide range of abilities and competencies of individuals with mental retardation, not all implications are pertinent in all cases. On the other hand, teachers should make an effort to carefully consider these theories, and when their application achieves positive results, they should apply them and evaluate them further.

■■ Assessment of Intelligence

For the past 100 years, all major definitions of mental retardation have included that the individual in question must exhibit subaverage intelligence. Other requirements have been added, such as deficits in adaptive behavior, but the one factor that is a *must* is subaverage intelligence, although how *much* below average has varied over the years. For example, several years ago, when working with pro-

grams for the mentally retarded in two adjacent states, we found that students who were mentally retarded in one state could regularly do much better in all academic subjects than students in the other state. One state used an IQ ceiling of 85, the other an IQ ceiling of 70. Moving across a state boundary could "cure" mental retardation. This variation is not surprising, considering that the AAMR has made the following changes, implemented when publishing new editions of its manual on terminology and classification:

1. In 1959, the IQ ceiling for identification was established at one standard deviation below the mean (approximate IQ of 85 or below).
2. In 1973, the IQ ceiling standard was lowered to two standard deviations below the mean (approximate IQ of 70 or below), omitting the borderline level of mental retardation (an IQ of about 70 to 85).
3. In 1983, the IQ ceiling standard remained two standard deviations below the mean, but the manual indicated that the ceiling might be raised to approximately 75 in individual cases, based on clinical judgment.

This is not to belittle either state education agencies or the AAMR. The fact is that the upper level established for identification as mentally retarded is, and always will be, arbitrary. The AAMR requirement (instituted in 1959) that individuals have *both* below-average IQ and specific deficits in adaptive behavior was a significant step in the right direction. Prior to that time most students were identified as mentally retarded and placed in special programs based on IQ test results alone, leading to some serious errors, especially with respect to minority students, and students from very deprived home environments.

So what is intelligence? An early description by Alfred Binet, who developed the first reasonably valid and reliable individual IQ test in 1905, stated that *intelligence* is a group of abilities, including good sense, initiative, judgment, and the ability to adjust to changes in environment (Venn, 1994). Wechsler, who developed the other individual tests of intelligence in most common use (which we briefly describe in the next section), believes that ability to adjust to changes in environment is a major indicator of intelligence, but also emphasizes ability to act purposefully. Wechsler views intelligence as a more global ability, as opposed to a group of abilities. The following description of the Wechsler Intelligence Scale for Children—Third Edition (WISC-III), is of value in understanding the tasks that test developers believe will indicate an individual's level of intelligence. In Chapter 12 we further discuss this and other tests of intelligence.

General Description of the WISC-III

The WISC-III has two major sections; the verbal scale and the performance scale.

Verbal Scale
(students answer questions which are asked verbally)

Subtest	Description
General information	Questions requiring factual knowledge, including those that relate to general life experience and those reflecting formal education
General comprehension	Problem situations whose solutions require the ability to evaluate past experiences
Arithmetic	Practical arithmetic problems
Similarities	Identifying similarities or commonalities of word pairs
Vocabulary	Defining or describing the meaning of words in a list of increasing difficulty
Digit span (supplementary)	An "alternative test" that may be substituted for others, involving immediate recall of orally presented digits

Performance Scale
(requires visual reasoning and fine motor skills)

Subtest	Description
Picture completion	Identifying missing elements in pictures; may test ability to differentiate essential and nonessential
Picture arrangement	Placing picture parts in sequence so as to "tell a story"; may test knowledge of social situations and understanding of logical sequence of events
Block design	Copying designs through block arrangement; may assess ability to analyze and synthesize
Object assembly	Assembly of puzzle pieces; provides opportunity to observe student's task approach and reaction to mistakes
Coding	Matching symbols by reference to a code
Mazes (supplementary)	"Finding the way out" of a maze; may indicate planning ability
Symbol search (supplementary)	Searching for/identifying a target symbol in a search group

Assessment of Adaptive Behavior/Skills

After many years of using the term *adaptive behavior* in the definition of mental retardation, the AAMR 1992 definition changed the terminology to *adaptive skills*. The definition requires a limitation in two or more adaptive skill areas: communication, self-care, home living, social skills, community use, self-direction, health and safety, functional academics, leisure, and work. This change, according to the AAMR manual, is not intended to refute the previous term, but is in part a response to the charge that it has been too conceptually tied to the content of existing, commercial adaptive behavior scales. The AAMR suggests the use of multiple assessment techniques, including assessment scales completed by (at least two) third-person raters, further interviews with service raters, self-reports of adaptive skills, and existing tests of adaptive behavior. The manual's authors note that the development of additional measures is essential for the current (1992) definition to be fully and properly operationalized.

Despite potential shortcomings of existing tests of adaptive behavior, we believe an outline of the domains included in such tests will assist the reader to better understand the nature of adaptive skills and behavior. Figure 9–1 outlines the domains of the AAMR Adaptive Behavior Scales—School (second edition) (Nihira, Lambert, & Leland, 1992).

Beirne-Smith et al. (1994, pp. 118–135) review the major issues relating to the use of adaptive behavior measures in identification of mental retardation. They note, for example, that adaptive behaviors may be less a function of the person than of the social unit to which they belong. They believe that "while experts in the field appear to have reached relative

agreement on the definition of adaptive behavior, and perhaps even on the skills that are believed to comprise it, the actual components of effective adaptive functioning remain much more puzzling" (p. 123). They further note that although adaptive behavior "has emerged as an important index in identification of mental retardation, in practice, its usage has been limited because of its imprecision" (p. 133).

What then, may educators conclude about adaptive behavior and its importance as a concept in mental retardation? Polloway, Payne, Patton, and Payne (1985) note a historical emphasis on social concerns in both defining and understanding mental retardation. However, they say, "throughout the middle of the 20th century the emphasis moved toward intellectual and academic factors. The increased reliance on intelligence in defining retardation is an example of how the initial concept of social incompetence was replaced by one of intellectual subnormality" (p. 365). They do not suggest a shift to some exclusive personal–social focus but remind teachers that "a total emphasis on academics can lead to isolated teaching of the 3 Rs with no relevance for the real world" (pp. 365–366).

We believe this point of view to be of great importance. Personal–social skills alone have limited value. Academic skills alone have limited value. Students with mental retardation require both if they are to function with maximum effectiveness as adults. Students with mental retardation will not learn personal–social skills as readily as other students; thus, they require specific instruction. This instruction, however, must be individualized, just as academic instruction must be individualized. Fortunately, the past decade has witnessed a resurgence in interest in the teaching of personal–social skills, and special education resource personnel should be able to provide specific suggestions for specific needs at specific age levels.

Part One (addresses coping skills and personal independence: an examination of extent of positive behaviors)

Domain 1: Independent Functioning. Pertains to eating, toileting, appearance, care of clothing, dressing and undressing, use of public facilities (emphasizing travel).

Domain 2: Physical Development. Relates to both sensory and motor development.

Domain 3: Economic Activity. Relates to money handling, shopping, and general financial management.

Domain 4: Language Development. Examines expression, comprehension, and social language abilities.

Domain 5: Numbers and Time. Assesses basic mathematical competencies.

Domain 6: Prevocational/Vocational Activity. Examines ability to function in settings essential to successful job or school performance.

Domain 7: Responsibility. Examines the individual's ability to be accountable for actions, belongings, and duties.

Domain 8: Self-Direction. Examines the extent to which an individual is active or passive in lifestyle.

Domain 9: Socialization. Examines ability to successfully interact with others.

Part Two (addresses social adaptative and maladaptive behavior: an examination of behaviors which might negatively influence successful integration and normalization)

Part Two includes seven areas (domains):

Domain 1: Violent and antisocial (physically or emotionally abusive) behavior

Domain 2: Rebellious behavior

Domain 3: Untrustworthy (stealing, lying, cheating) behavior

Domain 4: Stereotyped and hyperactive behavior

Domain 5: Eccentric (bizarre) behavior

Domain 6: Withdrawal

Domain 7: Disturbed (annoying personal) behavior

Figure 9–1
AAMR Adaptive Behavior Scales—School (second edition)

A Note Regarding Terminology

As discussed earlier in the chapter, the 1992 AAMR definition implemented a change in classification of levels of mental retardation from mild, moderate, severe, and profound, to mental retardation with need for intermittent, limited, extensive, or pervasive support. For the remainder of this chapter, we will sometimes consider the needs of individuals with mental retardation with respect to different levels of mental retardation. Because any research we may cite, or instructional suggestions, made as a result of demonstrated success with individuals with mental retardation, will relate to the classification terminology in use for the past many years, we will employ the former terms. If we were to cite research conducted with students with "mild," "moderate," "severe," or "profound" mental retardation, and arbitrarily interchange terminology, we would be doing exactly what the discussion accompanying the 1992 definition said we should not do.

Characteristics of Mental Retardation

The following discussion of characteristics should provide a general or global view of mental retardation, but it must be remembered that not all individuals with mental retardation will display all of these characteristics. If accepted definitions and identification procedures are used in verifying the existence of mental retardation, individuals will exhibit some of the characteristics associated with below-average mental ability, and some deficits in some adaptive behavior/skills, with considerable variation in the types of behavior and degree of deficit. It is also important to

note that with milder forms of mental retardation, deficits or differences in behavior or cognitive ability may be such that they will not be noticed until the child enters the school setting. He or she will then be asked to complete tasks requiring cognitive ability, and will be daily compared with other children of about the same age. Children with more severe degrees of mental retardation will usually be recognized at a much earlier age.

The following summary will follow the categories of characteristics suggested by Bierne-

Learning by doing

Smith et al. (1994): demographic; motivational and sociobehavioral; learning; speech and language; and physical health.

Demographic Characteristics

- More males than females are identified as having mental retardation, especially the milder levels of mental retardation. Such gender differences have been reported ever since such studies were initiated, and are verified in more recent studies (Wagner, Newman, & Shaver, 1989). This difference is not as evident with respect to individuals with more severe levels of mental retardation.
- A disproportionate number of nonwhite and ethnic minority children have been labeled mentally retarded since at least the 1960s (Bierne-Smith et al., 1994). This fact was the major focus of much of the early litigation cited in Chapter 1.
- There is a higher prevalence of milder forms of mental retardation among children from low income/lower socioeconomic level families. This has been recognized by the AAMR by its inclusion of environmental influences and "psychosocial disadvantage" as etiological classifications (potential causes) of mental retardation.

Motivational and Sociobehavioral Characteristics

- Individuals with mental retardation are more likely than those in the general population to be undermotivated, and may expect to fail. They may also be more likely to rely on situational cues or external forces for guidance in problem solving; a behavior sometimes called *outerdirectedness* (Bybee & Zigler, 1992). These characteristics apply to some extent to all levels of mental retardation.

- Children, adolescents, and adults with more severe levels of mental retardation are more likely to exhibit social and behavioral problems than those with more mild levels of mental retardation.

Learning Characteristics

Learning characteristics might be summarized by stating that individuals with mental retardation learn more slowly and inefficiently than their nondisabled peers. This difference applies to most types of learning, but is particularly notable with respect to what is often called academic learning, and/or learning through the interpretation of symbols (i.e., reading). The following learning processes are more likely to be a problem with individuals with mental retardation.

- Memory, especially short-term memory, may be an area of particular difficulty (Borkowski, Peck, & Damberg, 1983; Ellis, 1970). Long-term memory may approach normal.
- Ability to generalize and apply previous learning to new situations may be less than normal for age (Polloway & Patton, 1993).
- Executive control and metacognition (ability to consciously think through a problem, plan how to solve it, and monitor progress) may not be spontaneously employed (Sternberg & Spear, 1985).

Speech and Language Characteristics

Speech and language problems are a predictable characteristic, given the accepted correlation between language development and cognitive ability (Bierne-Smith et al., 1994). Below-average levels of language development may be related to many other factors; hearing impairments, learning disabilities, or lack of opportunity to develop language due to environmental factors, but students with mental retardation almost always exhibit below-average (for age) language ability. Exceptions to this generalization are students with milder levels of mental retardation who may enter school with near-normal language ability. In such cases, it will usually become lower than that of the normal peer group over a period of time.

Physical Health Characteristics

- The physical health of individuals with milder levels of mental retardation will not likely be much different from that of the general population; however, physical health problems are much more likely among those with more severe mental retardation. For example, individuals with Down syndrome, the most common clinical cause of mental retardation (Manfredini, 1988), often have congenital lung or heart defects, and tend to have respiratory infections, obesity, and hearing impairments. Other clinical types of mental retardation may also have related physical disorders.

- The physical appearance of many students with mild levels of mental retardation is little different from that of the general population. There is, however, a general tendency toward less developed motor skills.

- The physical appearance of students with more severe levels of mental retardation may be quite different from the general population. The most commonly recognized example is Down syndrome, in which the student will more often be short in stature, and have a flat, broad face, small nose and ears, short, broad hands, upward slanting eyes, and a protruding tongue. Students whose mental retardation relates to other genetic disorders or chromosomal deviations will also often exhibit unique appearance characteristics.

 ## Educational Programs for Students with Mental Retardation

The Board of Directors of the Division of Mental Retardation and Developmental Disabilities of the Council for Exceptional Children approved a statement on program design for students with mental retardation that "affirms the importance of what students need to learn within and outside the school setting as the basis for determining curriculum and instruction for the individual" (MRDD, 15 April 1992). In this statement, the board reaffirms the need for "specialized programs, such as community-based instruction, [which] may take precedence from time to time, particularly at the secondary level." In a discussion and amplification of this statement, Smith and Hilton (1994) note that "program design for students with mental retardation should be based on the unique attributes of each student, which should be reflected in the student's individual educational program (IEP). Program decisions should never be based on clinical labels, needs of the school, needs of teachers, or needs of parents" (p. 4).

The regular classroom teacher may be responsible for a major part of the educational program, particularly with students with milder levels of mental retardation, and must carefully attend to the information included in the student's IEP. If guidelines are unclear, special educators should be asked for clarification. However, within these guidelines, there will always be a great deal of leeway for individual initiative on the part of the teacher.

In the lower grades, many students may continue to make satisfactory progress in many aspects of their program. They may require individual help in the resource room, in their development of basic reading and number skills, and the regular classroom teacher and special educator can collaboratively determine the most effective approaches to use in the regular class. When students continue to have significant academic difficulties, there is a growing discrepancy between their level of achievement and that of their age peers. The use of high-interest, low-vocabulary level materials permits the teaching of many essential concepts, but some additional curriculum modification becomes inevitable if education is to remain meaningful. For some students, the program should emphasize social skills, habits, attitudes, and the understandings that will later maximize the ability of the student to obtain and keep employment. Students at the secondary level may have less involvement in regularly structured, regular class programs.

Students with more severe levels of mental retardation will require a more radically modified educational program. Learning social skills in interactions with nondisabled peers remains of value, but Beirne-Smith et al. (1994) indicate that to provide individuals at this level of mental retardation the best opportunity to enjoy a satisfactory adult life, their curriculum must emphasize: (a) functional activities, (b) community-referenced activities, and (c) age-appropriate activities. In brief, this means activities that the student must do, or have someone do for him (practical, essential to everyday functioning), activities required or common to life in the home in which the individual lives and the community in which she now functions or will likely function in the future, and activities that "fit" the individual's chronological age (*not* activities that are generally associated with much younger individuals). As examples of inappropriate, nonfunctional activities for a 17-year-old individual with severe mental retardation, they cite putting pegs in pegboards, matching shapes and colors, stringing beads, and completing

worksheets. As an example of age-inappropriate activity they cite adolescents or adults putting together Big Bird puzzles. They believe that instruction must be developed to enhance the individual's probable future success in the vocational, domestic living, community living, and recreation/leisure domains.

When students functioning at this level of mental retardation are in the regular classroom, the teacher must depend on guidelines provided in the IEP, and insights gained through conferences with special educators who also work with the student. Social goals will assume major importance. However, as individual decisions about instructional alternatives must be made, *functionality* is the key concept.

A variety of supportive services should be available to regular classroom teachers as they collaborate with special educators in providing an appropriate educational program for students with mental retardation. Although the purpose of this text is to assist regular classroom teachers as they teach exceptional children, we urge them to be aware of the need for special assistance, to be certain that such needs are reflected on the IEP, and to demand such assistance, as required by IDEA and state regulations. To do less would contradict both the spirit and the letter of the law, as well as what we know about the needs of students with disabilities.

Career Education

In 1974, the Office of Career Education was established within the U.S. Office of Education. Its purpose was to promote national awareness of the need for career education for all students. Kokaska and Brolin (1985) note that one of the major problems experienced with this terminology has been that too many educators have tended to consider *career* as synonymous with *occupation*, which is inaccurate. They indicate, "Career education is the process of systematically coordinating all school, family, and community components together to facilitate each individual's potential for economic, social, and personal fulfillment and participation in productive work activities that benefit the individual or others" (p. 43). They further note, "Career education does not de-emphasize the fundamentals. Rather, it brings meaning to the curriculum by making individuals more aware of themselves, their potentials, and their educational needs" (p. 43).

In 1976, in recognition of the importance of the concept of career education for individuals with disabilities, the Council for Exceptional Children established a new division, the Division on Career Development (DCD). Since that time, special educators have evolved various curriculum models to guide the development of career education efforts for students with disabling conditions. One of the leading advocates of career education for students with disabling conditions, Donn Brolin began the development of the Life-Centered Career Education (LCCE) model in the early 1970s. Figure 9–2 presents the competencies targeted in the 1993 LCCE model. The LCCE model is referenced by many other authors, and apparently, it is widely accepted for its provision of 22 major competencies and 97 subcompetencies. It is obvious that to achieve these competencies, close cooperation must be maintained among the school, the family, and the community.

White and Biller (1988) note that there are two major ways to approach planning for career education programming. These are: (a) separate content—perhaps a short unit to teach such competencies as money skills and check writing—or (b) infusion—that is, integrating career education concepts with other subject matter. They suggest that either approach has certain merits, but that a combination of the two may be best. Factors such as

severity of disabling condition and age or grade level tend to favor one approach over the other. Whatever the approach they use, most educators agree that all students need some degree of career education, and special educators feel that students with disabling conditions have a particularly critical need. Educators also agree that unless the curriculum is specifically planned, important aspects may be missing from it. Regular class teachers should be aware of this emphasis and provide for development of career-related skills and understandings whenever possible.

The career education concept is particularly applicable to students with mental retardation, and was given additional emphasis in 1990, with the passage of IDEA, as a result of the specific requirement for transition planning. We discuss transition planning for individuals with mental retardation in the following section.

Planning for Successful Transitions

Transition planning is a required part of the IEP (mandatory at age 16, desirable at younger ages in specific cases), and to some extent had been a part of long-range planning for students with mental retardation long before it was mandated by IDEA. For example, the LCCE program developed by Brolin, noted in the preceding section, was first published in 1978. With its emphasis on daily living skills, personal-social skills, and occupational guidance and preparation, it is clearly oriented toward easing the transition from school to home, community settings, and the workplace. However, transition planning requires more than the LCCE emphasis. Bierne-Smith et al. (1994) emphasize the potential need for linkages with various other community agencies, to provide needed, ongoing support services. This might include short-term services, such as postsecondary

Figure 9–2
The Life-Centered Career Education Curriculum (LCCE)*

Daily Living Skills Domain
1. Managing personal finances
2. Selecting and managing a household
3. Caring for personal needs
4. Raising children and meeting marriage responsibilities
5. Buying, preparing, and consuming food
6. Buying and caring for clothing
7. Exhibiting responsible citizenship
8. Utilizing recreational facilities and engaging in leisure
9. Getting around the community

Personal-Social Skills Domain
10. Achieving self-awareness
11. Acquiring self-confidence
12. Achieving socially responsible behavior
13. Maintaining good interpersonal skills
14. Achieving independence
15. Making adequate decisions
16. Communicating with others

Occupational Guidance and Preparation Domain
17. Knowing and exploring occupational possibilities
18. Selecting and planning occupational choices
19. Exhibiting appropriate work habits and behavior
20. Seeking, securing and maintaining employment
21. Exhibiting sufficient physical-manual skills
22. Obtaining specific occupational skills

* These 22 competencies are targeted in the LCCE curriculum. The complete LCCE training package includes lesson plans, assessment batteries, a videotaped training program for teachers, and other related materials.

vocational training or assistance from vocational rehabilitation, or ongoing services such as various kinds of support in employment. Their emphasis, and the emphasis of most discussions of transition planning is this school-to-postschool life planning. On the other hand, Gearheart et al. (1993) note the possible need for systematic planning for (a) transition (for very young children) from parental care to care by others, (b) transition between school levels, (c) transition between special and regular class, and (d) transition from school to community integration. Planning at each of these levels may be of great importance to certain students with mental retardation.

Although most planning for specific transitional emphases will involve special educators to a much greater extent than the regular classroom teacher, it is important for the regular classroom teacher to understand the need for such efforts. One of the major goals of transition planning is some type of employment following completion of the formal public school program. We discuss potential employment options in the following section.

■■ Adult Employment Options and Living Arrangements

Potential employment options and living arrangements must be considered at two levels. As indicated at the start of this chapter, some individuals with mild mental retardation "disappear" into the mainstream of society as adults. They are not likely to earn top-level wages, but have steady employment at economically lower- to middle-level jobs and live in homes consistent with their income.

Individuals with more severe levels of retardation will not be able to compete in the workplace (will not have "competitive" employment), and will be unable to live with complete independence in the community. However, because some type of regular work activity is highly important to personal feelings of success and self-worth, other work options have been developed, and are being continually reevaluated and improved. Descriptions of five possible employment options follows.

Competitive Employment

Competitive employment is the most desirable goal for individuals with mental retardation. This may be part-time employment, and may involve support from friends, family, or some community agency. This often involves unskilled work such as housekeeping tasks or lawn care.

Supported Employment

Supported employment, encouraged by federal legislation, involves competitive employment, an integrated work setting, and ongoing support services. Work crew programs, often supported by a local social service agency are one common means to provide supported employment, but the individual placement model is most prevalent (Test, Keul, Williams, Slaughter, & Allen, 1992). Supported employment is preferable to sheltered employment because it involves work alongside nondisabled employees and may serve as part of a preparation for transition to competitive employment (Gearheart et al., 1993).

Sheltered Employment

Sheltered employment involves work in an activity center or sheltered workshop, alongside other individuals with disabilities. Some type of training is provided, but disadvantages include tolerance of behavior that would not be permitted in higher-level employment and a tendency to keep good workers rather than attempt to move them on to less segregated levels of employment.

Unpaid Employment

Unpaid employment may be the only option for some individuals for certain time periods of their life. This may include volunteer work, which can be of value due to the employment-related skills that it helps build.

Permanent Nonemployment

Permanent nonemployment is a reality for some individuals whose need for support is so pervasive that other options will not work.

Whatever the employment option in place (if less than full, competitive employment) the goal is movement on the continuum, toward full-time, competitive employment.

Living Arrangements

Living arrangements are at least equally important to employment variables. If individuals cannot or do not live completely on their own, other possibilities include apartment living with limited support, boarding homes licensed to care for individuals with disabilities, group homes, and various versions of intermediate care facilities. One of the less restrictive settings is in apartment clusters, in arrangements which pair individuals with mental retardation with nondisabled adults (Gearheart et al., 1993).

■ Early Childhood Programs

Public Law 99–457, the 1986 amendments to the Education for All Handicapped Children Act (EHA) established the framework for providing services to pre-schoolage children at risk, or those with identified disabilities. Its focus was prevention, and it authorized programs for the birth through age 2, and the 3-through-5 populations. The eligibility requirements focused on developmental delays rather than categorical labels, and the family was a major part of targeted interventions (see the discussion of the Individual Family Service Plan (IFSP) in Chapter 2). It did, however, provide for service to children with a "diagnosed physical or mental condition which has a high probability of resulting in developmental delay" (PL 99–457, Sec. 672).

Early intervention programs for children with confirmed mental retardation, such as those with Down syndrome, have been supported, and often provided by parent groups for many years, but with the encouragement of PL 99–457, the number of programs has significantly increased. Some programs are provided directly through the public schools, and housed in the public school facilities. Others are provided by various community agencies. Whatever the arrangement, students with mental retardation, and those with other dis-

abilities, have benefited greatly. In addition, children at risk, especially those where environmental factors seem to have a major influence, are now included in a wide variety of publicly funded programs. Regular classroom teachers will become involved with various facets of such programs primarily as young children with mental retardation make the transition from such programs to kindergarten or first grade.[2] This should happen with all children in such programs who have continuing special needs, because the Individual Family Service Plan requires delineating specific steps and using them to transfer young children to services provided through IDEA, if the need for services continues. The major advantages to kindergarten or first-grade teachers are many. They will, for example, deal with parents and other family members that are already accustomed to working with professionals in program planning for their child. They will also receive information as to previous successes, and failures, in various behavioral and educationally related strategies, and the child will have had the benefit of considerable help before entrance to kindergarten or grade one. The result will be the ability to more immediately and effectively plan instruction that will benefit the child.

■ Suggestions for Regular Classroom Teachers

Before discussing instructional options and strategies, it is essential that we call attention to the variations which can exist between stu-

---

[2]In this discussion, *regular classroom teachers* means teachers of kindergarten and upward through the school system. Teachers of various early intervention programs may be employed directly by the schools, but are, in essence, special education teachers.

dents who can look alike "on paper." It is altogether too easy to classify students on the basis of their IQ and the academic difficulties supposedly generated as a result of this IQ. It is particularly important to encourage teachers to use their own considerable abilities and instincts in teaching students classified as having mental retardation.

We will illustrate the variation possible by comparing MariAnn and Susan, two 16-year-old students with mental retardation (Figure 9–3). In spite of their "on paper" similarities, with respect to IQ and educational history, these two students have quite different educational program needs. The predictable likelihood of such differences makes it imperative that educators consider students and plan programs on an *individual* basis, not on the basis of scores, labels, or classifications.

Many of the instructional strategies outlined in Chapter 3 have direct applicability to teaching students with mental retardation.

For example, peer systems (peer buddies, advocates, tutors) have been found to be effective at various age and cognitive ability levels of mental retardation. For students with milder levels of mental retardation, they may be effective in learning both academic and social skills. For older students with more severe levels of mental retardation, they may be most effective in relation to learning acceptable social skills. In all cases, they must be planned by the teacher (not just "allowed to happen") to meet identifiable instructional goals. In a similar manner, suggestions for planning to enhance motivation, and those relating to classroom management will be of value, and modeling, cueing, and providing positive reinforcement appear to be quite effective with many students with mental retardation. Various suggestions related to teaching and encouraging language development from chapters 6 and 10 may be appropriate, as will a number of other suggestions

Success experiences are important.

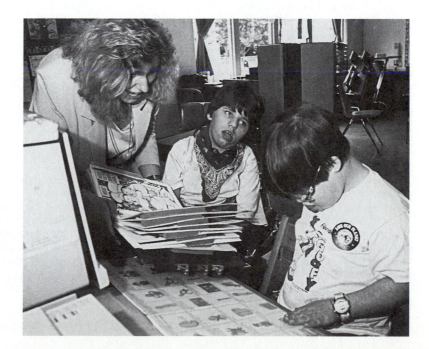

Susan
Age: 16 years
Program: first year in senior high special program, with limited enrollment in adapted regular classes
Years in school: 11
Physical health: good
Full-scale WISC–R IQ: 65

MariAnn
Age: 16 years
Program: first year in senior high special program, with limited enrollment in adapted regular classes
Years in school: 11
Physical health: good
Full-scale WISC–R IQ: 66

Based on these data, Susan and MariAnn might be expected to be relatively similar in school performance. Each was referred as a result of significant academic problems near the close of the third year in school (second grade). At that time, Susan's IQ was recorded as 62, MariAnn's as 68. Measures of adaptive behavior supported identification of both girls as educable mentally retarded. Each was placed in a special program at the start of third grade. During their elementary school years, each spent approximately 2 hours each day in a special resource room and the remainder of the day in the regular class.

Susan and MariAnn have lived in the same city throughout their 11 years of school attendance and have been in the same school and same resource room program since they moved to middle school. Other information indicates that the program quality in the two different elementary schools that they attended was essentially the same.

There are no known serious family problems in either family, and parents have been generally cooperative with school officials through the years. Both girls are from white, middle-class families.

But here the similarity ends.

Susan is reading at the upper fourth-grade level, according to standardized achievement tests. She can recognize the words included in the special program reading curriculum (relating to employment, voting, family responsibility, and practical, daily living skills), and next year will move into phase one of the work experience program with excellent preparation. She is successful in the adapted vocational education program taught by a regular class teacher and is as skilled as most other students in her school, including nondisabled students, in interpersonal relations. She has learned that she will be rejected or ignored by some students but does not make an issue of their behavior. Susan's speaking vocabulary is somewhat below that of other students her age but not notably so in most normal social situations. (This discrepancy would be noticeable if she were enrolled in some of the advanced classes in her school, but she is not.) In most respects, in the large school Susan attends, she does not appear different.

MariAnn is reading at the middle second-grade level, according to standardized achievement tests. She has difficulty in reading approximately 50% of the words included in the special program reading curriculum, and she will not likely be ready for phase one for the work experience program for at least 2 years. MariAnn experiences her greatest difficulty in the adapted vocational education program, where the teacher says, "She has difficulty reading our low vocabulary materials, but her biggest problem is understanding the concepts involved." MariAnn socializes with a few students in the special program but is not well accepted, even by many of the special program students. She has essentially no acceptance by nondisabled students. MariAnn's speaking vocabulary is very limited, and she has often attempted to become part of a conversation only to be rejected because her comments make her appear different. Even with specific suggestions from her teacher, she cannot seem to anticipate such situations.

Perhaps the most important understanding to be gained from the comparison of Susan and MariAnn is that students classified as EMR may perform very differently in regard to both academic achievement and social competence, regardless of similarity of test scores or other variables generally recognized as important. As such students progress through their educational program, projections of educational and social ability and success may become more reliable, but at ages 6, 7, and 8, predictions of future success may be inaccurate. Certain generalizations may be made based on valid test results and environmental and sociological data, but these are only generalizations. Variations in performance are undoubtedly just as great among students diagnosed as EMR as they are among the so-called normal student population.

Figure 9–3
Susan and MariAnn, two 16-year-old students

from Chapter 10, depending on a given student's age and ability level.

Counteracting Failure Expectations

Certain characteristics of individuals with mental retardation may reduce the effectiveness of learning in both classroom and social settings. One cluster of such characteristics relates to high failure expectation (due to repeated failures), a tendency to rely on external cues or instructions (often called *outerdirectedness*), and the belief that they have little control over their environment (an external locus of control). If teachers cannot help students overcome these attitudes and tendencies, the effectiveness of other instructional strategies may be greatly diminished.

Patton, Beirne-Smith, and Payne (1990) provide several suggestions for strategies to counteract these tendencies. For example, with respect to an external locus of control, instruction may deliberately associate actions with their consequences. Then, students may be taught to anticipate possible consequences, so that they choose appropriate behaviors. (Note here that most students with normal learning abilities learn this relationship in the process of daily living, *without* specific instruction. The key to effective instruction of students with mental retardation is understanding that such students often do not learn automatically from their environment as do most other students.) Another suggestion is use of a social learning contract. In such a contract, which may be established in writing or in pictures, various behaviors may be linked to possible positive, negative, or neutral outcomes.

Expectations of failure may be reduced by establishing reasonable, reachable goals and utilizing very small learning steps. A system of positive rewards for the achievement of each step can help students develop confidence in their ability to succeed and, thus, overcome the failure syndrome.

The tendency to rely on external cues may be overcome in a variety of ways that reward inner-directed behaviors. For example, a student may be taught to try to find two or three ways to solve a problem and then to try them out. Eventually, the student may generalize this approach to new situations.

Suggestions for Use in Nonclassroom Settings

Although the major concern of regular class teachers may be how to more effectively teach and manage behavior in the classroom (academic) setting, such teachers must also consider nonclass settings, like the playground, cafeteria, and hallways. These are important in the total spectrum of opportunities for learning for students with mental retardation.

Nonconforming behavior is a predictable concern for many teachers. Besides applying common sense, teachers should attempt to gain more information about the students who are of particular concern. This information may be available from the teacher who is responsible for the student for the majority of the day or from the special educator (resource room teacher or consultant). Information about management techniques that work in other settings may also be of great value here. Information about level of language, ability to understand rules, response to aggressive behavior on the part of other students, and similar aspects can be invaluable. Suggestions in Chapter 11, such as the use of reinforcers or contracts, or the principles of assertive discipline may also be helpful.

In addition to concerns about management of behavior, teachers should remember that students with mental retardation have great need for social learning, that is, learning to act in a normal manner and react to problems so as to not appear different. Commercial materials described in Chapter 11 may provide suggestions for teaching social skills, even if not used as an entire "curriculum."

Playgrounds, cafeterias, and halls are good places to learn normal behavior. Therefore, it is the responsibility of teachers to promote learning in these settings, regardless of the type of learning involved. Simply being aware of these opportunities may lead to effective use of learning situations as they develop.

Suggestions for Use in Classroom Settings

Most regular classroom teachers are concerned about meeting the unique needs of students with mental retardation in their classrooms, and apply teaching techniques and strategies that have worked for other students. However, the following suggestions, along with those provided in other chapters, may assist teachers in their ongoing attempts to maximize classroom learning.

Attend to the Possibility that Students May Not Fully Develop the Piagetian Concepts that the Average Child Appears to Learn Informally from Environmental Interaction

If mental retardation is a type of developmental delay, then students may not develop concepts such as classification, seriation, and number conservation to the degree present in age peers, and this lack of development may inhibit other learning. McCormick, Campbell, Pasnak, and Perry (1990) had considerable success in teaching concrete operational concepts to students with mild mental retardation in a relatively short period of time. Teachers may provide specific training in classification, seriation, and number conservation skills by using variations or expanded versions of the following techniques.

Classification may be taught by showing sets of objects (four or five per set) and asking the child to name the one that "does not fit." Verbal classification may be taught by following a similar procedure, except that objects are only named. Verbal teacher approval and a reward system involving points may help further motivate the students.

Seriation training may involve arranging objects in order of length, height, thickness, or some combination of these dimensions. Depending on the age and readiness of students, this process may start with three, four, or five objects, and proceed to eight or nine objects. A parallel procedure involves naming objects and asking the child to seriate them (place them in order). Repetitive reading of the objects may be necessary. Rewards provide useful motivation.

Number conservation training might involve the moving (expanding and compressing) of matched rows of items, while the student(s) watch, showing that the number in the group remains the same, unless items are added or subtracted. This training requires considerable explanation from the teacher, and questioning of students to be certain that the desired learning is taking place.

Be Aware of Skills, Information, and Concepts that Are Prerequisites to New Learning Tasks, and Do Not Attempt New Tasks Until These Prerequisites Are Part of the Learning Repertoires of the Students

It is likely that there will be gaps in skills or basic information not present with nondisabled students. These areas must be identified and when possible developed before initiating new learning tasks. In some cases, when such prerequisite learning cannot be accomplished in a reasonable amount of time, teachers must substitute assignments and establish modified goals. In any event, just as learning long division in the traditional manner requires understanding of subtraction, there are prerequisites in other subject and skill areas. In some cases, the prerequisite is a specific skill; in others, it is information; and in still others, it is a concept. Prerequisites may be particularly important in science and social studies, because most students learn many concepts in these areas in the course of daily living. However, students with mental retardation may require specific teaching, and it is important that teachers be aware of this possibility.

Be Aware of a Variety of Possible Readiness and Ability Levels, Both Across and Within Subject Areas. Modify Assignments as Necessary in Recognition of These Variations

The use of multiple reading groups at the elementary level is common, and most elementary teachers have learned to manage this instructional practice. Students with mental retardation may require adjustments for some aspects of reading instruction beyond the traditional three groups but may be able to participate in many reading group activities if other facets of their reading assignments are modified. Similar modifications may be necessary in other subject or skill areas. The nature of such modifications varies among students. Teachers must be alert to the likelihood that students may benefit from the content of group reading (what they hear other students reading) and group discussion even if their own reading ability does not permit fluent reading of the material.

At the secondary level, particularly in senior high, it is more likely that students with mental retardation are in specially scheduled class groupings, but for classes in which there is no special grouping, the same principle applies. In some schools, teachers use simplified versions of reading materials (similar concepts and content, but simplified written form). In other instances, it is a matter of maximizing the learning that can take place through group work. In all cases, if students can learn *without* modifications and adapta-

tions, this approach is most desirable. Yet, if learning without modifications is possible in most areas of the school curriculum, it is likely that the student has been misclassified.

Be Alert to Special Needs in the Abilities to Generalize and Conceptualize

Two abilities, generalization and conceptualization, are among the more significant factors in learning as measured by individual intelligence tests. Therefore, by definition, students with mental retardation have lower than average ability in these two important areas. A young student may recognize the plus sign in a mathematical equation but have difficulty understanding that the word *and* (as in "6 and 7 equals 13") has the same meaning as the plus sign. The student may understand and follow the rules governing behavior in the cafeteria line but have difficulty relating the same rules to another situation, such as the recess line. Teachers must specifically point out how one principle may apply in other academic or social situations.

Through practice with generalization and conceptual skills, students acquire repertoires of experiences that promote maximum development of these abilities. Ability to generalize and conceptualize is the basis for skills related to successful employment and participation in the adult world, but such skills are regularly overlooked or underemphasized in favor of specific facts or improvement in basic skills such as reading. It is doubtful whether, for example, an increase of 1 year in a student's basic reading level will be as important to the student as development of the ability to generalize in social situations or conceptualize the requirements of various job-related tasks. It is difficult to demonstrate that any specific area of learning is more important than any other, but generalization and conceptualization are certainly among the most important for students with below-average intellectual ability.

Create Opportunities for Verbal Expression

Students with mental retardation are often less adept at self-expression than are nondisabled students. The effects of below-average learning ability are cumulative and are readily seen when students attempt broad verbal expression. Some teachers may be concerned about negative effects on self-concept or become discouraged and thus avoid attempts to encourage students to engage in further self-expression, but teachers must use both structured, individually planned experiences and incidental opportunities to encourage students to improve language development. Language development requires experience, and students with mental retardation require more experience with language to develop a given level of language ability than do students with average or above-average intellectual ability.

Finally, if earlier school experiences and provisions have been inconsistent with the level of readiness, students may be even more retarded in language development than their intellectual level would indicate. A further complication is the effect of bilingual or bicultural influences. Teachers must be alert to provide all possible opportunities for verbal expression and general language development and to make these opportunities interesting and appropriate to the present level of development. Such opportunities are important at both the elementary and the secondary level.

Use Concrete Rather Than Abstract Examples Whenever Possible

For example, in teaching that 4 plus 3 equals 7, it would be better to ask, "How many oranges would I have if I had four oranges in this hand and three oranges in this hand?" This approach helps students visualize the situation and the adding process, making it easier to visualize the answer. The student might have much more difficulty with the question in the abstract, but after learning the process with concrete objects, the student may find it easier to learn on the abstract level. Making learning concrete also includes the principle of relating new learning to familiar experiences.

Make Maximum Use of Group Experiences as Vehicles for Learning

Good readers sometimes learn more efficiently when left alone to read new material, but students with mental retardation are more likely to benefit from oral input when learning new concepts or basic information. This does *not* mean that individualized planning and individual efforts in respect to basic skills may be overlooked or shortchanged. It means that teachers must involve students in group experiences whenever possible, especially when covering basic information or introducing new concepts.

Use a Variety of Techniques to Support or Simplify Learning Tasks

Following are several suggestions:

1. Reduce distractions in the learning environment whenever possible.
2. Provide for frequent review.
3. Simplify instructions.
4. Introduce new vocabulary words *before* making new assignments (experience indicates which words are more likely to cause difficulty—there is no rule or list of difficult words applicable to all students).
5. Assign problems in smaller clusters.
6. When practical, use peer tutors (the viability of peer tutors varies considerably from subject to subject, grade to grade, and student to student).
7. Whenever possible, use filmstrips or films to introduce broad new concepts, such as the tropics or the polar

regions, or to introduce topics such as novels or classics that the class will discuss for a considerable period of time.

8. Provide an outline of important points of reading assignments.
9. Use color coding when appropriate.
10. Use pictures and arrows on direction sheets or other written assignments.
11. Avoid true-false tests that require an understanding of language that the student may not have (otherwise, the test results reflect the language level of the student rather than actual knowledge of the subject).

These general suggestions are a brief sample of ideas that have worked with some students. Resource room specialists should be able to provide many more, including ideas that have developed out of the more individualized work taking place in the resource room. In many instances, alternate approaches are a part of the IEP or the extended ideas that grow out of the IEP. Especially in the lower grades, activities used with other students in regular class work also with only minimal modifications for students with mental retardation.

The preceding suggestions are applicable at the elementary level, and many are applicable at the secondary level, but education in regular classrooms at the secondary level remains more difficult. This greater difficulty may occur because educational retardation is cumulative—students fall farther and farther behind their peers as they go through their school program—or because secondary curriculum planners tend to assume basic reading, language, and mathematics skills when they plan course goals and content. In any event, it is likely that the secondary curriculum planned for students with mental retardation will be more separate than it is for students with most other disabling conditions.

Secondary School Programs

It is possible that some students with mental retardation can complete an adapted version of the secondary school program with minimal assistance from special education personnel. When a student can achieve at least modest success, such programming may be the best possible alternative. It certainly is consistent with the concept of education in the least restrictive environment. On the other hand, as long as the student is having educational difficulties and is classified as a student with a disabling condition, programming decisions must be made by the IEP committee, and social, educational, and career goals must be carefully considered.

If students are ready for more normal school programs, enrollment in one or two special class sections taught by the special education teacher may still be necessary, but the best or more appropriate program is strictly an individual matter. Sometimes, in large high schools, class sections are taught by nonspecial educators for students who are academically less ready than other students. Such classes may include some students who are considered part of the special education program and some who are not. The major common characteristic of students in such classes may be, for example, reading competency at the third- or fourth-grade level. Therefore, adapted materials may be used with the entire class.

In other programs, central, vocational training facilities are established primarily for nondisabled students but include students with mental retardation. In some such programs, a special education coordinator helps students learn specialized or technical vocabulary or complete reading assignments that are too difficult. This coordinator also usually provides assistance to students with learning disabilities, hearing impairment and others with disabilities.

When adaptations of existing programs do not meet the needs of students who are disabled, educators must provide more specialized programs. Morsink (1984) suggests that a work-study or work experience program is "an excellent way to provide a transition for the student from the sheltered school environment to the competitive world of work" (p. 336). For many students with mild mental retardation, complete self-support (as adults) is possible if appropriate work training is provided.

Regular classroom teachers may play roles in secondary programs primarily oriented to work-study by providing instruction in areas such as typing, home economics, driver education, and other practical secondary school subjects. Assignment to such classes is ordinarily determined on an individual basis.

Work-study coordinators, often working in conjunction with vocational rehabilitation counselors, find employment sites and supervise students on the job. With guidance from work-study coordinators, teachers may play significant roles in remedying difficulties that students experience in the workplace (Morsink, 1984).

As described by Mercer and Payne (1975), the five major phases of a work-study program are vocational exploration, vocational evaluation, vocational training, vocational placement, and followup. In this sequence, students (a) become familiar with the nature of the required skills, (b) are provided guided experience with job skills, thus permitting instructors to determine abilities and preferences, (c) receive broad training in a wide variety of vocational areas, (d) are assisted with placement in an actual job, and (e) are assisted with on-the-job difficulties. Vocational rehabilitation personnel employed by rehabilitation services agencies are important in this process, especially in the last two steps.

Work-study programs vary widely, but the goal is the same in all instances. The role of regular classroom teachers varies with the ability level of the students and the defined roles of special education and rehabilitation personnel. Retish, Hitchings, Horvath, & Schmalle (1991) indicate that students in work-study programs may be in self-contained, integrated, or resource class programs, but through work-study, may receive pay, work experience, and graduation credits. They view "work-study" as a description of class content, not a type of organization.

The CEC Division on Mental Retardation & Developmental Disabilities addressed the unique problems of secondary education programs for students with mental retardation in a 1994 position paper entitled, "Dealing with Secondary Curricula and Policy Issues for Students with MR/DD" (MRDD, 1994, pp. 3–4). The paper's authors wrote, "Appropriate curricula in schools should include a deemphasis on regular academic tracks and an increased opportunity for experiences such as job exploration and job shadowing that can lead to competitive employment for many of these individuals." It also noted, "Many young adults with mental retardation and developmental disabilities may lack the functional living skills that are necessary for independent living. This may be the result of being forced into an academic curriculum during their school years, or the simple fact that the school did not have a functional curriculum" (1994, p. 3).

Where appropriate special programs are offered, special educators and rehabilitation personnel will likely retain primary responsibility, but whatever the program structure, regular classroom teachers at the secondary level will undoubtedly have increasing contact with students with mental retardation, playing various roles, depending on program organization and content.

■: Alternative Sites and Activities

In their review of instructional planning and implementation for students with disabilities, Snell and Brown (1993) state, "For most students with disabilities, there are instructional needs or personal management skills that require an *alternative* activity not scheduled for the regular class" (p. 104). They note that the intensity of such need will normally increase in relation to age and severity of the disability. Though regular classroom teachers will not directly provide such instruction, they will need to understand its purposes, and be prepared to support and reinforce it as appropriate in the regular class environment.

One of the most common sites for learning experiences essential to adult life is an actual employment setting. Polloway and Patton (1993) note that community employers, as an element for developing vocational preparation, can perform several essential services. First, they can provide valuable information about employment, and may be involved in such activities as explaining about the operation of their business to small groups of students, or giving group tours of their plant or shop. Second, they offer a site where students will receive specific skill training. In this setting, students will need the assistance of an employment specialist (job coach), and can also benefit

Leisure activities are part of education.

from a variety of support activities in the school (for example, simulations of various kinds). Special educators may supply other, community-based instruction to help students learn to be better shoppers, cooks/food managers, and may also teach other essential life skills. In their discussion of community-based instruction, Browder and Snell (1993) note that "in the past decade, community-based instruction has received increasing attention, including more widespread practice. Most recently, however, with increases in school integration, many teachers and parents have tried to balance teaching time in the community so that adequate time with peers during school is possible" (p. 510). The regular classroom teacher's role is to assist in making such inschool time of maximum value.

The most restrictive educational alternative for students with mental retardation is the 24-hour residential facility. This may be used when there are severe, multiple disabilities. The number of students in such settings is very small, and the role that the regular classroom teacher might play with respect to such programs is when students are to be moved from these programs into the regular school program. Such a move should be preceded by considerable information sharing (information from residential facility personnel), and specific assistance from regular education personnel from within the school district.

Summary

In this chapter, we defined mental retardation and its relationship to developmental disabilities. We discussed the 1992 AAMR classification system, which emphasizes systems of support, and the implications of the work of Piaget, Inhelder, Luria, and Vygotsky. We outlined characteristics associated with mental retardation, considered under the categories demographic, motivational and sociobehavioral, learning, speech and language, and physical and health. We reviewed an individual test of intelligence, the WISC-III, and discussed assessment of adaptive skills/behavior, outlining the concept of adaptive behavior.

We discussed at length curriculum planning for students with mental retardation, providing career education guidelines, emphasizing the importance of transition planning, and discussing adult employment options. We noted the current federal emphasis on early childhood programs. We offered suggestions for the regular classroom teacher, including both general strategies, such as counteracting failure expectations, and more specific strategies, such as ways to promote the development of the ability to generalize and conceptualize. We then separately discussed secondary school level work-study programs, emphasizing the potential of alternative sites and activities.

chapter 10

- Why were learning disabilities identified and named so much later in history than was mental retardation?

- What definitional disputes continue in the field of learning disabilities? What differences would it make if the definition required proof of a central nervous system disorder?

- Can a learning disability be caused by inappropriate teaching practices? If so, how might this happen?

- How can the assessment team differentiate between learning disabilities and behavior disorders when the student's behavior is common to both diagnoses?

- In how many ways may attention deficits affect learning? What can teachers do to reduce the negative effects of attention deficits?

- Can you describe your own cognitive learning strategies? How might a better understanding of your learning strategies help you learn more efficiently?

- In what ways has technology been particularly helpful in the education of students with learning disabilities? How might its misuse prove to have negative results?

Teaching Students with Learning Disabilities

by **Barbara Garralda Rhine**

■■■■■■■■■■

Learning disabilities is an umbrella term coined in 1963 to cover a wide range of learning difficulties. Almost one hundred different characteristics have been described as fitting under the label of learning disabilities (Freiberg, 1994). This diversity of characteristics and learning problems results in learning disabilities being the category most used in providing special education services. Half of all children receiving special education services are identified as learning disabled (U.S. Department of Education, 1993). Although some students with severe learning disabilities are in self-contained programs, most are in general education classrooms for much of the school day and, therefore, are taught primarily by regular classroom teachers. This chapter provides information to help general education teachers understand the nature of learning disabilities and to work collaboratively with specialists in providing the best possible educational programs for students identified as having learning disabilities.

■■■■■■■■■■■

■ Learning Disabilities: Definition and Discussion

People with learning disabilities process incoming information in ways that are different from their peers. These differences in processing have an adverse effect on their achievement in academic areas. This concept is a constant in efforts to define learning disabilities, but attempts to clarify the differences and effects have not resulted in useful definitions.

The federal definition given in PL 94–142, and now a part of IDEA, is the definition that states must use in identifying and providing services to students with learning disabilities.

Specific learning disability means a disorder in one or more of the basic psychological processes involved in understanding or in using language, spoken or written, which may manifest itself in an imperfect ability to listen, think, speak, read, write, spell, or to do mathematical calculations. The term includes such conditions as perceptual disabilities, brain injury, minimal brain disfunction, dyslexia, and developmental aphasia. The term does not apply to children who have learning problems that are primarily the result of visual, hearing, or motor disabilities, of mental retardation, of emotional disturbance, or of environmental, cultural, or economic disadvantage. (CFR 300.7[10], 1993)

The federal definition lacks specificity for identifying and providing services to students with learning disabilities and states have implemented the definition using widely varying standards and procedures (Moats & Lyon, 1993). This has resulted in variation in number and characteristics of students served in different states, and even within states. Dissatisfaction with the federal definition has resulted in continuing efforts to clarify the definition of learning disabilities.

Concerned about the large number of students identified as learning disabled, the U.S. Congress requested a clarification of the definition. In 1987, the federal Interagency Committee on Learning Disabilities (ICLD) proposed the following:

Learning Disabilities is a generic term that refers to a heterogeneous group of disorders manifested by significant difficulties in the acquisition and use of listening, speaking, reading, writing, reasoning, or mathematical abilities or of social skills. These disorders are intrinsic to the individual and presumed to be due to central nervous system dysfunction. Even though a learning disability may occur concomitantly with other handicapping conditions (e.g., sensory impairment, mental retardation, social and emotional disturbance), with socioenvironmental influences (e.g., cultural differences, insufficient or inappropriate instruction, psychogenic factors), and especially attention deficit disorder, all of which may cause learning problems, a learning disability is not the direct result of those conditions or influences. (1987, p. 222)

This definition was not endorsed by the Department of Education because of concern that including "social skills" would add to the confusion of identification and result in even more students being identified as learning disabled.

The National Joint Committee on Learning Disabilities (NJCLD) reached agreement on the following definition, which appears to have current consensus among those who are active in the field of learning disabilities:

Learning disabilities is a generic term that refers to a heterogeneous group of disorders manifested by significant difficulties in the acquisition and use of listening, speaking, reading, writing, reasoning, or mathematical abilities. These disorders are intrinsic to the individual, presumed to be due to central nervous system dysfunction, and may occur across the life span. Problems in self-regulatory behaviors, social perception, and social interaction may exist with learning disabilities but do not by themselves constitute a learning disability. Although learning disabilities may occur concomitantly with other handicapping conditions (for example, sensory impairment, mental retardation, serious emotional disturbance) or with extrinsic influences (such as cultural differences, insufficient or inappropriate instruction), they are not the result of those conditions or influences. (1989, p. 1)

The NJCLD definition modifies the federal definition by emphasizing the heterogeneous nature of learning disabilities, including a statement that learning disabilities may occur across the life span, and recognizing that problems in self-regulatory behaviors, social perception, and social interaction may coexist with learning disabilities.

Elements common across the definitions are (a) neurological involvement, (b) a discrepancy between ability and achievement, and (c) the exclusion of sensory disabilities, mental retardation, emotional disturbances, and extrinsic factors as primary causal factors. Kavale, Forness, and Lorsbach (1991) point out that all three definitions are descriptive renderings of what learning disabilities are perceived to be but lack the absolute criteria for easy identification.

To provide guidance in the implementation of IDEA, federal regulations specify criteria to determine the existence of a specific learning disability (Figure 10–1). These criteria do not include diagnosis of the processing component identified in the federal definition and do not indicate what constitutes a significant discrepancy between achievement and intellectual ability. States trying to meet the federal regulations have used various discrepancy models. Two common approaches have been to use a percentage of educational lag or deficit (for example, 40% or 50%) or a grade equivalent discrepancy in one or more of the academic skill areas (for example, a fifth-grade student must score below the 2.5 grade-equivalent level in one of the academic areas).

This difficulty in accurate classification has resulted in too many students being identified as learning disabled (Raab & Steele, 1993). This overidentification occurs for several reasons. School identification teams sometimes use the less stigmatizing label of *learning disabilities* rather than *mental retardation* or *emotional disturbance*. This label is also used to provide additional services to students with academic difficulties due to other reasons (such as cultural/linguistic differences or experiential deprivation) when other services are not readily available. Though school personnel do this with the best of intentions, such a practice often does not provide appropriate services and may in fact have a negative effect on services provided to students with actual learning disabilities.

Because learning disabilities interfere with academic achievement, the federal regulations for implementing IDEA have additional procedures for evaluating children with specific learning disabilities (Figure 10–2). The expertise of the general education classroom teacher is necessary in the diagnostic process if a learning disability is suspected. The child's regular teacher or a qualified appropriate teacher must be a part of the multidisciplinary team making the identification and the child's academic performance must be observed in the regular classroom setting. An identification of learning disabilities cannot be made if the student's functioning in the classroom is not included in the information gathered by the team.

Attention Deficit Disorders (ADD)/Attention Deficit Hyperactivity Disorders (ADHD)

The definition and identification of learning disabilities is further confused by the condition commonly known as attention deficit disorder (ADD). Like learning disabilities, ADD is plagued by numerous definitional and diagnos-

Figure 10–1
Criteria for determining the existence of a specific learning disability

§ 300.541 Criteria for determining the existence of a specific learning disability.

(a) A team may determine that a child has a specific learning disability if—

   (1) The child does not achieve commensurate with his or her age and ability levels in one or more of the areas listed in paragraph (a)(2) of this section, when provided with learning experiences appropriate for the child's age and ability levels; and

   (2) The team finds that a child has a severe discrepancy between achievement and intellectual ability in one or more of the following areas—

      (i) Oral expression;
      (ii) Listening comprehension;
      (iii) Written expression;
      (iv) Basic reading skill;
      (v) Reading comprehension;
      (vi) Mathematics calculation; or
      (vii) Mathematics reasoning.

(b) The team may not identify a child as having a specific learning disability if the severe discrepancy between ability and achievement is primarily the result of—

   (1) A visual, hearing, or motor impairment;
   (2) Mental retardation;
   (3) Emotional disturbance; or
   (4) Environmental, cultural or economic disadvantage.

(Authority: 20 U.S.C. 1411 note)

tic problems (Reid, Maag, & Vasa, 1994). *Attention deficit disorder* is a generic term for a group of heterogeneous, pervasive, and long-term characteristics believed to have a neurological etiology. The characteristics fall into three areas: (a) an inability to attend, (b) impulsivity and (c) inappropriate overactivity (hyperactivity). The variety of designations for the condition has revolved around the degree of specification of hyperactivity. The designations used in the *Diagnostic and Statistical Manual of Mental Disorders* (DSM-III) (American Psychiatric Association, 1980) were attention deficit disorder with hyperactivity (ADD/H)

and attention deficit disorder without hyperactivity (ADD/WO). The terms were revised in 1987 (DSM-III-R) to attention deficit hyperactivity disorder without distinctions among attention deficits, impulsivity, and hyperactivity. The 1994 revision (DSM-IV, 1994) identifies three subtypes of attention deficit hyperactivity disorder: predominately inattentive, predominately hyperactive-impulsive, and combined. Regardless of the particular terms used, many students with the characteristics of this disorder have difficulty in school.

Characteristics of inattention are seen as the student finds it difficult to pay close atten-

Figure 10–2
Additional procedures for evaluating children with specific learning disabilities

§ **300.540   Additional team members.**

In evaluating a child suspected of having a specific learning disability, in addition to the requirements of § 300.532, each public agency shall include on the multidisciplinary evaluation team—

(a) (1) The child's regular teacher; or
     (2) If the child does not have a regular teacher, a regular classroom teacher qualified to teach a child of his or her age; or
     (3) For a child of less than school age, an individual qualified by the SEA to teach a child of his or her age; and

(b) At least one person qualified to conduct individual diagnostic examinations of children, such as a school psychologist, speech-language pathologist, or remedial reading teacher.

§ **300.542   Observation.**

(a) At least one team member other than the child's regular teacher shall observe the child's academic performance in the regular classroom setting.

(b) In the case of a child of less than school age or out of school, a team member shall observe the child in an environment appropriate for a child of that age.

(Authority: 20 U.S.C. 1411 note)
(Approved by the Office of Management and Budget under control number 1820–0030)
[57 FR 44798, Sept. 29, 1992, as amended at 58 FR 13528, Mar. 11, 1993]

tion to details and has difficulty sustaining attention. The student may have difficulty following directions, finishing tasks, and organizing activities. They often appear forgetful, lose things and appear to be lazy. Hyperactivity-impulsivity is exhibited as the student fidgets, squirms, moves about, and talks excessively for her or his age level. This student finds it difficult to wait during an activity and will often talk or act out of turn.

Medications are often prescribed as a part of the management of ADHD. Commonly used drugs are stimulants (e.g., Ritalin, Dexedrine, and Cylert) and antidepressants (e.g., Imipramine). These drugs lower the quantity and intensity of motor activity, increase attention, and improve compliance in many children and adults, leading to improved achievement. Drug treatment is not effective for all children and must always be accompanied by a plan for developing academic and self-control strategies.

Advocacy groups proposed that ADHD be added as a disability category to IDEA because these characteristics of ADHD do interfere with educational performance (Aleman, 1991). After a study conducted by the U.S. Department of Education, students with ADHD were declared eligible for special education services under the existing categories of

"Other Health Impaired," "Learning Disabled," and "Emotionally Disturbed." This does not mean all students identified as having attention deficit hyperactivity disorder are eligible for services in special education. If the condition does not have a significant impact on the student's education, special services are not required.

Because of the difficulty in defining and identifying both learning disabilities and ADHD, it is difficult to establish the frequency of co-occurrence of the two conditions. Elbert (1993) states that estimates have ranged from 10 to 90 percent, but a conservative estimate indicates that between 19 and 26 percent of students with ADHD also have learning disabilities with academic needs. Regardless of the label(s), each student found to have a disability must have an individual plan based on a careful assessment of abilities and needs, both academic and behavioral. It is essential to realize that labels do not dictate specific means of meeting a student's needs.

■■ Characteristics of Students Who Have Learning Disabilities

All students who have learning disabilities display a significant discrepancy between learning potential and actual level of learning, as well as learning processes and strategies different from those seen in most peers. The actual characteristics may vary widely. Remember that this is a heterogeneous group and each student is unique. The following characteristics are often observed in students who have learning disabilities:

1. Significantly different classroom behaviors
   a. Difficulty in beginning or finishing tasks
   b. Difficulty in organizing
   c. Inconsistency in behavior
   d. Difficulty in peer relationships
2. Significantly below-average performance in auditory comprehension and listening
   a. Difficulty in following directions
   b. Difficulty in comprehending or following class discussions
   c. Difficulty in retaining information received aurally
   d. Difficulty in understanding or comprehending word meanings
3. Significantly below-average performance in spoken language
   a. Use of incomplete sentences or an unusual number of grammatical errors
   b. Use of immature or improper vocabulary or very limited vocabulary
   c. Difficulty in recalling words for use in self-expression
   d. Difficulty relating isolated facts; scattered ideas
   e. Difficulty in relating ideas in logical sequence
4. Significant academic problems
   a. Difficulty in reading fluency
   b. Difficulty in associating numbers with symbols
   c. Difficulty in associating sounds with letters
   d. Incorrect ordering of letters in spelling
   e. Avoidance of reading
   f. Confusion of math concepts—addition, multiplication
5. Orientation difficulties
   a. Poor time concept, no grasp of meaning of time
   b. Difficulty in "navigating" around building or school grounds
   c. Poor understanding of relationships (big, little, far, close, under, on, near)

d. Inability to learn directions (right, left, north, south)
6. Motor disabilities or significant under-development for age
   a. Poor coordination, clumsiness
   b. Awkward, poorly developed manipulative or manual dexterity
   c. Lack of rhythm in movements

All students display some of these characteristics some of the time. It is the interaction of a number of characteristics that results in a pervasive impact on the functioning of the student. It should be understood that a learning disability is a real disability with lifelong consequences. The characteristics continue across the life span and adults continue to struggle with inefficient and ineffective strategies when learning and applying knowledge (Ryan & Price, 1992).

An additional problem relating to the identification of learning disabilities results from the use of the discrepancy model. Because a severe discrepancy must exist before identification, severe failure must occur before special education interventions can be provided. This can create lifelong problems of damaged self-concept. It is important to remember that an individual with a learning disability is not stupid or lazy. The disability cannot be overcome if the student or teacher just "works harder"; rather, they both must "work smarter." The following story illustrates the influences of a learning disability.

Living and Learning with Sally[1]
Sarah Levine and Sally Osbourne

I remember kindergarten being a lot of fun, but school wasn't fun from the first grade on. My first-grade teacher used to walk by our house every week to drop off a bunch of flash cards. My mother was supposed to go over them with me until I learned the words. But it was so hard. I'd look at a word and wouldn't know it. When my mother told me what it was, I would repeat what she said. But then we'd go to the next word, and I'd forget the first one. It was frustrating.

I was in the seventh grade when my teacher asked me to stand up and read. I stood up, but I couldn't recognize even one word on the page. After what seemed an eternity, the teacher got angry and told me to go into another classroom where I was to write, again and again: "I am stupid because I cannot read."

I didn't say a word. But I couldn't do what the teacher wanted, because I couldn't spell. So I just sat and waited until a friend came in at the end of the day to collect the assignment. After she had spelled it out for me, I wrote it over and over again. Then I gave it to the teacher and went home.

That was the end of it. The teacher never helped me with my reading or writing before or after that time.

Students with learning disabilities often become frustrated with their inability to learn in school. Some become behavior problems to divert attention from their academic performance; others try to behave perfectly and hope that adults won't notice them. Sally adopted the latter strategy, always smiling and pretending that she was happy. "It was much easier to make believe that everything was fine than it was to admit that I did not understand," she says.

Sally knew very early in her school career that something was wrong. There had to be a reason why she couldn't learn when all her friends were learning. She decided there was something wrong with *her*. She decided that she was *dumb*.

In elementary school, when one of Sally's friends asked to have Sally sit near her, she was told that Sally was retarded and needed to sit next to the teacher.

What seems strange to Sally today is the fact that most adults in the schools simply ignored her. Once, when she was called on to read and couldn't, the teacher told her mother that Sally needed glasses. When that didn't work, the teacher moved Sally from the lowest reading group to the highest reading group— and never asked Sally to read again. Of course, Sally couldn't even read the book in the lowest group, but, wherever the teacher told her to sit, Sally sat and continued *not reading*.

In high school, Sally's guidance counselor told her that she was "not college material." But Sally's mother insisted that she was. After a heated argument, Sally was placed in the vocational track, to satisfy the guidance department—*and* in the college-preparatory track, to satisfy her mother. She had no free periods, she had twice as much work, and she was under a lot more pressure to hide her differences.

From first grade through high school, Sally did not experience academic success. For the most part, teachers returned her smile but were content to ignore her learning problem. Always, her mother encouraged her. And Sally kept wondering what was wrong. Gradually, she became convinced that she was not stupid. The way she was treated and the results of all her efforts in school, however, offered powerful evidence to the contrary.

College was a struggle from the start. I remember fighting my way through freshman registration lines, asking other students where to go. I felt ashamed because I couldn't read the signs posted on the walls or the forms I held tightly in my hand. Had anyone asked why I was having so much trouble, I was prepared to say that I was a foreign student.

When I did register, it was for classes that had oral tests, projects, or papers. I could not take a written exam.

Four years later, I earned a bachelor's degree—or perhaps I should say my mother and I earned one. She read many of the textbooks to me; she transcribed the ideas from my head onto paper; she pushed me to accept new challenges. I remember how she smiled when I received an A in a class in which she had once received a B. She danced with delight when she saw my first grade report with a B+ average. She cried when my name appeared on the dean's list.

Sally graduated from college with a teaching certificate and found a job teaching first and second grades in a rural school. Sally's ingenuity paid off in the classroom. She had second-graders teach first-graders, even though some of the children refused to believe her when she said she didn't know the answers to their questions. When she read a book and came to a part she couldn't remember, she would close the book and ask the class, "What might happen next?"

Sally and her students did a lot of hands-on learning. Since they were out in the country, they could go for long walks. She used these times to demonstrate, and this is how they did math and science. Inside, they also learned by doing; they did a lot of cooking, for instance. Parents were frequently invited to visit and help with the class, and Sally had an aide who could teach the children phonics.

The test scores of Sally's students improved. And it is interesting that her alternative and expanded strategies for teaching and learning were the products of her ostensible *limitations*. Perhaps all teachers could do more for students by doing less traditional teaching. Certainly, most teachers could profitably expand their repertoire of teaching methods.

A year later, Sally agreed to take over a friend's special-needs classroom in another state. Her friend, a teacher of the learning disabled, suspected that Sally had learning difficulties and encouraged her to take the position, which would also require Sally to enroll in an intensive summer course. As Sally learned about teaching dyslexic children, her own reading and writing abilities gradually improved. For Sally, both the learning experience and the discovery that she had a learning disability were revelations.

One of Sally's enduring qualities is her tendency to set high personal standards. She is bent on proving her capabilities to the world (and to herself). After years of teaching kindergarten, she wanted a new challenge. She began by taking several graduate courses. Then she decided to go back to school full-time. She applied to the Harvard Graduate School of Education, and she was accepted.

At Harvard, Sally's insecurity about her disabilities resurfaced with fierce intensity. She did not want anyone to know that she was dyslexic, to make concessions for her, or to decide that she didn't belong. She lived by herself in a dormitory room, telling no one of her learning disabilities for the entire first term. One can only imagine how difficult it must be for someone with severe dyslexia to cope in such a highly conceptual environment, in which reading and writing are so important.

Sally started her papers months before they were due. In one course, she joined every available study group, so she could hear the readings discussed over and over again. She repeatedly turned down opportunities to go out. Her friends were limited to the students who could help her learn. She slept an average of four or five hours a night. By the start of winter, she was on the brink of exhaustion.

Only a marginal grade on a term paper drove Sally to seek help. Thinking she had failed, Sally went to an office at the university that was specially designed to help students with reading and writing. Even then, she initially told the counselor that she was seeking information to improve her teaching. Desperation—more than courage—finally motivated Sally to tell her story and agree to be tested. Two weeks later, Sally received the first official description and diagnosis of her learning disabilities: she was the most severely dyslexic student that the specialist had seen in his many years at the university. . . .

She was referred to an office for student services in the Harvard Graduate School of Education, where she learned that the university would pay for someone to tape her assignments, read to her, and edit her written work. She also discovered other resources: a university support group for learning-disabled students and a student organization that sponsored monthly speakers on learning disabilities.

During her second semester at Harvard, Sally told her story—to teachers, to classmates, and to friends. To her surprise, most of them were empathic. None lowered their expectations for Sally's performance, but many developed a new appreciation for diverse learning needs. Several teachers were especially helpful. One offered the services of his teaching assistants as well as his own time to read assignments, to review papers, and to discuss the readings. Sally took advantage of this offer and talked to the teacher about specific readings. Understanding Sally's preference for visual learning, this teacher made a point in class of drawing figures and diagrams on the chalkboard and pausing after a question to give students time to formulate their responses.

Not all of Sally's teachers were comfortable with her disclosure. Sally noted in one class that her fast-paced instructor consistently overlooked her raised hand, which Sally interpreted as an effort to protect her. In fact, it exaggerated her sense of isolation, of being different.

Today, Sally believes that the services she received from the university markedly strengthened her ability to read and write, but she is convinced that the most critical factor in her growth was her enhanced feeling of self-worth. "Once I began to feel good about myself," she says, "I could start learning. And now that I'm learning, I never want to stop."

Sally's story raises some important questions: How is it possible for a student to go through school without learning to read and write with proficiency? How can educators pass over, ignore, or deny learning difficulties? Why are there so many schools in which only a very narrow range of learning styles is rewarded?

Sally's story also teaches many lessons—some of them painful, but most of them promising. Sally's gains have not been without cost. In order to keep up with her schoolwork and to keep her disability a secret, Sally distanced herself from the activities and friendships that most of us take for granted. A person who likes people, Sally found it especially difficult to maintain this social isolation.

Sally's story dramatizes the essential role of parents in personal development and in schooling. Sally's mother contributed to Sally's success in tangible and intangible ways. Without her support and encouragement, Sally would not have believed in herself or experienced success.

Sally's story also dramatizes the power of individual initiative, courage, and resilience. Despite constant obstacles, Sally refused to accept defeat. In fact, the obstacles only sparked her desire to triumph.

Sally's experience at Harvard illustrates the importance of special services for learning-disabled students. It shows the positive influence of knowledgeable and understanding teachers, as well as the need to reeducate those teachers who may be unfamiliar or uncomfortable with learning handicaps.

Finally, Sally's story reminds us that learning disabilities may be constructively thought of as learning *differences*. Children and adults with dyslexia and other learning handicaps often demonstrate talents in the visual arts, athletics, music, and math. Rather than dismiss learning-disabled students, teachers can identify their strengths and can capitalize on them.

---

[1] From "Living and Learning with Sally" by S. Levine and S. Osbourne, April 1989, *Phi Delta Kappan, 70*. pp. 594–598. Reprinted by permission.

[2] The term *dyslexia* was used to identify Sally's difficulties. Dyslexia has been popularized as a condition of seeing print as reversed or a "mirror image". Actually, the term is defined as a learning disability manifested by difficulty in learning to read and write despite adequate intelligence, instruction, and opportunity. There appears to be a genetic basis with possible structural differences in the brain. The National Advisory Committee on Dyslexia and Related Reading Disorders (1969) stated that the term *dyslexia* is a medical term and does not appear to be a useful term in education. The preferred term is *severe reading disability*.

■■■■

■ Identification and Program Planning

When a classroom teacher suspects that a student has a learning disability, the teacher should hold a prereferral meeting with a building-based teacher support team or child study team. This team uses a collaborative problem-solving approach and usually consists of both general and special education teachers. The team meets to discuss approaches already used to meet the needs of a particular student and to generate possible additional approaches to be used without special education intervention. If it appears that the student's needs cannot be met without additional support, the regular classroom teacher may make a formal, written referral to the individual at the school who is designated to receive such referrals (principal, counselor, special education teacher, etc.).

This referral is an important part of planning assessment and services and should be precise and complete. The teacher should indicate the specific behaviors, both academic and social, that are concerns. As assessment information is gathered, the general education teacher has a responsibility (as specified in IDEA) to serve on the multidisciplinary team and to provide information of both social and academic functioning. Also, another member of the team must observe the student in the general education classroom. This focus on classroom functioning reflects the emphasis on academics in the definition of learning disabilities. After gathering the assessment information, the identification and IEP development procedure outlined in Chapter 2 is followed.

The education of students with learning disabilities is a joint responsibility of both general education and special education teachers at every grade level. These students have

the same needs as all students—to acquire the basic components needed to be adjusted, contributing, responsible adults. All instruction should be focused toward this end goal. The unique needs of each student should be met through collaborative effort by all involved. In addition to understandings, information, and skills, it is important that teachers realize that students with learning disabilities must also develop self-determination (Durlak, Rose, & Bursuck, 1994). Self-determination includes characteristics of assertiveness, self-advocacy, creativity, and independence. These characteristics, essential for successful adult functioning, are not developed by simply writing transition goals into an IEP. The planning of every educational activity, at every grade level, should seek to answer the questions, "How will this help this unique student with learning disabilities become an adjusted, contributing, responsible adult?" and "Where does this fit into the rest of his or her life?" The services provided must consider the unique needs of each student and how the needs can be met, utilizing the expertise of both general and special education teachers who jointly plan the activities and modifications.

The movement toward full inclusion or integration of all students with disabilities into the regular classroom is a popular element of school reform. The professional organizations in the field of learning disabilities favor the inclusion of a student with learning disabilities, but caution that the population of students identified as having learning disabilities is so diverse, that a full continuum of services must be available (LDA, 1993; CLD, 1993; NJCLD, 1993).

Some needed services may be such that the student should be removed from the regular classroom for a period or more during the day and instructed one to one or in a small group. This might be necessary when the methods or materials used would embarrass the student

Abstract concepts can be difficult for some students.

or disrupt the learning of other students in the general education classroom. If the discrepancy between the student's abilities and the content are so great, and the modifications so extensive that they are difficult to provide in the general education classroom, the student might be pulled out for that particular content.

If instruction is to be successful in the general education classroom, the learning of all students must be facilitated and enriched, and the integrity of the content must be maintained (Bulgren, Schumaker, & Deshler, 1994). Regular education and special education teachers must collaborate in planning and presenting the modifications and adaptations for instruction in the general education classroom. General education teachers rate

the adaptations of providing reinforcement and encouragement, establishing a personal relationship with the student, and involving the student in whole-class activities as being the most feasible for them to provide (Schumm & Vaughn, 1991).

When students leave the regular classroom for services, general education and special education teachers must plan for the student to become reoriented to the activities of the classroom when they reenter. Such plans should consider the student's needs and abilities, the characteristics of the classroom, and teacher expectations (Lazzari & Wood, 1993). Plans should include methods for orienting the student in activities at the time of reentry, informing the student of missed activities, and alleviating student embarrassment when entering and leaving. Depending upon the abilities, age, and level of the student, possible strategies include a checklist; a reorientation interval conducted by a paraprofessional, teacher, or student; and careful scheduling of periods out of the room and not holding the student responsible for general education classroom activities occurring during that time.

Most students with learning disabilities need modifications and support in the regular classroom, specific to their abilities and needs. They do not need a separate curriculum. In the following sections we present teaching suggestions to stimulate the thinking of teachers when planning and modifying instruction for students with learning disabilities.

■ Suggestions for Regular Classroom Teachers

Reading, Writing, and Language Development

Students with learning disabilities experience many different problems in reading. They often have difficulty in developing an understanding of the correspondence of sounds to written letters; learning to recognize words by sight; sounding out and blending words; understanding the meaning of what they read; developing fluency in both reading and writing; organizing when writing; and using conventional grammar, spelling, and punctuation in writing.

The philosophy of whole language for literacy learning emphasizes integrating the four language processes of reading, writing, listening, and speaking with content curriculum areas in authentic settings. This approach is effective when used with students with mild to severe learning disabilities (Englert, Raphael, & Mariage, 1994; Scala, 1993; Zucker, 1993). However, there must also be

appropriate, supplemental instruction provided with a variety of techniques based on individual need (Mather, 1992). Students with learning disabilities often have difficulty with both incidental learning and generalization across contexts. For this reason, specific instruction should be embedded in the whole language activities.

An example of a whole language program adapted for students with learning disabilities is the Early Literacy Program (ELP), an integrated literacy program developed by Englert, Raphael and Mariage (1994). The ELP uses whole language oral, reading, and writing activities integrated in thematic units. Oral activities are oral storytelling, story dictation, and listening to oral stories. Reading and writing activities are undisturbed silent reading, teacher-led group reading/rereading and writing, individual reading/rereading and writing, partner reading/rereading and writing, sharing chair, morning news, story-comprehension discussion, and author's center. Needed specific skill instruction is embedded in these activities.

Another important feature of the ELP is strategy instruction. Teachers model strategies and involve students in the use of strategies during the activities. An example is the use of semantic mapping, a technique for organizing information. Thematic units are introduced through pictures and picture books. A brainstorming session is used to activate background knowledge, generate questions, and make predictions. Initially, the teacher should write the students' contributions on the board, a chart, or an overhead projector, allowing the students to concentrate on the organization and content.

Semantic mapping is used to organize the brainstorming session (Figure 10–3). Semantic maps, webs, or graphic organizers are visual organizations of information. The structure of the map varies with the ability level of the stu-

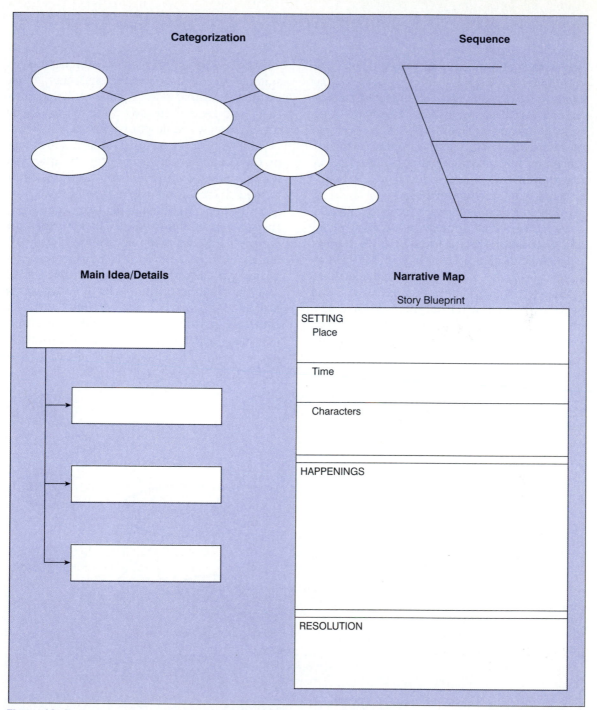

Categorization

Sequence

Main Idea/Details

Narrative Map

Story Blueprint

SETTING
  Place

  Time

  Characters

HAPPENINGS

RESOLUTION

Figure 10–3
Ideas for visual organizers

dents, the genre used, and the complexity of the material. A simple map consists of the main idea with subunits of supporting information. More subunits are added with more complex material. Figure 10–4 is an example of a semantic map used to organize student responses after a thematic unit about modes of transportation was introduced to a second-grade class using a picture book.

Modeling techniques are used as the teacher demonstrates each strategy by thinking aloud and discussing relevant features of the process with students (Englert & Mariage, 1991). The teacher is explicit with "think-alouds" such as, "One way I remembered that is. . . . " Prods such as, "Can you tell us more about that?" are used to help students generate more conceptually related information. As students

develop the semantic map, the teacher makes statements and asks directed questions: "That is connected to . . . "; "Where will that idea fit?"; and "Are there any other parts of our information we could put with this?"

Following brainstorming, students read text or trade books, and then alter the maps to include new or corrected information. After guided discussion to generate summaries, monitor understanding, and clarify confusion, the teacher guides students in strategies for writing using the mapping. The teacher models and thinks aloud while writing the first paragraph, discussing explicitly mechanics and organization of the paragraph during this process. The teacher and students together finish the writing. They then edit the draft for communication and mechanics, illustrate it,

Figure 10–4

Sample classroom-generated semantic web

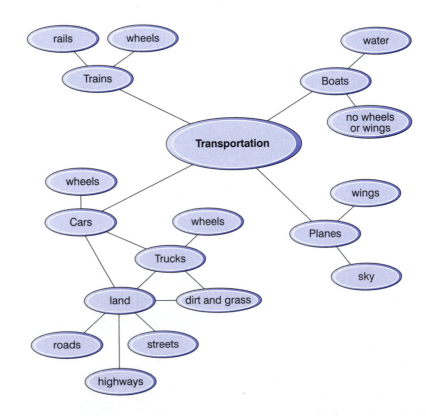

and publish it. Over time, the teacher shifts the writing to the students to develop self-regulated use of the strategies by each student.

Language Experience Activities (LEA) are well suited for individualizing within a group activity at any grade level. A variation that enhances oral language abilities of students with learning disabilities is to use semantic mapping while tape recording the oral discussion (Kaderavek & Mandlebaum, 1993). Students first participate in an experience. The teacher then presents an experience-related word or question to the group (or student) and the students make contributions while the teacher writes them down. The teacher and students organize the contributions into a map. Using sheets of paper to record student contributions and attaching them to the larger sheet with nonpermanent glue allows moving the contributions around for a more organized map. The teacher and students discuss the semantic map while tape recording. Students then listen to the taped discussion to evaluate the completeness and clarity of their story or report both at the sentence level and at the full report level.

Another variation of the Language Experience Approach, first advocated over 50 years ago, is still in use today. Developed by Grace Fernald (1943, 1988), the method is a multisensory approach. The first step is to explain to the student that this is a new way of learning words that really works. The student is told that others have had the same problem and were able to learn using this method.

The second step is to ask the student to select any word he or she wants to learn, regardless of length, and then to teach the student to write and recognize (read) it, using the following method:

1. Write the word chosen by the student, usually with a crayon in plain, blackboard-size cursive writing. In most cases, regardless of age, cursive writing is used rather than manuscript because the student tends to see and feel the word as a single entity rather than a group of separate letters.

2. Have the student trace the word with his or her fingers in contact with the paper, saying the word at the same time. Repeat this step as many times as necessary, until the student can write the word without looking at the copy.

3. Have the student write the word on scrap paper, demonstrating to himself or herself mastery of the word. Teach several words in this manner, taking as much time as necessary for the student to completely master them.

4. When the student has internalized the fact that he or she can write and recognize words, encourage the student to start writing stories. Let the student's stories be whatever the student wishes them to be at first, and give the student any words (in addition to those mastered) necessary to complete the story.

5. After the story is written, type it and ask the student to read it in typed form while it is still fresh. It is important that this reading be done immediately.

6. After the story is completed and the new words have been used in a meaningful way, have the student write the new words on cards that the student files alphabetically in an individual word file. In addition, use this word file to teach the alphabet without undue emphasis on rote memory.

This procedure is often called the Fernald tracing method because the tracing is an added feature in contrast to the usual methods of teaching reading or word recognition. However, note that the student is simultaneously *feeling, seeing, saying,* and *hearing* the word. Thus, the approach is truly multisensory.

Carefully observe the following points for maximum success:

1. Each word should be selected by the student.
2. Finger contact is essential. The student may use either one or two fingers.
3. The student should write a word, after tracing it several times, without looking at the copy.
4. In case of error or interruption in writing, the word should be crossed out and a new start made.
5. Each word should be used in context.
6. The student must always say each word aloud or to himself or herself while tracing it and writing it.

Teachers may use a modification of repeated reading to support students with learning disabilities in the development of a sight word vocabulary and letter–sound correspondence. Highly predictable materials are read chorally, independently after modeling, and with oral cloze until the student can "read" the material from memory. Specific words, letters, and high-frequency subword units can be discussed during this process. The reading is then reproduced in an individual size and cut first into sentence strips and later into word units for reassembly. This serves to focus attention on word units. The words can be written on file cards and word boxes made.

Onsets and rimes are used to extend and generalize patterns found in the sight words. *Onsets* are both single consonants such as *c, r, t,* and *b,* and consonant blends such as *ch, tr, dr,* and *st. Rimes* are vowel and constant(s) units that are found in groups of like-sounding words. Rimes with the highest frequency of occurrence are as follows:

-ack	-all	-ain	-ake	-ale	-ame
-an	-ank	-ap	-ash	-at	-ate
-aw	-ay	-eat	-ell	-est	-ice
-ick	-ide	-ight	-ill	-in	-ine
-ing	-ink	-ip	-ir	-ock	-oke
-op	-ore	-or	-uck	-ug	-ump
-unk					

Onsets and rimes are combined to form words such as *bill, hill, mill, chill, drill,* and *still.*

The teacher selects words from the student's well-learned predictable reading to use in extending to new words with rimes and onsets. For example, a teacher may use the words *hop, top,* and *pop* to introduce new words. The teacher would highlight the rime, *-op,* and discuss the grapheme–phoneme correspondence. Students say the words and the rime. The teacher and students would then form new words using constants and consonant blends, such as the words *stop, mop, hop,* and *drop* (new words formed should be in the student's speaking vocabulary). These words are then used in further reading and writing activities. Building display lists of words assists children in using the patterns when reading and spelling. The patterns of the rime must be highlighted in the activity with interactive discussion.

Blending is a critical step when using rimes and onsets and must be explicitly taught (Grossen & Carnine, 1993). An effective way to teach blending of onsets and rimes is to model by pointing to the onset for two seconds and saying the sound; then pointing to the rime and saying the sound for two seconds with no break in the sound. Students then blend the sounds as the teacher points, and finally perform the blending independently. The patterns should then be extended to other reading in trade books and basal readers. Extensive practice is necessary for students with learning disabilities to develop reading skills.

Teachers may use the following three-step sequence of activities to improve vocabulary, fluency, and comprehension. It involves pairs of readers; one more able and one less able.

1. *Text Reading and Rereading.* The more able reader of the pair models by reading for five minutes with the less able reader as tutor. Then, the less able reader rereads the same text for five minutes with the more able reader as tutor. Students are trained as tutors to point out a missed word and ask the reader to "figure it out." If the reader cannot do this in five minutes, they are instructed to read the sentence again. If this does not help, the reader is given the word and told to read the sentence again with the word. The teacher may have to give the word if neither of the pair knows it.

2. *Comprehension Activities of Retell and Shrink.* After both students in the pair have read the same text, the less able reader retells what they have read. The readers then do paragraph shrinking. The first step is naming the *who* or *what* and then telling the most important part about the *who* or *what*. With this information, the reader then says the main idea in ten words or less. Mapping may be integrated into this step.

3. *Predict and Check.* The last part of the activity is to predict what will be on a half page of text, read the text and check the prediction. Prompt cards, adjusted to grade level, can be used to guide students through the entire process by listing the steps and roles.

When students have difficulty with basic sight vocabulary words, such as *and, if, from, was,* and *going,* prepare audiotapes of stories or selections. Choose short and interesting passages (about 15 minutes each) at the listening level of the students and record the pas-

sages on tape. Be sure to include cues such as page numbers and times to turn pages. (Either teachers or good readers can prepare tapes.) Then, have the students listen to the tapes while following the printed versions of the passages, listening and simultaneously reading as many times as necessary to recognize all of the words. When the students recognize all of the words within a passage, listen to them read the passage without the tape. The purpose of this activity is to help students recognize the printed versions of words in their speaking vocabularies. In addition, the activity provides appropriate models for oral reading.

Teachers may employ Peabody Classwide Peer Tutoring (Mathes, Fuchs, Fuchs, Henley, & Sanders, 1994) to provide practice in reading for students with learning disabilities in the general education classroom. The development of comprehension strategies is embedded in the practice. Students are paired by ranking students by ability and dividing the list in the middle. The top students on each list are paired and the matching continues until each pair contains a higher and lower ability level student. Two teams are formed, with pairs assigned to the teams. Each pair earns points for the team based on engagement in reading and appropriate behavior.

Because students with learning disabilities have difficulty organizing for writing, preplanning structures are useful at all grade levels. Maps are useful organizers during the preplanning stage. Cue cards or sheets with sections for the elements of the story grammar are helpful. Checklists for students to use in monitoring their planning and writing provide the structure needed for many students (Figure 10–5).

Because character development is frequently lacking in student narrative writings, explicit instruction is important. The narrative planning formats of planning sheets, display charts, or cue cards, containing such

Figure 10–5
Narrative writing checklist

1. Story

    I have included:

    Setting: Time _____   Place _____

    Characters: Main person   Others

          appearance   _____   _____

          actions   _____   _____

          dialogue   _____   _____

    Problem/conflict   _____

    Attempts to resolve   _____

    Problem solution   _____

2. Process

    I brainstormed before I started to write.   _____

    I organized my ideas to follow a plan.   _____

    I had someone edit it:

        makes sense   _____

        is interesting   _____

3. Form

    I checked for complete sentences. _____

    I checked for spelling.   _____

    I checked for punctuation:

        periods, etc.   _____

        quotation marks   _____

        commas, etc.   _____

    I checked for capital letters:

        proper nouns   _____

        first of sentence   _____

    I checked for neatness.   _____

questions as What does my character look like?; What does my character do and say?; and What does my character think and feel? assist the students. Brainstorming possibilities for each question on large sheets of paper provide ideas for the students to incorporate in their writing (Montague & Leavell, 1994). These techniques should be directly taught using modeling and interactive discussion.

Spelling

Spelling is a difficult subject for many students with learning disabilities. Effective approaches to instruction use words from the student's reading and writing. The words should always be in the student's speaking and listening vocabulary. Priority should be given to the high-frequency words that account for most adult writing.

A test-study-test approach with students studying only words they do not know how to spell is preferable to the single and total list approach. Students should correct their own spelling with teacher assistance. This can be done by having the student write the correct spelling directly under the misspelled word. Attention should be focused on the correct letters and the points of error. Usually, students have most of the letters in the word correct and will be more motivated to see that they "know more than they don't know." This metacognitive approach creates an awareness of patterns and problems in spelling.

Board games and electronic games can be used to encourage practice in spelling. Computer software often provides motivating formats for practicing spelling.

Technology in Reading and Writing

Students with learning disabilities benefit from available technologies at all grade and ability levels. Software is available for reading readiness, beginning sight words, phonics skill, reading comprehension, and whole language activities. Built-in computer speech synthesizers expand the usefulness of the software. Many programs feature excellent graphics. CD-ROM reading programs add animated graphics to motivate reluctant readers. The teacher may adapt many programs for specific skills. By careful selection and use, a computer can be of great benefit in reading instruction for students with learning disabilities.

Computer-based readers are systems that scan a printed page of text in a book and speak the words while displaying them onscreen. The program highlights the text while vocalizing it, text and the reading speed is adjustable. Dictionaries that provide meanings and syllabication are a part of these programs. These are valuable aids for students with disabilities in content classes.

Independent or self-contained optical character recognition systems, originally designed for use by people who are blind, can read text print aloud while scanning. Some units attach to a tape recorder to feed the scanned print onto an audiocassette so that texts can be taped for later use by the student. Variable-speed tape players allow the student to adjust the recording and playback rate. Some adjustable-speed tape players can only play a tape back at the speed of recording and should be avoided, as this does not provide the needed flexibility.

Students with learning disabilities benefit from writing on word processors, either independent units or computer-based systems, as both writing and reading skills improve. Word processors simplify both the composing and the editing processes, as the student can insert, delete, and move text about. Software for outlining and brainstorming assists the student in planning and organizing writing. Graphics can be utilized to add structure and to motivate production. Most programs have proofreading programs to check for grammar and punctuation as well as spelling. These are not foolproof, but do help students. Papers are neater and more legible than handwriting. With the labor thus less intensive, students can focus on the communication aspects of their writing.

Some programs provide the useful features of abbreviation and expansion; students only need to type part of frequently used words. Software is also available that will supply possible words for the student to consider. Many computers now have speech synthesis capabilities. These are very useful for students with learning disabilities. As the text is read by the computer, students can find errors and monitor meaning by listening. Spelling choices given by the spell checker become easier as the student hears the pronunciation to help determine which of the suggested words is correct. Hand-held spell checkers are also available, with some models having dictionar-

What is puzzling her?

ies and speech synthesizers. Such multisensory input, with words spelled correctly, can help improve students' spelling abilities.

Though still expensive, voice-activated systems are becoming more affordable. These convert oral dictation to print and are useful when a student's oral language exceeds written language abilities.

Software of the drill and practice variety for mechanics and spelling can be useful for some students. As with reading, it is important to remember that this type of software is most effective when used to reinforce already developing skills.

Mathematics

Interventions for students with learning disabilities have placed greater emphasis on reading than on mathematics, although most students with learning disabilities have difficulties in mathematics as well. These deficiencies in mathematics are often as disabling as a reading deficiency (Bartel, 1990). Traditionally, programs to address mathematical deficiencies have emphasized drill, practice, and memorization. These programs may actually exacerbate the difficulties students with learning disabilities have with math learning (Scheid, 1994). The focus of mathematics instruction should be to help students relate math to their real world and to connect concepts and skills. In this section, we offer considerations and suggestions for use in general education classrooms to help students with learning disabilities develop an understanding of mathematics.

Cawley, Baker-Kroczynski, and Urban (1992) state that teachers working to help students with disabilities should have a clear understanding of the developmental characteristics and levels as children acquire mathematical knowledge and processes. They should also have a commitment to the meaning of mathematics rather than the routines and memorization of procedures and basic facts. The ultimate goal should be to help students apply the process and skills of mathematics to everyday settings.

The following suggestions are organized around guidelines for incorporating cognitive principles into instruction (Scheid, 1994). These are useful when planning mathematical instruction for students with, and without, learning disabilities in general education classrooms at all grade levels.

1. Order and careful planning are essential. Identify the underlying concepts and relationships and explicitly teach them to students. Then, be certain that the activity and materials used in the lessons accurately reflect the mathematical concepts and relationships. Computation accuracy and proficiency should be secondary to concept development.

2. Use the understandings students already have to introduce new concepts and relationships. Present instruction in the context of familiar activities and situations. Problems related to the real lives of the students should be the base of instruction with the language of the students being used to develop the concepts and formal language of mathematics. Mathematical activities are most effective when they can be integrated across the curriculum.

3. Actively engage students in a problem-solving structure to lead them to higher levels of understanding and performance. Because learning is not always efficient for students with learning disabilities, during an activity, plan for flexible time, repeated activities, and variation of activities. Don't be too quick to show students the "correct procedure" or "right answer."

4. Teach strategies as students are engaged in problem solving. Use a variety of instructional techniques. Show the students how to use strategies in the process of working problems with students. Use the "think aloud" technique of saying, for example, "If I draw a picture, it may help me understand the problem better," to help students realize the purpose and process of the strategy. Use direct instruction when necessary, such as when teaching specific steps of a process. Be careful that the strategies do not violate concepts or are advanced beyond the student's understandings. For example, teaching students to use cue words rather than concepts to signal an operation shortchanges the student; real-life situations do not come with cue words. Also, teaching a procedural strategy before students have the conceptual understanding will often interfere with the development of understanding.

5. Rely heavily on questioning using "how" and "why" questions. Then listen to ascertain whether the students understand the concepts, relationships, processes, and procedures. Resist the urge to correct or instruct until students communicate their level of understanding. The students' informal procedures and incomplete/incorrect understandings are the foundation for further planning of instruction.

6. Use learning groups. Communication during problem solving helps integrate new knowledge into what students already know. Students learn as they hear other students explain and as they organize their own thinking through explaining their actions and reasoning.

7. Explicitly teach that it is smart to ask questions about what you do not understand, that errors are natural, and that informal knowledge from daily living is

relevant to formal school mathematics. Figure 10–6 presents ideas for activities incorporating these guidelines.

Students with learning disabilities have great difficulty using formal symbols to represent a mathematical situation (Montague, Applegate, & Marquard, 1993). Teachers should introduce the concept of symbols in activities familiar to the students. Students with learning disabilities will need a number of activities, each with slightly different contexts and materials. Then, the teacher should explicitly develop an abstract representation of the problem with mathematical symbols, at all grade levels, using a continuum from the concrete to the abstract extending from (a) the actual real-life activity and objects to (b) the use of counters such as blocks or chips that can be moved about to (c) the use of pictures/drawings to (d) representations such as tallies or partitioned units (e.g., the "fraction pie") to (e) the formal written symbols and algorithms. The movement along the continuum must be carefully planned and nonlinear. Students should learn to move back and forth between all points on the continuum as they develop concepts and skills. Algorithms should be developed from activities and object displays and activities and object displays should be developed from algorithms with both oral and paper–pencil solutions.

Students with learning disabilities often continue to rely on external representations such as manipulatives or drawings rather than internalize the representations. For this reason, teachers should not use external manipulatives in all activities. Fingers, however, are natural counters for all children in the developmental process and should be allowed. Because the student is limited to ten counters at a time, fingers are important links in the shift to internalization.

As students are developing concepts, allow alternatives to the conventional procedures of solving the problem. Once students understand the relationships, the conventional procedure or computation can be taught as the more efficient. However, the relationship—not the procedure—should always be given precedence. Performance of a conventional learned procedure or computation does not always indicate understanding. Students should also be allowed to use calculators for computations once a concept is learned, with occasional checks of paper and pencil calculations. Schooling must be relevant to life for students with learning disabilities and calculators are standard for adults in real life.

Automaticity or rapid recall of learned facts is a component of many school programs and is reflected in timed tests of basic facts in the four operations. Automaticity increases ease of calculation and does have value; but memorization of facts as isolated rote information is not a useful approach, particularly for students with learning disabilities. A student who views $2 + 5$ as unrelated to $5 + 2$ is not actually learning, but is only acquiring bits of information. Facts can be learned as statements of relationships of parts and the whole. Repeated activities in which students subdivide given numbers of objects into all possible subgroups and record those subgroupings by picture and diagrams, will help students understand the concepts related to basic facts. When working with basic facts, many students with learning disabilities do not use the facts they know to compute the facts they do not know. Understanding the interrelationships of parts and wholes can facilitate their development of this useful strategy.

Once a student understands the relationships of the parts and the whole, five to ten minutes of concentrated practice each day with flash cards, paper and pencil computations, and computer programs can help develop automaticity. A limited group of facts, rather than all of the facts of an operation, should be the

1. You may use histograms associated with daily activities to develop understandings of *more* and *less*, addition and subtraction concepts, and graph meanings. Attach magnetic tape with adhesive backing to one-inch blocks. Give each student a block to place in the row of their choice on a chalkboard during activities of voting and lunch count. Some possible voting activities could be to name a classroom pet, decide on a story to read, or to select a favorite story among three or four. Point graphs can be drawn on the chalkboard to extend graphing skills.

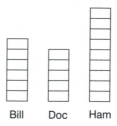

Bill   Doc   Ham

2. Use interlocking blocks to build number rods for showing simple addition and subtraction problems. For simple addition problems, students build number rods of blocks equal to each of the two numbers. The written number to symbolize the number of blocks in each rod is written on a removable label on the top block of each rod. The two rods are then joined; the total number of blocks is counted; and that number is written on a different color label on the bottom end of the rod. Be careful to maintain the concept that the two subsets are joined to comprise the whole quantity. Do not have students with learning disabilities represent the whole quantity with a separate rod containing the total number. They can confuse the total number they see as being a resultant quantity. One boy insisted 1 + 2 was 6 in "school arithmetic" because the teacher represented the answer with a separate grouping of three blocks, resulting in a total of six blocks in front of him.

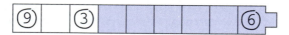

3. Time is often a difficult concept for students with learning disabilities. Try putting the entire calendar for the year on display in sequence around the room. This can help build an understanding of past and future in a way that the usual classroom calendar of only the current month cannot do. Mark important dates (including the students' birthdays) and note interesting class events. Students can review and build a sense of time. Also, throughout the year, use the calendar to illustrate such discussion topics as the months of the year, the days of the week, the recurring pattern of weekdays, and number of days in the month.

4. Number lines mounted vertically match informal understanding more closely than number lines mounted horizontally. Going up is intuitively matched with an increase in quantity and going down is matched with a decrease in quantity. Negative numbers are also easier to understand with a second number tape mounted under the zero line.

5. Students with learning disabilities may have difficulty when writing numbers. They may instead use a set of plastic numbers as an alternative to writing the numbers, or as a model to follow when writing the numbers. Help the student learn to organize by keeping the numbers in sequential order for easy access.

Figure 10–6
Mathematics activities

6. Give students stickers of dinosaurs, cars, animals, etc. to use when writing problems. Have them write a word problem; illustrate the problem with the stickers; and then write the number sentence. This is a good activity for pair work.

7. Have a math journal time. Near the end of the day, students write a math story about something that happened during the day. Students can trade journals and work each other's problems.

8. Students with learning disabilities often have difficulty when working with simple algebra equations, such as $a + 6 = 13$. The use of a letter variable with numbers is confusing for them. Cooperative group work with boxes can help clarify the concept of an unknown quantity. Obtain several costume jewelry boxes and write the letter used in the equation on the box lid. Put pennies equal to the unknown amount into the box and put the lid on the box. Lay the number of pennies in the other set on the table and tell the students, "There are ___13___ pennies altogether. How many pennies are in the box?" Ask for explanations as students explain how they figured it out. Then, take the lid off and have them verify their answers. Have group members devise and set up problems for one another. Gradually move to including the equation in the activity. Be very careful to avoid the too early introduction of the procedure of "doing the same operation on each side of the equation."

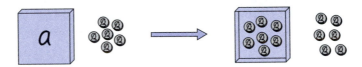

9. Have a "Problem Please" activity each day. This activity can be adjusted to any age group and any content area and is well suited as a transition activity. Using natural situations or content information, write a math activity on the board. With younger children, use pictures or read the problem to them. It is often motivating to include the students' input when generating the problem. Students solve the problem in group activity and each member of the group must be able to explain the group's solution. Encourage students to use alternative ways to show their understandings. The following is an example of a Problem Please for a third-grade classroom:
   a. How many letters in each student's name?
   b. What is the difference in the number of letters in the longest name and the shortest name?
   c. What is the average length of a name in your group?
   d. Does anyone have a name that is the average length?

10. Use literature to develop and reinforce mathematical concepts. Many possibilities can be generated using a collection of buttons and the story "The Lost Button" from *Frog and Toad Are Friends* by Arnold Lobel (New York: Harper & Row, 1970). Children can count buttons, group buttons into three groups and then regroup into four groups with justification for groupings, write and solve addition and subtraction problems with the buttons, graph numbers of buttons in each grouping, determine average number across groups, and even calculate what fractional part each group is of the whole. As the story is read, children sort by attributes and can then paste the buttons on coats they cut from fabric or paper. Other stories about buttons can be read and children can write button stories to extend a thematic unit.

Figure 10–6, *continued*

focus at any one time. The student should go through the group and answer all as quickly as possible. Review those facts that require deliberation or are incorrect by relating them to a known fact ("I know that 5 groups of 6 is 30, so 6 groups of 6 would be 6 more so it is 36. 5 times 6 is 30, 6 times 6 is 36").

When a student can quickly give an answer to a fact, that fact should be included only once a week in the practice group. It is important to periodically review all known facts to maintain the automaticity.

The following exercise is one way to reinforce the relationships of basic facts. Students can make their own flashcards of interrelated facts using four- by six-inch index cards. Cut the cards in triangle shapes by cutting off two corners. The related basic facts are written on the cards.

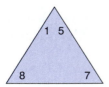 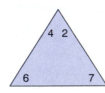

The student can cover one of the three corners, answer, and then immediately check the accuracy of the answer.

Students with learning disabilities can develop the understandings and skills necessary for lifetime functioning through participation in general education mathematical programs. Teachers who use conceptually based programs and embed needed specific instruction facilitate this development.

Technology in Mathematics

The National Council of Teachers of Mathematics (1989) has taken the position that calculators should be a part of every math program. For students with learning disabilities this is very important, as they can concentrate on the concepts rather than on rote computations during problem-solving activities.

Computer software is plentiful for skill and drill activities in computations. The additional sound and animated graphics motivate students and help them practice for automaticity. Readiness skills, such as counting, matching, and number recognition are also available. Much of the available computer software to enhance problem solving is not particularly applicable to students with learning disabilities because of the reading skills necessary to use the software. Teachers should carefully preview software for use by a student with learning disabilities and then monitor as the student uses the software, so that the student benefits from the use.

Other Content Areas

Students with learning disabilities have difficulty in content area classes at all grade levels. The difficulty is not only because of reading difficulties but because they also lack effective strategies for organizing and retaining the concepts and information of content areas.

A variety of techniques—cognitive training, metacognition, and cognitive behavior modification—involve training students to monitor and modify their cognitive strategies. Such approaches are applicable from elementary grades through high school. The premise underlying these approaches is that some students do not produce effective strategies for learning; therefore, their learning processes are ineffective and disorganized. The strategies that tend to require remediation are the plans, actions, steps, and processes that result in inefficient learning or problem solving.

Meichenbaum (1983) suggests that teachers examine their own cognitions before attempting to teach thinking skills to students. His guidelines follow:

1. *Try out* target behaviors yourself to determine all of the steps. Ask students

who perform well, and those who don't, to help analyze the task.

2. *Tune in* to students as they perform tasks. Be especially attuned to hesitation or confidence expressed verbally and nonverbally.

3. *Choose as a training task an actual task the students perform* (or something similar). Otherwise, the students will be unable to generalize.

4. *Ask for students' advice* in devising the training. Use the actual words of the students whenever possible.

5. *Train subtasks and metacognitive skills at the same time*; otherwise, the students may develop separate skills. Subtasks are the skills needed to perform the task, and metacognitive skills include skills such as self-questioning.

6. *Provide specific feedback*, indicating how the use of the strategy leads to improvement. The goal is not to use the metacognitive skills but to improve performance.

7. *Teach generalization* by using the strategy under new circumstances. Use a variety of persons in a variety of settings.

8. *Provide a coping model* by demonstrating what happens when the strategy is not used and how to cope with that failure.

9. *Review the strategy* on a planned basis. Provide for reteaching specific skills.

Modifications and supports for students with learning disabilities are essential in content areas. General suggestions for teachers follow.

1. Be well organized. Provide verbal or written overviews of units or chapters and review key points after the completion of chapters or units. Begin each class period with a short overview of that class period and its relationship to the whole unit. Review important information at the close of the class.

2. Break tasks into subparts. For example, visualize an oral or written report on energy problems as follows: (a) traditional energy resources, (b) cost of energy, (c) alternative forms of energy. Demonstrate how to take notes for each of the main ideas and how to organize them prior to writing or orally presenting the report. Likewise, shorten reading assignments. Secondary school students who have learning disabilities may read less than one-third as much as their peers in the same amount of time.

3. Use direct questions when you give both reading and writing assignments. Emphasize and review key questions until they become automatic. Vary questions according to subject area, but try to include the following: Who is important? What has happened? When did it happen? Where did it happen? Why did it happen? What will happen next?

4. Type assignments, tests, advance organizers, vocabulary lists, and similar materials that you give to students—typing is much easier to read than handwriting. Provide clear, well-spaced materials. Leave space to write directly on the page, and draw lines for responses. Some students may need wide spaces in which to write.

5. Model or demonstrate the use of preview, self-questioning, and review techniques. For consistency, modify commercially prepared work sheets or handouts to reflect the same techniques.

6. Whenever possible, provide information using more than one sense. For example, use diagrams, pictures, or slides as you discuss a concept. Pro-

vide tapes for the students to listen to while they are reading, so that the students receive the information auditorily as well as visually. Such dual presentation helps slow or otherwise inefficient readers. Likewise, use films and visuals to reinforce key concepts.

7. Use peer tutors in many ways and in a variety of subject areas. Alternately, use computer tutorials to allow students to repeat the critical information addressed in class. Use cooperative learning groups or practice tests to provide opportunities to study and review for tests.

8. Provide wait time for students to formulate responses, and provide informational and motivational feedback to allow students to modify their responses.

9. For students with poor writing ability, allow other options for demonstrating knowledge, such as oral reports, artwork, photographic essays, and dioramas.

10. Arrange tests sequentially from easiest to most difficult, and test major concepts rather than details. Use visual cues, such as diagrams, on the test paper itself or on the chalkboard.

11. Allow more time for the completion of tests, or give one section one day and another the next day. Give students a choice regarding the place they will take tests—in the resource room, in a carrel, or in the library (if there is supervision). Alternately, allow students to take their tests on a computer.

The Recall Enhancement Routine is an example of a modification designed for use in general education classes to support students with learning disabilities using many of the above suggestions. This approach enhances the retention of targeted information by associating mnemonic devices with information (Bulgren, Schumaker, & Deshler, 1994). The mnemonic enhancement can be used during the initial delivery and/or the review. The teacher identifies the factual information the students are to remember and designs a mnemonic device of one of three types to be used with the information: (a) first-letter acronym (b) mental imagery, and (c) keyword. An example of an acronym is *HOMES* used to remember the Great Lakes—the letters stand for *H*uron, *O*ntario, *M*ichigan, *E*rie, and *S*uperior. Mental imagery can be used to enhance recall of the fact that the Copperheads supported the Confederacy by having students build a mental image of a Confederate soldier with a shining copper head waving a Confederate flag. Keywords are slight alterations of the actual words to words that are more familiar and that create a somewhat ridiculous picture. An example of this device is to enhance the recall of the fact that Hearst covered the war in Cuba by having students form a visual image of a large, black shiny hearse (Hearst) with a large ice cube (Cuba) sitting on top.

During the lesson presentation, the teacher follows a five-step procedure:

1. Cues the students that the information to follow is important
2. Cues the students to take notes about the information and the device
3. Tells the students which type of device is to be used
4. Presents the information and the mnemonic, writing or sketching on the board
5. Reviews the mnemonic at the end of the period

This process brings the important information to the students' attention and provides elaboration to increase retention and recall.

Another technique for elaborating information is a more indirect approach of elaborative interrogation with systematic questioning and coaching. This is used so that students use their prior knowledge to provide rational explanations for information (Scruggs, Mastropieri, & Sullivan, 1994). After presenting a content area fact, the teacher asks a student to provide an explanation about why the fact would make sense. The teacher uses further structured questioning to activate prior knowledge if the student is unable to provide a correct explanation. By linking new information to current knowledge, the student is able to actively construct new understandings and elaborate and integrate them to retain the new information.

The POSSE instructional program is another program designed to involve students with learning disabilities in active construction of content area meaning (Englert, Tarrant, Mariage, & Oxer, 1994). Prior to reading in the content area, the teacher guides the group in predicting what ideas will be in the text and organizing background knowledge. To predict, students gather cues from titles, headings, pictures, and introductory paragraphs to predict what will be in the text by brainstorming, using prior knowledge. The teacher asks students to link specific cues from the preview of the text to their predictions. The brainstormed ideas are organized by grouping similar ideas in a semantic map with the teacher as scribe. Students then read short segments and summarize by identifying the main idea. The teacher records the main idea on a second semantic map. The teacher or a student restates the main idea in the form of a question and elicits relevant details, which the teacher records on the semantic map. Everyone then compares and discusses the two semantic maps, explaining unfamiliar vocabulary or unclear information. Predictions are made about the next section and the process

repeated. The leadership of the POSSE is reciprocal, with the teacher turning the responsibility of directing the strategies over to students so that all become teachers and active mediators of learning using prior knowledge, social dialogue, and effective strategies.

Within content areas, students with learning disabilities often need a systematic sequencing of organizational supports. These often need to be highly structured, and the student will require instruction in their use. An example of this type of systematic sequencing of supports is the use of *Who*, *What*, *Where*, *When*, and *Why* while taking notes, reading, and writing in a content area. The first step is to use an external, high-support organizational sheet, containing areas for each key element and a brief definition (Figure 10–7). The teacher interacts with the students, using modeling, think aloud, and direct explanation to organize a selected reading using the sheet. After several readings with the sheet, the teacher fades the support and gradually turns the activity over to the students. The sheet is then used with readings in other content areas, and as a guide for prewriting organization in the content areas.

The teacher then fades the external support sheet to a sheet without the boxes and with only the named areas. After students are able to easily use this format, the teacher modifies the support sheet so it has the listing of *Who*, *What*, *Where*, *When*, and *Why* at the top of the sheet. The next modification is to write only *The 5 W's* at the top. Finally, the teacher fades all external prompts. Teachers must observe and monitor student use of this procedure so that they may withdraw (and possibly reintroduce) the support appropriate to the students' acquisition of the strategy.

To help students with note taking, divide 5-by-8-inch cards into three spaces, as shown in Figure 10–8. Alternately, direct the students to divide each notebook page into four

Figure 10–7
High-support organizational
sheet—The five W's

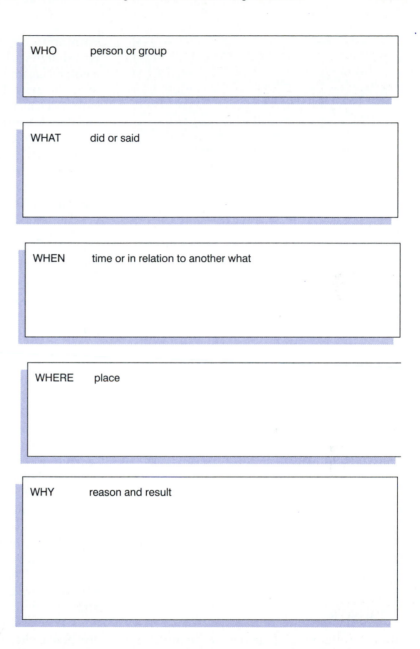

WHO   person or group

WHAT   did or said

WHEN   time or in relation to another what

WHERE   place

WHY   reason and result

columns going down the page. Tell the students to label the columns "Vocabulary," "People," "Places and Dates," and "Ideas and Discoveries." At the top of the notebook pages, have the students write the headings that are in bold print or color. (Several notebook pages may be necessary for each chapter.) Teach the students to fill in the columns as they read the chapter. The labels for the columns may be modified to reflect the rele-

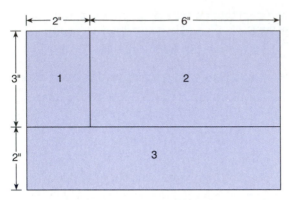

Note: Space 1 is for major ideas and topics, space 2 is for supporting information, and space 3 is for a summary or questions.

Figure 10–8
Diagram for note taking

vant aspects of the various content areas or the particular chapters within a specific book.

Some students require specific teaching regarding the use of organizational aids and cues. Teach students the names and uses of the specific parts of a book, such as the index, glossary, and table of contents. Also teach students how to identify and use headings, sub-headings, italics, color, and bold print. In addition, content area materials often depend on graphics and illustrations to present important information. Because such characteristics of content area materials can be problematic for students, teach students to recognize such organizational cues.

Social Skills

Many students with learning disabilities exhibit significantly poorer social skills than their peers. Though most of these students have the necessary knowledge to handle social situations, they are often unable to use the knowledge appropriately (Tur-Kaspa & Bryan, 1994). A social environment is necessary for

learning to use appropriate social skills and, for students, the social environment is the regular classroom. State rules for the classroom clearly. Teach them to all students, making clear the consequences of misbehavior. Apply these consequences consistently and fairly. Role play and frequent review may be necessary for a student with learning disabilities to really understand the rules. Behaviors, both appropriate and inappropriate, of the student and others ought to be discussed in terms of the classroom rules.

The general education teacher should provide activities that include students with disabilities as contributing members of groups. Many students with learning disabilities have strengths in specific areas or knowledge about special interests that may authentically contribute to group efforts. Pairing a student with learning disabilities and a popular student in classroom activities can both provide modeling of appropriate social interactions and build a sense of acceptance and inclusion. Friendships often develop that extend to activities outside of the classroom.

Responsibilities are a means of including a student in classroom membership, so students with learning disabilities should be a part of routine classroom responsibilities. When possible, having a student tutor a younger student or teach class members about an area of interest or expertise can provide for opportunities to practice social interactions. Give specific feedback to the student, in a positive way, about observed behaviors. Note and reinforce appropriate behaviors and discuss inappropriate behaviors, suggesting acceptable alternative behaviors.

Students with learning disabilities may have a poor self-concept and may experience peer rejection because of low academic achievement. Individually competitive activities can highlight the low achievement of these students and should be kept to a mini-

Reading is often difficult for students with learning disabilities.

mum. Even the bulletin board display of ice cream cones with a scoop for each book read can send negative messages about a student with learning disabilities and result in lowered social interaction ability. Using alternative methods for demonstrating achievement and understanding will benefit all students.

In Chapter 11, we further discuss approaches and commercial materials for teaching specific social skills. As with all areas of education, the social characteristics of students with learning disabilities are diverse and the educational plan for an individual student must address that student's specific needs.

■ Summary

In this chapter, we reviewed several definitions of learning disabilities and presented characteristics of students with learning disabilities. After outlining the identification process, we discussed certain unique needs of students with learning disabilities. We offered teaching suggestions for use by the regular classroom teacher, with emphasis on the areas of reading, writing, language development, and mathematics. We discussed programs such as the Early Literacy Program, and two language experience approaches, and emphasized the importance of learning strategy instruction.

We provided suggestions for incorporating cognitive principles into mathematics instruction, highlighting the potential of technology in teaching students with learning disabilities. We offered a series of general instructional suggestions, applicable to many different subject content areas, emphasizing the importance of attention to social skills development.

chapter 11

- Under what conditions might unacceptable behavior be an indication of behavior disorders? When might it not be an indication of behavior disorders?

- Why might some students be considered to have a behavior disorder in one school and not considered to have a behavior disorder in another school? How are such decisions made?

- Why is there such variety in approaches to treatment of behavior disorders?

- What is the ecological approach to the treatment of students with behavior disorders? How does it differ from the behavioral approach? How does it differ from the psychodynamic approach? Which might you more likely use to deal with a 10-year-old child who is exhibiting acting out behavior and identified as having a behavior disorder?

- How do logical consequences and punishment differ? How are they similar?

- How are juvenile delinquency and behavior disorders related? To what extent are they synonymous?

- How may child abuse be related to behavior disorders?

Teaching Students Who Have Emotional and Behavior Disorders

■■■■■■■■■■

Emotional and behavior disorders are among the most troubling disabilities for many teachers. When students are disruptive and interfere with the learning of others, the result is troubled students, and concerned teachers and parents. When it appears that a student has the ability to "behave" but won't, many adults lose patience.

There have been many discussions among professionals regarding acceptable definitions of emotional and behavior disorders and related terminology. Such discussions will likely continue as our understanding of child development and psychology grows. Definitions of terms such as *immature, disruptive, socially maladjusted, delinquent, withdrawn,* and *aggressive,* all used to label students with emotional and behavior disorders, will continue to be refined and modified.

Teachers are somewhat less concerned about such discussions and want information regarding ways to prevent inappropriate behavior and how best to manage it in the event that it occurs (and it will if the student has an emotional and behavior disorder). In this chapter, we address these issues as well as other topics that are related to, but not synonomous with, emotional and behavior disorders.

■■■■■■■■■■■

Definitions of Emotional and Behavior Disorders

There have been several attempts to find a single definition of emotional or behavior disorders that would be satisfactory to the various disciplines such as education, psychiatry, psychology, medicine, and sociology involved with this disability. The federal definition uses the term *serious emotional disturbance* and makes the following statement:

The term means a condition exhibiting one or more of the following characteristics over a long period of time and to a marked extent, which adversely affects educational performance.

An inability to learn which cannot be explained by intellectual, sensory, or health factors;

An inability to build or maintain satisfactory relationships with peers and teachers;

Inappropriate types of behavior or feelings under normal circumstances;

A general pervasive mood of unhappiness or depression;

Or a tendency to develop physical symptoms or fears associated with personal or school problems.

The term includes children who are schizophrenic. The term does not include children who are socially maladjusted unless it is determined that they are seriously emotionally disturbed. (34 CFR 300.7 (9), 1993)

Many educators and specialists have criticized this definition, particularly because of the ambiguity of such terms as "seriously," "over a long period of time," and "to a marked degree." Also, it would seem, according to this definition, that if students were to experience the characteristics listed but maintain average educational performance they would not be eligible for services. Further, the exclusion of students who are "socially maladjusted" appears to suggest that they would not exhibit any of the characteristics listed and may arbitrarily exclude students who need services (Bower, 1982; Cline, 1990; Kauffman, 1993a).

Representatives from various professional organizations and disciplines combined to form the National Mental Health and Special Education Coalition and developed a definition they hope will be adopted at the federal level (Forness & Knitzer, 1991). This proposed definition includes the following:

1. Disorders that are behavioral as well as emotional
2. Behavioral and emotional responses that are so different from those appropriate to age, culture, or ethnic norms that they adversely affect academic, social, vocational, or personal performance
3. Responses that are more than temporary and expected as a result of stressful events in the environment
4. Consistent problems in an environment in addition to school
5. Persistent disorders despite ordinary interventions
6. The possibility of behavioral or emotional disorders with other disabilities
7. A full range of disorders related to emotions and behavior such as schizophrenia, anxiety, affective, conduct, or adjustment (Adapted from Forness & Knitzer, 1991)

The American Psychiatric Association *Diagnostic and Statistical Manual of Mental Disorders*, used by psychiatrists, psychologists and other health care workers, provides a classification system that includes terms such as disruptive behavior disorders, oppositional-defiant behaviors, over-anxious disorder, elective mutism, organic disorders due to brain pathology, substance-use disorders, and disorders of sociocultural or psychological origin (no known organic pathology). Other authors and sources use classification systems that include terms such as conduct disorders, aggressive behavior, antisocial behaviors, social isolation, compulsive, psychotic, and personality disorders (Bullock, 1991; Paul & Epanchin, 1991; Nelson & Pearson, 1991; Newcomer, 1993; Haring, McCormick, & Haring, 1994).

While other professionals may debate the merits of definitions and terminology, teachers have "little difficulty identifying the student with emotional problems" (McDowell, Adamson, & Wood, 1982, p. 3). Normal behavior is often considered as a range of behaviors along a continuum. The limits of normal or acceptable behavior are based on subjective judgments related to environmental, cultural, and situational factors. Teachers who observe various levels or stages of development each day are able to recognize students with emotional and behavioral problems (Lourie, 1991).

On the other hand, teachers should not assume that a student has emotional or behavior disorders based on arbitrary or capricious factors. The behaviors must be present over a period of time, be of sufficient intensity (clearly different from normal), occur frequently, and not be ameliorated through usual disciplinary or assistive practices. All students experience emotional crises that may be minor or severe; however, they are usually transitory. The frequency of occurrence, duration, and degree of severity form the guidelines for teachers in determining which students to refer for special assistance.

Prereferral and Referral

Teachers who are aware of student behavior sufficiently different from normal and that occurs frequently over a period of time should request a prereferral conference, for the purpose of consultation or for suggestions regarding interventions, as described in Chapter 2. Depending on local school practices, the spe-

Classroom activities can enhance self concept.

cialist who teaches students with emotional or behavior disorders may observe the student in the classroom to complete a checklist or rating scale of classroom interactions (Figure 11–1) and may ask the teacher also to complete a checklist (Figure 11–2). More formal checklists include *The Walker Problem Behavior Identification Checklist* (Walker, 1983), which lists observable behaviors that are rated by the teacher; *Burks Behavior Rating Scales* (Burks, 1977), which require ratings by the teacher; the *Systematic Screening for Behavior Disorders* (Walker & Severson, 1990), which uses teacher judgment and observations to determine further steps to be taken; the *Child Behavior Checklist* (Achenbach & Edelbrock, 1991), used for a teacher report; the *Social-Emotional Dimension Scale* (Hutton & Roberts, 1986), which has items related to the five behavioral characteristics of the federal definition; the *Behavior Rating Profile* (Brown & Hammill, 1983), for which teachers, peers, and parents provide ratings; and the *Hahneman High School Behavior Scale* (Spivak & Swift, 1972), which measures ability to cope with the pressures of the secondary school system. These, and other similar measures may be completed by the classroom teacher or the behavior disorders teacher/specialist. Following the procedures and/or interventions as described in Chapter 2 in relation to prereferral may result in resolution of the emotional or behavior problem. If not, a referral may be initiated and conducted. It is particularly important that cultural differences do not unfairly bias the assessment or judgments related to the assessment. The Council for Children with Behavioral Disorders (1989)

Behaviors	Date	Length of observation	Mark each time behavior occurs	Comments
Student uses profanity				
Student must be told more than once to begin work				
Student destroys property				
Student talks out inappropriately				
Student makes inappropriate noises				
Student moves around aimlessly				
Student is out of seat				
Student does not follow teacher directions				
Student interrupts others				
Student is verbally abusive to others				
Student becomes angry with little provocation				

Figure 11–1
Sample items from a checklist used by an observer

Behaviors	Frequency			Under what circumstances does the behavior occur?	Comments
	Daily	Weekly	Monthly		

Student's name: _____ **Date:** _____

Birth date: _____ **School:** _____

Please check the areas that are applicable. If you wish to make comments, please do so.

Behaviors	Daily	Weekly	Monthly	Under what circumstances does the behavior occur?	Comments
Needs close supervision					
Destroys property					
Throws temper tantrums					
Displays erratic, unpredictable behavior					
Indicates poor self-concept					
Appears angry or hostile					
Isolates self					
Appears out of touch with reality					
Does not achieve at expected academic level					
Seeks inordinate amount of attention					
Interferes with learning of others					
Makes inappropriate noises					
Threatens to injure self or others					
Does injure self or others					
Verbally assaults others					
Physically assaults others					
Avoids eye contact					
Cries inappropriately					
Refuses to talk with teacher					
Refuses to talk with others					
Seems to daydream					

Figure 11–2
Sample items from a checklist used by the regular classroom teacher

370

published guidelines related to assessment, including the following recommendations:

1. Focus on classroom and learning environments that may foster behavior problems, attending to observable teacher and student behavior and the conditions under which these occur.
2. Attend to predisposing factors that may play a role in the student's behavior such as family conditions, prior experiences with learning, culture, cultural and family expectations, and tolerance levels.
3. Focus evaluation practices on the instructional process such as teaching procedures, instructional organization, and instructional support.
4. Avoid placing all of the responsibility for learning or performance failure on the student.

If a referral is made and the student is found to be eligible for special education services, the involved parties develop and implement an IEP for that student. For some students the least restrictive placement may be a special class or even a residential facility. This type of placement may be necessary when the student is self-injurious, suicidal, psychotic, or injurious to others. Most students remain in regular classes with support from consulting/special education teachers.

Collaboration Among Teachers

Regular classroom teachers may find it relatively easy to individualize instruction and provide effective learning interactions with students who have learning disabilities or make accommodations for students who have hearing impairments or low vision.

However, the same teachers may implement a variety of modifications to address the needs of students who have behavior disorders and feel as if they are making little or no progress. The disruptive nature of behavior disorders may lead teachers to discouragement and doubt about their teaching ability. Therefore, a mutual support system between consulting teachers or teachers of students who are behavior disordered and classroom teachers may be necessary. By sharing frustrations, disappointments, and successes, teachers can regain perspective and renew their enthusiasm.

Special education teachers provide suggestions relating to management of behavior problems and remedial academic assistance. They also teach social skills to small groups of students, provide a place for students to cool off, and temporarily remove students from the regular classroom for intense discussions relating to behavior. In general, the assistance occurs in response to requests or mutually agreed-upon plans. In some cases, psychologists, psychiatrists, or counselors provide therapy for students on a regular basis.

It is essential that teachers of regular classes and specialists discuss what methods they are to use. Because there is such a variation in theories about the causes of emotional or behavior disorders and, therefore, a wide variation in treatments, the teachers involved must agree theoretically and personally how best to proceed. Students who have behavior disorders are often manipulative. They use ambiguities on the part of the teachers to their fullest advantage. For example, if a specialist believes that the student's difficulties are caused by internal hostility and pent-up anger and thinks the way to deal with them is to provide a warm, accepting environment and to allow acting out or aggression so that the student can work through them, then treatment is based on this premise. If, on the other hand, the regular classroom teacher cannot allow such acting out in the classroom or cannot tolerate barrages of obscene language, the two different approaches will lead to ambiguity or dissension.

A second example involves a specialist who believes in counting and observing every behavior. The specialist also believes that the student has learned inappropriate behaviors and therefore must learn new behaviors to function successfully in regular classes. This philosophy is reflected in the specialist's suggestions for treatment. However if, in this scenario, the regular classroom teacher believes in allowing students to express themselves freely and personally believes in "flowing with the students," allowing them many choices in what and how to study, both teachers will be frustrated and the student will take advantage of the situation.

Regular class teachers and specialists must arrive at some general agreement, and each must be somewhat comfortable with the other's approach to the treatment. Few teachers are able to teach consistently in manners inconsistent with their personalities. For example, teachers who are extremely creative, take almost all their cues from the students, and plan on a minute-by-minute basis are not usually comfortable with a structured, precise behavior modification approach. This is not to say that either approach is better or more effective but only that they are different. Both teachers must recognize and acknowledge their unique teaching styles and know how they teach most comfortably and effectively. Then, during the writing of the IEP, each style must be considered when developing the best educational plan for the student. This cooperation requires discussion and compromise, but it is at this point—the writing of the IEP—that various potential conflicts must be resolved.

 Major Theoretical Approaches

Definitions of emotional and behavior disorders vary among the disciplines, such as psychiatry, social work, and education, concerned with student behavior. Each discipline's unique orientation to the cause of the disorder provides the basis for that discipline's proposed treatments or interventions to ameliorate the problem. Table 11–1 and the following discussion indicate the key aspects of these approaches and provide insight into the manner in which teachers may modify these approaches for classroom use.

Behavior Modification

In the early 1960s, the term *behavior modification* was introduced (and later the same decade, the term *applied behavior analysis* was used) to emphasize the application of behaviorist principles to real-life settings. Usually, the term *applied behavior analysis* refers to a more stringent relationship between the behavior changed and the intervention (Alberto & Troutman, 1990). Applied behavior analysts use the principles of specific data collection, reinforcement, and observation of change in a manner similar to that of behaviorists (Ysseldyke & Algozzine, 1984). In the interest of simplicity, this chapter uses the term *behavior modification*. As a general rule, in journal articles or other books, *behavior modification* is defined more generally and *applied behavior analysis* somewhat more rigorously, but both deal with behavior change.

With students who are verbally or physically aggressive, some variation of behavior modification is ordinarily attempted first. Many educators believe it to be the quickest, most efficient technique to reduce or eliminate inappropriate behaviors (Alberto & Troutman, 1990; Walker & Shea, 1991).

Table 11–1

Theoretical approaches to emotional and behavior disorders

Approach or Conceptual Model	Causes of Emotional and Behavior Disorders	Treatment Indicated
Biophysical	Internal causes, such as chemical imbalances, genetic deficiencies, poor nutrition, disrupted sleep patterns, brain injury.	Use medication like tranquilizers, stimulants, or antidepressants and/or apply behavior modification.
Behavioral	External causes, such as inappropriate behavior learned, reinforced, and maintained by others in the environment.	Remove reinforcers that maintain inappropriate behavior, reinforce appropriate behavior, teach acceptable behavior.
Psychodynamic	Internal causes, such as unsuccessful negotiation of psychological stages, internal conflicts, guilt feelings.	Allow free expression of feelings, provide accepting warm environment, avoid too many demands.
Sociological	External causes, such as society's labeling as deviant, factors "forcing" rule breaking, lack of social rules that serve as behavior inhibitors.	Modify society, teach alternate behaviors, help the individual establish rules for himself or herself.
Ecological	Internal and external causes, that is, interaction between feelings, needs, and desires and society's norms, demands, and responsibilities.	Aid adjustment of the individual, the environment, or both; manipulate either the individual or the environment for the benefit of both.

As noted in Table 11–1, behaviorists assume that inappropriate behaviors have been learned and are being maintained by reinforcement. The keys to this approach are determining the nature of the reinforcement and eliminating it or using a more powerful reinforcer to bring about desired behavior. Teachers become manipulators of the environment of students, and by such manipulation, they systematically plan changes in behavior.

In practice, teachers observe students, count the inappropriate behaviors (which have been stated specifically), and attempt to determine what precedes and follows the behav-iors. Observing and counting provide information regarding how frequently the behaviors occur, as well as show the seriousness of the behaviors. By noting what precedes and follows behaviors, teachers may gain clues concerning what reinforces them. After obtaining a count and noting possible reinforcers, teachers carefully select reinforcers to apply when students exhibit desired behaviors after a given time period or a given number of appropriate responses.

For example, a student uses obscene language at the slightest provocation. The teacher defines the behavior precisely. Then, the teacher counts the number of times this behavior occurs during a class period, during a particular time of the day, or during an entire day. This count is usually taken for 3 to 5 days to establish a baseline (Figure 11–3). The teacher may also note that after each occurrence, some or all of the class laughed or that the teacher said something about the language to the student.

At this point, the teacher selects an intervention. In this example, if the student seems to enjoy the attention and social rewards of attention from the class and the teacher, the teacher may decide to provide attention when

the student does not use obscene language. This, then, is the intervention. Watching for times when the student is working or paying attention, the teacher may praise the student at least three times during every hour. During this period of intervention, the teacher keeps careful records to note whether the obscene language is decreasing, increasing, or remaining the same (see Figure 11–3). If the behavior is decreasing, the positive comments may be considered successful.

If the behavior is not decreasing, the reinforcer is not powerful enough and another must be selected. This new reinforcer is then

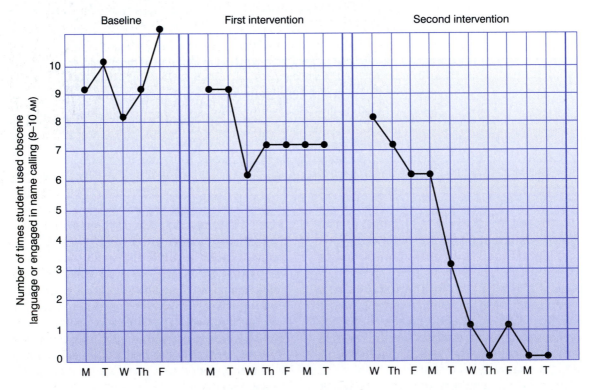

Note: The first intervention decreased the behavior but not to an acceptable level, and another intervention was attempted.

Figure 11–3
Sample teacher record of frequency of a student's verbal abuse

tried, records are kept to determine whether the behavior is decreasing, and if necessary, still another reinforcer is selected. The process continues until the appropriate reinforcer is found and the behavior is decreased to an acceptable level or eliminated; then the reinforcers are phased out.

In other situations, the objective may be to increase a desirable behavior. For example, the objective may be to increase the number of times the student volunteers a response during a class discussion. The same principles of obtaining a baseline, attempting an intervention, and noting the results apply, except that in this case, the teacher notes whether the behavior is increasing. Completion of work, time spent on tasks, cooperative efforts with peers, and effective use of study time are other behaviors that teachers ordinarily want to increase.

Reinforcers

There are a variety of ways to find out what is reinforcing, such as by observing what students do during free time or asking what they would enjoy doing. Reinforcers can be tangible items, tokens, social reinforcers, or special privileges (Figure 11–4).

The goal of teachers should be to choose reinforcers that are useful with all students. For example, a teacher should not give cookies to a ninth grader to eliminate tardiness if providing 10 minutes at the end of the class period to begin homework is sufficient reinforcement. If the principal of a school does not allow students on the playground or in the student lounge except at designated times, then the teacher cannot use free time in such locations as reinforcers. If the teacher has a personal aversion to using food, free time, or any other particular reinforcer, these obviously should not be used.

Time Out

Sometimes, students who have behavior disorders require a period of time during which they are separated by some physical space in the room. When this separation seems advisable, the teacher can physically move the desk of a student to the front, back, or side of the

Figure 11–4

Reinforcers

Source: Based on *Behavior Management: A Practical Approach for Educators* (pp. 98–99) by J. E. Walker & T. M. Shea, 1991, Englewood Cliffs, NJ: Merrill/Prentice Hall.

1. *Tangible reinforcers.* Peanuts; personal grooming aids; special materials, such as felt pens and colored pencils; toys; models.

2. *Token reinforcers.* Individual behavior charts; achievement charts; checks; points; happy faces; stars; trading stamps.

3. *Social reinforcers.* Verbal praise; clapping or cheering from others; display of work or projects; helping the librarian, school secretary, nurse, cooks, custodian, or counselor; tutoring younger children.

4. *Special privileges.* Exemption from an assignment, homework, or a test; extra time before or after recess; taking class roll; distributing or collecting materials; serving as secretary for class meetings; operating the slide, movie, or filmstrip projector; leading or organizing an event, such as a class raffle or auction; reading a message over the intercom; washing the chalkboard; watering the plants; feeding the fish or other animals.

room to provide physical space between the student and the rest of the class. The purpose of the removal varies. Sometimes, it is to reduce the amount of reinforcement from other students (if the student is in the back of the room or over to one side, antics are not so visible). Being very near the teacher often prevents the student from annoying others. However, a student may refuse to move, thereby creating a new problem for the teacher—a test of wills. Alternately, the student may create more commotion as he or she moves than the move is worth. The student may bang desks; knock books, pencils, or papers off desks; and move slowly to lengthen the time of the chaos. The teacher must determine whether asking the student to move is advisable.

In another form of time out, the teacher physically marks out a specific place (for example, bookcases arranged to form an enclosed corner). In this area, a rug or pillows may be available along with reading materials or anything else the teacher and students arrange. A class discussion should be held about the purpose of such a space. The teacher may suggest that a student go to the space to gain control, or the student may go independently for the same reason. Be sure that this place is seen as a safe haven, not punishment, so that time out is a way to reduce tensions that arise from having to deal with pressing problems.

Regardless of whether the teacher suggests that a student go to the space or the student selects it, the student should come out only when he or she chooses to. It is important that the teacher explain that using this space does not absolve the student from responsibility for assignments or homework. This explanation should prevent abuses and misunderstandings. If a student does abuse the privilege, and it is to be expected that students who are behaviorally disordered will try, discuss the guidelines with the offending student—and discuss them again and again.

Contracts

No discussion of behavior modification, however brief, should omit the principle of contracting. Contracts are agreements that specify in exact terms what the student must do and what the teacher will do *after* the student has completed his or her portion of the agreement. This sequence is essential, particularly with students who have behavior or academic problems. The teacher would be in an untenable position if the student were to receive the reward before performing his or her portion of the contract, an approach analogous to saying, "You can have the ice cream first if you promise to eat your spinach afterward."

Contracts may be informal verbal agreements, simple written statements, or sophisticated written and witnessed agreements (Figures 11–5 and 11–6). Which is most useful depends primarily on the needs of the student. Secondary students often respond more favorably to written agreements. Sometimes, a teacher may want the parents to sign the contract, especially if the task being negotiated is one involving homework. By asking the parents to sign, the teacher is ensuring their awareness. Of course, teachers must realize, particularly with the parents of disruptive students, that the parents' awareness does not ensure follow-through or cooperation.

The following contract guidelines are based on Homme, Csanyi, Gonzales, and Rechs (1979). The guidelines provide a useful summary of the characteristics of proper contracting.

1. Performance should come before rewards.
2. Rewards should immediately follow performance in the beginning.
3. Rewards should be provided frequently and for each approximation.
4. Rewards should be provided for accomplishment rather than obedience. The

CONTRACT

This contract is between _____ and

_____

I (student) agree to do the following:

_____

_____

_____

When I do I will be able to:

_____

_____

_____

And I (teacher) agree to help by:

_____

_____

_____

Student signature _____ Teacher signature _____

Date signed _____ Date to be renegotiated _____

Figure 11–5
Sample contract

tone of the contract should be, "When you do this, you can . . . " rather than "If you do this, then I will allow you to. . . . "

5. Contracts should be fair and honest. Teachers and students must agree that the rewards are appropriate for the tasks completed. After completion of the tasks, teachers must follow through with the rewards. If for some unforeseen reason teachers cannot provide the rewards, students should be allowed to choose alter-

nate rewards or be given the rewards specified at the earliest possible time.

6. The terms of the contract should be clear. A statement like "if you behave during class" is not clear. Teachers may have definite standards in mind, but students may interpret *behave* in an entirely different manner.

7. Contracts should be positive. This quality is especially important for students who have a history of conflict with authority figures. Positive statements

Figure 11–6

Sample contract

Source: From *It's Positively Fun* (p. 27) by P. Kaplan, J. Kohfeldt, & K. Sturla, 1974, Denver: Love. Reprinted by permission.

avoid the threat of punishment and contribute to positive educational experiences.

8. Contracts should be used systematically. Teachers might ask themselves what the payoff is for the student. Does the student achieve a sense of satisfaction from appropriate behavior, or will the student gain satisfaction from being able to have free time? Will this change become the first of a series of small but ever closer approximations to the desired goal of appropriate behavior in the classroom?

For teachers unfamiliar with negotiating contracts, it may be best to begin with a simple format. Teachers should use the following contract checklist when first making contracts.

1. Explain contracts and contracting.
2. Show an example of a contract.
3. Discuss possible tasks and list student-suggested and teacher-suggested tasks.
4. Agree on a task.
5. Suggest reinforcers or ask the student to suggest them.

6. Negotiate the ratio of the task to the reinforcer.
7. Identify the time allotted for the task.
8. Identify the criterion or achievement level for a task completion.
9. Agree on the method of evaluation.
10. Negotiate the delivery of the reinforcer.
11. Set a time or date for renegotiation.
12. Sign the contract and have the student sign it.

Once familiar and comfortable with contracting, teachers may omit or combine various steps.

Teachers may also employ combinations of contracts, point systems, or tokens. Students and teachers should negotiate the items and the possible points or tokens to be earned.

The points or tokens can then be traded for free time or other reinforcers (Figure 11–7). By arranging the value of the reinforcers with students (the three cards alluded to in Figure 11–7) some allowance is made for students who find it extremely difficult to perform the tasks required. They have goals for which to strive yet receive something for less successful efforts. There should be a lower limit (145 points in Figure 11–7) below which no reinforcement is given.

There is an element of risk in using this type of contract and point system. If a student views something on card 2 as desirable, the student may reach exactly the points necessary to receive it and thereafter be uncooperative, knowing that he or she will still receive the reward. If teachers anticipate this problem, they should not use the varying reinforcer sys-

Name: _____		Date: _____				
5 points possible for each	**Mon.**	**Tues.**	**Wed.**	**Thurs.**	**Fri.**	**TOTAL**
Promptness						
Preparedness (book, paper, pencil)						
Completed homework						
Use of time						
Effort						
Cooperation						
Attitude						
Bonus points for extra effort, extra neat homework						

GRAND TOTAL: _____

175 points or above: Choose from card 1
160–174 points: Choose from card 2
145–159 points: Choose from card 3

Figure 11–7
Points or tokens that can be traded for reinforcements

tem. However, if students discuss the issue in good faith but manipulate it to advantage, teachers should point out the change and use a more direct system of contracting.

Modeling

Research indicates that children imitate the behavior they observe; however, they are not always discriminating in what they imitate. Thus, teachers may want to seat certain students in close proximity to students who model specific behaviors (such as seating a student behind one who usually does raise his or her hand and waits to be called on). Yet, teachers must keep in mind elements that can affect the results. In its simplest form, modeling perhaps works best with young students. Still, for a variety of reasons, some students do not receive sufficient reinforcement merely in the example of a model. In addition, the mere fact that a teacher sees a student as a model does not mean that other students view him or her in the same manner. To them, a model may seem too good, too bright, the teacher's pet, or simply obnoxious. Thus, it may be a violation of peer-group norms to imitate this student in any manner whatsoever. When such is the case, the model may be subjected to taunts and ridicule outside of class, and more aggressive students may not wait until after class to begin their jeers.

At the secondary level, guiding students in discussion of problems is generally more productive than is modeling. In discussion, help students (a) define a problem precisely, (b) establish appropriate goals, and (c) find solutions to the problem. With this approach, peer pressure may be a powerful influence on students who have emotional and behavior disorders.

Ethics

One additional concern related to behavior modification must be addressed—the ethical aspects of manipulating another person's behavior. The following guidelines for teachers who are considering the use of behavior modification are loosely based on Walker and Shea (1991):

1. Consider why you want or feel a need to change the behavior of another person. Is it to create a positive learning environment for all students? Or is it some inner need to exert control or demonstrate power?

2. Attempt to understand the problems of students, not merely control. Discuss the behavior you deem inappropriate to gain insights with regard to the behavior. If you learn through such discussions that the student throws a pencil because he or she observes a parent throwing dishes when angry or frustrated, you can better decide if or how to use behavior modification.

3. Determine whether the behavior change will help the student better understand himself or herself or the environment. Manipulating behavior merely for the sake of conformity is not defensible.

4. Be aware that your knowledge of human behavior is in a continuous stage of development and that students change and develop. Keep abreast of developing information in regard to how and why people behave as they do.

Teachers should also consider the following questions with respect to the use of behavior modification:

1. Will intervention help this student be viewed as more normal in this environment?

2. Will a change in the student's behavior lead to greater acceptance by peers?

3. Is this intervention fair to the student?

4. Does the intervention demonstrate respect for the student as an individual?
5. Does this intervention allow the student to maintain dignity?

Psychodynamic Approach

As a treatment for mental illness, psychodynamic therapy is used in mental health settings such as hospitals (Rich, 1982). In schools, psychologists and psychiatrists may use it in conjunction with other types of therapy or may adapt it to meet the needs of students. Ethical considerations that relate to required training and expertise with guidance from qualified supervisors contraindicate use of the psychodynamic approach by teachers, but regular classroom teachers may find some variations and adaptations useful. As noted in Table 11–1, the psychodynamic approach includes certain basic assumptions in regard to the cause of inappropriate behavior.

If a student is extremely angry with himself or herself, peers, the teacher, the school, and the whole world, then expressing the anger in an acceptable manner may serve as a release to the student. Drawing, painting, or writing may be used as a medium for expression of feelings, as may dance, drama, or role playing. Teachers must decide how and when to use this method. Often, the medium depends on the age of the student, the structure of the classroom, and the school system. In lower grades, because the classrooms are essentially self-contained, teachers have more latitude in the selection of the time and means of implementation. In the upper grades, when teachers have each group of students for only a relatively short time (a 40- to 50-minute period), implementation is much more difficult.

In primarily self-contained rooms, a portion of the room can have an easel, paints, tapedeck, or whatever else is necessary for various types of therapy. After the teacher knows the student well enough and thinks that one or more of the expressive media may be helpful, the teacher can discuss with the student when, how, and under what conditions the student may use the materials. When the school system is departmentalized and students move from room to room, it is usually necessary to make arrangements with the specialist. In the resource room, the materials may be readily available. Again, it is necessary to determine the guidelines for the use of the materials.

The emphasis with art, music, or dance is conveying feelings in a nonverbal manner, not the production of masterpieces. Teachers should not be shocked at the pictures or gestures that may result from therapeutic activities. Sometimes, the intent is to shock, and on other occasions, the work may reflect confusion, anger, or guilt.

Puppetry and role playing may also be used to help students express their feelings. Puppetry allows for verbal expression without face-to-face contact. Sometimes, shy or withdrawn students participate in this form of expression while hiding behind the stage. Depending on the age of the students involved, puppet shows may be given to other class members or to younger students. Beginning with nonthreatening materials such as fairy tales usually enables students to gain sufficient self-confidence to attempt shows that depict situations more true to life.

Often more successful with older students, role playing is very similar to puppetry. Again, by beginning with nonthreatening situations, students gain the motivation they require and can later attempt sensitive forms of dialogue. Generally, it is necessary to discuss the feelings that specific roles engender. The use of situations that are part of life can teach students alternate coping strategies. During both the role playing and the discussion that follows, the student can learn new strategies concerning effective ways to handle this problem.

The psychodynamic approach has many variations. It cannot be overemphasized, however, that teachers must not experiment with the emotions of students. It is a wise policy to discuss with the school psychologist, psychiatrist, or specialist what is best for each student before implementing the psychodynamic approach in the classroom.

Biophysical Approach

As noted in Table 11–1, the biophysical approach assumes the cause of behavior problems to be internal, that is, the result of genetic defects, chemical imbalances, brain injuries, nutritional deficiencies, and so on. Obviously, diagnosis of such causes of behavioral disorders is out of the realm of education; therefore, a physician is involved. The medical role is dominant in the biophysical approach to behavioral disorders. Parents and teachers must work in cooperation with the medical professionals to ensure the best possible results.

Some of the more commonly prescribed medical interventions include stimulants that are intended to increase the attention of the student and decrease the need for teacher control, antidepressants intended to increase attention and communication, tranquilizers or antipsychotics that are meant to decrease aggression and hallucinations and increase socialization, and anticonvulsants that decrease the frequency of seizures. Many possible medications may be prescribed, with more being introduced regularly as a result of research in this area.

When a student is taking prescribed medication the teacher should know the dosage, the times of the day when the medication is to be taken, the behavioral changes expected, and the possible side effects. The parents or physician should provide such information in writing and if they do not, it is the responsibility of the teacher to seek such information

(Barkley, 1991). Teachers are often asked to record information regarding the attention of the student, acts of aggression, occurrences of communication, or similar behaviors to determine whether the medication is producing the intended effects. The teacher is also likely to be one of the sources of information regarding the presence of side effects. Such information is vital for the physician to know when to adjust the dosage, to change the medication, or to discontinue the prescription altogether.

School policy must be followed regarding the storage and administration of medication in school. In some cases the medication is stored in a locked desk or cupboard in the classroom or in the nurse's or principal's office. The student may take the medication in the presence of the teacher, nurse, or principal at the prescribed times. Written information related to the dosage, prescribed times for administration, and possible side effects must be stored with the medication.

Some teachers appear to have a bias against medication for emotional or behavior disorders (Forness & Kavale, 1988), but Singh (1993) suggests that teachers should remember that "medication does not teach the student any new skills; good teachers do" (p. 196). He further suggests that medication that reduces or controls emotional or behavior disorders provides the teacher the time and opportunity to teach the skills necessary for improved, more appropriate social and academic functioning. According to Singh, some emotional and behavior disorders are so complex that behavioral interventions alone are simply inadequate. For example, students who are severely depressed, suicidal, or extremely violent may require medication and additional interventions for an amelioration of the disorders. Biological factors that affect emotions and behavior also interact with environmental influences and, as research continues, medications will likely be introduced that treat underlying symptomology but will not affect the influence of environment.

Sociological and Ecological Approaches

From a sociological and ecological perspective, behavior disorders are a result of rule breaking, social disapproval, and lack of harmonious interaction between individuals and the environment. Regular classroom teachers must be aware of the various backgrounds of their students and of the powerful influence of background.

The socialization process that takes place in the home is influenced by the socioeconomic level, type of discipline employed by the parents, parental presence and absence, television viewing, number and ages of siblings, geographic location, minority or majority status, and numerous other factors that are so entwined that it is virtually impossible to separate them; yet teachers must consider as many as possible (Leone, McLaughlin, & Meisel, 1992; Kozol, 1992; Gadow & Sprafkin, 1993; Cullinan & Epstein, 1994). For example, when youngsters learn in the home or neighborhood that the way to get things is to steal them and that their peers will think them inept if they get caught, it is not surprising if others soon report stolen jackets, money, school assignments, or other desired objects. Teachers cannot allow the stealing to take place, but may acquire insight into how to treat the problem by understanding that it is a learned behavior, perhaps a valued behavior in the home or neighborhood milieu, rather than an experimental transgression on the part of a student.

Students who have emotional or behavior disorders are frequently in conflict with school, home, neighborhood, and various other social environments. In school, they may be in conflict with teachers, the principal, cafeteria workers, and others. It is possi-

Physical restraint may at times help students regain control.

ble that a major part of the conflict is caused by a mismatch between the student and one particular environment in the school. For example, lack of structure plus noise level plus horseplay with other students may lead to conflict in the cafeteria. A careful analysis of the subenvironments in school may indicate major trouble areas. Discussion and scheduling adjustments may alleviate major stress areas and lead to improved behavior.

Within a classroom, conflict may result from a mismatch between the student's skills, the teaching style, and peer relationships. Careful analysis of all of the factors pertinent and adjustment (as required and possible) may reduce stress and improve behavior.

A word of caution is necessary: the solution is not always an adjustment on the part of teachers and the school. Students must develop coping skills, which will be important not only in the school and during school years, but also for the rest of life. The ecological approach leads to an examination of interaction between a student and the various environments that exist in school. Whenever possible, this examination should be expanded to include other environments, but educators must focus first on the school environment. To apply this approach effectively, educators must be careful to arrive at a solution that will lead to a reduction of conflict, not place blame.

The sociological approach seeks to provide assistance in all parts of the environment. The dynamics of the family may need to be examined and supportive therapy provided. Teachers may be the most effective persons for this task, or individuals more skilled in counseling techniques may need to intervene.

When a student's behavior problems are sociological or ecological, it is essential that all appropriate personnel (social worker, parole officers, principal, and so on) be involved. Because the sociological and ecological causes of behavior problems involve the values and mores of society and changing interrelationships, a wide range of expertise must be involved in effecting behavior changes. Working with allied professionals, classroom teachers may be the catalysts to change and improve the environments of students who have behavior disorders.

Other Approaches

Some approaches that may be valuable to teachers but are not readily categorized under the other major approaches follow.

Rudolf Dreikurs

Dreikurs and Cassel (1972), noted psychiatrists, identify several goals of students that are generally at cross-purposes with those of teachers. Students who have behavior disorders often demonstrate behaviors associated with one or more of these goals. Dreikurs suggests various methods of counteracting these undesirable behaviors. Table 11–2 indicates these goals, the behaviors that students demonstrate in attempting to reach the goals, and possible alternatives for teachers.

Dreikurs believes that in attempting to achieve these goals, students operate with faulty logic. With attention getting, students feel worthwhile only if people pay attention to them; therefore, the students extract that attention at any price. Students must be made to feel worthwhile when not seeking attention so as to realize that they are valuable.

With power, the faulty logic is "Unless I win or get you to do what I want, I am not worthwhile." Any teacher soon recognizes that students do have power and that if they are determined, they can "win." One need teach only a few months to realize that a teacher seldom can force students to do anything they do not want to do. When a student is seeking power, the best, most disarming device is simply to give it. There are many legitimate ways to do this: give the student the power to choose what and when to study, enlist the student's cooperation (power) in formulating rules, or provide the student with leadership positions.

One of the most disarming statements a teacher can make is simply "I know I can't *make* you do anything, I know you don't *have* to do anything, but I'm asking you to please do this." Often, after such a statement, the teacher can observe in the student physical changes, such as a reduction of tension in the shoulders and a less defiant stance. At this time, one can make use of the student's willingness and quickly move on to the task at hand; it is *not* the time for teachers to flaunt their own power!

Table 11–2
Counteracting student goals associated with behavior disorders

Goal	Behavior Demonstrated	Teacher Alternative
Attention getting	Attempts to get teacher's attention, shows off, asks useless questions, disturbs others	Ignore misbehavior if possible, do not show annoyance, give much attention for appropriate behavior, select student as a helper
Power	Contradicts teacher and other students, deliberately disobeys rules, dawdles, lies, has temper tantrums	Recognize student's power, give power as much as possible, give student choices, do not argue, avoid struggle for power, ask student for help, make contracts with student
Revenge	Steals, hurts others, acts sullen or defiant, makes others dislike him or her, retaliates	Apply natural consequences, persuade student that he or she is liked, enlist a buddy to befriend the student, do not show the student that you are hurt or disappointed, enable other students to support him or her
Display of inadequacy or hopelessness	Demonstrates inferiority complex, will not try, is discouraged before attempting new activity, gives up too easily, refuses to get involved	Do not support inferiority feelings, be constructive, get class cooperation, praise student, provide ways for student to demonstrate ability

To some students, the world and all the people in it seem so hurtful that students feel the only thing to do is to gain revenge. Such students feel disliked by all, distrusted by all, and vulnerable. Such students see the world as unfair. Teachers must attempt to help such students see that there are persons who can be trusted, that there are places in which one can be safe, and that people can care. This process is difficult to accomplish because students often view such attempts with suspicion and lack of trust.

When a student displays vengeful behavior, the teacher must take care that the remainder of the class does not turn against the student, thus confirming the student's belief in the absence of goodness. Punishing a student may further entrench this belief, so the application of logical consequences can be a valuable procedure with this student. At times, it may help to encourage a promising friendship between a vengeful student and another student.

Some students become so discouraged that they seem to give up all hope—they no longer attempt to get even. Their faulty logic may lead to display of inadequacy or hopelessness, which includes the building of a protective shield of despair. The shield is reinforced by a display of ineptitude, so that nothing is expected of the student. When confronted with this type of behavior, teachers may also be tempted to give up. Usually, such students are not disruptive, do not demand anything from teachers or classmates, and can easily be allowed to "vegetate." However, such students may have the greatest need for attention. Attempts to achieve in any arena must be encouraged, and highly motivating activities must be used. Students who are demonstrating hopeless behavior must receive much praise—but it must be honest praise. Mistakes must be handled as learning experiences. At times, it is helpful for teachers subtly to admit mistakes that they make in the presence of the entire class, saying, for example, "Did you see how I spelled that today? Didn't I spell it differently yesterday?" and then correcting the error.

Young children usually easily reveal their behavior as goal seeking. The older the students, however, the more effective they are in camouflaging their goals. Often, these goals are also intermingled with desire for excitement, behaviors resulting from drug use, or other contaminating factors. In short, it may be fairly difficult for teachers to sort out just which goal or combination of goals students are seeking.

Since Dreikurs discussed logical consequences, as early as 1964 (Dreikurs & Saltz, 1964), the term has often been used in suggestions for classroom discipline. This concept involves teacher attitudes more than actual disciplinary measures. Teachers must believe the basic tenets of this philosophy before they can make the method of logical consequences workable in the classroom.

The first of these tenets is that the classroom is a replica of the democratic system that is an essential aspect of life in the United States. A democratic classroom implies that both teacher and students are working toward a common goal and that no one has more power than anyone else. This principle rules out punishment, because punishment is meted out by someone in authority. Clearly,

the teacher is the adult in the classroom, the teacher does have various responsibilities to ensure learning, and the teacher is not just another child or adolescent. However, even though the teacher has responsibilities and is not another child, according to this philosophy, the teacher does not have the right to sit continually in judgment, to hand out punishments, or to be a dictator. (The teacher *can* do these things but will pay the price with students who retaliate.)

The democratic classroom consists of teacher and students who choose rules for the common good and goals to pursue. Within this context, the method of natural or logical consequences can become appropriate. If the natural flow of events is allowed to take its course, natural consequences become learning tools. For example, if a student forgets his or her lunch money, the natural flow of events is that with no lunch money the student gets no lunch; therefore, the teacher does not rescue the student, does not scold, does not discuss it. The natural consequence of going without lunch will teach the student to remember to bring lunch money.

At times, of course, the safety of a student does not permit the teacher to allow natural consequences to occur. There are also times when natural consequences simply are not present, so the method of logical consequences may be useful. Logical consequences are structured and arranged by the teacher and *must be experienced by the student as logical;* that is, the student must see the relationship between his or her actions and the consequences. This awareness is absolutely necessary—it is not enough for the teacher alone to see the relationship.

Logical consequences can often be arranged through the manner in which the teacher makes a statement. For example, the statement, "when you are finished with your assignment, you may leave for free time" provides for logical consequences. The responsibility is placed on the student. A student who does not finish in time may miss free time. This approach does not set the teacher up as the authority, handing out privileges or punishments, as the student may perceive in the statement "I will let you go for free time when you finish the assignment."

In another example, if two students engage in a fight, the teacher can step in to settle the fight or simply say, "We decided in this room that fights are not allowed and that whoever fights will not be able to go to the gym," and then walk away. Of course, the teacher cannot allow students to be hurt, but a reminder of the consequences chosen by the group along with the lack of attention given the inappropriate action often defuses the situation. If not, and if the students are in danger of being hurt, the teacher may need to ask the rest of the class what was decided about fighting. When they state the consequences, much of the punitive aspect and imposition of authority by the teacher are removed from the consequences. The teacher may need to step between the students to stop the fight. Again, this action should be performed with as little imposition of authority as possible. When it is time for the class to go to the gym, the students who were fighting are asked, "What are the consequences for fighting?" When they answer, the rest of the class can be taken to the gym.

The purpose of the use of logical consequences is to help students be responsible for their own actions with a minimum of conformity for the sake of conformity. The teacher first asks, "What is likely to happen if I don't intervene?" The answer is usually the natural or logical consequence. The teacher then asks, "What consequence would the student most likely see as a result of his or her actions?" That consequence is the one to use.

Dreikurs and Cassel (1972) suggest several reasons for considering the use of logical con-

sequences: they are learning processes, they are related to inappropriate behavior, they involve distinctions between the student and deeds of the student, and they reflect the reality of social order rather than the whim of an adult. Teachers must be educators who are sympathetic and understanding, who are interested in situations and the outcomes, who are objective, and who provide a choice of continuing a behavior or experiencing the consequences.

A thorough understanding and acceptance of the principles of natural and logical consequences may provide imaginative teachers with a variety of methods to promote a cooperative attitude. Interested readers may refer to the references to locate more of Dreikurs's valuable suggestions concerning discipline in the classroom.

William Glasser

William Glasser (1965, 1992) developed a type of individual therapy or counseling that with modification may be useful in classrooms. The basic tenet of this therapy is that all persons attempt to fulfill various needs even though it may be difficult to interpret the need when the behavior appears irrational or inadequate. The basic needs are (a) to love and (b) to feel worthwhile to others—to be loved. Glasser believes that all races and cultures have these two needs in common and that all people strive to meet them. How an individual behaves is often the key to whether or not that person elicits love from others. Being loved by others is the result of appropriate behavior. When an individual acts in a manner that causes discomfort in others, they find it difficult to demonstrate their love.

Glasser suggests that only by taking responsibility for one's actions can one be lovable. The key to his therapy therefore is to cause persons to be responsible for their actions. In other words, the right way is to help individuals gain self-respect and the closeness with others by saying in essence, "I care enough about you to force you to act in a better way, a way whereby you will learn through experience to know what I already know" (p. 19).

Glasser is a firm believer in the rightness or wrongness of actions—for instance stealing is always wrong, regardless of the reasons for doing it—and this moral value must be taught to students. Only when students behave "rightly" do they develop self-respect. Readers interested in further information regarding reality therapy as well as specific techniques for classroom meetings and helping students develop more responsibility for their actions should consult Glasser's text, listed in the references.

Lee and Marlene Canter

In the mid 1970s, an assertive discipline approach was developed and advocated by Lee and Marlene Canter (1976, 1989). The basic premise of the approach is that students learn more effectively when teachers are clearly in charge and the students clearly understand what is expected of them. The Canters believe that their approach provides teachers with effective means of managing inappropriate behavior constructively while providing a warm, caring atmosphere.

The Canters suggest that many teachers labor under several misconceptions regarding discipline, such as the notion that firm control is stifling rather than liberating, that students neither need nor deserve firm discipline, and that teachers who are assertive are necessarily authoritarian and dogmatic in their approach. According to the Canters, teachers must believe that they have rights, like the right to determine what behaviors are appropriate, to expect those behaviors from students, and to provide consequences when students do not exhibit appropriate behaviors. These rights provide teachers with opportunities to establish environments most conducive for learning. On the other hand, students have basic rights also. They have the right to a teacher who supports them when their behavior is appropriate, to receive assistance in controlling inappropriate behavior, and to choose their behaviors with full knowledge of the consequences of their choices.

The basic needs of the students and teachers are met through the use of assertive discipline. Teachers never violate the needs of students or the best interests of the entire class, but they do communicate unequivocally their expectations in relation to behavior and consistently follow through with the predetermined consequences.

Teachers following the assertive discipline approach:

1. Clearly identify expectations; that is, they go over the day and determine the acceptable and unacceptable behaviors related to each activity (for instance, the amount of talking appropriate when small groups are working as differentiated from working at an interest center or the computer). They discuss these expectations with the students more than once. Students learn these expectations by repetition and practice, just as they learn multiplication or correct letter-writing form.

2. Understand the difference between nonassertive, hostile, and assertive responses to the behavior of students. Nonassertive teachers are generally unable or unwilling to place demands on students, or if they do, they retreat at the first sign of opposition. In general, they accept the decisions of the students. This is clearly not a situation conducive to learning. Hostile teachers usually feel out of control and resort to threats and irrational punishments that infringe on

the right of students to have teacher assistance in limiting their behavior and to choose their behavior with complete knowledge of the consequences.

Assertive teachers clearly indicate expectations and insist on compliance. The teachers' words are always backed up by actions, appropriate behaviors are supported, and inappropriate behaviors are quickly and efficiently followed by predetermined consequences. The Canters suggest that teachers practice assertive responses until they come naturally. Following are examples of the three types of responses in two different situations.

1. *Behavior: not paying attention*
   Nonassertive: "Won't you please listen?"
   Hostile: "Are you ever going to learn to pay attention? I've asked ten times already this morning!"
   Assertive: "Listen to what I say since I won't repeat it."
2. *Behavior: fighting on the playground*
   Nonassertive: "It would be better if you tried not to fight anymore."
   Hostile: "You always pick on someone. Why don't you grow up!"
   Assertive: "The rule is we don't fight. Stand here until you are ready to obey the rule."

These examples illustrate clear disapproval of the action, unambiguous statements of what consequences follow, and the behaviors expected of the students. Assertive responses deliver the expectation that students can and will choose appropriate behavior. It is essential that teachers recognize the appropriate behavior in the same assertive manner: "You did listen and now you know what to do" or "You did stand here. Are you ready to join the group and follow the rules?"

Canter and Canter also suggest that teachers make assertiveness plans in much the same manner as they do lesson plans for reading, history, or math. This planning is to be accomplished prior to the beginning of the school year and repeated as often as necessary during the school year. The guidelines for assertiveness planning include (a) determining inappropriate behaviors that are occurring or the potential for them, (b) identifying the specific behaviors that students are to engage in, and (c) determining positive and negative consequences and deciding on implementation of consequences.

An aid for assertiveness plans may be constructed, duplicated, and used for as many activities as necessary (Table 11–3). This type of planning requires visual and mental preparation for both appropriate and inappropriate behaviors, as well as consequences for both (Charles, 1989). Some teachers may wish to rehearse verbally what they will say so that when the need actually arises, assertive responses will feel natural.

The assertiveness approach borrows from several other approaches. For more information on this and other models of discipline, see the Canter and Canter (1976), Canter (1989), and the Charles (1989) references for additional insights.

■■ Suggestions for Regular Classroom Teachers

Teachers who have students with emotional or behavior disorders in their classroom often say these students are the most difficult to accommodate. This is not surprising, because by definition these students exhibit behaviors that are significantly different from normal. Other students in the classroom may also find these students more difficult to accept.

Table 11–3
Assertiveness planning table

Activity	Acceptable Behaviors	Consequences	Unacceptable Behaviors	Consequences
Music class (large group)	Playing instruments	At least four comments per class recognizing good behavior	Playing instruments while I'm talking	Saying to the student, "We don't play when I'm talking, so I'll take the drumsticks" and taking them until I'm finished

Classroom Dynamics

Whenever inappropriate behavior occurs in the classroom, teachers must decide quickly whether it is an individual or a group problem. At times, a problem in class dynamics, such as a lack of unity, low morale, or negative reactions, contributes to the difficulties of students who have behavior disorders. It is mandatory for regular classroom teachers to examine the dynamics of the class as a whole and take effective steps for correction if they find problems. However, it is also mandatory that individual problems receive prompt attention. It is a matter of correcting both areas of concern simultaneously, not one first and then the other. Johnson and Bany (1970) list a number of observable behaviors that teachers may use for determining whether the general atmosphere of the classroom is a factor further compounding the problem of a student who is disruptive (Table 11–4).

Some techniques can temporarily address the needs of a student or prevent further problems among other students as a result of contagion. Long and Newman (1980) describe several:

1. *Hurdle lessons*. Provide individual attention to the student's academic needs in order to get past some difficult hurdle. Be alert to determine when to provide this assistance.
2. *Restructuring the classroom routine*. Although students generally benefit from routine, a sensitive teacher may see that the students need a change of pace. For example, a student has just had an emotional outburst, which the entire class has witnessed. Break the class into groups instead of continuing with the lecture or vice versa.
3. *Direct appeal to values*. Get students to thinking by asking questions as, "Do you realize that if you don't finish this, you will not be able to go to cheerleader practice?" or "What do you think _____ (best friend) will say?" Long and Newman suggest that the trick is to learn how to say *no* without being angry and how to say *yes* without feeling guilty.
4. *Removal of seduction object*. It is often easier to remove an object from sight than it is to manage the behaviors related to the object. For example, place a toy or pencil on a shelf or in a container. An interesting science project does not have to lose its appeal just because the bell rings for another class.

Table 11–4
Observable behaviors when the classroom atmosphere compounds disruptive behavior

Classroom Problems	Observable Characteristics
Ease of distraction	Undue attention to visitors, noises, movements outside windows, etc.; inability easily to return to task when distracted, almost as if looking for diversions; frequent squabbles over books, pencils, chairs, etc.
Lack of cohesion	Division into subgroups: boys vs. girls, minorities vs. majority, various cliques; frequent arguments between subgroups over usual competitive aspects of classroom, such as grades, games, differentiated assignments
Lack of conformity to normal standards	Excessive noise and talk in routine situations, between classes, going to assembly, etc.; more than usual noise in activities such as handing back papers, correcting work, and completing assignments; nonadherence to rules of quiet talk when in small groups, committees, or ability groups
Put-down of individuals	Active hostility or aggressiveness toward one or two students; ridiculing, ignoring, criticizing, or refusing to work with certain students, hiding books or papers of disliked students and attempting to trip them or make them appear clumsy, dumb, different
Resistance and hostility toward teacher	Slowdowns or work stoppages created by certain groups' "losing" things, asking for assignments to be repeated, or asking obviously irrelevant questions; accusations of other students that are clearly a challenge to the teacher
Rigidity	Unusual restlessness, argumentativeness, or disagreeability when schedules are changed, when a substitute is present, or when different types of assignments are given or classroom activities are varied
Support for misbehavior	Encouragement of acting out, talking back, or clowning around; suggesting disruptive activities to individuals; attention to any misbehavior

Source: Adapted from *Classroom Management: Theory and Skill Training* (pp. 46–47) by L. Johnson & M. Bany, 1970, London: Collier-Macmillan.

Discuss the project for a few minutes and then remove all equipment related to it in order to reduce the seduction it might continue to produce.

5. *Tension reduction by humor.* Many potentially explosive situations are defused by a humorous comment; however, such comments must never be at the expense of a student. Teachers who are self-confident are able to use humorous comments at their own expense.

Most teachers practice a number of variations of these techniques, having learned them through experience. However, if teachers understand the principles, when to use them, and how to use them, the principles are far more powerful.

Further thoughts about the social atmosphere of the classroom that may prevent rather ordinary conflicts from escalating into more serious problems are presented in Figure 11–8. They also could be stated as principles for teacher thinking and behavior.

The following "things to think about" list provides ideas and principles that may help prevent unacceptable or inappropriate behaviors, help teachers understand the origins of certain behaviors, and prevent situations from becoming unmanageable.

1. Know the background and both personal and academic problems of each student. Knowledge will aid in prevention.

2. Cultivate a demeanor that is friendly, but demands respect.

3. Disciplinary actions are most effective when they are quick, fair, consistent, and inevitable. If punishment is necessary, make it fit the individual, not the crime.

4. Group punishment for inappropriate behavior generates ill will among all students.

5. Look at the situation from the student's point of view. What were his reasons and motivations?

6. Model effective, cooperative working relationships with co-workers: fellow teachers, secretaries, maintenance personnel, the principal, kitchen employees.

7. Redirection, diversion, and provision of alternatives are nonpunitive ways of addressing minor misbehavior.

8. Be aware that students have bad days just as adults do, and have constructive, alternative activities or tasks available for such days.

9. Actively "listen" to students, especially to the nonverbal messages.

10. Well-planned lessons with a variety of activities (group work, lecture, independent work, research, problem solving, etc.) allow the teacher to concentrate on teaching and behavior, rather than on what or how to teach.

11. Understand fads and phases, even if they seem silly. They are part of growing up and developing a self-identity.

12. Don't make deals or compromise your standards but be fair and remember that students are in your class to learn how to be authoritative and how to live with authority.

13. Avoid anything that humiliates a student. No matter how angry you are, allow yourself time to cool off.

14. Recognize that some discipline problems are related to situations beyond your control. If appropriate, discuss these with the student, even if it is just to show that you understand.

Figure 11–8
Things to think about

15. Strike a balance between encouraging students to make decisions and you making all the decisions.

16. All persons in the class are human. Recognize that teachers also err, and be mature enough to admit it. This also provides the students with a positive model.

17. Repeated discussions about the student's past mistakes or failures rarely accomplish anything except make the teacher feel better.

18. Recognize that undisciplined, aggressive behavior is rarely directed at the teacher personally, but is directed at the symbol of authority.

19. If there is a disturbance, try to stop it immediately. Usually, the longer you wait, the more difficult it is for the student to remove him/herself from the disturbance.

20. Try to help students feel liked and appreciated. Make a conscious effort to find reasons to praise students. Most students with behavior problems receive a great deal of negative interaction with the teacher. Reward the absence of disturbing behavior; reward for not swearing, hitting, or interrupting. Try to "catch students" being good.

21. Be consistent. Don't make threats if you don't plan to carry through. It may take only three or four times of being consistent and following through for the student to know that you mean what you say.

22. Videotape or audiotape students so you can show them their behavior. Turn on the recorder (without their knowing) when they are noisy or disruptive. Later, play it back to them. Many students don't realize how noisy and disturbing they are.

23. If a student uses abusive language, refuse to be shocked. Ask the student to define the term. Let the student know that you don't approve of his/her language.

24. Don't tell a student that an assignment or required behavior is "easy," and that you know he/she can do it. It may not be easy for the student—and if the student does complete it, you have belittled the task.

25. Begin each day with a clean slate—for yourself, and for each student.

26. Remember that students will not likely treat you any better than you treat them.

27. Look into the mirror each day and say something good about yourself and your teaching.

Source: The authors wish to thank Dr. Clifford Baker for these "Things to Think About." From "257 Things to Do About Behavior Problems" by Clifford Baker. Selected portions are reprinted by permission.

Stress

Regular classroom teachers may have feelings of inadequacy and frustration when it appears that their attempted interventions seem useless (Mueller, 1993). It may be helpful to reflect on the various aspects of behavior that are not under the control of the teacher. Students may be experiencing stress from normal developmental stages, ranging from the kindergartener who is being separated from mother for the first time to the high school student concerned about graduation and choosing a career. In addition to these rather normal types of stress are those related to physical or sexual abuse, poverty, inadequate nutrition, living with parents who are substance abusers or are violent, inadequate housing, lack of privacy, early parenthood, and limited opportunity to participate in social activities. Some students are told they are or were unwanted, that they are a burden, that they are dumb, troublemakers, or useless (Wood & Long, 1991; Johnson, 1993). Still others experience stress that may seem minor to teachers or other adults, such as severe acne just before an important date, a friend who accidentally spills soda on an assignment, or a trusted friend telling another what was to have been a secret.

Any one of these types of stress can lead to what Long and Fagen (1981) refer to as a stress cycle. The student experiences a stressful situation that leads to a variety of feelings. The student may feel uncomfortable with these feelings, thinking that they are unacceptable or wrong. Attempting to deal with the feelings, the student engages in some sort of behavior that is an honest reflection of the feelings or an attempt to cover these up. A student who verbally attacks the teacher because of an incomplete assignment may have strong feelings of inadequacy or inferiority because of lack of study time or of a place

to study or because the student was fighting with a drunk parent when he or she should have been finishing homework. The behavior that the student demonstrates leads to an environmental reaction. Other students observe the outburst, and the outburst evokes feelings in the teacher. At this point, a power struggle may be initiated. The teacher may feel threatened by the student's verbal abuse and react in an authoritarian manner: "You will not speak to me that way!" or "Take your things and go to the principal's office immediately!" In such cases, there is no winner. Rather, both the teacher and student are acting immaturely. The teacher must be the responsible professional and attempt to interpret the student's actions.

Long and Fagen (1981) suggest a series of guidelines for teaching students how to cope with various kinds of stress:

1. Be attentive to nonverbal communication. Many students learn early that what they say can be held against them and that speaking evokes angry responses from adults. Therefore, they may refrain from verbal communication. However, tense muscles, clenched fists, rapid breathing, jerky body movements, and looks in the eyes can tell observant teachers much about the anger or frustration students are experiencing.

2. Attend as much to *how* students speak as to *what* they say. The tone or short, clipped statements may be more important than what is actually said. A *yes* or *no* said through clenched teeth indicates far more than agreement or disagreement.

3. Label and accept the feelings of students. As teachers hear what is really being said through nonverbal and verbal communication, they can label the feelings for students: "You are really angry about this,

aren't you?" As teachers reach out to students in this way, the first hesitant step toward a relationship is made. For students, labeling feelings is one matter, but accepting those feelings is far more complex. Teachers must indicate that the feelings are legitimate even though acting them out is not always acceptable: "I know you are angry, but I cannot allow you to hit another student" or "You have a right to be upset about what she said, but you cannot destroy her property." The process of labeling and accepting feelings while rejecting specific behaviors is difficult for students to learn. Teachers need to repeat this process time and time again.

In providing students with a supportive, helping environment, teachers must be certain that the students take responsibility for changing their behavior. Sometimes, teachers become too sympathetic and actually support or contribute to inappropriate behavior. Students may begin to feel put upon and feel that because of stress, they have a right to act inappropriately. The questions or comments of teachers should lead students to examine the behaviors that contributed to problems and what they can do to change the situations. Teachers must be aware of and support the students' attempts—however feeble or unsuccessful—to change situations. Most students do not suddenly begin to have behavioral problems; therefore, changing behavior for the better is also generally slow and painful. Teachers who understand this difficulty can provide encouragement as students develop the skills necessary to change their behavior.

Exploration of Feelings

Students who are disruptive and withdrawn often find it difficult to describe or evaluate their own behavior. Teachers may find it helpful to discuss their behavior with them on a daily basis, usually at the close of the day or the close of a class. Recalling specific circumstances or events one at a time in a factual manner and asking students to monitor them is often effective. If students find this method too threatening, describing real events in imaginary settings can objectify them.

For example, the teacher may describe an incident this way: "There was a fourth-grade boy who cheated in the ball game. He did not follow the rules of the game, so everyone else got mad and made him get out of the game. He then called them names and they began hitting him. There was a big fight and the teacher had to come over and tell them all to stand by the wall. What really started the fight? Why did the others get so mad? If this boy had played by the rules, how would the story end? If the boy didn't like the rules, what two things could he have done?"

With students who have sufficient writing skills, ask them to write what took place in a particular situation. After an angry student has written his or her account of the event, the anger may be sufficiently diffused and the entire matter can be dropped. At other times, written accounts can be matters for discussion. Discussion can be used to teach alternative behaviors rather than to argue concerning the accuracy of perceptions.

To allow students opportunities to identify their own moods or feelings and to indicate them to others, a "feelings board" may be developed with or by the students. Teachers can hold a discussion of the wide variety of emotions, such as disappointment, happiness, excitement, and anger. Students can then make cards with appropriate descriptions on them. Each day, as the students come into the classroom, they choose the cards that best express their feelings and place them on the bulletin board. For some students, this choice is difficult, because they are unaware of their feelings. As frequently as desired by the teacher or students, hold discussions to explore why students feel the way they do, whether these reasons are under their control, and so on.

Sometimes, students do not want to publicize their emotions; therefore, alternately, allow them to place their cards on their desks or in their notebooks. Some students find that their moods change during a class period or during the day, in which case they may change their cards to indicate the current mood. The overall guiding purpose is to help students recognize their feelings and, when appropriate, consider why they feel as they do. When students recognize the how and why of their emotions, they can explore alternative solutions to problems and ways to change moods or to gain control over them.

Figure 11–9 illustrates an end-of-the-school-day evaluation that includes clearly positive and potentially negative aspects. The

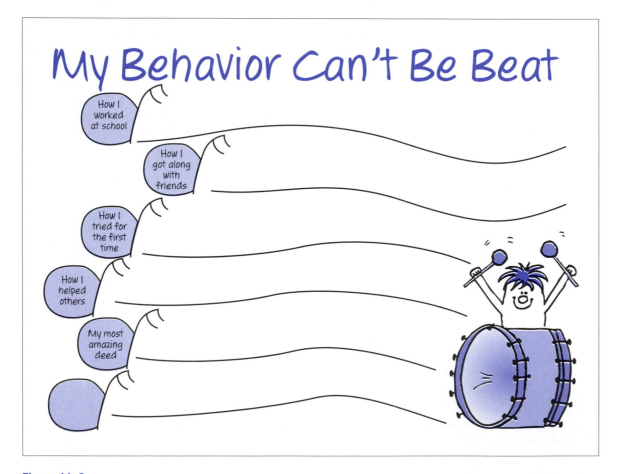

Figure 11–9
Behavior self-evaluation
Source: From *It's Positively Fun* (p. 29) by P. Kaplan, J. Kohfeldt, and K. Sturla, 1974, Denver: Love. Reprinted by permission.

student may not be able to make truthful positive statements concerning the first two items; however, the next three are stated so that the student's response is positive. The last space can be used by the teacher to include an item to which the student responds, or it can be filled in with a positive statement of something the teacher observed. This evaluation, too, may be used for discussion, taken home, or placed in the "good deeds" scrapbook.

Stories

Creating stories may serve as an outlet for a variety of feelings and emotions. The emphasis should be on expression rather than grammar, spelling, or punctuation; however, these aspects of communication should be taught and reinforced in other writing activities. Allow students to explore a range of feelings and to examine alternatives for problem solving. If stories often repeat similar themes, an atmosphere of openness and acceptance can encourage exploration of other, perhaps more sensitive, issues of concern to students.

If students find the whole blank sheet of paper intimidating, have them fold it into fourths. The first block is for the beginning, the two middle blocks are for elaboration, and the final block is for an ending. At times, students need to be prompted. Suggest, for example, "Write a story with a car as the main character" or "Using these words, write a story" or "Using this picture, describe what happened before and what you think will happen next." Encourage students to use one-word sentences or pictures if their writing skills are insufficient to permit them to do more.

After the stories are written, discuss them. However, allow individual students to decide whether or not to discuss their stories. Some students are reluctant or unable to verbalize the feelings about which they have written.

When students become secure and proficient in writing stories, introduce the concept of alternative solutions. Have one student write the beginning and middle of the story while two or three classmates write endings. When all are completed, have the students discuss the various solutions or outcomes. Gradually, students may generalize to other areas of life the reflective thinking and understanding of choices and consequences that they applied in writing (Dehouske, 1982).

Drama

Using facial expressions, pantomime, or charades is a nonthreatening form of releasing feelings or emotions (Necco, Wilson, & Scheidemantal, 1982). When students are comfortable with these techniques, let them act out original skits, stories, and real-life events, such as what happened on the playground or on a date. Hold a discussion of the emotion, story, or event with all members of the class. This provides an opportunity for reflection and careful consideration of all facets of the situation. As the discussion progresses, ask for volunteers to take the part of certain characters or to discuss with individuals what they would do. When there are volunteers to play the part of each character, let them reenact the story. If the drama begins to deteriorate or when it has served its purpose, hold another discussion. The entire class should participate, emphasizing the critical feelings, solutions, and alternatives demonstrated. Gradually, as the students are able, guide the discussion in such a manner that reenactment can be applied to real-life situations. The purpose is to enable the students to recreate feelings and emotions while exploring a variety of solutions to their own problems in a nonthreatening atmosphere.

Recognition

Certificates of recognition for working cooperatively with another student may positively influence the behavior of a student who has behavior problems (Figure 11–10). The opportunity to share a reward may be an incentive for some students (Figure 11–11). "Renting" popular playground balls, bats, gloves, or areas like a basketball court or softball field is also a powerful incentive for some students (Figure 11–12). However, take care in arranging such rentals so that only objects that can be replaced are used and that the students demonstrate some responsibility for the property of others. Realize that some students are much too destructive to be entrusted with the property of others.

Another incentive is free class time, that is, time in which a student has no specific assignment (Figure 11–13). In addition, gaining cooperation of members of the class can be a method of reducing the frequency of disruptive behaviors. Certificates such as those in Figures 11–10 and 11–14 may be used to recognize the effort of members of the class when they demonstrate cooperative behavior or ability to accommodate difficult situations.

Because students with behavior problems often receive minimal praise, teachers may use certificates similar to those illustrated in

_____ and _____
have shown that

in

ON THIS MEMORABLE DAY   AS WITNESSED BY

_____   _____

Figure 11–10
Certificate of recognition
Source: From _Positive Pitches_ (p. 27) by P. G. Kaplan and A. G. Hoffman, 1981, Denver: Love. Reprinted by permission.

Figure 11–11
Rental card to share
Source: From *It's Positively Fun* (p. 16) by P. Kaplan, J. Kohfeldt, and K. Sturla, 1974, Denver: Love. Reprinted by permission.

Figure 11–12
Rental card
Source: From *It's Positively Fun* (p. 16) by P. Kaplan, J. Kohfeldt, and K. Sturla, 1974, Denver: Love. Reprinted by permission.

Figures 11–10 to 11–14 to provide significant positive recognition. Some students attempt to moderate their behavior to receive them. Other students do not actually work *for* them but are exceptionally pleased if teachers surprise them with certificates after situations that are particularly trying. Depending on the reaction of parents to such reinforcement, students may want to take certificates home for additional praise. In other situations, students may not take certificates home, but they are additionally rewarded if the certificates receive prominent placement on a bulletin board or in a scrapbook.

Disruptive students are commonly unaware of the progress they have made, perhaps because after the students have not demonstrated a particular behavior for a time, teachers select another behavior that is disruptive and begin working on it. Thus, students may

be deprived of opportunities to enjoy their success. The perception may be that they are always working at something (this may be true in regard to academic areas also) and are not making progress.

To provide opportunities for students to note their successes or achievements, keep a "good-deeds" or "good-work" scrapbook. The scrapbook may be purchased or made of construction paper together with a cover. Achievement certificates awarded to students may be glued into it along with math, handwriting, or any other academic work sheets. When appropriate, a student may page through and recall the reasons for different awards and note the progress he or she has made. Such books can stimulate positive discussions between teachers and students, which can be rewarding in and of themselves. Scrapbooks can also be used at parent-teacher conferences.

BULLS EYE !

_____ has earned

_____ minutes of free time

Figure 11–13
Free-time card
Source: From *It's Positively Fun* (p. 18) by P. Kaplan, J. Kohfeldt, and K. Sturla, 1974, Denver: Love. Reprinted by permission.

TO:
_____

Some things are hard to ignore. . .

By turning your back you were a. . .

Many thanks for
_____
_____
_____

_____
Official Appreciator

_____
Special Day

Figure 11–14
Certificate for cooperation
Source: From *Positive Pitches* (p. 27) by P. G. Kaplan and A. G. Hoffman, 1981, Denver: Love. Reprinted by permission.

Structure

The academic needs of students must receive attention along with the behavioral needs. A variety of suggestions related to academic help described in other chapters may be useful with students who have behavior disorders. For example, some of the materials designed for use with students who have low vision may provide sufficient tactile stimulation to capture and maintain the attention of students who have behavior disorders. Similarly, materials developed for use with students who are hearing impaired may provide visual representations helpful in presenting concepts related to various content areas. Many of the suggestions for academic remediation provided in Chapter 10 are appropriate for students with behavior disorders, since many such students are not successful in academic arenas. Erickson (1987) suggests that for some students, success in academic work must precede any expectations for behavior change.

Generally, if teachers are organized, they can help students structure or organize their day. (On the secondary level, this process is accomplished to some extent by the existing organization of the school day.) Simple cards or sheets on which assignments are written by either students or teachers provide a minimum of organization (see Figure 11–15). The use of columns allows for a record of what is not yet begun, what is begun but not completed, and what is completed. Either teachers or students may use the comments column.

Teachers may peruse the work and make comments, or students may make notes, such as "need history book" or "ask about this."

In addition to organizing the day or week, teachers may call attention to specific goals or qualities (see Figure 11–16). During the time allotted for completion, teachers monitor behavior according to the attributes listed. At the end of the period or class, teachers can quickly indicate either a grade or the points received. Such records help students note the progress they are making. If students do not make progress, the reasons for lack of progress may be the basis for discussion. Rating cards or sheets may be useful for either upper-elementary or secondary students. The students use one card for each class. Some specialists want to collect the cards so that they, too, may understand the progress.

At times, the assignment given to a student may seem overwhelming, either because of the task itself or because the student lacks organizational skills. Figure 11–17 illustrates one way that a task can be subdivided to make it more manageable. Subdividing is especially appropriate for assignments like themes, because the various elements of research, outlining, writing, proofreading, editing, and revising can be slices. Indicating intermediate dates for completion also helps students organize long-term assignments. Likewise, an hour period to work on assignments may be sliced into 5- or 10-minute portions.

Most students with behavior problems need help in structuring their day, assignments, and activities. The need for structure is indicated by their inability to begin a task or to make the transition from one task to another (for example, science to history or physical education to math) or from one type of activity to another (small-group work to individual work or lecture to independent

Name:		Date:	
Activities, assignments, or page numbers	**Started**	**Completed**	**Comments**

Figure 11–15
Format for organizing a student's day

Assignments	Good attitude	Showed effort	Used time wisely	Completed work	Comments
Mon.					
Tues.					
Wed.					
Thurs.					
Fri.					

Name: _____   Week: _____

Teacher's signature: _____

Figure 11–16
Format for rating specific goals or qualities

work). Some students even have difficulty moving from one type of response to another within the same task or class (subtraction to multiplication or written response to verbal).

Another common difficulty with students who have behavior problems is their inability to wait quietly for teacher assistance when they encounter a problem and the teacher is not able to assist them immediately. A sign, as shown in Figure 11–18, can be attached to the top of a pencil or dowel, which may be placed in a spool or a mound of clay. Such a sign serves as a silent signal that the student requires assistance. By using such a nondisturbing system, the teacher also reinforces the idea that study or independent activity time is a time to be quiet. Note, however, that it is unrealistic to place a restriction such as being quiet on a student simply because he or she tends to be disruptive and not impose the restriction on the entire class.

Alternative Assignments

Incentives that may be extremely motivating are modified assignments based on recognition of the feelings of the student. The teacher may say, for example, "I see you are really angry about the fight you had and that you still think it wasn't your fault. For now, why don't you write the answers to only these two rows of problems, skip this one, and do the last. As soon as you are finished, you can paint. That will cheer you up, won't it?" In this scenario, the teacher is acknowledging the student's feelings and his or her right to them and is demonstrating a flexibility in assignments and an alternative for changing the feelings. After an exchange such as this, the student often begins the assignment. The student hears the lesson about redirecting feelings, but being excused from a part of the assignment provides incentive to complete the

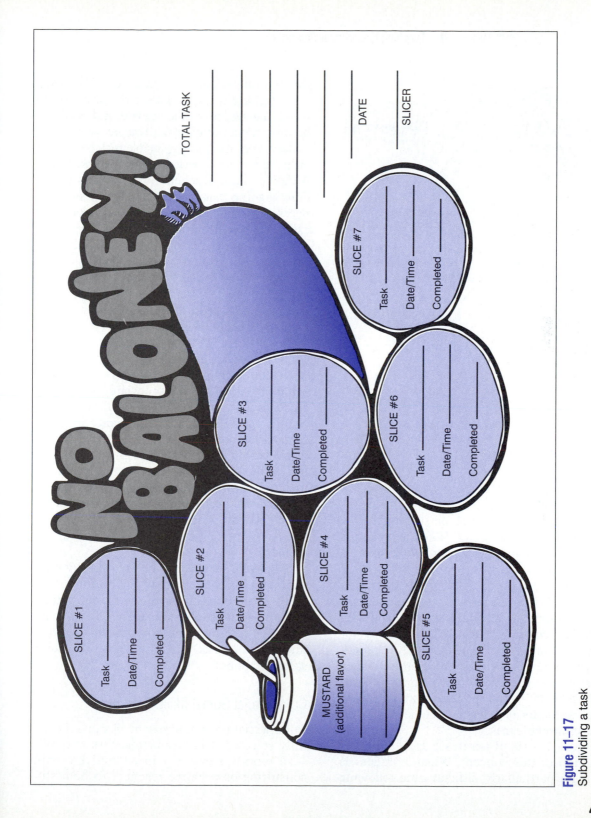

Figure 11-17
Subdividing a task
Source: From *Making It Positively Clear* (p. 40) by P. G. Kaplan and A. G. Hoffman, 1981, Denver: Love. Reprinted by permission.

Figure 11–18

Need-help sign

Source: From *It's Positively Fun* (p. 7) by P. Kaplan, J. Kohfeldt, and K. Sturla, 1974. Denver: Love. Reprinted by permission.

task instead of dwelling on the unfairness of the fight and its aftermath.

The method of crossing out some problems or exercises may be useful. When a student is finding it extremely difficult to work, explain why the modifications are made ("I can see that you are having trouble concentrating today" or "I realize that you are upset because Tom said some awful things to you") and with a magic marker or red pen boldly cross out some portion of the assignment. Alternately, tell the student, "Do only the even-numbered questions at the end of the chapter in your science book." Used sparingly, this technique helps students begin what seemed to be an insurmountable task.

Figure 11–19 illustrates a more complex variation of this concept. When a student is having a particularly difficult time following

through on assignments on a given day, such an assignment sheet makes the work seem more manageable to the student and need not be time consuming for the teacher. At the secondary level, the same principle may be applied either for a class period or for an entire day. Although some teachers object to this procedure, arguing that every problem or exercise is necessary, other teachers argue that not every exercise is essential and that they can determine the competency of the student with fewer exercises. All teachers must decide this matter for themselves. If daily homework is required or expected in a particular school, allowing one free night as a reward is a powerful reinforcer for some students (Figure 11–20).

Variations of obtaining baseline data, as in the behaviorist approach, can often be useful with disruptive students. Discussing the behaviors that are inappropriate and having students who are disruptive keep a card tally of each time they call out or engage in unacceptable behavior often reduces the behavior immediately. Such students may cheat and not mark the card, but they are still aware of their behavior. After class, discuss the number of marks on a card and point out how disruptive the behavior has been, the effect it has on the class, and some possible solutions to the problem.

The same system can be associated with a contract or reward system; for example, say, "If there are no more than two marks, you do only the even-numbered math problems." If a reward is contingent on no marks or a certain number of marks, then students must keep accurate counts.

Commercial Social Skills Programs

Commercial programs may be of value if carefully selected. Classroom teachers may use such programs alone or in conjunction with consulting or resource teachers to help stu-

Name: _____		Date: _____	
Must Do	**Should Do**	**Do If There's Time**	**Do Not!**
Reading workbook, p. 37, nos. 1, 3, 5, 7, 8	Use colored pencils to circle the correct answers.	Nos. 6 and 9	Do nos. 2 and 4 on p. 37
Math, pp. 142–143, all even numbers		The odd-numbered ones that have a 4 in them	Do numbers that have a 3 in them
Take 10 minutes and listen to your favorite record.	Use the earphones so no one knows you are doing it.		Let anyone know you are taking a break
Write 2 paragraphs about your hobby.	Read the rules for a good paragraph before you begin. Write neatly.	Draw a picture that illustrates your hobby.	Write more than 2 paragraphs
Work on the mural for social studies.	Take time to think about where you finished last time. Decide what you want to put on it today.	Color what you drew.	Do any more than you want
Read pp. 105–110 in your reader.	Read carefully. Watch for the new words. (They are on the chalkboard.) Write down any word that gives you trouble.	Write *your* ending to the story.	Read more than 5 pages or write more than 1 sentence for your ending

Figure 11–19
Assignment priority schedule

dents identify and/or accept feelings and learn new skills. These programs may use puppetry, sociodrama, role playing, group discussions, or art in the various suggested activities. Commercial programs may be used as complete curricula for affective needs or to address specific needs. Many of these programs are available in most schools. Some examples follow:

1. *Contract Maturity: Growing Up Strong* (1972). This program is written for junior and senior high school students with a low reading level. It uses posters, pictures, short stories, and open-ended stories to stimulate discussion and help clarify values.

2. *ACCESS* (Walker, Todis, Holmes, & Norton, 1988). This program may be used to develop relationships with peers or adults, and self-management skills with students of middle school or high school age. It provides suggestions for

Figure 11–20

No homework permit

Source: From *It's Positively Fun* (p. 17) by P. Kaplan, J. Kohfeldt, K. Sturla, 1974, Denver: Love. Reprinted with permission.

grouping students, procedures for teaching, and teaching scripts.

3. *The Coping With Series* (Wrenn & Schwarzrock, 1984). This series contains four sets of five books, each addressing concepts related to such themes as personal identification, human relationships, facts and fantasies, and teenage problems. The program is designed for use with students in upper elementary and early senior high school.

4. *Social Skills and Me* (Crane & Reynolds, 1983). This program contains 100 lessons, which focus on skills in communication, responsibility, assertiveness, and problem solving for the first through sixth grades. It includes individual and group activities.

5. *Developing Understanding of Self and Others—Revised (DUSO—R)* (Dinkmeyer, 1982). This program includes

DUSO I, which is for students in kindergarten through third grade, and DUSO II, which is for third and fourth graders. The program contains discussion, poetry, music, and stories relating to independence, choices and consequences, stress, and personal motivation.

6. *ACCEPTS Program* (Walker et al., 1983). This is a social skills curriculum for students from kindergarten through sixth grade. It uses an instructional approach in which social skills are defined, modeled, and role played, and homework assignments provided. Videotapes demonstrating appropriate and inappropriate examples of the social skills are also available.

7. *Cognitive-Behavioral Therapy for Impulsive Children* (Kendal & Braswell, 1985). This program uses a four-step process to teach impulsive students self-talk that enables them to internalize control. The steps include (a) recognition of a problem, (b) generation of strategies to alleviate the problem, (c) consideration of the consequences of the possible solutions, and (d) acting on the best solution. Students are taught how to reward themselves after using the process.

8. *Getting Along with Others: Teaching Social Effectiveness to Children* (Jackson, Jackson, & Monroe, 1983). This program contains activities designed to teach skills such as compromising, following directions, problem solving, and how to handle name calling and teasing. The program contains scripts for the teacher and students, examples and nonexamples of the skills, and directions for practicing the skills at home and in the community.

Commercial materials are also available to assist teachers to better understand and manage student behaviors. An example is *Choices* (National Information Services Institute, 1989), which provides a description of such behaviors as fighting, truancy, talking out, and substance abuse; abstracts of current research relating to the problems; and "Outlines of Action" (which include suggestions for alleviating the problems). *Choices* is produced on disks for IBM, IBM Compatible, Macintosh, Apple IIE, and Apple IIGS computers.

Verbal or Physical Aggression

Students with emotional and behavior disorders may be verbally or physically aggressive toward other students or the teacher. Such behavior is troublesome to the teacher because of the disruption and possibility of contagion. It is to the teacher's advantage to prevent such behaviors when possible by following the suggestions in chapters 3 and 4 and elsewhere throughout this text that relate to classroom organization and preparation. Specific, fair discipline practices and other reinforcement principles described in various sections of this chapter may be preventive in nature. Additional general, preventive guidelines follow.

- Develop an attitude of trust in the classroom emphasizing mutual respect between teacher and students and among the students. Correct infractions consistently and teach appropriate behavior.
- Develop the characteristic of "withitness," defined as a teacher's ability to pay attention to more than one thing at a time (Kounin, 1977). Teachers with the characteristic of withitness are always aware of what is happening in their classroom and are able to overlap instruction with monitoring behavior. They can alter their instruction when the first signs of confusion or restlessness become evident and if minor disruptions between students take

place they take immediate action to prevent it from growing, without interrupting the teaching/learning process. Teachers who have developed withitness are able to communicate with the students through eye contact, facial expressions and gestures. Such a teacher is able to continue teaching while gesturing to a group of students who need redirection or standing next to an overactive student who needs to refocus on the task at hand.

- Examine the physical organization of the classroom with particular attention to seating arrangements and the movement patterns of the students and the teacher. Some students may need additional space around them or can engage in academic tasks with fewer distractions if seated in rows for part of the class period. When the teacher moves around the room, inappropriate behavior decreases, the teacher usually praises students more, and positive interactions between teacher and students and among students increases (Good & Brophy, 1987; Foster-Johnson & Dunlap, 1993).
- Develop a small number of rules in clear, positive (rather than negative) statements, indicating what students should do rather than stating only what they should not do. Include statements regarding physical or verbal aggression, for example, "Only kind words spoken here," or "Treat every person with respect."
- Define consequences for compliance and for infractions that allow for the students to save face and self-respect. Involve the students in the development of both rules and consequences. Post the rules in a conspicuous place.
- If necessary, teach appropriate behavior through the use of examples and role playing. Be sure the students understand the consequences for appropriate and inappropriate behavior.

- Consistently and unemotionally enforce the rules. Model calm and composed behavior in the face of inappropriate behavior. Do not make threats or argue with the student and avoid power struggles. Avoid discussions when enforcing consequences.
- Discussions regarding the specific behavior should take place after the consequences have been implemented, when the student is calm, with the focus on the "what" of the behavior not the "why" ("What did you do?" not "Why did you do it?").
- Reteach appropriate behavior, with a discussion of the consequences.

Preventive measures may not be sufficient to ensure that inappropriate behavior does not escalate into aggressive behavior since by definition students with emotional and behavior disorders do not always respond to ordinary measures. Therefore, for students with a history of verbal or physical aggression, those involved should develop and state on the IEP procedures to implement during a crisis situation. These procedures should center around the types of aggressive behavior that have occurred in the past, what events preceded them, the time of day they occurred, what previous measures were taken, their effectiveness, and what steps will be taken in the future. Such plans are individualized for the student. If necessary, identify additional personnel (the counselor, teacher of students with emotional and behavior disorders, social worker, another teacher, or principal) who may be called for immediate help. The crisis plan should be clearly understood and agreed upon, particularly by those responsible for implementation.

During the crisis it is important that the teacher remain calm. An angry or fearful teacher communicates these same emotions to the student and other members of the class, thus likely escalating the problem. In a calm manner the teacher should implement the crisis plan, sending for help if necessary, issuing directives or requests or providing a rationale for stopping the behavior in a clear authoritative voice. The teacher should avoid invading the student's physical space unless another student is in danger. The teacher should use as little physical action as possible because the student may interpret this as physical aggression and react more aggressively (Calvin, Sugai, & Patching, 1993; Shores, Gunter, Denny, & Jack, 1993; Gilliam, 1993).

A crisis plan may identify personnel qualified to physically restrain or control a student. Although there are safe and effective techniques for physically controlling an individual, these must be used only as a last resort and administrative procedures and policies must be followed. Similarly, interventions such as exclusion time out, suspension, or expulsion may be viable options. Such extreme measures must always follow established policies and when they are included in the IEP, parents must sign to indicate their approval.

Suspensions

We have deliberately placed this discussion last in the consideration of suggestions for the regular classroom teacher, because although such measures may be required, they take place under only certain conditions and as a last resort. In general, suspensions relate to the safety of a student or the safety of others. All other methods and techniques must be used first. No teacher would suggest suspending a student because the student could not see or hear, because these are conditions for which the student is not responsible. However, it seems there is no such clear recognition in relation to behavior disorders, which relate to interactions with others and beliefs regarding the ability of students to become socialized and to control their behavior. Many people think that behavior disorders are merely the result of a lack of self-discipline, lack of discipline on the part of parents, poor parenting, or such factors as poverty, culture, dysfunctional families, and drug abuse. Such factors may be related to behavior disorders, but designating cause-and-effect relationships is too simplistic.

Historically, schools have used suspension from school to coerce students into modifying their behavior (Barnetti & Parker, 1982). Students may be truant, do something that is prohibited (such as smoke), or fail to do something required (such as hand in homework). In accordance with school policy, they are suspended, meaning not allowed to come to school for a specified number of days. The underlying assumption is that students want to be in school and will change their behavior so that they can attend. The procedure is valid if students want to be in school, but it is not if students do not value school attendance. Not being allowed to be present in a place in which one does not want to be in the first place does not likely motivate change in behavior. Thus, suspension may not be effective in all cases. Furthermore, if a student has a condition or a disability identified as a behavior disorder, to prevent the student from receiving services by suspension from school seems to be punishing the student for something for which he or she is not entirely responsible.

Inschool suspensions consist of removal of the student from the classroom to another room, usually the resource room, the counselor's room, an unused room, or a similar place in the school building. Supervision of the student is provided and the length of time spent in the room must be a previously specified, short duration. Specific behaviors that lead to inschool suspension are discussed with the student and with the parent (usually during the development of the IEP). Counsel-

ing by the special education teacher, counselor, or consulting teacher should be provided at some time during the inschool suspension so that the student is learning and gaining insight regarding the behavior, the consequences, or other factors necessary to reduce the likelihood of additional need for this type of suspension. Most schools have policies regarding inschool suspensions, and teachers should be fully informed about them.

Inschool suspensions are used for only extremely serious problems. If a student is frequently being placed in an inschool suspension, it would seem that the placement of the student might need to be reconsidered. The authors of IDEA recognized that the needs of students range from all services being provided in regular classrooms to hospital services, homebound services, and 24-hour care (see Chapter 2). The principle of least restrictive environment must be followed, but the fact remains that for some students, self-contained classrooms or even more restrictive placements are the most appropriate. Such changes of placement require reconvening the staffing team and parental consent.

■ Related Considerations

Several issues in students' lives are of increasing concern to teachers. Some are associated with or related to emotional and behavior disorders, but others are not. Adolescence is a normal stage of development but, for some students, may be a very difficult time. Students with emotional or behavior disorders may experience extremely difficult adolescent years. Youngsters who commit illegal acts are referred to as *juvenile delinquents*. They may be gifted, identified as emotionally or behavior disordered or learning disabled, considered members of gangs (Bunsen & Hurley, 1993), classified as dropouts (Steinberg & Knitzer, 1992), or considered habitual criminals or youngsters caught in the first illegal act of their lives (McIntyre, 1993). Students who are involved with substance abuse may or may not be considered to have emotional or behavior disorders. Depression is a characteristic of emotional and behavior disorders and is often associated with suicide. In general, students who are severely depressed are considered to have emotional and behavior disorders, but they may not be identified because no one has noticed the depression (Maag & Forness, 1991). Students with emotional and behavior disorders may commit suicide; however, not all students who commit suicide are identified as having emotional or behavior disorders nor are they considered so by their friends, parents, or teachers (Guetzloe, 1989). Students who have been or are being abused or neglected may sometimes exhibit behaviors that are similar to those associated with emotional and behavior disorders (Karlin & Berger, 1992). The following discussion is provided to help teachers note the relationships that may exist between these factors and emotional and behavior disorders, and also to help them make distinctions between them.

Adolescence

Because of a variety of factors, an acceptable definition of what constitutes emotional and behavior disorders in adolescents has been even more elusive than has a definition for younger students. One factor in this definition problem is the lack of a clear definition of what is acceptable behavior in normal adolescents. It is generally agreed that adolescence is a time of transition (Schiamberg, 1988; Kashani, Orvaschel, Rosenberg, & Reid, 1989). It involves the passage of an individual from a position of dependence to one of independence. This passage may be initiated at various chronological ages and lasts a varying number of years. The transition involves both physiological and psychological stages.

Physiological changes include the production of hormones that lead to the development of secondary sex characteristics and the ability to reproduce. During these changes, adolescents begin to look more to peers than parents for approval and have increasing concern for physical appearance. At the same time that adolescents look at peers for approval, peers seem to seek some indefinable standard of how one should look and act. Any deviations are subject to taunting by peers. Being too tall, too short, too thin, or too fat is a relative characteristic, but for many adolescents, these factors have great significance. Rarely are adolescents satisfied with their physical appearance, but such dissatisfaction does not always lead to severe crisis.

Adolescents must cope with physical maturation, the emergence of new cognitive abilities, dating, changes in family dynamics, moves to more complex school settings, and societal demands to become more responsible and assume more adult roles, among other challenges. Sigelman and Shaffer (1991) describe several psychological changes that adolescents experience. Although described here separately, they are closely interwoven.

1. *Status*. Status involves how one is perceived by others. For adolescents, how one is perceived by peer groups is far more important than how one is perceived by parents or relatives. This perception by others is closely allied with self-concept. Status may be conferred by others, as in the case of a class clown, who is designated after one or two incidents and then accepts the role as a way to gain status.

2. *Identity*. Identity is generally developed in two areas: (a) identity with a group

such as a gang, club, or team and (b) self-identity, which is reflected by a knowledge of who one is, what one believes in, and what one represents. The development of an identity usually involves an element of breaking away from family ties.

3. *Independence*. The degree to which an individual is self-sufficient reflects the independence of the individual. Striving for independence involves testing limits, establishing an identity, and redefining relationships. Perhaps one of the most difficult aspects of gaining a sense of independence is being expected to act as an adult but enjoying few of the privileges of the adult. In attempting to solve the dilemma, adolescents may disregard authority, resulting in conflicts in school as well as at home.

4. *Relationships*. Although they vary from interactions with strangers to intimate interactions, relationships are a vital part of life. Early adolescence involves seeking out of a same-sex best friend or friends. Later, this interaction expands to include members of the opposite sex. As adolescents strive for identity, independence, and status, they gradually grow away from family support systems, which are replaced by other relationships. Unless various other relationships are developed, adolescents suffer from alienation and feelings of loneliness and inadequacy, which adversely affect development in other areas.

5. *Sex*. Although much has been written recently concerning sex-role stereotypes, the development of a sexual identity is a major issue that adolescents must resolve. Any interference with the development of a sexual identity may have lifelong effects. Adolescents must learn about the potential functions of their bodies and how to use them. Religious beliefs, parental attitudes, and peer knowledge affect this development in a positive or negative fashion.

6. *Values*. One's identity generally reflects one's values, which often become the criteria by which one is judged. Often, adolescents seem to reject the values of their parents as they strive for independence and identity. Because they may be unwilling to live by the values taught by their parents, required by religion, or expected of younger individuals and yet have not developed workable, consistent values of their own, adolescents find themselves in a dilemma. The inconsistency in judgment and behavior of adolescents often reflects this seemingly unsolvable puzzle.

7. *Decision making*. The ability to examine alternatives, choose among them, and live with the consequences is important for successful adult living. Objectively examining alternatives is often difficult for adolescents. As a general rule, adolescents are more concerned with immediate goals than long-range ones, and this concern often leads to decisions that may be seen as not appropriate in hindsight. Effective, appropriate decision making is a skill that must be developed and practiced. Often, adults significant to adolescents are impatient with the inability to make effective decisions. Peers, a lack of acceptable models, and need for independence may influence adolescents to make poor decisions that have lifelong effects.

One or any combination of the seven psychological changes to which adolescents must adjust may cause short-term or lifelong crises. For a variety of reasons, which usually can be determined only case by case if at all, some adolescents experience problems far beyond those considered normal. Such adolescents may turn to drugs, alcohol, crime, or in extreme cases, suicide. This is not to say that every adolescent who experiments with drugs, alcohol, sex, or criminal acts is suffering from a behavior disorder. The problem depends on the frequency, the severity, and the dependence of the behavior.

Teachers of adolescents must be aware of the normal behaviors of adolescents to be able to help students with special needs. Teachers can employ a variety of approaches that enhance the opportunities of adolescents for successfully negotiating this important stage in life:

1. An open, honest, respectful relationship with their students
2. Challenging, motivating activities
3. Frequent and positive attention
4. Fair and firm limits
5. Involvement in goal setting in both academic and behavioral areas
6. Acceptance of students as individuals while not reinforcing inappropriate or self-defeating behavior
7. Learning environments that ensure considerable success

Juvenile Delinquency

Juvenile delinquency is often associated with emotional and behavior disorders and learning disabilities; however, there is no established causal relationship. Most of the data related to the relationship between these disorders and juvenile delinquency is based on incarcerated youth (Leone, Rutherford, & Nelson, 1991; Waldie & Spreen, 1993). It is likely that confusion will persist because the popular press frequently uses the terms interchangeably (Cole, 1992). Further, data does indicate that individuals identified as having a learning disability or an emotional and behav-

ior disorder, or being socially maladjusted are likely to have criminal records within a few years of either dropping out of school or graduating (Allen, 1992; Steinberg & Knitzer, 1992; Cole, 1992; McIntyre, 1993; Brier, 1994). Our discussion of juvenile delinquency in this chapter is merely one of convenience, it would be as appropriately addressed in the chapter concerning learning disabilities.

Legal definitions of juvenile delinquency relate specifically to acts that are against the law. These include criminal offenses such as stealing, destruction of property, causing injury to another person, and killing. These are called *index* crimes. Other offenses are illegal only if the offender is within a specific age range, for example, running away from home, truancy, buying alcoholic beverages or cigarettes, or sexual promiscuity. These are called *status* crimes. Both types of crimes carry penalties upon conviction (Cole, 1992).

Students who have been convicted of either type of crime and are attending school may be on probation and be considered juvenile delinquents. A probation officer may be involved with the school if the terms of the probation relate to attending school or maintaining certain grades. The role of teachers may vary widely. Students convicted of a crime may be model students in every other way. In such cases, the role of teachers relates to the provisions of the IEP and the provisions of the probation. Usually, an individual at school is designated to be the contact person for the probation officer—the counselor, special education teacher, social worker, principal, or homeroom teacher. The role of that person is determined by the provisions of the probation and the circumstances of the student in school.

Substance Abuse

Substance abuse includes the use or abuse of either legal or illegal substances, including alcohol, nicotine, glue, paint thinner, heroin, cocaine, crack, LSD, PCP, and marijuana. Use induces a psychological or physiological change that has a therapeutic purpose. Abuse may cause health risks, psychological dysfunction, or other adverse consequences. Abuse of substances does not seem to be associated with a particular disability, since many "normal" persons abuse drugs (Maag, Irvin, Reid, & Vasa, 1994). Because of the number of students involved in substance abuse nationwide, it would not be uncommon for a class to include students who are at least experimenting with drugs and other substances subject to abuse (Devlin & Elliott, 1992; Kress & Elias, 1993).

Teachers must be aware of the progression from experimentation to dependency, while also remembering that not every student who experiments becomes dependent (Karacostas & Fisher, 1993). A brief description of the increased involvement that can occur follows. Experimentation is trying out or infrequent use, often with a variety of substances. Situation-specific, or social, use reflects attempts to conform. The individual feels "I can handle it—no big deal" but experiences some guilt. Such use varies from once to several times per week. With habitual use, the individual looks for or needs the euphoria, feels guilt and depression when not using, and uses or tries to use the substance daily. With dependency, the individual feels uncomfortable if drugs are not available, committing other crimes to get them. The individual demonstrates erratic, disorganized thought processes or behavior, sometimes suicide. Such an individual uses several times daily if possible.

Miksic (1987) describes the changes in behavior often associated with substance abuse. At the experimental stage, little change is noticeable; however, by the social stage, teachers may note more association with others who use drugs, a withdrawal from productive activities outside school, or a decrease in academic performance. If students reach the habitual stage, teachers may notice decreased interest in school, frequent unexplained absences, family problems related to usage, and mood swings or impulsiveness. When students are dependent on drugs, there is usually only sporadic school attendance, a change in physical appearance through weight gain or loss, and a somewhat unkempt look due to a loss of concern regarding personal appearance. There may also be aggressive behavior, betrayal of friends, lying or stealing to obtain drugs or money for them, and depression, paranoia, or suicidal thoughts.

Most schools have drug awareness and prevention programs and policies and procedures to follow in cases of suspected drug use, actual use, intoxication, or withdrawal crisis (Elmquist, 1991). Teachers must be aware of such policies and procedures, and depending on their own knowledge, they may offer to teach or otherwise participate in awareness or prevention programs. Primarily, however, teachers should know the procedures indicated by the school, effectively manage students during a crisis, maintain a calm and nonjudgmental attitude, and refer students to proper authorities in accordance with school policy.

Depression and Suicide

Childhood and adolescent depression as a disorder differentiated from adult depression has only recently become a topic of study (Rutter, 1991). The *Diagnostic and Statistical Manual of Mental Disorders* (American Psychiatric Association, 1994) describes several problems that must be exhibited most of the day, nearly every day over a 2-week period before a clinical diagnosis of depression can be made. They include changes in appetite and weight; irregularities in sleep patterns; physical agitation or lethargy; inability to experience pleasure; inordinate feelings of guilt or inadequacy; lack of ability to concentrate or make decisions; and thoughts, threats, or attempts of suicide. The reasons that students may become depressed are unclear, although there are several theoretical views. Forehand, McCombs, and Brody (1987) suggest that depression in the family can be a factor; however, the distinction between genetic predispositions and the family relations that develop because of depression is not clear. Depressed parents may set unrealistic goals for their children, lack effective parenting skills, be unable to provide sufficient support, and overly emphasize punishment. Depression may also be related to low self-esteem, low social competence, lack of self-control, or a belief that all negative things that happen are one's own fault (Kaslow & Rehm, 1991).

When a psychologist or psychiatrist makes a diagnosis of depression, several interventions are possible. Antidepressant drugs may require careful monitoring of behavior changes. Training in social skills may also be indicated on the IEP. Such training is usually implemented by consulting teachers or specialists and may be directed toward the student in question or a small group. It is critical that classroom teachers be fully aware of the goals and provide support for newly emerging social skills. Interventions may also center on cognitive modification, which is designed to alter negative beliefs. Classroom teachers are expected to provide support and encouragement as students modify their manner of thinking.

Suicide and depression are closely related, but not all students who threaten or attempt suicide are depressed. Although IDEA recognizes "a general pervasive mood of unhappiness or depression" as a characteristic of severe emotional problems, it does not specifically include threats of suicide. School administrators are divided in their beliefs about providing suicide prevention programs. Some schools do, while others fear that discussions and awareness programs create a climate in which students are tempted to think about or attempt suicide (Guetzloe, 1989; 1991).

The problem of suicide cannot be ignored. Suicide rates have steadily increased even though many actual suicides are not reported (Muse, 1990). Researchers have noted higher rates of suicide in exceptional students than in the normal population. The highest rates of suicide among exceptional individuals are among those identified as having emotional and behavior disorders or as being gifted (Blumenthal, 1985; Willings & Arsenault, 1986; Guetzloe, 1991).

Causes of suicide may be a genetic predisposition to schizophrenia, alcoholism, or substance abuse; birth trauma; or extreme stress (Hawton, 1986; Pfeffer, 1986; Gottesman, 1991).

Most authorities believe that it is impossible to identify with precision the students who might attempt suicide (Muse, 1990). There are, however, warning signs and risk factors that should receive attention:

1. Behavior or emotional problems
2. Depression, including expressed feelings of unhappiness, helplessness, inadequacy, or sadness
3. Drug or alcohol abuse, including intoxication, which decreases inhibitions
4. Familiarity with suicide, including suicide threats or attempts, attempted or completed suicide in the family, or recent, publicized suicide in the community
5. Severe stress from any of a variety of sources, such as death in the family, loss of friends, family violence, parental divorce, parental loss of employment, public humiliation, poor achievement, sexual abuse, or other physical abuse

6. Severe mood changes
7. Poor concentration
8. Frequent accidents
9. Unusual fatigue or anxiety
10. Poor self-esteem, including inability to tolerate any flaws in oneself or to accept compliments or negative comments
11. Sudden changes in friends
12. Preoccupation with death as evidenced by actions that have an aspect of finality, including giving away prized possessions, notes of farewell, repeated apologies, plans for the future that do not include the individual, or frequent discussions about the desirability of death

Teachers who become aware of such indications should immediately report such information to the proper authorities. Because of controversy related to the contagion factor (students who discuss suicide or know of someone who committed suicide), many schools do not have established policies or procedures related to the prevention of suicide. As a result, teachers may be unsure of appropriate actions. In the absence of established policies, teachers should contact the principal, counselor, psychologist, nurse, or social worker. Some schools have incorporated assessment of potential for suicide in the overall assessment completed prior to staffing for students who have behavior disorders. The results of such assessment are incorporated into the IEP, and resources for the family, including agencies outside the school, are identified so that the interventions available can be incorporated into the plan (Minneapolis Public Schools, 1986). The goal in relation to suicide is prevention. Teachers should always take threats or talk about suicide seriously, attempt to maintain or establish communication, provide emotional support, and seek immediate help from other professionals.

Unusual talent may coexist with behavior disorders.

Child Abuse and Neglect

The Child Abuse Prevention and Treatment Act defines *child abuse* and *neglect* as the "physical or mental injury, sexual abuse or exploitation, negligent treatment, or maltreatment of a child . . . by a person who is responsible for the child's welfare, under circumstances which indicate that the child's health or welfare is harmed or threatened" (PL 93–247, as amended by PL 95–266, 1978, Sec. 3). All 50 states have procedures for reporting suspected child abuse and neglect by any citizen, and schools have specific guidelines and policies for school personnel to follow. It is imperative for teachers to know the policies and procedures for their state and school.

Some of the characteristics of abuse and neglect are similar to the behaviors of individuals identified as having emotional and behavior disorders (Sigelman & Shaffer, 1991). The two situations are not the same, but are often closely related. Karlin and Berger (1992), Sigelman and Shaffer (1991), Stronge (1992), and Eddowes (1992) suggest that there are a number of behavioral indicators that youngsters who are abused or neglected may exhibit. The following personality characteristics are similar to those of students identified as having emotional or behavior disorders.

- *The shy or fearful child.* Whether a child is fearful or is shy can be determined by becoming aware of what and whom the child fears. The fearful child is usually afraid or fearful of many persons and things; the fear is generalized. The shy child differs in that the fear is related more to contact with people. The shy child usually speaks in a low voice, sits with head lowered to avoid eye contact, and declines participation in group activities. The shy child may be modeling parental behavior or may be the victim of excessively critical parents, who expect perfection. Since the child cannot meet this standard, he or she hesitates to attempt any task.
- *The careless child.* Messy papers, desk, and physical appearance are hallmarks. Often, the teacher is unable to decipher the work of the child to evaluate it. Other children trip over the books, papers, and boxes strewn around the child's desk. The child seems to stumble through life. This careless attitude may be the result of parents who place little value on orderliness or organization, or the child may adopt this pattern of behavior because of excessive demands made by the parents.
- *The aggressive child.* This child is quarrelsome and bullying. He or she may have a pattern of behavior learned from parents who express themselves with physical punishment when they are displeased.

- *The disobedient child.* This child is an insolent, disrespectful child, who never seems to hear directions and who engages in a continuing power struggle with authority. A lack of recognition in the home may lead to the child's extreme attempts at gaining attention. Parental attitudes toward authority, especially school, may also influence the child's attitudes toward teachers.
- *The child who cheats, lies, or steals.* Infrequent occurrence of such behavior, especially in young children, is usually not a cause for alarm, but repeated activities of this nature often reflect hostility toward family or authority. They can also indicate a need for attention or may result from modeling behaviors in the home.
- *The unkempt child.* This child's dirty face, matted hair, and soiled clothing may result from a lack of proper facilities for bathing or laundering clothing but also from carelessness of the parent. Such a child does not feel valued and feels little or no personal pride. Both feelings are reflected in the child's work.
- *The show-off.* This child is an extreme extrovert, identified by clowning in class and inability to wait, both behaviors masking insecurity and feelings of inferiority, feelings that may be the result of little or no warmth or attention from the parents.
- *The child nobody likes.* This child is often listless, sometimes destructive, seemingly incapable of forming satisfying relationships. Commonly, this student is absent from school or is a dropout. The home environment may lack warmth or satisfying relationships. Family members may live isolated lives; therefore, the child has not learned the skills necessary for productive interactions.

Alert teachers may discern many forms of mistreatment including abandonment, emotional abuse or neglect, physical abuse and neglect, and sexual abuse (Eddowes, 1992; Stronge, 1992). Abandonment occurs when children are simply left behind. Even when children are left with an adult but no provisions are made for their continued support, they have been abandoned.

Emotional abuse and neglect often result in extremely low self-concept and inappropriate attempts to seek attention. Young females may turn to promiscuous behavior in efforts to receive love and attention. Young males may turn to vandalism, drugs, or gangs to feel of value to others or themselves. Emotional abuse may take the form of ridicule for failing to achieve the goals parents set. In such cases, the normal parent–child relationship of unconditional caring is either absent or destroyed. Some children withdraw from contact with others because their normal family relationships have been so devastating. Others are so convinced that they are worthless that they begin to act out behaviors that confirm their worthlessness. Emotional neglect reflects lack of involvement by parents. It is a fault of omission rather than commission. The parents may provide the basics of food, clothing, and shelter, but seem unable to provide any of the warmth and caring essential for the development of children (McWhirter, McWhirter, McWhirter, & McWhirter, 1993).

Physical abuse and neglect are other forms of child abuse. Physical neglect occurs when the physical needs of food, clothing, general care, supervision, or shelter are not met. The actions of children, such as stealing food or articles of clothing, may seem inappropriate, but they may be the attempts to meet basic needs. In cases where poverty causes the neglect, social agencies are usually available to assist. Yet, poverty is not the reason some parents neglect their children. Some parents are barely able to meet their own emotional needs and have little time or concern for their offspring.

Physical abuse is the most often reported and most easily recognized form of maltreat-

ment. The various forms of physical abuse can generally be observed by teachers. Signs of possible physical abuse include (a) abrasions in various stages of healing; (b) burns shaped like objects such as cigarettes or utensils or burns that indicate immersion in hot water or of having had water poured on parts of the body; (c) injuries that suggest an imprint of belts, clothes hangers, hose, hand, teeth, or rope; injuries on parts of the body inconsistent with a fall; injuries of peculiar sizes or shapes; or injuries around the head; and (d) bruises of different colors, indicating they were received over time. Children are often reluctant to discuss why or how they received injuries that result from physical abuse. Victims of physical abuse show fear of adults that is manifested when they protect their heads with their hands or use other forms of apparent self-defense when approached suddenly or unexpectedly by adults. Sexual abuse involves a range from exposure, to fondling, to rape, to incest and may occur from infancy through adolescence. Generally, it is not a one-time event except in the case of strangers. Because a sexually abused child generally exhibits no physical signs, the abuse is frequently undetected. Sometimes, teachers observe a sudden change of behavior that occurs at the onset of the abuse or when the child becomes aware that such treatment is not normal among peers. Many sexually abused children attempt to hide the mistreatment because they recognize they are participants in activities that are unacceptable in society. They submit to abuse because of fear of punishment or withdrawal of love, because of desire for some promised reward, or because they are physically forced to submit. At times, the burden of undeserved guilt becomes so great that the child turns to a trusted adult. This confidence must not go unheeded. Although extremely personal, the matter must be investigated. Teachers need to be aware of the proper procedures for reporting suspected sexual abuse.

■ Summary

Definitions of emotional and behavior disorders have been subject to controversy for many years, as have the various approaches through which professionals have attempted to provide effective educational interventions. In this chapter, we gave the federal definition for serious emotional disturbance and a revision proposed by a coalition of most of the professional groups whose members attempt to assist individuals with emotional and behavioral disorders. We outlined the process through which regular classroom teachers might refer students with suspected emotional/behavioral disorders, emphasizing the importance of collaboration among teachers.

We discussed four major theoretical orientations—behavior modification, psychodynamic, biophysical, and sociological/ecological—along with the educational interventions that grow out of these orientations. We presented alternate approaches by Dreikurs, Glasser, and the Canters.

We offered practical suggestions for classroom teachers, including the use of such techniques as monitoring and modifying class dynamics, reducing stress, exploring feelings, and using alternative assignments. We explored other issues of concern, including juvenile delinquency, substance abuse, depression, and child abuse, and noted that although they seem at times related to and/or associated with emotional and behavior disorders, they cannot be assumed to be the cause of such disorders.

chapter 12

- How are giftedness, creativity, and talent interrelated? How are they different? Can one exist in the absence of the others?

- Why is it difficult to discover giftedness among some students from culturally diverse populations? How might the situation be remedied? What are the pitfalls in any attempted remedy?

- Under what conditions might separate schools for students who are gifted be justifiable? How would opponents of such schools support their position?

- How may a future studies program benefit students who are gifted? How might the benefits be expanded beyond the students enrolled in the program?

- What is Bloom's taxonomy? How is it useful in planning programs for students who are gifted?

Teaching Students Who Are Gifted or Talented

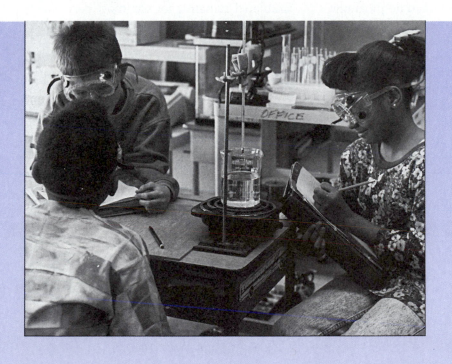

■■■■■■■■■■

Special educational programs for students who are gifted and talented are not mandated by the federal government (as is the case for students with disabilities), and in many states, such programs receive considerably less special funding from state-level sources than do programs for students with disabilities. In the United States, the federal report, *National Excellence: A Case for Developing America's Talent* (1993) led to a flurry of additional interest in programs for gifted and talented students; however, the report concluded that "although effective programs do exist, many are limited in scope and substance" (p. 2). Yet, despite this apparent lack of support, parent and advocacy groups have kept programs alive, and "interest in the education of the gifted and talented is steadily growing worldwide" (Clark, 1992, p. 166).

Whatever influences have contributed to the variation in the breadth and depth of programs, we believe that students who are gifted have special needs, and deserve additional interest and attention. The question of how this additional interest and attention may be stimulated remains, for the most part, unanswered. In addition to the variation in the degree and types of programming now provided for students who are gifted and talented, there is only limited consensus concerning which students to include in such special programs. To a considerable extent, this relates to disagreement and ambiguity in various definitions of the terms gifted, talented, and creative, which in turn, leads to questions about the procedures for identifying students for special educational assistance. We address all of these concerns in this chapter, beginning with a review of definitions.

■■■■■■■■■■

■■ Definitions

The wording of definitions of *giftedness, talent*, and *creativity* may have a great deal of influence on the type of program developed to serve students so identified. Percentage-based definitions and regulations (for example, serving the top 2 or 3 percent of students, according to some academic achievement criteria) may target a different group of students than IQ-based definitions. And talent-based definitions, which consider demonstrated talent in one or more areas (for example, in music, art, or dance), target another group of students. State level definitions vary, but since the early 1970s, many have followed the general structure of the first widely recognized national definition, articulated in 1972 by Sydney Marland, then commissioner of the U.S. Office of Education. Marland included his definition in a report to Congress, entitled *Education of the Gifted and Talented* (Marland, 1972):

1972 Marland Definition (Public Law 91–230, section 806)

Gifted and talented children are those identified by professionally qualified persons, who by virtue of outstanding abilities are capable of high performance. These are children who require differentiated educational programs and/or services beyond those normally provided by the regular school program in order to realize their contribution to self and society.

Children capable of high performance include those with demonstrated achievement and/or potential ability in any of the following areas, singly or in combination:

1. general intellectual ability,
2. specific academic aptitude,
3. creative or productive thinking,
4. leadership ability,
5. visual and performing arts,
6. psychomotor ability.

It can be assumed that utilization of these criteria for identification of the gifted and talented will encompass a minimum of 3 to 5 percent of the school population.

The Marland definition was revised by succeeding federal pronouncements. For example, Public Law 97–35, the Education Consolidation and Improvement Act (1981), refers to "children who give evidence of high performance capability in areas such as intellectual, creative, artistic, leadership capacity, or specific academic fields, and who require services or activities not ordinarily provided by the school in order to fully develop such capabilities" (Sec. 582). This definition is consistent with earlier modifications of Marland's original definition in that it does not mention psychomotor ability.

The Javits Act Definition

The Jacob K. Javits Gifted and Talented Students Education Act, passed in 1988, included a modified definition of gifted and talented: "The term 'gifted and talented students' means children and youth who give evidence of high performance capability in areas such as intellectual, creative, artistic, or leadership capacity, or in specific academic fields, and who require services or activities not ordinarily provided by the school in order to fully develop such capabilities" (Sec. 4103).

The *National Excellence* Definition

In 1991, an advisory group to federal leadership administering the Javits Act proposed revising the definition of gifted and talented. After considerable discussion, the following definition was included in the report, *National Excellence: A Case for Developing America's Talent* (1993, p. 26). Note that the emphasis has shifted to "outstanding talent," and that although the term *gifted* appears in some of the discussion, it does not appear in the basic definition.

Neuroscience and cognitive psychology provide us with new insights into what it means for children and youth to be outstanding talents and require us to develop a new definition of this population. The term "gifted" connotes a mature power rather than a developing ability and, therefore, is antithetic to recent research findings about children. The following definition, based on the definition used in the federal Javits Gifted and Talented Education Act, reflects today's knowledge and thinking:

Children and youth with outstanding talent perform or show the potential for performing at remarkably high levels of accomplishment when compared with others of their age, experience, or environment.

These children and youth exhibit high performance capability in intellectual, creative, and/or artistic areas, possess an unusual leadership capacity, or excel in specific academic fields. They require services or activities not ordinarily provided by the schools.

Outstanding talents are present in children and youth from all cultural groups, across all economic strata, and in all areas of human endeavor.

To put this definition into practice, schools must develop a system to identify gifted and talented students that

- Seeks variety—looks throughout a range of disciplines for students with diverse talents;
- Uses many assessment measures—uses a variety of appraisals so that schools can find students in different talent areas and at different ages;
- Is free of bias—provides students of all backgrounds with equal access to appropriate opportunities;
- Is fluid—uses assessment procedures that can accommodate students who develop at different rates and whose interests may change as they mature;

- Identifies potential—discovers talents that are not readily apparent in students, as well as those that are obvious; and
- Assesses motivation—takes into account the drive and passion that play a key role in accomplishment.

The various federal definitions have influenced state definitions and the regulations through which special state funding (if any) is provided to local education agencies (LEAs). These definitions, and state definitions and regulations, have also provided various degrees of direction to the manner in which local school districts provide special services for students who are gifted and/or talented. Other definitions or conceptualizations of giftedness and talent also have influenced the manner in which LEAs attempt to serve the needs of students. We here present three such conceptualizations.

Gagné's Concept of Giftedness and Talent

Francoys Gagné (1990, 1992) has proposed a model of talent in which talent is considered "the developmental product of an interaction between aptitudes and intrapersonal and environmental catalysts" (1990, p. 66). He considers giftedness as the aptitude for achievement in various fields of talent. In this conceptualization, giftedness domains include intellectual aptitude, creative aptitude, socioaffective aptitude, and sensorimotor aptitude. Fields of talent might include, for example, talent in arts (either visual or expressive), athletics and sports, communications, business and commerce, science and technology, and education.

Gagné suggests that we must recognize talent in fields such as cooking, gardening, teaching, and others, in addition to the traditional professional fields such as medicine and law. Piirto (1994) believes that Gagné's model has had considerable influence on the latest thinking in the area of development of talent.

Renzulli's Operational Definition

A recognized definition of giftedness is provided by Renzulli and Smith (1980) and Renzulli, Reis, and Smith (1981). Their definition, which they consider an operational definition of giftedness, reflects their belief that the categories in the federal definition often overlap to a considerable extent. Renzulli et al. suggest three generalizations. First, three traits are common to all truly gifted individuals: (a) above-average intellectual ability, (b) task commitment, and (c) creativity. They suggest that no single trait should be used to identify giftedness, since it is the interaction of these traits that leads to what we commonly call giftedness. The second generalization is that giftedness should be recognized in relation to all socially useful areas of performance. The third generalization is that there is great need to increase efforts to measure or assess a broad range of abilities or potential abilities in addition to those of general intellectual ability.

Clark's Definition of Giftedness

Clark (1992) proposes another definition, based on her interpretation of brain research and the belief that in gifted individuals, there is advanced, or accelerated, brain function development:

Giftedness is a biologically rooted concept that serves as a label for a high level of intelligence and indicates an advanced and accelerated development of functions within the brain, including physical sensing, emotions, cognition, and intuition. Such advanced and accelerated function may be expressed through abilities such as those involved in cognition, creativity, academic aptitude, leadership, or the visual and performing arts. Gifted individuals are those who perform, or who show promise of performing, at high levels in such areas and who, because of such advanced and accelerated development, require services or activities not ordinarily provided by the schools in order to develop their capability more fully. (p. 8)

How Definitions and Regulations Influence Identification

Definitions and related regulations have a profound influence on the identification of those who are to participate in programs for the gifted, talented, or creative. For example, in a number of states, despite philosophical statements to the contrary, identification relates primarily to two factors, IQ and achievement. Such definitions and regulations ignore artistic or creative talents unless the student who is artistic or creative also has a high IQ. Such definitions also tend to discriminate against individuals who are poor, who underachieve on achievement tests, or who are from culturally diverse populations.[1] If state and local education agencies can develop creative, effective ways to implement the suggestions made as an adjunct to the 1993 federal definition of children with outstanding talent, stated previously, a great deal of this discrimination and bias may be avoided. However, authors of texts that address this concern regularly provide only a few suggestions, and include some statement

---

[1]One exception applies in relation to students from one culturally diverse group. The federal report, *National Excellence: A Case for Developing America's Talent* (1993), notes that in a recent national study of students served in programs for gifted and talented, although most minority racial and ethnic groups were underrepresented, a higher percentage of Asian students were served than any other racial or ethnic group, including white, non-Hispanics.

to the effect that there are, at present, a limited number of options and that professionals must continue to develop and test new measures and procedures (Baca & Cervantes, 1989; Ewing & Yong, 1992; Venn, 1994). This is not to suggest that serious efforts have not been undertaken, but rather that implementing the suggestions included in the federal definition is a complex process.

■■ Characteristics

Because nomination for possible inclusion in programs for students who are gifted or talented plays such an important role in the identification process, teachers must be aware of various characteristics of such students. This is particularly important in instances where students do not give evidence of their abilities in their academic work. Figure 12–1 indicates three general categories for students who are intellectually gifted: (a) general behavioral characteristics, (b) learning characteristics, and (c) creative characteristics (Whitmore, 1985). Recent investigations of characteristics provide remarkably similar results to earlier studies, particularly when intellectual talent (as opposed to talent in some performance area such as music, art, or athletic ability) is the major concern (Scott, Peron, Urbano, Hogan, & Gold, 1992; Piirto, 1994). Such studies seem to indicate that Hispanic and African American children, and children from other minority populations who are identified and included in programs for the gifted and talented have similar characteristics, but they are not identified in numbers reflecting their proportion in the general population (Serwatka, Deering, & Stoddard, 1989).

Characteristics of intellectually gifted or talented students are generally accepted; characteristics of students with unusual creative potential are more subject to debate. In part, this relates to lack of agreement with respect to various tests purporting to measure creative potential (more about this later in this chapter), but in part it relates to the nebulousness of the term *creativity*. The difficulty of assessing creative potential and the potential for lawsuits in relation to identification is discussed by Piirto (1994) who suggests a way to sidestep the pitfalls inherent in such assessment. Her suggestion is to identify for specific talent, or judge products for their creativity, and not attempt to identify for "creative ability." Perhaps Clark (1992) was right when she stated, "Creativity is a very special condition, attitude, or state of being that nearly defies definition" (p. 47). However, we will attempt to shed further light on the nature of, and characteristics associated with creativity in the following paragraphs.

Torrance (1974) developed one of the leading measures of creativity (Tests of Creative Thinking). He noted that creativity can be defined in terms of (a) product (invention and discovery), (b) process, and (c) characteristics of the individual who is considered to be creative. His concept of creativity includes many elements that others ascribe to intelligence but also includes sensitivity to deficiencies, gaps in knowledge, and disharmonies.

A more traditional concept of creativity relates to bringing something new into existence, literally creating something new. This concept recognizes that creative individuals work with given physical or mental materials but shape these materials into something new. Common-use definitions relate creativity to inventiveness and seem to view creativity primarily as the making of a product. However, most authorities agree that creativity, like intelligence, is a good thing, even if the general population has widely varying concepts.

If the concept of creativity is limited to creativity resulting in a product, there is a degree

General Behavioral Characteristics

- Many typically learn to read earlier with a better comprehension of the nuances of the language. As many as half of the gifted and talented population have learned to read before entering school. They often read widely, quickly, and intensely and have large vocabularies.

- They commonly learn basic skills better, more quickly, and with less practice.

- They are better able to construct and handle abstractions than their age mates.

- They are frequently able to pick up and interpret nonverbal cues and can draw inferences which other children have to have spelled out for them.

- They take less for granted, seeking the "hows" and "whys."

- They display a better ability to work independently at an earlier age and for longer periods of time than other children.

- They can sustain longer periods of concentration and attention.

- Their interests are often both wildly eclectic and intensely focused.

- They frequently have seemingly boundless energy, which sometimes leads to a misdiagnosis of "hyperactive."

- They are usually able to respond and relate well to parents, teachers, and other adults. They may prefer the company of older children and adults to that of their peers.

- They are willing to examine the unusual and are highly inquisitive.

- Their behavior is often well organized, goal directed, and efficient with respect to tasks and problems.

- They exhibit an intrinsic motivation to learn, find out, or explore and are often very persistent. "I'd rather do it myself" is a common attitude.

- They enjoy learning new things and new ways of doing things.

- They have a longer attention and concentration span than their peers.

Learning Characteristics

- They may show keen powers of observation, exhibit a sense of the significant, and have an eye for important details.

- They may read a great deal on their own, preferring books and magazines written for youngsters older than themselves.

- They often take great pleasure in intellectual activity.

Figure 12–1
Characteristics of intellectually gifted children

of agreement that invention of such things as the electric light bulb, the telephone, and the zipper reflects creativity. Yet, is it possible to predict that a child will later become such a creative inventor? How can educators and parents encourage such potential creativity in children? The answers are not clear cut, but there are possible indicators of creativity and ways to encourage creativity if the potential is present.

A potentially creative individual might have any of the following characteristics:

1. Unusual curiosity
2. Unusual persistence
3. Unusual imagination
4. Originality

A fifth characteristic is sometimes included with these four: restlessness. This may not be

- They have well developed powers of abstraction, conceptualization, and synthesizing abilities.
- They generally have rapid insight into cause-effect relationships.
- They often display a questioning attitude and seek information for the sake of having it as much as for its instrumental value.
- They are often skeptical, critical, and evaluative. They are quick to spot inconsistencies.
- They often have a large storehouse of information regarding a variety of topics which they can recall quickly.
- They show a ready grasp of underlying principles and can often make valid generalizations about events, people, or objects.
- They readily perceive similarities, differences, and anomalies.
- They often attack complicated material by separating it into its components and analyzing it systematically.

Creative Characteristics

- They are *fluent* thinkers, able to produce a large quantity of possibilities, consequences, or related ideas.
- They are *flexible* thinkers, able to use many different alternatives and approaches to problem solving.

- They are *original* thinkers, seeking new, unusual, or unconventional associations and combinations among items of information. They also have an ability to see relationships among seemingly unrelated objects, ideas, or facts.
- They are *elaborative* thinkers, producing new steps, ideas, responses, or other embellishments to a basic idea, situation, or problem.
- They show a willingness to entertain complexity and seem to thrive in problem situations.
- They are good guessers and can construct hypotheses or "what if" questions readily.
- They often are aware of their own impulsiveness and the irrationality within themselves and show emotional sensitivity.
- They have a high level of curiosity about objects, ideas, situations, or events.
- They often display intellectual playfulness, fantasize, and imagine readily.
- They can be less intellectually inhibited than their peers in expressing opinions and ideas and often exhibit spirited disagreement.
- They have a sensitivity to beauty and are attracted to aesthetic dimensions.

Figure 12–1, *continued*

Source: From "Characteristics of Intellectually Gifted Children" by J. R. Whitmore, 1985, ERIC Digest, 344.

seen until after the child's entrance into school and is usually a reaction to meaningless, repetitive tasks, which are not challenging to creative students.

Most children show some degree of curiosity, persistence, and imagination. Potentially creative children, however, have

an unusually high degree of these characteristics compared to age peers. Originality may be the distinguishing characteristic, but originality is easy to overlook, probably because originality in children generally does not produce products as obvious as the light bulb, the telephone, and the zipper. Originality in

Dramatic talent is one dimension of giftedness.

children relates to their age and experience. It involves something that would not be expected from an individual of that age or level of experience.

For example, a very young child might use a self-constructed lever arrangement to lift something when the child has had no specific experience that would lead to understanding the lever and has not observed someone using a lever. Of course, many people use levers, but most have seen someone else do so or have had a sequence of experiences that led to understanding the mechanical properties of levers. Whatever the child might demonstrate, the question of originality is a matter of whether it is usual or normal for someone of that age and experience to demonstrate that ability, understanding, or insight.

The efforts of J. P. Guilford deserve special mention in any discussion of creativity. In fact, Guilford deserves equal mention for his efforts related to understanding general intelligence, giftedness, and creativity. He developed a three-dimensional conceptual model called the "structure of intellect," with which he predicted the existence of at least 120 distinct types of intellectual ability (Guilford, 1959a). This model played a major role in triggering debate and research related to "convergent" and "divergent" thinking. Guilford's consideration of divergent thinking, now usually related to creativity, has led to continuing speculation about the true nature of creativity, but leaves unanswered questions.

Facilitating the development of creativity is the teacher's responsibility. Such facilitation requires both an accurate general concept of the nature of creativity and some specific ideas and skills. Table 12–1 presents a brief sample of factors and conditions that may facilitate or inhibit creativity. Teachers who want to encourage creativity should think in terms of both "what I should do" and "what I should avoid doing," since many schools encourage teachers to follow practices that may inhibit creativity. Although there is disagreement in the identification of creativity, most teachers indicate an interest in promoting it. With continuing attention to the behavior of individual students, regular classroom teachers can become facilitators rather than inhibitors of creative efforts.

Table 12–1
Factors and conditions that may facilitate or inhibit creativity

Facilitating	Inhibiting
Spontaneous participation and expression	Requirement of unquestioning obedience to authority
Encouragement of many questions and acceptance of divergency from plan	No deviation from preestablished lesson plan
Openness to unevaluated practice and experimentation	Evaluation of all student work—a grade for everything
Encouragement of imagination, make-believe, fictional discussion, and writing	Discussion of real, practical ideas only
Encouragement of problem solving at all age levels	Emphasis on memorizing "correct" answers
Openness to new ideas and a self-concept relatively independent of student comment and behaviors	Requirement that students recognize teacher "rightness" regularly

■ Identification

As might be deduced from the earlier discussion of characteristics, identification of students for programs for the gifted, talented, or creative, is a subject of considerable debate, and the reader of journals or texts relating to education of gifted, talented, or creative students might well think that there is undue emphasis on identification. But with no federal mandate relating to identification procedures, and with a variety of agendas on the minds of parent and educator advocates as they work for better educational programs, identification procedures vary considerably. However, there is some agreement as to what *should be*, even if the procedures agreed upon are not often followed.

Tyler-Wood and Carrie (1991) noted that although research literature consistently recommends the use of multiple measures of assessment in the identification of gifted children, "many school systems still base identification of gifted students primarily on one measure of cognitive ability because using a single measure is less costly and consumes less time even though each test may operationally define cognitive ability differently. It is possible, therefore, that we fail to identify many gifted students using a single measure of cognitive ability, particularly if the cognitive measure employed does not maximize a child's best abilities" (p. 63). They voice this opinion in relation to their study of the effectiveness of four different measures of cognitive ability, which indicated that different tests may tap different types of information. They concluded that when the program is based primarily on a single test, "the population of gifted students identified will vary greatly, depending upon which test is used" (p. 64).

The federal report, *National Excellence: A Case for Developing America's Talent* (1993), contains the following discussion of identification procedures:

Most states and localities have developed definitions of gifted and talented students in order to identify such students for special programs. Many of these definitions are based on the definition in the 1972 Marland Report to Congress on gifted and talented education. . . .

A large gap exists, however, between the Marland definition and the way most districts identify gifted students. The definition suggests that districts consider a broad range of talents, but most continue to restrict participation in programs for the gifted largely to those with exceptional intellectual ability. . . . Most mainly use tests and teacher recommendations to admit students to gifted and talented programs, limiting participation to students with high general intelligence and good school records and missing many outstanding students with other talents. This practice ignores extensive evidence from psychologists and neuroscientists that youngsters can be intelligent in many different ways, all of which schools can help to develop.

Several categories of talented children are particularly neglected in programs for top students. These include culturally different children (including minority and economically disadvantaged students), females (who are underserved in mathematics and science programs), students with disabilities, high potential students who underachieve in school, and students with artistic talent. Some schools are discouraged from serving these students by state laws or regulations which require the schools to use certain IQ cutoff scores or specific levels of performance on standardized tests if they wish to receive state funding for gifted and talented programs. However, even in states that do not have test score cutoffs, local schools often choose to use test scores because they are easier to determine and "safer" than more subjective procedures. While state and local definitions display good intentions, the practices used to assess and identify students are often unsatisfactory. (pp. 15–16)

Unfortunately, affirmation and reiteration of this state of affairs can be found from many sources.

Steps in the Identification Process

The term *multidimensional* is a key word in relation to any acceptable plan through which students are to be identified for programs for the gifted, talented, or creative. In the following paragraphs, we outline a sample identification process and the program placement that may follow.

Step One: Initial, Multidimensional Screening
1. Nomination procedures (by teachers, administrators, counselors, parents, the student's peers, or the student)
2. Review of existing records (cumulative files, anecdotal records, group or individual test results)
3. Use of some type of behavioral checklist or standardized form to gather additional behavioral information from teachers
4. Samples of products of performance (particularly in the case of programs targeting specific talents)
5. Developmental portfolios

Certain of the elements named above might be given more weight than others in specific cases. For example, samples of art work would be of primary importance in a program developed to encourge the work of students with apparent high potential in this field. This might include samples produced over as long a period of time as possible, and in various media. In another example, early childhood developmental portfolios may be essential in identification of young, economically disadvantaged, potentially gifted students (Wright & Borland, 1993). Such portfolios might include, for example, audiotapes, videotapes, samples of the children's work, and, most importantly, careful, sequential observations by the teacher, and where possible, by the parents. Various research projects, such as Project Synergy at Teachers College,

Columbia University, have developed extensive guidelines for the use of such portfolios for purposes of identification, curriculum development, and placement of young students who are potentially gifted or talented.

Step Two: Compilation of Information and Additional Assessment as Indicated

After collecting initial information, a committee or designated coordinator reviews it, deciding whether further assessment is indicated. If so indicated, additional tests, often either individual tests of intelligence or of creativity, will be administered. If the student appears to be a potential candidate for any existing program, or some program that might be developed, he or she will be referred to a formal meeting with other staff members and the parents.

Step Three: Formal Identification and Placement Decision

In a formal meeting, parents and committee members review the information compiled in steps one and two, and program options are discussed. If the parents agree to programs and/or placements suggested, the process continues.[2]

Step Four: Optional Interim Step

Often some additional assessment is required, to answer questions raised in step three, before a final decision regarding placement can be made. After such data is gathered, parents and school staff decide, in another formal

---

[2]Unlike program planning for students with disabilities, where a full continuum of services is mandated, it is altogether possible that some student might have potential talent that should be encouraged, but no program is available. Where no appropriate program is available, a decision must be made as to whether one might be initiated (often difficult to "sell" if it involves additional cost), or whether the student might be made to "fit" into another program.

meeting, actual placement and more detailed educational plans (in some LEAs this is called an IEP, in others it is not). When program choices are obvious in step three, the IEP is developed there, and this step is eliminated.

Step Five: Special Program Implementation

The student begins the program on the basis of earlier planning. Procedures and results are reviewed on an established basis by school staff and parents.

The preceding process may be subdivided into more steps, but represents a relatively simple procedure through which objective decisions can be made with respect to identification, and program placement. One of the weakest links in this process relates to the reliability and validity of the assessment instruments, which may have already been a part of the student's cumulative record, those used in step two, or those sometimes used in step four. It is beyond the scope of this text to discuss these instruments in detail, but the following overview may be of value in providing a better general understanding of tests and other assessment tools that might be used.

Tests and Other Assessment Tools Used to Identify Students with Intellectual Ability or Creativity

We should note at the outset that for the most part, the assessment instruments reviewed in this section purport to measure *potential* intellectual ability or creativity, not developed ability or talent. The extent to which they actually do so is one major concern of many of their detractors. A second concern is that different tests of cognitive ability measure different abilities or potential abilities.

One report of the practical results of this fact is that of Tyler-Wood and Carrie (1991). In their study, four different measures of cognitive ability were used with students already selected for a special program for gifted students in Georgia. To be eligible for gifted placement, students in grades 3 to 12 were required to have a mental abilities score at the 96th percentile or higher. Twenty-one students, ranging in age from 7 to 12 years, were randomly selected from 45 program participants. Over a 6-week period, these students took a battery of four tests: the Stanford-Binet (LM), the Stanford-Binet (Fourth Edition), the Otis-Lennon School Abilities Test, and the Cognitive Abilities Test. (Each of these tests is used as a measure of intellectual ability in various parts of the United States and may in some cases be the only measure of intellectual ability used.) Seventeen of the 21 students would have been ineligible for placement in Georgia, depending on the test used, and only five met the state's criteria on all tests administered. These results certainly support the authors' conclusion, "If the identification criteria for a program for the gifted is based primarily on a single test, the population of gifted students identified will vary greatly depending upon which test is used. To facilitate appropriate and consistent identification, multiple criteria for identification should be used" (p. 64).

Individual Tests of Intelligence

Rightly or wrongly, programs for gifted or talented students are often based primarily on a presumption that the student has above-average intelligence or intellectual ability. How much above average (required to be eligible for some given program) depends on state regulations or guidelines, but whatever the requirement or cutoff point, administrators must use some type of score. The basic question with reference to testing for intelligence, or cognitive ability is, "What is intelligence?" Venn (1994) answers with the following questions about defining *intelligence*: "Is it the ability to change behavior based on experience? Is it

what intelligence tests measure? Is it a complex theoretical concept developed to explain certain types of behavior? Is it a score on an IQ test? Is it the measurement of one general trait or the separate measurement of different traits or characteristics? What makes a person intelligent? How should intelligence be measured?" (p. 92). Whatever the theoretically correct answers to these questions, for practical purposes, what the schools most often deal with in relation to programs for the gifted is a score, or scores, from some assessment instrument. The individual assessment tools mentioned in the remainder of this section are among the most commonly used individual measures of intelligence.

The Stanford-Binet Intelligence Scale IV (1986) is the most recent version of a test first published by Binet and Simon in 1905. According to Venn (1994), Binet believed that intelligence may be considered as a group of abilities, including initiative, judgment, good sense, and the ability to adjust to changes in the environment. Two versions of the Stanford-Binet remain in common use to identify children with high level intelligence, the Stanford-Binet Intelligence Scale IV (1986), and the Stanford-Binet Intelligence Scale Form L-M (1973). Psychologists and educators of gifted students can make a case for the use of either version (Robinson, 1992; Silverman & Kearney, 1992), and both have very good overall technical qualities.

The three Wechsler tests, particularly the Wechsler Intelligence Scale for Children—Third Edition (WISC-III), (Wechsler, 1991) are also widely used to identify gifted and talented students. The WISC-III is for students from age 6 to 16 years, and has two scales, verbal and performance, which test quite separate abilities or potential abilities. The verbal subtest relies heavily on understanding of oral questions and a variety of verbal language behaviors. The performance subtest has minimal dependence on verbal ability, relying on perceptual abilities and fine motor skills. This permits certain special applications of the WISC-III, for example, use of the performance test alone in cases where verbal abilities are obviously poor predictors of overall ability. (See description of the WISC-III on page 308.) Two other Wechsler tests, the Wechsler Preschool and Primary Scale of Intelligence—Revised (WPPSI-R) (Wechsler, 1989) and the Wechsler Adult Intelligence Scale—Revised (WAIS-R) (Wechsler, 1981), are used for the age spans below and above the range of the WISC-III. In contrast to the basic premises underlying the Stanford-Binet, the Wechsler tests are based on the assumption that intelligence is a global ability to think reasonably, to act in a purposeful manner, and to successfully and appropriately adjust to changes in the environment (Sattler, 1992).

Kaufman, following a positive review of the WISC-III and WPPSI-R as evaluative instruments for identification of gifted children, notes that these batteries "have much to recommend them for gifted assessment, but they also have aspects that call out for caution. Above all, using the WPPSI-R or WISC-III or any intelligence test for gifted assessment requires the examiner to go beyond the simple IQs, and try to make sense out of WHY the child scored the way he or she did. And proper use of IQ tests with gifted or potentially gifted children demands that they be used in conjunction with other tests and criteria" (1992, p. 158).

Other individual tests of intelligence may sometimes be used to determine whether a student is intellectually gifted or talented; however, if they are used as the primary test, it is likely to be because of a special circumstance such as limited English language proficiency or a profound hearing impairment. Individual tests may be used to further investigate findings of the Stanford-Binet IV or the

WISC-III, especially when those findings are borderline and when there are clinical indications that they may be an underestimate of potential ability.

Group Tests of Intelligence

Several group tests have been used to establish eligibility for inclusion in programs for the gifted and talented. Although some are well constructed, most are too dependent on factors such as already developed reading ability, general ability in the English language, and motivation to take a group, pencil and paper test. They may be of value as a screening tool, but will "overlook" many students who are potentially gifted or talented.

Assessment of Creativity

Creativity tests are among the most controversial of those used in identification for special programs. Guilford (1959b) states a view of creativity still regularly used in discussions of its traits. He speaks of four dimensions of creative behavior: fluency, flexibility, originality, and elaboration. By their very nature, these are difficult traits to measure. Torrance (1962, 1965) offers additional insight into creativity, and a number of measures of creativity. The following brief description of one such measure, Thinking Creatively in Action and Movement (TCAM), (Torrance, 1981) shows how one may attempt to measure creativity in children ages 3 through 8. It also provides some insight into the type of behaviors that may characterize creativity.

Thinking Creatively in Action and Movement (TCAM) has four subparts. A description of the first two subparts follows.

1. How Many Ways? is scored for originality and fluency with respect to the various ways the child may "invent" to move across the floor. The originality score is the total of points assigned to

particular responses, rated from 0 to 3. For example, goose-stepping is rated 3, duck-walking is rated 2, jogging is rated 1, and simple crawling is rated 0. The fluency score is the total of the number of ways and the combination of ways.

2. Can You Move Like? provides a score for imagination. One question asks "Can you move like a tree in the wind? Imagine you are a tree and the wind is blowing very hard." Children are then asked to show how many different ways a tree in the wind can move. Responses on each of the six questions on this part of the TCAM are rated from 1 to 5, according to an established scale.

The TCAM, and other tests of creativity, are much more subjective than most other instruments used to assess the intellectual ability of gifted or talented students, despite attempts to develop concise instructions for administration and scoring.

Portfolio Assessment

We discuss portfolio assessment in some detail in Chapter 3 (see also Stiggins, 1994). Such an assessment tool may be particularly important in assessment of the gifted minority student (Barken & Bernal, 1991; Hadaway & Marek-Schroer, 1992). For children with limited English proficiency, the inclusion of art work, for example, "provides a powerful nonverbal way to communicate" (Hadaway & Marek-Schroer, 1992, p. 76). In a similar way, many other components of broad-scope portfolios can be particularly valuable in the assessment of children from minority groups. Like tests of creativity, evaluation of portfolios can be very subjective. However, if they are part of a truly multidimensional assessment, there can be little question of their value.

Gifted Females and Other Special Populations

Many authors and researchers concerned with identification and education of gifted students have identified certain at-risk or special populations of such students (Clark, 1992; Sisk, 1987; Smutny & Blocksom, 1990; VanTassel-Baska, Patton, & Prillaman, 1991). Most would include students from low-income families whose parents' educational level and occupational status are commensurately low, students from dysfunctional family backgrounds, students from racial or cultural backgrounds different from the mainstream, students of limited English proficiency, students who have physical or learning disabilities that mask their potential, and those with a combination of these characteristics. As indicated in various sections throughout this chapter, such students are less likely to be identified for programs for the gifted, and if identified, the program may be inappropriate, unless modified or individualized in recognition of their special needs. Their special status requires specific consideration in the planning and implementation of programs for students who are gifted or talented.

Another group, comprising approximately half of the total potentially gifted student population, is also at risk in relation to both initial identification and to the provision of a program meeting their special needs (Clark, 1992; Piirto, 1994; Sisk, 1987). This group is comprised of gifted females.

Why are gifted females underidentified, or, when identified, do not appear to benefit from existing programs in the same manner as gifted males? And why do they not experience professional "success" and recognition in the same proportion as males, after completion of formal educational programs? Many theories purport to explain this phenomenon. Most who have studied this question believe that it a matter of the interaction of a variety of factors:

1. Lack of encouragement of females to enter certain professional or vocational fields
2. A shortage of nontraditional female role models
3. The social unacceptability (among both female and male peers) of high-level academic achievement by females
4. Gender bias (favoring males) built in to many achievement tests, including college admission, graduate record examinations, and similar tests
5. Gender differences in interests (i.e., presumptions that females are less interested in physics and chemistry, more interested in writing, music, drama, foreign language, etc.), which may contribute to test and achievement biases
6. Adult women realize they are childbearers, and are influenced by what some call the "motherhood, home, and hearth" mandates
7. Societal sex-role stereotyping

There seems to be general agreement with regard to most of the listed factors except number four, gender bias in various achievement tests. This issue remains under study, and although test developers may discard items that can be shown to have gender bias, males may do better than females because most such tests are power tests, and males tend to do better on power tests (Piirto, 1994; Stanley, Benbow, Brody, Danber, & Lupowski, 1992).

Other factors, related to values, may lead to gender differences, which in turn lead to career and choice differences (Eccles, 1985). For example, girls appear to be more interested in social goals, while boys are more interested in power and achievement goals (Brown & Gilligan, 1992; Higham & Navarre,

1984). This can lead to lack of motivation to achieve in areas that lead to inclusion in programs for the gifted.

Prevalence

Estimations of the prevalence of gifted, talented, or creative students vary widely, and depend primarily on the concepts and definitions used by those providing those estimates. The Marland report to Congress (1972) estimated that 3 to 5 percent of the total student population would be considered gifted or talented, using the criteria included in that report. Other federal estimations have accepted this prevalence estimate. Some state regulations have defined the gifted as those in the top 2 percent, and other estimates have ranged as high as 10 percent. Until we have a generally accepted national definition, it is impossible to acquire authoritative prevalence data.

School Organization and Program Options

Gifted students are not served consistently throughout the nation. Some regular classroom teachers receive essentially no assistance or guidance from specialists; some receive only limited consultative help; and others have both consultative assistance and special materials for students who are gifted. Still other teachers work with gifted students in some type of ability grouping. When regular classroom teachers have the advantage of continuing consultation with a specialist in the education of students who are gifted, their role is primarily that of cooperative planning and implementation of ideas. Such a role requires day-to-day modifications of instructional activities, but most teachers soon develop the ability to meet the educational needs of students who are gifted.

The instruction provided by regular classroom teachers is greatly influenced by the local organizational plan for education of students who are gifted. The three major organizational plans utilized on behalf of gifted students are (a) ability grouping, (b) enrichment, and (c) acceleration.

Ability Grouping

Grouping in separate, special classes or special schools often means that regular classroom teachers are involved only in relation to identification and referral of students who are gifted. Alternately, some schools provide special classes but integrate students into several regular classes. Still other schools supplement regular classes with special, pullout programs for part of the school day. Clustering several gifted students in one regular class allows interactions between students who have a broad range of abilities. Various combinations of ability grouping are utilized, and any groupings in which regular class teachers are active may be valuable, but in each arrangement, teachers must recognize and plan to meet the needs of students who are gifted.

Enrichment

Enrichment may be the most utilized program for gifted students. At least, it is among the most often mentioned when school administrators are asked how they serve gifted students in their district. *Enrichment* is an umbrella term that includes a variety of provisions for extra, broadened educational experiences. In the ability groupings mentioned in the preceding section, it is assumed that enrichment is taking place. However, school district practice with respect to serving stu-

dents who are gifted is often enrichment with no special grouping. This means differentiated learning opportunities for gifted students, but authorities disagree as to the effectiveness of enrichment without ability grouping.

Acceleration

Acceleration moves students who are gifted more rapidly through the regular program of the public schools. This may mean early school entrance, the skipping of grades, early or advanced placement in college, or a combination of procedures that lead to completion of the regular school program in less time than is normally required. Although perhaps not so popular today as in the past, research seems to support the general effectiveness of acceleration on an individual basis (Clark, 1992; Piirto, 1994).

In summarizing their followup study of young adults who had experienced acceleration, Noble, Robinson, and Gunderson (1992, p. 130) note the following:

1. "Accelerating one's secondary education is as healthy a decision for many highly capable students as remaining with age-mates" (as regards social and emotional development).
2. "Acceleration can be particularly beneficial for gifted young women because it allows them to by-pass a social milieu which is often destructive to female intellectuality."
3. "Acceleration in whatever form can prevent bright young people from turning off to school before they have had a chance to experience the joys and possibilities of their intellectual potential."

They also note, however, that "radical acceleration is not an option that will work for all gifted students."

Program Options

In general, special provisions for students who are gifted, talented, or creative, may be considered within the general categories of ability grouping, enrichment, acceleration, or some combination of these three. There are, however, many program components through which special assistance may be provided. Cox, Daniel, and Boston (1985), in a study designed to determine the program variations in use, included the following options:

1. Enrichment in regular classrooms
2. Appropriate pacing (content and pace of curriculum matched to student needs/abilities)
3. Guidance and counseling (to assist in development of high-level abilities and plan for future)
4. Within-class cluster-grouping
5. Across-class subject matter grouping
6. Regular enrichment classes during school day
7. Saturday enrichment programs
8. Summer enrichment programs
9. Resource room programs (part-time special program to small groups of gifted or talented students)
10. Seminars/convocations/workshops
11. Competitions
12. Acceleration (early entrance, grade skipping, subject matter acceleration, combined classes, self-paced instruction, concurrent enrollment, and others)
13. Honors classes
14. Advanced placement
15. Mentorships
16. Internships
17. Special schools

There may be a good deal of overlap between various of these programs. We will briefly describe several of these options in a later sec-tion of this chapter. Obviously, many of these options are available for students who are gifted and talented only if the school district makes provision for them; the regular classroom teacher cannot simply "do" them. However, as more educators are aware of the possibilities inherent in such program options and actively advocate for them, more options will become available.

■ Curriculum Guidelines

Teachers must adapt and modify teaching methods and curriculum content to meet the special educational needs of gifted and talented students. This is true, even when using an acceleration program, comprised mainly of grade skipping. In some schools, help is available from other educators who have specialized training and skills in this area, but if such help is not available, the guidance provided in Figures 12–2 and 12–3 should be of value. Figure 12–2 indicates the abilities and types of thinking advocated in the literature as important to promote critical thinking; Figure 12–3 lists "shoulds" and "should nots" that should be observed in developing a differentiated curriculum for students who are gifted, talented, or creative. In total, the information in these two figures may be a starting point for planning, but the most useful guide to planning for any student or group of students is a comprehensive assessment and analysis of their individual needs.

A basic tenet of this text is that exceptional students should be educated in the most normal way possible, consistent with meeting established educational goals. To the extent that educators can help exceptional students become more effective learners in the mainstream, the efforts are successful. Most authorities in the education of students who

The gifted student should become skilled at:

Distinguishing between verifiable facts and value claims

Determining the reliability of a claim or source

Determining the accuracy of a statement

Distinguishing between warranted and unwarranted claims

Detecting stated and unstated assumptions

Determining the strength of an argument

Detecting bias

Recognizing logical inconsistencies in a line of reasoning

Remaining open minded

Taking a position when the evidence and reasons are sufficient to do so

Taking into account the total situation

Being well informed

Seeking as much precision as the subject permits

Dealing in an orderly manner with the parts of a complex whole

Looking for alternatives

Seeking reasons

Seeking a clear statement of the issue

Using credible sources and mentioning them

Remaining relevant to the main point

Keeping in mind the original and/or basic concern

Remaining sensitive to the feelings, levels of knowledge, and degree of sophistication of others

Grasping the meaning of a statement

Judging whether there is ambiguity in a line of reasoning

Judging whether certain statements contradict each other

Judging whether a conclusion follows

Judging whether a statement is specific enough

Judging whether a statement is actually the application of a certain principle

Judging whether an observation statement is reliable

Judging whether an inductive conclusion is warranted

Judging whether the problem has been identified

Judging whether something is an assumption

Judging whether a definition is adequate

Judging whether a statement made by an alleged authority is acceptable

Understanding the difference between a conclusion which **might** be true and one which **must** be true

Questioning everything which does not make sense to him or her

Avoiding common mistakes in reasoning

Avoiding arguing about something he or she knows nothing about

Separating emotional thinking from logical thinking

Understanding and using external feedback

Recognizing problems

Formulating hypotheses

Gathering pertinent facts or data

Testing and evaluating

Drawing sound conclusions

Willing to question one's deepest beliefs and prejudices

Listening to another person's presentation of opinion or argument, no matter whether he or she agrees or not

Using specific terminology to refrain from overgeneralizations and supporting assumptions with valid data

Assessing the views of others and one's own views according to acceptable standards of appraisal

Figure 12–2

Critical thinking abilities students should become skilled at using

Source: From "We Can Agree After All! Achieving Consensus for a Critical Thinking Component of a Gifted Program using The Delphi Technique," by N. Stahl & R. Stahl, 1991, *Roeper Review, 14*(2), 81. Copyright 1991 by the *Roeper Review*, Bloomfield Hills, MI.

1. The curriculum *should* be planned and sequentially organized to include specific expectations for the acquisition of subject matter, mastery of skills, creation of products, and development of attitudes and appreciations related to self, others, and the environment.

    The curriculum *should not* be a potpourri of learning activities that are disjointed and haphazardly selected without reference to specified criteria.

2. The curriculum *should* place emphasis on the interdependence of subject matter, skills, products, and self-understanding within the *same* curricular structure.

    The curriculum *should not* focus on the attainment of cognitive competencies in isolation from the development of affective competencies. Nor should the curriculum focus on affective development without concern for cognitive growth.

3. The curriculum *should* include provisions to meet the need for some type of instructional pacing by any or all of the following means:
    a. Making it possible to accomplish a range of learning experiences in a shorter span of time using a continuous progress curriculum
    b. Assigning students to curricula at levels beyond those expected at the students' age/grade level
    c. Eliminating from the curricula what is already learned and substituting curricula more appropriate to student interest, abilities, and needs.

    The curriculum *should not* penalize students for being gifted or talented, through restricting their opportunities to learn by ignoring those characteristics that define their giftedness.

4. The curriculum *should* allow for the expression of some aspect of the individual's interests, needs, abilities, and learning preferences. The curriculum *should* be organized to allow for some individualization and self-selection.

    The curriculum *should not* be without defined expectations and clearly expressed opportunities for teacher-directed as well as student-selected learning activities.

Figure 12–3
The shoulds and should nots of an appropriately designed differentiated curriculum

are gifted or talented accept the idea that students who are gifted should be educated along with students who are not gifted as long as this achieves the desired results. However, most of these same authorities recognize that the unusual abilities of students who are gifted increase the likelihood that such students will require different learning environments and different teaching approaches. Educators of students who are gifted and talented endorse the goal of development of normal social skills and competence in interpersonal relationships, but in the learning arena, educational success accentuates differences. In some instances, such differences dictate removal from the mainstream.

A number of factors make any consideration of education of students who are gifted or

5. The curriculum *should* provide opportunities to learn to reconceptualize existing knowledge, to perceive things from various points of view, and to use information for new purposes or in new ways.

    The curriculum *should not* stress the accumulation of knowledge or reinforce mastery without simultaneously encouraging students to be productive thinkers.

6. The curriculum *should* provide learning experiences for students to address the unresolved issues and problems of society and apply personal and social data to analyze, clarify, and respond to such issues and problems.

    The curriculum *should not* focus only on knowledge of the world as it is, but should encourage the development of perceptions of the need to invent in order to restructure the world into what it ideally could be.

7. The curriculum *should* incorporate learning experiences that foster the development of the complex thought processes that encourage the creation of unique products and develop strategies of productive thought. The curriculum *should* teach both fundamental and higher-level thinking skills as integral parts of every learning experience.

    The curriculum *should not* overemphasize mastery of fundamental basic skills, nor should it exonerate gifted/talented students from mastering these. The curriculum *should not* ignore the development of fundamental or basic skills for the mastery of higher-level thinking skills.

8. The curriculum *should* provide opportunities for students to practice leadership and followership skills and appropriate and varied forms of communication skills and strategies.

    The curriculum *should not* be based on the assumption that gifted/talented students can assume positions of leadership without the development of skills and understandings that promote this end.

Source: Reprinted with permission of Merrill, an imprint of Prentice Hall Publishing Company, from *Growing Up Gifted*, 4th ed. (pp. 259–261) by Barbara Clark. Copyright © 1992, 1988, 1983, 1979 by Merrill/Prentice Hall Publishing Company.

talented different from that of students with disabilities. For example, educators must be careful about *over*inclusion of economically deprived or culturally diverse students in programs for students with disabilities. In contrast, educators must be alert to the possibility of *under*inclusion of gifted students in these groups. In addition, educators may initially provide quite different programs for economically deprived and culturally diverse gifted students than for gifted students from the middle class and above. Because there is less certainty about identification of students who are gifted than there is for students with disabilities, a specific educational practice may be appropriate for students identified as gifted in one area but inappropriate for many students identified as gifted in another area.

■■ Suggestions for Regular Classroom Teachers

The role of the regular classroom teacher will vary considerably in relation to whether special provisions exist for students who are gifted, and if so, the nature of those provisions. If there is a special teacher of the gifted and talented, or a consultant with whom the teacher can plan and collaborate, this is the best way to proceed. Even in this instance, however, an understanding of the principles reflected in the information in Figures 12–2 and 12–3 is essential. In this section, we will consider several ideas, methods, and approaches for the teacher who must plan for gifted students with little or no regular assistance from other professionals. The teacher may implement some of these methods with minimal assistance from others, and with little more than approval from the school principal. Some, such as the use of mentors, require specific approval from parents, the superintendent of schools, and the local school board.

Bloom's Taxonomy as a Basis for Instruction

Bloom (1956) conceived of thinking as a multilevel process. His conceptualization, known as Bloom's taxonomy, has been used extensively by researchers and theorists. The taxonomy describes six levels of thinking, which, from highest to lowest, are (a) knowledge, (b) comprehension, (c) application, (d) analysis, (e) synthesis, and (f) evaluation. This taxonomy addresses the needs and characteristics of all students, and has been used as a basis for curriculum planning for individuals and groups, at all age and grade levels. In a given classroom, a teacher may be working with one or two gifted students, twenty or more typical learners, and one or two students with disabilities. In this

situation, Bloom's taxonomy may be quite valuable in planning differentiated instruction.

In addition to its value to teachers, the taxonomy can build students' awareness that they think at these various levels. Many gifted students will quickly respond to the challenge to "think at a higher level." Teachers can find various ways (appropriate to age and grade level) to display the levels of thinking and the verbs associated with each level on some type of chart or mobile. This may remind both teacher and students to use higher levels of thinking. It should also remind the teacher to structure activities to promote higher levels of thinking. Table 12–2 lists key verbs and various classroom products related to Bloom's six levels. Figure 12–4 illustrates ways in which such "reminders" might be displayed in the classroom. Creative teachers, with the help of students, will find many more ways, appropriate to the age level of students in the class.

Bloom's Taxonomy as a Basis for Questioning

Teachers may write specific or general questions relating to Bloom's taxonomy to correspond to specific books, or general questions to be used with a number of books. Questions may cover the categories of humor, adventure, science, fiction, animals, distant lands, historical fiction, fantasy, tall tales, biography, folktales, fairy tales, and myths. Leiker (1980) lists generic questions corresponding to the six levels of Bloom's taxonomy, as shown in Figure 12–5. These may be applied to most books in the areas indicated in the figure (science fiction, adventure, fantasy, and biography), and are an excellent example of a way in which a regular classroom teacher may adjust and differentiate curriculum. Most authors in the field of education of the gifted have used Bloom's taxonomy as a basis for planning curriculum for students who are gifted (Clark, 1992; Maker, 1982;

Table 12–2
Verbs and classroom products related to Bloom's taxonomy

Areas	Definition	Key Verbs	Classsroom Products
Knowledge	Knowing and remembering facts	Match, recognize, identify, list, describe, name, define, show, record, select	Report, worksheet, chart, map
Comprehension	Understanding	Explain, locate, inquire, demonstrate, discover	Diagram, model, game, picture, teach a lesson, diorama, time line
Application	Doing, making use of what is known	Model, apply, code, collect, organize, construct, report, experiment, sketch, paint, draw, group, put in order	Survey, diary, mobile, scrapbook, photographs, stitchery, cartoon, model, illustration, sculpture, learning center, construction
Analysis	Explaining what is known	Categorize, take apart, analyze, separate, dissect, compare, contrast	Graph, survey, report, questionnaire, time line, family tree, commercial, fact file
Synthesis	Putting together the known into something new	Add to, create, imagine, combine, suppose, predict, role-play, hypothesize, design, [ask] what if...? invent, infer, improve, adapt, compose, change	Story, poem, play, song, pantomime, news article, invention, radio show, dance, mural, comic strip
Evaluation	Judging the outcome	Justify, debate, solve, recommend, judge, criticize, prove, dispute	Editorial, survey, panel, self-evaluation, letter, conclusion, recommendation, court trial

Source: From *An Affordable Gifted Program That Works* (p. 39) by M. Leiker, 1980, Denver: Coronado Hills School, Adams School District No. 12. Adapted by permission.

Piirto, 1994; Sisk, 1987), and Piirto (1994) notes that gifted students need few knowledge and comprehension questions, but will quickly move to the levels of application, analysis, synthesis, and evaluation. When teaching in a classroom that includes students with a variety of ability levels, the teacher who understands Bloom's taxonomy can tailor questions to challenge all students in the class.

Reading

According to Baskin and Harris (1985, n.p.),

Reading is the single most important component in any curriculum for gifted children. Not only is that skill essential for the mastery of all other subjects, but it allows youngsters to pursue their intellectual interests both inside and outside the classroom. Researchers continue to report reading as an activ-

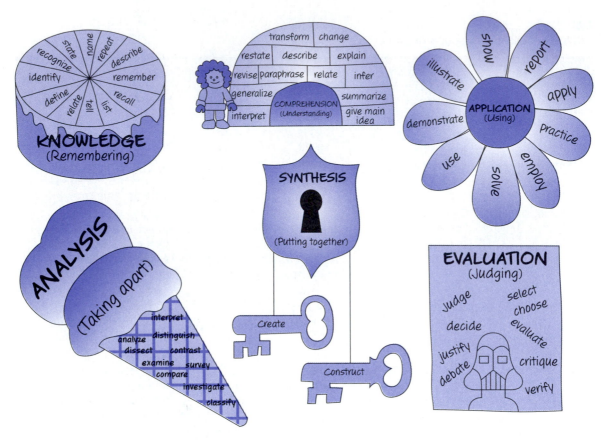

Figure 12–4
Examples of mobiles and displays of Bloom's taxonomy

ity of singular importance in the lives of gifted youth who, through books, can control the depth, pacing, direction, sequence, quantity, quality, and complexity of their learning. Books remain the most accessible, affordable, and pleasurable tool for fostering cognitive growth and independence. Reading surpasses even direct experience in this task since such knowledge is obviously limited by time, place, accessibility, and the like.

Gifted children often come to school reading at a much higher level than age peers, and care must be taken to provide reading material that will tap and extend this potential (Clark, 1992). It is therefore important for teachers to encourage a range of reading experiences and to monitor and guide the student's selection of reading materials. Students should develop skimming strategies, meaning-related strategies (such as making predictions and drawing inferences from materials read), and reasoning-related strategies (such as generalizing). Gifted students may develop these competencies on their own, but if they do not, teachers should help them. A second-grade teacher, for example, may need to obtain assistance from a fifth- or sixth-grade teacher with respect to strategies that are not ordinarily considered with respect to second-grade students.

Science Fiction

Knowledge:	**1.** What is the *setting* of the story? List the main characters.
Comprehension:	**2.** What was the main idea or theme of the story?
Application:	**3.** Draw a picture of the *setting* of the story.
Analysis:	**4.** Compare the environment *(setting)* in this story to your own *setting.* List the things that are the same and those that are different.
Synthesis:	**5.** Choose one thing from the story that you feel could benefit our world if it existed. Write a short story explaining how you would make it a part of life today.
Evaluation:	**6.** Anticipate problems. List the major hurdles you would encounter in selling the idea to others.

Adventure

Knowledge:	**1.** Locate by page number a place in the book that shows *action, conflict, suspense.*
Comprehension:	**2.** What was the *main bold idea* in the story? What was one exciting event that made you nervous until you knew the ending?
Application:	**3.** List in order what happened in the story. Put a star next to the most exciting event.
Analysis:	**4.** In adventure stories, there are *usually two forces* (people or things) *working against each other.* What were they in this story?
Synthesis:	**5.** Write an adventure story about an event in your life. Be sure to include action, conflict, suspense, and two forces working against each other.
Evaluation:	**6.** Evaluate your story. Give one point for each of the points in Question 5. How did you score?

Fantasy

Knowledge:	**1.** Who are the main characters in the story? Where did it take place?
Comprehension:	**2.** What *extraordinary* thing happened in the story?
Application:	**3.** In fantasy STRANGE things happen. List 4 things that could never *really* happen.
Analysis:	**4.** Choose the one thing out of the 4 above that you feel shows the *greatest imagination.*
Synthesis:	**5.** Write down the thing in your life that you feel is an example of your own imagination at work.
Evaluation:	**6.** What effect does your imagination have on your life?

Biography

Knowledge:	**1.** Whose life is the book about? What type of work did the author have to do before writing the book?
Comprehension:	**2.** *What makes you feel you really know what the person in the book was like?*
Application:	**3.** Make a diary of the person's life. List only major events.
Analysis:	**4.** *What emotions did you feel toward the person in the book?* When did you feel these emotions?
Synthesis:	**5.** How could the author have improved this book? Be specific.
Evaluation:	**6.** Do you feel biographies are important types of books? Should they be published before or after a main character's death? Why?

Figure 12–5

Generic literature questions

Source: From *An Affordable Gifted Program That Works* (p. 63) by M. Leiker, 1980, Denver: Coronado Hills School, Adams School District No. 12. Reprinted by permission.

Because students who are gifted may be ready and able to grasp relatively complex concepts for their age, teachers must remember that their reading materials must be qualitatively different from those used with age peers. Gifted children are often interested in topics that are usually considered inappropriate for their chronological age. For example, a third-grade student interested in paleontology may demonstrate advanced reading ability and understanding of complex vocabulary plus understanding of concepts far beyond the readiness of other third graders. If there is no readily available consultative help from a specialist, the school librarian may be of assistance. Parents can also help in relation to areas of interest.

Education of students who are gifted requires a differentiated, individualized program. Modifications or adaptations of the standard reading program at the elementary school level are often inadequate, and the normal wide reading program at the secondary level may be unchallenging. If there is a nearby college or university, or a major library, include it in the planning for secondary school students.

Learning Centers

Learning centers may address any subject or topic, and teachers may use learning centers in the classroom to individualize instruction and better serve students who are gifted. Thus, teachers may develop activities and materials based on student needs and objectives, and they may use learning centers to introduce, reinforce, review, or enrich concepts.

Bloom's taxonomy may be used in the development of learning centers. For example, teachers may code file folders by color and develop questions for each of the six levels of thinking. Numerous books on the market offer ideas and patterns for learning centers; however, teachers must exercise creativity and originality in the development of learning centers to meet the needs of specific situations.

Autonomous Learning

The autonomous learner model is based on the belief that students who are gifted should become responsible for the development, implementation, and evaluation of their own learning. This, of course, is the eventual goal of the program. Figure 12–6 illustrates the five dimensions of the autonomous learner model: (a) orientation, (b) individual development, (c) enrichment activities, (d) seminars, and (e) in-depth study. Figure 12–7 illustrates the individual development dimension of the model. Figure 12–8 is Betts's (1985) description of the five dimensions of the model.

Biographical Research

It is important for gifted students to understand their attitudes, needs, and drives. Biographical (or autobiographical) research can help develop understandings of the characteristics, attitudes, needs, and motivations of various eminent persons, and thus provide insight regarding personal attitudes, needs, and drives. This may be particularly valuable if students can research the lives of persons who have followed paths or professions of personal interest. Initial teacher guidance is important in biographical research, but once started, students may go a long way on their own.

Bibliotherapy

Bibliotherapy has been advocated as a procedure to help improve self-concept, modify attitudes, and contribute to better mental health, but the concept also has applicability to enriching the educational program. In bibliotherapy, individuals use books and other reading materials to help in problem solving.

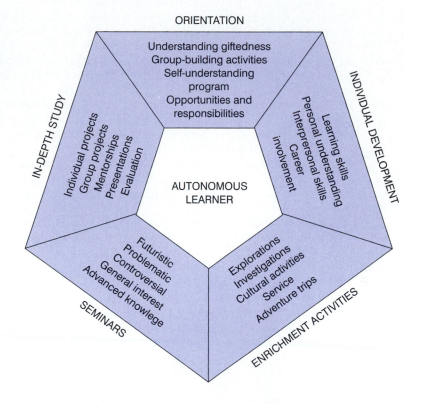

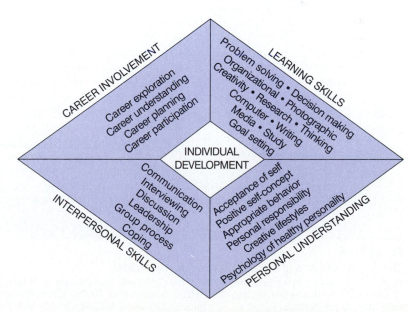

The Orientation Dimension of the model provides students, teachers, administrators and parents the opportunity to develop a foundation of information concerning the program. Emphasis is placed on understanding the concepts of giftedness, creativity and the development of potential. Students learn more about themselves, their abilities and what the program has to offer. Activities are presented to give students an opportunity to work together as a group, to learn about group process and interaction, and to learn more about the other people in the program.

During the Orientation Dimension of the program, a series of inservices are presented for teachers, administrators, parents and involved community resource people. Again, emphasis is placed on the opportunities possible for students, the responsibilities for students and involved personnel, and information given regarding the overall format of the program.

The Individual Development Dimension of the model provides students with the opportunity to develop the cognitive, emotional and social skills, concepts and attitudes necessary for life-long learning: in other words, to become autonomous in their learning.

The Enrichment Activities Dimension of the model was developed to provide students with opportunities to explore content which is usually not part of the everyday curriculum. Most content in the schools is prescribed. Someone beyond the student is deciding what is to be learned, when it is to be learned, and how it is to be learned. Within the Enrichment Activities Dimension students are able to begin explorations into their major area(s) of emphasis, related areas of interest, and new and unique areas. Students decide what they want to pursue, how it is going to be arranged, and where and when the learning will take place. Gifted and talented students need responsibility in selecting what they are going to study and how they are going to learn.

The Seminar Dimension of the model is designed to give students, in small groups of three to five, the opportunity to research a topic, present it as a seminar to the rest of the group and other interested people, and to evaluate it by criteria selected and developed by the students. A seminar is essential because it allows students the opportunity to move from the role of a *student* to the role of a *learner*. If students are to become learners, they must have an opportunity for independent individual and group learning, which means having a structure which allows and promotes the development of knowledge by the individuals.

The In-Depth Study Dimension of the model allows learners to pursue areas of interest through the development of a long-term small group or individual in-depth study. The learners determine what will be learned, how it will be presented, what help will be necessary, what the final product will be and how the entire learning process will be evaluated. In-Depth Studies are usually continued for a long period of time. Plans are developed by learners, in cooperation with the teacher/facilitator, content specialists, and mentors. The plans are then implemented and completed by the learners, with presentations being made at appropriate times until the completion of the project. A final presentation and evaluation is given to all who are involved and interested.

Figure 12–8

The five dimensions of the autonomous learner model

Source: From *Autonomous Learner Model for the Gifted and Talented* (pp. 3–4) by G. T. Betts, 1985, Greeley, CO: Autonomous Learning Publications & Specialists (ALPS). Copyright 1985 by ALPS. Reprinted by permission.

Clark (1992) believes that the technique has special advantages in use with gifted students. Through bibliotherapy, abilities that are usually strengths (ability to conceptualize, generalize, and deal with abstractions) can be used to promote areas identified as targets for additional development. Like most strategies, this must be individualized and part of an overall educational plan.

Individual Projects

Individual projects are units of learning designed by students who are aided by teachers as facilitators. Individual projects may take on a variety of forms and be applicable to many areas. Thus, each student is afforded the opportunity to pursue individual interests and use his or her own learning. For example, a student interested in computers planned and participated in a project to investigate computer applications in the field of art. After learning the techniques of programming, the student created a cartoon using the graphic capabilities of the computer.

On the other hand, a student may earn specific course credit for developing new fields of interest. In this case, the student, a facilitator, and a content area teacher negotiate a project that fulfills the objectives and requirements for a particular course. Then, the student goes beyond the regular classroom activities and independently pursues an interest in depth. As an example, a student was interested in the study of anatomy. After consulting with a biology instructor, the student produced a comparative anatomy study of a shark, a cat, a pig, and a snake, making evolutionary comparisons and highlighting contrasts. The student presented the results in a formal paper and gave a slide presentation to diversified audiences, including biologists, college students, and persons in the medical field.

The ability to learn independently is often a characteristic of students who are gifted.

Group Projects

Group projects differ from individual projects. In a group project, two or three students develop the project rather than a single individual. The project is broader in scope but still reflects the interests of each student involved. For example, three students were interested in working together on a project. One student wrote poetry and short stories; another enjoyed working with lasers and photography; and still another was proficient in computer programming. The result of combining these three talents was an original planetarium show, controlled by a computer and incorporating photographs, poetry, and laser techniques.

Simulation

When properly developed and focused, simulation can be a powerful learning tool for all students, but it may be particularly stimulating to students who are gifted. Sisk (1987) believes that simulation builds on curiosity, requires keen observation skills, affords opportunities for the use of inquiry skills, and requires the use of problem-solving abilities. Use simulation to lead to better understanding of the feelings of others, such as a student who has AIDS, or some real-life process, such as a meeting of the state senate.

Brainstorming

Brainstorming may be of particular value to gifted students, but it requires careful handling by the facilitator (usually the teacher). In the initial stage, warn against judgmental comments, such as "that doesn't make sense," "that wouldn't work," or "that's been done before." The goal is to solicit ideas without evaluation. Terms such as *freewheeling* (relating to the way in which individuals contribute suggestions) and *hitchhiking* (relating to the building on the ideas of others) are often used in characterizations of successful brainstorming.

In a typical brainstorming session, the facilitator establishes a problem and members of the group suggest solutions. In most cases, the facilitator records the solutions on the chalkboard so that others can see them. This encourages hitchhiking on the suggestions made by others. Only after the collection of ideas is complete (some suggest a time limit of 15 to 20 minutes for the initial collection of ideas) are the ideas evaluated or discussed in any manner. Even at this point, avoid having any student feel put down by another student, or this may influence the manner in which students contribute at the next brainstorming session.

Futuristics

Future studies (futuristics) are part of the curriculum in many school districts. Aspects of future studies have often become parts of the sciences and social sciences, but they may be integrated with almost any subject. Futuristics is based on the concept that students will live in a future quite different from the world as it exists today and even more different from the world as it existed when their parents and teachers were children. According to Clark (1992), "A futurist must deal comfortably with uncertainties, open-ended situations, and vastly divergent possibilities" (p. 358). It would seem that gifted individuals would be uniquely able to help forecast events and needs, and prepare members of society to live in the world as it will exist in the future. Sisk (1987) believes that a futuristic point of view must be adopted as a teaching philosophy and applied in teaching all subject areas. She feels that this philosophy is particularly essential in education of students who are gifted "if gifted students are to use their ability to help create the future" (p. 118).

In recognition of this need, Torrance, Blume, Maryanopolis, Murphey, and Rogers (1980) and Torrance and Torrance (1981) initiated the Future Problem Solving Program for gifted students in grades 4 through 12. This project involves students throughout the United States and consists of a variety of curriculum activities, group and individual involvement, and state and national competition. (To learn more about this program, write to Future Problem Solving Program, Nebraska Department of Education, Lincoln, Nebraska 68508.)

Established programs such as the Future Problem Solving Program can be valuable to regular classroom teachers in planning for gifted students, but other strategies may be of equal value. For example, teachers may develop and write scenarios as starting points for thinking about the future: "As I was unplugging the overnight regenerator on my nuclear hovercraft, I realized that someone or something must have used it last night. The trip odometer, which is automatically reset each night as it regenerates, read 125,310 ergometers. And the seat had been readjusted to be closer to the steering control, and much higher than I had left it. I sensed a strange sickly-sweet odor, and felt a prickly sensation at the back of my neck. Then, it happened . . . " Teachers can then encourage students to develop the next scenes and discuss alternatives. This may be accomplished as individual projects or small-group efforts. Either way, futuristic scenarios promote creative thinking and the use of creative language. Develop similar scenarios about environmental concerns, space stations, and world conflicts.

Mentors

The use of mentors to provide learning opportunities for gifted students has proved successful in many programs. Mentor programs may use interested professionals from the community, high school students with special talents (to mentor gifted students in grade school), and senior citizens. Such programs

may be essentially informal, as when a student is linked with a resource person on an individual basis (observing proper cautions, orientation, parent involvement, and so on) or part of formal, planned enrichment programs. Runions and Smyth (1985) discuss the significance of mentorships and provide guidelines for developing them in local school districts (Figure 12–9). Although mentorship can be a valuable part of an enrichment program, it should not be considered *the* program. Mentorships involve unique, meaningful, experientially based learning opportunities, but like all successful educational program components, they require consistent monitoring and involvement by responsible educators.

Social Development

Schneider (1987) believes that "two types of myth impede objective reasoning about social relations of the gifted" (p. 1). The first is that they are destined to be social outcasts; the

Mentorships provide significant enrichment experiences.

Why Are Mentorships Significant in the Education of the Gifted and Talented?

Mentorships provide a creative and viable means of differentiating programs for gifted and talented learners:

- By creating opportunities for learner access to professional expertise in the community to pursue in-depth career and academic interests at competent levels.
- By offering real-life experiences that support the growth of the learner's self-concept through the acquisition and application of life skills.
- By facilitating the cooperative use of community resources in more effective and efficient ways.
- By establishing a network of community resource people available to all members of the school community.
- By offering the learner more responsibility in the learning process.

- By providing an experientially-based framework for enriching the curriculum.
- By involving the learner in the application of networking skills necessary for an information society.
- By providing leadership opportunities through cross-age tutoring between and among elementary and secondary school students.
- By presenting traditional and nontraditional role models of competence in the pursuit of and commitment to excellence.
- By supporting the development of independent and interdependent learning skills in real life situations.

How Are Mentorships Developed?

In selecting the strategy for your school and community to use in developing a mentorship program, the following suggestions may be helpful:

- Select students who have the intensity of interest and commitment to explore learning beyond the classroom.
- Select school and community resource people interested in pursuing mentorships.
- Develop program and curriculum guidelines flexible enough to accommodate mentorships.
- Orient all participants (student, teacher, mentor) to their redefined roles—students as co-learners, teacher as facilitator, mentor as networker.
- Develop communication skills—telephone skills, interview skills, small group process skills, letter writing skills, contract learning skills, and journal writing skills.
- Develop community research skills—data collection, analysis, and presentation.
- Develop self-directed learning skills—decision making, problem solving, critical think-

ing, creative thinking, effective communication, and self-evaluation.
- Establish a community-based component of linking agencies (volunteer bureaus) that can facilitate access to available and receptive people and print resources.
- Make evaluation a shared process among the learner, the mentor, and the teacher, with clear and precise guidelines mutually agreed upon. Both the program and process should be evaluated on an individual and group basis, using the techniques of quantitative and qualitative evaluation, as well as summative and formative evaluation. Because mentorships are a personal learning experience, self-evaluations can play an important role in communicating the value of the experience.

Figure 12–9

Mentorships

Source: From "Mentorships for the Gifted and Talented" by T. Runions and E. Smyth, 1985, ERIC Digest, 346.

second is that they are "destined to succeed in all areas of functioning" (p. 3). Schneider makes the case that both ideas are myths. Often, they are based on case histories of a limited number of gifted individuals, without proper attention to all of the others who do not fit these stereotypes. Schneider reviews a number of studies of the social development of gifted students and concludes that although sometimes special programming for students who are gifted seems to correlate with the establishment of parallel social systems, one that includes primarily gifted students and one that includes primarily nongifted students, this is certainly not always the case. He concludes that although "insensitivity to, and outright rejection of, young gifted peers are not unknown . . . such treatment cannot be seen as the prevalent state of affairs" (p. 102).

Meaningful, satisfying social development of students who are gifted appears to be specific to the type and structure of special programming (if it exists) and the personality of individual students. Teachers must understand that peers may be threatened by students who are gifted and may not understand the near-adult-level concern that gifted students express with social causes, environmental concerns, and so on. On the other hand, gifted students may ignore social learning and the social rules of age peers, and thus become outcasts. Alternately, they may be unusually sensitive to the feelings of age peers and attempt to hide their cognitive abilities, so they will be like other students, and thus be accepted. In either case, teachers must nurture the characteristics essential to the social development of students who are gifted. This is most effectively accomplished in an environment where every child is considered unique. Then the gifted child will have much less cause to feel out of place (Clark, 1992).

Legal Issues Relating to Education of Students Who Are Gifted

Many legal issues relate to the rights of gifted children to appropriate education, and such issues are usually settled at the local and state levels. Karnes and Marquardt (1991) note that at least one-half of the states have some sort of legislation that "requires" that the public schools in that state meet the needs of gifted and talented students. However, this does not necessarily mean that those schools provide an appropriate education. According to Karnes and Marquardt, "Even in such states, not every gifted and talented youngster is identified, and even fewer have access to apropriate and challenging programs of high quality" (p. 16).

Litigation relating to programs for the gifted has taken place with regard to a number of admission issues, including early admission to school, admission and gender, and admission and race. Such cases have questioned due process, the validity of IQ tests, various criteria for eligibility and admission, and the right of the school to say that although a given student is qualified, there is "no room" in existing classes. Litigation has also targeted the question of appropriateness of education once a student is admitted to a program. In contrast to court cases relating to students with disabilities, which frequently include objections to placement in special classes, cases relating to the gifted often are to obtain placement in special classes (often called "pullout" classes). Such cases, if settled in federal courts, might have a profound influence on education of students who are gifted, but when they are state cases, they have precedential impact only in the jurisdiction in which they are decided.

Advocates of better, more comprehensive programs for students who are gifted or talented may improve the quality of programs in their state by attending to the elements of the statutes governing the provision of such programs. Karnes and Marquardt (1991) suggest that key components of such statutes include the following:

1. The definition of gifted and talented
2. Identification procedures
3. Provisions for development of an IEP
4. Program options and pertinent related services
5. Procedures for program evaluation
6. Provisions for diplomas for early high school graduates
7. Certification/qualifications of school personnel
8. Transportation
9. LEA responsibilities
10. Provision for financial encouragement of programs
11. Guidelines for procedural due process, mediation, and impartial due process hearings

The question of due process is particularly important with respect to improving educational opportunities for students who are gifted or talented through legal action. In states where education of students who are gifted is part of an "exceptional children" division (one including students who are gifted and those with disabilities), state-imposed due process procedures established for students with disabilities may apply to students who are gifted. Sixteen states and the District of Columbia report that state-imposed due process guidelines apply to students who are gifted (Karnes & Marquardt, 1991). Though the power of a federal mandate and federal government and Supreme Court decisions is not available, decisions in state courts, favor-

ing appropriate educational programs for students who are gifted and/or talented, are helping move the cause forward. As parent groups share information and ideas, leading to additional local and state level pressure through litigation, and as more favorable state legislation is enacted, educational programs for the gifted will be expanded and improved.

■ In the Final Analysis

It is important to ask whether research supports the effectiveness of special programs for students who are gifted or talented, and whether such programs are satisfying from the gifted individual's point of view.

As for program effectiveness, a number of studies suggest that special programs for students who are gifted pay big dividends both to the individuals involved, and to society. The first major longitudinal study, by Lewis Terman (1925), left little question about the success of the individuals identified as gifted. A followup study (Terman & Oden, 1959) reviewed the accomplishments of 1528 subjects who had been identified as intellectually gifted 35 years earlier. The results indicated, for example, very low incidence of crime and delinquency, and a low mortality rate, compared to general population of the same age. As a group, they earned nearly double the average income of others in the same vocational categories. In addition, 71 of the men were listed in *American Men of Science* and 31 in *Who's Who in America*. Together, they had produced 60 books and monographs, 2000 scientific and technical papers and articles, 33 novels, and 375 short stories. Followup data for women were analyzed separately, because the majority of the women were not employed outside of the home (note the date of the followup); however, seven of the women were listed in *American Men of Science* and two in *Who's Who in America*. At least 230 patents had been granted to members of the total group. It might be argued that these individuals would have made these accomplishments without their special program, but they believed that the program made a difference. Certainly the societal benefits were obvious.

Another study, by Noble, Robinson, and Gunderson (1992), gives a somewhat different perspective. This study involved a comparison of a group of gifted individuals who had participated in a program of "radical acceleration" with others who had qualified for the program but rejected it, and with a third group, of nonaccelerated National Merit Scholarship finalists. The study focused on both academic success and the effect on social and emotional adjustment, the concern often used to discourage programs for gifted students, particularly those involving acceleration. All three groups were very successful academically. As for social and emotional adjustment, the results of this study were consistent with those reported by Noble and Drummond (1992): The social and emotional development of a majority of the students had not been compromised, but rather, according to the students themselves, it had been enhanced.

Despite the apparent success and acceptable social and emotional adjustment of gifted students, parents and educators should consider the feelings and concerns of students who are gifted, related to the fact that they know they are gifted (have different learning characteristics than other students). Most of these concerns have implications whether or not a special program is provided. Kunkel, Chapa, Patterson, and Walling (1992) conducted a study in which they asked a group of gifted seventh- and eighth-grade students, "What's it like to be gifted?" Although they received both positive and negative responses, they were most concerned with negative responses or concerns. The following were the major concerns expressed by these students:

1. *Confusion*. Students didn't like the word *gifted*, were not sure what it meant, felt that being gifted, although "special" was also "wierd," felt being "gifted" didn't feel different from being "nongifted."
2. *Boredom*. Classes are boring because students already know what is being taught, giftedness makes one lazy
3. *Ridicule*. Everyone talks about someone, people call them a "snob," people think they are a nerd, or they are disliked by others because they are gifted.
4. *Loneliness*. It's hard to have friends that are not gifted because individuals don't understand each other, others are jealous, others don't think of them as a friend, but only as a source of information.
5. *Uniqueness*. A student may try to convince others that they are not "special"; they are asked how it feels to be gifted and don't want to talk about it.
6. *Burdened*. Being gifted means lots of extra work, it's hard to keep up a reputation (for giftedness) and still have an active social life and be popular, people look up to such students and give them too much responsibility.

The major, overriding theme of these students' responses was confusion about giftedness and the implications of giftedness in their lives. There was an expression of discomfort with their uniqueness, and in some cases shame when they did not fulfill the high expectations of others. It would appear to be very important for both parents and educators to consider the possibility that gifted students have such feelings and concerns, regardless of effectiveness of their educational programs. Teachers must address these concerns in whatever manner is appropriate to the student's age and educational environment. Kunkel et al. (1992) suggest that students be asked about, and given ample opportunity to express, both positive and negative feelings or concerns. This may then permit parents and educators involved in their educational programming to address them.

Summary

In this chapter, we presented several definitions of giftedness, noting the present federal emphasis on "talent" as opposed to "giftedness." We discussed both characteristics usually associated with giftedness and the difficulty in defining and identifying creativity. We reviewed tests and other assessment tools used to identify students with unusual intellectual ability or creativity and considered briefly legal issues associated with education of students who are gifted.

We discussed in detail program options, including ability grouping, enrichment, and acceleration, also considering general curriculum guidelines. We provided specific suggestions for the regular classroom teacher, emphasizing the use of Bloom's taxonomy as a basis for instruction. We outlined other options, such as the use of mentors, bibliotherapy, simulation, brainstorming, and futuristics, and discussed student social development. Several special, underserved populations were outlined. Finally, we presented data from followup studies indicating the considerable success of gifted students who have been provided special programs, and quoted examples of the feelings and concerns of such students.

Books About Exceptional Individuals

This appendix contains two sections of books about exceptional individuals: (a) books for children and youth and (b) books for adults. The section on books for children and youth is divided into the following classifications (listed alphabetically): behavior disorders, giftedness and talents, hearing impairment, learning disabilities, mental retardation, orthopedic and health impairments, and visual impairment. The books within the individual classifications are listed alphabetically according to author.

Books for Children and Youth

Written for children and youth, the following books provide information about exceptional individuals. The annotated listing is based on areas of exceptionality. Age ranges are provided to help in determining the approximate reading level; however, some books for older students may still be profitably read to younger students.

Behavior Disorders
Please Don't Say Hello by Phyllis Gold, Human Sciences Press, 1975.
  A boy who is autistic and his family move into a new neighborhood and face the problems of acceptance by their new neighbors. This is a sensitive story of real experiences, written by the mother of a severely disturbed, autistic boy. Ages 10 and up.

Gifted/Talented
Daniel's Duck by Clyde Robert Bulia, Harper & Row, 1979.
  Daniel, a Tennessee mountain boy of the early 1900s, learns about creative talent, pride, and false pride. Ages 5 to 8.
No Good in Art by Miriam Cohen, Greenwillow Books, 1980.
  Jim, a talented boy, learns to overcome the negative kindergarten experience that convinced him he was "no good in art." Ages 5 to 8.
Carol Johnston: The One-Armed Gymnast by Pete Donovan, Children's Press, 1982.
  This is the true story of a Canadian gymnast who won All-American honors despite the fact that she was born with just one arm. This is more a story of talent than an account of disability. Ages 8 to 12.
The Gifted Kids Survival Guide for Ages 10 and Under and *The Gifted Kids Survival Guide for Ages 11–18* by John Galbraith, Free Spirit, 1983 and 1984.
  These books are not about exceptional students in the usual sense of the word but are for gifted students to read in order to learn more about themselves. The ages are in the titles.

Jemmy by Jon Francis Hassler, Atheneum, 1980.
Jemmy, a half-Chippewa high school senior, is told by her father to quit school in October of her senior year. Initially, she accepts this situation, but through a series of experiences, she discovers both her Native American heritage and great artistic talent. Ages 12 and up.

Hearing Impairment

The Secret in the Dorm Attic by Jean Andrews, Gallaudet University Press, 1990.
This mystery involves strange happenings in the attic of a school for the deaf. As the story proceeds, readers learn about the deaf culture in addition to enjoying an exciting mystery story. Ages 8 and up.

My Sister's Silent World by Catherine Arthur, Children's Press, 1979.
Heather's eighth birthday as told by her older sister. Heather has a hearing aid and can distinguish sounds but not words. Ages 5 to 9.

The Waiting Game by Anne Evelyn Bunting, J. B. Lippincott, 1981.
Three high school seniors (one of them deaf) anticipate possible offers of college football scholarships. Ages 10 and up.

Burnish Me Bright by Julia Cunningham, Pantheon Books, 1970.
This is a story of friendship between Auguste, who is deaf and mute, and Monsieur Hilaire, who is a mime. Through mime, Auguste is accepted by the village and becomes very close to Monsieur Hilaire. Ages 8 to 12.

Gallaudet, Friend of the Deaf by Etta DeGering, McKay, 1964.
This is a biography of a man who was instrumental in the education of the deaf in America. Ages 9 to 11.

Meet Camille and Danille: They're Special People by Margaret H. Glazzard, H.&H. Enterprises, 1978.
A very simple book explains how people who are deaf communicate and understand others. It also explains how people who can hear should communicate with those who have hearing impairments. Ages 8 to 12.

What Is the Sign For Friend? by Judith E. Greenberg, Franklin Watts, 1985.
This is a story of a boy who is deaf. The text is "real" and includes signs. Ages 8 and up.

Breakaway by Ruth Hallman, Westminster, 1981.
Rob, a 17-year-old who is almost totally deaf as a result of a diving accident, has many difficulties in adjusting to his situation. His overprotective and domineering mother is one of his major problems. Ages 12 and up.

The Swing by Emily Hanlon, Bradbury Press, 1979.
This books tells how two children—one deaf—learn from each other. Their bonds are their mutual love of animals and the swing that stands between their two houses. Ages 10 to 12.

Silent Dancer by Bruce Hlibok, Julian Messner, 1981.
A youngster who is deaf finds pleasure and confidence in her ballet school classes, which have been adapted to accommodate students who are deaf. Ages 8 to 11.

Child of the Silent Night by Edith Fisher Hunter, Dell Publishing, 1963.
This is the story of Laura Bridgman, who suffers an illness that leaves her blind and deaf. She is sent to the Perkins Institute, where she is taught to see and hear. Ages 7 to 12.

Lisa and Her Soundless World by Edna A. Levine, Human Science, 1984.
This book teaches nondeaf children about their peers who are deaf and shows chil-

dren who are deaf how they can successfully participate in the social environment
around them. Ages 8 to 13.

Annie's World by Nancy Smiler Levinson,
Gallaudet University Press, 1990.
*A 16-year-old girl is mainstreamed after 9
years in a private school for the deaf. This
story includes elements of mystery and
romance, along with valuable understandings about deafness. Ages 12 and up.*

Words in Our Hands by Ada Bassett Litchfield,
Whitman, 1980.
*Three children with normal hearing com-
municate with their parents who are deaf.
In addition to building understanding of
communication with individuals who are
deaf, there is a good deal of specific information, such as the alphabetic, fingerspelling symbols. Ages 12 and up.*

Albert Whitman & Company by Ada B. Litchfield, Whitman, 1982.
*Michael has two sisters and a mom and
dad. There is only one difference between
Michael's family and other families.
Michael's parents are deaf. He explains
what their family life is like and the special
gadgets used in their house to help his parents function better. The book also provides
a fingerspelling chart. Ages 8 to 12.*

I Have a Sister: My Sister is Deaf by Jeanne
Whitehouse Peterson, Harper & Row, 1977.
*This story is about a little girl whose sister
is deaf. The girl believes her sister is exactly
the same as anyone else except she cannot
hear and explains the similarities instead of
the differences. Ages 8 to 12.*

Apple is My Sign by Mary L. Riskind,
Houghton Mifflin, 1981.
*An interesting, historically pertinent story
about a boy who is deaf at the turn of the
century. This story includes factual material
about various sign languages and shows the
evolution of sign language. Ages 10 to 14.*

David in Silence by Veronica Robinson, J. B.
Lippincott, 1966.
*David, born deaf in a small town in Eng-
land, is harassed by children of his own age.
His efforts to make friends result in disaster.
David proves his competence and courage
in a hair-raising trip through an abandoned
tunnel and then finds acceptance and
friendship. Ages 9 to 13.*

Just Like Everybody Else by Lillian Rosen,
Harcourt Brace Jovanovich, 1981.
*This is the first-person story of a teenager
who loses her hearing. This book contains
factual information but also manages to
maintain interest and promote understanding of the considerable affective needs of
individuals who are deaf. Ages 11 and up.*

Child of the Arctic by Hubert C. Woods, Fol-
lett, 1962.
*A child's deafness makes other Eskimos
suspect him until he becomes hero of the
village. Ages 8 to 12.*

Learning Disabilities

Do Bananas Chew Gum by Jamie Gilson,
Lothrop, Lee & Shepard, 1980.
*A boy has repeated failures in school until
he is diagnosed as learning disabled and is
provided the special help he needs. Ages 9
to 11.*

*Will the Real Gertrude Hollings Please Stand
Up?* by Sheila Greenwald, Little, Brown,
1983.
*This is the story of Gertrude, a teenage girl
who has learning disabilities, and her
cousin Albert, a straight-A overachiever.
Albert learns a great deal from Gertrude.
Ages 11 and up.*

Tuned In-Turned On by Marvell Lo Hayes,
Academic Therapy, 1974.
*This is a book for kids with learning disabil-
ities about kids with learning disabilities.
Ages 7 to 11.*

Sue Ellen by Judith Fisher Hunter, Houghton Mifflin, 1969.
> *Sue Ellen has a learning disability and is surprised and happy with her new special class. This is the touching story of a child who is finally given the opportunity to learn. Ages 8 to 12.*

He's My Brother by Joe Lasker, Whitman, 1974.
> *This is a simplified explanation of a little boy who has learning disabilities. Ages 5 to 8.*

Putting Up with Sherwood by Ellen Matthews, Westminster, 1980.
> *Diane, a fifth grader who feels sorry for herself, is asked to tutor Sherwood, who has a learning disability. Sherwood helps her toward a happier life. Ages 9 to 11.*

Running Scared by Jane Morton, Elsevier/Nelson, 1979.
> *This is the straightforward story of a boy's frustration with his inability to achieve in school. Ages 10 to 14.*

The Whales to See by Glendon & Kathryn Swarthout, Doubleday, 1975.
> *A special class of students who have learning disabilities goes out to sea to watch the semiannual whale migration, and a class of "normal" students happens to be on the same ship. This story provides an interesting view of attitudes. This was written before mainstreaming but still has validity. Ages 10 and up.*

Mental Retardation

Love Is Like Peanuts by Betty Bates, Holiday House, 1980.
> *A 14-year-old girl takes a summer job caring for a girl who is brain-damaged and mentally retarded and has a handsome 18-year-old brother. This story mixes romance with understanding of the condition of mental retardation. Its value is enhanced by characterizations of the manners in which different persons respond to mental retardation. Ages 11 to 14.*

Nancy and Her Johnny-O by Bianca Bradbury, Washburn, 1970.
> *An adolescent girl and her family respond in different ways to 5-year-old Johnny, who is mildly retarded. Ages 9 and up.*

For Love of Jody by Robbie Branscum, Lothrop, Lee & Shepard, 1979.
> *This story, which takes place during the Depression on an Arkansas farm, presents an interesting picture of how Jody, a child who is severely mentally retarded, changes the life of one family. Age 9 to 12.*

The Child Who Never Grew by Pearl Buck, John Day, 1950.
> *This is a moving account of a parent's personal experience in rearing a child who is severely retarded. Miss Buck has successfully portrayed the problems of many parents. Ages 15 and up.*

Our Jimmy by Ruth K. Doorly, Service Associates, 1967.
> *A father talks with his two children about their younger brother, who is retarded, explains the special needs, and explains ways in which they can help him learn. This is a warm and loving book for parents and children. Ages 5 to 13.*

One Little Girl by Joan Fassler, Behavioral Publications, 1968.
> *Because she is somewhat retarded, grownups call Laurie a slow child, but Laurie learns that she is slow in doing only some things. Ages 6 to 12.*

Alice with Golden Hair by Eleanor Means Hull, Atheneum, 1981.
> *Alice, who is nearly 18 years old, has been in institutions for individuals who are mentally retarded since early childhood. This book provides a rare, interesting insight into the thinking of individuals who are mildly mentally retarded. Ages 11 and up.*

Deep Search by Theodore Koob, J. B. Lippincott, 1969.

A 16-year-old girl finds herself in the midst of her parents' disagreement about the future of her 10-year-old brother, who is mentally retarded. Ages 9 to 13.

She's My Sister: Having a Retarded Sister by Jane Claypool Miner, Crestwood House, 1982.

A 16-year-old has great difficulty with the fact that her sister, who is retarded, is coming home from her special school and that they will be attending the same public school. Ages 11 and up.

Clunie by Robert Newton Peck, Alfred A. Knopf, 1979.

A teenage girl who is retarded, overweight, and poorly accepted by many of her peers has a variety of difficulties and a generally unhappy life. This story tells a great deal about "how it really is" for many persons who are retarded. Ages 12 and up.

Show Me No Mercy: A Compelling Story of Remarkable Courage by Robert Perske, Abingdon, 1984.

Twins, one with Down syndrome, share their lives and discuss some of the unique challenges they face. Ages 10 and up.

In My Sister's Eyes by Grace Posner, Beaufort, 1980.

The story is about a sister who has mental retardation who is at times considered the "skeleton in the closet." Ages 12 and up.

My Brother Is Special by Maureen Crane Wartski, Westminster, 1979.

A teenage girl loves her brother, who is retarded. She can't understand people who think of individuals who are retarded as "creatures from another planet." Ages 10 to 13.

My Sister Is Different by Betty Ren Wright, Raintree, 1981.

Carlo has a sister who is retarded. Sometimes he resents her greatly and sometimes he loves her. This is a realistic picture for young readers. Ages 6 to 9.

A Racehorse for Andy by Patricia Wrightson, Harcourt, Brace, 1968.

This is a sensitive portrayal of the desire of a boy who is retarded to be included in his friend's games. Ages 8 to 15.

Orthopedic and Health Impairments

Anna Joins In by Katrin Arnold, Abingdon, 1982.

Anna, who has cystic fibrosis, deals with peer influence regarding the taking of her medicine. She visits a doctor and participates in many activities. This is a descriptive and frank discussion of Anna's illness. Ages 9 and up.

Crazylegs Merril by Bill J. Carol, Steck, 1969.

This is the story of a lad who has had polio and his success with friends and football. Ages 12 to 14.

Angie and Me by Rebecca Castaldi Jones, Simon & Schuster, 1981.

A girl with severe juvenile rheumatoid arthritis has a terminally ill roommate. Ages 9 to 11.

Accident by Hila Crayder Colman, William Morrow, 1980.

The first date between two teenagers leads to a tragic motorcycle accident. The story provides a look at the slow rehabilitation process and related feelings of anger, hopelessness, and guilt. Ages 11 and up.

Darlene by Eloise Greenfield, Methuen, 1980.

A 6-year-old girl confined to a wheelchair has problems with attitudes. Ages 5 to 7.

Alesia by Eloise Greenfield, Philomel, 1981.

Entries in Alesia's diary provide an intimate look at the daily activities of a teenage girl who overcomes her physical limitations with courage and good spirit. Ages 10 to 14.

Circle of Giving by Ellen Howard, Atheneum, 1984.

Marguerite learns more about a neighbor with cerebral palsy and becomes friends with her in the process. Through this process, Marguerite learns to overcome some of her own fears. Ages 9 and up.

Laura's Gift by Dee Jacobs, Oriel, 1980.

This is a story about twins and muscular dystrophy. Ages 11 and up.

Karen by Maria Killilea, Dell, 1952.

This book tells what can be done for a child who has spastic cerebral palsy and the emotional trauma involved. Ages 13 and up.

With Love from Karen by Marie Killilea, Dell, 1963.

This is the continuing true story of Karen. It tells how Karen grew up. Ages 9 to 12.

Wren by Marie Killilea, P. H. Dell, 1968.

This is the story of a child born with cerebral palsy. She is helped by the patience, love, work, and faith of her family. Ages 8 to 12.

You Can't Catch Diabetes from a Friend by Lynne Kipnis, Triad, 1979.

This is a well-done presentation of the problems of juvenile diabetes. It emphasizes the problems of the family. Ages 7 to 12.

Nick Joins In by Joe Lasker, Whitman, 1980.

This is the story of a 7-year-old in a wheelchair, his fear of school, and the growing ability of his classmates to make him a part of the group. It provides a hopeful look at mainstreaming. Ages 5 to 8.

It's a Mile from Here to Glory by Robert C. Lee, Little, Brown, 1972.

Early MacLaren, the school's star runner, is temporarily disabled by a freak accident. His struggles and what he learns about being a person versus being a star makes this book valuable. Ages 9 to 13.

Go Toward the Light by Chris Oyler, Harper & Row, 1988.

This is an account of the experiences of a child who has AIDS. This real-life story may help students better understand the feelings of children who have AIDS. Ages 10 and up.

Only Love by Susan Diana Sallis, Harper & Row, 1980.

This story has sorrow and reality. All does not end on a happy note. It's the first-person narrative of an English girl, a paraplegic who has lived in institutions since she was abandoned as a child. It's a sad love story that may be of value in special circumstances. Ages 12 and up.

On the Move by Harriet M. Savitz, John Day, 1973.

After becoming involved with other disabled youths, a formerly sheltered paraplegic girl realizes that she can also learn to lead an independent life. Ages 8 to 12.

Run, Don't Walk by Harriet Savitz, Watts, 1979.

After Samantha is told that she cannot enter the marathon because she is confined to a wheelchair, she realizes why Johnny Jay, another wheelchair student, is determined to fight for what he wants. Ages 8 to 12.

Shutterbug by Lou & Zena Shumsky, Funk & Wagnalls, 1970.

An eighth-grade boy becomes stricken with rheumatic fever. Ages 7 to 11.

Martin Rides the Moor by Vian Smith, Doubleday, 1965.

Gail is struck down by polio, and her recovery is almost halted until a horse brings back her desire to walk. Together, the girl and the horse triumph over fear and pain. Ages 10 to 12.

Let the Balloon Go by Ivan Southall, Bradbury, 1985.

This book tells of the decision of a boy with spastic cerebral palsy to no longer accept the words "you can't do that." Ages 9 to 16.

About Handicaps by Sara Bonnet Stein, Walker, 1974.

An interesting story explains "extraordinary ways that ordinary children between 3 and 8 years of age attempt to make sense of difficult events in their lives." The story is about a boy and his friend with cerebral palsy. It is well written, and the photographs are excellent. Ages 12 and up.

My Name is Jonathan (and I Have AIDS) by Jonathan Swain and Sharon Schilling, Prickly Pair Publishing, 1989.

This is a first-person account of the experiences of a child who has AIDS. It is an excellent way to help build understanding of the unusual emotional impact of AIDS. Ages 10 and up.

Be Not Afraid by Robin White, Berkley Medallion, 1972.

This is the true story of Checkers, who at 8 years of age received a blow on the head that led to incapacitating epilepsy. The story, told by the father, tells much about severe epilepsy but even more about a family's love and compassion. Ages 9 and up.

Marathon Miranda by Elizabeth Winthrop, Holiday House, 1979.

Miranda tells her story and explains some of the problems experienced by children who have severe asthma. Ages 9 to 11.

Visual Impairment

The Blind Connemara by G. W. Anderson, Simon & Schuster, 1971.

A beautiful white pony is going blind. Rhonda knows that a sightless horse is dangerous to himself and his rider. She cannot stand the thought that he might have to be put away. When Pony is given to her, she is overjoyed. With patience and devotion, she begins to gain his trust and to teach him to move with confidence again. Ages 8 and up.

Gift of Gold by Beverly Butler, Dodd, Mead, 1973.

A young girl is determined to prove she can succeed as a speech therapist despite her blindness. Ages 9 to 15.

Light a Single Candle by Beverly Butler, Dodd, Mead, 1964.

A girl finds she must face a very different way of living when she loses her sight at age 14. The greatest challenges are in the attitudes of other people rather than in her physical disability. Ages 8 to 12.

A Girl and Five Brave Horses by Sonora Carver, Doubleday, 1961.

A young lady is injured riding stunt horses and learns to ride again even though blind. Ages 11 and up.

See You Tomorrow, Charles by Miriam Cohen, Greenwillow, 1983.

A boy must learn to cope with his blindness after an accident. Ages 8 to 11.

Finding My Way by Borgheld Dahl, E. P. Dutton, 1962.

In an autobiography, a well-known author gives a gripping account of her day-to-day experiences learning to live with total blindness, continuing her career, and leading a full life. Ages 12 to 15.

Helen Keller by Margaret Davidson, Hastings, 1970.

This excellent book tells the courageous story of Helen Keller and her teacher, Anne Sullivan. Ages 7 to 10.

Seeing Finger, Louis Braille by Etta DeGering, McKay, 1963.

This book tells how the French inventor of a system of reading for the blind adjusted to his own disabilities. Ages 9 to 12.

About Glasses for Gladys by Mark K. Ericsson, Melmont, 1962.

After getting glasses that are just right, Gladys no longer is teased by her classmates about her nearsighted way of reading. Ages 7 to 12.

The Seeing Summer by Jeanette Hyde Eyerly, J. B. Lippincott, 1981.

A 10-year-old is upset when her new neighbor turns out to be blind, but she eventually adjusts to the situation. A kidnapping and adventure are wrapped into this fast-paced story. Ages 8 to 10.

Follow My Leader by James Garfield, Viking, 1967

This story of an 11-year-old boy who is blinded in an accident describes how he overcomes this blindness and uses a Seeing Eye dog. Ages 9 to 12.

Half the Battle by Lynn Hall, Charles Scribner's Sons, 1982.

An 18-year-old who is blind and his sighted brother make a grueling, 100-mile trip on horseback. The trip highlights their conflict and their genuine affection for each other. Ages 11 and up.

Mary Lou and Johnny: An Adventure in Seeing By Mildred Hart, Watts, 1963.

When Mary Lou befriends her young neighbor, who is blind, he helps her with her problems. They brighten life for each other and for their friends in a story that emphasizes the importance of not feeling or expressing pity for individuals with disabilities. Ages 8 to 11.

Sound of Sunshine, Sound of Rain by Florence Heide, Parents' Magazine Press, 1970.

With feeling and sensitivity, this book communicates the world of a child who happens to be blind. Ages 5 to 7.

What's That? by Virginia Jensen, Collins, 1979.

This book is about the adventures of imaginary characters. The book can be used with all children, but it is especially designed for children who are visually impaired or blind. The design of the book is tactual, so children can use the sense of touch to actually feel the characters of the story. Ages 5 to 7.

The Rose-Colored Glasses by Linda Leggett and Linda Andrews, Human Sciences, 1979.

Melanie loses most of her vision in a car accident and must wear "ugly" glasses to aid her vision. The story describes the initial reaction of her classmates and tells how the teacher, Melanie, and a friend help the class understand Melanie's situation. Ages 7 and up. Note: this book is a bit harsh and sarcastic.

Through Grandpa's Eyes by Patricia Maclachlan, Harper & Row, 1980.

This book can be used to help children understand the aging process or to help children understand the world of someone who is blind. In this story, Grandpa is blind and his grandson John attempts to understand the world as his grandpa does—through using his other senses. Ages 8 to 12.

Stevie's Other Eyes by Lois Eddy McDonnell, Creative Educational Society, 1962.

A boy who is blind learns about the outside world and teaches something to his sighted companions. He proves that he can do many of the things they can do and earns their respect and admiration. Ages 7 to 11.

"Seeing" in the Dark by Elizabeth Rider Montgomery, Garrard, 1979.

A young girl who is blind moves to a new home and must adjust to a new teacher and new classmates. This mainstreaming success story emphasizes her strengths and the generally helpful attitudes on the part of classmates. Ages 5 to 7.

Jennifer Jean, the Cross-Eyed Queen by Phyllis Naylor, Lerner, 1967.

This story is about a cross-eyed girl and how she avoids ridicule even when her eyes are in the process of being straightened (she has to wear glasses and a patch). Ages 5 to 12.

Triumph of the Seeing Eye by Peter Putnam, Harper & Row, 1963.

A man who is blind writes of the history and workings of the Seeing Eye and explains the great love between a Seeing Eye dog and his master. Ages 12 and up.

My Mother Is Blind by Margaret Reuter, Children's Press, 1979.

In this story, a family must adjust to a parent's blindness. Ages 5 to 8.

Blind Outlaw by Glen Harold Rounds, E. P. Dutton, 1981.

A blind horse and a teenager who cannot speak respond to each other and form a lasting bond. Ages 9 to 12.

To Catch an Angel by Robert Russell, Vanguard, 1962.

This autobiography was written by a man who was blinded at the age of 5 yet proceeded to become a great scholar, fine wrestler, and finally an associate professor, all through his determination. Ages 8 to 13.

The Road to Agra by Aimee Somerfelt, Criterion, 1961.

A village boy walks nearly 300 miles with his 7-year-old sister to a hospital where her blindness may be cured. Ages 8 to 12.

The Cay by Theodore Taylor, Doubleday, 1969.

This story is about Phillip, who loses his sight from a blow to the head. He and Timothy find themselves cast on an island after the freighter on which they were traveling is torpedoed. The book tells of their struggle for survival and of Phillip's effort to adjust to his blindness and overcome learned prejudice. Ages 12 to 15.

The New Boy Is Blind by William E. Thomas, Julian Messner, 1980.

This books tells what individuals who are blind and individuals who are nondisabled can learn from each other. Ages 6 to 10.

Window for Rosemary by Marguerite Vance, Harcourt Brace, 1965.

Blind from birth, Rosemary enjoys all of the ordinary childhood activities because her parents' loving, unsentimental attitude toward her gives her a sense of security and independence. Her sighted brother is a good friend. Ages 8 to 12.

Run with the Ring by Kathryn Vinson, Harcourt Brace, 1965.

This book tells the painful struggles of an intelligent boy to accept the limitations imposed by sudden blindness. Ages 13 and up.

The Lake Is on Fire by Maureen Crane Wartski, Westminster, 1981.

An auto accident blinds Ricky and kills his best friend. Ricky is deeply depressed and attempts suicide. This story outlines his comeback and includes adventure. Ages 10 to 13.

Dead End Bluff by Elizabeth Wetheridge, Atheneum, 1965.

Despite his blindness, Quig wants to be as much like other boys as he can be, but an overprotective father prevents it. A summer job tests and proves Quig's capabilities and shows his father that Quig can climb and swim like other boys. Ages 9 to 11.

Second Sight for Tommy by Regina J. Woody, Westminster, 1972.

This is a story of bravery, discovery, blindness, life, death, love, and loneliness. Ages 10 to 14.

Books for Adults

The following books were written primarily for adults, but they are about children and youth who have severe behavior disorders and may be of value to teachers and high school-age youth who have an interest in behavior disorders. The books in this section are listed alphabetically according to author.

Dibs: In Search of Self by Virginia Axline, Ballantine, 1976.

> *This is an account of a young autistic-like child, Dibs, who is involved in play therapy sessions. It provides insight into the nature of autism and the process of play therapy. Ages 14 and up.*

I Never Promised You a Rose Garden by Hannah Green, Signet, 1964.

> *This is a novel about Deborah, a 16-year-old who spends 3 years in a mental hospital. This classic work provides valuable insights into the world of a girl who is psychotic, life in a mental hospital, and the difficult road back to reality.*

A Child Called Noah by Josh Greenfeld, Pocket Books, 1970.

> *This true story of raising a child who is autistic provides a realistic picture of the anger and despair of parents who find little real help in their quest for understanding of Noah's condition.*

A Place for Noah by Josh Greenfeld, Pocket Books, 1978.

> *The continuing story of Noah is told by his father, who rejects the term autistic in favor of brain damaged. Noah is 11 years old, and his father feels even more anger in the lack of viable programs and services for Noah. This story provides additional insight into the relationships between Noah, his parents, and his brother.*

One Child by Torey Hayden, Avon, 1980.

> *This is the story of 6-year-old Sheila, who was placed in a class for individuals who are mentally retarded after she committed a serious act of violence against a 3-year-old. Sheila had been abused by her father, abandoned by her mother, and was apparently without emotion. This is another story of the triumph of a teacher's persistence and love.*

Lovey: A Very Special Child by Mary MacCracken, Signet, 1976.

> *This is the story of Hannah, a child who is behaviorally disordered, and a teacher who was able to reach her. This true story provides a glimpse of the success that may be found with some children who are behaviorally disordered.*

Lisa, Bright and Dark by John Neufeld, Signet, 1969.

> *This is a novel about a 16-year-old who thinks she is crazy, and three friends who try to serve as her therapists when her parents choose to ignore her plea for help.*

Professional Organizations, Advocacy Groups, and Other Sources of Information

Administration on Developmental
  Disabilities
200 Independence Avenue, S.W.
Washington, DC 20201

Alexander Graham Bell Association for the
  Deaf, Inc.
3417 Volta Place, N.W.
Washington, DC 20007

American Academy for Cerebral Palsy and
  Developmental Medicine
2405 Westwood Avenue
P.O. Box 11083
Richmond, VA 23230

American Association of the Deaf-Blind, Inc.
814 Thayer Avenue
Silver Springs, MD 20910

American Association for Gifted Children
15 Gramercy Park
New York, NY 10003

American Association on Mental Retardation
1719 Kalorama Road, N.W.
Washington, DC 20009

American Association of Psychiatric Services
  for Children
1133 Fifteenth Street, N.W., Suite 1000
Washington, DC 20005

American Association of School
  Administrators
1801 North Moore Street
Arlington, VA 22209

American Bar Association Child Advocacy
  Center
1800 M Street, N.W., Suite 200
Washington, DC 20036

American Cancer Society
777 Third Avenue
New York, NY 10017

American Cleft Palate Association
331 Salk Hall, University of Pittsburgh
Pittsburgh, PA 15213

American Coalition of Citizens with
  Disabilities
1012 14th Street, N.W., Suite 901
Washington, DC 20005

American Council for the Blind
1010 Vermont Avenue, N.W., Suite 1100
Washington, DC 20005

American Diabetes Association
1819 H Street, N.W., Suite 1200
Washington, DC 20006

American Epilepsy Society
179 Allyn Street, Suite 304
Hartford, CT 06103

American Foundation for the Blind
15 West 16th Street
New York, NY 10011

American Heart Association
7320 Greenville Avenue
Dallas, TX 75231

American Juvenile Arthritis Organization
1314 Spring Street, N.W.
Atlanta, GA 30309

American Lung Association
1740 Broadway
New York, NY 10019

American Occupational Therapy Association
1383 Piccard Drive, P.O. Box 1725
Rockville, MD 20850

American Physical Therapy Association
1111 N. Fairfax Street
Alexandria, VA 22314

American Printing House for the Blind
1839 Frankfort Avenue
Louisville, KY 40206

American Psychiatric Association
1400 K Street, N.W.
Washington, DC 20005

American Psychological Association
1200 Seventeenth Street, N.W.
Washington, DC 20036

American Society for Deaf Children
814 Thayer Avenue
Silver Spring, MD 20910

American Speech-Language-Hearing
    Association
10801 Rockville Pike
Rockville, MD 20852

Apple Computer's Office of Special Education
    Programs
20525 Mariani Avenue
Cupertino, CA 95014

Association for Children and Adults with
    Learning Disabilities
4156 Library Road
Pittsburgh, PA 15234

Association for Educational Communications
1025 Vermont Avenue, N.W.
Suite 820
Washington, DC 20005

Association for Persons with Severe
    Handicaps
7010 Roosevelt Way, N.E.
Seattle, WA 98115

Association for Retarded Citizens of the
    United States
2501 Avenue J
Arlington, TX 76006

Association for the Education and
    Rehabilitation of the Blind and Visually
    Impaired
206 North Washington Street, Suite 320
Alexandria, VA 22314

Association of Birth Defects Children, Inc.
3526 Emerywood Lane
Orlando, FL 32806

Attention Deficit Disorder Association
8091 South Ireland Way
Aurora, CO 80016

Attention Deficit Disorder Advocacy Group
8091 South Ireland Way
Aurora, CO 80016

Autism Society of America
1234 Massachusetts Avenue, N.W., Suite 1017
Washington, DC 20005

Braille Circulating Library
2700 Stuart Avenue
Richmond, VA 23220

Children with Attention Deficit Disorders
499 N.W. 70th Avenue, Suite 308
Plantation, FL 33317

Clearinghouse on the Handicapped, Office of Special Education and Rehabilitation Services
330 C Street, S.W., Switzer Building
Washington, DC 20202

Clearinghouse and Research in Child Abuse and Neglect
P.O. Box 1182
Washington, DC 20013

Coalition on Sexuality and Disability, Inc.
853 Broadway, Suite 611
New York, NY 10003

Committee for Promotion of Camping for the Handicapped
2056 South Bluff Road
Travers City, MI 49684

Council for Disability Rights
343 South Dearborn, Suite 318
Chicago, IL 60604

Council for Exceptional Children
1920 Association Drive
Reston, VA 22091

Cystic Fibrosis Foundation
6931 Arlington Road
Bethesda, MD 20814

Disability Law Center, Inc.
11 Beacon Street, Suite 925
Boston, MA 02108

Disability Rights Center, Inc.
1616 P Street, N.W., Suite 435
Washington, DC 20036

Epilepsy Foundation of America
4351 Garden City Drive, Suite 406
Landover, MD 20785

Federation for Children with Special Needs
312 Stuart Street
Boston, MA 02116

Gallaudet University Press
800 Florida Avenue, N.E.
Washington, DC 20002

Gifted Child Society, Inc.
190 Rock Road
Glenrock, NJ 07452

IBM National Support Center for Persons with Disabilities
P.O. Box 2150
Atlanta, GA 30055

Juvenile Diabetes Foundation International
60 Madison Avenue
New York, NY 10010

Kurzweil Computer Products
33 Cambridge Parkway
Cambridge, MA 02142

Leukemia Society of America
733 Third Avenue, 14th Floor
New York, NY 10017

March of Dimes Birth Defects Foundation
1275 Mamaroneck Avenue
White Plains, NY 10605

Muscular Dystrophy Association
810 Seventh Avenue
New York, NY 10019

National Aid to the Visually Handicapped
3201 Balboa Street
San Francisco, CA 94121

National Association for Creative Children
and Adults
8080 Spring Valley Drive
Cincinnati, OH 45236

National Association for the Deaf-Blind
12573 S.E. 53rd Street
Bellevue, WA 98006

National Association for Down Syndrome
P.O. Box 4542
Oak Brook, IL 60521

National Association for Gifted Children
5100 N. Edgewood Drive
St. Paul, MN 55112

National Association of Parents of the Deaf
814 Thayer Avenue
Silver Spring, MD 20910

National Association of the Deaf
814 Thayer Avenue
Silver Spring, MD 20910

National Association for Parents of the
Visually Impaired
P.O. Box 180806
Austin, TX 78718

National Association of School Psychologists
1511 K Street, N.W., Suite 716
Washington, DC 20005

National Association for Sickle Cell Disease
3460 Wilshire Boulevard, Suite 1012
Los Angeles, CA 90010

National Association of State Directors of
Special Education
2021 K Street, N.W., Suite 315
Washington, DC 20006

National Association for the Visually
Handicapped
22 West 21st Street
New York, NY 10010

National Braille Press
86 St. Stephen Street
Boston, MA 02115

National Center for Education in Maternal
and Child Health
38th and R Streets, N.W.
Washington, DC 20007

National Center for Stuttering
200 East 33rd Street
New York, NY 10016

National Council for the Handicapped
800 Independence Avenue, S.W.
Washington, DC 20008

National Cued Speech Association
P.O. Box 31345
Raleigh, NC 27622

National Down Syndrome Congress
1800 Dempster Street
Park Ridge, IL 60068

National Easter Seal Society for Crippled
Children and Adults
2023 West Ogden Avenue
Chicago, IL 60612

The National Foundation for Ileitis and
Colitis
444 Park Avenue South
New York, NY 10016

National Handicapped Sports and Recreation
Association
1341 G Street, N.W., Suite 815
Washington, DC 20005

The National Hemophilia Association
The Soho Building
110 Greene Street, Room 406
New York, NY 10012

National Information Center for Handicapped
  Children and Youth
P.O. Box 1492
Washington, DC 20013

National Kidney Foundation
2 Park Avenue, Suite 908
New York, NY 10016

National Library Services for the Blind and
  Physically Handicapped
Library of Congress
1291 Taylor Street, N.W.
Washington, DC 20542

National Mental Health Association
1021 Prince Street
Alexandria, VA 22314

National Multiple Sclerosis Society
205 East 42nd Street
New York, NY 10017

National Rehabilitation Information Center
4407 Eighth Street, N.E.
Washington, DC 22990

National Retinitis Pigmentosa (RP)
  Foundation, Inc.
1401 Mount Royal Avenue
Baltimore, MD 21217

National/State Leadership Training Institute
  on Gifted and Talented (NS/LTI/GT)
Ventura County Superintendent of Schools
535 East Main Street
Ventura, CA 93009

National Society for Children and Adults with
  Autism
1234 Massachusetts Avenue, N.W., Suite
  1017
Washington, DC 20005

National Tay-Sachs and Allied Diseases
  Association
92 Washington Avenue
Cedarhurst, NY 11516

The Orton Dyslexia Society
724 York Road
Baltimore, MD 21204

Parent Information Center
P.O. Box 1422
Concord, NH 03301

Parents Helping Parents, Inc.
535 Race Street, # 220
San Jose, CA 95126

President's Committee on Employment of the
  Handicapped
1111 20th Street, N.W., Room 600
Washington, DC 20036

President's Committee on Mental
  Retardation
Regional Office Building, #3
7th and D Streets, S.W., Room 2614
Washington, DC 20201

Recording for the Blind, Inc.
215 East 58th Street
New York, NY 10022

Scoliosis Research Society
444 North Michigan Avenue
Chicago, IL 60611

Special Olympics, Inc.
1350 New York Avenue, N.W., Suite 500
Washington, DC 20005

Speech Foundation of America
5139 Lingle Street, N.W.
Washington, DC 20016

Spina Bifida Association of America
1700 Rockville Pike, Suite 540
Rockville, MD 20852

Stuttering Foundation of America
P.O. Box 11749
Memphis, TN 38111

Telecommunications for the Deaf, Inc.
814 Thayer Avenue
Silver Spring, MD 20910

The Candlelighters Childhood Cancer
   Foundation
1901 Pennsylvania Avenue, N.W., Suite 1001
Washington, DC 20006

United Cerebral Palsy Association
66 East 34th Street
New York, NY 10016

appendix C

Journals and Newsletters

American Annals of the Deaf. Conference of Educational Administrators Serving the Deaf & Convention of American Instructors of the Deaf, 814 Thayer Avenue, Silver Spring, MD 20910

American Journal on Mental Retardation. American Association on Mental Retardation, 1719 Kalorama Road, N.W., Washington, DC 20009

Behavioral Disorders. Council for Children with Behavior Disorders of the Council for Exceptional Children, 1920 Association Drive, Reston, VA 22091–1589

Beyond Behavior. Council for Children with Behavior Disorders of the Council for Exceptional Children, 1920 Association Drive, Reston, VA 22091–1589

Computers in the Schools. 12 West 32nd Street, New York, NY 10001

Disability Studies Quarterly. Department of Sociology, Brandeis University, Waltham, MA 02254

Disabled USA. President's Committee on Employment of the Handicapped, 1111 20th Street, N.W., Suite 600, Washington, DC 20036

Education and Training of the Mentally Retarded. Division on Mental Retardation and Developmental Disabilities of the Council for Exceptional Children, 1920 Association Drive, Reston, VA 22091–1589

Education & Treatment of Children. PRO-ED, 8700 Shoal Creek Boulevard, Austin, TX 78758–6897

Electronic Learning. Scholastic Inc., 555 Broadway, New York, NY 10012

Exceptional Children. Council for Exceptional Children, 1920 Association Drive, Reston, VA 22091–1589

The Exceptional Parent. Psy-Ed Corporation, 1170 Commonwealth Avenue, Third Floor, Boston, MA 02134

Focus on Exceptional Children. Love Publishing Co., 1777 South Bellaire Street, Denver, CO 80222

Gifted Child Quarterly. National Association for Gifted Children, 1155 15th Street, N.W., #1002, Washington, DC 20005

Gifted Child Today (formerly *G/C/T*). GCT Inc., 350 Weinacker Avenue, Mobile, AL 36604

Intervention in School and Clinic. PRO-ED, 8700 Shoal Creek Boulevard, Austin, TX 78758–6897

Journal for the Education of the Gifted. Association for the Gifted of the Council for Exceptional Children, 1920 Association Drive, Reston, VA 22091–1589

Journal of Creative Behavior. Creative Educational Foundation, Inc., State University College, 1300 Elmwood Avenue, Buffalo, NY 14222

Journal of the Association for Persons with Severe Handicaps. The Association for Persons with Severe Handicaps, 7010 Roosevelt Way, N.E., Seattle, WA 98115

Journal of Early Intervention. Division for Early Childhood of the Council for Exceptional Children, 1920 Association Drive, Reston, VA 22091–1589

Journal of Educational Multimedia and Hypermedia. Association for the Advancement of Computing in Education, P.O. Box 2966, Charlottesville, VA 22902

Journal of Learning Disabilities. PRO-ED, 8700 Shoal Creek Boulevard, Austin, TX 78758–6897

The Journal of Special Education. PRO-ED, 8700 Shoal Creek Boulevard, Austin, TX 78578–6897

Journal of Speech and Hearing Disorders. American Speech-Language-Hearing Association, 10801 Rockville Pike, Rockville, MD 20852

Journal of Visual Impairment and Blindness. American Foundation for the Blind, 15 West 16th Street, New York, NY 10011

Journal of Vocational Rehabilitation. Andover Medical Publishers, Inc., 80 Montvale Avenue, Stoneham, MA 02180

Language, Speech, and Hearing Services in the Schools. American Speech-Language-Hearing Association, 10801 Rockville Pike, Rockville, MD 20852

Learning Disabilities Focus. Division for Learning Disabilities of the Council for Exceptional Children, 1920 Association Drive, Reston, VA 22091–1589

Learning Disabilities Research. Division for Learning Disabilities of the Council for Exceptional Children, 1920 Association Drive, Reston, VA 22091–1589

Mental Retardation. American Association on Mental Retardation, 1719 Kalorama Road, N.W., Washington, DC 20009

Perspectives in Education and Deafness. Gallaudet University, 800 Florida Avenue, N.E., Washington, DC 20002

Rehabilitation Literature. National Easter Seal Society, 2023 West Ogden Avenue, Chicago, IL 60612

Remedial and Special Education. PRO-ED, 8700 Shoal Creek Boulevard, Austin, TX 78758–6897

RE:view (formerly *Education of the Visually Handicapped*). Association for Education and Rehabilitation of the Blind and Visually Impaired, 206 North Washington Street, Room 320, Alexandria, VA 22314

Roeper Review. Roeper City and Country Schools, 2190 North Woodward, Bloomfield Hills, MI 48013

Teaching and Computers. Scholastic Magazine, P.O. Box 2040, Mahopac, NY 10541–9963

Teaching Exceptional Children. Council for Exceptional Children, 1920 Association Drive, Reston, VA 22091–1589

The Volta Review. Alexander Graham Bell
Association for the Deaf, 3417 Volta Place,
N.W., Washington, DC 20007

Topics in Early Childhood Special Education.
PRO-ED, 5341 Industrial Oaks Boulevard,
Austin, TX 78735

Young Children. National Association for the
Education of Young Children, 1834
Connecticut Avenue, N.W., Washington,
DC 20009

Glossary

AAMR   The American Association on Mental Retardation. An organization of individuals from many professional disciplines, concerned with mental retardation. For the most part, the AAMR is an organization of professionals. (Most other groups organized on behalf of individuals who are mentally retarded include primarily parents and laypersons.)

absence seizures   Epileptic seizures of short duration (5 to 20 seconds) that may occur as many as a hundred times a day. An individual may become pale and stare into space, his or her eyelids may twitch, and he or she may demonstrate jerky movements.

academic planning meeting   Group meeting in which the students and teacher plan the academic program.

acceleration   A process leading to a student's accelerated movement through the various grade levels, including early entrance to school, skipping grades, and early or advanced college placement.

acuity   Acuteness or keenness, as of hearing or vision.

adaptive behavior   Ability to meet standards set by society for a cultural group. The American Association on Mental Retardation considers three areas of performance in assessing adaptive behavior: maturation, learning, and social adjustment.

adaptive physical education   Physical education programs designed to meet the specific needs of students who have disabilities.

adaptive skills   Those skills which, in composite, permit an individual to function successfully in his or her environment, including self-help, communication, social, health care, consumer, and vocational skills.

Adlerian theory   Theory suggesting that schools must become truly democratic, with students playing an active role in the process of their education. One advocate is Rudolph Dreikurs.

advocates   Those who plead the cause of others or take actions to attempt to improve the life and/or opportunities of others.

ambulation   Walking without assistance from others. It may include the use of crutches, a cane, or other mechanical aids.

aphasia   Loss or impairment of the ability to use oral language.

articulation problems   Most common type of speech problem including addition (*buhrown* for *brown*, *cuhow* for *cow*), distortion (*shled* for *sled*), omission (*pay* for *play*, *cool* for *school*, *ift* for *lift*), substitution (*dat* for *that*, *wabbit* for *rabbit*, or *thum* for *some*).

assertive discipline   An approach to classroom management that encourages teachers to be in control of classrooms through clear identification of expectations plus an understanding of how to respond to student behavior assertively but without hostility. Lee and Marlene Canter are leading advocates of this approach.

athetoid cerebral palsy   A type of cerebral palsy that involves recurring, slow worm-like movements of the hands and feet.

at risk (infants or children)   Infants or children who are not currently identified as having a disability, but who, for socioeconomic, environmental, physiological, or genetic reasons have a greater than usual chance of developing a disability. *At risk* may be more specifically defined in legislation.

audiogram   Graph on which results of audiometric evaluation are charted to indicate the ability of each ear to hear tones at each of the presented frequencies.

audiologist   Hearing specialist who administers an audiometric examination.

audiometer   Instrument that produces sounds at varying intensities (loudness) and varying frequencies (pitch) for testing purposes.

audiometric evaluation   A hearing test using a series of carefully calibrated tones that vary in loudness and pitch. This evaluation assists in determining the extent and type of hearing loss so that proper remedial or medical steps can be taken to overcome the problem.

augmentative and alternative communication   Methods, strategies, and approaches used to enhance the communication abilities of individuals whose speech is unintelligible or nonexistent.

aura, epileptic   Subjective sensation that precedes and marks the onset of an epileptic seizure.

autism   Disorder which may render an individual noncommunicative and withdrawn, or self-stimulating and aggressive.

behavior modification   Techniques offering tools and systematic procedures that teachers may implement to change or modify unacceptable or defiant behavior and encourage more acceptable and appropriate behavior.

behaviorism   A school of psychology that explains causes of emotional disturbance and behavior disorders in terms of learned behavior. Treatment is then based on behavioral principles and methods.

biophysical theory   A theory that attempts to explain causation of emotional disturbance and behavior disorders on the basis of biologic factors.

blind   A general term that can refer to either no vision or to limited vision, although *visual impairment* is the preferred term for the latter condition. (See also *legally blind*.)

braille   A system of raised dots used by persons who are blind to read and write. Braille is named after Louis Braille, its developer.

brainstorming   A problem-solving process in which a group of individuals attempt to find solutions to a specified problem. Brainstorming sessions typically involve verbalizing and recording in some brief written form a variety of solutions. No judgment or initial evaluation of solutions is made by either the facilitator or participants, thus encouraging innovative ideas. After a preset time period (15 to 20 minutes in many settings), evaluation and discussion take place.

cane technique   Use of a cane as an aid to mobility.

career education   The combination of experiences through which one acquires the attitudes, knowledge, and skills required for successful community living and employment. *Career education* is much broader than a series of courses in vocational or occupational areas.

CD-ROM (compact disc—read-only memory) Digitally encoded information permanently recorded on a compact disc.

CEC The Council for Exceptional Children.

central nervous system (CNS) That part of the nervous system to which the sensory impulses are transmitted and from which motor impulses originate. In vertebrates, the brain and spinal cord.

cerebral palsy A group of conditions that may seriously limit motor coordination. Cerebral palsy is commonly present at birth but may be acquired any time as the result of head injury or infectious disease. The conditions are characterized by varying degrees of disturbance of voluntary movement.

class-action suit Litigation instigated on behalf of a group of individuals in a common situation (such as students with similar disabilities).

classification Indicating, as a matter of written record, that a committee of professionals has determined a specific type of disability, based on the use of appropriate testing, data gathering, and group consideration and discussion.

cleft lip or palate Congenital fissure of the palate or lip that can cause articulation errors and problems with nasality. Normally corrected by surgery.

cognition The process of comprehending and understanding information. The term *cognitive development* is perhaps more often used than cognition and includes efforts to learn new facts and develop new understandings and concepts. Most cognitive development is believed to be a result of relating new experiences to previously developed knowledge and understandings.

colostomy Surgical procedure in which an artificial anal opening is formed in the colon.

complex partial seizures Complex seizures that affect motor systems and mental processes and are manifested by peculiar behavior, such as licking or chewing of lips or purposeless activities. May last for a few minutes or several hours.

computer-assisted instruction Direct instruction to learners, which allows them to interact with instruction programmed into the computer system. Information presented purely for passive reception by the student is *not* computer-assisted instruction.

computer hypermedia system An integrated system of computer hardware and software that allows the composition and display of nonsequential documents. This may include text, audio, and visual information.

computer-managed instruction Management through use of the computer of information about student performance and learning resources, so as to control individual lessons.

conductive hearing loss Hearing loss caused by interference with the transmission of sound from the outer ear.

congenital Present in an individual at birth.

consent decree Formal approval by the court of an out-of-court agreement reached by plaintiffs and defendants. It ends litigation, thus saving time and cost.

continuum of alternative placements Full spectrum of services that may be tailored to the needs of each student at any time during the student's educational career.

contracture Condition of muscle characterized by fixed high resistance to passive stretch and generally caused by prolonged immobilization.

control braces Braces to prevent or eliminate purposeless movement or to allow movement in only one or two directions.

cooperative plan   Plan in which the student is enrolled in a special class but attends a regular classroom for part of the school day. The student's homeroom is a special class.

corrective braces   Braces for prevention and/or correction of deformity during a child's rapid growth.

crisis, or helping, teacher   Teacher who provides temporary support and control to troubled students when they are unable or unwilling to cope with the demands of the regular classroom.

decibel (dB)   Unit of measurement of the loudness of sound.

defiant behavior   Stubborn or aggressive behavior resulting from forces within a student or the environment, including interactions with significant others.

delayed speech   Condition wherein a child does not talk by the time when normal developmental guidelines would indicate that he or she should be talking.

diabetes   Metabolic disorder wherein the individual's body is unable to utilize and properly store sugar. It is the result of the inability of the pancreas to produce a sufficient amount of the hormone insulin.

diabetic coma   Condition caused by too much sugar (too little insulin), resulting from failure to take insulin, illness, or neglect of proper diet.

diagnosogenic theory   Theory that sees the cause of stuttering as the labeling of normal disfluencies by individuals in a child's early environment.

direction taking   Travel method employed by individuals who are visually impaired. It involves using an object or sound to establish a course of direction toward or away from an object.

disability   Objective, measurable lack of function; lowered capacity or incapacity.

Down syndrome   A clinical type of mental retardation related to an abnormal arrangement of chromosomes.

Duchenne (childhood) muscular dystrophy   Generally fatal disease characterized by slow deterioration of the voluntary muscles and ending in a state of complete helplessness.

due process   In general, the right of a citizen to formally protest any action that may result in deprivation of constitutional rights. With respect to students with disabilities (and their parents or guardians), a set of legal procedures and policies established to ensure appropriate educational opportunities.

dyslexia   Severe reading disability accompanied by visual perceptual problems.

efficacy studies   Research specifically established to determine the extent to which given educational practices or procedures achieve the desired effects.

electronic mobility devices   Devices to enhance hearing efficiency, detect obstacles, enable an individual to walk in a straight line, or reveal specific location of obstacles in the environment.

enrichment   An educational approach that emphasizes extra, broadened educational experiences, above and beyond those that are a part of the standard curriculum. Enrichment is advocated by some educators of students who are gifted.

environmental factors   Variables such as poverty, racial discrimination, school pressures, and deteriorating families, considered when evaluating students.

epilepsy   Not a disease in itself but a sign or symptom of some underlying disorder in the nervous system. Convulsions or seizures are the main symptoms related to this term.

etiology   The study of causes or origins of a disease or condition.

fluency disorders   Inappropriate pauses, hesitations, or repetitions that interrupt the natural, fluent flow of speech.

FM amplification systems   A wireless amplification system that transmits an FM radio signal to a combination hearing aid/FM receiver, bypassing environmental sounds.

frustration theory   Theory about the cause of stuttering, based on the idea that a student may have an unusual need to be listened to. In the drive to keep the listener's attention, normal disfluencies cause the speaker to become more and more frustrated.

generalized tonic-clonic seizures   Major seizures, usually involving loss of consciousness, general convulsive movements, and at times, frothy saliva from the mouth. The individual may also lose control of his or her bowel and bladder.

glad notes   Notes given to students or parents by teachers for positive actions by students.

hearing loss   Inability to perceive sounds.

hertz (Hz)   Unit of measurement used to express frequency of sound.

hospital-bound and homebound   Terms used for students who have conditions requiring long-term treatment in a hospital or at home. Such students receive special instruction from homebound or itinerant special education personnel.

hostile aggressiveness   Behavior characterized by violence toward teachers, peers, and parents, including kicking, hitting, biting, and fighting.

humanistic approach   Approach that involves the acceptance of a student's behavior and the reflection of that behavior back to the student. This direct and uncomplicated framework encourages the student to learn, to express, and to better understand his or her feelings in a caring, reflective environment.

hyperactivity   Condition characterized by incessant motion or activity that interferes with learning.

hypoglycemia   A condition in which there is an unusually low level of circulating glucose in the blood. This may lead to lethargy and be related to learning disabilities.

incontinence   Lack of bowel or bladder control.

inclusion   This term, and the concept involved, has in many respects replaced the term *mainstreaming*. Some would differentiate between *inclusion* and *total inclusion*, with inclusion meaning about the same as mainstreaming, with perhaps more emphasis on needed special education assistance, and total inclusion meaning *all* class time is spent in the regular class. There is some question as to whether the concept of total inclusion meets the requirements of IDEA.

individualized education program (IEP)   A written plan that specifies short-term educational objectives, long-term educational goals, how they will be accomplished, who will carry them out, and applicable dates. It is a planning tool, required by IDEA, to help assure appropriate educational programs for students with disabilities. It must be signed by both parents and educators.

individualized family service plan (IFSP)   A parallel to the IEP, first required by PL 99–457, and designed to ensure effective coordination of early intervention services for infants or toddlers with disabilities. The IFSP requires more ongoing parent involvement than does the IEP.

inschool suspension   A procedure in which a student is removed from his or her assigned classroom to another room (such as an unused room or the counselor's room) on a temporary basis. Ordinarily, such suspensions are the result of certain specified behaviors. Such suspensions must be supervised and should be for specified time periods.

instructional technology According to the Association for Educational Communications and Technology, it is "a complex, integrated process involving people, procedures, ideas, devices, and organization, for analyzing problems and devising, implementing, evaluating, and managing solutions to those problems in situations in which learning is purposive and controlled."

insulin Protein hormone produced by the pancreas and secreted into the blood, where it regulates carbohydrate (sugar) metabolism. Used in treatment and control of diabetes mellitus.

interactive media A media format that allows or requires some physical activity from the user, which in some manner alters the presentation.

interactive video Computer-controlled video playback that includes a means for users to control the presentation in some manner.

itinerant teacher Traveling teacher who works with a student on a regularly scheduled basis depending on the student's needs at a particular time.

kinesthesis The sense by which movement, weight, position, and so on are perceived.

kyphosis Curvature of the spine; hunchback.

language nonfluency General lack of smoothness in language production.

learning lab Diagnostic and prescriptive center designed to meet the needs of each student.

legally blind Category of individuals having central visual acuity of 20/200 or less in the better eye after correction, or visual acuity of more than 20/200 if there is a defect in which the widest diameter of the visual field subtends an angle no greater than 20 degrees.

listening helper or buddy Peer in the classroom who helps a student who is hearing impaired in such things as turning to the correct page, taking notes, or adjusting to a new class or school.

litigation Carrying on a suit in a court of law.

low vision A classification of impaired vision in which the individual's corrected vision is lower than normal but still significantly usable. Visual tasks are performed with reduced precision and endurance and at reduced speeds.

magic circle Technique used by elementary school teachers to help students dispel the feeling that they are significantly different from those around them. The teacher attempts to foster an atmosphere of warmth and honesty, in which each student contributes his thoughts and feelings and listens respectfully to peers.

mainstreaming Maximum integration of students with disabilities into regular classrooms, consistent with provision of the most appropriate educational program. Mainstreaming requires close collaboration between regular and special educators, and may require various types of special services, as indicated by the disability and the unique needs of the student. (See also *inclusion*.)

manual communication A method of communication in which fingerspelling or sign language is used in place of speech.

mental retardation Significantly subaverage general intellectual functioning existing concurrently with deficits in two or more adaptive skills areas and manifested before age 18.

misclassification   Inaccurate classification (see *classification*). Misclassification of many minority students was a major factor in the litigation against school districts that contributed to the move toward mainstreaming.

mobility   Individual's movement from one point in his or her environment to another.

mobility training   Training provided for individuals with visual impairments that enables them to detect obstacles in their environment and thus to safely move from place to place.

modeling   Providing a demonstration of some particular behavior.

multimedia system   Audio and video media integrated into a systematic, structured presentation.

muscular dystrophy   A progressive condition in which the muscles are replaced by fatty tissue.

myelomeningocele   Type of spina bifida in which a sac containing part of a malformed spinal cord protrudes from a hole in the spine.

near-point vision   Ability to see at close range, as in reading.

occupational therapy   Therapy directed at upper extremities, emphasizing activities of daily living, such as tying shoes and eating.

ophthalmologist   Medical doctor specializing in the diagnosis and treatment of diseases of the eye; licensed to prescribe glasses and contact lenses. Also called an oculist.

Optacon   Device that converts printed material to either a tactile or auditory stimulus.

optician   Technician who makes glasses and contact lenses and fills the prescriptions of ophthalmologists and optometrists.

optometrist   Specialist in eye problems who does not possess a medical degree. Licensed to measure visual function and prescribe and fit glasses and contact lenses.

oral communication   Approach to teaching students who are hearing impaired. Communication is carried on through spoken language, such as speechreading, listening, and writing without sign language or fingerspelling.

orientation   Blind or visually impaired individual's use of the remaining senses to establish position and relationship to objects in the environment.

orthopedic impairments   Physical impairments related to disorders of the joints, skeleton, or muscles. Students with orthopedic impairments make up one major part of the more general classification *physically disabled*; the other major part relates to health impairments, such as asthma and diabetes.

orthoptist   A nonmedical technician who directs prescribed exercises or training to correct eye-muscle imbalances and generally works under the direction of an ophthalmologist.

osteoarthritis   Degenerative arthritis usually confined to one joint.

otologist   Medical doctor specializing in diseases of the ear.

overattention   Condition in which an individual focuses on one particular object and seems unable to break the focus.

paralysis   Loss or impairment of function in a part of the body.

paraplegia   Paralysis of the lower limbs or lower section of the body.

partially sighted   Category of individuals whose visual acuity is better than 20/200 but is still significantly impaired.

pedagogy   The art, science, or profession of teaching.

perceptual disorders   Disorders involving visual, auditory, tactile, or kinesthetic perception.

perfectionism   Extreme fear of failure or criticism, sometimes seen in students who are troubled.

perseveration   Persistent repetition without apparent purpose.

physical therapy   Therapy directed at the lower extremities, emphasizing posture, gait, movements, and the prevention of contractures.

plus factors   Additional instruction that students who are visually impaired might need in nonacademic areas, such as braille, orientation and mobility, and typewriting.

poliomyelitis   Acute viral disease characterized by involvement of the central nervous system. Sometimes results in paralysis.

postlingual deafness   Deafness occurring after the development of speech and language.

prelingual deafness   Deafness that is present at birth or develops in early life, before the development of speech and language.

prereferral intervention   A system in which special consultive help is requested, with the hope that formal placement within the framework of special education services might never be required. Prereferral intervention is based on the principle of prevention.

pressure theory   Theory that views the cause of stuttering as developmental pressure that promotes disfluency.

problem-solving meeting   Group meeting in which students learn to examine situations, propose solutions, and evaluate the results.

prosthesis   Artificial arm or leg to replace an amputated part of the body.

psychoanalytical approach   Approach to troubled students in which teachers provide ways for the students to bring into consciousness their unconscious repressions. All program cueing comes from the students. Used in residential schools and not readily adaptable to public schools.

quadriplegia   Paralysis affecting both arms and both legs.

readability level   Indication of the difficulty of reading material by the grade level at which students might be expected to read it successfully.

referral   In most cases, a formal request for assistance in planning a more meaningful educational program for a specific student. This usually means completing a form providing certain basic information on the student, including reason(s) assistance is required. (See also *preferral intervention*.)

Regular Education Initiative (REI)   The name given a movement to promote restructuring of the special education–regular education relationship. The REI has been defined and interpreted differently by various special educators.

rehabilitation   Restoring to a former capacity. For example, a student may suffer damage to a limb and, through therapy, the limb may be restored to good condition and use. The term is commonly applied to a variety of services that are designed to help individuals overcome disabilities, especially in preparation for employment—such services are referred to as vocational rehabilitation services.

remediation   Correction of a deficiency. Often refers to correction of academic deficits, such as problems in reading.

residential, or boarding, school   School established for students who are visually or hearing impaired, emotionally disturbed, or mentally retarded because local school districts did not offer the services needed. Usually provides 24-hour care and treatment.

residual hearing　Individual's remaining hearing after some hearing loss.

resource room teacher　Teacher who provides supplemental or remedial instruction (usually daily) to a child enrolled in a regular classroom. The assistance is regularly scheduled in a room that has been specifically designated for that purpose.

responsibility-oriented classroom　Classroom in which students are responsible for their own behavior, academic success, and failure. They cannot blame the environment, parents, or peers; they have the ability to choose. The classroom is neither a teacher-dominated nor a student-controlled room, but rather is a joint effort to learn, relate, and experience. One advocate is William Glasser.

rheumatoid arthritis　Systemic disease characterized by inflammation of the joints and a broad spectrum of other manifestations involving destruction of the joints and resultant deformity.

rubella　German measles.

scoliosis　Abnormal lateral curvature of the spine (C curve).

screening　Broad scale assessment, usually of groups of children, to determine those who may merit more intensive, individual assessment. Vision and hearing screenings are the most common such processes.

seizures　Excessive electrical discharges released in some nerve cells of the brain, resulting in loss of control over muscles, consciousness, senses, and thoughts.

sensorineural hearing loss　Hearing loss associated with damage to the sensory end organ or a dysfunction of the auditory nerve.

sheltered workshop　A structured work setting in which low skill level work is provided for individuals who are not presently capable of competitive employment. For some individuals this will prove to be terminal employment; for others this will provide training for later competitive employment.

sighted-guide technique　Technique in which an individual who is visually impaired grasps the arm of a sighted person just above the elbow, enabling him or her to "read" any movement of the guide's body.

Snellen chart　Chart consisting of letters, numbers, or symbols of graduated sizes to be read at a distance of 20 feet to determine field visual acuity. A special Snellen chart to be read at a distance of 14 inches may be used to measure near vision.

sociometry　A technique used to measure the social structure of a group or class.

spastic cerebral palsy　A condition characterized by jerky or explosive motions when an individual initiates a voluntary movement.

special education　A subsystem of the total educational system for the provision of specialized or adapted programs and services or for assisting others to provide such services for exceptional youth and children.

special educator　One who has had specialized training or preparation for teaching children with disabilities; works collaboratively with general educators.

speech compression/speech expansion　A means whereby the intelligibility of speech, recorded at normal speed, is maintained when played at faster (compression) or slower (expansion) speeds.

speech compressor　A modified tape recorder on which the pause between each recorded word is electronically removed, thereby compressing the material and speeding up the listening process without changing the pitch.

speech disorder　Speech that (a) interferes with communication, (b) causes the speaker to be maladjusted, or (c) calls undue attention to the speech as opposed to what is said.

speechreading   A highly important skill for individuals who are hearing impaired. Individuals learn to observe lip movements, facial gestures, body gestures, and other environmental clues, to supplement whatever degree of residual hearing is present. The term *speechreading* has, for the most part, replaced the term *lipreading*, which emphasized only one part of this skill.

speech synthesizer   A device attached to a computer that audibly reads numbers and words displayed on the computer screen.

spina bifida   Serious birth defect in which the bones of the spine fail to close during the 12th week of fetal development, resulting in a cyst or sac in the lower back that is generally surgically treated during the child's first 24 to 48 hours of life. Varying degrees of paralysis in the lower extremities are generally observed.

tactile   Pertaining to the sense of touch.

task analysis   Breaking a skill into smaller parts.

taxonomy   A classification system.

TDD   A device that allows a telephone conversation to be typed rather than spoken.

teacher-move analysis   Tool that evaluates interaction between teacher and student by placing teacher behavior into eight categories, called teacher moves.

tinnitus   Hearing noises within the head.

total communication   Total-language approach for individuals who are hearing impaired, in which there is equal emphasis on speech, auditory training, and a system of visual communication.

trailing   To follow lightly over a straight surface with back of fingertips to locate specific objects or to get a parallel line of direction.

transition programs   Programs that help prepare students for successful transition to the next level or type of educational program, or to adult life, employment, and independent or semi-independent living. Such programs require careful planning and cooperation on the part of school personnel, parents, and the various agencies who may be involved.

traumatic brain injury   An injury to the brain caused by an external physical force or by an internal occurrence such as stroke or aneurysm, producing a diminished or altered state of consciousness.

visual acuity   Measured ability to see.

voice disorders   Disorders of pitch, intensity, quality, or flexibility of the voice.

References

Achenbach, T. M., & Edelbrock, C. S. (1991). *Manual for the Child Behavior Checklist/4–18 and 1991 Profile*. Burlington, VT: University of Vermont, Department of Psychiatry.

Adger, C. T., Wolfram, W., & Detwyler, S. (1993). Language differences. *Teaching Exceptional Children, 26*(1), 44–47.

Alberto, P. A., & Troutman, A. C. (1990) *Applied behavior analysis for teachers* (3rd ed.). Englewood Cliffs, NJ: Merrill/Prentice Hall.

Aleman, S. R. (1991). *Special education for children with attention deficit disorders: Current issues*. Congressional Research Service (Report No. 91-862 EPW). Library of Congress. (ERIC Document Reproduction Service No. ED 343 319)

Allen, R. (1992). Asking the experts: Students' views on delinquency. *Beyond Behavior, 3*(2), 21–23.

American Academy of Pediatrics. (1984). Administration of medication in school, *Pediatrics, 74*, 433.

American Association on Mental Retardation. (1992). *Mental retardation: Definition, classification and systems of supports* (9th ed.). Washington, DC: Author.

American Psychiatric Association. (1980). *Diagnostic and statistical manual of mental disorders* (3rd ed., DSM-III). Washington, DC: Author.

American Psychiatric Association. (1987). *Diagnostic and statistical manual of mental disorders* (3rd ed. rev., DSM-III-R). Washington, DC: Author.

American Psychiatric Association. (1994). *Diagnostic and statistical manual of mental disorders* (DSM-IV). Washington, DC: Author.

American Speech-Language-Hearing Association. (1982). Definitions: Communicative disorders and variations. *ASHA, 24*, 949–950.

American Speech-Language-Hearing Association. (1983). Position paper: Social dialects. *ASHA, 25*, 23–24.

American Speech-Language-Hearing Association (ASHA), Committee on Language. (1983). Definition of language. *ASHA, 25*, 44.

Americans with Disabilities Act (Public Law 101–476). (1990). Office of the Federal Register, Washington, DC: U.S. Government Printing Office.

Anthony, D. (1971). *Seeing essential English*. Anaheim, CA: Anaheim School District.

Aronson, E. (1978). *The jigsaw classroom*. Beverly Hills, CA: Sage.

Artiles, A. J., & Trent, S. C. (1994). Overrepresentation of minority students in special education: A continuing debate. *The Journal of Special Education, 27*(4), 410–437.

Babad, E., Bernieri, F., & Rosenthal, R. (1991). Students as judges of teachers' verbal and nonverbal behavior. *American Educational Research Journal, 28,* 211–234.

Baca, L. M., & Cervantes, H. T. (Eds.). (1989). *The bilingual special education interface.* Englewood Cliffs, NJ: Merrill/Prentice Hall.

Ballard, J., & Zettel, J. (1977). Public Law 94–142 and section 504: What they say about rights and protections. *Exceptional Children, 44,* 177–185.

Barken, J. H., & Bernal, E. M. (1991). Gifted education for bilingual and limited English proficient students. *Gifted Child Quarterly, 35*(3), 144–147.

Barkley, R. A. (1991). Foreword. In L. Braswell & M. L. Bloomquist (Eds.), *Cognitive-behavioral therapy with ADHD children: Child, family and school interventions.* New York: Guilford.

Barnetti, S. M., & Parker, L. G. (1982). Suspension and expulsion of the emotionally handicapped: Issues and practices. *Behavioral Disorders, 7*(3), 173–179.

Baron, R. M., Tom, D. Y. H., & Cooper, H. M. (1985). Social class, race, & teacher expectations. In J. B. Dusek, V. C. Hall, & W. J. Meyer (Eds.), *Teacher expectancies.* Hillsdale, NJ: Erlbaum.

Baroody, A. (1993). Introducing number and arithmetic concepts with number sticks. *Teaching Exceptional Children, 26*(1), 7–11.

Barraga, N. (1983). *Visual handicaps and learning* (rev. ed.). Austin, TX: Exceptional Resources.

Barraga, N., & Erin, J. (1992). *Visual handicaps and learning.* Austin, TX: PRO-ED.

Bartel, N. R. (1990). Problems in mathematics achievement. In D. D. Hammill & N. R. Bartel (Eds.), *Teaching students with learning and behavior problems* (5th ed.). Boston: Allyn & Bacon.

Baskin, B., & Harris, K. H. (1985). Reading for the gifted. *ERIC Digest, 362.* Reston, VA: Council for Exceptional Children.

Bateman, B. (1994). Who, how and where: Special education's issues in perpetuity. *Journal of Special Education, 27*(4), 509–530.

Behrman, R. E., Vaughan, V. C., & Nelson, W. E. (1987). *Nelson textbook of pediatrics* (13th ed.). Philadelphia: W. B. Saunders.

Berger, G. (1987). *Crack, the new drug epidemic.* New York: Impact.

Berko Gleason, J. (Ed). (1993). *The development of language* (3rd ed.). Englewood Cliffs, NJ: Merrill/Prentice Hall.

Bernstein, D. K., & Tiegerman, E. (1993). *Language and communication disorders in children* (3rd ed.). Englewood Cliffs, NJ: Merrill/Prentice Hall.

Betts, G. (1985). *Autonomous learner model for the gifted and talented.* Greeley, CO: Autonomous Learning Publications and Specialists.

Betts, G., & Knapp, J. (1981). Autonomous learning and the gifted: A secondary model. In *Secondary programs for the gifted/talented.* Ventura, CA: National/State Leadership Training Institute on the Gifted and Talented.

Bierne-Smith, M., Patton, J. R., & Ittenbach, R. (1994). *Mental retardation.* Englewood Cliffs, NJ: Merrill/Prentice Hall.

Bigge, J. L. (1991). *Teaching individuals with physical and multiple disabilities.* Englewood Cliffs, NJ: Merrill/Prentice Hall.

Biklen, D. (1992). Typing to talk: Facilitated communication. *American Journal of Speech-Language Pathology, 1*(2), 15–17.

Biklen, D., & Schubert, A. (1991). New words: The communication of students with autism. *Remedial & Special Education, 12*(6), 46–51.

Bloom, B. (Ed.). (1956). *Taxonomy of educational objectives: The classification of edu-*

cational goals: Handbook 1: Cognitive domain. New York: McKay.

Bloom, B. S. (1971). Mastery learning. In J. H. Block (Ed.), *Mastery learning: theory and practice*. New York: Holt, Rinehart & Winston.

Bloom, L. (1970). *Language development: Form and function of emerging grammars*. Cambridge: MIT Press.

Blumenthal, S. (1985, April 30). *Testimony before the United States Senate on juvenile justice*. Washington, DC: U.S. Department of Health and Human Services.

Borkowski, J. G., Peck, V. A., & Damberg, P. R. (1983). Attention, memory, and cognition. In J. L. Matson & J. A. Mulich (Eds.), *Handbook of mental retardation*. New York: Pergamon.

Bornstein, H. (1974). Signed English: A manual approach to English language development. *Journal of Speech and Hearing Disorders, 3*, 330–343.

Bower, E. M. (1992). Defining emotional disturbance: Public policy & research. *Psychology in the Schools, 19*, 55–60.

Brier, N. (1994). Targeted treatment for adjudicated youth with learning disabilities: Effects on recidivism. *Journal of Learning Disabilities, 27*(4), 215–222.

Bristol, M. M., & Schopler, E. (1989). The family in the treatment of autism. In *Treatments of psychiatric disorders*. (Vol. 1). Washington, DC: American Psychiatric Association.

Brolin, D. (1982). Life-centered career education for exceptional children. *Focus on Exceptional Children, 14*(7), 1–15.

Brophy, J. E., & Good, T. L. (1974). *Teacher-student relationships*. New York: Holt, Rinehart & Winston.

Browder, D., & Snell, M. (1993). Daily living and community skills. In M. Snell (Ed.), *Instruction of students with severe disabilities* (4th ed.). Englewood Cliffs, NJ: Merrill/Prentice Hall.

Brown, C. (1993). Assistive computer technology: Opening new doorways. *New Directions in Student Services, 64*, 89–102.

Brown, L., & Gilligan, C. (1992). *Meeting at the crossroads: Women's psychology and girl's development*. Cambridge, MA: Harvard University Press.

Brown, L. L., & Hammill, D. (1983). *Behavior Rating Profile*. Austin, TX: PRO-ED.

Bruner, J. (1974). The organization of early skilled action. In M. P. M. Richards (Ed.), *The integration of a child into a social world*. London: Cambridge University Press.

Bruner, J. (1975). The ontogenesis of speech acts. *Journal of Child Language, 2*, 1–19.

Buell, C. (1950). *Motor performance of visually handicapped children*. Unpublished doctoral dissertation, University of California, Berkeley.

Bulgren, J., Schumaker, J., & Deshler, D. (1994). The effects of recall enhancement routine on test performance of secondary students with and without learning disabilities. *Learning Disabilities Research and Practice, 9*, 2–11.

Bullock, L. M. (1991). *Exceptionalities in children and youth*. Boston: Allyn & Bacon.

Bunsen, T. D., & Hurley, B. (1993). Kids dropping out—and into gangs. *Beyond Behavior, 4*(3), 4–8.

Burks, H. F. (1977). *Burks Behavior Rating Scales*. Los Angeles: Western Psychological Service.

Bybee, J., & Zigler, E. (1992). Is outerdirectedness employed in a harmful or beneficial manner in students with and without mental retardation? *American Journal on Mental Retardation, 96*, 512–521.

Calculator, S. (1992). Perhaps the emperor has clothes after all: A response to Biklen (1992). *American Journal of Speech Language Pathology, 1*(2), 18–20.

Calvin, G., Sugai, G., & Patching, B. (1993). Precorrection: Instructional approach for managing predictable problem behaviors. *Intervention in School and Clinic, 28*(3), 143–150.

Canter, L. (1989). Assertive discipline . . . more than names on the board and marbles in a jar. *Phi Delta Kappan, 71*(1), 57–61.

Canter, L., & Canter, M. (1976). *Assertive discipline: A take-charge approach for today's educator.* Seal Beach, CA: Canter & Associates.

Carrol, C. (1989). Larry Stewart: Reverse mainstreaming trend. *The Deaf American, 39*(3), 11–18.

Carter, J. F. (1993). Self-management. *Teaching Exceptional Children, 25*(3), 28–31.

Cartledge, G., & Milburn, J. F. (1986). *Teaching social skills to children* (2nd ed.). New York: Pergamon.

Cartwright, G. P., Cartwright, C. A., & Ward, M. E. (1984). *Educating special learners.* Belmont, CA: Wadsworth.

Cawley, J., Baker-Kroczynski, S., & Urban, A. (1992). Seeking excellence in mathematics education for students with mild disabilities. *Teaching Exceptional Children, 24*(2), 44–46.

Centers for Disease Control. (1989). Guidelines for prevention of transmission of immunodeficiency virus and hepatitis B virus to healthcare and public-safety workers. *Morbidity and Mortality Weekly Report, 38.*

Chapman, W. (1991). The Illinois experience. *Phi Delta Kappan, 72*(5), 355–358.

Charles, C. (1989). *Building classroom discipline* (3rd ed.). White Plains, NY: Longman.

Chomsky, N. (1957). *Syntactic structures.* Houston, TX: The Hague.

Chomsky, N. (1965). *Aspects of the theory of syntax.* Cambridge: MIT Press.

Chrispeels, J. H. (1991). District leadership in parent involvement. *Phi Delta Kappan, 72*(3), 367–371.

Cicchelli, T., & Ashby-Davis, C. (1986). *Teaching exceptional children and youth in the regular classroom.* Syracuse, NY: Syracuse University Press.

Clark, B. (1992). *Growing up gifted* (4th ed.). New York: Merrill/Macmillan.

Cleary, M. E. (1976). Helping children understand the child with special needs. *Children Today, 5,* 24–31.

Cline, D. H. (1990). A legal analysis of policy initiatives to exclude handicapped/disruptive students from special education. *Behavioral Disorders, 15,* 159–173.

Clymer, E. W., & Parrish, R. (1994). Productive administration applications of computers in schools programs for deaf students. *American Annals of the Deaf, 139* (special issue), 3–66.

Code of Federal Regulations (CFR), 34 (1993). Office of the Federal Register. Washington, DC: U.S. Government Printing Office.

Cole, G. F. (1992). *The American system of criminal justice* (6th ed.). Pacific Grove, CA: Brooks/Cole.

Coleman, M. C., & Gilliam, J. E. (1983). Disturbing behaviors in the classroom: A survey of teacher attitudes. *Journal of Special Education, 17,* 121–129.

Contact maturity: Growing up strong (1972). Englewood Cliffs, NJ: Scholastic Book Services.

Conture, E. G., & Fraser, J. (1991). *Stuttering and your child: Questions and answers.* (Publication no. 22). Memphis, TN: Stuttering Foundation of America.

Costa, A. L. (1987). Thinking skills: Neither an add-on nor a quick fix. In M. Heiman & J. Slomianko (Eds.), *Thinking skills instruction: Concepts and techniques.* Washington, DC: National Education Association.

Costa, A. L. (1991). *The school as a home for the mind*. Palatine, IL: Skylight.

Council for Children with Behavior Disorders. (1989). Best assessment practices for students with behavioral disorders: Accommodation to cultural diversity and individual differences. *Behavioral Disorders, 14*, 263–278.

Council for Learning Disabilities. (1993). Concerns about the "full inclusion" of students with learning disabilities in regular education classrooms. *Learning Disabilities Quarterly, 16*, 126.

Cox, J., Daniel, N., & Boston, J. B. (1985). *Educating able learners: Programs and promising practices*. Austin, TX: University of Texas Press.

Crane, J. C., & Reynolds, J. (1983). *Social skills and me*. Houston, TX: Reynolds.

Creasy, R. K., & Resnick, R. (1989). *Maternal-fetal medicine: Principles and practices* (2nd ed.). Philadelphia: W. B. Saunders.

Cronin, M. E., Slade, D. L., Bechtel, C., & Anderson, P. (1992). Home-school partnerships: A cooperative approach to intervention. *Intervention in School & Clinic, 27*(5), 286–292.

Culatta, R., & Culatta, B. K. (1985). Communication disorders. In W. H. Birdine & A. E. Blackhurst (Eds.), *An introduction to special education* (2nd ed.). Boston: Little, Brown.

Cullinan, D., & Epstein, M. H. (1994). Behavior disorders. In N. Haring, L. McCormick, & T. G. Haring (Eds.), *Exceptional children and youth* (6th ed.). Englewood Cliffs, NJ: Merrill/Prentice Hall.

Cummings, C. (1980). *Teaching makes a difference*. Edmonds, WA: TEACHING.

Cummins, J. (1989). A theoretical framework for bilingual special education. *Exceptional Children, 56*(2), 111–119.

D'Angelo, D. A., & Adler, C. R. (1991). Chapter 1: A catalyst for improving parent involvement. *Phi Delta Kappan, 72*(5), 350–354.

Daniels-Mohring, D., & Lambie, R. (1993). Dysfunctional families of the student with special needs. *Focus on Exceptional Children, 25*(5), 1–11.

Davila, L., Williams, M., & MacDonald, R. (1991). *Special education for children with attention deficit disorder: Current issues*. (Report No. 91-862 EPW). Library of Congress: Congressional Research Service. (ERIC Document Reproduction Service No. ED 343 319)

Davis, J. M., Elfenbein, J., Schum, R., & Bentler, R. A. (1986). Effects of mild and moderate hearing impairments on language, educational, and psychosocial behavior of children. *Journal of Speech and Hearing Disorders, 51*(1), 53–62.

Dean, A. V., Salend, S. J., & Taylor, L. (1993). Multicultural education. *Teaching Exceptional Children, 26*(1), 40–43.

Dehouske, E. (1982). Story writing as a problem-solving vehicle. *Teaching Exceptional Children, 1*(1), 11–17.

Delquadri, J., Greenwood, C., Whorton, D., Carta, J., & Hall, R. (1986). Classwide peer tutoring. *Exceptional Children, 52*, 535–542.

Devine, T. G. (1987). *Teaching study skills: A guide for teachers* (2nd ed.). Boston: Allyn & Bacon.

Devlin, S. D., & Elliott, R. N. (1992). Drug use patterns of adolescents with behavior disorders. *Behavior Disorders, 17*(4), 264–272.

DeVries, D. L., & Slavin, R. E. (1978). Team games tournament: A research review. *Journal of Research and Development in Education, 12*, 28–38.

Dinkmeyer, D. (1982). *Developing understanding of self and others—Revised*. Circle Pines, MN: American Guidance Service.

Dreikurs, R., & Cassel, P. (1972). *Discipline without tears*. New York: Hawthorn.

Dreikurs, R., & Saltz, U. (1964). *Children: The challenge*. New York: Hawthorn.

Dunn, L. M. (1968). Special education for the mildly retarded: Is much of it justifiable? *Exceptional Children, 35*, 5–22.

Dunn, R., & Dunn, K. (1992). *Teaching elementary students through their individual learning styles*. Boston: Allyn & Bacon.

Durlak, C., Rose, E., & Bursuck, W. (1994). Preparing high school students with learning disabilities for the transition to postsecondary education: Teaching the skills of self-determination. *Journal of Learning Disabilities, 27*, 51–59.

Eby, J. W., & Kujawa, E. (1994). *Reflective planning, teaching, and evaluation: K–12*. Englewood Cliffs, NJ: Merrill/Prentice Hall.

Eccles, J. (1985). Why doesn't Jane run? Sex differences in educational and occupational patterns. In F. D. Horowitz & M. O'Brien (Eds.), *The gifted and talented: Developmental perspectives*. Washington, DC: American Psychological Corporation.

Eddowes, E. A. (1992). Children and homelessness. In J. H. Stronge (Ed.), *Educating homeless children and adolescents*. Newbury Park, CA: Sage.

Edgar, E., & Polloway, E. (1994). Education of adolescents with disabilities: Curriculum and placement issues. *Journal of Special Education, 27*(4), 438–452.

Eichinger, J. (1990). Goal structure effects on social interaction: Nondisabled and disabled elementary students. *Exceptional Children, 56*(5), 408–416.

Eichinger, J., & Woltman, S. (1993). Integration strategies for learners with severe disabilities. *Teaching Exceptional Children, 26*(1), 18–21.

Elbert, J. (1993). Occurrence & pattern of impaired reading and written language in children with attention deficit disorders. *Annals of Dyslexia, 43*, 26–43.

Ellis, N. R. (1970). Memory processes in retardates and normals. *International Review of Research in Mental Retardation, 4*.

Elmquist, D. L. (1991). School-based alcohol and other drug prevention programs: Guidelines for the special educator. *Intervention in School and Clinic, 27*(1), 10–19.

Englert, C., & Mariage, T. (1991). Share understandings: Structuring the writing experience through dialogue. *Journal of Learning Disabilities, 24*, 330–342.

Englert, C., Raphael, J., & Mariage, T. (1994). Developing a school-based discourse for literacy learning: A principled search for understanding. *Learning Disability Quarterly, 17*, 2–32.

Englert, C., Tarrant, K., Mariage, T., & Oxer, T. (1994). Lesson talk as the work of reading groups: The effectiveness of two interventions. *Journal of Learning Disabilities, 27*, 163–187.

Epstein, J. L. (1991). Paths to partnership. *Phi Delta Kappan, 72*(5), 344–349.

Erickson, M. T. (1987). *Behavior disorders of children and adolescents*. Englewood Cliffs, NJ: Prentice-Hall.

Evans, R. J. (1984). Fostering peer acceptance of handicapped students. *ERIC Digest, 1406*. Reston, VA: Council for Exceptional Children.

Ewing, N. J., & Yong, F. L. (1992). A comparative study of the learning style preferences among gifted African-American, Mexican-American, and American-born Chinese middle grade students. *Roeper Review, 14*(3), 120–123.

Fad, K. S., & Ryser, G. R. (1993). Social/behavioral variables related to success in general education. *Remedial and Special Education, 14*(1), 25–35.

Federal Register. (1977, 23 August). Rules and regulations for the implementation of part B of PL 94–142. Washington, DC: U.S. Government Printing Office, 42474–42515.

Fernald, G. (1943). *Remedial techniques in basic school subjects*. New York: McGraw-Hill.

Fernald, G. (1988). *Remedial techniques in basic school subjects: Methods for teaching dyslexics and other learning disabled persons*. Austin, TX: PRO-ED.

Feuer, M. J., & Fulton, K. (1993). The many faces of performance assessment. *Phi Delta Kappan, 74*(6), 478–483.

Fiedler, C. R., & Simpson, R. L. (1987). Modifying the attitudes of nonhandicapped high school students toward handicapped peers. *Exceptional Children, 53*, 343–349.

Field, S., LeRoy, B., & Rivera, S. (1994). Meeting functional curriculum needs in middle school general education classrooms. *Teaching Exceptional Children, 26*(2), 40–43.

Figueroa, R. A. (1989). Psychological testing of linguistic-minority students. *Exceptional Children, 56*, 145–153.

Forehand, R., McCombs, A., & Brody, G. H. (1987). The relationship between parental depressive mood states and child functioning. *Advances in Behavior Research and Therapy, 9*, 1–20.

Forest, M., & Lusthaus, E. (1989). Promoting educational equality for all students. In S. Stainback & W. Stainback (Eds.), *Educating all students in the mainstream of regular education*. Baltimore: Paul H. Brookes.

Forest, M., & Lusthaus, E. (1990). Everyone belongs with the MAPS action planning system. *Teaching Exceptional Children, 22*(2), 32–35.

Forness, S. R., & Kavale, K. A. (1988). Psychopharmacological treatment: A note on classroom effects. *Journal of Learning Disabilities, 21*, 144–147.

Forness, S., & Knitzer, J. (1991). *A new proposed definition and terminology to replace "serious emotional disturbance" in Individuals with Disabilities Education Act*. Alexandria, VA: National Mental Health & Special Education Coalition.

Foster, G., Algozzine, B., & Ysseldyke, T. (1980). Classroom teacher and teacher-in-training susceptibility to stereotypical bias. *Personnel and Guidance Journal, 59*, 27–30.

Foster-Johnson, L., & Dunlap, G. (1993). Using functional assessment to develop effective, individualized interventions for challenging behaviors. *Teaching Exceptional Children, 25*(3), 44–50.

Fox, C. L. (1989). Peer acceptance of learning disabled children in the regular classroom. *Exceptional Children, 56*(1), 50–59.

Fraser, K. (1989). *Someone at school has AIDS*. Alexandria, VA: National Association of State Boards of Education.

Freeman, Y. S., & Freeman, D. E. (1992). *Whole language for second language learners*. Portsmouth, NH: Heineman.

Freiberg, K. L. (Ed.). (1994). *Educating exceptional children* (7th ed.). Guilford, CT: Duskin Publishing Group.

Gable, R. A., & Warren, S. F. (Eds.). (1993). *Strategies for teaching students with mild to severe mental retardation*. Baltimore: Paul H. Brookes.

Gadow, K., & Sprafkin, P. (1993). Television "violence" and children with emotional and behavioral disorders. *Journal of Emotional and Behavioral Disorders, 1*, 54–63.

Gagne, F. (1990). Toward a differentiated model of giftedness and talent. In N. Colangelo & G. Davis (Eds.), *Handbook of gifted education*. Boston: Allyn & Bacon.

Gagne, F. (1992, November). *Talent identification and development as an alternative to gifted education*. Paper presented at the

National Association for Gifted Children Conference, Los Angeles, CA.

Gayeski, D. M. (Ed.). (1993). *Multimedia for learning: Development, application, evaluation*. Englewood Cliffs, NJ: Educational Technology Publications.

Gaylord-Ross, R. (Ed.). (1989). *Integration strategies for students with handicaps*. Baltimore: Paul H. Brookes.

Gearheart, B. (1974). *Organization and administration of educational programs for exceptional children*. Springfield, IL: Charles C. Thomas.

Gearheart, B. R., & Litton, F. (1979). *The trainable retarded: A foundations approach* (2nd ed.). St. Louis: C. V. Mosby.

Gearheart, B. R., Mullen, R. C., & Gearheart, C. J. (1993). *Exceptional individuals*. Pacific Grove, CA: Brooks/Cole.

Gearheart, C., & Gearheart, B. (1990). *Introduction to special education assessment: Principles and practices*. Denver: Love.

Gersten, R., & Woodward, J. (1994). The language-minority student and special education: Issues, trends, and paradoxes. *Exceptional Children, 60*(4), 310–322.

Gilliam, J. E. (1993). Crisis management for students with emotional/behavioral problems. *Intervention in School and Clinic, 28*(4), 224–230.

Glasser, W. (1965). *Reality therapy*. New York: Harper & Row.

Glasser, W. (1992). *The quality school* (2nd ed.). New York: Harper Collins.

Goldstein, A., Sprafkin, R., Gershaw, N., & Klein, P. (1980). *Skillstreaming the adolescent: A structured learning approach to teaching prosocial skills*. Champaign, IL: Research Press.

Goldstein, H. (1993). Use of peers as communication intervention agents. *Teaching Exceptional Children, 25*(2), 37–40.

Goldstein, H., Moss, J., & Jordan, L. (1965). *The efficacy of special class training on the development of mentally retarded children* (U.S. Office of Education Cooperative Project No. 619). Urbana, IL: University of Illinois.

Gollnick, D. M., & Chinn, P. C. (1994). *Multicultural education in a pluralistic society* (4th ed.). Englewood Cliffs, NJ: Merrill/Prentice Hall.

Good, T. L. (1987). Teacher expectations. In D. C. Berliner & B. V. Rosenshine (Eds.), *Talks to teachers*. New York: Random House.

Good, T. L., & Brophy, J. E. (1987). *Looking in classrooms* (4th ed.). New York: Harper & Row.

Goor, M. B., & Schwenn, J. O. (1993). Accommodating diversity and disability with cooperative learning. *Intervention in School and Clinic, 29*(1), 6–16.

Gottesman, I. I. (1991). *Schizophrenia genesis: The origins of madness*. New York: W. H. Freeman.

Gresham, F. M. (1982). Misguided mainstreaming: The case for social skills training with handicapped children. *Exceptional Children, 48*, 422–433.

Gronberg, G. (1983). *Attitude responses of nonhandicapped elementary students to specific information and contact with the handicapped*. Unpublished doctoral dissertation, University of Northern Colorado.

Gronlund, N., & Linn, R. (1990). *Measurement and evaluation in teaching*. Englewood Cliffs, NJ: Merrill/Prentice Hall.

Grossen, B., & Carnine, D. (1993). Phonics instruction: Comparing research and practice. *Teaching Exceptional Children, 25*(2), 22–25.

Guetzloe, E. C. (1989). *Youth suicide: What the educator should know*. Reston, VA: Council for Exceptional Children.

Guetzloe, E. C. (1991). *Depression and suicide: Special education students at risk*. Reston, VA: Council for Exceptional Children.

Guilford, J. P. (1959a). Three faces of intellect. *American Psychologist, 14,* 469–479.

Guilford, J. P. (1959b). Traits of creativity. In H. H. Anderson (Ed.), *Creativity and its cultivation.* New York: Harper.

Gustason, G., Pfetzing, D., Zawolkow, E., & Norris, C. (1972). *Signing exact English.* Rossmore, CA: Modern Science.

Hadaway, N., & Marek-Schroer, M. F. (1992). Multidimensional assessment of the gifted minority student. *Roeper Review, 15*(2), 73–77.

Hallenbeck, M. J., & McMaster, D. (1991). Disability simulation for regular education students. *Teaching Exceptional Children, 23*(3), 12–15.

Hamayan, E. V., & Damico, J. S. (1991). *Limiting bias in the assessment of bilingual students.* Austin, TX: PRO-ED.

Hanson, V. (1983). Juvenile rheumatoid arthritis. In J. Umbreit (Ed.), *Physical disabilities and health impairments* (pp. 240–249). Englewood Cliffs, NJ: Merrill/Prentice Hall.

Haring, N. G., McCormick, L., & Haring, T. G. (Eds.). (1994). *Exceptional children and youth* (6th ed.). Englewood Cliffs, NJ: Merrill/Prentice Hall.

Hawton, K. (1986). *Suicide and attempted suicide among children and adolescents.* Beverly Hills, CA: Sage.

Heiman, M., & Slomianko, J. (Eds.). (1987). *Thinking skills instruction: Concepts and techniques.* Washington, DC: National Education Association.

Heller, H. W., & Schilit, J. (1987). The regular education initiative: A concerned response. *Focus on Exceptional Children, 20*(3), 1–7.

Hendrickson, J., & Frank, A. (1993). Engagement and performance feedback: Enhancing the classroom achievement of students with mild mental disabilities. In R. A. Gable & S. F. Warren (Eds.), *Strategies for teaching students with mild to severe mental retardation.* Baltimore: Paul H. Brookes.

Heron, T. E., & Harris, K. C. (1987). *The educational consultant* (2nd ed.). Austin, TX: PRO-ED.

Higham, S. D., & Navarre, J. P. (1984). Gifted adolescent females require differential treatment. *Journal for Education of the Gifted, 8,* 43–49.

Hildreth, B. L., & Candler, A. (1992). Learning about learning disabilities through general public literature. *Intervention in School and Clinic, 27*(5), 293–296.

Homme, L., Csanyi, A. P., Gonzales, M. A., & Rechs, J. R. (1979). *How to use contingency contracting in the classroom.* Champaign, IL.: Research Press.

Hoover, J. J. (1988). *Teaching handicapped students study skills* (2nd ed.). Lindale, TX: Hamilton.

Hunter, M. (1994). *Enhancing teaching.* Englewood Cliffs, NJ: Merrill/Prentice Hall.

Hutton, J. B., & Roberts, T. G. (1986). *Social-emotional dimension scale: A measure of school behavior.* Austin, TX: PRO-ED.

Inhelder, B. (1968). *The diagnosis of reading in the mentally retarded.* New York: John Day.

Interagency Committee on Learning Disabilities. (1987). *A report to the U.S. Congress.* Bethesda, MD: National Institutes of Health.

Irwin, R. B. (1955). *As I saw it.* New York: American Foundation for the Blind.

Itard, J. M. G. (1962). *The wild boy of Aveyron.* New York: Appleton-Century-Crofts.

Jackson, N. F., Jackson, D. A., & Monroe, C. (1983). *Getting along with others—teaching social effectiveness to children.* Champaign, IL: Research Press.

Jenkins, J. R., Jewell, M., Leicester, N., O'Connor, R. E., Jenkins, L. M., & Troutner, N. N. (1994). Accommodations for individual differences without classroom ability groups: An experiment in school restructuring. *Exceptional Children, 60*(4), 344–358.

Jensen, A. (1969). How much can we boost IQ and scholastic achievement? *Harvard Educational Review, 39*(1), 1–24.

Johnson, D. W., & Johnson, R. T. (1975). *Learning together and alone: Cooperative, competitive, or individualized.* Englewood Cliffs, NJ: Prentice-Hall.

Johnson, D. W., & Johnson, R. T. (1986). Mainstreaming and cooperative learning strategies. *Exceptional Children, 52,* 553–561.

Johnson, H. L. (1993). Stressful family experiences and young children: How the classroom teacher can help. *Intervention in School and Clinic, 28*(3), 165–171.

Johnson, L., & Barry, M. (1970). *Classroom management: Theory and skill training.* London: Collier Macmillan.

Kaderavek, J., & Mandlebaum, L. (1993). Enhancement of oral language in LEA: Improving the narrative form of children with learning disabilities. *Intervention in School and Clinic, 29,* 18–25.

Kaiser, A. P., & Goetz, L. (1993). Enhancing communication with persons labeled severely disabled. *Journal of the Association for Persons with Severe Handicaps, 18,* 137–142.

Kameenui, E. J., & Simmons, D. C. (1990). *Designing instructional strategies.* Englewood Cliffs, NJ: Merrill/Prentice Hall.

Kanner, L. (1964). *A history of the care and study of the mentally retarded.* Springfield, IL: Charles C. Thomas.

Kaplan, H. (1987). Assistive devices for the hearing impaired. *The Hearing Journal, 40*(5), 13–18.

Karacostas, D. D., & Fisher, G. L. (1993). Chemical dependency in students with and without learning disabilities. *Journal of Learning Disabilities, 26*(7), 491–495.

Karlin, M. S., & Berger, R. (1992). *Discipline and the disruptive child.* Englewood Cliffs, NJ: Parker.

Karnes, F. A., & Marquardt, R. G. (1991). *Gifted children and the law: Mediation, due process, and court cases.* Dayton, OH: Ohio Psychology Press.

Kashani, J. H., Orvaschel, H., Rosenberg, T. K., & Reid, J. C. (1989). Psychopathology in a community sample of children and adolescents: A developmental perspective. *Journal of the American Academy of Child and Adolescent Psychiatry, 28,* 701–706.

Kaslow, N. J., & Rehm, L. P. (1991). Childhood depression. In T. R. Kratochwill & R. J. Morris (Eds.), *The practice of child therapy* (2nd ed.). New York: Pergamon.

Kaufman, A. S. (1992). Evaluation of the WISC-III and WPPSI-R for gifted children. *Roeper Review,* 154–158.

Kauffman, J. M. (1993). *Characteristics of emotional and behavioral disorders of children and youth* (5th ed.). Englewood Cliffs, NJ: Merrill/Prentice Hall.

Kavale, K., Forness, S., & Lorsbach, T. (1991). Definitions for learning disabilities. *Learning Disabilities Quarterly, 14,* 257–266.

Kellough, R. D. (1994). *A resource guide for teaching: K–12.* Englewood Cliffs, NJ: Merrill/Prentice Hall.

Kendall, P. C., & Braswell, L. (1985). *Cognitive-behavioral therapy for impulsive children.* New York: Guilford.

Kennedy, J. (1992, October). Outcome based education (OBE) and the high ability student. *North Carolina Association for the Gifted and Talented Newsletter,* 16–17.

Keogh, B. K. (1988). Improving services for problem learners: Rethinking and restructuring. *Journal of Learning Disabilities, 21,* 19–22.

King, J. F. (1991). The misinterpretation of PL 94–142. *Perspectives in Education and Deafness, 10*(2), 20–21.

Kirk, S. A., & Gallagher, J. J. (1989). *Educating exceptional children*. Boston: Houghton Mifflin.

Kleinberg, S. (1982). *Education of the chronically ill child*. Rockville, MD: Aspen Systems.

Kohler, F. W., & Strain, P. S. (1993). The early childhood social skills program. *Teaching Exceptional Children, 25*(2), 41–42.

Kokaska, C., & Brolin, D. (1985). *Career education for handicapped individuals* (2nd ed.). Englewood Cliffs, NJ: Merrill/Prentice Hall.

Kounin, J. (1977). *Discipline and group management in classrooms*. New York: Holt, Rinehart & Winston.

Kozol, J. (1992). *Savage inequalities: Children in America's schools*. New York: Harper Collins.

Kraemer, M. J., & Bierman, C. W. (1983). Asthma. In J. Umbreit (Ed.), *Physical disabilities and health impairments* (pp. 159–166). Englewood Cliffs, NJ: Merrill/Prentice Hall.

Kress, J. S., & Elias, M. J. (1993). Substance abuse prevention in special education populations: Review and recommendations. *The Journal of Special Education, 27*(1), 35–51.

Kretschmer, R. R., & Kretschmer, L. N. (1978). *Language development and intervention with the hearing impaired*. Baltimore: University Park.

Kunkel, M., Chapa, B., Patterson, G., & Walling, D. (1992). Experience of giftedness: Eight great gripes six years later. *Roeper Review, 15*(1), 10–14.

Kurlychek, K. (1993). Software—at your service. *Perspectives in Education and Deafness, 12*(2), 22–23.

Lancelotta, G., & Vaughn, S. (1989). Relation between types of aggression and sociometric status: Peer and teacher perceptions. *Journal of Educational Psychology, 81*, 86–90.

Langdon, H. W. (1989). Language disorder or difference? Assessing the language skills of Hispanic students. *Exceptional Children, 56*, 160–167.

Lazzari, A., & Wood, J. (1993). Reentry to the regular classroom from pull-out programs: Reorientation strategies. *Teaching Exceptional Children, 25*(3), 62–65.

Learning Disabilities Association of America (1993). Position paper on the full inclusion of all students with learning disabilities in the regular education classroom. *Journal of Learning Disabilities, 26*, 594.

Lee, C., & Antia, S. (1992). A sociological approach to the social integration of hearing impaired and normally hearing students. *The Volta Review, 94*(4), 425–434.

Leerhsen, C., & Schaefer, E. (1989, July 31). Pregnancy + alcohol = problems. *Newsweek,* 57.

Leiker, M. (1980). *An affordable gifted program that works*. Denver: Adams School District No. 12.

Leinhardt, G., & Pallay, A. (1982). Restrictive educational settings: Exile or haven? *Review of Educational Research, 52*, 557–578.

Lenz, B. K., Clark, F. L., Deshler, D. D., Schumaker, J. B., & Rademacher, J. A. (Eds.), (1990). *SIM Training library: The strategies instructional approach*. Lawrence, KS: University of Kansas Institute for Research in Learning Disabilities.

Leone, P. E., McLaughlin, M. J., & Meisel, S. M. (1992). School reform and adolescents with behavior disorders. *Focus on Exceptional Children, 25*(1), 1–15.

Leone, P. E., Rutherford, R., & Nelson, M. (1991). *Special education in juvenile corrections*. Reston, VA: Council for Exceptional Children.

Levine, S., & Osbourne, S. (1989). Living and learning with Sally. *Phi Delta Kappan, 70*, 594–598.

Lewis, B. L., & Doorlag, D. (1991). *Teaching special students in the mainstream* (3rd ed.). Englewood Cliffs, NJ: Merrill/Prentice Hall.

Lewis, D. E. (1992). FM systems. *Ear and Hearing, 13*(5), 290–293.

Lewis, R. B. (1993). *Special education technology: Classroom applications*. Pacific Grove, CA: Brooks/Cole.

Light, J., & McNaughton, D. (1993). Literacy and augmentative and alternative communication (AAC): The expectations and priorities of parents and teachers. *Topics in Language Disorders, 13*, 33–46.

Lobel, A. (1970). *Frog and toad are friends*. New York: Harper & Row.

Long, N., & Fagen, S. (1981). Therapeutic management: A psychoeducational approach. In G. Brown, R. McDowell, & J. Smith (Eds.), *Educating adolescents with behavior disorders*. Englewood Cliffs, NJ: Merrill/Prentice Hall.

Long, N. J., & Newman, R. G. (1980). Managing surface behavior of children in schools. In N. J. Long, W. C. Morse, & R. G. Newman (Eds.), *Conflict in the classroom* (4th ed.). Belmont, CA: Wadsworth.

Long, S. H. (1994). Language and children with autism. In V. Reed (Ed.), *An introduction to children with language disorders* (2nd ed.) Englewood Cliffs, NJ: Merrill/Prentice Hall.

Long, S. H., & Long, S. T. (1994). Language and children with mental retardation. In V. Reed (Ed.), *An introduction to children with language disorders* (2nd ed.). Englewood Cliffs, NJ: Merrill/Prentice Hall.

Lourie, I. S. (1991). What I learned from teachers. *Beyond Behavior, 2*(4), 3–6.

Lowenthal, B. (1992). Collaborative training in the education of early childhood educators. *Teaching Exceptional Children, 24*(4), 25–29.

Luckner, J. L., & Humphries, S. (1992). Picturing ideas through graphic organizers. *Perspectives in Education and Deafness, 11*(2), 8–22.

Luetke-Stahlman, B., & Luckner, J. (1991). *Effectively educating students with hearing impairments*. New York: Longman.

Luria, A. (1961). *The role of speech in the regulation of normal and abnormal processes in the child*. Baltimore: Penguin.

Luria, A. (1963). *The mentally retarded child*. Oxford: Pergamon.

Maag, J. W., & Forness, S. R. (1991). Depression in children and adolescents: Identification, assessment and treatment. *Focus on Exceptional Children, 24*(1), 1–19.

Maag, J. W., Irvin, D. M., Reid, R., & Vasa, S. R. (1994). Prevalence and predictors of substance abuse: A comparison between adolescents with and without learning disabilities. *Journal of Learning Disabilities, 27*(4), 223–234.

Maker, C. J. (1982). *Teaching models in education of the gifted*. Rockville, MD: Aspen.

Manfredini, D. (1988). *Down Syndrome*. Reston, VA: Council for Exceptional Children (ERIC Digest No. 457).

Marland, S. (1972). *Education of the gifted and talented: Report to the Congress of the United States by the U.S. Commissioner of Education*. Washington, DC: U.S. Government Printing Office.

Marsh, G., Price, B. J., & Smith, T. E. (1983). *Teaching mildly handicapped children: Methods and materials*. St. Louis: C. V. Mosby.

Mather, N. (1992). Whole language reading instruction for students with learning disabilities: Caught in the crossfire. *Learning Disabilities Research and Practice, 7*, 87–95.

Mathes, P., Fuchs, D., Fuchs, L., Henley, A., & Sanders, A. (1994). Increasing strategic reading practice with Peabody classwide peer tutoring. *Learning Disabilities Research and Practice, 9,* 44–48.

McCartney, B. (1984). Education for the mainstream. *The Volta Review, 86*(5), 41–52.

McCormick, L. P. (1986). Keeping up with language trends. *Teaching Exceptional Children, 18*(2), 123–129.

McCormick, P., Campbell, J., Pasnak, J., & Perry, D. (1990). Instruction of Piagetian concepts for children with mental retardation. *Mental Retardation, 28,* 359–366.

McDaniel, T. (1986). A primer on classroom discipline: Principles old and new. *Phi Delta Kappan, 68,* 63–67.

McDowell, R., Adamson, G., & Wood, F. (1982). *Teaching emotionally disturbed children.* Boston: Little, Brown.

McIntosh, R., Vaughn, S., Schumm, J. S., Haager, D., & Lee, O. (1993). Observations of students with learning disabilities in general education classrooms. *Exceptional Children, 60,* 249–261.

McIntyre, T. (1993). Behaviorally disordered youth in correctional settings: prevalence, programming, and teacher training. *Behavior Disorders, 3,* 167–176.

McLoughlin, J. A., & Lewis, R. B. (1990). *Assessing special students* (3rd ed.). Englewood Cliffs, NJ: Merrill/Prentice Hall.

McTighe, J. J. (1987). Teaching for thinking, of thinking, and about thinking. In M. Heiman & J. Slomianko (Eds.), *Thinking skills instruction: Concepts and techniques.* Washington, DC: National Education Association.

McWhirter, E. H., McWhirter, J. J., McWhirter, B. T., & McWhirter, A. M. (1993). Family counseling interventions: Understanding family systems and the referral process. *Intervention in School and Clinic, 28,* 231–237.

Mehring, T. A., & Colson, S. E. (1990). Motivation and mildly handicapped learners.

Focus on Exceptional Children, 22(5), 1–15.

Meichenbaum, D. (1983). Teaching thinking: A cognitive behavioral approach. In *Interdisciplinary Voices in Learning Disabilities and Remedial Education.* Austin, TX: PRO-ED.

Mercer, C., & Payne, J. (1975). Programs and services. In J. Kauffman and J. Payne (Eds.), *Mental retardation: Introduction and personal perspectives.* Englewood Cliffs, NJ: Merrill/Prentice Hall.

Miksic, S. (1987). Drug abuse management in adolescent special education. In M. M. Kerr, C. M. Nelson, & D. L. Lambert, *Helping adolescents with learning and behavior problems.* Englewood Cliffs, NJ: Merrill/Prentice Hall.

Miller, J. (1993). Augmentative and alternative communication. In M. E. Snell (Ed.), *Instruction of students with severe disabilities* (4th ed.). Englewood Cliffs, NJ: Merrill/Prentice Hall.

Minneapolis Public Schools (1986). *Student suicide prevention guidelines.* Minneapolis, MN: School Social Work Services.

Minner, S. (1982). Expectations of vocational teachers for handicapped students. *Exceptional Children, 48,* 451–453.

Moats, L., & Lyon, G. (1993). Learning disabilities in the United States: Advocacy, science, and the future of the field. *Journal of Learning Disabilities, 26,* 282–294.

Montague, M., Applegate, B., & Marquard, K. (1993). Cognitive strategy instruction and mathematical problem-solving performance of students with learning disabilities. *Learning Disabilities Research and Practice, 8,* 223–232.

Montague, M., & Leavell, A. (1994). Improving the narrative writing of students with learning disabilities. *Remedial and Special Education, 15,* 21–33.

Morganthau, T. (1989, September 11). Children of the underclass. *Newsweek,* 16–24.

Morsink, C. (1984). *Teaching special needs students in regular classrooms*. Boston: Little, Brown.

Morsink, C. V., Chase, T. C., & Correa, V. T. (1991). *Interactive teaming: consultation and collaboration in special programs*. Englewood Cliffs, NJ: Merrill/Prentice Hall.

Morsink, C., & Lenk, L. (1992). The delivery of special education programs and services. *Remedial and Special Education, 13*, 3334.

MRDD. (1992, 15 April). Minutes of meeting of Board of Directors. n.p.

MRDD. (1994). Dealing with secondary curricula and policy issues for students with MR/DD. Board of Directors Position Paper. *MRDD Express, 4*(3), 3–4.

Mueller, F. (1993). Teaching and stress: A personal view. *Beyond Behavior, 5*, 3.

Mulick, J. A., Jacobson, J. W., & Kobe, F. H. (1993). Anguished silence and helping hands: Autism and facilitated communication. *Skeptical Inquirer, 17*, 270–287.

Murray, C., & Herrnstein, R. (1994). *The bell curve: The reshaping of American life by difference in intelligence*. New York: Free Press.

Muse, N. J. (1990). *Depression and suicide in children and adolescents*. Austin, TX: PRO-ED.

Nagata, D. K. (1989). Japanese American children and adolescents. In J. Taylor & I. Nahme-Huang (Eds.), *Children of color: Psychological interventions with minority youth*. San Francisco: Jossey-Bass.

National Advisory Committee on Dyslexia and Related Reading Disorders. (1969). *Reading disorders in the United States*. Washington, DC: U.S. Department of Health, Education, and Welfare.

National Council of Teachers of Mathematics. (1989). *Evaluation standards: Curriculum and evaluation for school mathematics*. Reston, VA: Author. (ERIC Document Reproduction Service No. ED 304 336)

National Information Center on Deafness. (1991). *Mainstreaming deaf and hard of hearing students: Questions and answers, research readings and resources*. Washington, DC: Gallaudet University.

National Information Services Institute. (1989). *Choices, a classroom management and discipline system*. Phoenix, AZ: Classroom Management Systems.

National Joint Committee on Learning Disabilities. (1989, 18 Sept.). Modifications to the NJCLD definition of learning disabilities. Letter from NJCLD to member organizations.

National Joint Committee on Learning Disabilities. (1993). Providing appropriate education for students with learning disabilities in the regular education classroom. *Journal of Learning Disabilities, 26*, 330–332.

Necco, E., Wilson, C., & Scheidemantal, J. (1982). Affective learning through drama. *Teaching Exceptional Children, 15*(1), 22–25.

Nelson, C. M., & Pearson, C. A. (1991). *Integrating services for children and youth with emotional and behavioral disorders*. Reston, VA: Council for Exceptional Children.

Newcomer, P. L. (1993). *Understanding and teaching emotionally disturbed children and adolescents*. Austin, TX: PRO-ED.

NICHCY—National Information Center for Children and Youth with Disabilities. (1991). *General information about autism*. Fact Sheet No. 1. Washington, DC: Author.

Noble, K. D., & Drummond, J. E. (1992). "But what about the Prom?": Students' perceptions of early college entrance. *Gifted Child Quarterly, 36*, 106–111.

Noble, K. D., Robinson, N., & Gunderson, S. A. (1992). All rivers lead to the sea: A follow-up study of gifted young adults. *Roeper Review, 15*, 124–130.

Norton, D. (1989). *The effective teaching of language arts* (3rd ed.). Englewood Cliffs, NJ: Merrill/Prentice Hall.

Nowacek, E. J. (1992). Professionals talk about teaching together. *Intervention in School and Clinic, 27*, 262–276.

Oddone, A. (1993). Inclusive classrooms. *Teaching Exceptional Children, 26*(1), 74–75.

Owens, R. E. (1988). *Language development* (2nd ed.). Englewood Cliffs, NJ: Merrill/Prentice Hall.

Patton, J., Beirne-Smith, M., & Payne, J. (1990). *Mental retardation* (3rd ed.). Englewood Cliffs, NJ: Merrill/Prentice Hall.

Paul, J. L., & Epanchin, B. C. (1991). *Educating emotionally disturbed children and youth: Theories and practices for teacher* (2nd ed.).Englewood Cliffs, NJ: Merrill/Prentice Hall.

Pfeffer, C. R. (1986). *The suicidal child*. New York: Guilford.

Piaget, J. (1952). *The origins of intelligence in children*. New York: International University Press.

Piaget, J. (1954). *The construction of reality in the child*. New York: Basic Books.

Piaget, J. (1962). *Play, dramas, and imitation in childhood*. New York: W. W. Norton.

Piirto, J. (1994). *Talented children and adults: Their development and education*. Englewood Cliffs, NJ: Merrill/Prentice Hall.

Polloway, E. A., & Patton, J. R. (1993). *Strategies for teaching learners with special needs* (5th ed.). Englewood Cliffs, NJ: Merrill/Prentice Hall.

Polloway, E. A., Patton, J. R., Payne, J. S., and Payne, R. A. (1989). *Strategies for teaching learners with special needs* (4th ed.). Englewood Cliffs, NJ: Merrill/Prentice Hall.

Polloway, E., Payne, J., Patton, J., & Payne, R. (1985). *Strategies for teaching retarded and special needs learners* (3rd ed.). Englewood Cliffs, NJ: Merrill/Prentice Hall.

Prillaman, D. (1981). Acceptance of learning disabled students in the mainstream environment: A failure to replicate. *Journal of Learning Disabilities, 14*, 344–346.

Pritchard, D. G. (1963). *Education and the handicapped: 1760–1960*. London: Routledge & Kegan Paul.

Prizant, B., Audet, L., Burke, G., Hummel, L., Maher, S., & Theadore, G. (1990). Communication disorders and emotional/behavioral disorders in children and adolescents. *Journal of Speech and Hearing Disorders, 55*, 179–192.

Pueschel, S. M., Bernier, J. C., & Weidenman, L. E. (1988). *The special child*. Baltimore: Paul H. Brookes.

Putnam, J. W., Rynders, J. E., Johnson, R. T., & Johnson, D. W. (1989). Collaborating skills instruction for promoting positive interactions between mentally handicapped and nonhandicapped children. *Exceptional Children, 55*, 550–557.

Quigley, S., & Paul, P. (1984). *Language and Deafness*. San Diego, CA: College-Hill.

Raab, M., & Steele, J. (1993). Application of expert systems in the field of learning disabilities: Classification of instructional modifications. *LD Forum, 19*, 47–53.

Rakes, T. A., & Choate, J. S. (1989). *Language arts: Detecting and correcting special needs*. Boston: Allyn & Bacon.

Ramirez, J. D. (1992). Executive summary. *Bilingual Research Journal, 16*, 1–62.

Reed, P. R. (1991). *Traumatic brain injury, an educator's manual*. Portland, OR: Portland Public Schools and Oregon Department of Education.

Reed, V. A. (1994). *An introduction to children with language disorders* (2nd ed.). Englewood Cliffs, NJ: Merrill/Prentice Hall.

Reeve, P. T., & Hallahan, D. P. (1994). Practical questions about collaboration between general and special educators. *Focus on Exceptional Children, 26,* 1–12.

Reid, R., Maag, J., & Vasa, S. (1994). Attention deficit hyperactivity disorder as a disability category: A critique. *Exceptional Children, 60,* 98–124.

Rennie, J. (1993, August). Who is normal? *Scientific American,* pp. 14–17.

Renzulli, J., Reis, S., and Smith, L. (1981). *The revolving door identification model.* Mansfield, CT: Creative Learning.

Renzulli, J., & Smith, L. (1980). An alternative approach to identifying and programming for gifted and talented students. *Gifted/Creative/Talented, 15,* 4–11.

Research brief T1, social integration of handicapped students: Cooperative goal structuring. (1988). Reston, VA: Council for Exceptional Children.

Retish, P., Hutchings, W., Horvath, M., & Schmalle, B. (1991). *Students with mild disabilities in the secondary school.* New York: Longman.

Revkin, A. C. (1989). Crack in the cradle. *Discover, 10,* 62–69.

Reynolds, M. C., & Birch, J. W. (1982). *Teaching exceptional children in all America's schools* (rev. ed.). Reston, VA: Council for Exceptional Children.

Rich, H. L. (1982). *Disturbed students.* Baltimore: University Park.

Richards, W. (1986). Allergy, asthma, and school problems. *Journal of School Health, 56,* 151–152.

Roberts, C., & Zubrick, S. (1993). Factors influencing the social status of children with mild academic disabilities in regular classrooms. *Exceptional Children, 59,* 192–202.

Robinson, N. M. (1992). "Stanford-Binet IV, Of course! Time marches on." *Roeper Review, 15,* 32–34.

Rogers, J. (1993). The inclusion revolution. *The Research Bulletin, 11,* 1–6.

Rosenthal, R., & Jacobson, L. (1968). *Pygmalion in the classroom.* New York: Holt, Rinehart & Winston.

Rudman, M. K. (1984). *Children's literature: An issues approach* (2nd ed.). New York: Longman.

Runions, T., & Smyth, E. (1985). Mentorships for the gifted and talented. *ERIC Digest, 346.* Reston, VA: Council for Exceptional Children.

Rutter, M. (1991). Age changes in depressive disorders: Some developmental considerations. In J. Garber & K. A. Dodge (Eds.), *The development of emotion regulation and dysregulation.* Cambridge, MA: Cambridge University Press.

Ryan, A., & Price, L. (1992). Adults with LD in the 1990's. *Intervention in School and Clinic, 28,* 6–20.

Sabornie, E. J., & Beard, G. H. (1990). Teaching social skills to students with mild handicaps. *Teaching Exceptional Children, 23,* 35–38.

Saint-Laurent, L., Fournier, A., & Lessard, J. (1993). Efficacy of three programs for elementary school students with moderate mental retardation. *Education and Training in Mental Retardation, 28,* 333–348.

Salend, S. J. (1984). Factors contributing to the development of successful mainstreaming programs. *Exceptional Children, 50,* 409–416.

Salend, S. J. (1994). *Effective mainstreaming: Creating inclusive classrooms* (2nd ed.). Englewood Cliffs, NJ: Merrill/Prentice Hall.

Salvia, J., & Hughes, C. (1990). *Curriculum-based assessment: Testing what is taught.* Englewood Cliffs, NJ: Merrill/Prentice Hall.

Sattler, J. M. (1992). *Assessment of children* (3rd ed.). San Diego: Author.

Scala, M. (1993). What whole language in the mainstream means for children with learning disabilities. *The Reading Teacher, 47,* 222–229.

Scheffers, W. L. (1977). Sighted children learn about blindness. *Journal of Visual Impairment and Blindness, 71,* 258–261.

Scheid, K. (1994). Cognitive-based methods for teaching mathematics. *Teaching Exceptional Children, 26*(3), 6–10.

Schiamberg, L. B. (1988). *Child and adolescent development.* Englewood Cliffs, NJ: Merrill/Prentice Hall.

Schiff-Myers, N. B., Djukic, J., McGovern-Lawler, J., & Perez, D. (1994). Assessment considerations in the evaluation of second language learners: A case study. *Exceptional Children, 60,* 237–248.

Schlesinger, H. S. (1985). Deafness, mental health, and language. In F. Powell, T. Finitzo-Hieber, S. Friel-Patti, & D. Henderson (Eds.), *Education of the hearing impaired child.* San Diego: College-Hill.

Schloss, P., & Sedlak, R. (1986). *Instructional methods for students with learning and behavior problems.* Newton, MA: Allyn & Bacon.

Schneider, B. H. (1987). *The gifted child in peer group perspective.* New York: Springer-Verlag.

Schumm, J. S., & Vaughn, S. (1991). Making adaptations for mainstreamed students: Regular classroom teachers' perspectives. *Remedial and Special Education, 12,* 18–27.

Schwartz, L. L. (1984). *Exceptional students in the mainstream.* Belmont, CA: Wadsworth.

Scott, M. S., Peron, R., Urbano, R., Hogan, A., & Gold, S. (1992). The identification of giftedness: A comparison of white, Hispanic, and black families. *Gifted Child Quarterly, 36,* 121–139.

Scruggs, T., Mastropieri, M., & Sullivan, S. (1994). Promoting rational thinking: Elaborative interrogation for students with mild disabilities. *Exceptional Children, 60,* 450–457.

Seels, B., & Richey, R. (1993). *Instructional technology: The definition and domains of the field.* Washington, DC: Association for Educational Communications and Technology.

Semmel, M., Gottlieb, J., & Robinson, N. (1979). Mainstreaming: Perspectives on educating handicapped children in the public schools. In D. Berliner (Ed.), *Review of research in education* (Vol. 7, pp. 126–130). Washington, DC: American Educational Research Association.

Serwatka, T. S., Deering, S., & Stoddard, A. (1989). Correlates of the underrepresentation of black students in classes for gifted students. *Journal of Negro Education, 58,* 520–530.

Shames, G. H., Wiig, E. H., & Secord, W. A. (1994). *Human communication disorders: An introduction* (4th ed.). Englewood Cliffs, NJ: Merrill/Prentice Hall.

Sharon, S., & Sharon, Y. (1976). *Small-group teaching.* Englewood Cliffs, NJ: Educational Technology.

Sheinker, J., & Sheinker, A. (1989). *A metacognitive approach to study strategies.* Rockville, MD: Aspen.

Shores, R. E., Gunter, P. L., Denny, R. K., & Jack, S. L. (1993). Influences on aggressive and disruptive behaviors of students with emotional and behavioral disorders. *Focus on Exceptional Children, 26,* 1–10.

Shriner, J. G., Ysseldyke, J. E., & Thurlow, M. L. (1994). Standards for all American children. *Focus on Exceptional Children, 26,* 1–19.

Sicley, D. (1993). Effective methods of communication: Practical interventions for classroom teachers. *Intervention in School and Clinic, 29,* 105–108.

Sigelman, C. K., & Shaffer, D. R. (1991). *Lifespan human development.* Pacific Grove, CA: Brooks/Cole.

Silverman, L. K., & Kearney, K. (1992). The case for the Stanford Binet L-M as a supplemental test. *Roeper Review, 15,* 34–37.

Simpson, R. (1981). Further investigation and interpretation of the expectancy effect generated by disability labels. *Diagnostique, 17,* 101–108.

Simpson, R. L. (1990). *Conferencing parents of exceptional children* (2nd ed.). Austin, TX: PRO-ED.

Simpson, R. L., Whelan, R., & Zabel, R. (1993). Special education personnel preparation in the 21st century: Issues and strategies. *Remedial and Special Education, 14,* 7–22.

Singh, N. N. (1993). Personal reflections. In J. M. Kauffman (Ed.), *Characteristics of emotional and behavioral disorders of children and youth* (5th ed.). Englewood Cliffs, NJ: Merrill/Prentice Hall.

Sisk, D. (1987). *Creative teaching of the gifted*. New York: McGraw-Hill.

Skinner, B. F. (1957). *Verbal behavior*. New York: Appleton-Century-Crofts.

Slavin, R. E. (1978). Student teams and comparison among equals: Effects on academic performance and student attitudes. *Journal of Educational Psychology, 70,* 532–538.

Slavin, R. E. (1980). Cooperative learning. *Review of Educational Research, 50,* 315–342.

Slavin, R. E. (1986). *Using student team learning* (3rd ed.). Baltimore, MD: Center for Research on Elementary and Middle Schools, Johns Hopkins University.

Sleeter, C. E., & Grant, C. A. (1994). *Making choices for multicultural education* (2nd ed.). Englewood Cliffs, NJ: Merrill/Prentice Hall.

Smith, G., & Smith, D. (1989). Schoolwide study skills program: The key to mainstreaming. *Teaching Exceptional Children, 21*(3), 20–23.

Smith, M. D. (1990). *Autism and life in the community*. Baltimore: Paul H. Brookes.

Smith, T., & Hilton, A. (1994). Program design for students with mental retardation. *Education and Training in Mental Retardation and Mental Disabilities, 29*(1), 3–8.

Smutney, J. F., & Blocksom, R. H. (1990). *Education of gifted: Programs and perspectives*. Bloomington, IN: Phi Delta Kappa.

Snell, M. E. (Ed). (1993). *Instruction of students with severe disabilities* (4th ed.). Englewood Cliffs, NJ: Merrill/Prentice Hall.

Snell, M. E., & Brown, F. (1993). Instructional planning and implementation. In M. E. Snell (Ed.), *Instruction of students with severe disabilities* (4th ed.). Englewood Cliffs, NJ: Merrill/Prentice Hall.

Spivak, G., & Swift, M. (1972). *Hahneman High School Behavior Scale*. Philadelphia: Department of Mental Health Sciences, Hahneman Medical College & Hospital.

Stahl, N., & Stahl, R. (1991). We can agree after all: Achieving consensus for a critical thinking component of a gifted program using the delphi technique. *Roeper Review, 14,* 81.

Stainback, S., & Stainback, W. (1987). Integration versus cooperation: A commentary on educating children with learning problems, a shared responsibility. *Exceptional Children, 54,* 66–68.

Stainback, S., & Stainback, W. (1992). *Curriculum considerations for inclusive classrooms: Facilitating learning for all students*. Baltimore: Paul H. Brookes.

Stainback, S., Stainback, W., & Forest, M. (1989). *Educating all students in the mainstream of education*. Baltimore: Paul H. Brookes.

Stainback, W., Stainback, S., & Froyen, L. (1987). Structuring the classroom to prevent disruptive behaviors. *Teaching Exceptional Children, 19*(4), 12–16.

Stanley, J. C., Benbow, C. P., Brody, L. F., Danber, S., & Lupowski, A. E. (1992). Gender differences in eighty-six nationally standardized achievement tests. In N. Colangelo, A. Assoline, & D. Ambroson (Eds.), *Talent development*. Unionville, NY: Trillium.

Steinberg, Z., & Knitzer, J. (1992). Classrooms for emotionally and behaviorally disturbed students: Facing the challenge. *Behavior Disorders, 17*, 145–156.

Sternberg, R. J., & Spear, L. (1985). *Beyond IQ: A triarchic theory of intelligence*. New York: Cambridge University Press.

Stiggins, R. J. (1994). *Student-centered classroom assessment*. Englewood Cliffs, NJ: Merrill/Prentice Hall.

Strickland, B. B., & Turnbull, A. P. (1990). *Developing and implementing individualized education programs* (3rd ed.). Englewood Cliffs, NJ: Merrill/Prentice Hall.

Stronge, J. H. (1992). *Educating homeless children and adolescents*. Newbury Park, CA: Sage.

Stuckless, E. R. (Ed.). (1994). Education applications of technology for deaf students (symposium). *American Annals of the Deaf, 139* (special issue), 3–66.

Stuttering Foundation of America. (1993). *Did you know . . . ?* Memphis, TN: Author.

Sugai, G., & Tindal, G. (1993). *Effective school consultation an interactive approach*. Pacific Grove, CA: Brooks/Cole.

Tal, Z., & Babad, E. (1990). The teacher's pet phenomenon: Rate of occurrence, correlates, and psychological costs. *Journal of Educational Psychology, 82*, 637–645.

Taylor, R., Smiley, L., & Ziegler, E. (1983). The effects of labels and assigned attributes on teacher perceptions of academic and social behaviors. *Education and Training of the Mentally Retarded, 18*, 45–51.

Terman, L. (1925). Mental and physical traits of a thousand gifted children. In L. Terman (Ed.), *Genetic studies of genius* (Vol. 1, n.p.). Stanford, CA: Stanford University Press.

Terman, L., & Oden, M. (1959). The gifted group at midlife. Twenty-five year's follow-up of the superior child. In L. Terman (Ed.), *Genetic studies of genius* (Vol. 5, n.p.). Stanford, CA: Stanford University Press.

Test, D., Keul, P., Williams, B., Slaughter, M., & Allen, C. (1992). Evaluating performance in a workstation. *Education and Training in Mental Retardation, 27*, 335–344.

Thomas, R. (1989). *Taking back our rights*. Paper presented at the Annual Conference of the American Society for Deaf Children, Faribault, MN, June.

Thompson, T. (1993). A reign of error: Facilitated communication. *Kennedy Center News, 22*, 2–3.

Thorndike, R. L., Hagen, E., & Sattler, J. (1986). *Stanford-Binet intelligence scale* (3rd ed.). Chicago: Riverside.

Tiedt, I. M., Carlson, J. E., Howard, B. D., and Watanabe, K. S. O. (1989). *Teaching thinking in K–12 classrooms: Ideas, activities, and resources*. Boston: Allyn & Bacon.

Torrance, E. P. (1962). *Guiding creative talent*. Englewood Cliffs, NJ: Prentice-Hall.

Torrance, E. P. (1965). *Rewarding creative behavior*. Englewood Cliffs, NJ: Prentice-Hall.

Torrance, E. P. (1974). *Torrance tests of creative thinking technical manual*. Lexington, MA: Personnel.

Torrance, E. P. (1981). *Thinking creatively in action and movement*. Bensonville, IL: Scholastic Testing Services.

Torrance, E. P., Blume, B., Maryanopolis, J., Murphey, F., & Rogers, J. (1980). *Teaching scenario writing*. Lincoln, NE: Future Problem Solving Program, Nebraska Department of Education.

Torrance, E. P., & Torrance, J. P. (1981). Educating gifted, talented and creative students for the future. *American Middle School Education, 4*(1), 39–46.

Trueba, H. T. (1991). Learning needs of minority children: contributions of ethnography to educational research. In L. M. Malave & G. Duquette (Eds.), *Language, culture, and cognition*. Clevedon, England: Multilingual Matters, Ltd.

Tucker, B. F., & Colson, S. E. (1992). Traumatic brain injury: An overview of school re-entry. *Intervention in School and Clinic, 27*(4), 198–206.

Turnbull, A. P., & Turnbull, H. R., III. (1990). *Families, professionals, and exceptionality: A special partnership* (2nd ed.). Englewood Cliffs, NJ: Merrill/Prentice Hall.

Turnbull, H. R., III. (1993). *Free appropriate public education: The law and children with disabilities*. Denver, CO: Love.

Tur-Kaspa, H., & Bryan, T. (1994). Social information-processing skills of students with learning disabilities. *Learning Disabilities Research and Practice, 9*, 12–23.

Tyler-Wood, T., & Carrie, L. (1991). Identification of gifted children: The effectiveness of various measures of cognitive ability. *Roeper Review, 14*, 63–64.

U.S. Department of Education. (1993). *Fifteenth annual report to Congress on the implementation of the Individuals with Disabilities Education Act*. Washington, DC: Department of Education and U.S. Office of Special Education and Rehabilitative Services.

U.S. Department of Education, Office of Educational Research and Improvement. (1993). *National excellence: A case for developing America's talent*. Washington, DC: U.S. Government Printing Office.

VanBourgondien, M. E. (1987). Children's responses to retarded peers as a function of social behaviors, labeling, and age. *Exceptional Children, 53*, 432–439.

Van Dyke, D. C., & Fox, A. A. (1990). Fetal drug exposure and its possible implications for learning in preschool and school-age populations. *Journal of Learning Disabilities, 23*, 160–163.

Van Riper, C., & Emerick, L. (1990). *Speech correction: An introduction to speech pathology and audiology*. Englewood Cliffs, NJ: Prentice-Hall.

Van Tassel-Baska, J., Patton, J. M., & Prillaman, D. (1991). *Gifted youth at risk: A report of a national study*. Reston, VA: Council for Exceptional Children.

Vaughn, B., & Langlois, J. (1983). Physical attractiveness as a correlate of peer status and social competence in preschool children. *Developmental Psychology, 19*, 517–567.

Vaughn, S., McIntosh, R., Schumm, J. S., Haager, D., & Collwood, D. (1993). Social status, peer acceptance, and reciprocal friendships revisited. *Learning Disabilities Research and Practice, 8*, 82–88.

Venn, J. (1994). *Assessment of students with special needs*. Englewood Cliffs, NJ: Merrill/Prentice Hall.

Vygotsky, L. (1962). *Thought and language*. Cambridge, MA: MIT Press.

Wagner, M., Newman, L., & Shaver, D. (1989). *The National Longitudinal Transition Study of Special Education Students: Report on procedures for the first wave of data collection*. Menlo Park, CA: SRI International.

Waldie, K., & Spreen, O. (1993). The relationship between learning disabilities and persisting delinquency. *Journal of Learning Disabilities, 26*, 417–423.

Walker, H. M. (1983). *Walker Problem Behavior Identification Checklist* (rev. ed.). Los Angeles: Western Psychological Service.

Walker, H. M., McConnell, S., Holmes, D., Todis, B., Walker, J., & Golden, N. (1983).

The Walker social skills curriculum: The ACCEPTS program. Austin, TX: PRO-ED.

Walker, H. M., & Severson, H. H. (1990). *Systematic screening for behavior disorders (SSBD): A multiple gating procedure*. Longmont, CO: Sopris West.

Walker, H. M., Todis, B., Holmes, D., & Norton, N. (1988). *Walker social skills curriculum: The ACCESS program*. Austin, TX: PRO-ED.

Walker, J. E., & Shea, T. M. (1991). *Behavior management: A practical approach for educators*. Englewood Cliffs, NJ: Merrill/Prentice Hall.

Wallace, G., Cohen, S. B., & Polloway, E. A. (1987). *Language arts: Teaching exceptional students*. Austin, TX: PRO-ED.

Wallace, G., & Kauffman, J. M. (1986, 1990). *Teaching students with learning and behavior problems* (3rd & 4th eds.). Englewood Cliffs, NJ: Merrill/Prentice Hall.

Warner, I. (1991). Parents in touch. *Phi Delta Kappan, 72*, 372–375.

Wechsler, D. (1981). *Manual for the Wechsler adult intelligence scale—revised (WAIS-R)*. San Antonio, TX: Psychological Corporation.

Wechsler, D. (1989). *Manual for the Wechsler preschool and primary scale of intelligence—revised (WPPSI-R)*. San Antonio, TX: Psychological Corporation.

Wechsler, D. (1991). *Manual for the Wechsler intelligence scale for children (WISC-III)* (3rd ed.). San Antonio, TX: Psychological Corporation.

Welch, M., & Link, D. P. (1991). The instructional priority system: A method for assessing the educational environment. *Intervention, 27*, 91–96.

West, J. F., & Idol, L. (1990). Collaborative consultation in the education of mildly handicapped and at-risk students. *Remedial and Special Education, 11*, 22–31.

White, A., & White, L. (1992). A collaborative model for students with mild disabilities in middle schools. *Focus on Exceptional Children, 24*, 1–10.

White, W. J., & Biller, E. (1988). Career education for students with handicaps. In R. Gaylord-Ross (Ed.), *Vocational education for persons with handicaps*. Mountain View, CA: Mayfield.

Whitmore, J. R. (1985). Characteristics of intellectually gifted children. *ERIC Digest, 344*. Reston, VA: Council for Exceptional Children.

Wiggins, G. (1993). Assessment: authenticity, context, and validity. *Phi Delta Kappan, 75*, 200–214.

Will, M. (1986). Educating children with learning problems: A shared responsibility. *Exceptional Children, 52*, 411–415.

Willings, D., & Arsenault, M. (1986). Attempted suicide and creative promise. *Gifted Education International, 4*(1), 10–13.

Winter, R. J. (1983). Childhood diabetes mellitus. In J. Umbreit (Ed.), *Physical disabilities and health impairments* (pp. 195–205). Englewood Cliffs, NJ: Merrill/Prentice Hall.

Wishnietsky, D. H. (1992). *Hypermedia: The integrated learning environment*. Bloomington, IN: Phi Delta Kappa Educational Foundation.

Wood, J. (1984). *Adapting instruction to the mainstream*. Englewood Cliffs, NJ: Merrill/Prentice Hall.

Wood, J. (1989). *Mainstreaming: A practical approach for teachers*. Englewood Cliffs, NJ: Merrill/Prentice Hall.

Wood, M. M., & Long, N. J. (1991). *Life space intervention: Talking with children and youth in crisis*. Austin, TX: PRO-ED.

Worthen, B. R. (1993). Critical issues that will determine the future of alternative assessment. *Phi Delta Kappan, 74*, 444–456.

Wrenn, C., & Schwarzrock, S. (1984). *The coping with series*. Circle Pines, MN: American Guidance Service.

Wright, L., & Borland, J. H. (1993). Using early childhood developmental portfolios in the identification and education of young, economically disadvantaged, potentially gifted students. *Roeper Review, 15,* 205–210.

Yong, F. L., & McIntyre, J. D. (1992). A comparative study of the learning style preference of students with learning disabilities and students who are gifted. *Journal of Learning Disabilities, 25,* 124–132.

York, J., Doyle, M. B., & Kronberg, R. (1992). A curriculum development process for inclusive classrooms. *Focus on Exceptional Children, 25,* 1–16.

Ysseldyke, J. E., & Algozzine, B. (1984). *Introduction to special education.* Boston: Houghton Mifflin.

Zilboorg, G., & Henry, G. W. (1941). *A history of medical psychology.* New York: W. W. Norton.

Zirkel, P. A. (Ed.). (1978). *A digest of Supreme Court decisions affecting education.* Bloomington, IN: Phi Delta Kappa.

Zucker, C. (1993). Using whole language with students who have language learning disabilities. *The Reading Teacher, 46,* 666–670.

Name Index

Abbe de l'Epee, 6
Achenbach, T. M., 369
Adamson, G., 368
Adger, C. T., 211
Adler, C. R., 149, 151, 153
Alberto, P. A., 372
Aleman, S. R., 336
Algozzine, B., 128, 372
Allen, C., 317
Allen, R., 412
Anderson, P., 151
Anthony, D., 180
Antia, S., 183
Applegate, B., 354
Aronson, E., 144
Arsenault, M., 414
Artiles, A. J., 57
Ashby-Davis, C., 99
Audet, L., 214

Baca, L. M., 209, 210, 426
Baker, C., 131, 393
Baker-Kroczynski, S., 352
Ballard, J., 33
Barken, J. H., 435
Barkley, R. A., 382
Barnetti, S. M., 409
Baron, R. M., 129
Barraga, N., 227
Barry, M., 390, 391
Bartel, N. R., 352
Baskin, B., 443
Bateman, B., 48
Beard, G. H., 137
Bechtel, C., 151
Behrman, R. E., 288
Bell, A. G., 7
Benbow, C. P., 436
Berger, G., 289
Berger, R., 410, 416
Berko Gleason, J., 208
Bernal, E. M., 435
Bernier, J. C., 288, 289
Bernstein, D. K., 193, 207
Bentler, R. A., 163
Betts, G., 447, 448
Bierman, C. W., 275, 276
Bierne-Smith, M., 309, 312, 314, 315, 321
Bigge, J. L., 86, 290
Biklin, D., 221
Biller, E., 315

Binet, A., 307, 308
Birch, J. W., 185
Blockson, R. H., 435
Bloom, B., 99, 442, 444
Blume, B., 450
Blumenthal, S., 414
Bonet, J., 6
Borkowski, J. G., 312
Borland, J. H., 431
Bornstein, H., 180
Boston, J. B., 438
Bower, E. M., 367
Braswell, L., 406
Brier, N., 412
Bristoe, M. M., 222
Brody, G. H., 414
Brody, L. F., 436
Brolin, D., 314
Brophy, J. E., 129, 407
Browder, D., 328
Brown, C., 267
Brown, F., 327
Brown, L. L., 369, 436
Bruner, J., 195
Bryan, T., 362
Bulgren, J., 343, 359
Bullock, L. M., 368
Burke, G., 214
Burks, H. F., 369
Bunsen, T. D., 409
Bursuck, W., 342
Bybee, J., 312

Calculator, S., 222
Calvin, G., 408
Campbell, J., 322
Candler, A., 146
Canter, L., 388, 389
Canter, M., 388, 389
Carlson, J. E., 91
Carnine, D., 348
Carrie, L., 430, 432
Carrol, C., 165
Carta, J., 68
Carter, J. F., 87
Cartledge, G., 137, 148, 149
Cartwright, C. A., 183
Cartwright, G. P., 183
Cassel, P., 384, 387
Cawley, J., 352
Cervantes, H. T., 209, 210, 426
Chapa, B., 455, 456

Chapman, W., 153
Charles, C., 389
Chase, T. C., 137
Chinn, P. C., 210
Choate, J. S., 88
Chomsky, N., 194
Chrispeels, J. H., 149
Cicchelli, T., 99
Clark, B., 422, 425, 426, 435, 437, 441, 442, 444, 449, 450, 453
Clark, F. L., 148
Cleary, M. E., 146
Cline, D. H., 367
Clymer, E. W., 173
Cohen, S. B., 88
Cole, G. F., 412
Coleman, M. C., 128
Collwood, D., 140
Colson, S. E., 72, 73, 289
Conture, E. G., 202
Cooper, H. M., 129
Correa, V. T., 137
Costa, A. L., 91, 129
Cox, J., 438
Crane, J. C., 406
Cronin, M. E., 151
Csanyi, A. D., 376, 377
Culatta, B. K., 198
Culatta, R., 198
Cullinan, D., 383
Cummins, C., 99, 209

D'Angelo, D. A., 149, 151, 153
Damberg, P. R., 312
Damico, J. S., 208, 209
Danber, S., 436
Daniel, N., 438
Daniels-Mohring, D., 149
Davis, J. M., 163
Dean, A. V., 84, 210
Deering, S., 426
DeHouske, E., 397
Delguadri, J., 68
Denny, R. K., 408
Deshler, D., 148, 343, 359
Detwyler, S., 211
Devine, T. G., 90
Devlin, S. D., 413
DeVries, D. L., 143
Dinkmeyer, D., 406
Djukic, J., 210
Doorlag, D., 216

510

Subject Index